S0-AGY-122

Exceptional Children in Canada

Exceptional Children in Canada

Margret Winzer
Sally Rogow
Charlotte David

Prentice-Hall Canada Inc., Scarborough, Canada

Canadian Cataloguing in Publication Data

Winzer, Margret, 1940-
Exceptional children in Canada

Bibliography: p.
Includes index.
ISBN 0-13-293820-0

1. Exceptional children — Education — Canada.
I. Rogow, Sally M., 1930- II. David, Charlotte G., 1919- III. Title.

LC3984.W55 1986 371.9′0971 C85-099968-5

Prentice-Hall Inc., Englewood Cliffs, *New Jersey*
Prentice-Hall International, Inc., *London*
Prentice-Hall of Australia, Pty., Ltd., *Sydney*
Prentice-Hall of India Pvt., Ltd., *New Delhi*
Prentice-Hall of Japan Inc., *Tokyo*
Prentice-Hall of Southeast Asia (Pte.) Ltd., *Singapore*
Editora Prentice-Hall do Brasil Ltda., *Rio de Janeiro*
Prentice-Hall Hispanoamericana, S.A., *Mexico*
Whitehall Books Ltd., Wellington, *New Zealand*

ISBN 0-13-293820-0

Copy Editor: Janet MacLean

Production Editors: Heather Strongitharm/G.S. Fischer

Manufacturing Buyer: Matt Lumsdon

Anatomical Illustrations: Jane Wagner/Diagrams: Patrice Clarkson

Cover and Text Design: William Fox/Associates

Composition: DSR Typesetting Services

1 2 3 4 5 THB 91 90 89 87

Printed and Bound in Canada by
T.H. Best Printing Company Limited

This book is dedicated to those who paved the way
for special education in Canada — all those
first teachers of special classes who proved
that no child is uneducable — at a time
when it was not "fashionable";
and to the children who liven up the text.

TABLE OF CONTENTS

SECTION 2 CHILDREN WITH INTELLECTUAL DIFFERENCES

PREFACE

Exceptional children in Canada is designed to serve as a comprehensive introduction to exceptional children and special education. The text is intended to be practical and readily understandable to those who are studying the problems of exceptional children for the first time, as well as serve as a resource for more advanced students.

The text is useful for both education and psychology courses. It should interest students who are involved in special education, regular education, nursing, social work, and allied child-care disciplines such as audiology, speech therapy, and language pathology.

Because of the recent rapid advances in the Canadian special education complex, and because Canadian students require an intimate knowledge of the philosophies, policies and processes which determine the care and education of exceptional children in this country, we considered a Canadian text on exceptional children to be timely and important. These significant achievements tend to be obscured because there is no national office of education nor clearinghouse of information. We did not have the time or the resources to visit ministries of education in each of the provinces and search out the programs in the hundreds of school districts scattered across this vast land. And yet, as we attempted to seek out programs and services, we discovered that all across this country exceptional children are being served. Even in those regions where poverty is severe and resources diminished, efforts are being made to serve everyone, including the most disabled children. Lack of national surveys made it difficult to fully explore the incidence and prevalence of many types of exceptionalities in Canada or to accurately represent the many different types of services available. Nevertheless we tried to open a window on the Canadian experience and in doing so discovered the depth and breadth of care and concern for exceptional children in Canada. Efforts are being made to integrate exceptional children within the framework of public education. More and more disabled children are now able to remain at home with their families and attend school in their communities, both in small, remote communities as well as large urban centers.

Although the history and development of special education in Canada shares much with other countries, there are some unique and special features. We hope that we have at least captured the flavor of Canadian services and that our effort has given recognition to the considerable depth of the Canadian achievements in this field. Nonetheless, despite our Canadian focus, the text is widely applicable in an American context as well.

A categorical approach is adopted throughout the text. Not only is this the most practical and logical manner in which to organize such a huge body of information, but Canadian programs and research are still largely categorically oriented.

The reader will find an opening section that discusses issues central to the consideration of all special children. In this section the differences between normal and exceptional children are discussed, as well as the diagnosis of exceptional children, and the roles of the various disciplines involved with exceptional children. This section also discusses the families of exceptional children, and details the birth and development of special education. Major trends in special education also receive special attention — normalization, deinstitutionalization, mainstreaming, and recent regulatory legislation. These latter topics are further discussed throughout the text within the context of specific areas of exceptionality.

The following sections provide eleven chapters each dealing with specific populations of exceptional children. Although there is a good deal of overlap in both the characteristics and approaches to education among the various categories of exceptionality, each category receives separate, detailed treatment. These include children with intellectual differences including the gifted and talented, and the mentally retarded; children with communication exceptionalities including those with speech disorders, language differences, and learning disabilities; children with sensory handicaps (hearing handicapped and visually impaired); children with emotional disturbance such as those with personality and conduct disorders, delinquent youth, and severely and profoundly emotionally disturbed youngsters; children with neurological and health problems including such conditions as cerebral palsy, epilepsy, juvenile diabetes, muscular dystrophy, and orthopedic defects; multiply handicapped children, and culturally different pupils.

Throughout the text, a multidisciplinary approach is maintained; particular attention is paid to the psychological, medical, sociological and educational aspects of the various categories of exceptionality. Within each chapter the following material is discussed for each condition under consideration: definition and classification; prevalence and etiology; diagnosis and identification; developmental consequences, intervention, and implications for the immediate family.

Each chapter includes case studies or developmental profiles as concrete illustration of issues covered in the text. Glossary terms are marked for ease of reference.

Margret Winzer
Sally Rogow
Charlette David

ACKNOWLEDGEMENTS

Acknowledgements are due to the many people who contributed to the writing of this text. In particular, the teachers and their students whose composite profiles illustrate the text material and add a special quality to the explanations of the problems and their solutions. The parents and families of handicapped children who have shared their joys as well as their sorrows deserve a very special mention. Their stories add immediacy as well as reality, and highlight the personal courage as well as the anguish associated with severely disabling conditions. In particular, Dr. Rogow would like to express her personal gratitude to the parents of "Eddy". Their story is one of triumph, and shows once again that never giving up is the key to building a future for handicapped children. The authors would also like to thank the parents of the National Association of Parents of Visually Impaired Children and the International Institute for the Visually Impaired 0-7 Years for their generosity in sharing materials and insights, and the B.C. Association for Mentally Handicapped Persons for the pioneering work in the development of community life for severely disabled children and adults. Their dedication and persistence are building an active parent network and providing support. The authors would also like tothank their students for reading the material and providing helpful criticisms and suggestions. In particular, Ms. Sharon Paul, a Native indian student teacher contributed insight and understanding of the attitudes of Canada's Native people towards their handicapped members.

We would also like to thank the following for research help:

Jeanette Andrews, a member of the Faculty of Education at the University of British Columbia, was kind enough to write an autobiographical sketch of her experience of physical disability and its consequences.

Dr. Patricia Baird, Head of the Department of Medical Genetics at the University of British Columbia was kind enough to provide information about neural tube defects.

Elsie de Bruijn, Assistant Head of the Woodward Biological Medical Library at the University of British Columbia was very helpful in gathering material on the prevalence of a variety of conditions.

Collin Cox of the Brighouse School in Richmond, B.C., Don Dawson, Principal of Oakridge School in Vancouver, B.C., and G.E. (Bud) Phillips, Acting Executive Director of the Society for Crippled Children and Adults of Manitoba, contributed many appropriate photographs.

Karen Koch, a representative of Child Abuse Research and Education (C.A.R.E.) provided information on child abuse.

Margo Marshall and Louise de Chevigny, who are members of the National Film Board in Montreal, provided us with an extensive printout of appropriate films and tapes of exceptional children and adults.

Jo-Anne Naslund, reference librarian in the Curriculum Library at U.B.C., had been both helpful and supportive in the development of the text, and wrote the section on research guides for the Student Workbook.

Helen Adams, and the teachers and children at Jericho Hill School for the Deaf.

David Illerbrun, University of Saskatchewan, J.C. Croll, University of New Brunswick, and Denis Shackel, University of Toronto, reviewed all or part of the manuscript.

We would also like to thank the following individuals for their personal contributions: Marnie Darnforth, Donna Haqq, Betty Ife, Colin Laine, Perry Leslie, Linda Lewis, Tara Lynn Wilson.

Mrs. Margaret Baskette who typed multiple versions of the text merits a very special acknowledgement. With humor and graciousness, she spent countless hours typing and retyping. We thank her wholeheartedly. To the editors and publisher, we extend a special thanks for their patience, support and belief in the need to prepare a Canadian text.

1

Introduction and Overview

INTRODUCTION

All parents want their children to be born healthy, normal, and perfect. For most, the wish is fulfilled. Their children are born healthy and well-formed, even if perfection eludes them.

Some parents, however, must reduce the expectations they held for their new infant. These are the parents who face the tragedy of a handicapped child. Their children are not like other children. They are born with problems that potentially threaten their physical, intellectual, social, or emotional functioning.

About three percent of newborn infants have a handicap that can be considered a developmental delay or developmental disability. Another three percent are born with significant medical conditions capable of causing medical or social handicaps (Berlin, 1983). For other children, problems appear later as a result of childhood disease or accident. During the school years, approximately 15.5 percent of the Canadian school-age population will be considered exceptional. These children will require special education services for at least some part of their school career (Canada, Council of Ministers, 1983).

In the past few decades, the prospects for the exceptional child have altered dramatically. We have made major gains in our ability to provide sophisticated services for exceptional children. In medicine, great strides have been made in the prevention, intervention, and care of handicapping conditions. Technological advances have provided a variety of devices and aids to help exceptional children. In education, significant philosophical changes are being considered in the areas of school responsibility, program delivery, and program implementation for special education.

Today, special education is an exciting professional area, alive with new ideas. It is no longer an unknown quantity, a poor cousin of regular education. In the past few years, special education has come of age as a vital component of the public education system. It has broadened its scope and drawn many more children into the orbit of the public schools. It has also faced teachers with new challenges and assigned them new roles.

Outside the field of education, exceptional individuals are coming to be seen in a more positive light. Throughout Canada, public policies are changing, to develop potential and make better use of aptitudes among the handicapped population. A recent emphasis on the dignity and worth of each person is bringing wider acceptance of the exceptional individual in society.

CHAPTER ONE

Introduction to exceptional children

MARGRET WINZER

No longer can special education be regarded as an isolated sanctuary for a few children requiring protection from the demands of mainstream education. It is everybody's business – that of the regular classroom teacher no less than that of the specialist.

(Kendall, 1985)

In a philosophical and humanitarian sense, all children are special. All children have certain strengths and weaknesses. However, in most children, the strengths outweigh the weaknesses. In this text, we are concerned with the other children, those for whom the balance of strengths and weaknesses may tip the other way.

This book is about **exceptional children**, those who have difficulty in realizing their full human potential. Their intellectual, emotional, physical, or social performance falls below or rises above that of other children. The differences may be related to physical, psychological, cognitive, emotional, or social factors, or a combination of these.

Exceptional children require skilled intervention and special care from trained professionals. This is one reason why we recognize gifted and talented children as exceptional. They too need specialized help from professionals to fully develop their gifts and talents.

SPECIAL EDUCATION

In educational terms, children are only considered exceptional when their educational program must be altered to meet their unique needs. They must demonstrate a clear need for support services to reach their full human potential.

Special education means instruction that is specially designed to meet the unique needs of the exceptional child. The onus for direct instruction is placed on teachers, but they are not alone in their efforts. Psychologists, speech therapists, counsellors, and other professionals work with teachers to help them plan the best possible education for each exceptional child. These people form part of an interdisciplinary team to offer **related services**, those services that permit an exceptional child to benefit from special education. Related services include transportation, physical and occupational therapy, and diagnostic medical services.

THE MAJOR CATEGORIES OF EXCEPTIONALITY

A central theme of this book is that no two children are alike. Exceptional children should be viewed first as individuals, and then as people who differ from the norm in some way. A child's functional level and behaviour should be the critical components analyzed for intervention, but they should not supply a label that assigns the child to a specific category of exceptionality.

Despite our distrust of labels, however, this text is organized around categories of exceptionalities. These categories are widely used in Canada and offer the most efficient means of organizing the material. Moreover, much research is directed toward one or more of these categories. Therefore, although we distrust the traditional groupings, we are, to some extent, still bound by them.

There is relatively little standardization in the study of exceptional children. There is not a single consistent and universally accepted method of describing different kinds of children. Some assess differences according to how development deviates from the norm. Others classify differences in terms of some underlying organic or functional cause. Still others describe them in terms of educational functioning and achievement.

In general, the special traits of exceptional individuals fall into the following categories:

- Intellectual differences, which include children who are intellectually superior and those who are mentally retarded.

- Sensory handicaps, which include children with auditory impairments and those with visual problems.

- Communication disorders, which include children with speech and language problems and those with learning disabilities.

- Behaviour disorders, which include social maladjustment, emotional disturbance, and childhood psychoses.

- Physical handicaps and impaired health, which include children with neurological defects, orthopedic conditions, birth defects, developmental disabilities, and conditions that are the result of infection and disease.

- Multiple and severe handicaps, which include individuals with various combinations of impairments, such as cerebral palsy and mental retardation, or deafness and blindness.

CLASSIFICATION OF EXCEPTIONAL CHILDREN

Although conventional categories of exceptionality have evolved over the past thirty years, exceptional children are constantly being reconceptualized, reconsidered, and renamed. Many disciplines contribute to research and intervention for exceptional children — education, social work, medicine, genetics, and psychology are only a few. The professionals allied with special education all tend to have a different way of looking at the exceptional child. Therefore, they tend to use a slightly different framework for classification.

The use of discrete categories for exceptional children tends to oversimplify the facts. Although individual children may share a common exceptionality, they do not form a homogeneous group. Each disability ranges from mild to severe. A mildly mentally retarded child, functions quite differently than a child with severe mental retardation.

A subgroup of mildly mentally retarded children is extremely heterogeneous. The children exhibit different behaviours and are affected by the disability in various ways. On the other hand, children who are classified as having different disabilities often exhibit similar behaviour. For example, the mildly mentally-retarded child and the learning-disabled youngster may behave in much the same way.

Many exceptional children are difficult to classify because they do not fall easily into one specific category. This causes considerable overlap in the classification of handicapping conditions. Moreover, many exceptional children have more than one difficulty; according to conservative estimates, for example, twenty-five percent of all deaf children have at least one additional handicapping condition (Flathouse, 1979). Multiply handicapped children are often classified according to their primary disability. Therefore, a deaf child with an emotional problem is classified as hearing-impaired and may receive services designed for deaf children. The emotional problem is presumed to be secondary.

DEFINITIONS OF EXCEPTIONAL CHILDREN

Although exceptionality can be defined in many ways, some descriptors are more socially useful than others. *Exceptional* is an inclusive term, because it encompasses gifted children as well as those who function below the norm in some way. *Handicapped* is a term widely used by the general public. A **handicapped person** is one who has difficulty adjusting to the environment because of intellectual, physical, emotional, or social problems. Other terms include *disabled, impaired, atypical, dysfunctional,* and *special-needs.* The description *high-risk* is also gaining popular use.

Although they have slightly different meanings, all these terms are often used synonymously with *exceptional.* Generally, **disabled** refers to any person whose functioning is reduced as a result of a significant physical, learning, or social problem. *Disabled* is most commonly used to refer to physical problems such as the loss of a limb. *Impaired* and *dysfunctional* imply damage that will affect some area of functioning; they are usually applied to sensory problems, such as hearing loss. *Atypical* refers to the individual differing from the norm in some area. *Special-needs* is an educational term that generally refers to exceptional children who can profit from special education services. **High-risk children** are those who may, in future, develop some problem that will affect their functioning. For example, a pre-term infant who was born after a long and arduous labour would be considered high-risk.

Today's terminology, both specific and general, is relatively non-stigmatizing and gentle. We no longer use such terms as *deaf and dumb*, *feeble-minded*, or *idiot*, *imbecile*, and *moron*. We have adopted less emotionally laden terms that allow greater precision.

PREVALENCE OF EXCEPTIONAL CHILDREN

An estimated 500 to 600 million persons, approximately one-eighth of the world's population, can be regarded as disabled. Catastrophic as this figure seems, it may nevertheless be conservative. The incidence of largely preventable diseases, such as water-borne blindness, tuberculosis, and leprosy, may be much greater than present figures suggest. Millions more suffer from the chronic debilitating conditions that stem from malnutrition, impure water, and inadequate sanitation. In all, the number of persons, world-wide, with severe disabilities is simply staggering (Ward, 1984).

In recent years, many handicapping conditions have become preventable, or susceptible to treatment. *(origin unknown)*

In 1979, the Department of Health and Welfare estimated that there were approximately 2.3 million disabled persons in Canada. This figure represented about 9.8 percent of the Canadian population (Directions, 1982). In the United States, approximately 35 million people are considered exceptional.

A precise determination of incidence and prevalence rates for exceptional children and adolescents is very difficult. **Incidence** refers to the number of new cases of a particular condition ascertained over a given period of time, usually a year. **Prevalence** applies to the total number of existing cases, old and new. Prevalence is also used to refer to the percentage or proportion of the population that falls into a given category.

In general, estimates of the number of children with some identifiable special condition vary widely. In Canada figures are especially difficult to obtain. According to the Commission on Emotional and Learning Disorders in Children (Roberts and Lazure, 1970), one Canadian child in eight has an emotional or learning disorder that will prevent optimal development unless some intervention takes place. This meant that about 12 percent of the population up to nineteen years of age needed special help at some time during their school career. More recent figures (Canada, Council of Ministers, 1983) have raised the numbers to approximately 15.5 percent of the school age population. However, this figure varies greatly in cross-country estimates. Up to 20 percent of students in the Yukon may require some form of special education (Alberta 1980). Ontario figures, on the other hand, have been placed at 12 percent (Nikiforuk, 1981).

Exhibit 1-1 presents the estimated prevalence of children in Canada who belong to the major categories of exceptionality.

Exhibit 1-1 Prevalence of exceptional students by type of handicap

Type of Exceptionality	*Number of Students*	*Percentage of Special Education Total*	*Percentage School-age Population*
Mentally Handicapped	63 356	11.3%	1.75%
Learning Disabled	159 159	28.4%	4.41%
Behaviourally/ Emotionally Disabled	27 298	4.9%	0.78%
Speech Impaired	43 914	7.9%	1.22%
Sensorially Disabled, Visual	2 029	0.4%	0.06%
Sensorially Disabled, Hearing	5 231	0.9%	0.14%
Physically Handicapped	2 971	0.5%	0.08%
Multiple Handicapped	11 369	2.0%	0.31%
Other	244 390	43.7%	6.77%
Total	559 717	100.0%	15.50%

(Canada, Council of Ministers, 1983.)

Many factors contribute to the difficulty of obtaining accurate Canadian prevalence figures. Problems stem from the varying definitions and descriptions of disabilities, the methods of data collection, the interpretation of the data, and the lack of a national survey. In addition, social factors related to stigmatization and public perception inhibit accurate prevalence estimates.

Definition problems

When we discuss exceptional children, we face serious problems of definition. Not only do the disciplines allied to special education regard exceptional children in different ways, but special education itself uses many vague and inconsistent definitions. Without clear definitions it is almost impossible to estimate prevalence.

School systems tend to interpret a child's condition according to the services they provide. A child may be called learning-disabled in one school district, and counted as a low achiever in another.

Changing diagnoses

A diagnosis of a handicapping condition is not, nor should it be, immutable. A diagnosis that is correct today could easily be inappropriate tomorrow. Frequently, children who are handicapped by speech defects, behaviour disorders, or learning disabilities improve to such an extent that they are no longer considered disabled (Hallahan and Kauffman, 1982).

Multiple handicaps

Even if a clear definition of an exceptional condition could be agreed upon, confusion can still arise about the classification of particular children. Many children have more than one pertinent set of characteristics: a child might be mentally retarded and hearing-impaired, or speech-handicapped and blind. Such children are often classified according to their major handicap, although this is not always easy to ascertain.

Problems of early identification

Although some conditions, such as Down's syndrome, can be evident from birth, others do not manifest themselves until much later. Mild mental retardation, for example, may not be identified until the child has to confront the complexities of reading and writing in the classroom. Learning disabilities are most often identified in relation to academic functioning. As a result, estimates of mildly handicapping conditions are highest during the school years. These estimates drop as mildly handicapped individuals take their places as adults in the community.

The stigma of identification

Some parents are reluctant to have their child identified as exceptional. They may not report a condition, or they may opt for a different category. For example, many parents and teachers find the term *learning disability* far preferable to *mild mental retardation* or *brain damage*.

Survey problems and sampling errors

Survey problems result when researchers use varied definitions of an exceptionality. Surveys can also be misleading when figures from a small area are extrapolated to the rest of the country. In Canada, no national survey on the prevalence of exceptionalities has yet been undertaken.

Unidentified populations

Any attempt to estimate the incidence rate in a large birth cohort for a relatively common disorder amost invariably is based on results that do not take into account some affected individuals (Trimble and Baird, 1978). Low-incidence handicaps, such as severe retardation, serious physical impairment, or blindness, usually involve more professional intervention than high-incidence conditions, such as mild mental retardation. As a result, the low-incidence handicaps are more likely to be reported.

Given the geographical vastness of Canada, it is not surprising that many exceptional children go unreported. For example, hearing loss is endemic in the north, especially in the Eastern Arctic (Watters, 1980). However, these prevalence figures are not generally known or included in the estimates.

Lack of national survey

At this time, no truly national survey of the handicapped population has been undertaken. However, the Canadian government has recently begun to develop a data base and co-ordinate provincial estimates to analyze the characteristics of the disabled population. Statistics Canada has been making this information available since September 1985 (Secretary of State, 1982).

CHARACTERISTICS OF EXCEPTIONAL CHILDREN

Exceptional children are those who deviate in some way from what society calls normal. However, the norm itself encompasses a range of exceptionalities within which everyone deviates to some degree. No two individuals are exactly alike. We all have certain strengths, and we all have some limitations on our mental and physical abilities. Some of us have problems learning a foreign language, others forget directions or people's faces. For most of us, a perfect tennis backhand is an unreachable goal.

Like everyone else, exceptional individuals are unique. Exceptional children come in assorted shapes and sizes, and display various temperaments, personalities, abilities, and potential. At the same time, exceptional individuals share many attitudes, needs, and perceptions with everyone else. They desire acceptance, approval, and affection, as much as do their non-handicapped peers.

The degree to which an exceptional child can learn and participate in normal activity depends on a number of factors. Many of these are related less to the handicap than to forces outside the child. Factors include:

- The reaction of the child's nuclear and extended family to the condition, and the family's acceptance and willingness to focus on the child's positive potential.

- The time of diagnosis and intervention, and the appropriateness of intervention, whether medical, psychological, educational, or social.
- The related services available for both the child and the family.
- The amount of acceptance by the community.

Exceptional children, or adults, should not be treated with sympathy and pity. Instead, they should be accepted and recognized as individuals with certain limitations. Exceptional children derive little benefit from learning social skills if anxious neighbours will not let their children play with them. Training and encouragement must be reinforced by social acceptance.

SPECIAL EDUCATION IN CANADA

Special education exists to aid exceptional children in developing their full human potential. The past thirty years have witnessed a growing interest and involvement in the field. Today it is assuming increasing importance within education as a whole. At a time when school enrolments are declining, special education enrolments are on the rise.

In 1966, an estimated 2 percent of children across Canada were enrolled in special education programs (Statistics, 1966). The Commission on Emotional and Learning Disorders in Children (Roberts and Lazure, 1970) revealed the inadequacies of provisions for exceptional children in Canada. In 1971, further documentation found that the percentage of children served by the various provinces ranged from .4 to 6 percent. This compared poorly with the estimated 12 percent of children in need of services (Council for Exceptional Children, 1971).

The late 1960s and the 1970s saw a phenomenal growth of special education services in Canada. In British Columbia, between 1960 and 1970, special education grew 389 percent; this was six times the province's 64 percent growth in net enrolment (Ballance, Kendall, and Saywell, 1972). By 1976-77, 12.3 percent of all school-aged children in Ontario were receiving some type of special education (Reich, 1981). Between 1950 and 1979, ranks of special education teachers in Alberta swelled from 18 to 1,720 (Church, 1980). This vast increase arose largely because new provisions were made for mildly handicapped children who had previously received no special help at all (Kendall, 1980; Whyte, 1980).

The earliest expansion of special education was due to simple demographics. The post-war baby boom increased the number of handicapped children, and advances in medical technology kept more children alive and limited degrees of impairment. The polio epidemic of the 1950s and the rubella epidemic of the 1960s generated still more demand for special education. During these years, the concept of "learning disability" also began to be widely applied.

More recently, advances in special education have been assisted by continuing efforts by boards of education and other agencies to increase the universality of special education services. There has also been a trend toward earlier identification and intervention with exceptional children. Chiefly, however, advances in the 1970s resulted from changing social conceptions regarding the rights of the handicapped and their role in the community. This philosophy, called *normalization*, will be fully discussed in the next section.

Although major advances have taken place, special education in Canada has not yet fully emerged as a well-defined field. Few Canadians have a major interest in special education research. Canada's first full professor in special education was not appointed until 1959, at the University of British Columbia (Strothers, 1959). In 1980, the Canadian Society for the Study of Education, with a membership of about 1400, listed only 29 people who expressed a research interest in special education. Only 18 of these had doctorates and were employed in a university (Reich, 1981).

Special education draws heavily on knowledge and theories from a number of core disciplines. As an integrative professional area, it cuts across a spectrum of services. Special education makes use of many different fields of knowledge, and depends upon the techniques, the concepts, and the practices of several allied disciplines.

In Canada, special education has followed the American model (McMurray, 1980). Canadian educational issues, both administrative and curricular, are directly influenced by events, philosophies and pedagogy from the United States. As a result, Canadians have a touchstone against which to critically assess their progress, and greater freedom to meld practices and philosophies to Canada's unique educational system.

A field as diverse as special education is bound to reveal controversial issues and to reflect major trends and movements. The following is an overview of some of the issues, problems, and trends that characterize special education today. We will return to these concepts in greater detail in later chapters.

- Normalization, which advocates deinstitutionalizing children and returning them to their homes and communities.
- Mainstreaming, which promotes the educability of all children, and questions the effectiveness of special classes, labelling, and traditional classifications of exceptional children.
- Litigation and legislation directed toward the social and educational welfare of exceptional individuals.
- Early identification and early intervention for exceptional children and their families.
- The value and necessity of parents as partners in the education process.
- Helping exceptional children with teams drawn from a number of disciplines.

Changing ideas of exceptionality

Social attitudes concerning the education, care, and training of exceptional children generally reflect more general cultural attitudes concerning the obligations of a society to its individual citizens. Historically, special education has been a service-delivery system that adhered to contemporary social attitudes toward deviance. When the old adage "out of sight, out of mind" held sway, exceptional persons were placed in institutions for their care and training.

Traditionally, North American society has not demonstrated a high tolerance for exceptional persons. In the past, they were stigmatized and stereotyped by prevailing attitudes toward their disabilities. Many people were directed into roles that were thought to be consonant with their handicaps. Blind people were trained as piano tuners, deaf people for printing and cosmetology, crippled people for switchboards and answering-services, retarded people for janitorial jobs, and so forth.

Undoubtedly, there has been a significant increase in public awareness and understanding of exceptional individuals in recent decades. A newly evolving social philosophy has emphasized the value of the individual and the rights of every citizen. Most educators now agree that all children, exceptionality notwithstanding, have the right to an appropriate education at public expense.

In general, our society has shifted from qualitative to quantitative conceptions of exceptionality. The qualitative model held that the handicapped were different and deviant — they learned, perceived, and thought in ways that were unlike the normal. The quantitative model views these differences as a matter of degree, not kind — exceptional people develop and function much as others do, but their progress may be slower and their achievements more restricted. Today, most researchers agree that cognitive and linguistic development and functioning among the handicapped is qualitatively similar to that among the non-handicapped, but may take place at a slower rate (Telford and Sawrey, 1981).

Although major, positive changes have occurred in public attitudes toward exceptional people, there is still much to be done and few agencies to do it. In Canada, 1.4 million disabled Canadians are of working age. Of these, 45 000 are in institutions, 20 000 are in sheltered workshops, and 1.37 million are in the community. Over half of the disabled adults in the community are unemployed (Directions, 1982).

Prejudice and discrimination against mentally retarded people is ingrained in our culture. It cannot be overcome by simply providing more skills to the mentally retarded. At the structural level, changes are needed to ensure their economic stability. At the personal level, people must be taught to embrace those who are different (Lusthaus, Hanrahan, and Lusthaus, 1979). Unless a substantial portion of the public recognizes the needs of the exceptional, they will not be provided with the facilities, programs, and opportunities necessary to realize their potential.

Many Canadians are working toward greater acceptance and understanding. In June 1982, the Secretary of State announced major new strategies to help exceptional people. These included a new employment strategy and other expanded-aid programs aimed at removing social and economic barriers against disabled and handicapped people. These programs encompass:

- An integrated employment strategy for disabled persons. This is to include, in a five-year plan, the development of a disabled persons' directorate in Canada's Employment and Immigration National headquarters and the creation of specialized counselling centres in selected cities.

- Improvements to make dwellings more accessible to the handicapped. These are to be undertaken by Canada Mortgage and Housing Corporation.

- The expansion, under the Secretary of State, of existing technical and financial aid to organizations for the handicapped (Secretary of State, 1982).

Normalization

Of all the issues important today in the area of exceptionality, normalization is the most hotly debated. **Normalization** is the philosophical belief that all exceptional individuals, no matter what their levels and types of handicap, should be provided with an education and living environment as close to normal as possible. Advocates of normalization range from those who want to mainstream mildly handicapped children into regular classrooms to those who propose radical deinstitutionalization. Under deinstitutionalization, severely and profoundly handicapped people would be mainstreamed into the home and community rather than provided for in large residential institutions.

Today's efforts to provide surroundings, opportunities, and programs much like those provided for non-handicapped persons originated in Denmark. Normalization was first successfully implemented in the Scandinavian countries (Wolfensberger, 1972). Benge Nirje, who introduced the concept, defined normalization as "making available to all mentally retarded people patterns of life and conditions of everyday living which are as close as possible to the regular circumstances of society" (Nirje 1979, p. 173).

The normalization movement provides guidelines for the treatment of handicapped people, as well as concrete suggestions for action. Its adherents want society to regard handicapped persons as individuals and to treat them fairly and humanely. The major goal of normalization is a normal family and community life for all individuals. However, some limits must be recognized; these are determined by the availability of services for the handicapped, by community attitudes, and by the potential of each handicapped individual (Anderson, Greer, and Dietrich, 1976).

Deinstitutionalization

Normalization, as a process, is intended to replace institutionalization. Until recently, the primary mode of educating severely handicapped children was in the residential school. First established in Canada in the 1860s, these schools were referred to as asylums, institutions, colonies, or training schools. The establishment of special institutions for exceptional children was well-intentioned, but it served to remove exceptional persons from the mainstream of society. Moreover, institutionalization produced several negative by-products — regimentation; structured routines; impersonal treatment; lack of privacy; limited independence; and often loss of contact with the family.

Today we are rejecting the policies that once subjected the severely handicapped to life-long institutionalization. Instead, a normalization policy offers the handicapped the chance of a normal life routine, normal developmental experiences, independent choices, and the right to live, work, and play in normal surroundings. The handicapped are encouraged to remain in their own communities through the availability of foster homes, group homes, hostels, community-training centres, day-care facilities, and community-based social services.

Mainstreaming

The principle of normalization has been extended to the school-age child, resulting in a parallel educational process known as mainstreaming. The basic goal of mainstreaming is to provide the most efficient and appropriate education possible for each child.

Mainstreaming represents both an ideal and an ongoing process. It has been defined as "the temporal, instructional, and social integration of eligible exceptional children with normal peers based on an ongoing, individually determined, educational planning and programming process [that] requires clarification of responsibility among regular and special education administrative, instructional, and supportive personnel (Kaufman, Gottlieb, Agard, and Kukic, 1975 p. 47).

Mainstreaming and integration are two sides of one coin. The philosophy of mainstreaming is manifested in the process of integration. However, the two terms are often used synonymously, and are used this way in this text. Mainstreaming is the integration and instruction of children with learning, behaviour, physical, or other problems in regular classrooms. Children are released from alternate, segregated programs for short or long periods, depending on their capacities. Their progress is determined by their individual strengths and needs.

When special education was first initiated in Canada, exceptional children were educated chiefly in institutional settings. During the first decades of this century, special segregated classes were started in many schools, especially in urban centres. Children were labelled according to their disability, and then placed in special classes consistent with the classification. Segregation was rationalized on the grounds that:

- The public school system could not provide for grossly deviant children.
- The low incidence of certain disabilities in the population made it difficult to group children locally for educational purposes.
- Teachers needed very specialized training.
- Certain categories of exceptional children were happier with their own kind.
- Specialized equipment, such as braillers and hearing aids, could not easily be provided by the regular school system.
- Some children, such as the severely mentally retarded and the multiply handicapped, required custodial care (Roberts and Lazure, 1970).

Educators also believed that segregated classes could offer handicapped students the most benefits. A low student-teacher ratio could afford more individualized instruction for each child. Homogeneous groupings could enable the teacher to concentrate on fewer teaching strategies. Because the academic environment would be less competitive, the students' self-esteem would be improved. Segregated classes could also provide a remedial program to send some children into the regular classroom.

In reality, few children graduated to regular classrooms. By the late 1960s, educators expressed grave dissatisfaction with segregated schooling. Many questioned whether special classes could be justified for all exceptional children. In Canada, the philosophical underpinnings of desegregation appeared in the Hall-Dennis Report (1968); the Report of the Commission on Emotional and Learning Disorders in Children (Roberts and Lazure, 1970); the 1971 Report on Standards for Education of Exceptional Children in Canada (Hardy, McLeod, Minto, Perkins, and Quance, 1971); and the 1976 report on Canadian education prepared by the Organization for Economic Co-operation and Development (Csapo, 1984).

A number of other factors combined to bring about the current emphasis on mainstreaming. These include:

- A recognition that it is more humane to treat exceptional children as normally as possible.
- The failure of numerous research studies to establish the effectiveness of special classes for the handicapped (Bradfield, Brown, Kaplan, Rickert, and Stannard, 1973; Bruininks, Rynders, and Gross, 1974; Dunn, 1968; Gallagher, 1972; Myers, 1976; Reynolds and Birch, 1977).
- Realization that factors such as race, social class, personality, and managability had been operative in special-class placement.
- A recognition of the potentially pejorative effects of officially labelling and categorizing children.
- A growing awareness that the commonly used categories of exceptionality are inadequate for programming purposes.

The mainstreaming movement has drawn many more exceptional children into the orbit of the public schools. However, while many exceptional children can function in the regular classroom, others require a special setting. Before an exceptional child is placed in a regular education program, the special needs of the child must be carefully considered. One child may perform best by spending seventy percent of instructional time in a regular classroom. Another child might need to receive only five percent of instruction in a regular class and the rest in a special setting.

Children suffer from a wide range of handicapping conditions in varying degrees of severity. They also need different types and degrees of assistance at various age levels. As a result, many different kinds and combinations of assistance programs are required to meet their needs. Exceptional children need a continuum of educational services, a cascade that will accommodate all of them.

Figure 1-1 A diagrammatic model of a cascade of services.

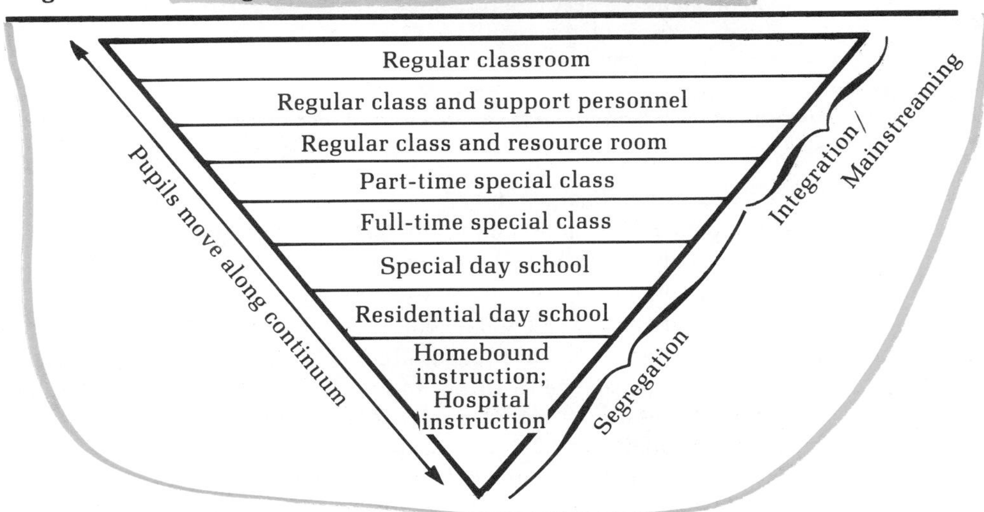

Although mainstreaming has become the dominant ideology in special education, no other concept seems so fraught with confusion and misconceptions. Exhibit 1-2 outlines the major points that define mainstreaming.

Exhibit 1-2 Mainstreaming.

Mainstreaming does:	*Mainstreaming does not:*
■ Attempt to place the exceptional child with peers as much as possible.	■ Eliminate all special classes and special education teachers.
■ Permit the exceptional child to receive necessary special help while enrolled in a regular class.	■ Get rid of special education support services.
■ Require the services of a number of professionals working together to assess the child's needs, plan the program, implement the program, evaluate its effectiveness, and make changes as needed.	■ Indiscriminately dump all children from special classes back into regular classrooms.
■ Permit modification to be made to the regular curriculum.	■ Stop at physically integrating exceptional children without trying to integrate them socially or intellectually.
■ Encourage special education teachers to adopt new roles as consultants to regular classroom teachers.	■ Force exceptional children to remain in regular classrooms without needed support services.
■ Unite the skills of regular education and special education so that all children have equal opportunities.	
■ Adapt itself to a variety of settings such as a combination of the regular classroom and the resource room.	

Integrating exceptional children

Under a policy of mainstreaming, special education stops functioning as a device for sorting exceptional children according to assigned labels. Instead, it offers a range of services that enable the tailoring of educational programs to meet individual needs. For mainstreaming to succeed, the regular classroom teacher requires many support personnel, and relies heavily on the special education teacher or the resource-room teacher. The classroom teacher can also look to support from the principal, the psychologist, the itinerant teachers, the speech therapist, the language therapist, and such allied childcare personnel as audiologists and school nurses.

Exhibit 1-3 shows the percentage of exceptional students enrolled in integrated programs as of 1983. Since that time, this percentage has steadily increased.

Exhibit 1-3 Percentage of exceptional students in segregated and integrated programs, by type of handicap.

Type of Exceptionality	*Segregated*		*Integrated*	
	Number	*Percentage*	*Number*	*Percentage*
Mentally Handicapped	48 802	77.0%	14 554	23.0%
Learning Disabled	39 041	24.5%	120 118	75.5%
Behaviourally/Emotionally Disabled	12 174	44.6%	15 124	55.4%
Speech Impaired	1 410	3.2%	42 504	96.8%
Sensorially Disabled, Visual	414	20.4%	1 615	79.6%
Sensorially Disabled, Hearing	1 917	36.6%	3 314	63.4%
Physically Handicapped	1 115	37.5%	1 856	62.5%
Multiple Handicapped	9 564	84.1%	1 805	15.9%
Other	15 633	6.4%	228 757	93.6%

(Canada, Council of Ministers, 1983.)

The mere physical presence of exceptional children in the regular classroom does not ensure their learning. Each child must be socially and instructionally integrated with other children. The exceptional child should be encouraged to participate in normal activities with non-handicapped peers, yet should not have to tackle experiences that are too difficult.

To integrate an exceptional child into the regular classroom, some modification to the regular curriculum must be made. Adding or reducing assigned tasks is not enough. Each child requires a unique plan of action, often called the Individual Education Plan, or IEP.

The Individual Education Plan is a management tool to ensure that each child's education program is appropriate to the child's specific needs. The IEP also ensures that the program is implemented and monitored. Simply stated, the IEP is a map that charts the child's progress. It outlines the child's short-term and long-term goals, and describes the methods and techniques that will be used to achieve them. The program also outlines the responsibilities of various people, such as the classroom teacher, the resource-room teacher, or the speech therapist, who will help the child along the way.

Individual Education Plans appear in many formats. Exhibit 1-4 outlines the components found in most plans.

Exhibit 1-4 Components of an Individual Education Plan (IEP).

The child's present level of functioning	Includes academic background, social adaptation, vocational skills, psychomotor development, and self-help skills.
Long-range (annual) goals	Broad statements that stress specific areas of need, the direction of desirable change, and an estimated level of accomplishment within a school year.
Short-term (weekly or monthly) goals	The steps that will be taken to accomplish the long-term objectives.
Related services	Lists special education and other related services needed by the child. The amount of time set aside for these services is usually specified.
Instructional materials	Includes special program kits, suggested approaches, and teaching techniques.
Date for services to begin	Includes the length of time anticipated for objectives to be achieved, and outlines details on program monitoring.
Educational environment	Tells who will be responsible for each component: the regular classroom teacher; the resource-room teacher; the school counsellor; and so on.
Evaluation	Evaluates the child's progress and development, as well as the usefulness and appropriateness of the selected program and related services. Through close monitoring, evaluation is an ongoing process.

Barriers to successful mainstreaming

The profound impact of mainstreaming has been met with relief by some groups and alarm by others. Even though mainstreaming seems the best way to normalize exceptional children, major barriers continue to exist. Some of these are simply physical, such as lack of school ramps or elevators for wheelchair-bound children. More problematic, however, are the barriers created by people's attitudes and actions.

Sometimes parents resist the notion of mainstreaming. The parents of non-handicapped children may believe their offspring are being denied teacher-time and instruction. Some may hold traditional prejudices about exceptional children. A few parents of exceptional children also oppose the idea of mainstreaming. They believe their children's needs can be better met in a segregated setting with a structured curriculum and a lower pupil-teacher ratio. Sometimes, they fear for the social consequences of integration, and anticipate stigmatization and rejection for their children.

The ultimate success of mainstreaming depends on the school staff, especially the regular classroom teachers. Classroom teachers carry the primary responsibility for the integration of the exceptional child. For most, the role of mainstreaming implementor is new. Teachers are expected to take on additional work loads and anxieties, and to devote extra time to assessment and referral. They must also find time to work with a team to develop, implement and evaluate mainstreaming programs.

If classroom teachers do not believe in the rationale behind mainstreaming, then the benefits are likely to be negligible. Research studies have demonstrated that classroom teachers are not overwhelmingly supportive of the concept of mainstreaming (Barngrover, 1971; Blazovik, 1972; Hudson, Graham, and Warner, 1979; Winzer, 1984a). A 1979 survey in the Yukon, for example, showed that, in general, one-third of regular classroom teachers rejected integration outright, another third lacked understanding of mainstreaming, and one-third accepted the idea with reservations (Albert, 1980).

Some classroom teachers feel that exceptional children will dilute their program (Bradfield, Brown, Kaplan, Rickert, and Stannard, 1973; Hudson, Graham, and Warner, 1979). Others believe mainstreaming will decrease their effectiveness (Major, 1961), cause classroom disruption (Hudson, Graham, and Warner, 1979; Vacc and Kirst, 1977), or demand a disproportionate amount of time (Brulle, Barton, Barton and Wharton, 1983). Teachers also seem to accept some exceptional children more easily than others. As a group, teachers are most supportive toward the integration of learning-disabled children, and least willing to accept mentally-retarded children in their classrooms. They are equivocal about those categorized as emotionally disturbed (Guerin, 1979; Hirshoren and Burton, 1979; Moore and Fine, 1978; Shotel, Iano, and McGettigan, 1972; Vacc and Kirst, 1977; Williams and Algozzine, 1979).

The attitudes that teachers hold toward exceptional children and mainstreaming are critical. These attitudes influence those held by non-handicapped children in the classroom (Lapp, 1957). They also influence the extent to which exceptional children are truly integrated with their class, and reap the concomitant academic, social, and emotional benefits (Baker and Gottlieb, 1980).

Lack of special education experience appears to contribute the most to fears held by educators (Kraft, 1973; Payne and Murray, 1974). As a large body of research shows, regular classroom teachers seem more willing to teach and program for exceptional children if they have information and training about exceptionalities or some previous exposure to exceptional people (Alexander and Strain, 1978; Leyser, Abrams, and Lipscomb, 1982; Payne and Murray, 1974; Sanche, Haines, and Van Hesteren, 1982; Stephens and Braun, 1980; Vacc and Kirst, 1977; Winzer, 1984).

Exhibit 1-5 presents some general tips for teachers of integrated children. It also offers some ideas for administrators and those in allied disciplines.

Exhibit 1-5 Tips for teachers, administrators, and allied professionals dealing with integrated special students.

Tips for teachers:

- Project a positive attitude when working with the child. Optimism is catching, as are negative attitudes.
- Avoid comparing the child to others. View the exceptional child as an individual, and praise all accomplishments.
- Encourage the child to talk to you. Show a genuine concern for the child's interests, aspirations, and fears.
- Reinforce behaviours that are not necessarily academic. Good manners, friendliness, and sharing also deserve positive comment.
- Assign responsibilities to the child. Encourage the child to become part of the class by helping in classroom chores.
- Use group work or the buddy system to involve the child with others in the class. Define success in terms of the individual child rather than intra-class competition. Stress that participation, fun, and sharing are more important than winning.

Tips for administrators and allied professionals:

- Design programs that allow exceptional pupils to truly participate in the instructional and social activities of the mainstream.
- Discuss the child's handicap with other children in the class, especially if some device such as a hearing aid is used.
- Remember that the degree to which exceptional children can be integrated is largely a function of the adaptability of the curriculum, the instructional materials, and the teaching procedures.
- Provide regular classroom teachers with in-service training before they are assigned exceptional students.
- Provide regular classroom teachers with support and encouragement.
- Make sure the classroom teacher and the special education teacher work co-operatively on designing programs.
- Remember that the regular classroom teacher is a vital part of the treatment team.
- Make record-keeping, monitoring of pupil progress, and reporting of results as simple as possible.

(Adapted in part from Karagianis and Nesbit, 1979, pp. 31-34.)

Non-categorical approaches

As special education embraces the concepts of normalization and mainstreaming, there is a movement away from categorizing children and slotting them into special classrooms. Special educators are now focusing on the individual needs of the child, rather than the child's category of disability. To do this, they depend upon a careful analysis of each child's overall academic, physical and personal pattern of strengths and weaknesses. For example, we used to describe a child as suffering from a profound bilateral sensori-neural hearing loss; this medically oriented diagnosis stressed the child's deficits, not educational and social needs. Now we are more likely to suggest that this child will process auditory information most successfully through the use of a visually coded system, such as sign language and finger spelling. This simple statement addresses the child's needs and takes the first step toward efficient programming.

Children with special needs, whether mental, physical, or emotional, usually have learning and development disabilities that extend across several categories of behaviour — physical, intellectual, linguistic, perceptual, social, or emotional. Disabilities are not mutually exclusive, but overlap. With this in mind, special educators are developing non-categorical, or cross-categorical, approaches.

A **non-categorical approach** implies that the functional behaviour of a child is the most important factor in the child's educational program. Educators look at the child's skill levels and decide what educational tasks are required to improve inadequate skills. Children who might previously have been categorized as learning-disabled, mildly mentally retarded, or mildly emotionally disturbed are freed from these labels. Instead, teaching is directed to their specific needs.

Labelling

Labelling refers to the categorizing of children on the basis of their primary disability. The practice evolved gradually; no one really planned it. Many of today's labels resulted from attempts by medical and psychological researchers to distinguish various handicaps.

Some system for the identification and classification of exceptional children would seem to be necessary. However, as we have already implied, the classification and labelling process is fraught with hazards. Although the labels broadly define categories of exceptionality, no one classification can adequately describe the social, psychological, and physical qualities of an exceptional individual. Moreover, there are clear disadvantages related to labelling which outweigh the advantages of the process.

Advantages of labelling

Labels can serve to simplify information for administrators, placement counsellors, educators, legislators, and parents. Within the school system, the label may be a necessary administrative lever to obtain funding for special services. Labels can also promote effective communication among agencies, services, and professionals that deal with exceptional children. Parents may find labels helpful, especially when a condition is initially diagnosed. For parents, the name of a handicap may seem to give them some control over it (Akerley, 1975).

A well-considered label can also result in increased visibility for groups of people with special needs. For example, many parents were eager for a more euphemistic label for their children than minimal-brain-dysfunction or neurologically handicapped. They readily adopted the designation of learning-disabled, and moved on to form the Association for Children and Youth with Learning Disabilities (ACLD) with chapters throughout Canada and the United States. As a highly effective lobbying group, the ACLD has gained substantial special provisions for children designated as learning-disabled.

Disadvantages of labelling

It is true that labelling permits us to identify children whose learning and behavioural characteristics cause them to require differentiated instruction. However, the benefits of labelling are of a general administrative nature. The practice offers few benefits to the labelled individual.

Too often, a label describes only the deficiencies of a person. It picks out a single quality, calls attention to it and stresses how this quality differs from the norm. The child's adherence to the norm and individual strengths are obscured by an over-simplified label.

In spite of the proliferation of labels among health and education professionals, they seldom adequately reflect a child's educational and therapeutic needs. Nor do they automatically result in better services for the child. Moreover, a label suggests a permanent disorder requiring long-term professional treatment. Children must wear their labels everywhere and all the time, although they may not apply in all situations. The child labelled mildly mentally retarded in the schoolroom, for example, may function very well at home and in the community.

According to researchers, many people tend to view a labelled person differently from a non-labelled one (Herson, 1974; Langer and Abelson, 1974; Salvia, Clark, and Ysseldyke, 1973). Labels accentuate stereotyping (Combs and Harper, 1967; Foster, Ysseldyke, and Reese, 1975; Gilling and Rucker, 1977; Shotel, Iano, and McGettigan, 1972). Labels also bias people's expectations of exceptional individuals.

Classroom teachers seem to be more willing to work with an unlabelled child than one to whom a label is attached (Gilling and Rucker, 1977). In the classroom, the label can predispose the teacher to expect behaviour consonant with the child's classification. Classroom teachers may use disability labels to explain their students' inability to learn. They may fail to see that inadequate teaching or inappropriate curricula are also to blame. Indeed, classroom teachers may feel that a labelled child does not belong in the regular classroom, but in segregated classes with a special education teacher (Chandler, 1981).

Labelling and enrolment in a special program may easily deflate a child's self-concept. This often aggravates the child's condition and increases vulnerability to ridicule and isolation from peers (Hallahan and Kauffman, 1982). The child may use the label as a rationale for surrendering personal responsibility, and may come to regard the future as beyond control (Jones, 1972).

Recent trends in classification

Clearly, then, the traditional system of labelling children by their primary disability is not always useful. Dangers include cultural bias, social stigma, distortion, and oversimplification. Administrators and professionals will likely continue to use categories of exceptionality. However, in the classroom, other approaches may serve exceptional children better.

The use of non-labelling, non-categorical approaches may do much to combat the stigmatization and stereotyping of exceptional individuals. Recently, these approaches have become much more popular. A 1979 survey indicated that most American states continued to use traditional, or similar, categories to identify exceptional children; rather than abandoning categorization, several states had developed new categories (Garrett and Brazil, 1979). By 1983, however, about half the states had adopted or were moving toward a non-categorical approach to the education of exceptional children (Mitchell, 1983).

Nevertheless, when Ontario legislators were creating mandatory special education legislation, they rejected non-categorical approaches on the grounds that they had not been conspicuously successful. The legislators decided to stay with traditional categories (Hodder, 1984). However, despite this decision, non-categorical approaches can offer educators a valuable means of conceptualizing special education services and the needs of exceptional children. In later chapters, this notion will be further discussed.

Litigation and legislation

Educational services are constantly changing, as are the ideas that shape them. Changing needs, or a changing conception of needs, lead to new policies and administrative arrangements. Court decisions and legislative actions can also have a dramatic impact on education. In the United States, the passage of Public Law 94-142, the *Education of All Handicapped Children Act*, made special education a national concern.

In Canada, special education is a key priority. Policies related to the rights of exceptional individuals are formulated at the federal, provincial, and local-district levels of government. The federal government is involved through Indian Affairs, National Defence, Manpower, Penitentiary Services, and Health and Welfare (Goguen, 1980). However, in Canada, except for the Declaration of Human Rights, there is no federal law to outline or guarantee the rights of exceptional children. More concern is shown at the provincial level, and several studies are currently in progress.

Further considerations regarding Canadian and American legislation for special education are addressed in Chapter Three.

MAJOR CAUSES OF EXCEPTIONALITY

As mainstreaming is introduced, teachers will encounter far more students with such medical problems as epilepsy, visual and auditory impairment, and orthopedic and urologic difficulty. Teachers therefore require basic training to help them cope with these medical problems. They also need to be sensitized to the social, emotional, and educational problems caused by the child's disabilities. For example, a child with spina bifida often requires an artificial bladder for urinary drainage. The clinical manifestation of the child's urologic difficulty (incontinence) and the need for medical management (the bag worn on the child's stomach or flank) may create practical and psychological problems for the child. If the teacher is unable to assist and reassure the child, then the child's medical problems may create learning difficulties (Freund, Casey, and Bradley, 1982).

The teacher must also be aware when certain activities are limited for an exceptional child. The teacher must know when to restrict the duration of an activity, or when to recommend an alternative learning experience. The teacher may also be involved in the monitoring of drug dosage.

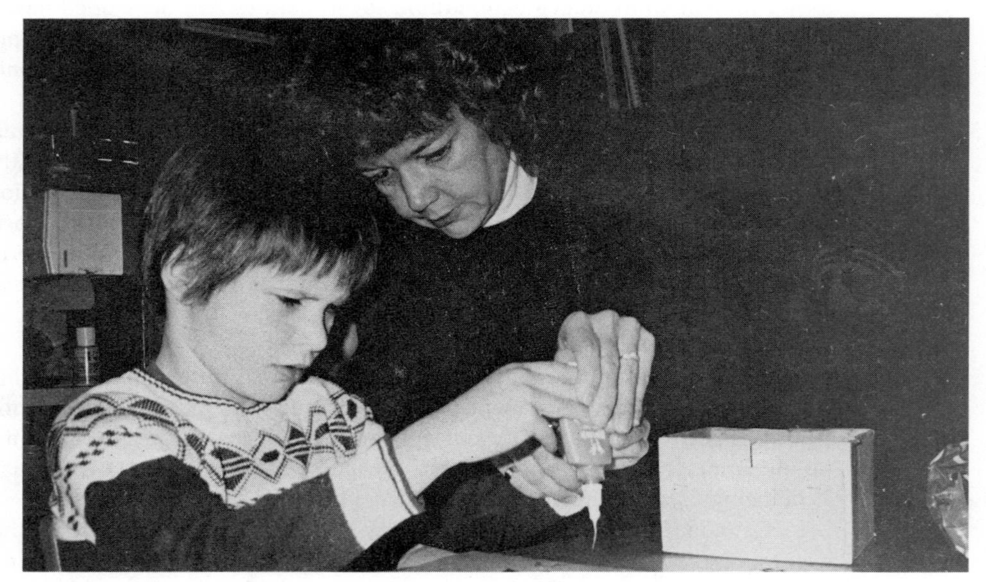

Teachers must be acutely aware of a child's strengths and limitations if they wish to tailor their teaching methods to meet specific needs.
(T. Wilson)

A huge variety of factors account for handicapping or potentially handicapping conditions in children. There are, for example, more than two hundred known causes of mental retardation and perhaps nearly two thousand inborn errors of metabolism (Berlin, 1983). However, despite all that is known, nearly half of all childhood exceptionalities are attributable to unknown causes.

Before the advent of antibiotics in the 1940s, diseases such as whooping cough, measles, smallpox, enteric fever, and scarlet fever seriously impaired, even destroyed, the vision or hearing of many children. Scarlet fever is one of the oldest known diseases and caused major sensory deficits even in pre-Christian times (MVD, 1925). Today, scarlet fever and other such conditions are virtually eliminated. Moreover, our medical technology helps children survive who, even twenty years ago, would not have lived.

For purposes of discussion, it is useful to group biological causes of exceptionality into specific developmental periods: the prenatal or gestation period; the perinatal, or delivery-and-birth period; the neonatal, or first two-week, period; and the postnatal period. In this section, we will briefly discuss some of the problems that can occur during each of these times. The etiology of specific handicapping conditions will be fully addressed throughout the following chapters.

Prenatal period

Life begins not at birth, but at conception. At the beginning of life, a human being is smaller than the period at the end of this sentence. The individual is a single cell, barely visible to the naked eye, a tiny drop of fluid made up mainly of non-living material surrounding a minuscule nucleus of living matter. By the time of birth, some thirty-eight weeks later, the individual weighs about 3.5 kilograms and contains 200 billion specialized cells (Montagu, 1977).

The prenatal period encompasses three stages. The first two weeks are known as the period of the ovum. Next, the period of the embryo lasts until the beginning of the third month. The remaining gestation time is known as the period of the fetus. The change of labels charts the organism's growth from a simple cell to a recognizable human creature.

From the moment of conception until delivery nine months later, the human being is more susceptible to environment than at any other time. The opening third of pregnancy, the first trimester, is the most important to development. During this time, major organs and basic tissues take shape and develop into their finished forms; after this stage, it is difficult to affect their growth in any fundamental way (Montagu, 1977). Specific changes occur to the developing human at specific times. Every cell, every tissue, and every organ has its own timetable for coming into existence, for developing, and for beginning to carry out its functions (Montagu, 1977).

Genetic and chromosomal differences

The human body is made up of billions of cells. Almost every cell contains a complete package of hereditary instructions for the characteristics that comprise the individual. These instructions are located in forty-six chromosomes, arranged in twenty-three pairs. Each pair carries one chromosome from each parent. The first twenty-two pairs are autosomal (identical) and determine the thousands of traits that make up a human being, whether male or female. The twenty-third pair determines the sex of the individual.

Each chromosome consists of thousands of genes, and each gene is made up of deoxyribonucleic acid (DNA). This DNA in turn consists of thousands of combinations of four chemical sub-units. The order in which these sub-units are joined together spells out the gene's message in the genetic code. Whether a particular cell will become facial skin or ankle-bone depends on which genes are "switched on"—a process that is still a mystery.

As the embryo develops, DNA directs the chemical processes within its cells. One tiny flaw in the genetic structure can have tragic results. A change in DNA may repair itself or lead to spontaneous abortion (miscarriage). However, the flaw may also create anomalies at birth, called **hereditary anomalies.**

Because hereditary anomalies are in the genes, they may be passed on to subsequent generations. For example, retinitis pigmentosa is a condition that affects the retina, the film-like layer in the back of the eye, and causes progressive visual loss. Retinitis pigmentosa is an inherited disease, transmitted through generations by a gene which may be recessive, dominant, or sex-linked. An estimated one person in eighty carries the gene for recessive retinitis pigmentosa. At present, it is rarely possible to detect the carriers (Children should see ..., 1980).

Another group of disorders carried by abnormal genetic material are known as **metabolic disorders**, or inborn errors of metabolism. In these disorders, the normal chemistry of the cell is altered by the inability to provide or dipose of a critical chemical or protein. Many of these conditions, such as phenylketonuria (PKU) and diabetes, can be treated or controlled. Others, such as Tay-Sachs—a fatal deterioration of brain function—are untreatable. Some genetic conditions are sex-linked—which means they are carried on the twenty-third pair of chromosomes. Hemophilia and colour blindness are examples of sex-linked genetic conditions.

Chromosomal problems occur when there is an extra chromosome, or when pieces or parts of chromosomes attach themselves to other chromosomes. The most common chromosomal aberration is Down's Syndrome, which occurs in approximately 1 in every 640 live births.

Scientists and researchers have looked for ways to locate and map defective genes to identify potential handicapping conditions before birth. The X chromosome has been most explored, and about 115, or ten percent, of its genes have now been mapped. About forty genetic conditions are now detectable through amniocentesis. This procedure involves extracting a small amount of amniotic fluid and then analyzing it for genetic and chromosomal anomalies.

Infections and intoxications

During pregnancy, the mother's adequate nutrition is vital to the development of the fetus. The ingestion by the mother of drugs and alcohol can harm the developing baby. Smoking by the mother may cause her to produce a baby with low birth-weight.

Maternal health is crucial during pregnancy. **Toxemia**, which refers to several common disorders of pregnancy, may well be related to maternal nutrition (Montagu, 1977). Toxemias appear in the first trimester of pregnancy and are characterized by edema (water retention), hypertension, and protein in the urine. Toxemias may impair normal fetal growth, and the drugs used to treat them may also harm the fetus (Berlin, 1983).

Of all the infections that threaten the fetus, five are especially damaging. These are rubella, syphilis, toxoplasmosis, cytomegalic inclusion disease, and herpes. Four of these infections are intra-uterine. Herpetic infections of the newborn, however, are acquired during passage through the birth canal (Berlin, 1983).

Birth and neonatal development

Birth takes place in three stages; labour, delivery, and afterbirth. It is a long process. An average first labour takes fourteen hours; the average for later labours is eight hours.

Birth is neither a beginning, nor an ending, but a bridge between two stages of life. Birth can be dangerous for the child or the mother. The fetus may be in an unusual position, such as breech or transverse presentation. The membranes may rupture too early, leading to infection. An incorrectly placed placenta may mean excessive bleeding. Drugs and forceps used during delivery may cause harm to the fetus.

When the time of birth draws near, the oxygen level in the placenta and in the child's circulatory system drops sharply. From that moment until birth, the child exists on a relatively small amount of oxygen. If the child is deprived of that oxygen, the condition is called **anoxia**. Prolonged oxygen deprivation can lead to irreversible brain damage, because destroyed brain cells cannot regenerate themselves. When a portion of the brain is damaged, the part of the individual that is controlled by that portion of the brain is also damaged. Anoxia may be a villian in cerebral palsy, some types of epilepsy, and some mental retardation. It can also produce other subtle forms of childhood disability.

Prematurity

The study of pre-term infants is marked by controversy at virtually every point. Standards detailing the criteria for prematurity have been in flux for more than thirty years (Mersils, Jones, and Strefel, 1983). **Premature babies** are generally defined as those born at less than thirty-seven weeks, a full week short of the full thirty-eight-week term. Premature babies generally weigh 2500 grams or lower, as compared to a usual birth weight of 3000 to 3500 grams. Prematurity occurs in ten or twelve births per hundred (Berlin, 1983). It is more likely to occur in multiple births.

The earliest stage possible for survival outside the womb is generally considered twenty-four weeks. About thirty percent of infants now born at this early point survive. These tiny infants may weigh only 500 grams and possess immature organs. Their eyes are still closed and their blood vessels appear clearly through their gelatinous-seeming skin. Children born after twenty-six weeks of gestation have a survival rate of sixty percent, and those born at twenty-eight weeks have an eighty-five to ninety percent chance to survive (Musgrove, 1984).

Research has clearly established that preterm infants have a higher incidence of developmental problems in childhood than full-term infants (Cohen, Parmelee, Sigman, and Beckwell, 1982). Extremely premature babies, rescued by agressive treatments that have only become available within the last decades, may face grave complications later in life. Possible complications include cerebral palsy, mental retardation, blindness, jaundice, collapsed lungs, infections, internal bleeding, and even a respirator-induced disease called broncho-pulmonary dysplasia (Musgrove, 1984).

In the early 1970s, some fifty to sixty percent of infants with birth-weights between 1 and 1.5 kilograms suffered from major handicaps. However, since intensive care has become available, only about fifteen to twenty percent have suffered any handicaps (Musgrove, 1984).

Apgar score

Every newborn baby is assigned an Apgar score. This is based on clinical observation of five areas of functioning – heart rate; respiratory effect; muscle tone; reflex irritability; and skin colour. The baby is evaluated one, three, and five minutes after delivery. Its responses are graded zero for absent, and one or two for normal, for an optimal score of ten. Most babies score in the eight to ten range. A score of seven or lower may be cause for concern.

Postnatal development

Child development might be seen as a series of patterned and predictable changes that foster the child's ability to cope with and master the external environment. Most children reach developmental milestones at roughly the same age. **Developmental milestones** are various critical behaviours, such as sitting, walking, and using first words, that children learn to perform. Children who fail to develop according to normal patterns are considered to be experiencing developmental delays or **maturational lags**.

Children who have **congenital conditions**, in which a disability is present at birth, will likely have problems reaching some of their developmental milestones. Their progress may not always be patterned or predictable. A variety of childhood diseases and infections can also hinder the child's progress. Meningitis and encephalitis, for example, can cause visual impairment, deafness, cerebral palsy, and other disabling conditions. Childhood accidents can also cause permanent disabilities, as can various forms of child abuse.

Environmental factors

Child development is a process influenced by a complex of interwoven factors. The psychological, social, and educational factors related to a disability cannot easily be separated from the biomedical causes. Every human life is a complex interplay of heredity and environment. The genes alone cannot produce a human being. An environment must also exist to provide nourishment, warmth, stimulation, and protection.

It is almost impossible to determine the relative influences of heredity and environment on human behaviour. The problem has been debated for centuries, first as "nativism versus sensationalism," and now as "nature versus nurture." However, we do know that hereditary and environmental factors are crucial to child development. A child's growth will be seriously hampered by restricted sensory stimulation, cultural deprivation and cultural impoverishment. The effects of the environment on child development will be addressed in greater detail in the following chapters.

DIAGNOSIS AND ASSESSMENT OF EXCEPTIONAL CHILDREN

Before we can help exceptional children, we must accurately pinpoint their problems. For each child, we need a detailed picture of strengths and weaknesses in a variety of domains. Only then can we develop an effective educational program.

Assessment is the process of determining whether a child exhibits a developmental problem, what the problem is, its causes, its potential course, its developmental consequences, and the best approaches to intervention and remediation. Assessment is not a single operation, but an ongoing process undertaken by a team of professionals, including classroom teachers, special education teachers, parents, psychologists, and counsellors. All these people provide information and opinions about the child, which can then be synthesized to plan an appropriate eucational program. In other words, assessment offers a bridge between the art of teaching and the psychological principle that each child is unique.

Assessment can be viewed in three stages — survey, or screening; specific, or diagnostic; and intensive, or medical and paraprofessional. Each of these stages involves vastly different strategies, and is undertaken by different professionals. All of them, however, focus on, developing an efficient educational program for the individual child.

Screening

Screening is the process of identifying children who are at-risk for an exceptional condition. Screening does not generate information to assist with placement or intervention services. Screening only provides enough information to determine that further diagnostic study is needed.

A primary screening test should be short and easily administered by a variety of professionals with minimal training. The scoring should be quick and simple. Screening procedures include first-hand observation, child and parent interviews, past records, developmental checklists, behaviour-rating scales, inventories, teacher-made tests, criterion-referenced tests, group-achievement tests, and error analysis.

On average, most screening identifies about eight-five percent of exceptional children (Lerner, Mardell-Czudnowski, and Goldenberg, 1981). However, some non-handicapped children may be identified (false positives), and some exceptional children may be missed (false negatives).

Diagnosis

Diagnosis is a term derived from the Greek roots *dia* (apart) and *gignoskien* (to know). By definition, diagnosis is the art of identifying disease from its symptoms. **Differential diagnosis** implies the precise specification that a given set of symptoms is indicative of one disorder rather than another.

Psychoeducational diagnosis provides further information on children who were identified as at-risk in their primary screening tests. The diagnostic process confirms or

Figure 1-2 Diagnosis, assessment and training viewed as a cycle with intermediate stages.

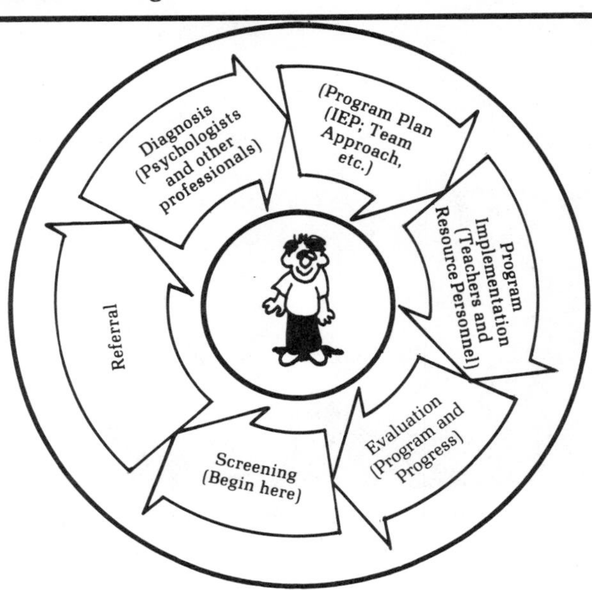

discounts the existence of a problem condition. It also helps to determine what treatment and intervention are needed. Figure 1-2 illustrates the steps involved in identification, referral, assessment, placement, and programming.

Diagnostic tests should be more detailed than screening tests, but still relatively easy to administer in various settings by a variety of professionals. To pinpoint areas of dysfunction, the tests should examine a spectrum of developmental domains, should test numerous skills within each domain, and should provide a profile of abilities in each domain. The tests should be administered by trained personnel only. Testing time should be longer and scoring more complex than for the primary screening tests (Brooks-Gunn and Lewis, 1983).

A psychoeducational assessment should provide information about:

- physical growth and development, including a medical history.
- Intellectual ability.
- Academic functioning in a variety of areas.
- Communication and language skills.
- Social and emotional development, including self-help skills.
- Fine and gross motor skills.
- Perceptual and sensory motor skills.
- Vocational interests and skills.

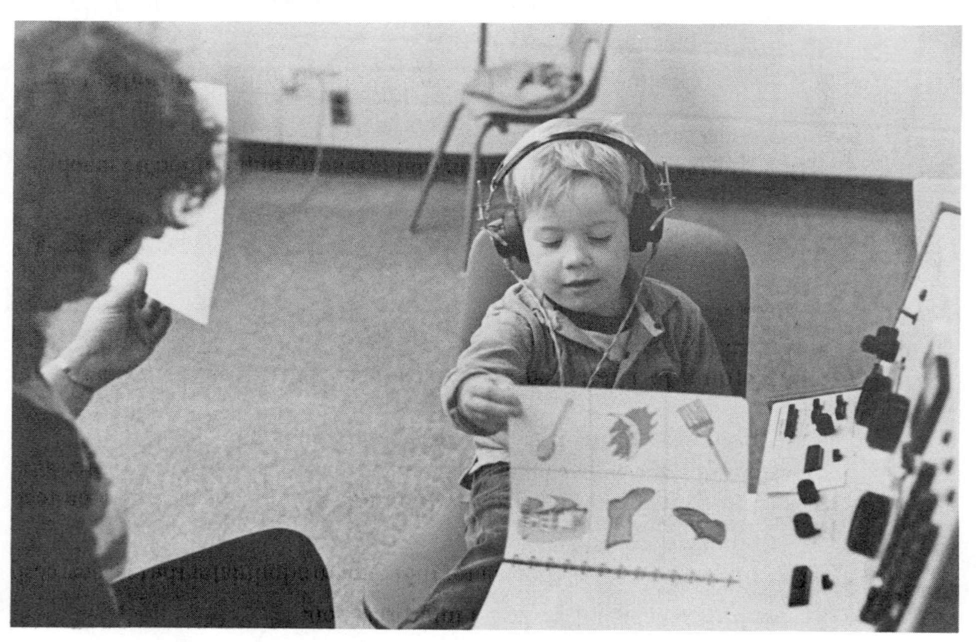

Diagnostic testing must be easy to administer, yet pinpoint problem areas precisely. This hearing-impaired child is being tested on language reception.
(T. Wilson)

As we have stressed, the assessment process functions primarily to develop a specific educational plan for the child. This plan is then verified or modified by the results of continuing evaluation as it is implemented (Keeton, 1980). Unfortunately, however, there is a growing awareness among parents and others that important educational decisions are being made on the basis of technically inadequate or inappropriately used tests (Hirshoren and McGuigan, 1984).

To be sound, diagnostic tests must meet six major criteria:

- **Validity** refers to the degree that a test actually measures what it claims to measure. For example, if a test purports to assess spelling skills, it should ask the child to actually spell words (Hirshoren and McGuigan, 1984).
- **Reliability** refers to the consistency of the test. The test should produce the same results on different occasions under the same circumstances.
- **Sensitivity** refers to the test's ability to discriminate among different levels of skill. For example, a test that measures ability in number facts should be able to distinguish between children who have mastered the facts and those who have only partly mastered them.
- **Objectivity** occurs when only one response is correct for each question. This leaves the scorer little chance for personal interpretation.
- **Clear guidelines** make it easier for the tester to administer the test correctly and use it in an appropriate context.
- **Feasibility** refers to the cost of obtaining, giving, and scoring the test (Fox, 1969). Shortcuts to save money must not be taken. These can jeopardize both the reliability and appropriateness of the test (Hirshoren and McGuigan, 1984).

According to Hirshoren and McGuigan (1984), there are also a number of less technical, more practical criteria for diagnostic tests. These include the following:

- Does the test reflect local curriculum expectations?
- Does the test reflect local and provincial guidelines for the placement of exceptional children?
- Does the test supply information that is readily understood by teachers, parents, and other concerned personnel?
- Does the test allow the student more than one opportunity to indicate mastery or lack of mastery of a skill?
- Does the test include more than one mode of collecting information for assessment?
- Does the test provide information that is useful in setting goals and establishing programs?

Early identification

One of the most interesting areas of special education concerns the early identification and prevention of developing disabilities. Clearly, the idea that potentially handicapping conditions can be detected and prevented, or at least ameliorated, is both rationally and emotionally appealing (Keogh, 1983).

The assessment of young handicapped children serves the following purposes:

- Identifies children who are at risk for handicapping condition.
- Diagnoses handicapping conditions.
- Predicts the child's future level of functioning.
- Prescribes treatment.
- Evaluates the child's success as a function of program variables and as a function of changes over time.
- Evaluates the success of the program. (Brooks-Gunn and Lewis, 1983.)

The early detection of a child's problems may prevent the development of more complex learning difficulties later in life. For infants and pre-schoolers, developmental screening is used to look for problems that can be improved through early intervention. In kindergarten, screening is used to identify children who do not have the readiness skills they need to perform well in a structured school environment.

Before examiners can assess a child, they must know what behaviours they expect to observe. To test a three-year-old, they must focus on behaviour usually exhibited by two- to four-year-olds. Such behaviour might include speaking in sentences of four to six words, building three-block pyramids, matching similar pictures, or buttoning. The examiners must choose tests appropriate to these behaviours (Fewell Du Bose, 1981).

To detect developmental and learning problems, examiners use such scales as the Denver Developmental Screening Test (Frankenburg, Dodds, and Fandal, 1975), the Boehm Test of Basic Concepts (Boehm, 1971), or the Metropolitan Readiness Test (Nurss and McGauvran, 1976). In Canada, the Denver Developmental Screening Test is widely used with children from one month to six years of age. The Denver Test surveys such areas of development as gross-motor skill, fine-motor adaptive skill, language behaviour, and psychosocial ability. A child's performance is measured against an age-scale that represents the functioning of normal children. By comparing the child's performance to the norm for each activity, examiners can estimate how delayed a child's development appears to be.

Examiners should use great caution, however, when using infant testing to predict future performance. It is very difficult to predict school achievement during the first three or four years of a child's life. In nonhandicapped children, the negligible correlation of early and later intelligence is well documented (Honzik, 1976). Infant testing simply tells us whether a child is reaching the developmental milestones within normal limits in a particular domain at a particular time.

Intensive testing

The final level of testing typically involves medical and paramedical professionals. A complete look at the child's health history and current medical status must form part of the child's total assessment. Suppose, for example, that a grade-one child, who appears bright and outgoing, cannot seem to comprehend such sound-symbol associations as "'S' is for snake." Before any specific psycho-educational diagnosis is undertaken, the child should be referred to an audiologist for a complete assessment of hearing acuity. Professionals involved at the medical level of assessment include the school nurse, the family doctor, the pediatrician, the neurologist, the audiologist, and the opthalmologist, to mention only a few.

SUMMARY

In recent decades, special education and society's treatment of exceptional people have changed dramatically. Special education has come to be seen as a means to provide better educational opportunities for exceptional children. Increasingly, special educators are attempting to decategorize exceptional children and encourage a view of them as individuals with special learning problems.

Society is now rejecting the closed-door policy that has traditionally placed the handicapped in segregated institutions. Today the watchwords of special education are normalization and mainstreaming. These widespread movements entail many different strategies, including deinstitutionalization, integration, non-categorical approaches to teaching, and a rejection of traditional labelling. All these strategies aim to provide exceptional individuals with an education and a life style as close to normal as possible.

BIBLIOGRAPHY

Akerley, M.S. (1975). Parents speak. *Journal of Autism and Childhood Schizophrenia*, 5, 373-380.

Albert, W. (1980). Special education in the Yukon territory. In M. Csapo and L. Goguen (Eds.), *Special education across Canada: Issues and concerns for the '80s*. Vancouver: Centre for Human Development and Research.

Alexander, C. and Strain, P.S. (1978). A review of educators' attitudes toward handicapped children and the concept of mainstreaming. *Psychology in the Schools, 16*, 390-396.

Anderson, R.M., Greer, J.G., and Dietrich, W.L. (1976). Overview and perspectives. In R.M. Anderson and J.G. Greer (Eds.), *Educating the severely and profoundly retarded*. Baltimore, MD.: University Park Press.

Baker, J.D. and Gottlieb, J. (1980). Attitudes of teachers toward mainstreaming retarded children. In J. Gottlieb (Ed.), *Educating mentally retarded persons in the mainstream.* Baltimore, MD : University Park Press.

Ballance, K., Kendall, D., and Saywell, D. (1972). Legislation for exceptional children in Canada, supplementary report. *Special Education in Canada, 47,* 19-32.

Barngrover, E.A. (1971). A study of educators' preferences in special education programs. *Exceptional Children, 37,* 754-755.

Berlin, C.M., Jr. (1983). Biological causes of exceptionality. In R.M. Smith, J.T. Neisworth, and F.M. Hunt (Eds.), *The exceptional child: A functional approach.* New York: McGraw-Hill.

Blazovik, R.R. (1972). The attitudes of teachers, parents, and students toward integrated programs for borderline educable retarded students. *Dissertation Abstracts International,* 127.

Boehm, A.E. (1971). *Boehm Test of Basic Concepts manual.* New York: Psychological Corporation.

Bradfield, R.H., Brown, J., Kaplan, P., Rickert, E., and Stannard, R. (1973). The special child in the regular classroom. *Exceptional Children, 39,* 384-390.

Brooks-Gunn, J. and Lewis, M. (1983). Screening and diagnosing handicapped infants. *Topics in Early Childhood Special Education, 3,* 14-28.

Bruininks, R.H., Rynders, J.E., and Gross, J.C. (1974). Social acceptance of mildly retarded pupils in resource room and regular classes. *American Journal of Mental Deficiency, 78,* 377-383.

Brulle, A.R., Barton, L.E., Barton, C.L., and Wharton, D.L. (1983). A comparison of teacher time spent with physically handicapped and able-bodied students. *Exceptional Children, 49,* 543-47.

Canada, Council of Ministers of Education. (1983), *Survey of special education in Canada, 1982-1983.* Winnipeg: Candid Research and Council of Ministers of Education, Canada.

Chandler, R.N. (1981). Teaching L.D. students in the public schools: A return to the closet? *Journal of Learning Disabilities, 14,* 482-485.

Children should see more and more each day. [1980.] Toronto: National Retinitis Pigmentosa Foundation of Canada.

Church, E.M. (1980). Special education in Alberta: Past accomplishments, present issues and future prospects. In M. Csapo and L. Goguen (Eds.). *Special education across Canada. Issues and Concerns for the '80s.* Vancouver: Centre for Human Development and Research.

Cohen, S.E., Parmelee, A.H., Sigman, M., and Beckwell, L. (1982). Neonatal risk factors in preterm infants. *Applied Research in Mental Retardation, 3,* 265-278.

Combs, R.H. and Harper, H.L. (1967). Effects of labels on attitudes of educators toward handicapped children. *Exceptional Children, 33,* 399-403.

Council for Exceptional Children. (1971). *Standards for education of exceptional children in Canada* (SEECC) *report.* Toronto: Canadian Committee and the National Institute for Mental Retardation.

Csapo, M. (1984). Segregation, integration, and beyond: A sociological perspective of special education. *B.C. Journal of Special Education, 8,* 211-229.

Directions: A report of the Canadian Organizing Committee for 1981, the International Year of Disabled Persons. (1982). Ottawa: Department of Health and Welfare.

Dunn, L.M. (1968). Special education for the mildly retarded—Is much of it justifiable? *Exceptional Children, 35,* 5-22.

Fewell Du Bose, R. (1981). Assessment of severely impaired young children: Problems and recommendations. *Topics in Early Childhood Special Education, 1,* 9-21.

Flathouse, V.F. (1979). Multiply handicapped deaf children and Public Law 94-142. *Exceptional Children, 45,* 560-565.

Foster, G.G., Ysseldyke, J.E., and Reese, J.H. (1975). "I wouldn't have seen it if I hadn't believed it." *Exceptional Children, 41,* 469-473.

Fox, D. (1969). *The research process in education.* New York: Holt, Rinehart and Winston.

Frankenburg, W.K., Dodds, J.B., and Fandal, A.W. (1975). *Denver Developmental Screening Test.* Denver, CO.: Ladoca Project and Publishing Foundation.

Freund, J., Casey, P.H., and Bradley, R.H. (1982). A special education course with pediatric components. *Exceptional Children, 48,* 348-351.

Gallagher, J.J. (1972). *The search for an educational system that doesn't exist.* Reston, VA.: Council for Exceptional Children.

Garrett, J.E. and Brazil, N. (1979). Categories used for identification and education of exceptional children. *Exceptional Children, 45,* 291-292.

Gillung, T.B. and Rucker, C.N. (1977). Labels and teacher expectations. *Exceptional Children, 43,* 454-465.

Goguen, L. (1980). Right to education for exceptional children in Canada: A growing national concern. In M. Csapo and L. Goguen (Eds.), *Special education across Canada. Issues and Concerns for the '80s.* Vancouver: Centre for Human Development and Research.

Guerin, G.R. (1979). Regular teacher concerns with mainstreaming learning handicapped children. *Psychology in the Schools, 16,* 543-545.

Hall, M. and Dennis, L. (1968), *Living and learning: The report of the provincial committee on aims and objectives of education in the schools of Ontario.* Toronto: Newton Publishing.

Hallahan, D.P. and Kauffman, J.M. (1982). *Exceptional children: Introduction to special education (2nd ed).* Englewood Cliffs, N.J.: Prentice-Hall.

Hardy, M.I., McLeod, J., Minto, H., Perkins, S.A., and Quance, W.R. (1971). *Standards for education of exceptional children in Canada: The SEECC Report.* Toronto: Leanord Crawford.

Herson, P.F. (1974). Biasing effects of diagnostic labels and sex of pupils on teachers' views of pupils' mental health. *Journal of Educational Psychology, 66,* 117-122.

Hirshoren, A. and Burton, T. (1979). Willingness of regular teachers to participate in mainstreaming handicapped children. *Journal of Research and Development in Education, 12,* 93-100.

Hirshoren, A. and McGuigan, C. (1984). Something isn't always better than nothing — On the use of educational and psychological tests. *B.C. Journal of Special Education, 8,* 99-106.

Hodder, C. (1984). The Education Amendment Act (Ontario) 1980: A review: *Interchange, 15,* 44-53.

Honzik, M.K. (1976). Value and limitations of infant tests: An overview. In M. Lewis (Ed.), *Origins of intelligence: Infancy and early childhood.* New York: Plenum Press.

Hudson, F.H., Graham, S., and Warner, M. (1979). Mainstreaming: An experimentation of the attitudes and needs of regular classroom teachers. *Learning Disability Quarterly, 2,* 58-62.

Jones, R.L. (1972). Labels and stigma in special education. *Exceptional Children, 38,* 553-564.

Karagianis, L.D. and Nesbit, W.C. (1979). *Perhaps I'll be in your class: Approaching integration.* St. John's, Nfld.: Council for Exceptional Children.

Kaufman, M.J., Gottlieb, J., Agard, J.A., and Kukic, M.B. (1975). Mainstreaming: Toward an explication of the construct. *Focus on Exceptional Children, 7,* 1-12.

Keeton, A. (1980). Policies and practices in Ontario special education: A time for change. In M. Csapo and L. Goguen (Eds.), *Special education across Canada: Issues and concerns for the '80s.* Vancouver: Centre for Human Development and Research.

Kendall, D.C. (1980). Developmental processes and educational programs for exceptional children: CELDIC Report, Public Law 94-142, Warnock Report. In G.M. Kysela (Ed.), *The exceptional child in Canadian education* (CSSE *yearbook*). Vancouver: Canadian Society for the Study of Education.

Kendall, D.C. (1985). Personal communication.

Keogh, B.K. (1983). Early identification: One component of comprehensive service for at-risk children. *Topics in Early Childhood Special Education, 3,* 7-16.

Kraft, A. (1973). Down with (most) special education classes. *Academic Therapy, 8,* 207-216.

Langer, E.J. and Abelson, R.P. (1974). A patient by any other name . . . Clinician group differences in labeling bias. *Journal of Consulting and Clinical Psychology, 42,* 4-9.

Lapp, E. (1957). A study of social adjustment of slow-learning children who were assigned to part-time regular classes. *American Journal of Mental Deficiency, 62,* 254-262.

Lerner, J., Mardell-Czudnowski, C. and Goldenberg, D. (1981). *Special education for the early childhood years.* Englewood Cliffs, N.J.: Prentice-Hall.

Leyser, L., Abrams, P., and Lipscomb, E. (1982). Modifying attitudes of prospective elementary school teachers toward mainstreaming. *The Journal for Special Educators, 18,* 1-10.

Lusthaus, E., Hanrahan, J., and Lusthaus, C. (1979). Issues in improving quality of life. *Mental Retardation/Deficience Mentale, 29,* 24-27.

Major, I. (1961). How do we accept the handicapped? *Elementary School Journal, 61,* 328-330.

McMurray, J.G. (1980). Learning disabled adolescents: Perspectives from Canadian principals, *Special Education in Canada, 55,* 10-14.

Mersils, S.J., Jones, S.N. and Strefel, G.S. (1983). Neonatal intervention: Problem, purpose and prospects. *Topics in Early Childhood Special Education, 3,* 1-13.

Mitchell, D.R. (1983). International trends in special education. *Canadian Journal on Mental Retardation, 33,* 6-13.

Montagu, A. (1977). *Life before birth.* New York: Signet Books.

Moore, J. and Fine, M.J. (1978). Regular and special class teachers' perceptions of normal and exceptional children and their attitudes toward mainstreaming. *Psychology in the Schools, 15,* 253-259.

Musgrove, P. (1984 November 21). Struggling to survive. Vancouver: *Sun,* pp. 1-2.

M.V.D. (1925). Routing an ancient enemy. *Volta Review, 27,* 81-85.

Myers, J. (1976). The efficacy of the special day school for EMR pupils. *Mental Retardation, 14,* 3-11.

Nikiforuk, A. (1981, August 10). Education bill called "not much of a law." Toronto: *Globe and Mail.*

Nirje, B. (1979). Changing patterns in residential services for the mentally retarded. In E.L. Meyen (Ed.), *Basic readings in the study of exceptional children and youth.* Denver, Co.: Love Publishing.

Nurss, J.R., and McGauvran, M.E. (1976). *Metropolitan Readiness Tests.* New York: Harcourt Brace Jovanovich.

Payne, R. and Murray, C. (1974). Principals' attitudes toward integration of the handicapped. *Exceptional Children, 41,* 123-125.

Reich, C.M. (1981). Special education. In J.H. Andrews and W.T. Rogers (Eds.), *Canadian research in education: A state of the art review.* British Columbia: University of British Columbia.

Reynolds, M.C. and Birch, J.W. (1977). *Teaching exceptional children in all America's schools.* Reston, VA.: Council for Exceptional Children.

Roberts, C.A. and Lazure. (Eds.). (1970). *One million children: A national study of Canadian children with emotional and learning disorders.* Toronto: Crainford.

Salvia, J., Clark, G.M., and Ysseldyke, J.E. (1973). Teacher retention of stereotypes of exceptionality. *Exceptional Children, 39,* 651-652.

Sanche, R., Haines, L., and Van Hesteren, F. (1982). Pre-service teacher preparation for mainstreaming: Attitude formation and measurement. *B.C. Journal of Special Education, 6,* 69-77.

Secretary of State Regan tables federal government's continuing response to Obstacles Report. (1982). *The Deaf Canadian, 7,* 6-9.

Shotel, J., Iano, R. and McGettigan, J. (1972). Teacher attitudes associated with the integration of handicapped children. *Exceptional Children, 38,* 677-683.

Statistics of special education for exceptional children. (1966). Ottawa: Dominion Bureau of Statistics.

Stephens, T.M. and Braun, B.L. (1980). Measures of regular classroom teachers' attitudes toward handicapped children. *Exceptional Children, 46,* 292-294.

Stothers, C.C. (1959). The first special education university course in Canada. *Special Education in Canada, 33-34,* 75-76.

Telford, C.W. and Sawrey, J.M. (1981). *The exceptional individual* (4th Ed.). Englewood Cliffs, N.J.: Prentice-Hall.

Trimble, B.K. and Baird, P.A. (1978). Congenital anomalies of the central nervous system: Incidence in British Columbia, 1952-72. *Teratology, 17,* 43-50.

Vacc, N.A. and Kirst, N. (1977). Emotionally disturbed children and regular classroom teachers. *Elementary School Journal, 77,* 309-317.

Ward, J. (1984). The rehabilitation of the disabled: A challenge for the '80s. *The Exceptional Child, 31,* 5-17.

Watters, B. (1980). Special education in the Northwest Territories. In M. Csapo and L. Goguen (Eds.), *Special education across Canada: Issues and concerns for the '80s.* Vancouver: Centre for Human Development and Research.

Whyte, L.A. (1980). Commentary. In G.M. Kysela (Ed.), *The exceptional child in Canadian education* (CSSE *yearbook*). Vancouver: Canadian Society for the Study of Education.

Williams, R.J. and Algozzine, B. (1979). Teachers' attitudes toward mainstreaming. *Elementary School Journal, 80,* 63-67.

Winzer, M. (1984a). Mainstreaming the handicapped child: Attitudes of teachers and non-teachers. *Canadian Journal for Exceptional Children, 1,* 23-26.

Winzer, M. (1984b). The effect of information on the attitudes of teachers and non-educators toward mainstreaming. *B.C. Journal of Special Education, 8,* 273-282.

Wolfensberger, W. (1972). *The principle of normalization in human services.* Toronto: National Institute on Mental Retardation.

CHAPTER TWO

Parents and families of exceptional children

MARGRET WINZER

The time immediately after the birth of my child with multiple congenital defects was the loneliest time of my life. I felt that neither encouraging family or friends nor competent and sympathetic doctors could really help, for none of them had ever given birth to such a child.

(Ouellett, 1972)

There are many apprenticeships available for professions and careers, but none for that most difficult job — parenting. There are no courses to teach really practical methods of child-rearing, or to teach parents how to weather the crises, frustrated ambitions, and periods of high stress that are common to most families. Nonetheless, most parents manage to raise their children remarkably well. They willingly endure many trials, problems, and moments of despair, secure in the hope that one day their children will become self-sufficient adults.

Like other parents, the parents of exceptional children must learn how to cope with problems in ways that will enhance rather than hinder the growth of their children. However, in addition to the usual stresses and strains, parents of exceptional children face other pressures. The discovery of a handicapped child creates intense and conflicting feelings among the members of a family. The family undergoes a crisis, the resolution of which determines whether they will live together in relative peace and contentment or in frustration, anger, and guilt.

The relationship between the exceptional child and the family is reciprocal; the child deeply affects the family climate, while the family, in turn, affects the child. Family problems that arise from the presence of a handicapped child require as much professional attention as the educational and medical treatment of the child. However, only during the past few decades have we begun to fully appreciate the parental pain and stress that accompany a handicapped child. Only recently have we come to realize the degree of courage and external support that parents need to retain their equilibrium.

Families often represent the only long-term, responsible, and caring people in the life of a handicapped child. The family is of vital importance: interaction with family members deeply influences the child's opportunities and barriers, challenges and expectations, ambitions and frustrations, and general quality of life. Whether the family is nuclear, single-parent, or extended, it plays a powerful role in the child's social, emotional, behavioural, and academic development and progress.

The handicapped child has a major impact on the family. Although this impact is not necessarily negative, it does require modification in family structure and roles. Parents and siblings are bound to find some problems, and may need to solve these with the aid of outside sources.

In this chapter, we present an overview of the dilemmas and stresses that may be faced by the families of exceptional children. As well, we will examine some of the types of intervention that are available to help parents cope with and enhance the prospects of normal development for their exceptional child. This help has been made possible through the caring and persistence of educators, advocates, and a wide range of allied child-care personnel.

FAMILY REACTIONS TO THE EXCEPTIONAL CHILD

Initial Response

Expecting parents have great dreams for their unborn child. They hope for intelligence and physical beauty, and plan ahead for later accomplishments and successes. When a handicapped child is born, these parental aspirations are shattered. The parents suffer a symbolic death of their hopes and dreams. A void is created that is only bridged as the family reformulates its expectations to accommodate reality.

As well as confronting the symbolic death of their expectations, parents must also be concerned with the provision of daily care for their child. They may need to provide immediate care, arrange transportation to treatment, alter methods of scheduling time, meet new financial costs, and assimilate technical information about the disability. At the same time, parents may have to confront cruel labels and stereotypes, a sense of isolation from others, and well-meaning but intrusive advice from friends. Parents may also have to provide support for other family members (Fortier and Wanlass, 1984).

The parents' history of dealing with problems will be reflected in their ability to cope with their handicapped child. If past crises have tended to produce major upheavals, then the discovery of a handicapped child will only add to already existing problems. But if the parents have been able to make healthy adjustments to past difficulties, they are more likely to find the route to acceptance more comfortable.

When first confronted with their child's condition, parents may show many patterns of reaction. Exhibit 2-1 outlines the possible range of these parental reactions. Not all parents pass through all of these stages, and each person works through them at a different rate of time. Parents are as unique as their children, and differ widely in their responses to their child's handicap. Some parents cope with steady resolve and competence; others barely manage to survive the daily routine.

Although parents respond differently, most pass through similar stages before they accept the reality of their child's condition (Chinn, Winn, and Walters, 1978). Acceptance does not come all at once; it begins fleetingly and goes on to fluctuate at different levels in different situations. Parental sadness may resurface at critical junctures in the life of the child and the family. A recurrence of sorrow and frustration may be triggered by milestones such as reaching school age, attaining puberty, and watching other children graduate from school or marry.

Exhibit 2-1 Parental reactions to the diagnosis of a handicapping condition.

Acute initial reactions	*Chronic adaptive reactions*	*Mature adaptation*
shock	withdrawal and isolation	refashioning expectations
denial and disbelief	depression	coping with everyday practical problems
anger	ambivalence	maximizing the child's potential
bitterness and shame, loss of self-esteem	rejection	protecting the interests of the whole family
inappropriate guilt, projection of blame	overprotectiveness; self-sacrifice, defensiveness	interaction with others
disappointment, sadness, grief bargaining	doctor "shopping"	

The impact of diagnosis

The age of the child at the time of diagnosis will vary. Parents may learn about a problem immediately after birth, as in the case of Down's Syndrome or they may discover a problem much more slowly as the child matures. Some children may not be handicapped by congenital conditions, but through childhood disease or accident.

It is impossible for parents to accept the diagnosis of their child's handicapping condition without reacting strongly. Immediately after the diagnosis, the first acute reactions are felt. When first presented with the problem, most parents react with shock, often accompanied by denial and disbelief. Their expectations are violated and their hopes shattered.

The period of shock is usually brief because of the necessity for making decisions regarding treatment. The period of denial may be more protracted, especially if the condition is not readily obvious to the parents. Denial may operate as a protective device, giving parents additional time to adjust to the pain and disappointment of lost expectations. Denial becomes maladaptive, however, when it results in the withholding of treatment necessary to ensure the child's optimal development. Unwittingly, family, friends, and even professionals, may support parental denial. Anxious to relieve the parent's worries, they suggest that the child will "grow out" of the condition, and may delay proper treatment as a result.

Parents may also feel anger when they learn of their child's condition. Initially they may direct this anger at the child as the obvious source of their frustration. When parents turn the anger inward, they can react with fear, guilt, and shame. Fear arises when parents hold misfounded apprehensions and incorrect information regarding the handicap, the implications, and the prognosis.

Parents may also feel profoundly alienated from others. They may believe that no one else has a problem like theirs. One mother's sense of alienation is succinctly expressed in the quote that opens this chapter.

Some parents feel guilt because they think the condition could have been avoided had they done something different. Others believe the handicap serves as retribution for some misdeed. Parents ask, "Why us?" and seek explanations. They consider factors such as marital discord, prenuptial pregnancy, unusual sex practices, use of drugs, and unusual events during pregnancy. Some parents worry that the handicap might be of a genetic nature. These parents worry about their future children, and sometimes view the handicap as a defect in themselves.

Parents who feel shame see their handicapped child as a threat to the family's prestige. They worry about the stigma attached to the handicap and anticipate social rejection.

Sometimes parents project guilt onto others. They direct resentment and hostility at their spouses, their other children, the doctor, the counsellor, society in general, even God. Some parents question their religious beliefs, others find solace in them. Although the evidence is somewhat inconclusive, some studies have found parents with a strong religious affiliation to be more accepting of their handicapped children (Boles, 1959; Zuk, 1962).

Mourning or grief is a natural reaction to the disappointment of having a handicapped child. Like anger, denial, and guilt, grief follows the initial diagnosis. For some parents, grief results in withdrawal and depression. Others take recourse in bargaining, or trying to make a deal with God, science, or society to cure their child.

Parents' initial grief may be more intense when the diagnosis is made well after the birth of the child. By this time, their hopes for the child have lasted longer and their bonds of affection have grown stronger (Fortier and Wanlass, 1984). Moreover, grief may continue to some extent throughout the parents' life, and may seldom disappear completely (Mindel and Vernon, 1971; Wikler, Wasow, and Hatfield, 1981).

Adjustment

Some parents are never able to completely accept their child's handicapping condition. They may accept the diagnosis but reject the prognostic implications. Such parents may embark on a trek from doctor to doctor and clinic to clinic. They may search for a more promising prognosis, miracle drugs, a new operation, a novel form of psychotherapy, or a radically new diet.

Some parents may reject the child as well as the condition. They may treat the child with open hostility, or use more subtle ploys, such as setting unrealistic goals or failing to praise positive behaviour. Other parents may develop positive and accepting attitudes, but nevertheless harbour resentment toward their child. Every parent must occasionally feel ambivalent about restricted activities, additional responsibilities, disappointments, and anxieties. If parents feel guilty about their ambivalent feelings, they may become overprotective and oversolicitous. They may try to compensate for their negative feelings with a life of martyrdom and self-sacrifice.

Parents may also foster an over-dependency in their child which eventually becomes circuitous. In the course of investing themselves emotionally in their child, these parents exaggerate the child's needs and promote an overly dependent attitude. Then, to prove their worth as parents, they allow their whole lives to become centred on the child. Such parents may actually resist attempts by others to ease the burden.

Acceptance

Many parents, of course, reach a stage of mature adaptation at which they can accept the child, the handicap, and themselves. They become reconciled to the fact that their child's condition deeply affects, and will continue to affect, the entire family. They hold a realistic hope that, despite hardship, the family can and will survive.

Mature adaptation is the end of the crisis period. At this stage, the family begins to mobilize its resources to adapt to their situation and cope with what is to come. Family solidarity also seems to emerge at this time, the close of the crisis period (Fortier and Wanlass, 1984).

PROFILE 2-1

Mrs. J. did not know she had contracted the rubella virus early in her third pregnancy. She felt healthy throughout the period and was not overly concerned when her infant arrived nearly a month before term. Labour was normal, of about fourteen hours' duration. The infant cried lustily, and Mrs. J. readily accepted the explanation that he was in neonatal intensive care only because he was of slightly low birth-weight.

Information about the true nature of the child's condition came quickly. Within twenty-four hours of the birth, the physician explained to both parents that the child, now named Stephen, was suffering serious defects as the result of the rubella virus. Examination had shown a defective heart and serious visual problems. The physician explained that other anomalies could emerge, possibly deafness and mental retardation. The physician urged the parents to think about institutional placement for Stephen if he survived his first month.

The parents' shock was soon displaced by grief and the necessity for making decisions about care. Mr. J. urged early institutionalization. Their oldest son had already been identified as learning-disabled, and Mr. J. perceived a seriously handicapped infant as potentially very disrupting to the family climate. Mrs. J., on the other hand, was determined not to accept the rather hopeless prognosis of the physician. She wanted to raise the child at home, to treat him, as far as possible, like the other children, and to seek support to assist in his development.

Stephen spent nearly three months in the neonatal unit. Once at home, he proved a fairly easy baby to handle. In fact, he was so docile and passive that this concerned his mother.

Mrs. J. became very active in seeking outside help. By the time Stephen was nine months of age, a visiting teacher was coming once a week. She worked with Stephen on various developmental tasks, especially in the motor area. Because language was a concern, she showed Mrs. J. how to stimulate Stephen's vocalizations, and gave hints about receptive language development.

By the time Stephen was sixteen months, a severe-to-profound hearing loss was confirmed. His vision was poor with a restricted visual field. However, with some complaint, he accepted both a hearing aid and glasses. He also reached some major developmental milestones — he walked and began to eat solid foods.

Throughout Stephen's pre-school years, Mrs. J. behaved toward him and disciplined him just as she did the older children. She accepted his multiple disabilities but held relevant expectations for his development. He became an integral part of the family circle. Sibling resentment was not directed at any special treatment Stephen received; it surfaced only when he got into the same type of mischief that any pre-schooler does. For both siblings, their proudest day was when Stephen marched off with them to his first day in the local public school.

THE FAMILY CLIMATE

Most observers conclude that rearing a handicapped child is often burdensome, tiresome, and frustrating. Families with handicapped children seem to be particularly vulnerable to stress (Fotheringham and Creal, 1974; Holroyd and McArthur, 1976). The presence of an exceptional child in the family circle not only creates stress, but can serve as a focus for existing stress. In some families, though, the handicapped child can provide a rallying point for increased family cohesion. This is illustrated by the family presented in Profile 2-1.

Some family stress results from the child's condition, but some is also influenced by the child-rearing practices and parent-child interactions prevalent in our culture. One dimension of stress appears to be related to the diagnostic category of the child. For example, one study assessed the amount of stress reported by parents of autistic children, Down's Syndrome children, and children who were outpatients in a psychiatric clinic. The parents showed different response patterns, but the parents of autistic children reported the most stress (Holroyd and McArthur, 1976).

Parents of handicapped boys report more stress than parents of girls. The age of the child may also be related to the stress felt by a family. As they grow older, children become harder to manage. At the same time, the gap between the progress of exceptional children and their peers becomes more noticeable (Bristol, 1979).

If a severely handicapped child does not develop sufficient independence and autonomy, that child may permanently occupy the social position of the youngest in the family. This easily becomes a source of conflict and difficulty. The child becomes a perpetual baby and never emerges from an infantile status (Hallahan and Kauffman, 1982).

Individual child characteristics interact with differing parental characteristics to produce a wide range of parent — child interactions and parenting styles. A high level of family stress may be created by a particular child's slower progress, more difficult temperament, lack of social responsiveness, adherence to stereotypic behaviour patterns, or additional or unusual caregiving needs (Beckman-Bell, 1981). Parents may become frustrated when their handicapped children do not respond in a normal manner, whether socially, behaviourally, or physically.

The attachment process between handicapped infants and their parents can be disrupted from birth. This disruption may arise from the medical needs of the child. Premature and handicapped infants may be kept in neonatal intensive care for up to twelve weeks, depending on birth weight, gestational age, physical anomalies, respiration, and weight gain. Such a separation naturally affects the bonding between parent and child. It may also adversely affect later parental-child interactions.

At home with their parents, children may display social, behavioural, and physical responses that create stress and worry. For example, children with problems such as Fetal Alcohol Syndrome, Down's Syndrome, and cleft palate may also have feeding problems. They may exhibit limited abilities to suck, bite, chew, or swallow. In some children, the delayed eruption of teeth may also prohibit the development of advanced chewing patterns (Mills and Hedges, 1983).

Robson and Moss (1970) found that about half of mothers' first positive feelings about their infants were associated with early communication responses — smiling, laughing, eye contact, and vocalization. The absence of such responses can disrupt the mother's relationship with her child. Because handicapped children often seem less responsive, parents need to work harder to focus their attention and generate smiles and contented vocalizations. Moreover, the stimulation threshold for these children is more difficult to judge and maintain. Once this is passed, the children fuss and cry and are harder to console (Field, 1983).

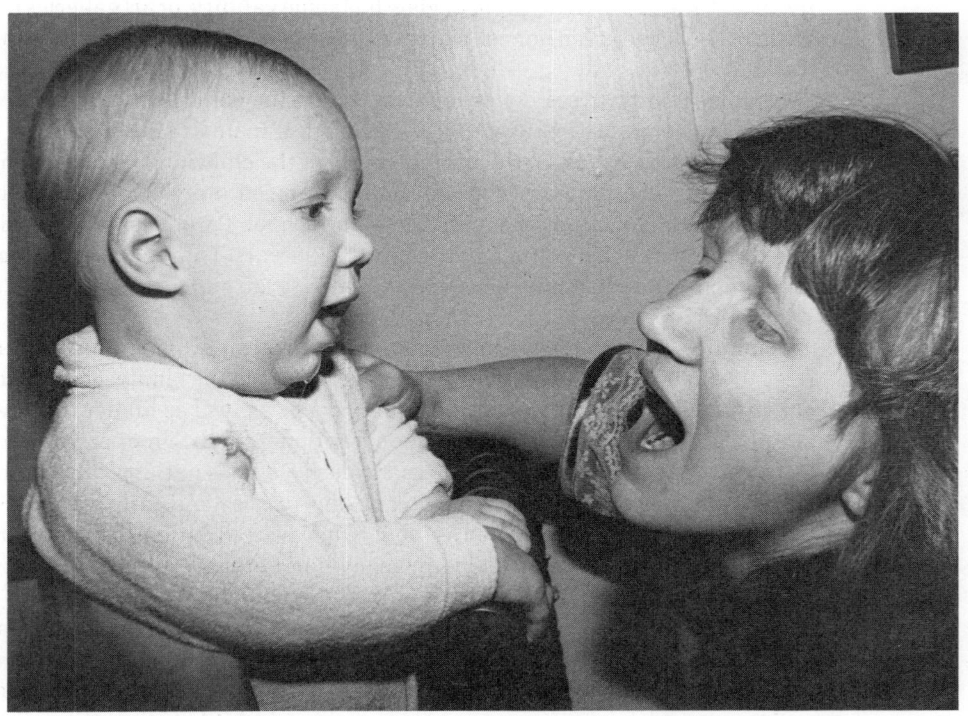

Early communication between parent and child is vital for healthy development. (M.C. Emme)

The presence of serious behaviour problems can be a source of great stress to the parents, both in the home and when visiting public places (Marcus, 1977). Behaviour problems may also make it difficult to find sitters and to maintain natural interaction with the neighbours. Negative behaviours may encourage parents to withdraw from outside social interactions. Parents may believe that negative societal reactions to their child's deviant behaviour reflects on their own capacity as parents, as well as their status in general. Not infrequently, parents interpret their child's negative behaviour as a verification of the handicap. For example, they often blame temper tantrums on the handicap rather than seeing them as a normal phase of emerging independence (Haggerty, 1980).

Fathers, more than mothers, are affected in the social domain. Fathers of mentally retarded children appear to suffer more from depression and lowered self-esteem (Cummings, Bayley, and Rie, 1976). They have more difficulty coping with the child and are more vulnerable to social stigma (Tallman, 1965). They also have more difficulty living with the uncertainty of the child's impairment and discussing the problem with friends (Erickson, 1976).

Fathers may be most affected because they often hold more specific and demanding expectations for their children. According to Akerley (1975), this can be seen in parents' different reactions to a pre-schooler's first painting of a horse. Dad points out that horses are not green and generally have four legs; Mom calls it beautiful and hangs it up for all the world to admire. Dad's point of view has some validity, or art galleries might be filled with three-legged green horses. However, his viewpoint also makes certain demands on the child.

Another family stress factor is the nature of the child's educational program (Gallagher, Beckman, and Cross, 1983). Although a mainstream placement in a regular school might clearly be in the best interests of the child, such a placement may cause problems for the parents. These parents are faced daily with reminders of the lag between their child and other children at the school. Parents may feel socially stigmatized by the handicap, and isolated from other parents. They may worry about the social adjustment of their child and the availability of support services (Turnbull and Blacher-Dixon, 1980).

As stated earlier, the handicapped child, regardless of ordinal position, is often relegated to the permanent status of youngest child in the family. This can cause family stress and disruption of the normal family cycle, as well as hinder the development of autonomous attitudes on the part of the exceptional child. Some parents allow two quite different disciplinary systems to run side by side — one for the non-handicapped children, and a more lenient, permissive system for the handicapped child. Some parents treat their handicapped children as though they were ill, giving them fewer responsibilities and placing fewer restrictions on behaviour. Parents are more tolerant of undesirable behaviour, often at the expense of the other siblings.

Other parents tend to be harsher with the exceptional child. Schlesinger and Meadow (1972) found that parents of pre-school deaf children gave more constant supervision, reported a narrower range of disciplinary techniques, relied more heavily on spanking, and expressed frustration about more areas of child-rearing than did mothers of pre-school hearing children. A substantial body of research evidence also indicates that handicapped children are at greater risk for child abuse (Embry, 1980). Mentally retarded children appear with disproportionate frequency in numerous studies of child maltreatment (Frodi, 1981). Increased family tensions and the child's decreased ability to perform acceptably, combined with the physical and financial burdens of raising a handicapped child, apparently lead to extremely harsh parental behaviour in many instances (Gaines, Sandgrund, Green, and Power, 1978; Gath, 1972; Schilling and Schinke, 1984).

To compound all these problems, financial burdens can cause parents constant concern and frustration. The need for special equipment, special medical care, and special programs often brings financial hardship (Holroyd, 1974; McAndrew, 1976; Meadow, 1980). Economic pressures can distort the parents' emotional response to their child, particularly in families with limited financial resources.

Marital stress and conflict

Research offers some support for the common-sense observation that an exceptional child adds greatly to the strain on a marriage. However, the findings in this area are conflicting. Although several studies report increased marital conflict (Farber, 1959; Holroyd, 1974; Marcus, 1977; Tavormina and Kralj, 1975), others indicate no increase in marital problems (Freeman, Malkin, and Hastings, 1975). A few studies even suggest that the presence of a handicapped child brings parents closer together (McAndrew, 1976).

Akerley (1975) contends that fifty-five percent of families with handicapped children break up completely. A recent review of the literature (Price-Bonham and Addison, 1978) found increased divorce rates among the parents of retarded children. However, in a study of the families of deaf children in Vancouver (Freeman, Malkin, and Hastings, 1975), no increased divorce rate was found among the parents. Another study compared families who kept their retarded child at home to those who institutionalized their retarded child. This study found that the presence of a severely retarded child in the home did not adversely affect marital integration. Most families who institutionalized their children had already been functioning poorly before the birth of their handicapped child. Moreover, institutionalization did not solve these families' problems (Farber, 1960; Fotheringham and Creal, 1974; Fowle, 1968).

From this conflicting evidence, we can only state that the presence of a handicapped child places a strain on the parents' marriage, and serves to underline already existing tension. However, in some families, the handicapped child may become the focus of increased family solidarity and cohesion.

Divorce is not the only way in which stress manifests itself. Both alcoholism and minor marital problems have been found to prevail among families with handicapped children (Block, 1978). Increased suicide rates have been discovered among parents of retarded children (Price-Bonham and Addison, 1978).

Siblings of handicapped children

Although no general picture of sibling reaction to the exceptional child has emerged, many siblings do respond negatively to the handicapped child. An early study reported that psychiatrists treated more siblings of handicapped children than the handicapped individuals themselves (Poznanski, 1969). More recent research indicates that siblings of handicapped children have a high incidence of emotional problems. These are related to feelings of guilt for being normal and to their parents' expectations that they will excel (Haggerty, 1980).

We have mentioned that parents may react differently to different diagnostic categories. The same may be true of siblings. When the attitudes of siblings of children with cerebral palsy, Down's Syndrome, blindness, deafness, and organic damage were compared, different attitudes emerged (Barsch, 1968). The siblings of deaf children showed a much larger proportion of negative attitudes: twenty percent of these siblings held negative attitudes as compared to an average of ten percent for the siblings of children with other kinds of handicap.

According to Trevino (1979), prospects for the siblings are most difficult when:

- There are only two children, one handicapped and one non-handicapped.
- The non-handicapped sibling is close in age or younger than the handicapped sibling.
- The non-handicapped sibling is the oldest female child.
- The handicapped and the non-handicapped sibling are of the same sex.
- The parents are unable to accept the handicap.

Females, especially oldest sisters, are more likely to be adversely affected by a handicaped sibling. Children younger than the handicapped child may also meet problems. Unlike older children, the younger siblings of a handicapped child have never had the experience of living in a "normal" family. They have probably not received a usual amount of attention because of the amount of adult time spent with the handicapped child (Akerley, 1975).

When non-handicapped siblings are required to supervise, care for, defend, and protect the handicapped child, resentment often develops. This resentment is aggravated when the handicapped child receives excessive attention and affection, or when additional care expenses deprive the others of educational and recreational opportunities. Sometimes, non-handicapped children are made to bear unrealistically high parental expectations. They may even be expected to repress their abilities so they do not perform better than the exceptional child. Some parents establish two different sets of rules, which may intensify sibling rivalry. The parents' attempts to protect the handicapped child may also result in various degrees of neglect for the other siblings.

The major concerns of siblings of handicapped children seem to be:

- The kind and amount of attention the disabled child requires of parents and siblings. This may interfere with the sibling's normal child-parent relationship, with family activity, and with social life outside the home.
- Disappointment at not having a normal sibling.
- The embarrassment of relating to the disabled sibling in the company of peers or in public.
- The heavy demands on normal siblings to care for the handicapped child.
- The pressure on the normal child to "make up" for the deficits in the disabled child.
- The concerns of adolescents about future genetic risks for themselves. (Schaffer, 1977.)

Although many siblings of handicapped childen react with resentment, guilt, and uneasiness, a significant number seem to reap benefits. Grossman (1972) found that many siblings of retarded children appeared to be more tolerant, more compassionate, and more aware of prejudice and its consequences.

The extended family

Handicapped children have a considerable impact on the extended family. At the same time, the extended family may influence the development of handicapped children through direct interactions and through the nature of the support provided to their parents (Cochran and Brassard, 1979).

In many ways, grandchildren provide a new lease on life for their grandparents (Benedek, 1970). The sense of surviving through the grandchild may help soothe the increasing infirmities of advancing age and the approaching reality of death. Grandchildren also allow grandparents to relive the joys of their own early parenthood. Playing with and caring for young grandchildren supplies grandparents with a revitalized feeling of importance and purpose in life (Gabel and Kotsch, 1981).

Like parents, grandparents hope for a healthy, normal baby. When the child is diagnosed as exceptional, they too may experience a death of expectations (Berns, 1980). This may leave them with a diminished capacity to provide support for the child's parents.

Grandparents pass through many of the same stages that parents do. They may feel angry when their grandchild is found to be handicapped. Some paternal grandmothers express their resentment toward their daughters-in-law (Farber and Ryckman, 1965). Pieper (1976) described how her mother-in-law lashed out in anger when presented with a handicapped grandchild. The grandmother blamed the daughter-in-law for having bad blood and burdening her husband with such a child.

DEALING WITH PROFESSIONALS

Parents' discovery of their child's handicapping condition brings them into the orbit of a number of professional disciplines. Many different people are available to support the parents and to help the child through various stages of development. Exhibit 2-2 shows a sampling of those who may intervene at some point with the child, the parents, or the family.

Few, if any, exceptional children will require all, or even most, of these professional services. However, the exceptional child certainly will meet some of these professionals at some time. A child diagnosed in infancy, for example, would encounter many of the medical personnel in hospital. Once the child was in the home, visiting personnel might provide infant stimulation, information for the parents, and the first steps for educational intervention.

The establishment of positive relationships between parents and professionals depends upon a number of factors. The professional must understand the parents' problems, must be flexible, and must appear open and empathetic. The professional's ability to communicate effectively with parents is of prime importance.

Exhibit 2-2 A sampling of disciplines involved with exceptional children.

Medical	*Paramedical*	*Educational*	*Psychological Social, Behavioural*
physician	audiologist	home-visiting teacher	intervenor
pediatrician	optometrist	infant stimulation therapist	social worker
neurologist	physical therapist	pre-school teacher	school social worker
otolaryngolist	occupational therapist	regular classroom teacher	child care worker
opthalmologist	public health nurse	special class teacher	guidance counsellor
dental surgeon	school nurse	remedial specialist	psychologist
psychiatrist		itinerant teacher	
nurse		learning assistant	
		school principal	
		speech therapist	
		language pathologist	

Parents and physicians

The ability of parents to cope with the initial diagnosis of their child's condition may be related to a variety of factors. These may include the informant's communication skills, the time when the diagnosis is presented, the nature and severity of the handicap, and the availability of outside resources. The socio-economic status and emotional stability of the parents may also be factors.

Pediatricians hold the primary responsibility for guiding parents through the first stages of the diagnostic process (Howard, 1982). Physicians and pediatricians are usually the ones to inform parents about their child's condition. In one survey, ninety-one percent of physicians claimed they were the first to inform the parents of a newborn about the existence of a handicap. A total of eighty-eight percent of the physicians informed the parents immediately after the birth, and provided specific diagnostic labels when possible (McDonald, Carson, Palmer, and Slay, 1982).

The initial diagnosis period is an emotionally vulnerable time for the family. Some parents deny the existence of a problem, while others acknowledge the handicap but insist that it is temporary. Some families pursue further medical opinions, while others resign themselves to the doctor's initial findings (Haggerty, 1980).

In the past, parents often voiced dissatisfaction regarding the manner in which they were told of their child's condition. They complained that the physician presented the initial diagnosis to only one parent, in an unsympathetic manner, using derogatory terms, or with inappropriate recommendations long after the parents already suspected a problem (Pueschel and Murphy, 1976). Some doctors have tended to be more pontifical than helpful; rather than providing specific information, they have generalized or offered vague hints and irrelevant observations. A physician's brusqueness or inability to communicate contributes to the parents' reaction of anger and hurt.

A physician's negative attitude may stem from a reluctance to be the bearer of bad tidings. Physicians, too, develop strategies to cope with stressful situations. They may appear cold and uncaring, when they are actually deeply concerned (Wolraich, 1982). Discomfort and a real sympathy for the family can cause them to reveal the diagnosis awkwardly and abruptly, sometimes causing the parents lasting bitterness. Despite these dangers, however, parents prefer to know the truth, however starkly stated (Steinberg, 1980).

Parents often turn to their pediatrician for assistance, guidance, and comfort during the diagnostic period. An informed and compassionate pediatrician can be invaluable in healing the emotionally distraught family (Clyman, Sniderman, Ballard, and Roth, 1979; Howard, 1982). Crucial factors include the pediatrician's attitude toward handicapped children, knowledge of the handicapping condition, and skill in communicating with parents (Wolraich, 1980, 1982). Pediatricians cannot rely on traditional medical models when dealing with the parents of handicapped children. They must keep up with current child-development information, and be willing to seek help from professionals in other disciplines.

Parents prefer to be told about their child's condition together, and as soon as possible. Parental aspirations for the newborn child crystallize within the first forty-eight hours after birth. Evidence suggests that aggression and resentment are more destructive in parents who have not known of handicaps from the earliest days (MacKay, 1976).

When presenting a diagnosis, physicians appear to take into account the severity of the condition and the emotional stability of the parents. One study found that physicians were more frank and informative to the parents of more severely retarded children (Lipton and Svarstad, 1977). These same doctors tended to give more information to parents they perceived as emotionally quite well adjusted. They were not highly informative to those parents viewed as below average in emotional adjustment.

Parental concerns include care of the infant, readjustment of family routines, possible neglect of other family members, the financial cost of special care, and disruptions to family integration (Howard, 1982). From the outset, pediatricians can help the parents overcome these problems. They can help the parents build a relationship with their child, and help them recognize the child's individuality and unique contributions to the family unit. They can provide information about the nature of the handicap and suggest management measures. Physicians can also advise the parents about other support services and resources.

Parent and family counselling

Before parents can effectively assist in the education of their handicapped child they need to overcome their own emotional reactions. Many parents seek counselling, especially in the period immediately following the initial diagnosis.

Counselling programs offer a range of approaches. However, although the programs impart different information and use different methods, their goals are essentially the same. Counselling should help parents understand the meaning of their child's diagnosis, and aid them in developing realistic expectations for their child. Counselling sessions also provide a forum in which parents can openly express and work through their feelings of anger, fear, and anxiety.

The counselling of families with handicapped children is really closer to social work than to psychotherapy. Counselling is not intended to change the personalities of family members. Rather, it should help the family to handle the special problems and environmental adjustments that accompany a handicapped child. The counsellor will stress immediate practical concerns and try to develop an approach that is appropriate for the family's individual needs, life style, and culture (Hoff, 1978).

Parents primarily seek information about their child's condition, capacities, and developmental needs. This is seldom enough. Parents also need help with their attitudes and feelings. When parents are encouraged to openly express their feelings, they can learn to appreciate their child's positive potential; this helps them to provide a niche for the child in their social system. This counselling may not be time-limited. Buscaglia (1975) stresses lifelong counselling to promote information and self-discovery for both the exceptional person and the family.

In many cases, the counselling sessions will actively involve siblings. One mother argues that any child over the age of two should be involved in solving family problems (Akerley, 1975). She urges that problems be explained simply and honestly to siblings, with a fair assessment of how the problems will affect family life. In instances when the child has a psychiatric or psychosomatic disability that appears to be maintained by the family system, instensive family therapy may be particularly valuable (Minuchin, Rosman, and Baker, 1978).

Parent self-help groups

In addition to counselling, parents should also be directed to parent and community groups involved with exceptional children. These groups promote understanding and offer parents therapeutic involvement with people with similar problems. The groups provide a forum in which parents can discuss their concerns and exchange ideas with each other. Parents can channel their frustrations and anxieties into positive action for their children, while gaining more realistic hopes for the future. Groups also help parents to develop a more positive sense of their parenting roles.

Across Canada, parent organizations exist at the local, provincial, and national level. Some of these groups are small, local, and casual; others are affiliated with professional organizations. Many parent organizations have lobbied successfully for improved educational, social, recreational, and vocational services for their children.

Through these groups, parents are increasingly acting as advocates for themselves and their handicapped children. Parents are starting to act as decision-makers and independent policy planners. The emerging role of parents as advocates and monitors of services is likely to have a considerable impact on special education (Mitchell, 1983).

Pilot Parents is an example of a parent-support group with chapters throughout Canada and the United States. The program was developed by parents of mentally handicapped children in order to offer support to parents of newly diagnosed retarded children. Support and sharing are the essential concerns of Pilot Parents, as they are for most other parent groups. More specifically, Pilot Parents is aimed at these objectives:

- To offer emotional understanding and practical support to new families during the initial critical period when a child's handicap has just been discovered.
- To provide new parents with factual information on mental retardation, community services, and other resources.
- To increase professional and public awareness of mental retardation.
- To promote acceptance of mentally retarded children in their own families and communities (Cameron, 1981).

Parent education

During the first years of a child's life, the parents assume the primary role of care and management. During these early years, the child's interpersonal relationships are vital to emotional and social development, and to the emergence of personality. Interaction with parents prepares the child to live in society by providing models of behaviour and easing the child's integration into the community. Recently, there has been a growing awareness that parents play a crucial role in facilitating and maintaining developmental gains in handicapped children. As a result, parents are becoming more involved as partners in the child's educational progress.

Recently, a wide range of parent education programs have been implemented. In the early 1960s, the impact of high-risk conditions upon children's later cognitive, linguistic, and social functioning led to the development and implementation of ameliorative programs for disadvantaged pre-schoolers across North America. As a result of these programs, the target population was expanded both vertically — to include toddlers and infants — and categorically — to include impaired and high-risk children (Kysela and Marfo, 1983).

Early and sustained educational intervention is vital to help exceptional children achieve some measure of independence. During the past fifteen years, interest in early intervention programs has increased dramatically. These programs try to enhance the child's development by helping the parents to become effective intervenors. Children seem to develop more quickly when parents are involved (Zigler and Valentine, 1979). Taking part in their child's education may also help parents to accept the handicapping condition. Parents' reactions may vary depending upon whether they think the condition can be improved and whether they feel they can participate successfully in the treatment program (Lavelle and Keogh, 1980).

Parents may be involved in educational or therapeutic interventions in home-based programs, classrooms, or other settings. Across Canada, there exists wide variability in the program options available for infants, toddlers, and pre-schoolers. Programs are administered by diverse organizations and different types of program are available in each community (Tobias and Kendall, 1984).

Parent training is as important for the success of early intervention programs as the training of their infants (Bricker and Bricker, 1976). The most successful programs have involved parent participation and have started before the child was two years old (Levenstein, 1970; Stedman, 1977). These programs are known as Infant Development Programs or "home-visiting programs." They offer parents intensive participation, and usually continue until the child is about three years of age.

Under an Infant Development Program, the teacher visits the home on a regular basis to help parents enhance their child's physical, self-help, academic, and language development. The parents of a hearing-impaired child, for example, are taught to appreciate their crucial role in communication development. They are shown how to provide models of language, how to motivate language through conversational exchange, and how to elicit vocalizations. The parents of a Down's Syndrome child may be shown how to stimulate motor activity. The parents of a child with cerebral palsy might learn how to hold or roll the infant. As well, the teacher provides general information to the parents and directs them to other community agencies.

Intervention should not become the sole concern of the mother. Parents can offer each other support and encouragement, and cope more effectively together with the stresses they face (Gallagher, Beckman, and Cross, 1983; Markowitz, 1984). Because the handicapping condition has an impact on the functioning of the entire family, siblings should also be included in the child's education. (Friedrich, 1977).

Occasionally, conflict arises between the professional and the parents concerning their different roles. The professional's efforts are devoted almost exclusively to the handicapped child. The parents must attend to the needs of the child, to other members of the family and to themselves. The professional may urge the parents to spend more time and effort on the child, but parents must weigh this against the needs of their family as a whole. When parents cannot participate fully, they risk guilt and criticism for appearing not to have their child's interests at heart (Akerley, 1975).

Exhibit 2-3 suggests some tips for working with parents.

Exhibit 2-3 Tips for working with parents.

- Respect the parents by not talking down to them. Respect the child as well.
- Listen carefully to parents.
- Be tactful and task-oriented when offering suggestions.
- Offer the parents help in locating additional services. Don't be territorial.
- Hope that parents will help to develop and maintain the child's potential, but don't expect them to fill the role of teacher.
- When you perform an activity with the child, explain why, how, and when.
- After you've explained or demonstrated an activity, let the parent take over.
- When possible, use items from around the house as toys. A coffee can and a wooden spoon make a wonderful drum.
- Include other members of the family, when possible.
- Stress the positive aspects of the child's development.
- Involve parents in all aspects of decision-making and planning.
- Be sensitive to, and honest about, the limitations of your own knowledge and abilities.
- Be sensitive to the child's individuality, but remember that parents are individuals too.
- Don't offend the parents by over- or under-dressing.

At three years of age, the child can generally be admitted to an available special program. Many special-needs pre-school programs serve a specific population of children, although most serve a variety of handicapping conditions. These pre-schools focus on stimulating and sustaining growth in those areas of development where a child has demonstrated a lag. The amount of parent participation in these classroom programs varies widely.

In the following chapters, special considerations in eduating pre-school age children with various handicaps are discussed.

INTERVENTION WITH EXCEPTIONAL CHILDREN

Intervention is a general term that refers to the application of professional skills to maintain or improve a child's potential and functioning. A number of programs are subsumed under the general rubric of intervention. **Therapy** implies the treatment of an illness or a disabling condition. **Rehabilitation** refers to procedures that endeavour to restore the individual to normal or optimal functioning. **Remediation** is an educational term that refers to helping the child to overcome, or compensate for, specific deficits in learning and development.

For the exceptional child, the major forms of intervention are medical, behavioural psychotherapeutic, educational, and social. These are not all the forms of intervention, but they do represent the basic approaches to care and education. Each allied discipline has developed its own form of intervention, diagnosis, and terminology to reflect its professional orientation and traditions.

Medical intervention

The medical intervention and treatment of exceptional children is a complex and highly sophisticated process. It involves a variety of specialists with unique skills. However, although medical treatment is extremely varied, the most common forms involve surgical procedures, the controlled use of medication, and supportive therapy (Suran and Rizzo, 1983).

Surgery

In recent decades, many forms of surgical treatment have emerged for exceptional children. Today, nearly half the admissions to children's hospitals are for surgical treatment (Owings, 1973). This has led to the development of subspecialties within the field of pediatric surgery (Wilkinson, 1975).

The most widely used surgical treatments currently include: reconstructive surgery, for repair of physical anomalies such as a cleft lip or palate; neurosurgery, for disabling conditions of the brain and spinal cord; and orthopedic surgery, for problems of the skeletal system that occur in youngsters with multiple physical anomalies (Suran and Rizzo, 1983).

Psychopharmacology

Of all the medical treatments for exceptional children, teachers are most likely to come into contact with psychopharmacology, or drug therapy. This treatment involves the administration of drugs that affect the central nervous system and cause changes in behaviour. Psychotropic drugs affect the cells in the nervous system (neurons) either by increasing or decreasing their excitability (Ross and Ross, 1982). The therapeutic use of such drugs presupposes some biochemical abnormality that is normalized by the drug action.

In general, such drugs are intended to manage problems of behaviour, activity level, emotion, or epilepsy (Simeonsson and Simeonsson, 1981). Teachers may take part in monitoring drug usage. Systematic monitoring of drug therapy is particularly important where multiple medications are used (Berman, 1976). When children receive medication over an extended period of time, teachers should also watch carefully for hidden long-term side effects (Yaffe, 1980).

In 1937, Charles Bradley was the first person to treat specific educational disabilities and hyperactive behaviour in school children with a stimulant drug, Benzedrine. Bradley noticed an overall improvement in the children's moods, activity level, and educational achievement (Bradley, 1937). Since Bradley's seminal work, psychopharmacological approaches to treatment have increased dramatically. Drug therapy is used extensively with handicapped children, because of their greater frequency of physical and neurological complications (Simeonsson and Simeonsson, 1981). Of children identified as hyperactive by parents, teachers, and physicians, an estimated eighty-six percent will use medication at some point between kindergarten and fifth grade (Lambert, Sandoval, and Sassone, 1979).

Drugs administered to children vary widely in purpose and pharmacological action (Simeonsson and Simeonsson, 1981). Medications, ranging from antibiotics to stimulants, have been administered to emotionally disturbed children, learning-disabled children, retarded children, bed wetters, children with behaviour problems, and others. Exhibit 2-4 shows the most common drugs used in pharmacological management.

The field of pediatric psychopharmacology is rife with uncertainties. The prediction of drug response is not an exact science. Much research is directed to the use of drugs with children. Children who are treated with psychoactive agents are in reality research subjects (Gualtieri, Golden, and Fahs, 1983). Studies have investigated the use of amphetamines for hyperactivity (Conners, 1972; Whalen, Henker, and Dotemoto, 1981); the use of tranquilizers to control aggressiveness in psychotic children (Eisenberg, 1968); and the use of antidepressants for enuresis (bed-wetting) (Halverstadt, 1976; Henderson, 1976) and for symptoms of depression (Frommer, 1967). Other researchers have studied the effects of medication on activity level, mood, and motor performance (Conners and Werry, 1979; Sprague and Werry, 1974).

Some researchers claim that drug therapy is effective with seventy percent of hyperactive children (White, 1975). Others claim immediate rates of improvement in the sixty to ninety percent range (Whalen, Henker, and Dotemoto, 1981). Some researchers, however, have found that drug therapy was enhanced when it was combined with behaviour therapy (Campbell and Small, 1978).

Drug therapy offers necessary and highly effective intervention for many types of behaviour and psychological disorders. However, serious questions have been raised concerning the ethics and advisability of using medication to control a child's behaviour (e.g. Offir, 1974; Sprague and Werry, 1974; Walker, 1974; Zentall, 1983). Many drugs

Exhibit 2-4 Drugs frequently used in pharmacological management of children and youth.

Classification	*Trade Name*	*Indication for Use*
major tranquilizers	Thorazine Mellaril	severe agitation, psychoses
minor tranquilizers	Librium Atarax	anxiety
antidepressants	Tofranil	mood elevation
stimulants	Dexedrine Ritalin	hyperactivity
anticonvulsants	Mysoline Dilantin Zorantin	anticonvulsant
drugs for specific problems	Toframil	enuresis
	Mellaril	nightmares, tics
	Benedryl	sedative

(Adapted from Simeonsson and Simeonsson, 1981.)

create side effects, which range from sleeplessness and loss of appetite to depressed growth and accelerated heart rate. These side effects will be discussed in detail when we readdress the question of drug therapy in later chapters.

Supportive therapy

Supportive therapy consists of a broad range of interventions to help children adapt to their particular disabilities. A child with poor articulation may require help from a speech therapist. A child who has lost a limb will need physical therapy. An adolescent with cerebral palsy may benefit from occupational therapy.

Psychotherapy and behaviour intervention

Psychotherapy is a common form of intervention for children who demonstrate emotional problems, severe behaviour disorders, or serious conflicts with people around them. Psychotherapeutic approaches stem from the contributions of Sigmund Freud, Carl Jung, Eric Erikson, Anna Freud and many others. There are numerous theoretical orientations and practical approaches to psychotherapy, but all are essentially designed to relieve the child's, distress and encourage development. For our purposes, individual, group, and family therapy represent the most important approaches. Family therapy has already been discussed earlier in this chapter.

Individual psychotherapy implies a transaction between the child and the therapist. In traditional techniques, this relies heavily on discussion and the probing of feelings and attitudes. Because young children communicate more easily through play than through

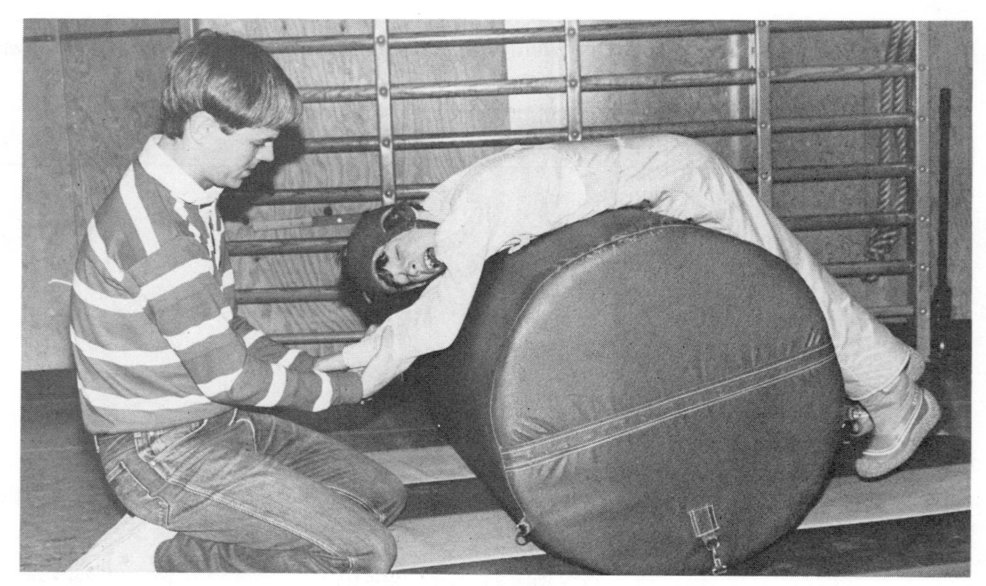

Help for special children is made possible by the care and persistence of parents, educators, and a wide range of child-care personnel.
(T. Wilson)

words, various forms of play therapy have evolved. In play therapy, the therapist creates an atmosphere where the child can freely express feelings, concerns, and conflicts. The therapist may assume the role of co-player, model, or observer. The therapist may interpret the child's play to find the source of fears and problems, or try to reflect back the feelings expressed by the child.

Group therapy implies the simultaneous treatment of several children, usually in the same age range. By treating children in a group, the therapist can use group processes and face-to-face peer interactions as primary vehicles for change (Suran and Rizzo, 1983). Group therapy makes use of modelling, play, verbal interaction, peer influence, socialization, experience, and mutual support.

All psychotherapeutic approaches search for the child's inner conflicts and motivations, while trying to explain current or past events. Behaviour therapy, or behaviour modification, is more concerned with producing desirable behaviour. Today's techniques owe their roots to the classic works of Pavlov, J.B. Watson, B.F. Skinner, and other pioneer behaviourists.

The behavioural approach maintains that all behaviour is caused and controlled by environmental events outside the child. All behaviour is therefore observable, measurable, and subject to change through a change in the environment. Examples of behaviour that can be modified include hyperactivity, aggressiveness, distractibility, bed wetting, excessive fearfulness, and harmful anxiety.

A number of techniques go under the general heading of behaviour therapy. Exhibit 2-5 outlines some of the more common of these.

Exhibit 2-5 Strategies for behaviour change.

positive reinforcement	The presentation of a positive reinforcer upon the occurrence of a specified response in the belief that this will encourage the recurrence of the appropriate response.
negative reinforcement	The halting of an aversive or unpleasant stimulus when a specified response occurs. For example, a child in detention may be allowed out to recess after giving an apology.
punishment	Not an effective technique. Punishment should only be used for serious behaviour problems, and only when positive procedures have been ineffective.
contingent observation	A child is removed from the group to observe, but not participate in, an activity.
time out	A child is completely isolated in order to decrease severe acting-out behaviours. Time out has proven effective in cases presenting a single behaviour problem (Hamilton, Stephens, and Allen, 1967). It is effective with aggressive behaviours, and provides feedback about appropriate as well as inappropriate behaviour (Matson, Ollendick, and DiLorenzo, 1980).
differential reinforcement of appropriate behaviour	Positive reinforcement is given to appropriate behaviour, so that less time is available to indulge in inappropriate behaviour.
differential reinforcement of incompatible behaviour	Positive reinforcement is given for a chosen behaviour that is physically incompatible with the inappropriate behaviour (Popovitch, 1981).
extinction	Positive reinforcement is withheld during an inappropriate behaviour. The reward must be withheld consistently. Extinction is most effective when positive reinforcement is given for the desired behaviour (Hallahan and Kauffman, 1976).
token reinforcement	In this technique, a child is rewarded for appropriate behaviour with some small thing such as a star, a check mark, or a poker chip. The tokens are then used to purchase reinforcers such as a special treat. This method has proven most successful in positively altering the behaviour of exceptional children (Axelrod, 1971).
response cost	This is used in conjunction with a token economy. A fine — the loss of a token — is levied for unacceptable behaviour.
overcorrection	During overcorrection, the child is prevented from engaging in inappropriate behaviour and is guided into the appropriate behaviour for the same situation (Foxx and Azrin, 1973; Popovitch, 1981).

contingency contracting	This involves a written contract that describes the child's goal, the steps for keeping to goal, and the reward. Both parties, such as a child and a teacher, sign the contract in the presence of witnesses, only after the child fully understands the obligations involved (Bond, 1981).

Educational intervention

Education for exceptional children may be provided through a variety of educational arrangements. The alternatives range from the regular classroom to the institution, and should be determined by the unique needs of the child. In chapter one, we outlined the cascade of educational services that are needed to achieve normalization and mainstreaming in our school system.

The following chapters discuss the educational arrangements available for exceptional children. Here we shall present an overview of placement options and personnel who are involved.

Learning environments

Regular classroom The regular classroom provides the exceptional child with the least restrictive environment and the maximum integration with non-handicapped peers. The classroom teacher holds primary responsibility for the child and must ensure that appropriate program and curriculum modifications are made. The classroom teacher also works with a number of professionals to tailor education to the needs of the individual child.

Itinerant teacher services Itinerant teachers are specially trained educators who give individual assistance to a child for specific periods during the normal school schedule. The type and intensity of itinerant intervention depend on the needs of the child. Some children may simply need tutoring to keep up in regular school subjects. Others may require a specific program in one area, such as speech and auditory training. Itinerant teachers may work with classroom teachers on program preparation, and offer in-service training to classroom teachers. They may also help prepare the exceptional child's classmates by explaining the child's disabling condition. In some instances, the itinerant teacher serves as an advocate to ensure that the special child receives the best education possible in the most appropriate environment.

Consulting personnel In general, a consultant has no teaching responsibilities. The consultant assists classroom teachers throughout a school district to maintain exceptional children in their regular school programs. As an indirect servicer of exceptional children, the consultant may serve as a diagnostician, a materials specialist, an administrator of varied services, and as an advocate.

Resource room The resource room helps children to bridge the transition between self-contained special classrooms and regular classrooms. Integrated exceptional pupils receive part of their education in the regular classroom and part of it in the resource room.

This allows some learning to take place in a less distracting, less intense, and less competitive environment than the regular classroom. The regular classroom teacher still carries primary responsibility for program design, but works in close co-ordination with the resource room personnel.

The resource room may also be used to tutor regular students who are meeting problems in academic, perceptual-motor, social, or emotional areas. In some Canadian provinces, however, this does not occur. Extra help for regular classroom students is provided in the Learning Assistance Centre (LAC), and the resource room is reserved for exceptional children.

Self-contained special classes For some exceptional children with severe problems, the self-contained special classroom is more appropriate than the regular classroom. Special classrooms are staffed by specially trained teachers and are located within the regular school. In these classrooms, children with similar disabilities are brought together for instruction and social interplay. Classes should follow the regular program closely enough to allow for partial integration when feasible.

Special schools

Special day schools provide special education services, usually to specific groups of exceptional children. Day schools allow a core of specially trained teachers and professionals to guide the child's education, while the child continues to live at home.

Special residential schools separate the child from the home. Large, provincially funded residential schools for hearing-impaired, visually handicapped, emotionally disturbed, and mentally retarded children still flourish across Canada. However, many of these have become residential/day schools, as more students have been encouraged to commute.

Homebound instruction For children who are unable to attend school for an extended period of time, many school boards provide homebound or hospital instruction. The child is individually tutored to maintain performance at an adequate level.

Social intervention

Social intervention covers a spectrum of services that can be grouped under the general category of child welfare. A primary concern is the care and treatment of the child within the family environment. A wide range of personnel are involved in social intervention — social workers, family counsellors, foster parents, child advocates, child care workers, probation officers, and so on. These people try to ensure that the child develops under the care of the family or surrogate family.

Child advocacy

Child advocacy can be defined as any social, political, or legal action that is intended to achieve a better life for children from infancy to late adolescence (Lourie, 1975). A child advocate is anyone who pleads a child's cause or defends a particular child-related cause.

Child advocacy is a wide-ranging movement that functions at several levels. It involves a spectrum of activities that identify the needs of children and try to rectify unsatisfactory practices. A major goal of advocacy is to stimulate public and professional response to child needs and abuses.

The advocacy concept is still evolving in Canada. Increasingly, advocates are playing an integral part in the education of exceptional children. As we have discussed, many parents and parent associations have become advocates to obtain better provisions for their exceptional children. Professional groups, such as the Canadian Association for the Mentally Retarded and the Association for Children with Learning Disabilities, also view advocacy as one of their primary functions.

SUMMARY

The discovery of a handicapping condition in a child causes great distress in many families. The impact of the diagnosis affects different families in different ways. Some families cannot handle the stress at all, and others find that it pushes already existing stress to the breaking point. In some families, however, a handicapped child unites family members, becoming a focus of family concern and cohesion.

The impact of their child's initial diagnosis is always traumatic for the parents. They grieve for their lost expectations, and pass through various emotional stages before they can reach acceptance. Counselling and parent-support groups help parents to gain information, express their concerns, and come to realize their child's positive potential.

Parents may become involved in therapeutic or educational programs designed to develop and maintain specific skills in their handicapped child. More and more, educators are appreciating the value of parent education. Various types of program are operating across the country, especially at the early childhood and pre-school level. Despite the unevenness of delivery systems across Canada, there has been a dramatic increase in the number of infants, toddlers, and pre-schoolers served by these programs.

In their search for assistance for their child and themselves, parents encounter a range of dedicated professionals. Intervention draws on a number of disciplines — medicine, education, social work, psychology, and paraprofessional occupations. A team approach has developed to allow these people to best accommodate the exceptional child.

BIBLIOGRAPHY

Akerley, M.S. (1975). Parents speak. *Journal of Autism and Childhood Schizophrenia, 5,* 373-380.

Axelrod, S. (1971). Token reinforcement programs in special classes. *Exceptional Children, 37,* 371-379.

Barsch, R.H. (1968). *The parent of the handicapped child: The study of child rearing practices.* Springfield, IL.: Charles C. Thomas.

Beckman-Bell, P. (1981). Child-related stress in families of handicapped children. *Topics in Early Childhood Special Education, 1,* 45-53.

Benedek, T. (1970). Parenthood during the life cycle. In E.V. Anthony and T. Benedek (Eds.), *Parenthood: Its psychology and psychopathology.* Boston: Little, Brown.

Berman, P.H. (1976). Management of seizure disorders with anticonvulsant drugs: Current concepts. *Pediatric Clinics of North America, 23,* 443-459.

Berns, J.H. (1980). Grandparents of handicapped children. *Social Work, 15,* 238-239.

Block, J. (1978). Impaired children. *Children Today, 7,* 2-6.

Boles, G. (1959). Personality factors in mothers of cerebral palsied children. *Genetic Psychology Monographs, 59,* 159-218.

Bond, D.E. (1981). Aspects of behaviour and management of adolescents who are hearing impaired. *British Teacher of the Deaf, 2,* 41-48.

Bradley, C. (1937). The behaviour of children receiving Benzedrine. *American Journal of Psychiatry, 94,* 577-585.

Bricker, D.D. and Bricker, W.A. (1976). Infant, toddler, and preschool research and intervention project report. In T.D. Tjassem (Ed.), *Intervention strategies for high-risk infants and young children.* Baltimore, MD.: University Park Press.

Bristol, M. (1979). *Maternal coping with autistic children: Adequacy of interpersonal support and effects of child characteristics.* Doctoral dissertation, University of North Carolina — Chapel Hill.

Buscaglia, L. (1975). *The disabled and their parents: A counselling challenge.* Thorofare, N.J.: Charles B. Slack.

Cameron, S.J. (1981). Pilot parents — Who are they? *Canada's Mental Health, 29,* 31-33.

Campbell, M. and Small, A.M. (1978). Chemotherapy. In B.B. Wolman, J. Egan and A.O. Ross (Eds.), *Handbook of treatment of mental disorders in childhood and adolescence.* Englewood Cliffs, N.J.: Prentice-Hall.

Chinn, P.C., Winn, J., and Walters, R. (1978). *Two-way talking with parents of special children.* St. Louis: C.V. Mosby.

Clyman, R., Sniderman, S., Ballard, R., and Roth, R. (1979). What pediatricians say to mothers of sick newborns: An indirect evaluation of the counseling process. *Pediatrics, 63,* 719-724.

Cochran, M.M. and Brassard, J.A. (1979). Child development and personal social networks. *Child Development, 50,* 601-616.

Conners, C.K. (1972). Psychological effects of stimulant drugs in children with minimal brain dysfunction. *Pediatrics, 49,* 702.

Conners, C.K. and Werry, J. (1979). Pharmacotherapy. In H.C. Quay and J.S. Werry (Eds.), *Psychopathological disorders of childhood* (2nd ed.) New York: John Wiley.

Cummings, S.T., Bayley, H. and Rie, H. (1976). Effects of the child's deficiency on the mother: A study of mothers of mentally retarded, chronically ill, and neurotic children. *American Journal of Orthopsychiatry, 36,* 595-608.

Eisenberg, L. (1968). Psychopharmacology in childhood: A critique. In E. Miller (Ed.), *Foundations in child psychiatry.* New York: Pergamon Press.

Embry, L. H. (1980). Family support for handicapped preschool children at risk for abuse. In J.J. Gallagher (Ed.), *New directions for exceptional children: Parents and families of handicapped children.* (Vol. 4). San Francisco: Jossey-Bass.

Erickson, G. (1976). The concept of personal network in clinical practice. *Family Process, 14,* 487-498.

Farber, B. (1959). Effects of a severely mentally retarded child on family integration. *Monographs of the Society for Research in Child Development, 24,* 2, Serial no. 71.

Farber, B. (1960). Family organization and crises: Maintenance and integration in families with a severely retarded child. *Monographs of the Society for Research in Child Development, 25.*

Farber, B. and Ryckman, D.B. (1965). Effects of severely mentally retarded children on family relationships. *Mental Retardation Abstracts, 2,* 1-17.

Field, T. (1983). High risk infants "have less fun" during early interactions. *Topics in Early Childhood Special Education, 3,* 77-87.

Fortier, L.M. and Wanlass, R.L. (1984). Family crisis following the diagnosis of a handicapped child. *Family Relations, 33,* 13-24.

Fotheringham, J.B. and Creal, D. (1974). Handicapped children and handicapped families. *International Review of Education, 20,* 355-369.

Fowle, C.M. (1968). The effects of the severely mentally retarded child on his family. *American Journal of Mental Deficiency, 73,* 468-473.

Foxx, R.M. and Azrin, N.H. (1973). The elimination of autistic self-stimulating behavior by overcorrection. *Journal of Applied Behavior Analysis, 6,* 1-14.

Freeman, R.D., Malkin, S. and Hastings, J.O. (1975). Psychological problems of deaf children and their families: A comparative study. *American Annals of the Deaf, 120,* 391-405.

Friedrich, W. (1977). Ameliorating the psychological impact of chronic physical disease on the child and family. *Journal of Pediatric Psychology, 2,* 26-31.

Frodi, A.M. (1981). Contribution of infant characteristics to child abuse. *American Journal of Mental Deficiency, 85,* 341-349.

Frommer, E.A. (1967). Treatment of childhood depression with antidepressant drugs. *British Medical Journal, 1,* 729-732.

Gabel, H. and Kotsch, L.S. (1981). Extended families and young handicapped children. *Topics in Early Childhood Special Education, 1,* 29-35.

Gaines, R., Sandgrund, A., Green, A.H., and Power, E. (1978). Etiological factors in child maltreatment: A multivariate study of abusing, neglecting, and normal mothers. *Journal of Abnormal Psychology, 87,* 531-540.

Gallagher, J.J., Beckman, P., and Cross, A.H. (1983). Families of handicapped children: Sources of stress and its amelioration. *Exceptional Children, 49,* 10-19.

Gath, A. (1972). The effects of mental subnormality on the family. *British Journal of Hospital Medicine, 8,* 147-150.

Grossman, F.K. (1972). *Brothers and sisters of retarded children: An exploratory study.* Syracuse, N.Y.: Syracuse University Press.

Gualtieri, C.T., Golden, R.N., and Fahs, J.J. (1983). New developments in pediatric psychopharmacology. *Journal of Development and Behavioral Pediatrics, 4,* 202-209.

Haggerty, R. (1980). Life stress, illness and social support. *Developmental Medicine and Child Neurology, 22,* 291-400.

Hallahan, D.P. and Kauffman, J.M. (1976). *Introduction to learning disabilities: A psychobehavioral approach.* Englewood Cliffs, N.J.: Prentice-Hall.

Hallahan, D.P. and Kauffman, J.M. (1982). *Exceptional children: Introduction to special education (2nd. ed).* Englewood Cliffs, N.J.: Prentice-Hall.

Halverstadt, D.B. (1976). Enuresis. *Journal of Pediatric Psychology, 4,* 13-14.

Hamilton, J., Stephens, L. and Allen, P. (1967). Controlling aggressive and destructive behavior in severely retarded institutionalized residents. *American Journal of Mental Deficiency, 71,* 852-856.

Henderson, W.A. (1976). A review of current medical aspects of enuresis. *Journal of Pediatric Psychology, 4,* 15-17.

Hoff, L.A. (1978). *People in crisis: Understanding and helping.* Menlo Park, CA.: Addision Wesley.

Holroyd, J. (1974). The questionnaire on resources and stress: An instrument to measure family response to a handicapped member. *Journal of Community Psychology, 2,* 92-94.

Holroyd, J. and McArthur, D. (1976). Mental retardation and stress on the parents: A contrast between Down's syndrome and childhood autism. *American Journal of Mental Deficiency, 80,* 431-436.

Howard, J. (1982). The role of the pediatrician with young exceptional children and their families. *Exceptional Children, 48,* 316-322.

Kysela, G.M. and Marfo, K. (1983). Mother-child interactions and early intervention programs for handicapped infants and young children. *Educational Psychology, 3,* 201-212.

Lambert, N.M., Sandoval, J. and Sassone, D. (1979). Prevalence of treatment regimes on children considered to be hyperactive. *American Journal of Orthopsychiatry, 49,* 482-490.

Lavelle, A.M. and Keogh, B.K. (1980). Expectations and attributions of parents of handicapped children. In J.J. Gallagher (Ed.), *New directions for exceptional children: Parents and families of handicapped children (Vol. 2).* San Francisco: Jossey-Bass.

Levenstein, P. (1970). Cognitive growth in preschoolers through verbal interaction with mothers. *American Journal of Orthopsychiatry, 40,* 426-432.

Lipton, H.L. and Svarstad, B. (1977). Sources of variation in clinicians' communication to parents about mental retardation. *American Journal of Mental Deficiency, 82,* 155-161.

Lourie, N.V. (1975). The many faces of advocacy. In I.N. Berlin (Ed.), *Advocacy for child mental health.* New York: Brunner/Mazel.

MacKay, R. (1976). *Mental handicap in child health practice.* London: Butterworths.

Marcus, L.M. (1977). Patterns of coping in families of psychotic children. *American Journal of Orthopsychiatry, 47,* 388-398.

Markowitz, J. (1984). Participation of fathers in early childhood special education programs: An exploratory study. *Journal of the Division for Early Childhood, 8,* 119-131.

Matson, J.L., Ollendick, T.H., and DiLorenzo, T.M. (1980). Time out and the characteristics of mentally retarded institutionalized adults who do or do not receive it. *Mental Retardation, 18,* 184-187.

McAndrew, I. (1976). Children with a handicap and their families. *Child: Care, Health and Development, 2,* 213-238.

McDonald, A.C., Carson, K.L., Palmer, D.J. and Slay, T. (1982). Physicians' diagnostic information to parents of handicapped neonates. *Mental Retardation, 20,* 12-14.

Meadow, K. (1980). *Deafness and child development.* Berkeley: University of California Press.

Mills, Y.L. and Hedges, C.A. (1983). The feeding process and the nutritional needs of handicapped infants and preschoolers. *Topics in Early Childhood Special Education, 3,* 33-42.

Mindel, E. and Vernon, M. (1971). *They grow in silence: The deaf child and his family.* Silver Spring, MD.: National Association of the Deaf.

Minuchin, S., Rosman, B., and Baker, L. (1978). *Psychosomatic families: Aneroxia nervosa in context.* Cambridge: Harvard University Press.

Mitchell, D.R. (1983). International trends in special education. *Canadian Journal on Mental Retardation, 33,* 6-13.

Offir, C.W. (1974). A slavish reliance on drugs: Are we pushers for our children? *Psychology Today, 8,* 49.

Ouellett, A.M. (1972). Michelle: A long way to kindergarten. *Exceptional Parent, 2,* 31-33.

Owings, R.S. (1973). *Nonoperative aspects of pediatric surgery.* St. Louis: Warren Green.

Pieper, E. (1976). Grandparents can help. *Exceptional Parent, 6,* 7-10.

Popovich, D. (1981). *Effective educational and behavioral programming for severely and profoundly handicapped students.* Baltimore, MD.: Paul H. Brookes.

Poznanski, E. (1969). Psychiatric difficulties in siblings of handicapped children. *Pediatrics, 8,* 232-234.

Price-Bonham, S. and Addison, S. (1978). Families and mentally retarded children: Emphasis on the father. *The Family Coordinator, 3,* 221-230.

Peuschel, S.M. and Murphy, A. (1976). Assessment of counselling practices at the birth of a child with Down's Syndrome. *American Journal of Mental Deficiency, 81,* 325-330.

Robson, K.S. and Moss, H.A. (1970). Patterns and determinants of maternal attachment. *Journal of Pediatrics, 77,* 976-985.

Ross, D.M. and Ross, S.A. (1982). *Hyperactivity: Current issues, research and theory (2nd. ed.).* New York: John Wiley.

Schaffer, E. (1977). *He's not so different, he's my brother.* Report, Workshop on Siblings, Meeting Street School, Providence, R.I.

Schilling, R.F. and Schinke, S.P. (1984). Maltreatment and mental retardation. In J.M. Berg (Ed.), *Perspectives and progress in mental retardation: Social, psychological and educational aspects (Vol. 1).* Baltimore, MD.: University Park Press.

Schlesinger, H.S. and Meadow, K.P. (1972). *Sound and sign: Childhood deafness and mental health.* Berkeley: University of California Press.

Simeonsson, R.J. and Simeonsson, N.E. (1981). Medication effects in handicapped preschool children. *Topics in Early Childhood Special Education 1,* 61-75.

Sprague, R.L. and Werry, J.S. (1974). Psychotropic drugs and handicapped children. In L. Mann and D.A. Sabatino, *The second review of special education.* Philadelphia: J.S.E. Press.

Stedman, D.J. (1977). Important considerations in the review and evaluation of educational intervention programs. In P. Mittler (Ed.), *Research to practice in mental retardation (Vol. 1).* Baltimore, MD.: University Park Press.

Steinberg, M.A. (1980). A message to special education from mothers of disabled children. *The Exceptional Child, 27,* 177-183.

Suran, B.G. and Rizzo, J.V. (1983). *Special children: An integrative approach (2nd. ed.).* Glenview, IL.: Scott, Foresman and Company.

Tallman, I. (1965). Spousal role differentiation and the socialization of severely retarded children. *Journal of Marriage and the Family, 27,* 37-42.

Tavormina, J.B. and Kralj, M.M. (1975). *Facilitating family dynamics: Family system issues in the overall management of the handicapped infant.* Paper presented at the Exceptional Infant Symposium, Charlottesville.

Tobias, E. and Kendall, D. (1984). British Columbia: Who is providing for the educational needs of preschoolers with special needs? *B.C. Journal of Special Education, 8,* 297-312.

Trevino, F. (1979). Siblings of handicapped children: Identifying those at risk. *Social Casework: The Journal of Contemporary Social Work, 60,* 488-493.

Turnbull, A.P. and Blacher-Dixon, J. (1980). Pre-school mainstreaming: Impact on parents. In J.J. Gallagher (Ed.), *New directions for exceptional children: Ecology of exceptional children (Vol. 1).* San Francisco: Jossey-Bass.

Walker, S. (1974). Drugging the American Child: We're too cavalier about hyperactivity. *Psychology Today, 8,* 43-48.

Whalen, C., Henker, B., and Dotemoto, S. (1981). Teacher response to methylphenidate (Ritalin) versus placebo status of hyperactive boys in the classroom. *Child Development, 52,* 1005-1014.

White, J.H. (1975). Current medical treatment of hyperkinesis. *Journal of Pediatric Psychology, 3,* 5-6.

Wikler, L., Wasow, M. and Hatfield, E. (1981). Chronic sorrow revisited: Parent vs professional depiction of the adjustment of parents of mentally retarded children. *American Journal of Orthopsychiatry, 51,* 63-70.

Wilkinson, A.W. (Ed.) (1975). *Recent advances in pediatric surgery.* London: Churchill Livingstone.

Wolraich, M.L. (1980). Pediatric practitioners' knowledge of developmental disabilities. *Journal of Developmental and Behavioral Pediatrics, 1,* 147-151.

Wolraich, M.L. (1982). Communication between physicians and parents of handicapped children. *Exceptional Children, 48,* 324-329.

Yaffe, S.J. (1980). Clinical implications of perinatal pharmacology. *European Journal of Clinical Pharmacology, 18,* 3-7.

Zentall, S.S. (1983). Effects of psychotropic drugs on the behavior of pre-academic children: A review. *Topics in Early Childhood Special Education, 3,* 29-39.

Zigler, E. and Valentine, J. (Eds.) (1979). *Project Head Start: A legacy of the war on poverty.* New York: Free Press.

Zuk, G.H. (1962). The cultural dilemma and spiritual crisis of the family with a handicapped child. *Exceptional Children, 28,* 405-408.

CHAPTER THREE

History of special education

MARGRET WINZER

History discusses our past, explains our present, and predicts our future.
(Old adage)

Special education exists to augment the regular education program so that all children can have a chance to become self-sustaining adults (Paul and Warnock, 1980). In the past twenty years, interest and involvement in special education has increased dramatically. Rapid growth in the field has been accomplished despite overlapping services, pseudo-scientific programs and projects, lack of proper co-ordination, inaccurate classification of children, and much literary licence concerning definitions (Frampton and Gall, 1955).

In the past, advances have been much slower. As a distinct category within general education, special education did not clearly emerge until 1901. In that year, the National Education Association (NEA) in the United States formed a specific Department of Special Education (NEA, 1901). In 1902, the NEA adopted a definite program for its newly formed department (NEA, 1902). In 1941, the Department of Special Education became the International Council for Exceptional Children. The Council for Exceptional Children was established in Canada in 1958. By 1968, it had a Canadian office with the potential to co-ordinate Canadian efforts on behalf of exceptional children (Hardy, McLeod, Minto, Perkins, and Quance, 1971).

Although special education has only been a distinct category during this century, the concepts underlying the care and training of exceptional children stem from a much earlier era. History records the existence of handicapping conditions within ancient cultures, but not until the mid-1700s did Europeans begin to systematically train and educate the handicapped. In 1817, special education began in the United States with the founding of an institution for the deaf in Hartford, Connecticut. Canada rapidly followed suit, and opened its first special school, again for the deaf, near Montreal in 1831. In both the United States and Canada, French philosophy and pedagogy exerted the major influence on special education (Winzer, 1985).

Exhibit 3-1 Progression of special education.

- Prior to 1750, the great majority of handicapped individuals were neglected, mistreated, and abused. Endeavours to educate them were few and scattered.
- From 1750 to 1820, a new humanitarian impulse altered public perception and sowed the roots of special education in Europe, especially France.
- Between 1820 and 1900, residential institutions were provided for the training and education of handicapped individuals.
- From about 1900 to 1950, special schools and special classes became more prevalent, while residential institutions continued to grow and expand.
- During the 1950s and 1960s, children with mild intellectual handicaps were placed more frequently in special classes, rather than special schools. During this time, there was a mounting dissatisfaction with the educational options available for exceptional children.
- Beginning mainly in the 1970s, there was a strong movement away from special classes and institutions. Wherever possible, exceptional children began to be educated in the regular school or classroom, with the help of support services.

In its development, special education has taken a fascinating journey. Its route has been illuminated by many brilliant and often controversial pioneers. The works of Itard, Seguin, Gallaudet, and their contemporaries have inspired countless followers with the romance, idealism, and excitement of their social experiments. The contributions of these educators laid the foundation for special education as it currently exists. Therefore, in order to better understand special education today, a brief consideration of its history and early contributions may prove useful.

Exhibit 3-1 shows a number of distinct stages in the development of Special Education.

EARLY HISTORICAL PRECEDENTS

Society's attitude toward the handicapped has always been complex, fashioned by its prevailing culture, religion, government, and economic condition. The care and training of exceptional individuals has followed historical trends, rather than creating them.

Although historical record is murky, it seems that from humanity's earliest beginnings, the handicapped have been grossly mistreated. For many ages, their condition was considered hopeless. In most cultures, they were scorned as degraded and inferior beings. Until the mid-1700s, handicapped individuals were rarely looked upon with humane concern.

From the writings of the past, we can assume widespread debilitating physical conditions as a result of unchecked virulent fevers and other illnesses. It is not possible to even estimate the numbers of handicapped individuals, but their visibility in society is confirmed by the number of laws that concerned them. The handicapped are mentioned in legal edicts and other writings by the Greeks and Romans, in the Bible, by the Catholic Church, and in the sixth-century legal Code of Justinian.

Primitive and ancient societies

In most early societies, it is unlikely that the handicapped survived. The severely impaired would have been incapable of enduring the hardships of nature, and unable to detect and ward off enemies. Moreover, if they could not hunt or forage for food, they woud have constituted an economic hazard to their group.

The oldest accounts of medical intervention come from ancient Egypt, where eye problems were apparently very common. An Egyptian treatise of about 1550 B.C. on eye diseases and remedies was later used by Hippocrates in Greece. Hippocrates (b. 430 B.C.) was concerned with etiology and medical intervention in a variety of handicapping conditions — visual impairment, deafness, epilepsy, and mental retardation.

Aristotle directed considerable philosophical enquiry toward the sensorily deprived. He viewed blindness as more serious, but less debilitating intellectually, than deafness. Aristotle characterized the deaf as "senseless and incapable of reason," and as "no better than the animals of the forest and unteachable" (McGann, 1888).

In Greece, handicapped children often did not survive infancy. In Sparta, newborn children were routinely brought before the elders to be examined for their fitness for citizenship. Under the laws of Lycurgus, imperfect children were exposed in a gorge in the Taygetus mountains or left in the wilderness. Under the laws of Solon, similar events occurred in Athens. Weak children were placed in clay vessels and left to die by the wayside (French, 1932).

Rome readily adopted the Greek attitude toward handicapped infants. Any child under three whc might someday become a burden on society was thrown into the Tiber. Those who survived infancy or suffered from acquired handicaps were generally treated with aversion. Deaf persons who could not speak were given guardians and deprived of the rights and responsibilities of citizenship. Blind boys were often trained to become beggars or sold as rowers; blind girls became prostitutes (French, 1932). Sometimes a wealthy family kept a mentally retarded person as a fool for the amusement of the household and its guests (Kanner, 1964).

Hebraic law concerning the handicapped represents a high point during this period. Under strictures outlined in Talmud and Midrash, the blind, the deaf, widows, orphans, and the needy were all treated with special consideration.

The Christian era

In the long, dark centuries between the fall of Rome and the flowering of the Renaissance, references to the handicapped are few and far between. Most of these are further obscured by an aura of the miraculous, and are of questionable accuracy. For example, Saint Nicholas Thaumaturgos, Bishop of Wyre in the fourth century, has been described as a protector of the feeble-minded. However, as Kanner (1964) points out, he was also the patron saint of children, sailors, and pawn-brokers, as well as the prototype of Santa Claus. Similarly, the Venerable Bede, in his seventh century *History of the Anglo-Saxon Church*, described how "Bishopp John cured a dumme man by blessing him." For this somewhat minor contribution, John of Beverly is today considered the patron saint of the deaf (Porter, 1847).

In general, superstition and myth prevailed, through the Middle Ages. The handicapped were regarded with fear and distaste, their afflictions looked upon as a visitation of divine or satanic powers. Blindness, for example, was long regarded as "one of those instruments by which a mysterious Providence has chosen to afflict man" (Address, 1836). Deafness was seen by many as "the hereditary transmission of moral turpitude" (Peet, 1855-1856). The mentally ill were believed to have been possessed by Satan, and were often cruelly persecuted (Payne and Thomas, 1978).

In some places, village folk protected their handicapped, believing that the divine retribution intended for all of them had been heaped on the exceptional person. Others regarded idiots superstitiously as blessed "infants of the good God," and allowed them to roam unmolested (Kanner, 1964). Some societies assigned distinct roles to specific handicaps, training blind children as oral historians or using retarded persons as court buffoons. However, life for most handicapped people was characterized by cruelty, mistreatment, and ignorance.

As time passed, the Catholic Church assumed some responsibility for exceptional people. The Church established hospices for the blind as early as the fourth century (Pritchard, 1963), and the clergy began systematically to provide asylums for the less fortunate members of society. Like monasteries, these asylums followed a cloistered routine and offered protection from the cruelty of the outside world. However, asylums cared for only a few of the handicapped; the rest led degraded lives as beggars and outcasts.

The Renaissance

The Renaissance ushered in a new and brighter era for the handicapped. The Renaissance concern with observation and scientific enquiry was accompanied by a new interest in education and humanitarianism. There was also a growing recognition of childhood as a special and distinct stage of development. During this time, the first known education of the handicapped was undertaken. Slowly, uncertain reports of miracles and legends gave way to authenticated records.

The first evidence of successful education of handicapped children dates from the late 1500s in Spain. There the monk, Ponce de Leon (1520-1584), successfully taught the deaf sons of some of Spain's wealthiest families to speak, read, and participate in the rituals of the Catholic church. De Leon's methods have been lost, but he may have employed a finger-spelling alphabet created by monks living under vows of silence.

By 1620, reports of De Leon's success found their way to England. There philosophers, avidly probing the origin and development of language, enlisted the deaf as natural recruits. The English philosophers taught speech to the deaf so successfully that John Bulwer, the first English writer on the subject, went so far as to plead for "an academy of the mute." However Bulwer achieved little in the face of the prevailing opinion that "original deafness and dumbness is not curable but by miracle" (Gordon, 1892, p. 20).

Throughout the 1500s and 1600s, there were many more authentic reports of educational intervention with the handicapped, and the needy. Teaching hospices were established for the blind and deaf, and industrial schools provided shelter and education to vagrant and neglected boys (Barnard, 1857). Conditions for the mentally ill, however, remained lamentably bad. At the Sâlpétrière and Bicêntre institutions in Paris, for example, the inmates were chained naked in rat-infested cellars and fed on bread and soup (Lane and Pillard, 1978). Such institutions also housed many epileptics, albinos, and mentally retarded people.

Although there were advances during this period, education was still only within the reach of a favoured few. Most of the handicapped were abandoned to their age-old condition of wretchedness and degradation. Most people continued to view handicaps through a moralistic framework as punishment for sin.

The industrial era

In the mid-1700s, Europeans turned for the first time to the systematic education of the handicapped. In France, a new Enlightenment social philosophy brought about educational advances. The social philosophers of France took as their major source the empirical philosophy of the English physician and thinker, John Locke (1632-1708).

Exhibit 3-2 Some major European pioneers in the early development of special education.

Ponce de Leon	1520-1584	Spain	Successfully taught speech and language to deaf students.
John Locke	1632-1708	England	Philosopher and physician whose ideas on sensationalism, language, and child development opened the way to major special education advances.
Jacob Periere	1715-1780	Spain/France	Devised effective methods to teach speech to the deaf. Exerted major influence on Itard and Seguin.
Michel de l'Epée	1712-1826	France	Devised the sign laguage for the deaf.
Phillippe Pinel	1765-1826	France	An early advocate of humane care for the mentally ill. Began the "moral treatment."
Valentin Huäy	1745-1822	France	Founded the first school for the blind in Paris.
Jean Marc Itard	1775-1858	France	Used structured sense-training methods with Victor, the "wild boy of Aveyron."
Eduard Seguin	1812-1880	France	Interpreted and expanded Itard's methods for use with mentally retarded children.
Louis Braille	1809-1852	France	Devised a method of raised dots by which the blind can read.
Maria Montessori	1870-1962	Italy	Developed approaches and methods to teach very young children. Used concrete experiences designed around special instructional methods and materials.

John Locke left his imprint on many eighteenth-century ideas. As a physician, he influenced many attitudes and practices concerning childbirth and child-rearing. In keeping with his philosophical regard for the rights of individuals, Locke believed that children should be raised with thought and care. He recognized the child as emotionally responsive, and he encouraged adults to strive for empathetic understanding of children (Illick, 1974).

Locke abandoned the notion that children were born with innate characteristics, imprinted on the soul before birth by God, nature, or the devil. Rather, he saw the child as a blank slate, a *tabula rasa* on which all experiences and sensations systematically made impressions. This philosophy of sensationalism was enthusiastically embraced in France by the major thinkers of the Enlightenment — Rousseau, Diderot, and Condillac.

Locke also studied the development of language. He argued that language was arbitrary — that the words we use to signify a thing have no intrinsic connection with the thing itself. This notion had a profound influence on the education of the handicapped, especially when combined with the use of such alternate sensory stimuli as sign language for the deaf and raised print for the blind.

SPECIAL EDUCATION IN EUROPE

Locke's empirical philosophy precipitated much of the thought of the broad intellectual movement known as the French Enlightenment (Seigel, 1969). The pioneer French educators adopted the concepts of sensationalism, arbitrary language, and alternate sensory stimuli, and joined them to new concepts of social equality and individual rights. These French educators took seriously the special needs of the handicapped. They were the founders of special education as we know it today (Winzer, 1985).

The first of these educators were members of the clergy, whose commitment arose from religious and humanitarian beliefs. They were soon joined by physicians, primarily young, ambitious men who challenged the wisdom of established authorities. Because we cannot discuss the contributions to special education of all these European pioneers, we shall outline only some of the contributions of the major figures.

Jacob Rodriguies Periere

Jacob Periere (1715-1780) was a Spanish Jew who fled the Inquisition and settled in Bordeaux, France. He studied anatomy and physiology, and eventually turned to the education of the deaf. Periere achieved remarkable success, and was the first to devise reliable methods for teaching speech. To accomplish this, he used the Spanish manual alphabet, and placed an innovative stress on the stimulation of residual hearing (Goldstein, 1920).

In accord with Locke's theories of sensationalism Periere also trained the other senses of his deaf students. He initiated what became known as physiological education, or education chiefly through the senses. Although Periere himself was later overshadowed by others, his physiological training had a profound impact on the education of the mentally retarded.

Michel Charles de l'Epée

Michel de l'Epée (1712-1789), a French priest, became the predominant French educator of the deaf. The Abbé's interest in handicapped children was piqued when he met a parishioner with two deaf daughters. In 1760, he opened a school in his own home in Paris. He taught chiefly the children of the poor, arguing that the rich could afford other educational means.

The Abbé knew little about the deaf, and studied his pupils closely. He soon noticed that, without any teaching or guidance, they evolved a language of simple signs by which to communicate. Building on these basic signs, the Abbé developed a system of what he called "natural signs." To teach his students metaphysical and abstract concepts, the Abbé also created a system of "methodological signs" (de l'Epée, 1860). This was the first use of an alternate method of sensory input to provide deaf children with information. He gave the deaf their own language of signs.

In 1789, the French government officially sanctioned de l'Epée's school. Soon after, the school was moved to a sequestered convent and renamed the National Deaf Mute Institute.

Phillippe Pinel

Phillippe Pinel (1745-1826), a French physician, is known as the father of psychiatry. In 1792, he was appointed director of the Bicêntre in Paris. He immediately threw out the whips, chains, and stocks used to restrain the inmates. Instead, he developed a *traitement moral* that used kindness, gentleness, and understanding. He provided patients with an orderly routine with structured activities and amusements (Carlson and Dain, 1960).

Pinel rejected the idea that madness was due to possession by evil spirits, witchcraft, or the effects of the moon. He was convinced that the mentally ill were diseased, rather than sinful or immoral. However, he did not fully accept causative factors that would later be propounded in the 1800s — masturbation, libertinism, and intoxicating stimulants (Hare, 1962).

Valentin Huäy

In 1784, Huäy (1745-1822) founded the first school for the blind in Paris in his own home. He had become interested in the work after witnessing the heartless exploitation of blind persons in the city streets. Huäy gained his inspiration from de l'Epée and his philosophy from the sensationalists. He was especially indebted to Diderot, who had carefully analyzed the thought processes of the blind and dropped hints concerning their education (French, 1932).

Huäy wanted to teach the blind to read so they could gain useful employment. To do this, he used raised-character print, as well as raised maps and musical notes. Huäy began teaching weaving, basket and mat making, chair caning, and the rope trade, so that his graduates could earn a living (Guillie, 1817).

Huäy had great success and prompted the government to establish the National Institute of the Blind. Later, in 1800, he displeased Napoleon and hastily left France. He then founded an institution for the blind in Russia, and laid the groundwork for a school in Berlin (Address, 1836; French, 1932).

Jean Marc Itard

Jean Marc Itard (1775-1858) was a French physician and student of Pinel's. In 1800, he joined the medical staff at the National Deaf Mute Institute in Paris. Soon after, reports reached Paris of a boy around twelve who was believed to have been raised by wolves in the woods near Aveyron. As soon as the boy was caught, Itard and other scholars were anxious to get him to the capital. They wanted to observe his behaviour before it became tamed through life in captivity.

Because the boy was mute, he was placed in the school for the deaf. Itard called him Victor, perhaps to anticipate the victory that education would achieve (Seguin, 1864). Victor was stunted in growth, with a light complexion and scarred, pockmarked skin — probably the result of the smallpox he had caught in captivity. A huge scar ran across his larynx, suggesting that his throat had been cut before he was abandoned in the forest (Lane and Pillard, 1978). Instead of resembling Rousseau's "noble savage," the boy was dirty, incapable of focusing attention, and insensitive to the basic sensations of heat and cold. He lapped his food, uttered inarticulate sounds, fixated on empty space, bit people who came too close, and spent most of his time sleeping or rocking back and forth.

Itard's old teacher, Pinel, observed Victor in the little attic where he was kept. Pinel saw a lad half-starved, crazed with fear, mute, and unkempt. He concluded that Victor's constitution was defective; the boy was not an idiot because he had been left in the wilds, but had been left in the wilds because he was an idiot.

Itard could not accept Pinel's diagnosis that Victor was irreversibly idiotic. Instead, Itard believed that Victor was mentally arrested due to social and educational neglect. He argued that Victor had acquired idiocy through isolation, suffering a sort of mental atrophy from disuse (Kanner, 1964). Despite Victor's appearance and lack of responsiveness, Itard believed that appropriate environmental conditions could humanize the boy. He decided to try to educate the child rather than sending him to an ayslum.

Like de l'Epée, Itard began his work with little concept of the complexities involved in working with a severely handicapped child. Using crude diagnostic methods, he determined that Victor's sense organs were intact, though "dull" or insensitive. Victor would not, for example, respond to loud noises, even to the sound of a pistol shot. On the other hand, he would react to such subtle signals as the cracking of a walnut.

Itard used a variety of means to make Victor aware of sensation — hot baths, massages, tickling, emotional excitement, even electric shock. Along with sensory stimulation and discipline, Itard presented Victor with a systematic series of specific sense-training activities designed to improve his visual, auditory, and motor skills. Itard taught the activities in order and at a variable rate tailored to fit Victor's progress.

After five years, Victor became moderately socialized but not, as Itard had naïvely hoped, normal. Victor's ability to communicate continued to increase, and he learned the basic skills of eating and dressing. However, when Victor died at around forty in 1818, Itard concluded that his work had been a failure.

Despite Itard's limited success, he willed to future educators one of the first documented accounts of work with a very special child. Itard's work had a wide influence on the use of sense training in Special Education. Itard also left to physicians a body of scientific research concerning hearing and otolaryngology.

Eduard Seguin

Although Itard was disappointed in his work with Victor, he maintained his interest in the education of "idiot" children. However, when Itard's health began to fail rapidly, he chose one of his students, Eduard Seguin (1812-1880), to carry on his work.

In 1837, Seguin opened the first school for mentally retarded children in France at the Bicêntre. Seguin believed that mental retardation, except in cases of brain damage, was caused by sensory isolation or deprivation. He viewed the mentally retarded brain as dormant, and capable of arousal by powerful motor and tactual stimuli. Using the sense-training techniques of Periere and Itard, Seguin created a structured and systematic program of education (Seguin, 1846).

Seguin met opposition from his powerful friend and mentor, Esquirol, who declared categorically that educational efforts for idiots were useless (Kanner, 1964). However, in 1842, a Commission of the French Academy declared that Seguin had definitely solved the problem of idiot education (Kanner, 1964). In 1848, distrustful of the new French regime, Seguin emigrated to the United States. In 1854 he opened a school for feeble-minded children in Syracuse, New York.

Louis Braille

The first embossed system of writing was invented by Charles Barbier, an engineer, inventor, philanthropist, and officer in Napoleon's army. In 1819, Barbier developed a system of raised dots that could be read by the fingers. Barbier intended this system as a form of night-writing for use in military ciphers. It was adapted for the blind by a young teacher in Paris, Louis Braille (1809-1852).

Louis Braille, the son of a shoemaker, was accidentally blinded at the age of three. His father kept him at home, fearing that he would become a beggar on the streets of Paris. Because Louis was an apt pupil, his father agreed to let him attend the Paris Institute for the Blind. Braille was an outstanding student and was soon appointed a teacher at the school.

After Braille had been teaching a few years, he heard of Barbier's military code. He reduced Barbier's twelve-dot cell to six dots, and developed an embossed system suitable for reading with the fingers. With his new system, Braille taught his students to read with more efficiency than was possible with embossed letters. Sadly, however, Braille's code did not come into popular use until two years after his death (French, 1932).

Maria Montessori

Early in the 1900s, Maria Montessori (1870-1962) began to work with retarded children in Italy. She drew heavily on the sense-training methods developed by Itard and Seguin (Lillard, 1972). She established a prepared environment in which the children were free to use materials of their own choice and at their own pace. Montessori wanted each of the materials to be used in a specific manner to provide a portion of the self-education that she envisioned. Her materials provided experience with length, breadth, height, colour, texture, weight, size, and form.

Montessori was instrumental in establishing educational and rehabilitation programs for retarded children. In addition, she demonstrated how these children could be helped to live fuller, more meaningful lives. Throughout this work, she insisted that mental retardation was an educational, not a medical, problem (Montessori, 1912; 1917).

SPECIAL EDUCATION IN THE UNITED STATES

So far we have mentioned only the European pioneers and reformers of special education. As we have seen, the first systematic approaches to special education took place in eighteenth-century France. These French efforts had great impact in North America on the education of the deaf, the blind, the mentally retarded, and the emotionally disturbed. French principles and philosophies were imported, and the first teachers in North American special schools were either French or trained in Paris. Before long, however, North Americans began to add their own important contributions to the growth of special education.

Thomas Hopkins Gallaudet

In 1817, education of the handicapped began in North America. Thomas Hopkins Gallaudet (1787-1851), a young American who trained at the National Deaf Mute Institute in Paris, and Laurent Clerc, a teacher from the Institute, opened the American Asylum for the Education and Instruction of Deaf and Dumb Persons in Hartford, Connecticut. At that time, except for a small asylum in Virginia, no facilities for the handicapped existed in North America. Once again, the deaf were the first handicapped group to be educated.

Gallaudet was an influential and energetic promoter of education throughout the first half of the 1800s. He worked in many different areas of exceptionality. Besides establishing the first school for the deaf, he was involved in educating the insane, building industrial schools for neglected and delinquent children, advancing the kindergarten movement, and promoting publicly funded schools. At the American Asylum, he founded the first teachers' school in North America. He was also a firm advocate of education of, and by, women (Winzer, 1981b).

In 1857, Thomas's youngest son, Edward, became president of the National Deaf Mute College in Washington, D.C. In 1864, the College, with Abraham Lincoln as patron, became a degree-granting institution, and in 1893, its name was changed to Gallaudet College. Today, Gallaudet College remains the world's foremost degree-granting institution for hearing-impaired students.

Samuel Gridley Howe

Samuel Gridley Howe (1801-1876), like Gallaudet, was a major educational reformer involved in a wide range of humanitarian, social, and educational movements. Howe's early life was a model of the Romantic tradition. Educated at Brown University and Harvard Medical School, he fought in the Greek war of liberation against the Turks for six years. He fought with Polish revolutionaries, was imprisoned for a time in Berlin, and opened a school for refugees in Crete. When he returned to the United States, he joined John Brown in the movement to emancipate the slaves.

(origin unknown)

(permission: Public Archives of Nova Scotia.)

(permission: Williams and Wilkins, Baltimore, MD.)

Samuel Grindley Howe made significant contributions to special education for both blind, deaf, and speech-impaired children. Frederick Fraser, founding principal of the Halifax School for the Blind. Alfred Binet, a French psychologist, developed the first formal quantified measures of intelligence.

In 1832, Howe became founding principal of the Perkins Institute at Watertown, Massachusetts. This was the first North American school for the visually impaired. Howe deplored the prejudices that labelled the blind as helpless and dependent. He believed that, instead of pity, the blind should be enabled to achieve dignity and usefulness through appropriate education (Address, 1836). Howe is probably best remembered for his work with Laura Bridgeman, a girl whose childhood infection had robbed her of sight, hearing, taste, and smell. Howe's extensive reports of her education and development left an outstanding legacy to the entire field of special education, and to teachers of the deaf-blind in particular (Hallahan and Kauffman, 1982).

Howe's educational endeavours were not confined to the blind. He was an adamant supporter of oralism — speech and lip reading — for deaf children, and supported the founding of the first North American oral school in 1867. He admired Eduard Seguin and convinced Massachusetts legislators that the training and education of the feeble-minded was a public responsibility. In 1848, he opened the Massachusetts School for Idiots and Feeble-Minded Youths at the Perkins Institution.

SPECIAL EDUCATION IN CANADA

Canadian developments in the education of the handicapped closely followed patterns established in the United States. Due to demographic, social, and economic factors, this education began somewhat later in Canada. Advances in Canadian education and social welfare took place only after the wealth of the provinces sufficiently increased. Canadians began to care for the handicapped and needy only after they felt they could afford to turn from their colonial preoccupation with survival and material development.

In the early colonial period, the care of the handicapped rested with the family. However, as Canadian social and economic patterns became more complex, many families grew less willing to care for handicapped children. In the late 1800s, residential institutions were created to serve the deaf, the blind, the mentally retarded, the insane, and neglected and delinquent children. Many of these schools were created by forceful personalities who drew mainly on charitable sources.

Although schools for the handicapped were not established until after 1850, the problem had for some time elicited concern. In Upper Canada in 1793, for example, town wardens collected statistics on the incidence of dependency, including an enumeration of the deaf and dumb (Splane, 1965). In the 1830s, Charles Dunscombe, a member of the Legislature of Upper Canada, directed his efforts to the education of the deaf, the blind, and the insane, and to the reform of prisons (Report, 1836). Many petitions on behalf of the handicapped were addressed to the government throughout the 1830s, and many more were drafted in the decades that followed (Splane, 1965).

Education of the deaf

Ronald McDonald

As in Europe and the United States, the education of the deaf was the first form of special education to be undertaken in Canada. In 1829, Ronald McDonald, a reporter with the *Montreal Gazette*, was sent by the government of Lower Canada to train with Gallaudet in Hartford. In 1831, McDonald opened a school for deaf children in Champlain, Quebec, but lack of funds closed the establishment after only five years. McDonald returned to reporting, and continually advocated education for the handicapped. He was influential in persuading the Catholic Church in Quebec to open schools for deaf boys in 1848 and deaf girls in 1851 (Clarke and Winzer, 1983).

John McGann

Possibly the most prominent pioneer in the early history of Canadian special education was John Barrett McGann (1810-1880). McGann arrived in Toronto from Ireland, via New York, in 1855. He discovered three hundred deaf people in the city, and many more scattered throughout the province (McGann, 1888). In 1858, McGann persuaded the City Council, the colonial government, and various social leaders to donate money for a school for deaf and blind children. His school opened in a spare classroom of the Phoebe Street School in Toronto that same year.

Between 1858 and 1869, McGann taught his deaf students while his daughter taught those who were blind. With the help of Egerton Ryerson, he also persuaded the Ontario government to found permanent institutions for the deaf and the blind. The Ontario Institution for the Education and Instruction of Deaf and Dumb Persons was established at Belleville in 1870, and the Ontario Institution for the Education and Instruction of the Blind was opened at Brantford in 1872 (Winzer, 1984).

McGann lent his influence to the development of other Canadian special schools. He helped J. Scott Hutton to develop the Halifax School for the Deaf, and helped Thomas Widd to found the MacKay Institution for the Deaf in Montreal. McGann was also active within the deaf community, and helped found the Ontario Deaf-Mute Association and the Ontario Mission of the Deaf (Winzer, 1984).

In all, twelve members of McGann's family became involved in special education in Canada and the United States. One daughter taught deaf and blind children in Ontario, a second taught deaf children in Michigan, and a third became principal of the McKay School for the Deaf in Montreal. A son-in-law founded the Manitoba School for the Deaf in 1886, as well as a similar institution in Washington state. Another son-in-law established a short-lived school for the deaf in Vancouver in 1888 (Winzer, 1984).

Education of the visually impaired

In the mid-1800s, very few, if any, blind persons had remunerative employment. The great majority were locked in asylums or begged in the streets. The general public was apathetic and indifferent to their fate (MacDonald, 1925).

John Barrett McGann was the first person in Canada to undertake the education of the blind. Beginning in 1861, he admitted blind children to his Toronto school where they were taught by his fifteen-year-old daughter, Effie (Winzer, 1984). In 1866, the Grey Nuns founded the Nazareth Institution in Montreal (Beggs, 1983; McLelland, 1934). Publicly supported institutions for the blind opened in Halifax in 1870 and Ontario in 1872.

Frederick Fraser became founding principal of the Halifax School for the Blind. Like McGann, Fraser worked to change public prejudices. He urged upon legislators the unassailable right of blind children to an education (MacDonald, 1925).

To demonstrate the viability of education of the handicapped, special-school promoters exhibited their students' achievements on legislature floors and in communities across the provinces. Many school principals and teachers devoted their summers to walking from village to village seeking handicapped children. They told parents of the importance of schooling, and described new employment opportunities for their children.

In the summer of 1875, J.M. Brown, a teacher from the Ontario School for the Blind, travelled over 3000 kilometres, 1300 of them on foot. On his return to school, poor Mr. Brown was "jaded and emaciated, and he was only two weeks in the classroom where he fell an easy victim to typhoid fever, which was prevailing in that portion of Brantford" (Ontario, Sessional Papers, 1875, pp. 257-258).

The care and education of the blind made rapid advances with the return of blinded soldiers from Europe after World War I. In 1917, a representative group of blinded soldiers and civilian blind met with women's organizations and businessmen. This meeting initiated the Canadian National Institute for the Blind (CNIB) (Canadian war blinded, 1942).

The mentally handicapped

The early treatment of mental retardation was hindered by a lack of definition concerning the nature of the condition. It seems probable that only the most severe types of retardation were reported and institutionalized (Penrose, 1963).

In the late 1800s, physicians sought more precise diagnostic classifications and tried to link retardation to organic pathology. In 1866, John Langdon Down described "the

Mongolian type of idiocy" by identifying one particular group of mentally retarded children. This study opened the way to more efficient classification. However, Down's contemporaries drew little distinction between mental handicap and mental illness. The psychotic child did not emerge as an object of study until much later (McMillan, 1960).

In the 1800s, the treatment of those labelled insane, which probably included many retarded persons, was reported as "exceedingly bad," and "entirely inadequate to the needs of that afflicted class" (Ontario Sessional Papers, 1878, pp. 1-2). Because no proper facilities were available, most retarded and insane people were confined in poorhouses, jails, and hospitals (Ontario Inspector of Prisons, 1871-72). In 1869 in Barrie, Ontario, of fourteen prisoners in the town jail, eight were considered "as dangerous lunatics, idiots, or imbeciles incapable of taking care of themselves." One inmate, afflicted with idiocy, epilepsy, and blindness, had been confined to the jail for eight years (Ontario Sessional Papers, 1869, p. 11).

The first asylums for the insane were not built until the 1850s. In 1876, the first Canadian institution for the mentally retarded opened in Orillia, Ontario, "with a capacity for serving 150 idiots" (Ontario Inspector of Prisons, 1876, p. 2). These efforts were motivated by humanitarian and economic concerns. Intervention improved the lives of the retarded and their families, and trained the retarded to require less custodial care and assistance (Ontario Inspector of Prisons, 1871-72).

In 1888, a proper school was organized at Orillia (Ontario Inspector of Prisons, 1888). Training involved a kindergarten program (one of the first in Canada), sense-training development as prescribed by Seguin, physical training, singing, and some academic schoolwork for the less retarded students (Hackett, 1969).

Delinquent, neglected, and vagrant children

In the 1800s, many Canadians were appalled by the numbers of neglected, vagrant, and delinquent children roaming the streets of the larger cities. Many of these youngsters drank, swore, pilfered orchards, played with catapults, harassed Salvation Army cadets, lit bonfires, stole newspapers, broke into letter boxes (Houston, 1982). For these, and more petty crimes, such as smoking or trampling strawberries, they were routinely committed to institutions.

In the early 1800s, neglected, vagrant, or delinquent children were committed to penitentiaries and common jails along with adult offenders. Between 1835 and 1857, some 683 persons between the ages of ten and twenty were sentenced to the penitentiary (Canada, Journals, 1858). Many reformers began to demand that children be exempt from the lash, wanton malnourishment, and association with hardened criminals. These efforts led to the establishment of reformatories in Canada East (Quebec) in 1858, Canada West (Ontario) in 1859, and Nova Scotia in 1864.

Reformers still complained that reformatories incarcerated children who had committed no other crime than being poor. In the 1870s, they began to agitate for alternative institutions to serve neglected children. In 1886, the Victoria Industrial School for Boys opened in Mimico, near Toronto. This residential institution accepted children between eight and fourteen on the principle that a change in environment might redeem a potentially criminal personality. Trade teaching was a vital component, and most school time was devoted to industrial training. Across Canada, the industrial school became an important way to handle potentially delinquent youth.

Exhibit 3-3 Early milestones in special education in Canada.

1830-1860	Orphanages to care for orphaned and dependent children were opened in Montreal, Kingston, Toronto, and Halifax.
1830	Legislation allowed the insane to be committed to common jails (Splane, 1965).
1831	Ronald McDonald opened a school for deaf children in Champlain, Quebec. This was the first special education venture in Canada.
1848	The Catholic Church in Quebec opened a school for Catholic deaf boys. This was followed by a school for deaf girls in 1851.
1851	The Toronto Asylum opened to care for the insane.
1856	Two deaf men established the Halifax School for the Deaf, with J. Scott Hutton as first official principal.
1858	In Toronto, John Barrett McGann opened a school to teach deaf children. In 1861, blind pupils were admitted.
1859	Canada West (Ontario) opened the Penetanguishene Reformatory. Although designed only for delinquent boys, it also admitted many young neglected children.
1866	The Grey Nuns opened a small private school for the blind in Montreal.
1870	Ontario opened a publicly supported institution for the deaf in Belleville. In Montreal, Thomas Widd established a school for Protestant deaf children, later named the MacKay School for Deaf and Crippled Children.
1872	Ontario opened a publicly supported school for the blind in Brantford.
1873	A public school for the blind opened in Halifax under Frederick Fraser.
1876	The first Canadian institution specifically for the mentally retarded opened in Orillia, Ontario. A school on the site opened in 1888.
1884	A son-in-law of McGann's, J.B. Watson, established the Winnipeg School for the Deaf.
1886	The first industrial school opened near Toronto to handle neglected, vagrant, and delinquent boys.
1888	Nova Scotia and Manitoba gave free education to deaf children.
1893	Children's Aid Societies were formed in Ontario. The model was adopted across Canada and the United States.
1898	British Columbia opened Woodlands, a facility for the mentally retarded.

Child welfare

By the late 1800s, Canadians recognized children as sensitive individuals, rather than chattels. A number of child-welfare reforms were passed, concerning orphans, child labour, truancy, apprenticeships, and so on (Spettigue, [1955]). In 1893, new legislation led to the formation of the first Children's Aid Societies. These reforms, together with the advent of free and compulsory education, offered all children a greater chance to develop to their full potential.

MAJOR HISTORICAL TRENDS

Much more could be said about the development of Canadian special education, and about the educators whose fascinating careers helped to shape its course. At this point, however, we will turn to a consideration of the major historical trends that led special education into the twentieth century.

Changing attitudes toward the handicapped

Throughout the short history of special education, two opposing philosophies have exerted a strong influence. Historically, these two threads were referred to as sensationalism and nativism. Today we call them environment and heredity, or nurture and nature.

For many centuries, superstitions and myths surrounded the handicapped. Exceptional conditions were seen as innate, imprinted before birth by God, nature or the devil. Educational intervention was not even considered as a possible option.

John Locke's philosophy of sensationalism opened a new era for the handicapped. The belief that handicaps were not innate led to an assumption that they could be partly overcome through education. This optimistic view predominated until the end of the 1800s. It underlay the thought and work of educators such as de l'Epée, Itard, and Seguin.

With the growth of genetics as a science, those who believed that handicaps were predetermined gained new support for their arguments. Proponents of the heredity theory of exceptionality gave much less credence to the value of education. Many believed the handicapped should be segregated in institutions, not only to protect them but to protect society. Views that focused on heredity were held by Samuel Gridley Howe, Alexander Graham Bell, and other prominent educators in the late 1800s (Howe, 1843; Mitchell, 1971).

Institutionalization

In the 1800s, special children were mostly educated in residential settings. In the United States and Canada, these special schools were divorced from the general educational system and administered along with prisons, asylums, and public charities. School superintendents were forced to act as general administrators of institutions, asylums, training schools, or colonies. Not until the early 1900s were special schools placed under provincial departments of education.

In the 1800s, a major problem for special schools was lack of clarity in the categorization of exceptional conditions. Because classification rested largely on personal observation of exceptional conditions. Because classification rested largely on personal observation, residential institutions often became dumping grounds for all sorts of misfits for the blind, the deaf, and neglected children contain many pleas for the removal of misplaced students, especially those judged to be feeble-minded.

Curricula in the institutions

As we have seen, education for the handicapped began as a philanthropic venture designed to enhance social welfare. Educators concentrated on providing industrial training so that handicapped children could attain some measure of economic self-sufficiency.

In most institutions, schooling took place for about three hours a day. The rest of the time was spent in upkeep of the institutions or in the practice of various trades. Blind boys at Brantford, for example, were taught chair caning and piano tuning. Deaf boys at Belleville and delinquent lads at Mimico made boots and shoes for the inmates of asylums and jails. The girls learned domestic science and performed all the mending and sewing in their institutions (Winzer, 1981a).

External influences

In the 1800s special education facilities in Canada formed part of North America's institutional complex. Canadian teachers trained in the United States, held office in American professional associations, and hosted North American professional conferences. Canada also recruited many personnel from American institutions.

Special education also developed within the larger context of education. Pioneers in special education forwarded arguments identical to those expounded by proponents of the public school system. Canadian special education owes much to educational reformers, such as Egerton Ryerson, John Langmuir, and J.J. Kelso (Winzer, 1981a).

Other disciplines, especially medicine, psychology, sociology, and social work, also contributed to special education. As the twentieth century opened, the emerging fields of psychology and sociology, and especially the widespread use of mental ability tests, had profound implications for special children and their education.

THE EARLY TWENTIETH CENTURY

The early years of special education were alive with energy, optimism, and the pulse of new ideas. In the early 1900s, however, special education lost much of its momentum in North America. Perceptions about special individuals were increasingly clouded by pessimism and fear, and coercive methods were developed to control deviant behaviour.

Public attitudes and assumptions contributed greatly to this decline. People increasingly believed that handicaps were genetically determined and not amenable to improvement through education. The enthusiasm generated by Seguin's training-school model faded, and institutions for the retarded sought only to provide a simplified and routine life-style for their inmates. The Orillia Institution, for example, almost closed in 1896 as a result of public criticisms regarding the cost and futility of education for idiots (Hackett, 1969).

Many other factors added to the problem. Overzealous professionals bickered among themselves and led the public to expect miraculous cures that never happened. Social Darwinists encouraged the public to reject the needs of the helpless. Industrialization, urbanization, and an influx of immigrants placed greater strain on social services.

Perhaps the most important factor in the decrease of social services was the eugenics or mental-hygiene movement. This movement received further impetus from the testing movement, which introduced quantitative methods of assessing intelligence.

The testing movement

By the early 1900s, schooling had become the social norm for most children in Canada. As the schools assumed public responsibility for socializing and educating huge numbers of children, they were faced with an unforeseen problem. How could schools best provide for those children who could not be handled in the regular classes? These difficult students were those labelled as feeble-minded. More severely handicapped children were still relegated to institutional settings (Hoffman, 1975).

In 1904, Alfred Binet (1857-1911) attempted to assess the intellectual ability of Paris school children. He wanted to devise a method for identifying children who could not adapt to school curricula and who thereby reduced the efficiency of their teachers and classmates. Binet invited a young colleague, Theodore Simon (1873-1961), to work with him. In 1906, Binet and Simon published the Binet-Simon Scale, the first formal instrument for assessing the intelligence of children.

The Binet-Simon Scale became the prototype for many later tests of mental ability. In 1910, Henry Goddard of the United States translated the Scale to English. In 1916, Lewis Terman's revision popularized the procedure.

When Goddard tested public-school children, he found at least two percent to be mentally retarded, unable to achieve in traditional classrooms. Goddard also tested representative samples of immigrants at Ellis Island. His results demonstrated that high numbers were feeble-minded and therefore prone to drunkenness, pauperism, vice, and criminality (Winzer and O'Connor, 1982).

Believing that mental retardation was a hereditary characteristic, subject to Mendelian laws, Goddard embarked upon a mission to warn the public against the "threat of the feeble-minded." Goddard's campaign spread panic throughout North American society. Professionals and politicians began to agree that the only way to save the world from hereditary defects was to isolate all defectives, prevent them from procreating, and remove them at birth to segregated settings. For those defectives who made contact with the normal community, sterilization was urged (Winzer and O'Connor, 1982).

The mainstay of Goddard's crusade was the IQ test. So great was public credulity that no one questioned the accuracy of these testing procedures. Not until the mid-1930s were doubts about the infallibility of IQ tests finally aired.

The eugenics, or mental-hygiene, movement

Goddard and the early proponents of IQ testing used intelligence tests in ways not envisioned by Binet and Simon. Goddard and his followers shifted the testing emphasis from the needs of the individual to the needs of society. They elevated the threat of the feeble-minded to the status of a national concern and triggered "a wave of eugenic alarm"

(Doll, 1967). They also increased national misgivings regarding the tides of immigrants then flooding into North America.

Francis Galton, a cousin of Charles Darwin, was the modern founder of the movement known as **eugenics**. To Galton and his disciples, eugenics consisted "chiefly in the sweeping away of a legion of ineffectives, and in introducing in very much greater proportion the number of men of independent and original thought" (Galton, 1873). They maintained that only society's superior classes should procreate. Those deemed unfit should be stopped by education, legislation, segregation, or even sterilization.

The hereditary nature of feeble-mindedness was given spurious support by ex post facto studies on two families — the Jukes and the Kallikaks. Dugdale (1877) conducted a genealogical survey on the Jukes, a fictitious surname derived from a generic term of reproach. Dugdale collected information on 709 of the 1200 descendants of the original Jukes, an American backwoodsman. Dugdale found that 140 had been imprisoned for crime, 200 were paupers dependent on public support, and most of the others possessed poor mental and physical abilities.

In 1912, Henry Goddard published his account of the Kallikaks. He told the story of Martin, a Revolutionary soldier who impregnated a feeble-minded tavern girl. Of the 480 descendants of this union, Goddard claimed that 143 were feeble-minded, 46 were normal, and the rest were undetermined. After leaving the army, Martin married a respectable girl. Through this second union came another line of descendants of a radically different nature. In this family were found none but respectable citizens, men and women prominent in every phase of social life (Kanner, 1964).

The name Kallikak, like Jukes, was invented. Goddard created it by combining two Greek words — *kalos* meaning attractive and *kakes* meaning evil. The name symbolized both branches of Martin's family — one made up of worthy members of society, and the other composed of criminals and deviants (Kanner, 1964). Only heredity was considered as a differentiating variable; the children's environment was not taken into account. The Kallikaks, said Goddard (1914), "were feeble-minded, and no amount of education or good environment can change a feeble-minded individual into a normal one, any more than it can change a red-headed stock into a black-haired stock" (p. 188).

Canadians were also warned of the dangers of the unchecked spread of feeble-mindedness. In 1918, a coalition of physicians, social workers, and wealthy patrons formed the Canadian National Committee for Mental Hygiene. The Committee began to exert pressure on the government for expanded custodial facilities. As well as protecting the mentally retarded, the new institutions would function to control retardation in order to protect the community.

The Committee warned Canadian legislators that feeble-mindedness arose from two factors. To begin with, eighty percent of all defectives spring from unsound stock." The spread of feeble-mindedness was also accelerated by "the admittance to the Dominion of degenerate immigrants" (Hincks, 1918). The Committee further claimed that:

> The feeble-minded are irresponsible mortals; that without supervision they cannot be trusted; that, unless special provisions are made for them, some will undoubtedly burn down buildings; others will spread venereal disease; others will bear illegitimate feeble-minded children; others will steal; others will become chronic paupers; others will retard whole classes in public schools and will poison morals; and others will commit murder (Hincks, 1919).

Eugenic beliefs, bolstered by IQ tests, caused the public to direct a general attitude of fear and alarm toward the handicapped. The mentally retarded were herded into institutions that were little more than warehouses for the storage of human beings. To a lesser extent, the deaf, the blind, and other exceptional groups were also caught in the eugenical net (Mitchell, 1971; Winzer and O'Connor, 1982).

A considerable amount has been written about this black chapter in Canadian history. Interested readers can refer to Baker (1980); Chapman (1977), Chase (1977, 1980); Christian (1974); Siegel (1939); and Winzer and O'Connor (1982).

The day school movement

When special education began in North America, exceptional individuals were thought to differ qualitatively from other people. They were thought to have traits and characteristics that made them fundamentally different from the general run of humanity. Because of this, and for reasons of economy and convenience, exceptional children were chiefly educated in institutional settings.

The concept of special segregated classes in regular schools was first introduced in the 1800s. Once again, educators of the deaf led the way. The first day-class for deaf children opened in Boston in 1869. In the 1870s, classes for the gifted opened in St. Louis. In 1896, classes for the mentally retarded opened in Providence, Rhode Island, and in 1900, classes for the blind opened in Chicago (Kirk and Gallagher, 1983). McGann's first school for the deaf in Toronto was essentially a segregated class. Moreover, in 1863, as a very early proponent of mainstreaming. McGann was advocating "the practicality of giving to all the deaf mutes of the Province at least two years' primary instruction in the common schools, situate in their respective districts" (McGann, 1863).

In the early 1900s, educators started special classes to extend schooling to larger numbers and a more varied clientele for longer periods. While Henry Goddard, Lewis Terman, and their associates were fostering national fear of the handicapped, others sought to improve their plight. Enlightened educators saw the handicapped as potentially productive citizens, whose problems most often stemmed from neglect, mistreatment, inadequate economic support, and inappropriate schooling. These educators called for the elimination of residential institutions, the introduction of courses to teach self-sufficiency, and the extension of equal educational opportunities to exceptional students.

In the early 1900s, American advocates of day classes in the public system focused on the mentally rather than physically handicapped. They urged that intellectually different children be provided with specially trained teachers and special classroom environments suited to their handicap. They sought to develop curricula suited to the children's needs, and to provide vocational training to render the children economically self-sufficient.

In Canada, the first special day classes were started for children with physical problems. In Montreal, the world's first organized movement on behalf of crippled children was started in 1906 by a group of educators at the Children's Memorial Hospital (Beggs, 1983). In 1908, the Hospital for Sick Children in Toronto began an open-air class on Toronto Island for children who were malnourished, sickly, or suffering from tuberculosis (McIntosh, 1977). These were followed by day classes for the mentally retarded, sight-saving classes, home instruction, speech correction, and lip reading

Exhibit 3-4 People who exerted major influence on the development of special education.

Thomas Hopkins Gallaudet (1787-1851)	An American Congregational minister who, after training in Paris, opened a school for the deaf in 1817. A widely influential promoter of all types of special and general education.
Samuel Gridley Howe (1801-1876)	An American physician who began the first North American school for the blind. Another influential special education advocate.
Alexander Graham Bell (1847-1922)	Inventor of the telephone, also involved in the education of the deaf. Bell believed that all deaf children could speak and fought to abolish sign-language use. An early promoter of eugenics, Bell published *Memoir upon the formation of a deaf variety of the human race* (1884).
Francis Galton (1822-1911)	A believer in eugenics. After studying genius, he decided it ran in families and its origins could be determined.
Alfred Binet (1857-1911)	A French psychologist who devised the first formal quantified measure of intelligence.
Theodore Simon (1873-1961)	Worked with Binet on the development of the Binet-Simon Scale, published in 1906.
Lewis Terman (1877-1956)	Popularized the use of intelligence tests in the United States. Used the measures to identify gifted children.

classes. There were also orthopedic classes, vocational and advancement classes, and remedial reading programs.

In 1910, Ontario's Special Classes Act permitted boards of education to legalize existing special classes. Teacher training began soon afterwards; in 1916, the first course for teachers of special classes was given at Wellesley School in Toronto (McIntosh, 1977). By the mid-1920s, special classes for exceptional children were a feature of urban education throughout Canada.

THE CURRENT ERA

By the late 1930s, special education had begun to overcome the inertia and repression of the previous thirty years. The important contributions of the 1940s and 1950s will be addressed in detail in the following relevant chapters. In general, however, there was a great extension of special education services, greater specialization of services, and an increased public involvement with all phases of training and care for exceptional children.

In the 1950s and 1960s, many educators began to seriously question the benefits of special education. Some claimed that special classes were too often used as dumping grounds. Gallagher (1972) pointed out that special education was often exclusionary rather than remedial; he also claimed that special education did not appear to be returning a significant number of children to the regular classroom. Educators also argued that special classes cast a stigma on exceptional children, provided low-quality education, and were often alotted inferior facilities and untrained teachers. Children from special classes, moreover, were barely tolerated by regular classroom teachers and administrators.

This grave dissatisfaction with special education was increased by numerous studies that compared the progress of exceptional children in segregated and regular classes. These studies found that children performed no better in special classes (Bradfield, Brown, Kaplan, Rickert, and Stannard, 1973; Bruininks, Rynders, and Gross, 1974; Dunn, 1968; Gallagher, 1972; Myers, 1976; Reynolds and Birch, 1977). In the 1970s, discontent with special classes continued to mount. Agitation by parent and professional groups led to new legislation and many of the changes that are apparent in special education today.

Parent pressure

Parent organizations have had a tremendous impact on special education, especially in the 1950s and 1960s. Parents have successfully agitated to expand special education services. They have formed groups to pressure governments, often in uneasy alliance with professional special educators. Parents have collected petitions, organized letter-writing campaigns, and placed public pressure on provincial ministers of education. Parent activists have fought court cases and pushed for legislation to bring about dramatic changes in the treatment of exceptional children.

Until recently, parents had little say in their child's classification and placement within the school system. Today, however, parents of exceptional children want to be involved in every issue affecting their child's education. In Canada parents of special children participate more in the school's decision-making process than do parents of regular children (Lusthaus and Lusthaus, 1982).

Parents have formed many organizations to increase social and educational opportunities for their exceptional children. In Ontario, for example, the Ontario Association for Children with Learning Disabilities (OACLD) pushed for the passage of Bill 82, the Education Amendment Act of 1980, which made special education mandatory (Winzer, 1982). In Quebec, since 1971, parents have successfully urged the government to pass legislation to increase parental involvement in the schools' decision-making process (Lusthaus and Lusthaus, 1982). In the United States, in 1963, parents helped to form the Association for Children with Learning Disabilities (ACLD). The efforts of this organization, supported by associations such as the Council for Exceptional Children, brought about the passage of the United States Learning Disability Act in 1969, signed into law in 1970 (Haring, 1983).

Litigation

In both Canada and the United States, parent activism has brought the plight of exceptional children to the courts. In general, parents have filed suits for two reasons.

Some have objected to the lack of special education services available for their children. Others have opposed the placement of their children in special classes that they consider inappropriate. For discussions of Canadian litigation and legislation, see Cameron (1979); Smith (1980); and Treherne and Rawlyk (1979). For summaries and discussions of American litigation, see Bateman and Herr (1981); Burgdorf (1979); Hallahan and Kauffman (1982); Hobbs (1975); Kuriloff, True, Kirp, and Buss (1974); Martin (1968); Turnbull (1981); and Zelder (1953).

Legislation

In Canada, special education is still very much in the legislative arena. Favourable court rulings have prompted legislators and advocates of the handicapped to press for new laws that ensure the rights of handicapped children in the public school system. Across the country, legislators and policy-makers are considering measures to compel respect for the unique needs of the exceptional child. In the United States, however, since the passage of PL 94-142, legislative involvement in special education appears to be growing less (Mitchell, 1983).

Public Law 94-142

In recent years, the most significant and influential legislation has been the United States Education for All Handicapped Children Act, Public Law 94-142. This bill was passed by Congress in 1975 and signed into law in 1977. Prior to its passage, an estimated four million of a total of seven million handicapped children in the United States were being inappropriately or inadequately educated (Meadow, 1980).

PL 94-142 has exerted a profound influence on special education, and its far-reaching effects have touched recent Canadian legislation. PL 94-142 altered the entire concept of special education in the United States. It introduced the principle of normalization, and insisted that children be taught in the least restrictive environment possible (Karagianis and Nesbit, 1981).

PL 94-142 is the broadest and most complex education law passed by the American government. Its terms are both specific and mandatory. PL 94-142 states that "in order to receive funds under the Act, every school system in the nation must make provision for a free, appropriate public education for every child... regardless of how, or how seriously, he may be handicapped."

PL 94-142 provides a formula by which the American government agrees to pay an increasing percentage of the costs associated with Special Education services. By subsidizing costs, the federal government attempts to ensure that exceptional children receive the special education programs they need from the state. PL 94-142 has brought many children into the orbit of the public schools, giving them attention they had previously been denied. However, the law was never intended to force schools to educate all exceptional children in the regular classroom (Abeson and Zettel, 1977). For many severely impaired and multiply handicapped children, the normal classroom is clearly inappropriate.

Exhibit 3-5 Basic provisions of PL 94-142, The Education for All Handicapped Children Act, United States.

Each state and local school system must have a plan that includes:

- Systematic procedures to screen and identify all handicapped children.
- An appropriate education at no cost for every handicapped child.
- The informed consent of the parents before the child is evaluated, labelled, or placed in special education.
- An impartial due-process hearing for parents if they disagree with the school's decision.
- Consultation with the child's parents or guardians concerning the child's education and placement and the school's educational plan for the child. A surrogate parent must be appointed to represent the child's interests if the parents or guardians are unknown or unavailable.
- A written individualized educational plan for each handicapped child.
- Education of each handicapped child in the least restrictive environment that is consistent with the child's educational needs.
- Placement of the child, to the furthest extent possible, in a classroom with nonhandicapped children.
- Evaluation of the child in all areas of suspected disability, and in a way that is not biased by language, cultural characteristics, or handicaps. The evaluation must be performed by a multidisciplinary team, and placement and planning must not be based on any single evaluation criterion.
- Information related to evaluation and placement must be kept confidential, and parents and guardians may have access to records regarding their child.
- Training for special teachers and other personnel, including in-service training for regular teachers.

(Adapted from Kneedler, Hallahan, and Kauffman (1984); and Lerner (1981).)

Like any far-reaching new law, PL 94-142 is not without critics. Hallahan and Kauffman (1982), for example, warn that PL 94-142 permits bureaucratic authorities to wield tremendous power in special education decisions. Another major problem has been the prescriptive nature of the Individualized Education Program (IEP). Under PL 94-142, the design of the IEP has become far more complicated.

Some teachers have complained that the new law requires them to spend too much time giving tests and filling out forms. The law interferes with teaching because so much time must be spent meeting detailed technical requirements (Katzen, 1980). One study found that, on average, a teacher spends about eleven hours formulating and writing each IEP (Safer, Morrissey, Kaufman, and Lewis, 1978).

Canadian legislation

Essentially, PL 94-142 gives exceptional children in the United States the right to a free, appropriate education in the least restrictive environment. In Canada, similar legislation rendering special education mandatory is now in progress. Parent groups, court decisions, escalating educational costs, and the example set by PL 94-142 are all exerting pressure on government. Stringent legislation is underway to guarantee equal access to education for all children, exceptionality notwithstanding.

In Canada, the right of every child to education is not entrenched by any constitutional provision. The 1867 British North America Act was chiefly concerned with protecting the education rights of linguistic and religious minorities, not handicapped children (Smith, 1980). In the absence of constitutional provisions, the responsibility for education rests entirely with provincial legislation.

Each of the ten provinces has its own school system based upon provincial education legislation. Only a few schools and institutions are controlled by the provincial governments directly, such as provincial resource centres for the deaf. The rest are administered through local school boards, each of which is responsible for a geographical school district. Funding stems from a combination of property taxes and provincial government grants, according to formulae that vary from province to province (Clarke and Kendall, 1976). Each provincial government can develop its own legislation, regulations, policies, and procedures to ensure that all children receive a free and appropriate education. The government may also selectively ignore the rights of some members of its population, such as exceptional students (Leslie and Goguen, 1984).

All the provinces and the two territories have some form of legislated responsibility for the education of exceptional children, but the breadth of services varies. In recent years, however, the concept of equal educational opportunities for exceptional children has become a dominant ideology. Provincial governments and local school boards have felt increasingly obligated to develop appropriate programs for the entire school-age population within the province.

Goguen (1980) reports that Newfoundland, Nova Scotia, Quebec, Ontario, Manitoba and Saskatchewan have some form of legislation to guarantee access to special education. The other provinces have permissive legislation; their school boards may provide services, but are under no legal obligation to do so. Currently, Quebec, Alberta, Saskatchewan, Nova Scotia and the two territories have a "zero-reject policy," which implies that no child is rejected by the schools.

More stringent legislation is in the making. In New Brunswick, the Correira-Goguen reports (1982, 1983) have made recommendations to expand and define the population of exceptional children. Correira and Goguen (1983) "recommend a revision of the Schools Act to provide the right to services and the funding for services for all exceptional children" (p. 3). New Brunswick intends to develop stronger policies by 1987. Manitoba has recently passed special education legislation and a task force is currently at work in Saskatchewan.

In Ontario, the most populous province, the first Canadian legislation along the lines of PL 94-142 has been introduced. Undoubtedly, interested parties in the other provinces are watching closely to see whether Ontario's mandatory legislation meets with success.

The Education Amendment Act, Ontario

Ontario's Education Amendment Act passed into law on December 12, 1980. The Act has been hailed as the most progressive piece of social legislation in recent memory (Hodder, 1984). It has been praised as a law "in tune with the times; its proposals timely and sound" (Ontario Teacher's Federation, 1982).

Under the Education Amendment Act, all school boards in the province of Ontario must provide special education to exceptional students (Green, 1983). Undoubtedly, the American bill PL 94-142 had considerable influence on the new Act. However, Ontario educators and legislators also had the chance to learn from PL 94-142 and avoid its major pitfalls. As Hodder (1984) points out, Ontario's legislation falls somewhere between PL 94-142 and no bill at all. Indentical in intent to the American law, Ontario's legislation has tried to avoid its prescriptive nature.

Under Ontario's new law, school boards can no longer exclude children on the basis of an exceptionality (Lane, 1981). School boards must enrol all children, regardless of condition, and provide them with "suitable programming" (*Hansard*, 23 May 1980). The legislation offers freely accessible, publicly funded education to all elementary and secondary students in Ontario.

The Education Amendment Act defines an exceptional pupil as "one whose behavioural, communicational, intellectual, physical, or multiple exceptionalities are such that he is considered to need a placement in a special education program by a committee" (1:20, a). Within this definition are included children with learning disabilities, emotionally disturbed children, children with behavioural disorders, the educable mentally retarded, and gifted and talented children. Because this definition was formulated for legislative, not educational, purposes it relies heavily on a categorical orientation. Non-categorical approaches were explored and rejected on the basis that attempts to eliminate labelling had not been very successful (Hodder, 1984).

As Exhibit 3-6 shows, five major principles are enshrined in the new legislation.

Exhibit 3-6 Five principles of The Education Amendment Act, Ontario.

- *Universal access.* All exceptional pupils have a right to appropriate educational programs.
- *Education at public expense.* Education is provided without additional fees charged to the pupil or the family.
- *Appeal process.* Exceptional children, their parents, and their advocates have the right to appeal identification and placement decisions, and to request a review hearing.
- *Appropriate program.* Exceptional pupils have the right to a program that states specific objectives and outlines the services that will meet their needs.
- *Ongoing identification, assessment and review.* Provisions are made for ongoing identification of students' needs, and continuous assessment and evaluation of their progress. The suitability of each placement is reviewed annually.

(Adapted from Keeton, 1983a, 1983b.)

Interlocking responsibilities reside with the Ministry of Education and individual school boards. The Ministry undertakes to ensure that all exceptional students have free and appropriate education, and that all boards implement early identification procedures. The Ministry defines exceptionalities and gives Roman Catholic boards the right to provide education for trainable mentally retarded students. In accordance with Ministry requirements, school boards of education must establish early identification programs, and provide appropriate education to special students. They must also establish programs for trainable mentally retarded pupils (Implications, 1981).

As we have stated, Ontario's legislation is identical in intent to PL 94-142, but not as prescriptive in nature. Unlike the American bill, Ontario's law does not insist on mainstreaming or provide for non-discriminatory, culturally-appropriate testing. In addition, the due-process provision is more broadly applied in the United States, allowing parents to more easily challenge the appropriateness of their child's educational program (Keeton, 1983b).

Although Ontario does not insist on mainstreaming or the "least restrictive environment," individual school boards are free to adopt this principle (Keeton, 1983b). Ontario's lack of guidelines for culturally unbiased testing seems unfortunate given the province's multi-cultural mix. Many new Canadian children may well be placed at a disadvantage, a topic that is further addressed in Chapter Fourteen.

SUMMARY

In this chapter, we have briefly explored the development of special education. Throughout most of history, exceptional conditions have been attributed to mystical and supernatural causes. In the eighteenth century, the French Enlightenment emerged, with a philosophical emphasis on rationalism, sensationalism, and social equality. During this period, the first systematic education of exceptional children began. The enlightened ideas of Locke, Rousseau, Diderot, and Condillac profoundly influenced the work of such special education pioneers as de l'Epée, Periere, Huay, Seguin, and Itard. These pioneers in turn influenced the principles, pedagogy, and philosophy of special education in Canada and the United States.

In the 1800s, special education grew rapidly in North America. During this period, it evolved from a philanthropic enterprise to an integral part of the continent's social-welfare complex. In the last decades of the nineteenth century, educators began to agitate for the inclusion of special institutions within departments of education. These attempts were defeated, however, by social leaders who preached the futility of education for the handicapped, most especially those labelled feeble-minded. These eugenists, who relied on spurious studies and the results of IQ tests, claimed that the handicapped genetically polluted society and should be segregated or sterilized.

As the eugenics scare faded in the 1930s, special education emerged revitalized. Special segregated classes developed to meet the needs of exceptional children. In the late 1960s, educators began to seriously question the viability of special classes. The concept of mainstreaming, or teaching exceptional children in the regular classroom, began to gain popularity.

At present special education is an exciting and expanding field, open to many new philosophies and approaches. Like the United States, Canada has adopted the principle of equal educational opportunity for all children, exceptionality notwithstanding. Throughout the country, legislators are moving, albeit cautiously, to make special education available to all exceptional children.

BIBLIOGRAPHY

Abeson, A. and Zettel, J. (1977). The end of the quiet revolution: The Education for All Handicapped Children Act of 1975. *Exceptional Children, 44,* 114-128.

Address of the Trustees of the New England Institute for the Education of the Blind to the public (1836). In *Report upon the subject of education made to the Parliament of Upper Canada, 25th February, 1836. Through the Commissioners, Doctors Morrison and Bruce, appointed by a resolution of the House of Assembly in 1835, to obtain information upon the subject of education, etc.* Upper Canada: M.C. Reynolds.

Baker, J.D. (1980). Remedies: Liabilities for wrongful sterilization. In *Sterilization and mental handicap.* Ontario: National Institute for Mental Health.

Barnard, H. (1857). *Reformatory education. Papers on preventative, correctional and reformatory institutions and agencies in different countries.* Hartford: F.C. Brownell.

Bateman, B.D. and Herr, C.W. (1981). Law and special education. In J.M. Kauffman and D.P. Hallahan (Eds.), *Handbook of special education.* Englewood Cliffs, N.J.: Prentice-Hall.

Beggs, R. (1983). A biographical history of education of the deaf in Canada. *The ACEHI Journal, 9,* 12-23.

Bell, A.G. (1884). *Memoir upon the formation of a deaf variety of the human race. (Rpt. ed.)* Washington, D.C.: A.G. Bell Association for the Deaf, 1969.

Bradfield, R.H., Brown, J., Kaplan, P., Rickert, E., and Stannard, R. (1973). The special child in the regular classroom. *Exceptional Children, 39,* 384-390.

Bruininks, R.H., Rynders, J.E., and Gross, J.C. (1974). Social acceptance of mildly retarded pupils in resource room and regular classes. *American Journal of Mental Deficiency, 78,* 377-383.

Burgdorf, R.L. (Ed.) (1979). *The legal rights of handicapped persons: Cases, materials, and text.* Baltimore, MD.: Paul H. Brookes.

Cameron, D.R. (1979). The right to education. *Mental Retardation/Defecience Mentale, 29,* 2-5.

Canada. *Journals.*

Canadian war-blinded. (1942). *Outlook for the Blind and the teacher's Forum, 36,* 281-286.

Carlson, E.T. and Dain, N. (1960). The psychotherapy that was moral treatment. *American Journal of Psychology, 117,* 519-524.

Chapman, T. (1977). Early eugenics movement in Western Canada. *Alberta History, 25,* 9-17.

Chase, A. (1977). *The legacy of Malthus: The social costs of the new scientific racism.* New York: Alfred Knopf.

Chase, A. (1980). History of involuntary sterilization. In *Sterilization and mental handicap.* Ontario: National Institute for Mental Health.

Christian, T. (1974). The mentally ill and human rights in Alberta. M.A. Thesis, University of Alberta.

Clarke, B.R. and Kendall, D.C. (1976). Communication for hearing-impaired people in Canada. In H.J. Oyer (Ed.) *Communication for the hearing handicapped: An international perspective.* Baltimore, MD.: University Park Press.

Clarke, B.R. and Winzer, M.A. (1983). A concise history of the education of the deaf in Canada. *ACEHI Journal, 9,* 36-51.

Correia, C.L. and Goguen, L.J. (1983). *Final report of a study concerning the Auxiliary Classes Act of New Brunswick submitted to the Honourable Clarence Cormier, Minister of Education.* New Brunswick: [University of Moncton].

Correia, C.L. and Goguen, L.J. (1982). *Report of a study concerning the Auxiliary Classes Act of New Brunswick: Discussion paper.* New Brunswick: [University of Moncton].

de l'Epée, M.C. (1860). The true method of instructing the deaf and dumb, confirmed by long experience. *American Annals of the Deaf and Dumb, 12,* 1-131.

Doll, E. (1967). Trends and problems in the education of the mentally retarded: 1800-1940. *American Journal of Mental Deficiency, 72,* 175-183.

Down, J.L. (1866). Observations on ethnic classifications. *London Hospital Report, 3,* 229-262.

Dugdale, R.L. (1877). *The Jukes: A study of crime, pauperism, disease and heredity.* New York: Punma.

Dunn, L.M. (Ed.). (1973). *Exceptional Children in the schools: Special education in transition (2nd ed.).* New York: Holt, Rinehart and Winston.

Dunn, L.M. (1968). Special education for the mildly retarded — Is much of it justifiable? *Exceptional Children, 35,* 5-24.

Frampton, M.E. and Gall, E.D. (1955). *Special education for the exceptional: Introduction and problems (Vol. 1).* Boston: Porter Sargent.

French, R.S. (1932). *From Homer to Helen Keller: A social and educational study of the blind.* New York: American Foundation for the Blind.

Gallagher, J.J. (1972). *The search for an educational system that doesn't exist.* Reston, VA.: Council for Exceptional Children.

Galton, F. (1873). Hereditary improvement. *Fraser's Magazine, 7,* 116-123.

Goddard, H.H. (1912). *The Kallikak family: A study in the heredity of feeble-mindedness.* New York: MacMillan.

Goddard, H.H. (1914). What it means. . . . In M. Rosen, G.R. Clarke and M.S. Kivitz (Eds.) (1976). *The history of mental retardation: Collected papers (Vol. 2).* Baltimore, MD.: University Park Press.

Goguen, L. (1980). Right to education for exceptional children in Canada: A growing national concern. In M. Csapo and L. Goguen (Eds.), *Special education across Canada: Issues and concerns for the '80s.* Vancouver: Centre for Human Development and Research.

Goldstein, M. (1920). An acoustic method. *American Annals of the Deaf, 65,* 472-481.

Gordon, J.C. (1892). *Notes and observations upon the education of the deaf, with a revised index to education of deaf children.* Washington, D.C.: Volta Bureau.

Green, Y. (September, 1983). Bill 82: Historical perspectives. *Federation of Women Teachers of Ontario Newsletter,* 30-31.

Guillie, D. (1817). *Essai sur l'instruction des aveugles ou expose analytique des procedes poiur les instruire.* Paris: Imprime par les aveugles.

Hackett, G. (1969). A history of special education for mentally handicapped children in the province of Ontario, 1850 to the present. Doctoral dissertation, University of Toronto.

Hallahan, D.P. and Kauffman, J.M. (1982). *Exceptional children: Introduction to special education (2nd ed.).* Englewood Cliffs, N.J.: Prentice-Hall.

Hansard. (1980). 23 May.

Hardy, M.I., McLeod, J., Minto, H., Perkins, S.A., and Quance, W.R. (1971). *Standards for educators of exceptional children in Canada: The SEECC Report.* Toronto: Crainford.

Haring, N.G. (1983). *Exceptional children and youth.* (3rd. ed.). Columbus, OH: Merrill.

Hare, E.H. (1962). Masturbatory insanity: The history of an idea. *Journal of Mental Science, 108,* 1-25.

Hincks, C.M. (1918). Feeblemindedness in Canada: A serious national problem. *Social Welfare, 1,* 29-30.

Hincks, C.M. (1919). Feeblemindedness in Canada. *Social Welfare, 1,* 103-104.

Hobbs, N. (Ed.) (1975). *Issues in the classification of children: A sourcebook on categories, labels, and their consequences (Vol. 2).* San Francisco: Jossey-Bass.

Hodder, C. (1984). The Education Amendment Act (Ontario) 1980: A review. *Interchange, 15,* 44-53.

Hoffman, E. (1975). The American Public School and the deviant child: The origins of their involvement. *Journal of Special Education, 9,* 416-423.

Houston, S. (1982). The "waifs and strays" of a late Victorian city: Juvenile delinquents in Toronto. In J. Parr (Ed.), *Childhood and family in Canadian history.* Toronto: McClelland and Stewart.

Howe, S.G. (1843). On the causes of idiocy. In M. Rosen, G.R. Clark, and M.S. Kivitz (Eds.) (1976), *The history of mental retardation (Vol. 1)*. Baltimore, MD.: University Park Press.

Illick, J.E. (1974). Child-rearing in seventeenth-century England and America. In L. de Mause (Ed.), *The history of childhood*. New York: Psychohistory Press.

Implications of Bill 82 and regulations pertaining thereof. (1981). *Ontario Education, 13*, 15-16.

Kanner, L. (1964). *A history of the care and study of the mentally retarded*. Springfield, IL.: Charles C. Thomas.

Karagianis, L.D. and Nesbit, W.C. (1981). The Warnock Report: Britain's preliminary answer to Public Law 94-142. *Exceptional Children, 47*, 332-336.

Katzen, K. (1980). An open letter to CEC. *Exceptional Children, 48*, 582.

Keeton, A. (1983a). *The five principles of Ontario's "Bill 82" and related regulations*. Paper presented at the Canadian Society for the Study of Education conference, Vancouver, June.

Keeton, A. (1983b). *A consumer's guide to Bill 82: Special education in Ontario*. Toronto: OISE Press.

Kirk, S.A. and Gallagher, J.J. (1983). *Educating exceptional children (4th ed.)*. Boston, MA.: Houghton Mifflin.

Kneedler, R.D. with Hallahan, D.P. and Kauffman, J.M. (1984). *Special education for today*. Englewood Cliffs, N.J.: Prentice-Hall.

Kuriloff, P., True, R., Kirp, D. and Buss, W. (1974). Law reform and educational change: The Pennsylvania case. *Exceptional Children, 41*, 35-42.

Lane, H. and Pillard, R. (1978). *The wild boy of Burundi*. New York: Random House.

Lane, M.E. (1981). The right to an appropriate education: An analysis of Ontario's Bill 82. *School Guidance Worker, 36*, 15-20.

Lerner, J. (1981). *Learning disabilities: Theories, diagnosis, and teaching strategies (3rd. ed.)*. Boston: Houghton Mifflin.

Leslie, P.T. and Goguen, L. (1984). British Columbia's education policies: A retrospective examination. *Special Education in Canada, 58*, 47-49.

Lillard, P.P. (1972). *Montessori: A modern approach*. New York: Schocken Books.

Lusthaus, C. and Lusthaus, E. (1982). Parents and their involvement in the educational process. *Canadian Journal on Mental Retardation, 32*, 18-21.

MacDonald, J.A. (1925). Our debt to the late Sir Frederick Fraser. Halifax School for the Blind, *Annual Report*.

MacMillan, M.B. (1960). Extra-scientific influences in childhood pscyhopathology. *American Journal of Psychiatry, 116*, 1091-1096.

Martin, E.W. (1968). Breakthrough for the handicapped: Legislative history. *Exceptional Children, 34*, 493-503.

McGann, J.B. (1863). *Home education for the deaf and dumb: First book of lessons.* Toronto: Printed for the author.

McGann, J.B. (1888). *The deaf mutes of Canada.* Toronto: C.J. Howe.

McIntosh, J. (1977). The evolution of a magazine: Special Education in Canada, 1925-1964. *Special Education in Canada, 52,* 22-25.

McLelland, M.C. (1934). Light from within. *Social Welfare, 15,* 31-32, 35-36.

Meadow, K. (1980). *Deafness and child development.* Berkeley: University of California Press.

Mitchell, D.R. (1983). International trends in special education. *Canadian Journal on Mental Retardation, 33,* 6-13.

Mitchell, S.H. (1971). The haunting influence of Alexander Graham Bell. *American Annals of the Deaf, 116,* 349-356.

Montessori, M. (1912). *The Montessori method.* A. George (Trans). New York: Stokes.

Montessori, M. (1917). *The advanced Montessori method: Scientific pedagogy as applied to the education of children from seven to eleven years.* London: Heinmann.

Myers, J. (1976). The efficacy of the special day school for EMR pupils. *Mental Retardation, 14,* 3-11.

National Education Association. (1901, July). *Proceedings: Fortieth Annual Meeting,* Detroit.

National Education Association. (1902). *Proceedings: Forty-first Annual Meeting,* Minneapolis, July.

Ontario, Inspector of Prisons, Asylums and Public Charities. *Annual Reports.*

Ontario. *Sessional Papers.*

Ontario Teachers' Federation, Learning Exceptionalities Committee. (1982). *Special needs— Special help.* Toronto: OTF, FED.

Paul, J.L. and Warnock, N.J. (1980). Special education: A changing field. *The Exceptional Child, 27,* 3-28.

Payne, J.S. and Thomas, C. (1978). The mentally retarded. In N.G. Haring (Ed.), *Behavior of exceptional children: An introduction to special education (2nd. ed.).* Columbus, OH.: Merrill.

Peet, I. (1855-1856). Inaugural address. *Medico-Legal Journal, 3,* 388-389.

Penrose, L.S. (1963). *The biology of mental defect (3rd. ed.).* New York: Grune and Stratton.

Porter, S. (1847). Review of *The Historie of the Church of England,* compiled by Venerable Bede, Englishman book V, Part 2). London: 1622. Thomas Stapleton (Trans.). In *American Annals of the Deaf and Dumb, 1,* 33-34.

Pritchard, D.G. (1963). *Education and the handicapped.* London: Routledge and Kagan Paul.

Report upon the subject of education made to the Parliament of Upper Canada, 25th February, 1836. Through the Commissioners, Doctors Morrison and Bruce, appointed by a resolution of the House of Assembly in 1835, to obtain information upon the subject of education, etc. (1836). Toronto: M.C. Reynolds.

Reynolds, M.C. and Birch, J.W. (1977). *Teaching exceptional children in all America's schools.* Reston, VA.: Council for Exceptional Children.

Safer, N.D., Morrissey, P.A., Kaufman, M.J. and Lewis, L. (1978). Implementing IEP: New teacher roles and requisite support systems. *Focus on Exceptional Children, 10,* 1-20.

Sarason, S.B. and Doris, J. (1979). *Educational handicap, public policy, and social history: A broadened perspective on mental retardation.* New York: Free Press.

Seguin, E. (1846). *Traitement moral, hygiene et education des idiots et des autres enfants erroires.* Paris: J.B. Brailliere.

Seguin, E. (1864). Origin of treatment and training of idiots. In M. Rosen, G.R. Clark, and M.S. Kivitz (Eds.) (1976). *The history of mental retardation (Vol. 1).* Baltimore, MD.: University Park Press.

Seigel, J.P. (1969). The Enlightenment and the evolution of a language of signs in France and England. *Journal of the History of Ideas, 30,* 96-115.

Siegel, M. (1939). *Population, race, and eugenics.* Hamilton, Ontario: Published by the author.

Smith, J.A.C. (1980). The right to an appropriate education: A comparative study. *Ottawa Law Review, 12,* 367-391.

Spettigue, C.O. [1955]. *An historical review of Ontario legislation on child welfare.* Toronto: Ontario Department of Public Welfare.

Splane, R.B. (1965). *Social welfare in Ontario, 1791-1893: A study of public welfare administration.* Toronto: University of Toronto Press.

Treherne, D. and Rawlyk, S. (1979). Canadian legislative processes: Special education. *McGill Journal of Education, 14,* 265-273.

Turnbull, H.R. (1981). Legal precedent and the individual case: How much can we generalize from court findings? *Exceptional Education Quarterly, 2,* 81-90.

Winzer, M.A. (1981a). An examination of some selected factors that influenced the education and socialization of the deaf in Ontario, 1870-1900. Doctoral dissertation, University of Toronto.

Winzer, M.A. (1981b). Talking deaf mutes: The special role of women in the methodological conflict regarding the deaf, 1867-1900. *Atlantis, 6,* 123-133.

Winzer, M.A. (1982). Bill 82: Ideal and reality. *B.C. Journal of Special Education, 6,* 159-169.

Winzer, M.A. (1984). Educational reform in Upper Canada: John Barrett McGann and the "deaf mutes." *The ACEHI Journal, 9,* 155-171.

Winzer, M.A. (1985). The French connection: Aspects of Enlightenment thought on the development of special education. Unpublished paper, University of British Columbia.

Winzer, M.A. and O'Conner, A. (1981). Eugenics: The threat of the feeble-minded. *B.C. Journal of Special Education, 6,* 217-229.

Zelder, E.Y. (1953). Public opinion and public education for the exceptional child — court decisions, 1873-1950. *Exceptional Children, 19,* 187-198.

2

Children with Intellectual Differences

INTRODUCTION

"Intellectual difference" is a category that includes two very different groups of children. Mentally retarded children are markedly slower than their agemates in using memory effectively, associating and classifying information, reasoning, and making judgements. Gifted children learn more, faster, and more thoroughly than their peers. Yet, both these groups are considered exceptional and require special education to develop to their full potential.

Throughout history, individuals have been seen to differ noticeably in intellectual capacity. Mental retardation has been acknowledged in literature for 2500 years. Hippocrates, for example, described several forms of mental retardation involving cranial anomalies. Confucius wrote about society's responsibility for the "weak-minded" (Scheerenberger, 1964). Interest was also shown in children possessing superior cognitive abilities. Plato believed that educators should recognize, train, and elevate to positions of leadership those children who possessed uncommon intelligence (Khoury and Appel, 1979).

In the past twenty years, education of the gifted and of the mentally retarded has advanced considerably. Positive changes have occurred in public perception, terminology, identification and assessment, educational administrative arrangements, and service delivery. However, a broad range of issues and problems remain to be solved.

Some of these problems are due to the lack of any universally accepted definition of either giftedness or mental retardation. Others are more complex and lie at the heart of our societal and personal values. For example, the major issue in the education of the gifted concerns whether an egalitarian school system should provide special services for children already well endowed. This single issue will determine the fate of education for the gifted.

In the field of mental retardation, educators are currently focusing on normalization. This philosophy advocates the provision of growth opportunities within a normal life-style rather than within the confines of a residential institution. Normalization and deinstitutionalization challenge our society to place new emphasis on the freedom of each individual life.

CHAPTER FOUR

Mental retardation

MARGRET WINZER

If a mentally retarded child is to be provided with the assistance he needs to face the problems of adult life and is to be given the opportunity to develop to his ultimate potential, he must at all times be given the greatest possible degree of participation in life. Society must maintain for him the maximum degree of normalcy in all of his experiences to allow him a happy and healthy development as a total person.

(Williston, 1971)

Throughout history, mental retardation has been misunderstood. In part, the confusion has arisen from ignorance concerning the characteristics, needs, and capabilities of mentally retarded people. The history of care for the mentally retarded has undergone sharp swings of mood between optimism and pessimism. It has encompassed humanitarian movements, biological theories of degeneracy, repressive theories of hereditary, and concern about civil and social rights.

Currently, attitudes toward the retarded are becoming more positive. As a result of new research, educators now entertain rising, but realistic, expectations for their mentally retarded students.

The field of mental handicaps has produced exciting advances in the last twenty years. However, in many respects, mental retardation is still a primitive field (Haywood, Meyers, and Switzky, 1982). Although our knowledge has increased a hundred-fold, we are still unable to answer some of the most fundamental questions about the handicap. We are frequently powerless to explain the condition of a retarded child.

Many ancient stereotypes regarding the mentally handicapped have disappeared. We no longer perceive the retarded child as a helpless, less-than-human creature. We have come to realize that the retarded person is an individual capable of growth and achievement. We know that the vast majority of the mentally retarded fall into the mild category; these individuals generally have no identifiable physical anomalies, but look like everyone else.

Much remains to be done, however, to improve public perception and awareness. For example, public confusion persists between mental retardation and mental illness, and the terms are often used synonymously. In 1979, a case before the Nova Scotia Supreme Court provided dramatic evidence of this confusion. A group home for the severely retarded had been denied a zoning application on the basis that proposed residents were "suffering from insanity or other mental diseases" (Nova Scotia Supreme Court, 1979). Fortunately, the judge disagreed with this statement and decided in favour of the home (MacLean, 1981).

Today much pejorative terminology has been abandoned. Many traditional labels are now seen to perpetuate confusion and offend the dignity of handicapped people. Until about 1945, such categories as feeble-minded, idiot, imbecile, and moron were common in North American literature. Today, terms such as retarded, mentally impaired, and mentally disabled are considered much more appropriate.

DEFINITIONS OF MENTAL RETARDATION

Although mental retardation has long been recognized as a condition, no universally accepted definition exists. Numerous attempts have been made to define retardation within various disciplines, including medicine, psychology, social work, and education. However, these definitions have not been standardized.

Definitions are not static. As more information becomes available, their meaning begins to shift. Past definitions of retardation have implied a condition intrinsic to the individual. In recent definitions, the emphasis has shifted to imply an interplay between the individual and the environment.

For example, at the beginning of this century, Tredgold (1908) defined mental retardation as "a state of incomplete mental development of such a kind and degree that the individual is incapable of adapting himself to the normal environment of his fellows in such a way as to maintain existence independent of supervision, external control, or support." During the same period, Binet characterized idiots as being unable to talk or to understand language (Peterson, 1925). In 1941, Edgar Doll defined mental retardation as encompassing six domains: social and occupational incompetence; inability to manage affairs at the adult level: mental subnormality; intellectual retardation from an early age; intellectual retardation during maturity; and incurability (Doll, 1941).

Today's definitions are much more flexible. They take into account that a person may be retarded at one time but not at another. They also recognize that a person can score in the low range on an intelligence test, but still be able to function adequately in society.

Today's primary definition of mental retardation is that proposed by the interdisciplinary American Association on Mental Deficiency (AAMD). Under the AAMD definition, **mental retardation** refers to significantly subaverage general intellectual functioning resulting in, or associated with, impairments in adaptive behaviour, and manifested during the developmental period (Grossman, 1977). Under this definition, mental retardation describes only the individual's behavioural and functional level, irrespective of etiology or incurability. Three factors must be present — subaverage general intellectual functioning, deficits in adaptive behaviour; and manifestation during the developmental period.

Subaverage general intellectual functioning

General intellectual functioning is measured by means of intelligence tests. Individuals are not considered retarded unless they score below 70 IQ; that is, two or more standard deviations below the norm. This procedure assumes that intelligence, as measured on standardized tests of mental ability, is normally distributed. A **normal distribution** is a continuum of scores that vary from the average score by predictable amounts.

Figure 4-1 shows the normal curve of intelligence, based on the scores of the Wechsler Intelligence Scale for Children — Revised (WISC-R) (Wechsler, 1974). This is the most widely used intelligence test for children, with an average score of 100. Each standard deviation, or 1σ, represents 15 points on this scale. Most people score around the middle of the curve, between 85 IQ and 115 IQ, or one standard deviation below or above the norm. Fewer individuals score in the lower or higher ranges. Students whose IQ scores fall between 85 (-1σ) and 70 (-2σ) are not considered mentally retarded, but as borderline subnormal, or slow learners. Those at or below 70 IQ (-2σ) are said to fall in the mentally retarded range.

Regular schools may require students who score less than 75 IQ to attend special classes for the mentally retarded (Kneedler, 1984).

Adaptive behaviour

Adaptive behaviour refers to how well a person is able to adapt to environmental demands. Grossman (1977) defines it as the degree and efficiency with which an individual meets "the standards of personal independence and social responsibility expected of his age or cultural group" (p. 11). In other words, adaptive behaviour differs according to the child's age group and particular situation. The pre-schooler needs sensory-motor skills, communication, self-help skills, and socialization to adapt to the environment. We do not expect the pre-schooler to be interested in vocational prospects and an expanded peer group; these are the adaptive concerns of the adolescent.

The two major elements of adaptive behaviour are the child's level of skill development and the relationship of skill development to developmental trends. The most significant skills are those the child needs to function independently and maintain responsible social relationships (Coulter and Morrow, 1978).

Adaptive behaviour is crucial to today's definition of mental retardation. In the past, children were identified as retarded solely on the basis of an intelligence test. Today, children must also show signs of poor adaptive behaviour before they are so classified. As a result, cases such as the "six-hour retarded child" can now be identified; this refers to a child who cannot cope with school but functions quite adequately in other environments.

Some children manifest deficits in adaptive behaviour but score within the normal range on IQ tests. These children are usually labelled emotionally disturbed or learning disabled (Reiss, Levitan, and McNally, 1982).

Developmental period

Under the AAMD definition, the developmental period refers to the time between the child's conception and eighteenth birthday.

Figure 4-1 The normal curve of intelligence based on WISC-R.

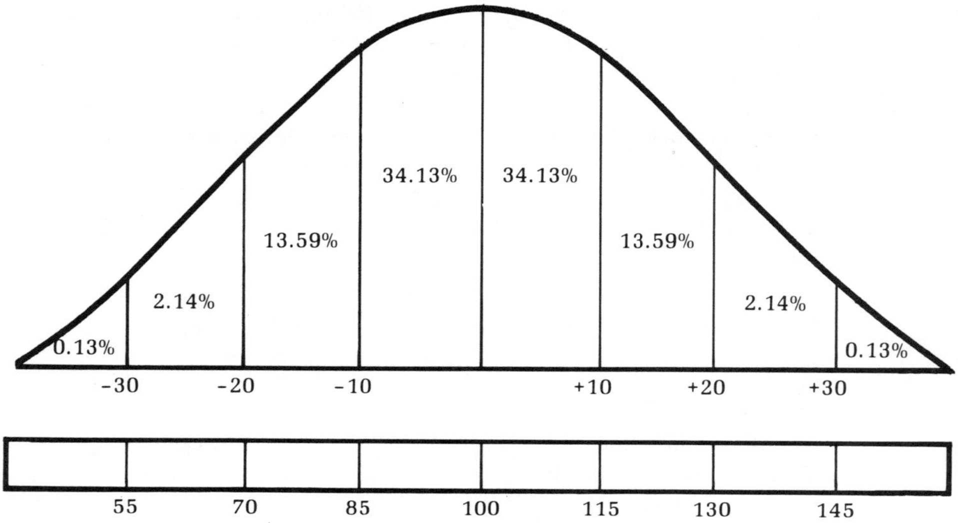

Alternate definitional approaches

Although the AAMD definition is the most commonly accepted, other workable definitions exist. Often these reflect the orientation of the researcher or organization that suggests them.

A number of researchers propose behavioural models for mental retardation. For example, Bijou (1966) suggests that retarded individuals are those who have a limited repertoire of behaviours shaped by events that constitute their history. Bijou views retarded behaviour as "a function of observable social, physical, and biological conditions, all with the status of individual variables" (pp. 2-3).

Mental retardation, as we know it, would not exist in a society that did not value intelligent, adaptive behaviour. Mercer (1973) holds that people's social systems often determine whether or not they are retarded. In the same vein, Sarason and Doris (1979) point out that "Mental retardation is not a 'thing,' not a set of characteristics inherent in an individual, but a concept that both describes and judges interactions of an individual, a social context, and the culturally determined values, traditions, and expectations that give shape and substance to the context at a particular time" (p. 17). According to this sociological perspective, then, the norms of society at a certain time determine whether an individual is retarded.

Although the AAMD definition is employed widely in Canada, the Canadian Association for the Mentally Retarded (CAMR), a strong advocacy group, uses a different definition. The CAMR suggests that a person who is mentally retarded "is anyone who has impaired intellectual ability. A retarded child learns more slowly and as an adult he may have difficulty in coping with some of the demands of daily life" (CAMR [1980]; MacLean, 1981).

CLASSIFICATION OF MENTAL RETARDATION

Most professionals classify the retarded according to the severity of their problems. The most generally accepted approach is to consider retardation along a continuum of scale of severity. Figure 4-2 presents two of the most common systems — that of the AAMD, and that employed by educators.

Figure 4-2 Two commonly used scales for classifying the mentally retarded.

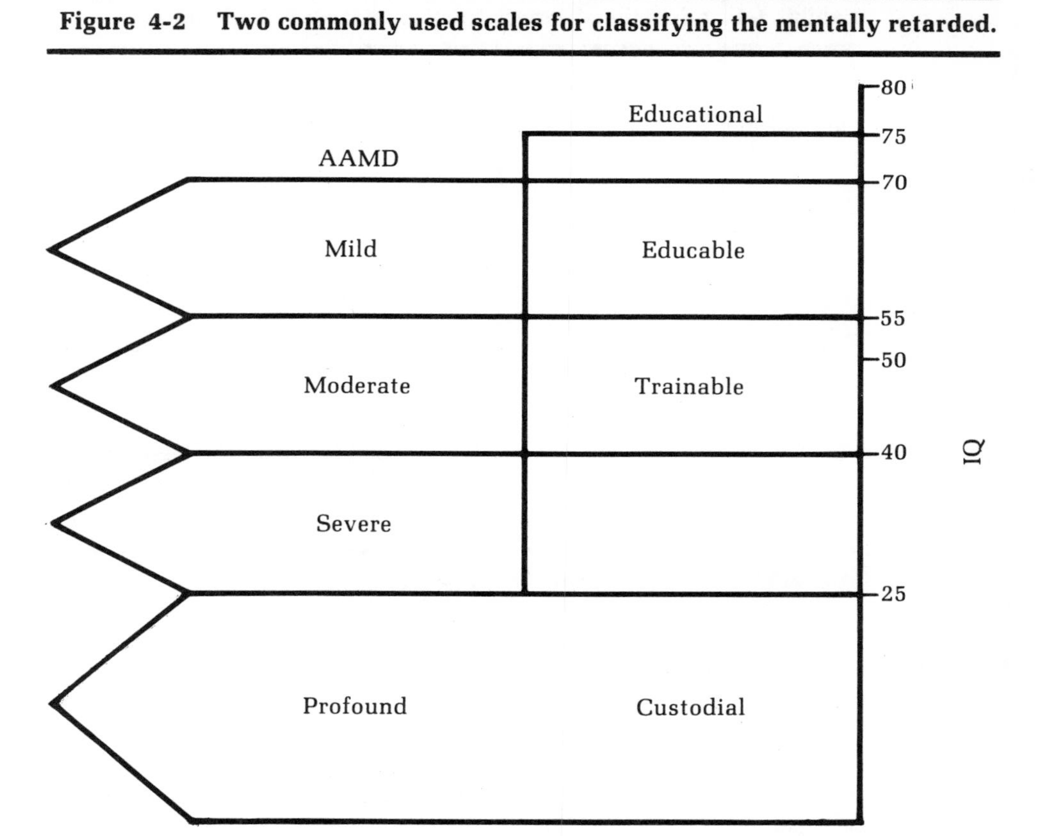

The AAMD system

Most professionals agree that the most useful system to measure the severity of retardation is that proposed by the AAMD. This is because the AAMD's terms — mild, moderate, severe, and profound retardation — describe the individual's functioning clearly and without negative stereotyping.

The educator's system

While many educators prefer the AAMD's classification system, others still opt for the terms "educable" and "trainable." Educators have used these categories over the years to try to describe the educational needs of retarded children. Educable students were those who could be educated, though at a less intensive level than regular students. Trainable children, on the other hand, could only be trained in lower-level skills to take care of their basic needs.

Exhibit 4-1 shows the level of educational expectation for each category.

Exhibit 4-1 Educational expectations for retarded children.

School Terminology	IQ *Level*	*Expectations*
Dull normal (not considered retarded)	75-90	Capable of competing in school in most areas except in abstract academic subjects, such as higher math.
Educable	50-75	Capable of basic academic subjects up to advanced elementary levels. General achievement ranges from second to fifth grade.
Trainable	25-49	Capable of attaining self-help skills, self protection, and social adjustment. Very limited achievement in areas considered academic. Can achieve later economic usefulness in sheltered workshops or in routine jobs under supervision.
Custodial	below 25	Usually unable to achieve basic skills.

(Adapted from Chinn, Drew, and Logan, 1979, p. 23.)

PREVALENCE OF MENTAL RETARDATION

Mental retardation is the largest category of lifelong handicap that affects the populations of developed countries (Baird and Sadovnick, 1985). However, it is extremely difficult to obtain true and accurate prevalence figures for mental retardation. This is because:

- Different IQ cut-off points are used.
- Methods of gathering data for prevalence studies differ.
- Different definitions of adaptive behaviour are used.
- Different regions and social classes show different prevalence. Because a majority of mildly retarded children come from a lower socio-economic bracket, large urban areas with a high lower-class population demonstrate a higher proportion of mental retardation.
- Different age groups show different prevalence figures, especially among the group classified as mildly mentally retarded. Prevalence is low in the pre-school years and high among school-age children, no doubt a reflection of the environmental demands of the school and the greater ease of case-finding among school-age children. As a result, the reported prevalence of retardation declines rapidly during late adolescence and young adulthood.

Given the normal curve, a theoretical 2.27 percent of the population might be expected to fall two or more standard deviations below the mean. In reality, this does not happen. Actual surveys show that about 3 percent of the population have IQs within the retarded range all across North America (Hallahan and Kauffman, 1982). In the 1976 Canadian census, just under 70 000 persons were reported as retarded (CAMR, 1980). Only a small number of Canadians are very seriously affected; most fall in the mild range.

Figure 4-3 illustrates the percentage of retarded persons in each severity group.

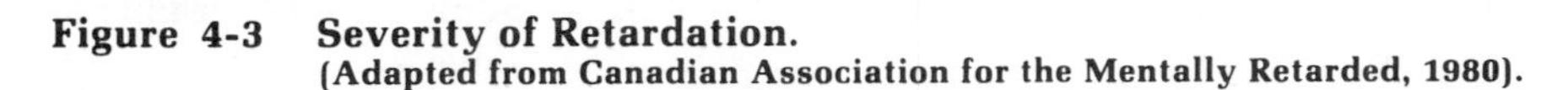

Figure 4-3 Severity of Retardation.
(Adapted from Canadian Association for the Mentally Retarded, 1980).

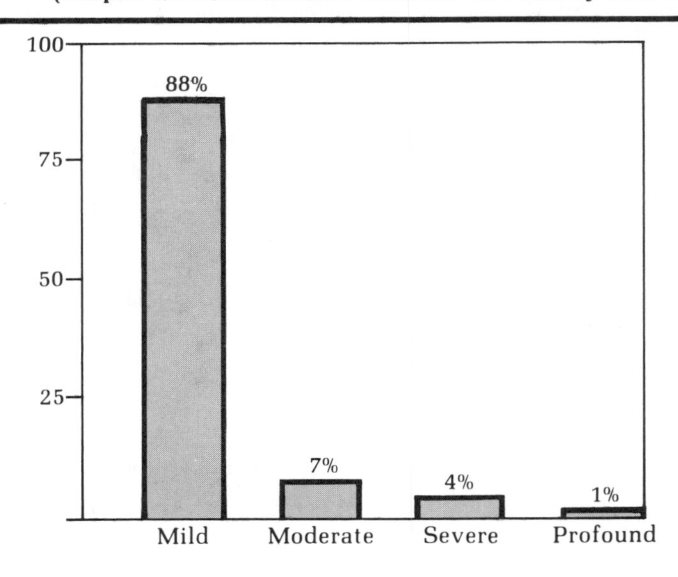

The difference between the expected 2.27 and the actual 3 percent may be due to the fact that a number of physical conditions, such as brain damage, can result in lowered intelligence. Postnatal accidents result in a slightly higher percentage of children in the retarded range, particularly at the severely and profoundly retarded levels (Hallahan and Kauffman, 1982).

ETIOLOGY OF MENTAL RETARDATION

Etiology has been prominent in the field of mental retardation, as in other areas of exceptionality. This reflects the medical orientation from which much work in the field has emerged. However, causes of retardation remain highly controversial. Although there are more than two hundred known causes of mental retardation, the etiology of a particular child's problem all too frequently remains obscure. In only about six to fifteen percent of cases can we actually specify the cause of retardation.

Generally, the etiology of mental retardation is divided into two broad categories — brain damage, and cultural-familial causes. When no clear-cut evidence of an organic cause can be found, the condition is referred to as non-specific mental retardation (Herbst and Baird, 1983). Most retarded children fall into this category. The majority of children with non-specific retardation are classed as mildly retarded. These children usually look the same as other children. In early childhood, they reach their developmental milestones, although often a little late. In most cases, the mildly retarded are not identified until they encounter reading, writing, and math at school.

Etiology is more easily determined for children who suffer from moderate, severe, or profound retardation. The condition of these children is more readily apparent and is frequently diagnosed before school entrance. Sometimes these children are diagnosed shortly after birth, as in the case of those with Down's syndrome.

The AAMD (Grossman, 1977) has proposed nine etiological categories for mental retardation: infection and intoxication; trauma or physical agent; metabolism or nutrition; gross brain disease; unknown prenatal influence; chromosomal abnormality; gestational disorder; retardation following psychiatric disorder; and environmental influence. In all, more than two hundred causes of mental retardation are known. Some of the causes of mental retardation are also the villians in other handicapping conditions. Rubella, for example, can leave the child with a range of handicapping conditions that affect almost every organ.

Exhibit 4-2 outlines a sample of etiologies, some common and some rare, that can lead to mental retardation (Aase, 1979; Grossman, 1977; Vitello and Soskin, 1985).

Infections and intoxication

Infections and intoxications that can lead to mental retardation can occur in the pregnant mother, the infant, or the young child. Rubella is a particularly dangerous virus. Rubella can enter the placenta and damage the developing fetus, especially during the first trimester of pregnancy. Mental retardation is only one of rubella's many damaging effects.

Exhibit 4-2 Some causes of mental retardation.

infections or intoxicants	*infections:* rubella; syphilis, toxoplasmosis; herpes simplex; bacterial infections; viral infections; parasitic infections. *intoxicants:* drugs; poisons; smoking; caffeine; alcohol; lead.
trauma or physical agents	anoxia, irradiation, trauma
metabolism or nutrition	*lipid storage diseases:* Tay-sachs disease; Hurler's; Hunter's. *carbohydrate disorders:* galactosemia; hypoglycemia. *amino acid disorders:* phenylketonuria. *endocrine disorders:* hypothyroidism. *other:* Prader-Willi syndrome; malnutrition.
gross brain disease	neurofibromatosis (von Recklinghavsen's disease); Sturge-Weber syndrome; tuberous sclerosis (epiloia); Huntington's chorea.
unknown prenatal influence	anencephaly; microcephaly; Apert's syndrome; meningomyelocele; hydrocephalus.
Chromosomal abnormality	*chromosomal aberration:* Down's syndrome; Klinefelter's syndrome; Cri-du-chat; fragile x syndrome. *Autosomal dominant gene disorders:* neuro-fibromatosis; tuberous sclerosis; Sturge-Weber syndrome. *autosomal recessive gene disorders:* phenylketonuria, congenital hypothyroidism; maple syrup urine disease; Tay-Sachs disease; Smith-Lemli-Optiz syndrome. *X linked disorders:* Lesch-Nyhan syndrome.
gestational disorders	prematurity; postmaturity; low birth weight.
psychiatric disorders	psychoses.
environmental influences	psychosocial disadvantage; sensory deprivation.

Syphilis in the mother is another disease that can cross the placental barrier and damage the fetus. Unlike rubella, syphilis is most dangerous after the fifth month of pregnancy. If the disease is controlled by penicillin before that time, only about two percent of fetuses will contract it. After the fifth month, uncontrolled syphilis will affect about forty percent of fetuses. An infant born with syphilis may suffer many handicaps including mental retardation, blindness, and deafness (Montagu, 1977).

Meningitis and encephalitis are two infections that can lead to mental retardation in the young child. Meningitis attacks the **meninges**, or coverings of the brain and spinal cord. It is accompanied by a high fever, and causes a range of problems, including mental retardation. Encephalitis can be caused by viral, bacterial, or parasitic infections. More encephalitic children suffer retardation than do meningitic children.

Intoxicants and poisons, in the pregnant mother or the child, can also cause mental retardation. Alcohol in moderate amounts used to be thought safe during pregnancy. We now realize that even small amounts can cross the placenta and damage the developing fetus. Although a precise threshold of safety has not been determined, research has shown that as little as three ounces of pure alcohol can harm the fetus (Nitowsky, 1979).

A mounting problem among heavily drinking mothers is Fetal Alcohol Syndrome (FAS). This syndrome has been recognized as the third leading cause of birth defects and mental retardation today (Edwards, 1981). Children with FAS may have physical stigmata, such as small eyes, a flat bridge of the nose, retarded growth, and a small head circumference, known as **microcephaly**. The more such physical handicaps are evident, the more severe the retardation is likely to be (Montagu, 1977). In Chapter 12, Fetal Alcohol Syndrome is discussed in greater detail.

Drugs are another potential cause of retardation in the child. One 1973 study found the average mother was taking 12.5 different drugs during pregnancy, thirty percent of which were self-prescribed (Montagu, 1977). Prescription drugs have been shown to have an adverse affect on fetal development (Bowes, Brackbill, Conway, and Steinschneider, 1970). There is also mounting evidence to indicate that pain-relieving drugs administered during labour and delivery can result in behavioural differences in infants (Aleksandrowicz and Aleksandrowicz, 1974; Rosenblith and Sims-Knight, 1985).

Trauma and physical agents

This category refers primarily to brain damage associated with extreme difficulty during labour and delivery. All infants are subject to varying degrees of oxygen deprivation during labour, but most tolerate this without difficulty. Sometimes, however, inadequate uterine environments pose additional risks, and the infant cannot tolerate the normal changes of labour. If supplies of oxygen to the nerve cells of the infant's brain are too greatly reduced, brain damage or death can result. Mild anoxia can produce irritability, muscular tension, rigidity, and motor defects (Graham, Matarazzo, and Caldwell, 1956; Lewis, Bartels, Campbell, and Goldberg, 1967). More serious results include mental retardation.

Childhood accidents involving cerebral assault or prolonged loss of consciousness can also cause brain damage that leads to retardation. Child abuse is increasingly being cited as another cause of brain damage. The implications of child abuse are more fully discussed in Chapter Twelve.

Metabolism and nutrition

Metabolic problems due to hereditary defects account for only a small percentage of mental retardation. However, the study of these disorders has provided valuable knowledge for the prevention and treatment of retardation due to other organic causes.

Phenylketonuria (PKU) is a genetically transmitted metabolic disorder. It is carried on a recessive gene by about 1 in every 600 people, so the chance of two carriers marrying is statistically 1 in every 3600. Phenylketonuria results in the body's inability to metabolize phenylalinine, an essential protein found naturally in many foods. The excessive build-up of phenylalinine in the infant's system produces brain damage that can result in severe mental retardation. Children with untreated PKU have intellectual levels below 50

IQ. They may also be subject to noisy and destructive psychotic episodes (Robinson and Robinson, 1976).

The effects of PKU can often be eliminated or diminished by early screening and a special diet. The screening procedure includes urinalysis and blood tests shortly after birth. Early detection of PKU is vital, because the infant must immediately be restricted to a diet low in phenylalinine.

Galactosemia is another metabolic disorder that can result in mental retardation. In this case, the child lacks the ability to metabolize galactose. As with PKU, successful treatment depends upon early detection and a special diet. Galactosemia and PKU are examples of genetic problems in which the most devastating consequences can be prevented by environmental intervention.

Inadequate nutrition can also affect the relationship between the body's biochemistry and the functioning of the brain. Severe malnutrition can stunt brain growth and produce a significant lowering of intellectual ability (Kaplan, 1972). The period of intra-uterine development and the first eighteen months after birth are crucial to the physiological development of every organ system. This is especially true of the brain.

Although the evidence is murky, children conceived during autumn and winter tend to be more favoured than those conceived during spring and summer. Cool-weather-conceived children tend to be heavier, healthier, more intelligent, and more likely to attend college. Conversely, a greater number of mentally deficient children are conceived during the spring and summer. Complications during pregnancy are also more frequent among this latter group (Montagu, 1977).

The basis of this phenomenon lies not in astrology, but in nutrition. In hot weather, pregnant women may feel uncomfortable and eat sparingly to keep their weight down. The resulting lack of nutrients may slow down fetal development, particularly if very hot weather coincides with a critical period of brain development (Montagu, 1977).

Postnatal malnutrition, especially during the first six months of an infant's life, is also a critical factor in brain development. Various important neural structures and interconnections between brain cells develop during this period. When prenatal and postnatal malnutrition both exist, problems are likely to be much more severe.

Gross brain disease

The category of gross brain disease includes a large number of hereditary disorders that are not well understood. One such disease is tuberous sclerosis, or epiloia. Tuberous sclerosis is characterized by the presence of tumours throughout the brain and other parts of the body, such as the face, kidneys, eyes, heart, lungs, and spleen (Gellis and Feingold, 1968). Although the severity of the disease varies, mild to severe retardation is inevitable. There is no known treatment or cure.

Unknown prenatal influence

This category is reserved for conditions present at or before birth for which there is no known cause. One such condition is microcephalus, a rare phenomenon in which brain development is impaired by an abnormally small cranium. Another condition, macrocephaly, refers to an enlargement of the head, most frequently caused by **hydrocephalus**, a build-up of cerebro-spinal fluid in the brain. Retardation may follow, but its severity can be reduced or eliminated by early diagnosis and treatment. To treat hydrocephalus, a shunt is surgically implanted to drain excess fluid away from the brain and into the vein behind the ear or in the neck.

Chromosomal abnormality

Chromosomal abnormalities include too many chromosomes, too few chromosomes, and chromosomes that are attached to one another. Abnormalities in the structure and number of chromosomes can be caused by natural mutation of genes, by radiation, and by a host of other factors that are only partly understood. Apart from Down's syndrome, the number of retarded children due to chromosomal abnormality is quite small. Nonetheless, there is considerable research in this area. Geneticists hope that the study of chromosomal abnormalities will eventually enable them to locate critical enzymes in the genetic structure (Cytryn and Lourie, 1975).

Down's syndrome is by far the most common and widely known form of chromosomal aberration. The condition occurs in about 1 in 640 births (Smith and Wilson, 1973). Down's syndrome can happen in any family, regardless of race, socio-economic class, or the education of the parents. It usually occurs only once in a family, and strikes most often when the mother is approaching the end of her child-bearing days (Pitt, 1979).

There are three major types of Down's syndrome — Trisomy 21, translocation, and mosaicism. In each type, the mental and physical problems of the afflicted child are caused by extra chromosomal material. Somehow this extra material disturbs the orderly development of the body and brain.

Trisomy 21 accounts for about ninety-five percent of children afflicted with Down's syndrome. There are actually fourteen different types of Trisomy 21, but they are all basically problems of dysjunction. In all of them, the twenty-first pair of chromosomes contains three chromosomes instead of two. This may result from a mistake in chromosomal distribution in the egg or sperm, or because the chromosomes were distributed unequally when the fertilized egg began to divide.

Mosaicism accounts for about two percent of Down's syndrome cases. This condition results when there is faulty distribution of chromosomes in later cell divisions. The afflicted child possesses some normal cells and some with a Trisomy condition. Any resulting physical and mental anomalies depend on the number of affected cells.

In **translocation**, some of the chromosomal material from the twenty-first pair of chromosomes attaches itself to another chromosome. Although the actual chromosome count is forty-six, the afflicted child suffers from the same overdose of chromosome twenty-one as the child with standard Trisomy. There may be a hereditary component in translocation.

The chances of having a Down's syndrome child increase dramatically with the age of the parents, particularly the mother. Very young mothers are also more likely to have a Down's syndrome baby. Women under thirty have a 1 in 1300 chance of bearing a Down's syndrome child. For the woman over forty, the chances increase to 1 in 80. For women over forty-five the chances are approximately 1 in 60 (Hansen, 1978).

Many authorities believe that Down's syndrome may result from a combination of two factors — chemical changes in the egg cells due to the mother's aging ovaries, and a reduction in the secretion of various hormones in older women (Montagu, 1977). However, the mother's age may not be the only variable. Researchers are discovering possible links between Down's syndrome and the amount of the mother's exposure to radiation and certain viruses. They are also exploring the role of the aging father, who contributes the extra chromosome in twenty to twenty-five percent of the cases (Abroms and Bennett, 1980; MacMillan, 1982).

A number of recent studies in Canada and the United States have found an increasing number of Down's-syndrome children born to women under thirty-five years of age. Canadian investigators suggest 1969 as the turning point at which Down's children began to be born to younger women with greater frequency (Zarfan and Wolf, 1979).

Down's Syndrome is the most common chromosomal aberration.
(T. Wilson)

Gestational disorders

Disorders due to abnormal length of pregnancy can also result in retardation. Infants born two weeks or more beyond the expected due-date are said to be **postmature**. These children are in somewhat greater danger from anoxia and cerebral hemorrhage than children born at the normal 266 to 270 days. They have a higher death rate and suffer more frequently from severe congenital anomalies. They also tend to have poorer general health in later years (Montagu, 1977).

Prematurity, which involves a shorter gestation period than normal, can also be potentially damaging. Indeed, "no single condition is more clearly associated with a wide range of insult to the nervous system than the too early expulsion into the world of a child scarcely able to function on an independent level as an independent organism" (Birch and Gussow, 1970). Many premature babies have a **low birth-weight** of less than 2500 grams. Babies may be of low birth-weight and not premature. However, both premature and small infants are candidates for a variety of physical and behavioural abnormalities, including retardation (Rubin, Rosenblatt, and Balow, 1973).

Psychiatric disorder

The relationship between mental retardation and childhood psychoses is obscure. It is extremely difficult, if not impossible, to determine whether the emotional disturbance caused the mental retardation, or vice versa. Children who are emotionally disturbed in early childhood may be deprived of the normal sources of intellectual and social development. Conversely, the retarded child may withdraw and display the behaviours characteristic of emotionally disturbed children. In Chapter 11, this problem will be further discussed.

Environmental influences

Known organic causes account for only a small percentage of retardation. As few as twenty to twenty-five percent of the total retarded population suffer from medical abnormalities caused by clear-cut organic conditions (Garrard and Richmond, 1975).

As we have stated, most retarded children are classed as mildly retarded due to "causes unknown." Because these children often come from deprived backgrounds, they are described as suffering from cultural-familial retardation. Many of their problems spring from psychosocial disadvantage, poverty, inadequate nutrition, family instability, lack of educational opportunity, or an unstimulating infant environment. Tarjan (1978) points out that:

> The children are often born unplanned and unwanted. They are reared in broken homes with absent fathers and physically or emotionally unavailable mothers. While the mothers struggle for mere survival, the children are left unattended without being cuddled or played with. The language they hear is simple, the vocabulary is limited, and the connotations of most adult communications are negative if not intimidating. Curiosity and exploratory behaviour are discouraged, with passivity if not apathy encouraged. Feelings of security and belonging are minimized, with early hopelessness and despair maximized.

Subtle genetic factors may interweave with socio-economic deprivation to further affect a child's development. In the case of mildly retarded children from deprived backgrounds the relative influence of genetic factors and environmental ones is unknown.

Most environmentally deprived children fall into the mildly retarded category. Moderate to profound retardation does not seem to be associated with economic status. Occurrence tends to be random rather than linked to any particular environmental variables (Robinson and Robinson, 1976).

PREVENTION OF MENTAL RETARDATION

Recent research suggests that post-natal causes account for about five percent of mental retardation, peri-natal causes for about fifteen percent, and pre-natal causes for about eighty percent (Milunsky, 1975). These estimates primarily refer to moderate, severe, or profound levels of retardation.

Various estimates claim that about twenty to thirty percent of mental retardation could be prevented with the intensive application of current knowledge (National Prevention Committee, 1982). Ideally, a preventive program would assure every child of a healthy central nervous system at birth, of early support for intellectual, emotional, and social growth, and of protection from damaging physical and psychological trauma (Tarjan, 1978). Although we are still far from realizing this ideal, some progress has been made in identifying contributing causes and developing preventive measures.

The prevention of mental retardation is usually classified as primary, secondary, or tertiary. Primary prevention refers to the establishment of medical and social programs to reduce the occurrence of diseases and conditions that cause retardation. Examples of primary prevention include measures to counteract poor nutrition, poverty, and prematurity (MacGregor, 1980). Genetic counselling and educational programs on conditions such as Down's syndrome are also part of primary prevention.

Secondary prevention refers to ascertaining, as early as possible, the evidence of disorders that may cause retardation. Once identified, the effects of a disorder may be inhibited, or at least minimized (MacGregor, 1980).

One form of secondary prevention is cytogenic screening to identify certain genetic and chromosomal aberrations. Cytogenic screening is performed by amniocentesis between the tenth and nineteenth week of fetal gestation. Amniocentesis can be used to prenatally detect about forty diseases (Rosenblith and Sims-Knight, 1985). In this procedure, a needle is inserted through the mother's abdominal wall to extract ten to twenty millilitres of amniotic fluid. A chromosomal analysis then checks whether free-floating fetal cells have karyotypes (genetic patterns) typical of specific handicapping conditions. In 1980, five thousand tests were performed in Canada, of which about fifty, or one percent, showed Down's syndrome.

Other screening procedures include ultrasonography and fetoscopy. Ultrasonography is used successfully in the pre-natal diagnosis of hydrocephaly, anencephaly, and other multiple congenital deformities. Fetoscopy is a procedure used to evaluate fetuses that are at risk for certain genetic diseases. A fetoscope, equipped with a fibre-optic lens for viewing the fetus, is inserted into the amniotic sac. This process can be useful in determining whether a fetus has a congenital malformation that may be associated with mental retardation (Vitello and Soskin, 1985).

Successful secondary prevention results in the limitation or even elimination of disabilities. As stated earlier, certain organic conditions that cause mental retardation can be successfully managed when identified early. The effects of PKU can be prevented or diminished if a low phenylaline diet is introduced in infancy. Hydrocephalus can be surgically treated, even in the fetus, by the insertion of a shunt to remove excess cerebrospinal fluid (Henig, 1982).

Tertiary prevention consists of intervention strategies for persons already recognized as mentally retarded. The object of tertiary prevention is to ameliorate, to the greatest extent possible, the impact of the handicap. Methods of intervention may be medical, psychological, social, or educational.

During 1981, five regional symposia on the prevention of mental retardation in Canada were held across the country. A number of critical issues related to prevention were forwarded. These included:

- The fragmentation of preventive services.
- The lack of regional availability of prevention services, such as genetic counselling, and the resulting increase in the risk of handicaps.
- The failure to apply preventive measures that are known to work effectively.
- The lack of public awareness of causes and preventions of mental retardation.
- The need for resources to promote the understanding and prevention of retardation.

(National Prevention Committee, 1982.)

A range of recommendations to reduce the incidence and severity of mental retardation in Canada also emerged from the symposia. Exhibit 4-3 presents a summary of prevention directions and programs.

Exhibit 4-3 Directions and programs for the prevention of mental retardation in Canada.

Prevention directions	*Prevention programs*
health promotion	■ immunization
	■ lifestyle modification
reproductive care	■ prenatal diagnosis and genetic counselling
	■ comprehensive pregnancy care.
developmental programs	■ early identification and intervention
	■ adolescent education in child care and parenting skills
	■ home-based parent training
	■ community living.

(National Prevention Committee, CAMR 1982.)

DIAGNOSIS AND ASSESSMENT OF MENTAL RETARDATION

Infant identification

In any handicapping condition, early identification is vital. Early identification leads to early intervention, which can ameliorate at least some of the child's problems.

The most pronounced cases of mental retardation are often accompanied by clear-cut organic or psychological signs. Children with Down's syndrome, for example, are frequently identified in the delivery room, or shortly afterwards. In infants with no physical anomalies, a low Apgar score may be an indication of damage. However, there are no tests available that adequately assess intelligence in the newborn or reliably predict later intellectual development (St. Clair, 1978). Standardized neurological tests of infant reflexes and basic behaviour are the most advanced assessment techniques currently available (Brazelton, 1973).

A number of tests have been designed to measure the infant's developmental state. Because children under two cannot solve complex cognitive problems, most scales make use of sensori-motor tasks. Gross-motor behaviour, vocalization, and language behaviour are studied in relation to basic sensori-motor aptitudes. The Bayley Scales of Infant Development (Bayley, 1965) and the Denver Developmental Screening Test (Frankenburg, Dodds, and Fandal, 1975) are both widely used. Children who are two and older can be assessed by more formal measures.

PROFILE 4-1

Bruce was diagnosed as mildly-to-moderately mentally retarded at the age of four. Bruce's mother first suspected a problem when he did not walk until nearly twenty months, or say his first word until two months after that. The family physician checked Bruce and found nothing amiss physically, but the parents were not reassured. They rejected the doctor's implication that they were overprotective and worrying unduly.

Bruce was bowel-trained by three years of age, but daytime and night-potty training was beyond him. Bruce's mother grew more concerned, especially when she observed other children of the same age. Finally, the parents contacted a clinical psychologist. The psychologist observed Bruce interacting with his younger sister and communicating with his parents, and gave him a battery of tests. Her findings indicated that Bruce had an intellectual handicap in the low mildly-retarded range. She also found that he had poor adaptive behaviour, delayed communication skills, and was very slow to meet his developmental milestones.

Although this diagnosis confirmed their suspicions, the parents were devastated. Bruce was the eldest son, and many hopes and dreams rode on his progress. Moreover, both sets of grandparents reacted very negatively. They unfairly attributed blame, even though the causes of Bruce's condition were unknown.

Bruce's parents found much-needed support in a community group of other parents of mentally retarded children. Talking to other families helped Bruce's parents to accept him as an individual with a problem. Bruce's placement in a nursery school for handicapped children was also a boon. Bruce's mother watched the teachers and learned some of their techniques for use at home. She recognized that Bruce could learn, even if more slowly than other children. The nursery school also freed Bruce's mother to devote more time to herself and the rest of her family.

Assessment of intelligence

In 1905, Alfred Binet devised the first real tests of mental ability. Since that time, these tests have remained the prime instrument in the measurement of intelligence. Although we no longer place uncritical faith in intelligence tests, they are still used with considerable success to predict academic achievement.

There are two broad categories of intelligence tests — those administered to groups, and those administered individually. Group tests are often used to screen out children who require further testing. Because individual IQ tests are very complex to administer, score, and interpret, they should only be given by qualified personnel.

Intelligence tests are merely one measure in the total assessment of the child. The score only reflects how well a certain child does on a certain day with a certain psychologist. Many things — a bad mood, no breakfast, fear or dislike of the tester — can influence scores. More will be said about intelligence testing in Chapter Five.

Assessment of adaptive behaviour

Numerous scales have been developed to measure adaptive behaviour. However, as in the case of intelligence, no simple, quantifiable, and reliable assessment procedures exist. One problem is the rather murky definition of adaptive behaviour. Another is the newness of the concept.

Exhibit 4-4 Major categories on AAMD Adaptive Behaviour Scale for Children and Adults, 1974 revision.

Part 1	*Part 2*
independent functioning	violent and destructive behaviour
physical development	antisocial behaviour
economic activity	rebellious behaviour
language development	untrustworthy behaviour
numbers and time	withdrawal
domestic activity	inappropriate interpersonal manners
vocational activity	unacceptable or eccentric habits
self-direction	self-abusive behaviour
responsibility	hyperactive tendencies
socialization	sexually aberrant behaviour
	psychological disturbances
	use of medications

Adaptive behaviour scales generally consist of lists or inventories of behaviour. These are completed by someone close to the child — a parent, teacher, or primary caregiver. Scales in common use include the Balthazar Scales of Adaptive Behaviour (Balthazar, 1973, 1976), the Adaptive Behaviour Checklist (Allen, Cortazzo, and Adams, 1970), and the Cain-Levine Social Competency Scale (Cain, Levine, and Elzey, 1963).

In Canada, the AAMD Adaptive Behaviour Scale (Nihira, Foster, Shellhaas, and Leland, 1974) is widely used to identify and place mentally retarded, emotionally maladjusted, developmentally disabled, and other handicapped persons. This comprehensive scale can be used to assess children from three years of age to adulthood. It examines critical development skills, such as eating, dressing, and peer relations, as well as fourteen areas of maladaptive behaviour. Exhibit 4-4 outlines the major categories of the two domains on this scale.

CHARACTERISTICS OF THE MENTALLY RETARDED

Until about the mid-1800s, idiocy was thought of as a more or less unitary condition. The work of John Langdon Down signified a major departure from the notion of the homogeneity of the mentally retarded population. However, Down's work had little impact at the time.

Mental retardation does not represent a homogeneous group of children, nor can it be considered a specific kind of disorder or disease. The field is so broad, and involves so many disciplines, that summary generalizations are nearly always superficial. Individuals who are described as mentally retarded vary widely in almost every aspect of human behaviour, human personality, and human temperament. Even when mentally retarded children are placed in homogeneous groupings for educational purposes, tremendous scholastic differences still exist within each class.

When discussing the mentally retarded, then, we must keep in mind the heterogeneous nature of the population. Categories of severity often overlap and are subject to change. Very early intervention allows teachers and parents to reduce the handicap's impact on child development. Recent use of early intervention with Down's syndrome children has shown that the condition need not always cause severe mental retardation. Some children with Down's syndrome approximate normal developmental patterns when intervention begins in infancy (Beers and Beers, 1980).

Mildly retarded children

Mildly retarded children are generally normal in appearance with no pathological signs of disease or injury. They show a wide diversity in academic and behavioural performance. Mildly retarded children learn at a rate of one-half to three-quarters that of normal children. They can usually reach the academic standards of the later elementary-school grades, and can be effectively educated in public-school settings. Mildly retarded children can develop and employ adequate social, personal, and communication skills. As adults they are perfectly capable of functioning well in a variety of contexts.

There is a higher percentage of boys than girls among the mildly retarded population. This may result from a higher probability of adverse biological factors affecting male children (Singer, Westphal, and Niswander, 1968). It may also result from the greater expectations placed on males (Kurtz, 1977), or from the greater aggressive behaviour among males, leading to the label of mental retardation (Ingalls, 1978).

Moderately retarded

Moderately retarded individuals have limited intellectual ability, difficulties in working with abstract ideas, and problems in generalizing learning to new situations. They are not ready for much academic work until their early teens. Moderately retarded students also have rather clearcut deficits in adaptive behaviour; they have problems with interpersonal relationships, social concepts, emotional instability, and communication. As moderately retarded children grow older, the progressive widening of their developmental lag tends to make their retardation more obvious. This is in contrast to the mildly retarded, whose condition become less obvious in adulthood.

Severely retarded

Traditionally, researchers and practitioners have tended to group the severely and the profoundly retarded together. In fact, severely and profoundly retarded persons differ from each other in several ways. Of course, the categories do sometimes overlap, as do severe and moderate retardation.

As retardation becomes more severe, the prevalence of additional handicapping conditions increases. These extra handicaps compound the original retardation. Severely retarded children may demonstrate poor speech, inadequate social skills, poor motor development or non-ambulation, incontinence, behavioural and psychiatric disorders, sensory impairments, seizures, and cerebral palsy. A severely retarded adult may learn to regulate toilet habits, to eat with a spoon or fork, to throw a ball at a target, to understand simple verbal directions, and to participate in simple play and games (Anderson and Greer, 1976).

Maladaptive behaviour is commonly found in both the severe and the profoundly retarded population. As with skill development, the frequency of maladaptive behaviour is extremely variable. Inappropriate behaviours might include aggression toward people and objects, tantrums, self-injury, and such stereotypic behaviour as meaningless repetitive movements, rocking, and hand-waving. Less common behaviours might include vomiting and rumination, disrobing, pica and coprophagy (eating inedible objects, including feces), stealing, and material hoarding (Whitman and Scibak, 1979).

Profoundly retarded

Profoundly retarded individuals are some of the most seriously impaired of all disabled people. The nature and degree of their handicap is so great that, without various forms of intensive training and therapy, they exhibit virtually no adaptive behaviour.

The profoundly retarded can be divided functionally into two groups (Miller, 1976). "Relative" profoundly retarded persons have less organic damage and are capable of some degree of ambulation, communication, and self-help skills. Persons who lack all adaptive behaviour and exist in a medically fragile state are called the "absolute" profoundly retarded.

Physical characteristics

As we have seen, additional handicapping conditions become more likely as the severity of retardation increases. Profoundly retarded persons have the highest incidence of devastating motor, sensory, and physical handicaps. A recent British Columbia study of nonspecific retardation (Herbst and Baird, 1983) found that 27 percent of mildly retarded people had additional handicapping conditions. Contrastingly, 73.1 percent of the profoundly retarded suffered additional handicaps. Survival rates also varied with the level of retardation. The death rate among the mildly retarded was twice as high as that of the general population. It was seven times higher among the severely retarded, and thirty-one times higher among the profoundly retarded.

The most prevalent conditions affecting the mentally retarded population are speech disorders (55 percent), lack of fine motor control of the upper limbs (44 percent), nonambulation (42 percent), lack of gross motor control of the upper limbs (42 percent), and behavioural and emotional disorders (42 percent) (Conroy and Derr, 1971). The special problems of the multi-handicapped population are more fully discussed in Chapter Thirteen.

Down's syndrome

Down's syndrome is characterized by physical and mental anomalies. Intellectually, the Down's child can fall anywhere in the spectrum from mild to profound retardation; most tend to be classed as moderately retarded. Down's individuals with normal intellectual development are almost exclusively those with the mosaic form of the condition.

More than fifty physical signs have been listed as characteristic of Down's syndrome. Some are apparent at birth, some appear much later, and some disappear with age. The number of physical features a child displays bears no relationship to the degree of retardation. Few children have all the characteristics typical of the syndrome. Exhibit 4-5 outlines the most common.

Down's syndrome was first described by Langdon Down (1866). The children's facial features prompted Down to refer to the condition as "mongolian idiocy." Down assumed that the condition represented a re-emergence of a more primitive evolutionary status, which he erroneously believed to be occupied by the Mongolian race (Blanton, 1975). The Mongolian resemblance, however, is due simply to the development of a fold in the upper eyelid not usually found among Caucasoids. In Down's children this fold is caused, not by inheritance, but by the failure of the root of the nose to develop normally (Montagu, 1977).

Today we have discarded the term "mongoloid" as demeaning and developmentally inappropriate. Asians are rightfully offended by the terms — indeed, some Japanese profess to see in their Down's children a resemblance to Europeans (Montagu, 1977).

Down's syndrome was one of the first conditions to be linked to a genetic abnormality (Lejeune, Gautier, and Turpin, 1959). The major breakthrough came in 1959 when scientists discovered the extra twenty-third chromosome and associated it to the syndrome (Carr, 1975).

Apart from their physical stigmata, Down's children are prone to a range of other serious health problems. About forty percent of Down's syndrome children have

Exhibit 4-5 Some observable physical characteristics associated with Down's syndrome.

Head:
distinctive shape
skull rounded and small

Hair:
sparse, fine, and soft

Face:
flat profile

Eyes:
epicanthic fold
speckling of iris (Brushfield's spots)
strabismus and nystagmus common

Ears:
small and low-set
overlapping upper letices

Nose:
small and "pug"
flat bridge
undeveloped or absent nasal cartilage
mucous discharge common

Mouth:
high-arched
thick, fissured lips
narrow palate

Teeth:
small, irregularly aligned
late erupting.

Tongue:
coarse, protruding

Hands:
broad, stumpy, with short fingers
palmar crease (simian line) on one or both hands
incurved little finger (clinodactly)

Feet:
broad and short
excessive space between first and second toe

Muscles:
general hypotonia
flexible joints

Skin:
thick, dry, rough
mottled or flushed

Abdomen:
prominent
umbilical hernia common

Stature:
short
average male height — 5 feet
average female height — 4 feet, 7 inches

congenital heart disease, while structural defects such as atresias (closed opening) of the stomach, duodenum, and trachea are common. Down's children are highly susceptible to infections such as pneumonia and gastroenteritis. Their incidence of different types of leukemia is about fifteen times greater than in normal children (Whaley and Wong, 1979).

Only within recent years has the life span of Down's syndrome children begun to approach that of the general population. The mortality rate is still high, however, especially perinatally and in the first year of life; this is largely due to congenital heart conditions and increased susceptibility to infections (Burgio, Fraccaro, and Tiepolo, 1981). After age one, mortality is considerably reduced. Between ages five and ten, life expectancy is only six percent below normal.

PROFILE 4-2

Jane L. is seven years and ten months old. She was diagnosed as having Down's syndrome at birth. When she was six months old, she and her mother began to attend an infant stimulation program for developmentally delayed children and their families. At age three, Jane was enrolled in a nursery school for developmentally delayed children. During these pre-school years, her mother spent a great deal of time with her, carrying out the suggestions of the infant therapist and then the pre-school teachers.

A recent psychological testing of Jane indicates that, both cognitively and socially, she is functioning in the high end of the moderately retarded range. While Jane's verbal and non-verbal intelligence scores were similar, her social age was somewhat higher, as measured by the Vineland Social Maturity Scale. Her use of receptive language, measured by the Peabody Picture Vocabulary Test, was more advanced than her expressive language. Jane's language problems are compounded by speech problems associated with the physical anomalies of Down's syndrome.

Jane loves school. She attends the local public school in a self-contained special classroom. Her teacher is using a language-experience method to expand her receptive language vocabulary, Jane enjoys this approach, and also finds integrated activities great fun — simple non-cooked recipes, dusting, sweeping, and "playing house." Jane is less enthusiastic about her sessions on articulation with the speech therapist. However, she is always eager to attempt any of the motor tasks suggested by the physical therapist to improve the quality of her movements.

Jane's social aptitude serves her well. She is well-liked by the other children in the class, and could be considered the class leader. At first, on the playground, she was very shy of the other children in the school. Recently, however, she has begun to join the games of some of the kindergarten children, who accept her quite readily.

DEVELOPMENTAL CONSEQUENCES OF MENTAL RETARDATION

Physical maturation

We have already noted many of the physical attributes of different categories of retarded persons. We have also seen that, the more severely a child is retarded, the more likely the child is to have other handicapping conditions.

In the mildly retarded population, physical and health characteristics do not differ dramatically from those of nonhandicapped groups. Minor differences often exist, however, in measures of health, and of physical and motor performance. In early childhood, retarded children reach developmental milestones later; they may take up to nine months longer to learn to walk, talk, eat, and toilet themselves. Mildly retarded children are also likely to be somewhat below the comparative standards for height, weight, and skeletal maturity (Bruininks and Warfield, 1978). In motor areas, they perform below the standards of non-retarded children (Bruininks, 1977).

Physical impairments become more complex in moderately retarded children. These children tend to be markedly less able physically and more unco-ordinated. Severely and profoundly retarded individuals must often struggle to achieve ambulation and simple physical activities.

Learning and memory

Mental retardation implies, in essence, a slower rate of mental growth. Because the handicap is specifically a retardation in the development of intellectual and behavioural capacities, its most noticeable effects concern the child's ability to learn and to progress educationally. Mentally retarded children usually have a higher frequency of problems in such areas as learning and memory, ability to pay attention, verbal communication, motivation, ability to generalize, and ability to understand similarities and differences (Neisworth and Smith, 1978).

More and more research evidence indicates, however, that retardation is quantitative rather than qualitative. Retarded children pass through the same cognitive development stages in the same order and manner as non-retarded children. The retarded simply pass through more slowly and attain lower levels of achievement (Weisz and Zigler, 1979). This applies even to severely and profoundly retarded children.

Retarded children have particular trouble with memory, a key aspect of learning. They have the most difficulty with short-term memory, and do not use strategies for memory efficiently. They fail to use mediation techniques such as rehearsal and sub-vocalization, nor do they use other mnemonic strategies. Retarded children can learn to use mnemonic strategies if explicitly trained (Paris and Haywood, 1973), but the effects of training are usually limited to a particular training context (Kramer, Nagle, and Eangle, 1980). Retarded children find it harder to remember abstract ideas than concrete information. Their memory efficiency decreases as their level of retardation increases. However, once retarded children have thoroughly learned information, their long-term memory is comparable to that of non-retarded learners (Ellis, 1963).

Difficulties with memory are compounded by problems with organization, the efficient storing of information, and selective attention. Retarded children find it very hard to select learning tasks and attend to all their relevant dimensions. They also have difficulty paying attention and keeping to the task. In the classroom, they tend to be less attentive, spend less time on academic tasks, and spend more time out of their seats than non-retarded children (Finkelstein, Gallagher, and Farran, 1980; Krupski, 1979). They are also less able to apply knowledge or skills which they have learned to new tasks, problems, or stimulus situations (Stephens, 1972).

Motivation is a key factor in all learning and achievement. Retarded children appear less motivated to succeed. They don't seem to take the pleasure that non-retarded children do in manipulating and mastering their environments. This lack of motivation seems to be accompanied by an expectation of failure. As several studies have shown, retarded children tend to experience failure more often than other children, and therefore learn to expect it (MacMillan, 1971; MacMillan and Keogh, 1971). This process creates a self-defeating cycle. As children picture themselves as underachieving or non-achieving, they become passive and lose their initiative. They grow overly dependent on others to tell them what to do, surrendering control to an outward locus.

For severely and profoundly retarded children, problems with learning and memory are much more severe. However, learning is both possible and common for these children (Haywood, Meyers, and Switzky, 1982). Using classical and operant conditioning procedures, educators have taught many skills in the domains of adaptive behaviour,

Retarded children require specialized intervention and encouragement if they are to reach their full human potential.
(T. Wilson)

simple academics, and vocational skill formation to severely retarded, and some profoundly retarded, individuals. As stated earlier, many severely and profoundly retarded children go through the same stages of cognitive development in the same order as do non-retarded children, (Weisz and Zigler, 1979). The possible exceptions are children who suffer from demonstrable and pronounced brain injury.

Language and speech problems

The language level of mentally retarded children is typically below that of non-handicapped children. Moreover, the language level of retarded children is often below their general mental-age level. Language problems are not related to the etiology of the retardation, but to its severity. Mildly mentally retarded youngsters may be delayed in talking, but mutism is rare. The moderately mentally retarded use stereotypical language, rarely free of defects. Mutism is common among the severely and profoundly retarded, as are primitive levels of speech such as babbling and jabbering (Jordan, 1976).

Speech problems are also common among retarded individuals. In one study, Spradlin (1963) found that over half of institutionalized retarded persons suffered from speech defects.

Social adjustment

Many myths have arisen regarding the personalities of retarded persons. Perhaps the most prevalent is the myth that the retarded child is blissful, trusting, and complacently unaware of the complexities of life. The stereotypes regarding the unique personality patterns of Down's syndrome children are particularly persistent. Many people think of Down's children as loving, trusting beings with perpetually sunny temperaments.

Retarded children often have special personal and social problems. In general, they are not well accepted by the non-retarded (Corman and Gottlieb, 1978; Gottlieb, 1975). They are frequently the subject of teasing, which serves to diminish their self-concept. This tends to further compound the problems in self-esteem that accompany low achievement.

Academic achievement

In general, mentally retarded children do not achieve in school at a level commensurate with their intellectual potential (Kirk, 1964). They tend to underachieve in all academic areas. This underachievement is most pronounced in reading, particularly reading comprehension (Dunn, 1973). In arithmetic, retarded children generally possess adequate computation skills, but are deficient in arithmetic reasoning and problem solving (Dunn, 1973).

Vocational adjustment

Education of retarded children, particularly in the adolescent years, is currently placing increased emphasis on the acquisition of life and vocational skills. Training in these areas helps children to develop stronger self-concepts and to engage in self-supporting, productive work. Many mildly retarded adults are able to merge into the community and work at a variety of semi-skilled and service positions. Most can partially or totally support themselves. More severely handicapped people whose disabilities preclude competitive employment, may be able to earn income in the sheltered workshop.

In Canada, the term **workshop** is used to describe a wide range of work situations and vocational rehabilitation programs. These range from adult day programs to highly automated production factories. Approximately 25 000 people are involved in workshop programs in Canada; of these, seventy percent are described as mentally retarded (Zdriluk, 1983).

In their present form, sheltered workshops are commercial-industrial models of production. They serve to assess, improve, and stabilize vocational functioning, thus assisting a disabled person to progress to employment in the competitive labour market. Within the workshop, expectations are adjusted to each individual's abilities. The workers have constant input and supervision, and their personal differences are tolerated.

Several businesses in Canada, administered by provincial associations for the mentally handicapped, employ mentally retarded individuals only. Hero's restaurant in Vancouver is an excellent example. At Hero's, the food is prepared and served by paid employees who are mentally retarded.

PARENTING THE RETARDED CHILD

The discovery that a child is mentally retarded causes great stress for the parents and other family members. Parents must eventually confront three critical issues. They must decide whether to institutionalize the child, accept that the child may never be self-sufficient, and decide the child's future after they die.

In instances of clearcut organic damage, the child will probably be diagnosed at birth or shortly afterwards. The parents should then be informed as soon as possible. Parental aspirations for their newborn child crystallize in the first forty-eight hours following birth. There is evidence that aggression and resentment are more destructive in parents who have not known of the retardation from the earliest days (MacKay, 1976).

Parents appear to react differently to the diagnosis of their child on some domains. The subjective impact of the diagnosis tends to be greater when the retarded child is the first-born. Parents of retarded males feel a greater social stigma than parents of retarded females (Levinson, 1976).

In general a physician announces the child's condition to the parents. In the past, much criticism has been levelled at physicians for the manner in which they communicate this diagnosis (Denhoff, 1960; Zwerling, 1954). Physicians seem to be more pessimistic than other service professionals, such as educators, psychologists, or social workers, in their expectations of the attainable functioning levels of mentally retarded children (Wolraich, 1980). Hence, physicians have tended to recommend institutionalization, even for moderately retarded children (Kelly and Menolascino, 1975). Today, fewer parents are allowing the doctor's advice to influence their choice between home care and institutionalization (Springer and Steele, 1980).

When the problem is not detected at birth, parents may start to suspect some disability when their child is too slow in reaching developmental milestones. Broussard and Hartner (1971) found that babies who, as early as one month of age, were considered below average in development by their mothers, turned out to have more problems when they were four years old. Moreover, parents' estimates of their child's intelligence prior to evaluation have proven to correlate positively with the child's performance on an IQ test (Schulman and Stern, 1975).

The more stress that diagnosis places on the parents, the more likely parents are to choose institutional care for their child (Levinson, 1976). A small percentage of parents are simply unwilling or unable to sustain the additional stress of raising a handicapped child. Others lack the financial, social, and medical resources to keep the child at home. In general, a parent's decision to place a child in an institution comes about only after a wrenching struggle between what is best for the child and for the rest of the family. In time, most parents come to terms with the future and the institution's central position within it (Rosenau and Provencal, 1981).

The diagnostic crisis and the child's pre-school years are the most difficult for the parents. By the time the child reaches school-age, many sources of stress have subsided. The family is generally more secure, other siblings have accepted the child, and full-time school programs provide daytime relief. As the youngster reaches adolescence, however, other problems appear. Jaslow (1976) found that one of the greatest concerns of parents of mentally retarded adolescents is the fear of problems related to sexual matters.

INTERVENTION WITH THE RETARDED

Medical intervention

No surgical procedures or miracle drugs are known to actually improve intellectual ability or adaptive behaviour. In general, medical intervention attempts to prevent or correct the organic causes of retardation, rather than alleviate the condition itself. We have already discussed the value of screening in cases such as PKU, and of early surgery in hydrocephalus.

A full pediatric medical evaluation of the retarded child is vital to pinpoint secondary conditions. An evaluation also allows the physician to recognize and identify the child's strengths. The physician searches for whatever potentialities will help the child achieve more efficient functioning. This includes all the sensory and motor strengths that can be used for later training and development.

Surgical intervention has been used with Down's syndrome children in an effort to alleviate speech and eating problems, and to render their appearance more normal. Although the procedure has been successfully performed in Germany and Israel, results are still inconclusive in regard to the improvement of speech and respiratory problems.

Deeply philosophical and complex questions surround the issue of life-management practices with the profoundly retarded. These questions, which concern active and passive euthanasia, are beyond the scope of this text. Those interested might pursue the issue further through the following research: Duff and Campbell, 1973; Fletcher, 1968; Fletcher, 1973; Hardman and Drew, 1978; Horan and Mall, 1977; Rachels, 1975; Rickham, 1969; Tymchuk, 1976. Canadian perspectives are presented by Baker (1980, 1981); Dickin and Ryan (1983); and Downie and Snart (1983).

The introduction of voluntary or involuntary sterilization of the mentally retarded is another important and controversial issue. Many retarded people have normal sexual feelings, and many want to marry and have children. One study (Gan, Tymchuk and Nishihara, 1977) found that eighty-five percent of mildly mentally retarded people believed they should be able to marry, while sixty-one percent felt they should have children. However, although there are many legal, psychological, and ethical barriers (Bass, 1978), a large proportion of parents and professionals are in favour of making voluntary sterilization available to those who need and want it (Bass, 1967; Whitcraft and Jones, 1974). Society's concern for human rights has highlighted this issue. In Canada, doctors, lawyers, and even parents have been successfully sued by mentally retarded adults who were sterilized as minors (Law Reform Commission, 1980).

Mentally retarded persons have a high risk of psychiatric disorders (Rutter, 1971). These become more common as the retardation becomes more severe. Aggression, hyperactivity, self-injury, excitability, and screaming are relatively common, particularly among the severely retarded population. Many patients require pscyhotropic drugs for a long time. A significant number are maintained on medication indefinitely (Lipman, 1970; Tu, 1979), a situation of some concern to many physicians (Tu, 1979).

Technical aids

Technological advances have just begun to result in the development of devices designed specifically for the mentally retarded. Progress is now being made to assist cognitive development through instructional technology, and to promote independent functioning through the creation of aids for self-help skills and environmental control (Kneedler, 1984).

The new instructional technology for retarded children primarily involves microcomputers and innovative software. A number of devices have been created to enhance self-help skills. These include a device that provides a signal for the non-toilet-trained child to go to the bathroom, a self-feeding tray for the multiply disabled, and special bathing devices (Kneedler, 1984).

Teaching multiply-handicapped children is a particularly difficult challenge. (T. Wilson)

Advocacy groups

Advocacy groups of parents and professionals exist for the sole purpose of improving life conditions for the mentally retarded population. The Canadian Association for the Mentally Retarded (CAMR) has 10 provincial and approximately 380 local associations. It was created to promote the welfare and protect the rights of retarded persons and their families.

The CAMR performs the following functions:

- Encourages the acceptance of all mentally retarded people into the life of the community.
- Promotes the enactment and implementation of legislation to improve the welfare of retarded people.

- Promotes improved education and vocational training for retarded people.
- Furthers the education and training of personnel for work in the field of mental retardation.
- Provides centres for the gathering and distribution of information about mental retardation.
- Fosters research concerning all aspects of mental retardation.
- Develops better public understanding of retarded people and their needs. (CAMR, 1980.)

Living arrangements

Institutionalization

Until recently, parents have looked to professionals and institutions to care for their mentally retarded offspring. The institutions were designed to protect the rest of society from the deviant child, as much as to protect the children from an intolerant and prejudiced world. Today, the residential institution is no longer considered the sole option for care of the retarded individual. This change has resulted from advances in medicine, high institutional costs, a recognition of the problems of segregation, and a new emphasis on normalization.

Many people consider the institutionalization of retarded persons one of the great social crimes of the modern era. They decry the locking away of children in human warehouses to become victims of neglect and aggression. One Canadian study found that institutions encourage the development of apathetic behaviour, which renders inmates incapable of functioning in the outside world. As well, children's social skills are reduced, their language and communication are hindered, and their self-concept is lowered by social stigma (Laurendeau, Blanchet, and Coshan, 1984).

An institution is defined as a publicly supported, professionally managed facility housing 15 or more people with similar disabilities. In Canada, approximately 27 000 people labelled mentally retarded are living in institutions. Another 6 000 are housed in institutions of 6 to 14 residents (McWhorter, 1983). Although federal cost sharing arrangements are generally the same across Canada, some provinces are phasing out institutions while others are building new ones. In most instances, new institutions are being strongly resisted by citizens' groups, who are demanding community supports and services instead (McWhorter, 1982).

In general, long-range trends across Canada show a movement away from institutions and toward community living for the mentally retarded. Exhibit 4-6 illustrates the situation in Manitoba, where normalization is becoming the mode.

Those who oppose institutionalizing the mentally retarded argue for placement in small, community-based residences. These smaller institutions create a more home-like atmosphere and encourage the mastery of skills for effective living. Children can have their own rooms, non-institutional clothing, and maintain some level of independence while receiving a full range of services. These residences can also serve as halfway houses to more independent community living.

Exhibit 4-6 Placement of mentally retarded persons in Manitoba, 1982.

	Community living	*Institution*	*Total*
Borderline	1874	20	1894
Mild	1707	130	1837
Moderate	1355	400	1755
Severe/Profound	580	800	1380
	5516	1350	6866

(Fishbach and Hull, 1982, pp. 16-19.)

Community living

With the movement toward deinstitutionalization, one administrative arrangement that is growing in popularity is the group home. Mentally retarded persons live in houses of three to ten people, under the direction of house parents. Most homes focus on a specific age range — children, adolescents, or adults. The purpose of the homes is to teach living skills in a relaxed setting. Across the country, Community Living Boards function to facilitate this arrangement.

A key objective of the community residential movement is to enable mentally retarded persons to interact with the general community to the greatest extent possible. However, group homes often encounter opposition from neighbors, local officials, and others. People tend to express positive attitudes toward mentally retarded people concerning such general issues as human rights. However, they express less positive, even negative, attitudes toward programs and policies that bring them into close contact with the mentally retarded (Griffiths and Curtis, 1984).

Parents are also ambivalent about group homes. They express positive attitudes toward normalization, but are skeptical of their own child's ability to function independently of the institution. A recent study (Meyer, 1980) of 273 parents of institutionalized children found that eighty-three percent of them had chosen the institution as the most suitable setting for their own child.

Despite these barriers, deinstitutionalization can be successful. Gollay (1977) followed 440 mentally retarded persons from the institution into the community. He found that eighty-eight percent successfully adapted, while twelve percent returned to the institution. The largest percentage of the successfully integrated persons lived in group homes. Factors in successful integration included community preparation, parental willingness, appropriate facilities, adequate follow-up, and the long-term involvement of an independent advocate.

Educational intervention

Like other professionals, educators have recently embraced the philosophies of normalization, mainstreaming and integration. In education, normalization requires the involvement of mentally retarded children with their non-handicapped peers. Mentally retarded children can benefit from attending school at the same time as regular students, having access to school facilities, participating in extra-curricular activities, and following regular school rules and routines. Ideally, each child is provided the most beneficial services and a minimal amount of segregation. An array of legal precedents, moral mandates, and philosophical arguments supports the aim of providing the least restrictive environment possible to each mentally retarded child.

Mentally retarded children may be placed in regular classes, special self-contained classes, special day schools, or institutions. In each case, the child's degree of retardation and adaptive behaviour are the determining factors. Mildly retarded children are likely to be placed in the regular classroom, and to receive special help in the resource room. Moderately retarded children may learn in the regular class or in special self-contained classrooms; if the latter, they would still be able to integrate with their non-handicapped peers for such non-academic subjects as physical education and art. Severely and profoundly retarded children may learn in special classes, special schools, or in group homes. Fewer and fewer children are remaining in the institutions.

Education of the mildly retarded

The current trend is to mainstream the mildly retarded student to whatever extent is appropriate and yields success. Educational options depend on the child's unique set of strengths and weaknesses. A child's success in the regular classroom depends on such factors as support services, resource-room assistance, curriculum modifications, acceptance by the other students, the classroom teacher's experience with and exposure to exceptional children, and the availability of community resources.

Before the advent of resource rooms, mildly retarded children floundered in the regular classroom, were placed in special classes, or were even sent to special schools. The resource room is not a study room or a place to do homework. It is a facility run by a teacher who deals directly with specific learning problems or subject areas. Resource rooms support mainstreaming, while removing the stigma of segregation.

For mildly retarded children, areas identified as deficient — memory, attention, generalization, motivation — can be improved through appropriate instructional techniques. Exhibit 4-7 suggests various strategies for teaching mildly retarded children. These can be readily adapted for use with any child with learning problems.

In the early grades mildly retarded children are taught readiness skills, in such areas as math and reading. During these early grades, not many mildly retarded children have been diagnosed, however. These children are often not identified as mildly retarded until they have been in school for a few years (Robinson and Robinson, 1976).

At the intermediate school levels, educational emphasis is placed on activities for everyday life. These activities include functional reading, writing, and math.

At the secondary level, mildly retarded students are taught personal-social adjustment and occupational skills, along with basic academics. Work-study experiences play a major role in the secondary curriculum. Work-study is founded on the premise that there should be a close co-ordination between school work and vocational experience. Students are placed in work situations in the community, and their academic programs are oriented to supplement the work experience.

Exhibit 4-7 Tips for teachers of mildly retarded children.

- Present tasks in an uncomplicated, brief, and sequential fashion.
- Ensure mastery of new material through repetition and overlearning.
- Apply learning to other situations, objects, and problems in the learner's environment.
- Emphasize concrete, meaningful content in initial instructional presentations.
- Provide the learner with methods of verbal mediation.
- Increase interest by highlighting relevant dimensions and minimizing extraneous stimuli.
- Promote an atmosphere of success.
- Sequence tasks from the simple to the more complex.
- Employ a variety of methods to present material and to reinforce learning.

Education of the moderately retarded

In the past, moderately retarded children attended special schools. Although these schools provided an appropriate curriculum, a controlled learning environment, and a suitable daily schedule, they also presented the major drawback of segregation. More often today, students who need special educational arrangements outside the regular classroom are placed in small, self-contained special classes in the regular school. In these classes, they receive most of their academic instruction.

The ultimate goal in education for moderately retarded children is functional independence. In order to achieve this, the children need a variety of daily-living and job-related skills. Generally, their curriculum is less academically oriented than for the mildly retarded child.

Children are trained in such self-help skills as independent eating, dressing, toileting, washing, combing hair, brushing teeth, and using a handkerchief. They also learn simple homemaking skills, such as dusting, sweeping, setting and clearing the table, washing and drying dishes, washing and ironing, sewing, using simple tools, and telephoning. As well, children are taught the safety rules and how to use public transportation.

Communication training is designed to help the child develop the skills necessary for everyday communication. Personal and social skills include consideration for others, common courtesy, obedience, and self-judgement, Students also learn perceptual-motor and physical skills. These include sense training in the visual, auditory, and tactile modalities, eye-hand co-ordination, balance, and gross and fine motor movement.

In general, moderately retarded children do not learn to read beyond a first-grade level. Although academics are not stressed, children are taught to read names, directions, and labels, and to write relevant names and words. They are also introduced to numbers, time, and simple money exchange.

The functional nature of programming for moderately retarded pupils places great stress on simple vocational skills. Secondary education programs are more explicitly vocationally oriented and directed toward securing employment upon graduation. In many cases, such programs are operated in conjunction with sheltered workshops.

Education of the severely and profoundly retarded

Educators generally agree that mainstreaming is appropriate for mildly retarded and, to a lesser extent, moderately retarded children. However, no such agreement exists concerning severely and profoundly retarded children. Some educators argue that the limitations of these children prohibit normalized education and mainstream settings (Burton and Hirshoren, 1978, 1979a, 1979b). They maintain that severely and profoundly retarded youngsters are best served in settings in which their cognitive development and social limitations can be addressed more intensively. For example, severely and profoundly retarded children are unable to generalize a skill taught in one setting to apply it in another.

Opponents of regular school education for severely and profoundly retarded children view mainstream settings as potentially harmful. They argue that regular schools may inhibit the children's development by imposing educational models and social demands which do not meet their needs. Opponents of regular school education argue that skills should therefore be taught in the environment where they are most likely to occur — the community, home, or work setting.

Other educators do not believe in limiting the learning experience of severely and profoundly retarded children. They insist that these children are best served in integrated school and community settings (Sontag, Certo, and Burton, 1979). These educators argue that severely and profoundly retarded students should be educated in special classes throughout regular schools. This would integrate the children into all aspects of normal school and community life, offer them good role models, and foster their acceptance by normal peers.

For severely and profoundly retarded children, we must redefine the term education beyond its traditional academic limits. For these students, the major educational goals are to decrease dependence on others, increase awareness of environmental stimulation, teach basic communication and self-help skills, and push achievement levels higher. These children often require a range of other services, involving such professionals as doctors, speech therapists, social workers and psychologists.

The training of severely and profoundly retarded children begins with basic survival and self-help skills, along with the elimination of undesirable behaviour. At first, teachers focus on obtaining responses to environmental stimulation; these responses include head and trunk balance, sucking, swallowing and chewing, grasping, movement of body parts, and vocalization. Later training includes imitation, language acquisition, self-feeding, ambulation, dressing skills, toilet training, social and recreational behaviour, and functional academic skills (Stainback, Stainback, and Maurer, 1976). At present, however, there is a lack of operational curriculum for the severely and profoundly retarded. There exists virtually no systematic course of instruction.

Behaviour modification with retarded children

Although behaviour modification is used with virtually every type of handicapping condition, it is particularly useful in the education and training of severely and profoundly retarded children. Behavioural methods seem to succeed where other methods fail, and the behavioural emphasis on specific task analysis is particularly well-suited to the problems of the severely handicapped. Behaviour modification has been successfully used to teach a diverse array of skills, including self-help, eating, toileting, dressing, socialization, and language acquisition.

As we have seen, severely and profoundly retarded children are more likely to exhibit maladaptive behaviour than their less retarded peers. This maladaptive behaviour often takes bizarre forms. Some educators have reasoned that maladaptive behaviour may occur because of the absence of environmental prompts and reinforcements for appropriate behaviour. Hence, a range of behaviour modification techniques have been employed in the elimination of maladaptive behaviours.

THE MENTALLY RETARDED PRE-SCHOOLER

Early intervention is vital for mentally retarded children to help them to overcome the effects of developmental delays. Early intervention can accelerate development (Clunies-Ross, 1979) and encourage healthy parent-child relationships (Hanson and Schwarz, 1978).

The need to serve handicapped children early has been recognized in Canada. British Columbia has established infant-development and pre-school programs for children under five years old. Ontario has amended its Day Nurseries Act to permit grants to nursery schools for handicapped children and to provide developmental day-care centres for school-aged (six to eighteen) children. Quebec is establishing pre-school programs for four- and five-year-old handicapped children, New Brunswick provides education for special children at age three (Richler, 1981).

Infant stimulation programs focus on sensor-motor functions and intellectual development. Infants are trained in simple reflex activity and equilibrium reactions. Later training expands all areas of growth and development, following normal patterns. Pre-school programming stresses communication, sensory stimulation, socialization, and discipline.

Earlier in this chapter, we met Bruce, a retarded pre-schooler. Bruce now attends a nursery school for developmentally delayed youngsters five mornings a week. His teachers have identified his major needs as lying in the areas of expressive language, fine and gross motor skills, and socialization. Exhibit 4-8 shows the section of Bruce's individual educational plan that focuses on expressive language.

THE MENTALLY RETARDED ADOLESCENT

A major concern of those involved with mentally retarded adolescents concerns sexual awareness. The social and sexual needs of retarded persons do not differ significantly from those of the general population. However, retarded adolescents are less likely to have accurate information about sex, are more subject to fears and myths, and are more likely to be sexually exploited.

Exhibit 4-8 Individual educational program.

Student: Bruce.

Goal: Extension and improvement of expressive language.

Behavioural Objectives:	*Techniques:*
When presented with a visual stimulus, Bruce will be able to describe it using three-to four-word sentences with noun and verb combinations.	peek pictures, puppets, flannel board stories, playdough shapes.
When presented with a stimulus, Bruce will use prepositional phrases containing the prepositions on, off, over, under.	enactive stories (model to be manipulated and discussed)
Bruce will identify and express five of the following adjectives (in a noun phrase) when they are presented through concrete objects two at a time: big, little, red, blue, yellow, happy, sad.	playdough faces, mixing coloured water, painting, concrete objects for common animals.

If normalization is to succeed, this problem must be addressed. Sex education programs for retarded adolescents should include explanations of bodily functions, the mechanics of reproduction, social behaviour, and preparation for marriage and family.

TEACHERS OF THE MENTALLY RETARDED

Teachers working with mentally retarded children require a thorough knowledge of child development. They need to understand the theory of behaviour modification, and how to apply it with children. They need instructional skills in the area of self-help, and basic academic teaching skills in reading and arithmetic. They should also be prepared to work with a multi-disciplinary team, and have good communication skills with parents.

The more pronounced the disability, the more specific are the competencies required by the teacher. The teachers of severely and profoundly retarded children need a special range of teaching skills that are more developmental than academic. Special programs are offered at the University of Alberta and the University of British Columbia, for example, to prepare teachers who wish to embark on this very special form of education.

SUMMARY

Education for the mentally retarded has altered drastically in the past twenty years. Major changes have taken place in definitions, terminology, program options, and program delivery. Normalization, with its corollaries of deinstitutionalization and mainstreaming, has become the dominant ideology in the education and treatment of mental retardation.

For the mildly retarded, educational mainstreaming offers many advantages. Following graduation, many mildly retarded individuals blend into the social fabric of their neighbourhoods, holding jobs, marrying, and having families. Once that adjustment is made, they are no longer, according to the AAMD definition, retarded.

More and more moderately retarded children are also being educated in the regular schools, either in the regular classroom or in special self-contained classes. They, too, can learn to function in the community, and often find employment in sheltered workshops.

Much controversy still surrounds the education and socialization of the severely and profoundly retarded. Many barriers to normalization remain for these children, including the attitudes of the children's parents and of the general public.

The assault on the prejudices and negative stereotypes that confront retarded children is slow and halting. However, the outlook in Canada permits cautious optimism. Increasingly, we are coming to appreciate the inherent dignity of every individual, regardless of developmental disability.

BIBLIOGRAPHY

Aase, J.M. (1979). Environmental causes of birth defects. In A. Lane (Ed.), *Human growth and development of the exceptional individual.* CN.: Special Learning Corporation.

Abroms, K. and Bennett, J. (1980). Current genetic and demographic findings in Down's syndrome: How are they presented in college textbooks on exceptionality? *Mental Retardation, 18*, 101-107.

Aleksandrowicz, M.K. and Aleksandrowicz, D.R. (1974). Obstetrical pain-relieving drugs as predictors of infant behavior variability. *Child Development, 45*, 935-945.

Allen, R.M., Cortazzo, A.D., and Adams, C. (1970). Factors in an adaptive behavior checklist for use with retardates. *Training School Bulletin, 67*, 144-157.

Anderson, R.M. and Greer, J.G. (Eds.) (1976). *Educating the severely and profoundly retarded.* Baltimore, MD: University Park Press.

Baird, P.A. and Sadovnick, A.D. (1985). Mental retardation in over half-a-million consecutive live births: An epidemiological study. *American Journal of Mental Deficiency, 89*, 323-330.

Baker, J.D. (1980). Remedies: Liabilities for wrongful sterilization. In *Sterilization and mental handicap.* Ontario: National Institute for Mental Health.

Baker, J.D. (1981). Remedies: Liabilities for wrongful sterilization. *Canadian Journal on Mental Retardation, 31*, 23-28.

Balthazar, E.E. (1973). *The Balthazar Scales of Adaptive Behavior — Section II: The Scales of Social Adaptation.* Palo Alto, CA.: Consulting Psychologists Press.

Balthazar, E.E. (1976). *The Balthazar Scales of Adaptive Behavior — Section I.: The Scale of Functional Independence.* Palo Alto, CA.: Consulting Psychologists Press.

Bass, M.S. (1967). Attitudes of parents of retarded children toward voluntary sterilization. *Eugenics Quarterly, 14*, 45-53.

Bass, M.S. (1978). Surgical contraception: A key to normalization and prevention. *Mental Retardation, 16*, 399-404.

Bayley, N. (1965). Comparisons of mental and motor test scores for ages 1-15 months by sex, birth order, race, geographical location, and education of parents. *Child Development, 36*, 379-412.

Beers, C.S. and Beers, J.W. (1980). Early identification of learning disabilities: Facts and fallacies. *Elementary School Journal, 81*, 67-76.

Bijou, S.W. (1966). A functional analysis of retarded development. In N.R. Ellis (Ed.), *International review of research in mental retardation (Vol. 1)*. New York: Academic Press.

Birch, H.G. and Gussow, J.D. (1970). *Disadvantaged children: Health, nutrition and school failure.* New York: Harcourt, Brace and World.

Blanton, R.L. (1975). Historical perspectives on classification of mental retardation. In N. Hobbs (Ed.), *Issues in the classification of children (Vol. 1)*. San Francisco: Jossey-Bass.

Bowes, W.A., Brackbill, Y., Conway, M., and Steinschneider, A. (1970). The effects of obstetrical medication on fetus and infant. *Monographs of the Society for Research in Child Development, 35*, Series no. 137.

Brazelton, T. (1973). *Neonatal Behavioural Assessment Scale.* Philadelphia: J.B. Lippincott.

Broussard, E.R. and Hartner, M.S. (1971). Further considerations regarding maternal perception of the first born. In J. Hellmuth (Ed.), *Exceptional infant: Studies in abnormalities (Vol. 2)*. New York: Brunner-Mazel.

Bruininks, R.H. (1977). *Manual for the Bruininks-Oseretsky Test of Motor Proficiency.* Circle Pines, MI.: American Guidance Service.

Bruininks, R.H. and Warfield, G. (1978). The mentally retarded. In E.L. Meyen (Ed.), *Exceptional children and youth: An introduction.* Denver, CO.: Love.

Burgio, G.R., Fraccaro, M., and Tiepolo, L. (1981). *Trisomy 21.* Berlin: Springer-Verlag.

Burton, T.A. and Hirshoren, A. (1978). The focus of responsibility for education of the severely and profoundly retarded. *Psychology in the Schools, 15*, 52-56.

Burton, T.A. and Hirshoren, A. (1979a). The education of severely and profoundly retarded children: Are we sacrificing the child to the concept? *Exceptional Children, 45*, 598-603.

Burton, T.A. and Hirshoren, A. (1979b). Some further thoughts and clarifications on the education of severely and profoundly retarded children. *Exceptional Children, 45,* 618-625.

Cain, L.F., Levine, S., and Elzey, F.F. (1963). *Manual for the Cain-Levine Social Competency Scale.* Palo Alto, CA.: Consulting Psychologists Press.

Canadian Association for the Mentally Retarded. [1980]. *Questions and answers about mental retardation.* Pamphlet, n.p.: CAMR.

Carr, J. (1975). *Young children with Down's syndrome.* London: Butterworths.

Chinn, P.C., Drew, C.J., and Logan, D.R. (1979). *Mental retardation: A life cycle approach (2nd ed.).* St. Louis: Mosby.

Clunies-Ross, G.G. (1979). Accelerating the development of Down's syndrome infants and young children. *Journal of Special Education, 13,* 169-177.

Conroy, J.W. and Derr, K.E. (1971). *Survey and analysis of the habilitation and rehabilitation status of the mentally retarded with associated handicapping conditions.* Washington, D.C.: Department of Health, Education and Welfare.

Corman, L. and Gottlieb, J. (1978). Mainstreaming mentally retarded children: A review of research. In N.R. Ellis (Ed.), *International review of research in mental retardation (Vol. 9).* New York: Academic Press.

Coulter, W.A. and Morrow, H.W. (1978). The future of adaptive behavior: Issues surrounding the refinement of the concept and its measurement. In W.A. Coulter and H.W. Morrow (Eds.), *Adaptive behavior: Concepts and measurement.* New York: Grune and Stratton.

Cytryn, L. and Lourie, R.S. (1975). Mental retardation. In A.M. Freedman, H.I. Kaplan, and B.J. Sadock (Eds), *Comprehensive textbook of psychiatry (Vol. 1) (2nd ed.).* Baltimore, MD.: Williams and Wilkins.

Denhoff, E. (1960). The impact of parents on the growth of exceptional children. *Exceptional Children, 26,* 271-274.

Dickin, K.L. and Ryan, B.A. (1983). Sterilization and the mentally retarded. *Canada's Mental Health, 31,* 4-8.

Doll, E. (1941). The essentials of an inclusive concept of mental deficiency. *American Journal of Mental Deficiency, 46,* 214-219.

Down, J.L. (1866). Observations on ethic classifications. *London Hospital Report, 3,* 229-262.

Downie, D.D. and Snart, F. (1983). Bioethical considerations for teachers of the severe and profoundly retarded: A position paper. *Special Education in Canada, 58,* 3-4.

Duff, R. and Campbell, A. (1973). Moral and ethical dilemmas in the special-care nursery. *New England Journal of Medicine, 289,* 890-894.

Dunn, L.M. (Ed.). (1973). *Exceptional children in the schools: Special education in transition (2nd ed.).* New York: Holt, Rinehart and Winston.

Edwards, M.S. (1981). Fetal Alcohol Syndrome. *Journal of Nursing, 14,* 6-8.

Ellis, N.R. (1963). The stimulus trace and behavioral inadequacy. In N.R. Ellis (Ed.), *Handbook of mental deficiency.* New York: McGraw-Hill.

Finkelstein, N.W., Gallagher, J.J., and Farran, D.C. (1980). Attentiveness and responsiveness to auditory stimuli of children at risk for mental retardation. *American Journal of Mental Deficiency, 85,* 135-144.

Fishbach, M. and Hull, J.T. (1982). Mental retardation in the province of Manitoba: Towards establishing a data base for community planning. *Canada's Mental Health, 30,* 16-19.

Fletcher, G.P. (1968). Legal aspects of the decision not to prolong life. *Journal of the American Medical Association, 203,* 119-122.

Fletcher, J. (1973). Ethics and euthanasia. In R.H. Williams (Ed.), *To live and die: When, why, and how.* New York: Springer-Verlag.

Frankenburg, W.K., Dodds, J.B. and Fandal, A.W. (1975). *Denver Developmental Screening Test.* Denver, CO.: Ladoca Project and Publishing Foundation.

Gan, J., Tymchuk, A.J. and Nishihara, A. (1977). Mildly retarded adults: Their attitudes toward retardation. *Mental Retardation, 15,* 5-9.

Garrard, S.D. and Richmond, J.B. (1975). Mental retardation: Nature and manifestations. In M.F. Reiser and S. Arieti (Eds.), *American Handbook of Psychiatry (Vol. 4) (2nd ed.).* New York: Basic Books.

Gellis, S.S. and Feingold, M. (1968). *Atlas of mental retardation syndromes.* Washington, D.C.: U.S. Government Printing Office.

Gollay, E. (1977, April). Deinstitutionalized mentally retarded people: A closer look. *Education and Training of the Mentally Retarded,* 137-144.

Gottlieb, J. (1975). Public, peer and professional attitudes toward mentally retarded persons. In M.J. Begab and S.A. Richardson (Eds.), *The mentally retarded in society: A social science perspective.* Baltimore, MD.: University Park Press.

Graham, F.K., Matarazzo, R.G. and Caldwell, B.M. (1956). Behavioral differences between normal and traumatized newborns: Standardization, reliability and validity. *Psychological Monographs, 70* (5): 428.

Griffiths, J. and Curtis, C.K. (1984) Integrating deinstitutionalized persons into the community. *B.C. Journal of Special Education, 8,* 257-271.

Grossman, H. (Ed.) (1977). *Manual on terminology and classification in mental retardation.* Washington, D.C.: American Association on Mental Deficiency.

Hallahan, D.P. and Kauffman, J.M. (1982). *Exceptional children: Introduction to special education (2nd ed.).* Englewood Cliffs, N.J.: Prentice-Hall.

Hansen, H. (1978). Decline of Down's syndrome after abortion reform in New York State. *American Journal of Mental Deficiency, 83,* 185-188.

Hanson, M.J. and Schwarz, R.H. (1978). Results of a longitudinal intervention program for Down's syndrome infants and their families. *Education and Training of Mentally Retarded Children, 13,* 403-407.

Hardman, M.L. and Drew, C.J. (1978). Life management practices with the profoundly retarded: Issues of euthanasia and withholding treatment. *Mental Retardation, 16,* 390-396.

Haywood, H.C., Meyers, C.E. and Switzky, S.N. (1982). Mental retardation. *American Review of Psychology, 33,* 309-342.

Henig, R.M. (1982, February 28). Saving babies before birth. *New York Times Magazine,* 19-22.

Herbst, D.S. and Baird, P.A. (1983). Non-specific mental retardation in British Columbia as ascertained through a registry. *American Journal of Mental Deficiency, 87,* 506-513.

Horan, D.J. and Mall, D. (Eds.). (1977). *Death, dying and euthanasia.* Washington, D.C.: University Publications of America.

Ingalls, R.P. (1978). *Mental retardation: The changing outlook.* New York: John Wiley.

Jaslow, R.I. (1976). Extending family planning services to the mentally retarded. *American Journal of Public Health, 66,* 1049-1050.

Jordan, T.E. (1976). *The mentally retarded (4th ed.).* Columbus, OH.: Merrill.

Kaplan, B.J. (1972). Malnutrition and mental deficiency. *Psychological Bulletin, 78,* 321-334.

Kelly, N.K. and Menolascino, F.J. (1975). Physicians' awareness and attitudes toward the retarded. *Mental Retardation, 13,* 10-13.

Khoury, J.T. and Appel, M.A. (1979). Gifted children: Current trends and issues. In A. Lane (Ed.), *Readings in human growth and development of the exceptional individual.* CT.: Special Learning Corporation.

Kirk, S.A. (1964). Research on the education of the mentally retarded. In H.A. Stevens and R.F. Heber (Eds.), *Mental retardation: A review of research.* Chicago: IL.: University of Chicago Press.

Kneedler, R.D. with D.P. Hallahan, and J.M. Kauffman, (1984). *Special education for today.* Englewood Cliffs, N.J.: Prentice-Hall.

Kramer, J.J., Nagle, R.J. and Eagle, R.W. (1980). Recent advances in mnemonic strategy training wih mentally retarded persons: Implications for educational practice. *American Journal of Mental Deficiency, 85,* 306-314.

Krupski, A. (1979). Are retarded children more distractible? Observational analysis of retarded and non-retarded children's classroom behavior. *American Journal of Mental Deficiency, 84,* 1-10.

Kurtz, R.A. (1977). *Social aspects of mental retardation.* Lexington, MA.: D.C. Heath.

Laurendeau, M.C., Blanchet, A., and Coshan, M. (1984). Studying the effects of deinstitutionalization programs on mentally retarded persons. *Canadian Journal on Mental Retardation, 34,* 33-41.

Law Reform Commission of Canada. (1980). *Sterilization: Implications for mentally retarded and mentally ill persons.* Ottawa: Ministry of Supply and Services.

Lejeune, J., Gautier, M., and Turpin, R. (1959). Etudes des chromosones somatiques de neuf enfants. *C.R. Academie Sci, 248,* 1721-1722.

Levinson, R. (1976). Family crisis and adaptation: Coping with a mentally retarded child. *Dissertation Abstracts International, 36,* 8221.

Lewis, M., Bartels, B., Campbell, H., and Goldberg, S. (1967). Individual differences in attention. *American Journal of Diseases of Children, 113,* 461-465.

Lipman, R.S. (1970). The use of psychopharmacological agents in residential facilities for the retarded. In F.J. Menolascino (Ed.), *Psychiatric approaches to mental retardation.* New York: Basic Books.

MacGregor, D.L. (1980). Mental retardation and medical services. *Mental Retardation/Deficience Mentale, 30,* 3-10.

MacKay, R. (1976). *Mental handicap in child health practice.* London: Butterworths.

MacLean, I. (1981). Mental disorder — Mental handicap. *Canada's Mental Health, 29,* 26-27.

MacMillan, D.L. (1971). The problem of motivation in the education of the mentally retarded. *Exceptional Children, 37,* 579-586.

MacMillan, D.L. (1982). *Mental retardation in school and society (2nd ed.).* Boston, MA.: Little Brown.

MacMillan, D.L. and Keogh, B.K. (1971). Normal and retarded children's expectancy for failure. *Developmental Psychology, 4,* 343-348.

McWhorter, A. (1982). Community living: Assessing the situation. *Canadian Journal on Mental Retardation, 32,* 39-43.

McWhorter, A. (1983). Overcoming obstacles to community living: The random, the extreme, and the absurd. *Canadian Journal on Mental Retardation, 33,* 32-39.

Mercer, J.R. (1973). *Labelling the mentally retarded.* Berkeley, CA.: University of California Press.

Meyer, R.J. (1980). Attitudes of parents of institutionalized mentally retarded individuals toward deinstitutionalization. *American Journal of Mental Deficiency, 85,* 184-187.

Miller, C.R. (1976). Subtypes of the PMR: Implications for placement and progress. In C.C. Cleland, J.S. Swartz, and L.W. Talkington, *The profoundly mentally retarded.* Austin, TX.: Western Reserve Conference and Hogg Foundation.

Milunsky, A. (1975). The causes and prevention of mental retardation. In *The prevention of genetic disease and mental retardation.* Toronto: W.B. Saunders.

Montagu, A. (1977). *Life before birth.* New York: Signet Books.

National Prevention Committee, Canadian Association for the Mentally Retarded. (1982). *Final report to the Minister of National Health and Welfare on the five regional symposia on the prevention of mental retardation in Canada.* Ottawa: Health and Welfare.

Neisworth, J.T. and Smith, R.M. (Eds.). (1978). *Retardation: Issues, assessment, intervention.* New York: McGraw-Hill.

Nihira, K., Foster, R., Shellhaas, M. and Leland, H. (1974). AAMD *Adaptive Behavior Scale, 1974 revision.* Washington, D.C.: American Association on Mental Deficiency.

Nitowsky, H. (1979). *Alcohol syndrome. Rose F. Kennedy Center Notes.* New York: Albert Einstein College of Medicine. Nova Scotia Supreme Court, trial division. (1979, November 13). *Between* CAMR, *Nova Scotia division, Northside Branch, a body corporate (plaintiff) and the Town of Sydney Mines, a body corporate (defendant) before Honourable J. Burchell,* 7-8.

Paris, S.G. and Haywood, H.C. (1973). Mental retardation as a learning disorder. In H.J. Grossman (Ed.), *The Pediatric Clinics of North America, 20* (3), 641-651.

Peterson, J. (1925). *Early concepts of tests of intelligence.* Chicago, IL.: World Book.

Pitt, D. (1979). Your Down's syndrome child: You can help him develop from infancy to adulthood. In A. Lane, *Readings in human growth and development of the exceptional individual.* CT.: Special Learning Corporation.

Rachels, J. (1975). Active and passive euthanasia. *The New England Journal of Medicine, 292,* 78-80.

Reiss, S., Levitan, G.W., and McNally, R.J. (1982). Emotionally disturbed mentally retarded people. *American Psychologist, 37,* 361-367.

Richler, D. (1981). A decade of change: How far have we come? *Canadian Journal on Mental Retardation, 31,* 35-43.

Rickham, P.P. (1969). The ethics of surgery in newborn infants. *Clinical Pediatrics, 8,* 251-254.

Robinson, N.M. and Robinson, H.B. (1976). *The mentally retarded child: A psychological approach (2nd ed.).* New York: McGraw-Hill.

Rosenau, N. and Provencal, G. (1981). Community placement and parental misgivings. *Canadian Journal on Mental Retardation, 31,* 3-11.

Rosenblith, J.F. and Sims-Knight, J.E. (1985). *In the beginning: Development in the first two years.* Monterey, CA.: Brooks/Cole.

Rubin, R.A., Rosenblatt, C., and Balow, B. (1973). Psychological and educational sequelae of prematurity. *Pediatrics, 52,* 352-363.

Rutter, M.L. (1971). Psychiatry. In J. Wortis (Ed.), *Mental retardation: An annual review (Vol. 3).* New York: Grune and Stratton.

Sarason, S.B. and Doris, J. (1979). *Educational handicap, public policy, and social history: A broadened perspective on mental retardation.* New York: Free Press.

Scheerenberger, R.C. (1964). Mental retardation: Definition, classification and prevalence. *Mental Retardation Abstracts, 1,* 432-441.

Schulman, J.L. and Stern, S. (1975). Parents' estimates of the intelligence of retarded children. In J.J. Dempsey (Ed.), *Community services for retarded children: The consumer-provider relationship.* Baltimore, MD : University Park Press.

Singer, J.E., Westphal, M., and Niswander, K.P. (1968). Sex differences in the incidence of neonatal abnormalities and abnormal performance in early childhood. *Child Development, 39,* 103-112.

Smith, D.W. and Wilson, A.A. (1973). *The child with Down's syndrome.* Philadelphia, PA.: Saunders.

Sontag, E., Certo, N. and Burton, J.E. (1979). On a distinction between the education of the severely and profoundly handicapped and a doctrine of limitations. *Exceptional Children, 45,* 640-616.

Spradlin, J.E. (1963). Language and communication of mental defectives. In N.R. Ellis (Ed.), *Handbook of mental deficiency: Psychological theory and research.* New York: McGraw-Hill.

Springer, A. and Steele, M.W. (1980). Effects of physicians' early parental counselling on rearing of Down's Syndrome children. *American Journal of Mental Deficiency, 85,* 1-5.

Stainback, S., Stainback, W., and Maurer, S. (1976). Training teachers for the severely and profoundly handicapped: A new frontier. *Exceptional Children, 42,* 203-210.

St. Clair, K.L. (1978). Neonatal assessment procedures: A historical review. *Child Development, 49,* 280-292.

Stephens, W.E. (1972). Equivalence formation by retarded and non-retarded children at different mental ages. *American Journal of Mental Deficiency, 77,* 311-313.

Tarjan, G. (1978, August). *The prevention of psycho-social retardation.* Paper presented at the Ninth International Conference for Child Psychiatry and Allied Professions, Melbourne, Australia.

Tredgold, A.F. (1908). *Mental deficiency.* London: Balliere, Tidall and Cox.

Tu, J.B. (1979). A survey of psychotropic medication in mentally retarded facilities. *Journal of Clinical Psychiatry, 40,* 125-128.

Tymchuk, A.J. (1976). A perspective on ethics in mental retardation. *Mental Retardation, 14,* 44-47.

Vitello, S.J. and Soskin, R.M. (1985). *Mental retardation: Its social and legal context.* Englewood Cliffs, N.J.: Prentice-Hall.

Wechsler, D. (1974). *Wechsler Intelligence Scale for Children — Revised.* New York: Psychological Corporation.

Weisz, J.R. and Zigler, E. (1979). Cognitive development in retarded and non-retarded persons: Piagetian tests of the similar sequence hypothesis. *Psychological Bulletin, 86,* 831-851.

Whaley, L.F. and Wong, D.M. (1979). *Nursing care of infants and children.* St. Louis, MO.: C.V. Mosby.

Whitcraft, C.J. and Jones, J.P. (1974). A survey of attitudes about sterilization of retardates. *Mental Retardation, 12,* 30-33.

Whitman, T.L. and Scibak, J.W. (1979). Behavior modification research with the severely and profoundly retarded. In N.R. Ellis (Ed.), *Handbook of mental deficiency: Psychological theory and research (2nd ed.).* Hillsdale, N.J.: Lawrence Erlbaum.

Wolraich, M.L. (1980). Pediatric practioner's knowledge of developmental disabilities. *Journal of Developmental and Behavioral Pediatrics, 1,* 147-151.

Zarfan, D.E. and Wolf, L.C. (1979). Maternal age and the incidence of Down's syndrome. *American Journal of Mental Deficiency, 83,* 353-359.

Zdriluk, D.M. (1983). Workshops: A Canadian perspective. *Canadian Journal on Mental Retardation, 33,* 35-37.

Zwerling, I. (1954). Initial counselling of parents with mentally retarded children. *Journal of Pediatrics, 44,* 469-479.

CHAPTER FIVE

Gifted and talented children

MARGRET WINZER

Canada's greatest resource is not oil, or gas, or timber — it is our gifted and talented children. Our greatest failure could be our general blindness to this fact.

(Gutteridge)

Giftedness is a somewhat abstract term applied to people who, by virtue of outstanding abilities, are capable of high performance (Clark, 1979). The gifted have greater ability in some areas than most of us. Generally we admire such people, but occasionally we are a little envious of their talents and achievements. We seem to have to work much harder than they to achieve only mediocre results.

Society has always been interested in those who achieve very highly. Traditionally they have been labelled geniuses. Around 1920, the term **gifted** came into use in educational circles (Passow, 1981). Throughout the following years, behavioural scientists used "gifted" as the sole designation to describe people with high intelligence. Only recently have the constructs **talented** and **creative** also come into use.

Intellectual giftedness, creativity and talent interact with one another to a greater or lesser degree. Some individuals soar to great heights in the talent domain, others in intellectual ability, and still others in creative endeavours. A few individuals achieve remarkably high levels of behaviour and aptitude across several domains.

Gifted and talented students have special educational needs. To reach their full potential, they must be confronted with suitable challenges and stimulating educational experiences. A great deal of professional skill and sensitivity is required to identify those needs. The development of appropriate programs taxes the skill, resourcefulness, and empathy of teachers. There is a growing emphasis upon detecting and fostering gifted behaviour, rather than upon giftedness in the abstract (Burdikin, 1983-84).

Special education today attempts to provide for any child markedly different from the average, even if this difference is a positive one. However, the provision of special services to gifted and talented children poses many complex issues and problems for educators. In this chapter, we will discuss many of these issues. Ultimately, however, they will only be resolved by further research, a genuine regard for outstanding abilities, and a vigorous and optimistic commitment to the future.

HISTORICAL PERSPECTIVES

Cultural values have always influenced the attitudes of society toward its outstanding members. As history clearly shows, different cultural eras have valued achievement in different fields of endeavour. Ancient Greece admired the philosopher, Rome the soldier and engineer, and Renaissance Italy the artist.

Throughout recorded history, much honour has been paid to individuals who made significant contributions to their own or succeeding cultures. However, little systematic research has been conducted into the characteristics of, and developmental influences on, these people (Callahan, 1981). Throughout history, the notion of precocity has been shrouded in myth and mysticism. Genius has also been misunderstood. Even in the late 1800s, it was still popularly viewed as directly related to insanity (Khoury and Appel, 1979).

Historically, the fate of highly intelligent children depended largely on the whims and wishes of those close to them. Many suffered the indignity of exhibition as mental wizards or child prodigies. Mozart, for example, was forced by his father to perform at age seven to amuse the nobility and further the family's finances. However, other extremely gifted children were encouraged with early and intensive education. John Stuart Mill's father, an outstanding intellectual himself, began tutoring his son at the age of three. By the time the boy was eight, he had read many Greek authors and was starting to learn Latin, geometry, algebra, and calculus (Laycock, 1979). Mill later exerted powerful influence upon nineteenth-century social thought. His childhood precocity yielded remarkable contributions in maturity.

Early precocity was also seen in other people who advanced our culture. Beethoven performed in public at age seven, Thomas Jefferson began serious study at five, and Pablo Picasso drew before he could walk. In some other major historical figures, however, genius bloomed later.

Outstanding individuals have often had serious problems to overcome. Mozart endured constant pressure from his father, and lived in penury all his life. Vincent Van Gogh suffered crippling bouts of depression that eventually led to his suicide. Charles Dickens struggled with childhood poverty, and Winston Churchill was a sickly child with a speech impediment. Many gifted individuals also suffered some type of learning disability — Auguste Rodin, Albert Einstein, Igor Sikorsky, and Nelson Rockefeller, to mention a few.

Some singularly gifted individuals, then, have survived hardships and handicaps to attain pinnacles of achievement. However, these men and women constitute only a few amid the vast streams of humanity. We can only speculate on what society might be like had thousands of equally gifted people received encouragement and active support.

ISSUES AND PROBLEMS

Francis Galton, an English scientist and eugenics advocate, was one of the first to research and write about giftedness. Galton proposed that motivation to achieve was innate and inborn. He claimed that genius would actualize itself despite external circumstances (Galton, 1869). This position led to the myth that "the cream will rise to the top," regardless of difficulties or lack of environmental support.

Many still believe that gifted children are smart enough to make it on their own. Others support the idea that giftedness needs to be fostered and nurtured. They argue that gifted children have the same right as other children to develop to their full potential. Too often, gifted children are denied these rights because they deviate toward the high end of the intellectual scale.

Many of the leaders, scientists, and artists of the next generation are likely to emerge from the current crop of gifted and talented children. Most thinking individuals would agree that Canada's gifted and talented youth form one of its greatest undeveloped resources. Gutteridge (1980) makes this point succinctly in the quotation that opens this chapter.

Canadian educators have demonstrated a long-standing interest in, and commitment to, gifted and talented children. As Bain (1980) points out, one of the best examples of community-based gifted education occurred in London, Ontario, in the late 1920s. There, concerned parents and teachers worked together to design an enrichment program for the elementary grades. Over the decades, other programs have developed in Canada. Many have been based on the philosophy of Samuel Laycock of Saskatchewan. From the 1930s to the late 1960s, Laycock championed the cause of those exceptional children who were capable of creativity and leadership, but too often ignored by society.

The Enterprise Method and the Major Work classes are two models that have been used in Canada for education of the gifted and talented. The Enterprise Method developed on the Prairies, and trained students in learning and community-oriented group activities. The Major Work program was first adopted in Alberta, then flourished briefly across the country. It offered selected children greater intellectual stimulation, along with training in advanced creativity and problem-solving (Bain, 1980).

Compared to education for the handicapped, the education of the gifted and talented has only been on a small scale. In a 1980 cross-Canada study, Dow found that only twenty-seven percent of school boards had made provisions for gifted and talented children. Exhibit 5-1 breaks down this figure into provincial percentages. Dow also found that fewer than 15 000 Canadian elementary students were enrolled in special programs for the gifted (Dow, 1981).

There are a number of reasons why fewer educational provisions have been made for gifted and talented children. All are associated, to a greater or lesser extent, with the notion that the "cream will rise to the top." Gifted students typically do well in school, easily meet age- and grade-levels for achievement, tend to be well-behaved, and create few classroom disturbances. They demonstrate no immediate problems that can serve as a basis for an emotional appeal for special services. The child with outstanding abilities rarely arouses the same level of concern as the handicapped child. Gifted and talented children are not perceived as suffering from social stigma or unhappiness. Indeed, giftedness is considered highly desirable and is seen as a boon to social status.

Traditionally, special education has been viewed as a way to help children who perform poorly in school. Many educators feel that although we are morally obliged to help handicapped children, there is no moral necessity to help children who already have advantages. Some of these educators are concerned that special education for the gifted might jeopardize the principle of democratic education. They argue that special provi-

Exhibit 5-1 Percentage of school boards providing programs for the gifted in Canada, 1980.

Alberta	31.6%
British Columbia	42.9%
Manitoba	34.6%
New Brunswick	30.0%
Newfoundland	23.1%
Nova Scotia	38.0%
Ontario	60.8%
Prince Edward Island	33.3%
Quebec	15.8%
Saskatchewan	35.3%

(Dow, 1981)

sions for gifted and talented will create an elite or meritocracy within the school population.

Gallagher (1979) argues that North Americans have a strong love-hate relationship with the gifted. Our society celebrates the underdog and largely distrusts the elite. On the one hand, we revere the gifted individual who has risen from a humble background. We are proud to live in a society where talent can triumph over economic hardship. At the same time, we are suspicious of attempts to subvert our commitment to egalitarianism. We do not wish a new elite class to develop, and we distrust those whose special abilities places them above the norm.

Because of this attitude, we direct our special education programs, and the taxes that support them, largely into programs for the deaf, the blind, and the intellectually and emotionally handicapped. Our regular education programs serve the needs of average children. The gifted we leave to fend for themselves, even when this involves a waste of their potential.

This policy leaves educators with a philosophical and practical problem. How are they to adequately educate gifted children in a public education system that is philosophically and administratively egalitarian in nature? If education for the gifted is to survive, this issue will have to be resolved.

THEORIES OF INTELLIGENCE

Measures for quantifying human intelligence were not devised until the 1900s. Intelligence tests, or IQ tests, have traditionally served as the single measure to identify giftedness. As we saw in Chapter Four, they also served for many decades as the sole measure of mental retardation.

Alfred Binet, a French psychologist, constructed the first developmental assessment scale for children in 1905. Binet had been asked by the French government to devise a measure to separate the feeble-minded from the rest of the school population. Binet created his scale by observing the tasks that children could perform at various age levels. Binet sequenced these tasks according to age-appropriate levels. From this, the notion of **mental age** emerged.

Binet derived the mental age of a child by corresponding the tasks the child could perform to the age scale he had carefully developed. In 1912, William Stern, a German pioneer in differential psychology, first used the term **intelligence quotient** to match the developmental levels of Binet's test to the child's chronological age. Psychologists adopted the simple formula, and the term has entered the language of everyday life, though not always with precision (Laycock, 1979).

The intelligence quotient (IQ) is the relationship between a child's mental age (MA) and chronological age (CA); it reflects the difference between a child's performance on the test and the normative performance for the child's age level. Thus, if eight-year-old Jimmy takes the test and is assigned a mental age of eight, his IQ would be 100. The IQ is obtained by dividing a child's mental age by his chronological age, and multiplying the answer by 100:

$$\frac{MA}{CA} \times 100 = IQ \text{ or, in this case, } \frac{8}{8} \times 100 = 100.$$

If five-year-old Jane then takes the test and obtains the same score, she can be said to have a MA of 8. Her IQ would be:

$$\frac{8}{5} \times 100 = 160.$$

This would categorize her as intellectually gifted.

Lewis Terman, an American educator and psychologist, expanded the concepts and procedures developed by Binet. Terman believed that the Binet scale assessed a wide range of performance and could be adapted for use with high-functioning children. In 1916, he published the Stanford-Binet Individual Intelligence Test, in conjunction with Stanford University.

Lewis Terman believed that intelligence was manifested essentially in the ability to acquire and manipulate concepts. He defined the gifted as those who scored in the top one-percent level of general intellectual ability as measured by the Stanford-Binet Scale or a comparable instrument (Terman, 1926). Terman carefully distinguished giftedness from talent and creativity. He viewed talent as a potential for unusual achievement, but only when combined with high IQ scores. Creativity, he believed, was a personality factor, and thus different from both giftedness and talent (Wolf and Stephens, 1982).

In 1922, armed with the Stanford-Binet Test and a single-measure concept of intelligence, Terman embarked on a massive study of giftedness among California schoolchildren. The study, which included 1528 children, "was designed to discover what physical, mental, and personality traits are characteristic of gifted children as a class, and what sort of adult the typical gifted child becomes" (Terman and Oden, 1951, p. 21). Terman's work represented the first full-scale longitudinal study of the nature of giftedness. Its impact was profound and dispelled some traditional myths about the gifted. The findings supported special education for the gifted, and for three decades established the IQ test as the sole measure of giftedness. Many of Terman's findings remain remarkably relevant. So far, his study is unsurpassed in the field of giftedness.

To determine his population, Terman relied on teacher nominations and group intelligence tests. He identified gifted children as those scoring at or above 140 points on the Stanford-Binet Individual Intelligence Test. From his gifted sample, Terman found:

- Most came from a middle or high socio-economic group, with a low incidence of broken homes.
- Nearly half the children could read before entering kindergarten.
- One in five children skipped part or all of the first grade.
- On average, the children finished school fourteen percent faster than normal students.
- The children averaged forty percent higher than their age mates on achievement tests.
- They preferred abstract subjects, such as literary debate and ancient history, and were less interested in such practical concerns as penmanship and manual training.
- They read more and better books, made numerous collections, and had many hobbies.
- They were far superior to their age peers in general health, physique, mental health, and emotional adjustment.
- When retested as adults, they were found to have retained their intellectual superiority.
- As adults, they were ahead in terms of occupational status, earned incomes, publications, and patents (Callahan, 1981; Passow, 1981).

After Terman, the study of giftedness was dominated by the single-variable IQ. This complete reliance on IQ tests continued for thirty years, even though it was not clear which mental abilities and cognitive processes the tests actually measured. Only in recent decades have researchers determined that intelligence comprises a variety of distinct abilities and capacities. Single arbitrary IQ scores are no longer used to determine a child's intelligence. Instead, professionals make flexible judgements based on more comprehensive measures of talent and ability.

The psychologist, J.P. Guilford, was one of the key contributors to the multidimensional theory regarding intelligence. He developed a model, called the Structure of Intellect, that outlined many different types of intellectual ability (Guilford, 1967). Figure 5-1 presents a representation of Guilford's model.

Guilford's distinctive approach prompted researchers to reconsider intelligence as a diverse range of intellectual and creative abilities. Guilford also inspired interest in the characteristics of creative-thought processes and creativity tests. His contributions have been of major importance to the study of gifted, talented, and creative children.

Figure 5-1 Representation of Guilford's Structure of Intellect.

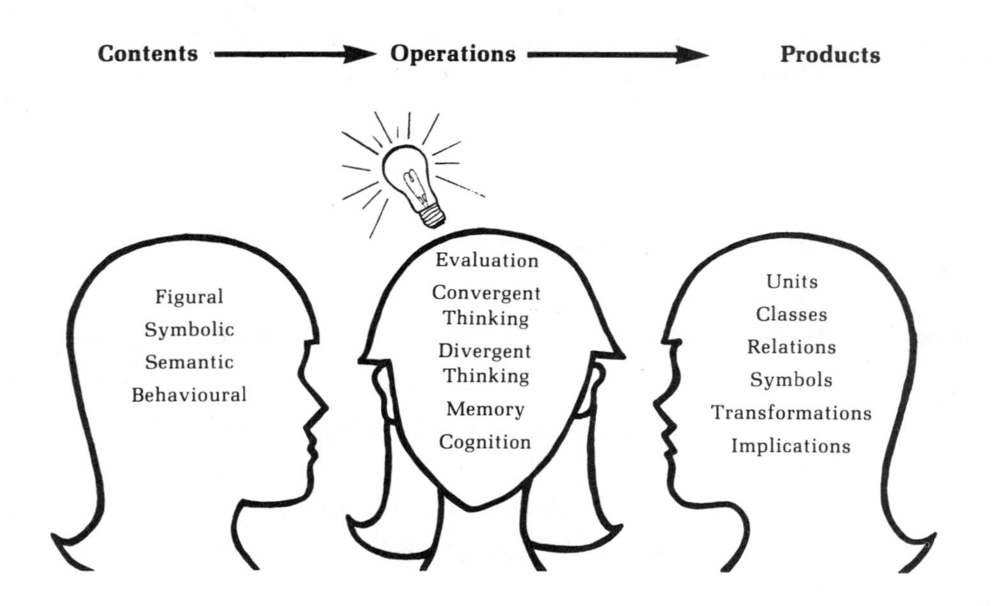

Guilford determined his Structure of Intellect by analyzing intelligence in terms of its specific skills. He divided intellectual performance into three dimensions, each of which encompasses several abilities.

Guilford's first dimension involves **operations**, or the methods people use to process information. The five operations are:

- *Cognition*, or the ability to recognize and comprehend data.
- *Memory*, or the ability to retain newly gained information.
- *Divergent production*, or the ability to generate logical alternatives and new ideas.
- *Convergent production*, or the ability to use information for problem solving.
- *Evaluation*, or the ability to make appropriate judgements.

Guilford's second dimension is known as **contents**. These have to do with how the learner classifies processed information. The four content areas are:

- *Figural contents*, or information about tangible objects derived through our senses.
- *Symbolic contents*, or information derived from symbols such as numbers, letters, musical notes, or formulae.
- *Semantic contents*, or information derived from language.
- *Behavioural contents*, or information involving human interaction.

Guilford called his third dimension **products**. These refer to the forms and structures that people use to organize information. There are six forms of product:

- *Units*, individual pieces of information.
- *Classes*, or objects that share some common attribute.
- *Relations*, or meaningful connections between items of information.
- *Systems*, or organized aggregates of information.
- *Transformations*, or modifications in existing information.
- *Implications*, or predictions, deductions, and conclusions about information.

DEFINITIONS OF GIFTEDNESS AND TALENT

Gifted children are superior in some way to average children of the same age. Beyond this almost meaningless statement, no definition of gifted children has been agreed upon. As we have seen, the concept of giftedness has only recently evolved from a singular IQ orientation to a multidimensional model that encompasses diverse intellectual abilities. In the course of this evolution a number of central issues concerning the nature of giftedness have been left unresolved. Exhibit 5-2 outlines some of these questions.

Exhibit 5-2 Issues in the definition of gifted and talented children

- Although many different gifts and talents have been identified, the gifted and talented typically are considered as a single category.
- Researchers have not yet determined the precise nature of intelligence and the role it plays in giftedness.
- Research has not yet determined the precise nature of creativity and the role it plays in giftedness.
- No consensus has been reached on whether to define giftedness in terms of potential or performance.
- Research has not yet shown the relationship of talent to giftedness.
- There is no consensus on how to measure superiority or how to recognize potential giftedness.
- There is no agreement on the degree to which a child must be superior to be considered gifted.

Although no definition of giftedness has been universally agreed upon, a plethora of definitions have emerged. One 1958 study found 113 different definitions in circulation (Abraham, 1958). Some definitions are narrow and restricted, relying on psychometric measures. Others are more comprehensive and include talent and creativity. Still others are extremely broad and global.

Khoury and Appel (1979) have identified five major classes of definition:

- Those that assign the term gifted to people who have attained outstanding achievements.
- Those that use an IQ cut-off ranging between 120 and 140 IQ.
- Those that base giftedness on an individual's consistently remarkable performance in some socially useful area.
- Those that restrict giftedness to a percentage of the population, ranging from the top one to twenty percent.
- Those that define giftedness partly or completely in terms of the individual's creativity.

A recent, widely employed definition defines gifted and talented children and youth as those

> who are identified at the pre-school, elementary, or secondary level as possessing demonstrated or potential abilities that give evidence of high performance capabilities in areas such as intellectual, creative, specific academic, or leadership ability, or in the performing and visual arts, and who, by reason thereof, require services or activities not ordinarily provided by the school (United States, Gifted and Talented Children's Act, 1978).

This definition manages to be inclusive, specific, and practical. It encompasses a wide range of gifts, talents, and creative aptitudes, and stresses the necessity for special education provisions. Many current definitions follow this model in stressing special programming and the diversity of the gifted population.

In Canada, definitional problems abound. Several provinces, including Newfoundland, Prince Edward Island, New Brunswick, Nova Scotia, Quebec, Manitoba, Saskatchewan, and the Northwest Territories, have no working definition of gifted and talented children (Lewis, 1984). Ontario has quite a specific definition that includes characteristics and programming (Ontario Ministry of Education, 1981). Alberta's 1983 Minister's Task Force on Gifted and Talented Pupils (Report, 1983) has recommended a similar definition. British Columbia has adopted an official definition (Manual, 1984), and the Yukon has adopted the model proposed by Renzulli (1978).

Definitions of gifted and talented children are based on the performance or assumed potential of school-age children. However, it is not always easy to recognize potential ability or leadership qualities. To overcome this problem, Renzulli (1977, 1978) devised a definition based on the characteristics of known gifted or talented adults. Renzulli found that all these adults demonstrated three qualities: high general abilities, high creativity, and high commitment to a task. All three characteristics were required for remarkable achievement.

Renzulli's definition (1978) states that:

> Giftedness consists of an interaction among three basic clusters of human traits — these clusters being above-average general abilities, high levels of task commitment, and high levels of creativity. Gifted and talented children are those possessing

> or capable of developing this composite set of traits and applying them to any potentially valuable area of human performance. Children who manifest or are capable of developing an interaction among the three clusters require a wide variety of educational opportunities and services that are not ordinarily provided through regular instructional programs (p. 261).

Renzulli (1978) claimed that his definition was an operational one, because it was based on research into gifted individuals and their characteristics. He believed his definition gave direction for developing instruments and procedures for educational plans. He also claimed his definition helped practitioners to focus their programs on the characteristics of giftedness essential for future achievements and contributions. However, Renzulli's definition does not satisfactorily resolve the problem of how to identify potential gifts and talents.

To compound definitional problems, a host of other terms are used to describe gifted individuals. Precocious, talented, creative, and genius are all used in reference to the gifted population. The terms gifted and talented are frequently used interchangeably.

Talent refers to a specific dimension of skill in an area such as music, visual arts, drama, athletics, or in particular academic domains. Although talent is not necessarily related to a child's more general abilities, most talented children are also intellectually gifted. Some children have unusual talents in one field and limited abilities in other areas. The direction of an individual's talent depends on many factors, such as experience, motivation, interest, emotional stability, hero worship, parental urging, and even chance.

Creativity is very difficult to define. It refers to the process of bringing unusual and unexpected responses to bear on a given situation. Some of the characteristics of creative thinking include:

- *Fluency of ideas*, or producing a number of responses to a given stimulus.
- *Flexibility*, or shifts in thinking from one category to another.
- Originality, or unusual or clever responses.
- *Elaboration*, or the addition of details to basic ideas or thoughts (Torrance, 1969).

Precocity refers to remarkable early development. Many highly gifted children show precocity in particular areas of development, such as language, music or mathematical ability. **Genius** has sometimes been used to indicate a particular aptitude or capacity. A more traditional term than giftedness, it has often been used to indicate extremely rare intellectual powers. **Atypical abilities** refer to outstanding strengths or abilities in a specific or narrow field.

Leadership is also a fairly abstract term. It can be defined as the ability to effect positive and productive change among other people that is self-enhancing or group-enhancing. Those with high leadership abilities demonstrate empathy and sensitivity, personality and proficiency. They also have charisma, the ability to actualize values to the extent that dynamic group change is effected (Lindsay, 1978).

PREVALENCE OF GIFTEDNESS

Because there is no universal definition of giftedness, it is very difficult to estimate its prevalence. However, we can reasonably assume that only a small percentage of a school population will require special programming for the gifted. In this general sense, then, giftedness is said to occur in two to five percent of the school-age population.

According to Dishart (1981), about half a million Canadians have IQs of 130 or above. In addition, there are at least another half million gifted academically, creatively, artistically, athletically, as leaders, or in psychomotor, sensory-perceptual, and psycho-social capacities. According to Dishart, then, by a very conservative estimate, there are over a million very gifted and talented Canadians. Thirty-two percent of them, or about a third, are of school-age or younger.

In Canada, there are currently around 3.5 million children enrolled in school. (Canada, Council of Ministers, 1983). However, Dow (1981) estimates that only 15 000 are enrolled in programs for gifted children.

FACTORS CONTRIBUTING TO GIFTEDNESS

Gifted and talented children appear in a wide array of shapes, colours, and sizes. They are found at every economic level and in every stratum of society, throughout all ethnic, cultural, and racial groups. However, we do not yet understand what contributes most to giftedness, or why some gifted children achieve eminence and others fade into obscurity. As Renzulli (1980) has stated, "We simply don't know what factors cause only a minuscule number of Thomas Edisons and Langston Hugheses or Isadora Duncans to emerge, while millions with equal "equipment" and educational advantages (or disadvantages) never rise above mediocrity."

We know that the effects of heredity and environment are both important in the development of the gifted and talented child. However, the relative contribution of genetic and environmental factors in not clearly understood. We know that genes carry potential for various characteristics from parent to child, down through the generations. However, the genes alone cannot produce a human being. Each of us is born into a unique environment in which conditions act and react with one another. The individual human being is the total expression of all these complex and constantly interacting forces.

Genetic factors

The proposition that intelligence and abilities are inherited is not very popular in our egalitarian society. Francis Galton and other early researchers maintained that most human traits were passed down through the generations on "germ-plasm." This argument provided fuel for such social movements as eugenics and social Darwinism, and became associated with an elitist view of society (Winzer and O'Connor, 1981). When the dangers of a purely genetic view of development became obvious, the pendulum swung toward a strong emphasis on environmental conditions, especially after the 1930s.

Although we no longer claim that giftedness springs entirely from the genes, it is only reasonable to assume that genetics do have some effect. A considerable body of child-development research suggests that, among Caucasian children in North America and Europe, half to three-quarters of intelligence variation is due to genetic factors (Eysenck, 1979; Newland, 1976; Scarr-Salapatek, 1975).

Research on **monozygotic** (identical) and **dizygotic** (fraternal) twins has illustrated that genetics does play some role. Fraternal twins are usually quite different from one another, while identical twins show a significantly higher correlation on measured intelligence (Montagu, 1977; Nichols, 1965). Genetics may also account for the emergence of children who, at very early ages, produce remarkable achievements. No set of experiences or activities could conceivably account for the child prodigy. These children offer the clearest evidence that some aspect of inherited constitutionality influences their development (Feldman, 1979).

The complex study of genetics has not yet revealed how genes influence giftedness (Eysenck, 1979). Moreover, even the strongest hereditarians acknowledge the great influence of environment on the development of intelligence (Laycock, 1979).

Environmental factors

Most educators agree that giftedness is a unique combination of genetic and environmental factors. These factors include:

- Genetically determined innate characteristics, such as intelligence, physical abilities, and so on.
- The unique development of these traits through specific interaction within the family units.
- Training and education (Eisenstadt, 1978).

Common sense tells us that a stimulating environment is important to child development. An environment that provides a child with little opportunity to learn is less likely to produce children who fulfil their potential for gifted behaviour.

The importance of nurturing has been clearly evidenced by many deprivational studies. These have demonstrated the negative effects of malnutrition and lack of stimulation on infant functioning. The high proportion of first-borns among the gifted population also suggests the importance of environment to the full development of intellectual potential (Laycock, 1979). Unlike younger siblings, first-borns receive full attention and much stimulation from their parents, even if only for a short time.

As stated earlier, no race, ethnic group, or culture holds a monopoly on giftedness. However, the statistical probability of giftedness increases when a child's parents have higher-than-average intelligence and provide a better-than-average, home environment. Brilliant children are most likely to be born to brilliant parents, although some gifted children are born to slow learners. Gifted children are also more likely to have parents of above-average income. Studies have found that the parents' superior social and educational background was the best correlate of superior intelligence (Fisch, Bilek, Horrobin, and Chang, 1976; Willerman and Fiedler, 1974).

A stimulating environment is essential in bringing out the potential in gifted children.
(Coquitlam, B.C. School Board)

In a recent Canadian study of gifted kindergarten children, Perks (1984) found that 59.5 percent of their fathers and 50 percent of their mothers had post-secondary education. This compared to 30.9 percent of fathers and 27 percent of mothers for non-gifted children. Perks compared the reading material available in the children's homes. She found that 61.9 percent of the families of gifted children had more than 300 books, as compared to 18.4 percent of families of non-gifted children. In other words, more highly educated parents were more likely to produce gifted children and to provide them with an enriching environment.

Beyond the obvious general advantages it is not known what specific factors of upper- and middle-class homes encourage giftedness (Hallahan and Kauffman, 1982). Certainly bright children come from lower socio-economic homes, but not as often as we would expect. Part of the reason may well be found in current identification procedures, teacher attitudes, and home and school expectations. Other factors may include lack of motivation, family expectations, neighborhood aspirations, and financial pressures.

The factors in the environment that seem most clearly to affect the development of giftedness are:

- The value and expectations of the culture.
- The socio-economic level of the family, with accompanying nutritional and other health variables, attitudes, and values.

- The position of the child in birth order and the number of children in the family.
- The presence of environmental stimulation (Eysenck, 1979; Laycock, 1979).

IDENTIFICATION AND MEASUREMENT OF GIFTEDNESS

Much of the success of programs for the gifted is contingent upon sound identification procedures. Clear descriptions or definitions are badly needed so that such children can be identified early and provided with appropriate educational experiences.

The issue of identification is a highly problematic one. Indeed, sometimes we seem to spend more time designing identification procedures than designing actual educational programs. Simpson (1984) succinctly expressed the difficulties and frustrations involved in identification of the gifted and talented:

> The literature and the experts shout the need for broad-based criteria using subjective nomination forms, standardized testing devices, matrices, weighing factors, and so on — altogether a time-consuming, paper-mountain, stress-inducing turmoil. Conversely, many trustees and administrators give credence to numbers only: "What is the student's rank, decile, percentile, stanine?" Many large school boards have encountered parents who will shop through the marketplace of independent psychologists until they find one who rates their offspring very highly, and then arrive at the education centre saying, "Here's an affidavit declaring my child has an IQ of 135. Is he/she in your gifted program, or do we go to court?"

Given the heterogenity of the gifted population, the plethora of available definitions, and the administrative problems, identification is particularly difficult and uncertain. In every generation, gifted children pass through school unidentified, their talents uncultivated. Prominent among those who go undiscovered are children who are culturally, ethnically, linguistically, socially, or economically different from the norm.

To fulfil their potential, gifted and talented children should be identified in the early years. During this critical period, their learning patterns are developed, their relationships are fostered, and the attitudes of their parents and teachers are formed (Perks, 1984). To minimize the effects of intellectual and emotional backsliding, identification should occur at the kindergarten level (Malone, 1975).

One difficulty in the early identification of gifted children concerns the number of areas to be assessed. At present, no single identification procedure or simple combination of procedures will effectively identify a high proportion of the gifted. The most effective identification procedures combine standardized tests of mental ability, standardized achievement tests, assessments of products and performance, and the use of rating scales that identify commonly observed performance characteristics of gifted children (Gallagher, 1975b). Other popular techniques include teacher nomination, parent nomination, peer nomination, previously demonstrated achievement, school grades, family histories, interviews, case studies, observation of physical, personality, and social traits, and tests of creativity.

Although no one criterion can be used to identify gifted and talented students, a reliable and comprehensive identification process should include:

- Early identification.
- A continuing search for gifted traits.
- Involvement of various professional personnel.
- Use of multiple resource materials.
- Thorough knowledge of the abilities of gifted and talented students (British Columbia, Ministry of Education, 1981).

In the past, individual intelligence tests, often accompanied by teacher nomination, were the primary method for the identification of gifted and talented pupils (Burdikin and Perry, 1975). Currently, teacher nomination, followed by a battery of measures that include individual intelligence tests, serves as the major identifying vehicle.

Tests of mental ability

Because giftedness has traditionally been defined on the basis of intelligence, identification procedures have typically involved some measure of intellectual ability. Some schools screen students with standardized **group intelligence tests**, because of their seeming objectivity, low expense, and ease of administration. However, all currently available group intelligence tests have a high prevalence of under-identification and over-identification of exceptional children, particularly with reference to creative divergent thinkers and very young children (Borthwick, Dow, Levesque, and Banks, 1980; Lichtenstein, 1982; Roedell, Jackson, and Robinson, 1980). Group intelligence tests also appear to penalize children from lower socio-economic and minority groups (Elkin, 1982). Moreover, Renzulli (1979) claims that, in many instances, these tests identify proficient test-takers at the expense of children who may score lower but think more creatively.

After screening takes place, promising students are given individual intelligence tests. These instruments appear to be the best predictors of giftedness (Gallagher, 1975a). They can identify even those gifted children who are underachieving. Assuming that motivation remains constant, these tests can reveal not only a child's present abilities, but those that will develop in the future.

Achievement tests

Achievement tests can be employed systematically to identify gifted and talented children who are already achieving at a high level. These tests have been used very successfully to identify school children performing at high levels in specific fields, such as mathematics (Stanley, 1979). However, tests of educational achievement do not detect the gifted child who is not achieving higher-than-average level. As a result, the use of achievement tests in the identification of gifted children remains a contentious issue.

Teacher nomination

Teacher nomination is an inexpensive screening method that has been used since gifted children were first formally identified. In Canada it has become the primary method of identification (Lewis, 1984). Teacher nomination is founded on the premise that teachers know their students well enough to spot gifted and talented children.

Unfortunately, however, teachers seem to be relatively poor at identifying gifted children. Estimates of teacher accuracy range from 9.5 to 57 percent (Perks, 1984). Teachers fail to recognize gifted and talented children most frequently at the primary level, where early identification is of the utmost importance (Khoury and Appel, 1979). Torrance (1965) pointed out that, as a rule, teachers do not nominate

> "the good guesser, the child who is courageous in his convictions, the emotionally sensitive child, the individual who regresses occasionally, ... the visionary individual, and the person who is unwilling to accept something ... without evidence. Instead, teachers choose those pupils who are courteous, prompt, obedient, popular, and willing to accept the judgement of authorities" (pp. 12-14).

Teacher accuracy in the identification of gifted and talented children can be improved up to forty percent if they are asked to identify children on the basis of clearly defined characteristics (Perks, 1984). Training programs, questionnaires, and rating scales can all increase effectiveness. Rating scales can be particularly helpful in objectifying teacher judgement. For example, the Scale for Rating Behavioral Characteristics of Superior Students (Renzulli, Hartman, and Callahan, 1975) is designed to obtain teachers' estimates of student traits in specific areas. The teacher is asked to rate each pupil on a series of four-point scales related to areas of learning, motivation, creativity, leadership, communication, and the arts. Separate weighted scores are obtained for each dimension, permitting emphasis on different areas of ability.

Parent nomination

Parent nomination questionnaires are another economical means of identifying gifted and talented children. Although studies have shown that parent accuracy varies from 11 to 76 percent (Khoury and Appel, 1979), parent nomination tends to be generally more accurate than teacher nomination (Ciha, Harris, Hoffman, and Potter, 1974).

Nonetheless, problems do exist. Parents from lower socio-economic neighbourhoods are more likely to report their child as gifted than are parents from higher socio-economic locales (Ciha, Harris, Hoffman, and Potter, 1974); this is partly because well-educated parents tend to set higher intellectual standards for their children (Roedell, Jackson, and Robinson, 1980). Parents may not always be aware of their child's outstanding abilities, especially if they have little chance to compare their child's accomplishments with those of other children of a similar age (Vernon, Adamson, and Vernon, 1977).

Measuring creativity

Gifted children may be identified by their high levels of ability, creativity, and motivation. If the measurement of intellectual ability is complex and difficult, then the assessment of creativity is even more so. Such an assessment presents a challenging paradox — how to devise a standardized means of identifying nonstandard behaviour.

One widely used device to assess creativity is the Torrance Tests of Creative Thinking (Torrance, 1966). The two Torrance Tests are subtitled "Thinking Creatively with

Words" and "Thinking Creatively with Pictures." The first of these measures verbal creativity in the forms of fluency, flexibility, originality, and elaboration.

Another measure is the SOI Learning Abilities Test (Meeker, Mestyanek, and Meeker, 1976). The SOI measures twenty-four of Guilford's intellectual capacities. Although it does not examine creativity per se, it has elements that indicate creative capacities such as divergent production, relationships, and transformations. The SOI tests a variety of abilities, and gives the non-verbal child as much opportunity to score in the gifted range as the verbal child. It also provides teachers and administrators with evidence of strengths and weaknesses, thus serving as a prescriptive as well as a diagnostic tool (Pearce, 1983).

A creativity measure enjoying some popularity in Canada is the Creativity Assessment Package (CAP) (Williams, 1980). CAP consists of two group tests for children: a Test of Divergent Thinking and a Test of Divergent Feeling. A third instrument, the Williams Scale, is a rating measure for parents and teachers. All three instruments can be used to screen, identify, and evaluate the most important factors of creativity found among all children.

One controversial issue concerning creativity is the question of hemisphericity. In brief, **hemisphericity** refers to a person's tendency to rely more on one cerebral hemisphere to process certain types of information. People seem to use their left cerebral hemisphere for logical, sequential processing, and to deal with verbal, analytical, abstract, temporal, and digital materials. The right hemisphere processes information nonlinearly, holistically and simultaneously. People tend to rely on it when dealing with non-verbal, concrete, spatial, analogic, emotional, and aesthetic materials.

There is some documentation to support the common notion that the right hemisphere is dominant in creative thinking (Kruger, 1976; Torrance and Reynolds, 1978). If this is the case, curricula might be designed to stimulate right hemisphere thought. However, accumulating evidence suggests that creative thinking and problem-solving require both left and right cerebral functions (Torrance and Mourad, 1979).

Leadership

Leadership does not describe inborn characteristics, but cumulative capabilities that result from an intermix of the child's innate ability and experience. To assess leadership, observation of performance together with some rating checklist is most appropriate. Children who display early leadership qualities will:

- Interact easily with a variety of people.
- Be sought out by others.
- Possess confidence.
- Establish the mood of the group.
- Be sensitive to the feelings of others.
- Show others how to improve on a task.
- Generate many ideas and solutions (Karnes and Strong, 1978).

Visual and performing arts

In this field, talent is still most often assessed by expert judges in an audition setting. Experts in the arts are not enthusiastic about the use of tests to determine artistic ability. Nevertheless, a range of measures are available to assess potential and aptitude, especially in the areas of music and visual art (Khatena, 1982).

Special problems in identification

In this chapter, we have presented some of the major measures used to identify gifted and talented children. Many others are in use. However, whatever method, or combination of methods, is employed, some special populations of children are often overlooked. Among these are gifted underachievers, gifted females, the gifted handicapped, and culturally different gifted children.

Gifted underachievers

Many gifted and talented children do not develop to their full potential. Sadly, about fifty percent of gifted children become non-active learners by age ten (Nolte, 1976). At the secondary level, about thirty percent of the top ten percent in intellectual capacity drop out of school, a rate that is about three times higher than the average (Banks, 1979; Gowan, 1968).

Gifted underachievers are often faced with a number of problems. They may be rejected by peers because they are gifted, and by teachers because they achieve at a low level. They may suffer from unfavourable self-concepts that distort their perceptions of the world and undermine their motivation and goal orientation (Zilli, 1971). They may feel that their creativity is stifled by the school's rigid schedule, restricted curriculum, and demand for conformity (Whitmore, 1979).

In some cases, underachievement may begin with learning not to learn. In the early years, the student needs to make little, if any, effort to make good grades. Consequently, when academic demands become greater, the student does not know how to apply effort. Self-esteem drops, and the underachiever may become disgusted with school (Banks, 1979).

Other factors may also come into play. Zilli (1971) identified five causes of underachievement in gifted and talented students:

- Inadequate motivation.
- Social pressure or maladjustment.
- Poor school environment, including inadequate curricula, poor teaching, lack of intellectual stimulation, and teacher emphasis on conformity.
- Personality characteristics.
- Home climate.

Profile 5-1 describes a child with high potential who became an underachiever by early adolescence. This child dropped out of school and seems fated not to use his unique gifts fully.

PROFILE 5-1

William was identified during fourth grade as a gifted child. On the WISC-R he scored 162 on the Verbal Scale and 108 on the Performance Scale, for a Full Scale of 134. Achievement testing showed his reading to be at grade-ten level, although his math was only at grade-four. During the testing sessions, William was resentful and manipulative, and stated that he "did not appreciate having his brain examined." He eventually complied with the examiner's requests and finally confided that: "When I was five I was an optimist; at seven a pessimist. Now I'm a cynicist."

Although William revealed outstanding abilities in verbal tasks and abstract thinking, he showed a severe defect in visual-motor dexterity functioning. He had an aversion to written classroom assignments, which had begun to significantly lower his achievement. William also had a tendency toward acting-out behaviours and poor peer relations, chiefly attributable to his bossy and directive attitudes. This was compounded by his inability or unwillingness to comply with expected school behaviour in matters of dress and personal hygiene.

William was accelerated and skipped grade six. At the same time, he was given special help to compensate for his visual-motor deficits. However, William increasingly failed to achieve at levels commensurate with his potential. By grade nine, he was functioning in a slow-moving junior-high-school stream.

When William was sixteen, he dropped out of school. Currently, he is unemployed with few prospects for work in the future.

Gifted females

More males than females are considered gifted and talented. By an overwhelming margin, men achieve high status and recognition more frequently than women of the same age. However, there is no conclusive evidence that this disparity is the result of biological differences. Available research points far more clearly to social and cultural expectations as an explanation for the disproportionate number of males recognized as gifted (Callahan, 1979, 1981).

Females have not been encouraged to enter those academic disciplines and careers historically dominated by males. Certainly, more women are entering such non-traditional professions as chemistry, engineering, dentistry, and physics, but the numbers are still very small. Once in the field, women are often rewarded inappropriately for their performance. They are assessed by irrelevant criteria, and rewarded with affection rather than promotion (Hallahan and Kauffman, 1982).

Girls generally begin to encounter problems in adolescence that obscure their giftedness (Dishart, 1981). The onset of underachievement in girls coincides with early adolescence, the age when sex roles are heavily reinforced by parents and peers (Handel, 1983). Gifted girls find it difficult to reconcile their academic interests with the areas of excellence traditionally seen by society as sex-roles appropriate for women (Schwartz, 1980). As high achievers, gifted girls are expected to be active, assertive, and exploratory. As females, they are encouraged to be nurturant, passive, and dependent (Handel, 1983).

In our society, it is considered neither proper nor advantageous for girls to be too superior. Girls who insist on their giftedness are encouraged to become musicians or artists, rather than physicists or engineers. Gifted adolescent girls have little opportunity to explore their true interests. They are placed under more pressure to conform, and are less likely than males to find learning opportunities with a supportive teacher, (Dishart, 1981).

Figure 5-2 illustrates how sex-role stereotyping, sex bias, and sex discrimination interact. A gifted female student has told her counsellor she is planning to run for class president. The barriers she meets effectively inhibit her ambition.

Figure 5-2 Factors that affect gifted females.
(Adapted from O'Brien Carelli, 1982).

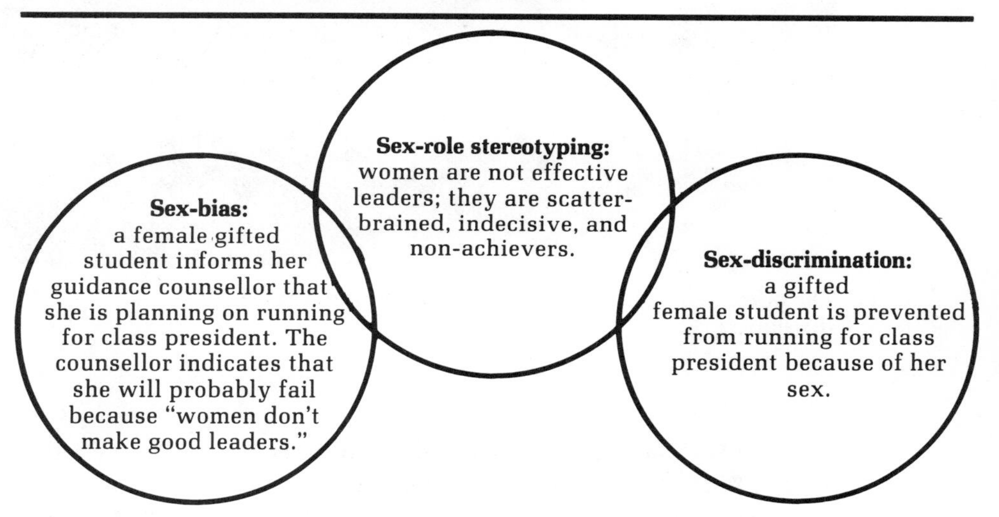

Even when gifted female students are encouraged to enter the fields of their choice, they meet further obstacles as adults. A woman's success is generally measured as a wife and mother, not as a professional. If she succeeds in all three roles, critics often insist that she is doing a poor job in one of them. She may be accused of using sexual favours to raise her professional status, or described as an exception to the rule (Schwartz, 1980).

The key to helping the gifted female fulfil her potential lies in better assessment, counselling, and career development. Specific strategies involve:

- A change in the opportunity structure of schools. This implies affirmative efforts to identify gifted and talented girls at an early age, and to continue the identification process throughout the school years.
- A reduction in barriers to advanced work by, for example, granting equal access to laboratories.
- Broadening the scope of counselling and guidance services to include such programs as achievement motivation and assertiveness training.
- The identification of successful female role models in the school and the community. (Rodenstein, Pfleger, and Colangelo, 1977).

The gifted handicapped are a minority within a minority.
(L. Snider)

The gifted handicapped

A substantial number of eminent people have been handicapped. Beethoven, Thomas Edison, Vincent Van Gogh, and Helen Keller, for example, overcame serious problems to make outstanding contributions to society. After an extensive review, Maker (1977) concluded that the prevalence of giftedness is the same in the handicapped population as in the total population. She observed that a gifted handicapped person "simply has both strengths and weaknesses that are very pronounced" (p. 7). Pledgie (1982) points out that the restriction on retarded children as gifted applies only in intellectual and academic fields. A retarded child may be gifted in an artistic or performing area.

Gifted handicapped children form a minority within a minority. Many teachers, administrators, students, and parents have trouble accepting that a handicapped child, may have outstanding abilities. They focus entirely on the child's handicap, to the exclusion of the child's individual potential and capabilities. In addition, the handicapped do not meet our stereotypic expectations of the gifted. They may exhibit developmental delays, or they may lack the opportunity to reveal superior mental or creative ability (Whitmore, 1981).

The abilities of non-handicapped gifted children are usually readily observable by their classroom teachers, parents, and peers. However, the abilities of gifted children who are blind, hearing-impaired, or learning-disabled may not be so easily apparent. No one instrument or checklist is capable of identifying the range of characteristics and conditions that may be present in a gifted handicapped child. In addition, observations of

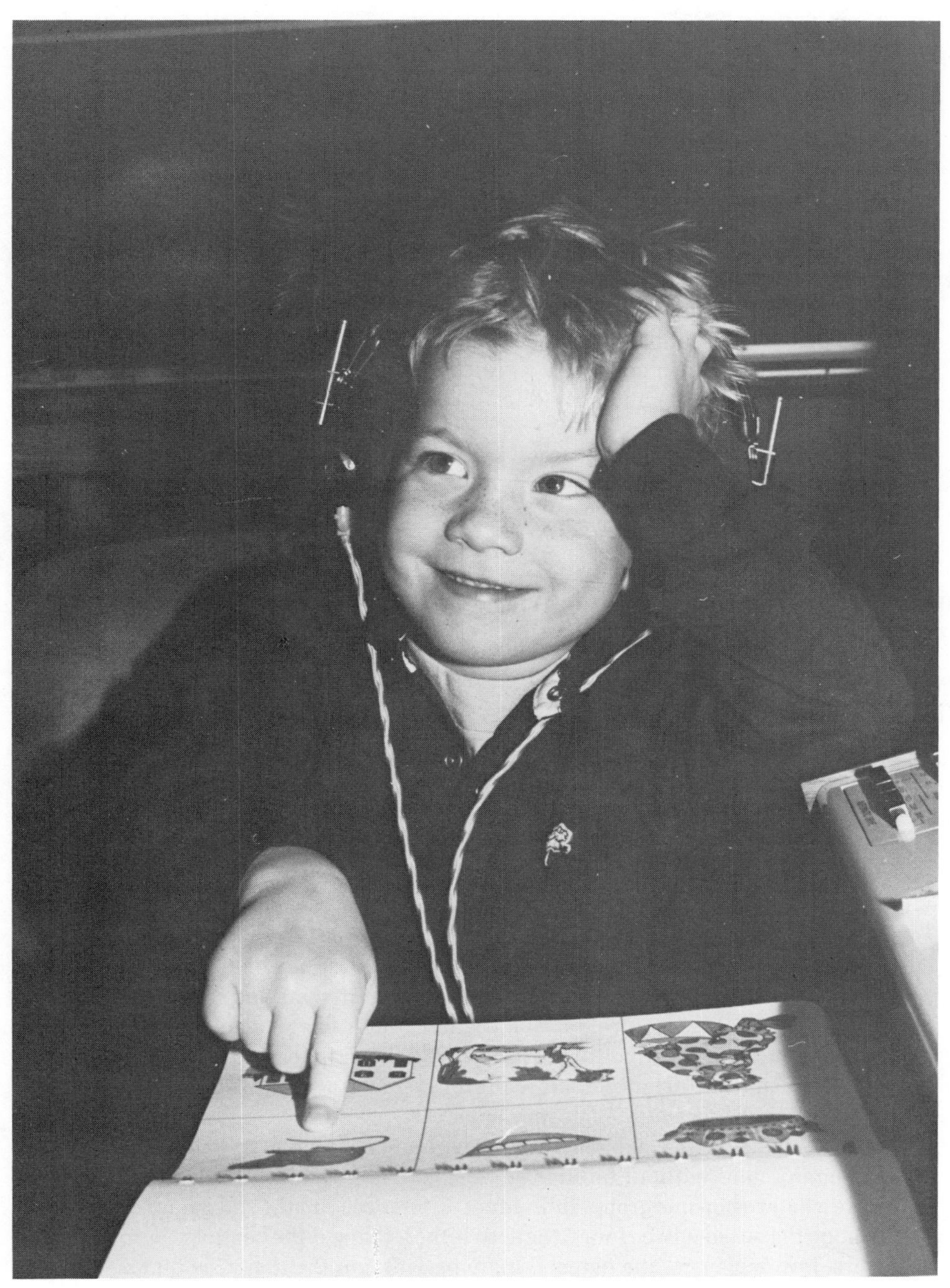

Children who are handicapped in one way may be exceptionally gifted in another area.
(T. Wilson)

the child's behaviour must be made over time rather than in isolation (Pledgie, 1982). This is true for all children, but even more important when identifying the gifted handicapped.

The culturally different gifted child

Children from other cultures are shaped by value systems that may be at odds with the dominant society (Parnell, 1976). Certain traits that define giftedness in the dominant culture may not even be allowed to appear. For example, White middle-class gifted children tend to display a high level of verbal ability. Native children, however, raised on reserves, are normally very quiet in accordance with the norms of their band. As a result, verbal ability would not be an indicator for gifted Native children (Haugen, 1981).

To assess giftedness in culturally different children, the examiner should look for certain traits. The gifted child should:

- Be able to meaningfully manipulate a symbol system held valuable in the culture.
- Think logically when given appropriate data.
- Use stored knowledge to solve problems.
- Reason by analogy.
- Extend or extrapolate knowledge to new situations or unique applications (Clark, 1979).

CHARACTERISTICS OF GIFTED AND TALENTED CHILDREN

Throughout recorded history, there has been a persistent stereotype of the gifted individual as an "egghead." According to this stereotype, the gifted person is physically weak, homely, timid, socially inept, narrow in interests, and prone to emotional instability. Terman's studies shattered this stereotype, and presented a much more positive image of the gifted.

Gifted children tend to be superior in every way. They are higher in intelligence and in achievement. They have a wider range of interests and special aptitudes. They are better adjusted socially, and enjoy more stable mental health. They are more popular, more socially responsible, and have a wider range of social interests and commitments. They are also more flexible, mature, tactful, realistic, and independent (Gallagher, 1966; Hollingsworth, 1942; Marland, 1972). In brief, the gifted appear to be precisely what the term implies — a group of individuals who are especially advantaged in confronting and resolving the challenges of life in every sphere.

In light of this evidence, we must take care not to develop another myth, that of the "superhuman" child without failings or defects. However, like every population, the gifted are a heterogeneous group. Individual differences run the full gamut of possibilities. Among the gifted will be found the active, the lethargic, the healthy, the infirm, high achievers, low achievers, the painstakingly patient and the lightning quick.

Exhibit 5-3 outlines some of the common characteristics of gifted, talented, and creative children. View this list with caution. Probably no child displays all these traits, and the great variance in the gifted population renders many other characteristics possible. The true extent of that variance is not even known because of our inability to identify all gifted children. This is especially true for children who are socially non-conforming, academically maladjusted, emotionally disturbed, culturally different, or physically handicapped.

Exhibit 5-3 Some common characteristics of gifted, creative, and talented children.

Traits common in gifted and talented children:

- Wide range of ability.
- Insatiable curiosity.
- Large vocabulary.
- Long attention span.
- Innovative, creative, divergent responses.
- Ability to synthesize large amounts of diverse information.
- Superior reading ability.
- Superior in height, weight, health, energy, and vitality.
- Ability to grasp and retain knowledge.
- Ability to convey ideas effectively.
- Ability to work independently.
- Ability to assume and discharge responsibility.
- Easy adjustment to new situations.
- Appreciation of social values.
- Establishment of favourable relationships.

Traits common in creative children:

- Tendency to ask many questions, often challenging the teacher and the textbook.
- Production of work that is off the beaten track, with much humour and playfulness.
- Boredom with recitation and memorization of facts; preference for talking about ideas and problems.
- Reputation among students and teachers for wild and silly ideas.
- Considerable energy.
- Unexpected answers on examinations.
- Pleasure in working alone.
- Apparent lack of hard work, coupled with good performance in examinations.
- Unusual capacity for originality, concentration, and hard work on special projects.

Traits common in talented children:

- Pronounced intuitive sense combined with a high degree of artistic integrity.
- Ability to interpret and interconnect to a refined degree.
- Use of technical ability as a foundation for reinterpretation, refocusing, and retranslation, chiefly for personal satisfaction.
- Ability to detach oneself from the surroundings and focus intently on the task at hand. This is especially true of auditory attention in musicians.

DEVELOPMENTAL CONSEQUENCES OF GIFTEDNESS

Physical development

As a group, the gifted tend to exhibit superior physical traits. The children in Terman's study were larger at birth, walked sooner, went through puberty earlier, had fewer diseases and operations, and reported less nervousness than average persons (Terman and Oden, 1959).

However, although gifted children tend to physically outstrip their age mates later on, their superiority is seldom detectable at birth or during the first year. Because there is also a sizable correlation between mental ability and socio-economic status, the apparent physical superiority of gifted children may be a result of nonintellectual factors (Hallahan and Kauffman, 1982).

Learning and memory

Gifted children learn more, faster, and more easily than do their age mates. They learn to read sooner and continue to read at a consistently more advanced level. They like learning, enjoy difficult subjects, and are willing to spend extra time on projects that stimulate their interest. Gifted children are also more adept at critically evaluating facts and arguments. Because they more readily recognize relationships and comprehend meanings, they can reason out problems more effectively.

All these factors place gifted children far ahead in academic achievement. They tend to be more advanced in reading than in areas that require manual dexterity, such as writing and art. They also tend to be more advanced in reading than in mathematics, which depends more on sequential development of concepts and skills (Gallagher, 1966). Many gifted children are younger than their classmates because they have been accelerated due to superior academic performance. Nevertheless, gifted children tend to receive more As and Bs, even when they are competing for grades with older classmates (Barnette, 1957; Shannon, 1957).

Gifted youngsters have often been depicted as bored with and antagonistic to school. In fact, studies have shown that most gifted children like school (Gallagher, 1966).

Social and emotional development

One common and persistent myth regarding the gifted, especially those in the arts, is that they are prone to mental disease. However, although problems do emerge, gifted children generally tend to be happy. They are emotionally stable, self-sufficient, and less prone to neurotic and psychotic disorders than average children. They also have wide and varied interests.

Gifted children tend to be well-liked by their peers. Tannenbaum (1962) reported that the bright students most favoured by peers were intelligent, athletic, and non-studious. The least-favoured gifted students were intelligent, studious, and non-athletic. When gifted students challenge teachers, discuss intellectual matters, and complete more difficult assignments, the less able students may interpret their behaviour as showing off (Pyryt, 1979).

During the pre-adolescent and adolescent years, group pressures to conform are at their peak. Gifted children may experience conflicts between their academic aspirations and a desperate desire to be liked. Sometimes such children decide to hide special talents and abilities behind a mask of mediocrity.

Moral and ethical development

The gifted tend to exhibit higher-than-average concern for moral and ethical issues. At an earlier age than most, gifted children tend to be concerned with abstract concepts of good and evil, right and wrong, justice and injustice (Hollingsworth, 1942; Terman, 1926). They tend to be particularly concerned with social problems and the ways they can be resolved.

PARENTING THE GIFTED CHILD

For the parents, the gifted child may be both a blessing and a burden. Although giftedness is socially acceptable, the child may cause disruption within the family. Many parents of gifted children are bewildered and frustrated about issues related to both home and school. They feel pressured to develop basic parenting skills and specific strategies for encouraging learning at home. They also want to make best possible use of community resources. Parents often feel inadequate in the management of their children, uncertain about programming and placement decisions, and unsure about how to stimulate their children in and out of school.

Ross (1979) hypothesized that the degree of a gifted child's impact on traditional family roles is directly related to the degree of discrepancy between the gifted child's intellectual capacity and that of other family members. Some of the problems encountered by families may include the following:

- The advent of a gifted child can alter normal family roles. Parents sometimes have difficulty clarifying the differences between parental and child roles. They wonder whether they should treat their offspring as a child or an adult.

- Gifted children can cause parents to question their capabilities and assume an added sense of responsibility.

- The family of a gifted child may be required to make special adaptations. These can include costly and time-consuming measures, such as special schools and extra equipment.

- When special adaptations are made for the child, sibling competition and jealousy may result. Siblings may resent the extra money and attention spent by their parents.
- The gifted child sometimes creates special family or neighbourhood problems, such as teasing and rejection by neighbour children.
- The gifted child sometimes creates special problems at school. These might involve unfounded criticism from teachers or interpersonal problems with school mates. (Hackney, 1981; Peterson, 1977; Ross, 1979; Thiel and Thiel, 1977)

INTERVENTION WITH GIFTED AND TALENTED CHILDREN

The basic educational goals for gifted and talented children are the same as for all other students: to develop their abilities in ways consistent with their personal needs and the best interests of society. Schools must develop mechanisms to identify gifted children and provide them with educational programs to help them fulfil their potential.

Gifted and talented children cannot just fend for themselves. They possess no magical ability to help them overcome the obstacles to their growth. Like other exceptional children, these youngsters need special assistance to fulfil their potential for achievement. Guilford (1975) argues that:

> of all children who become the responsibility of educators, the "gifted" ones have the most probable potential for becoming effective problem solvers. The general picture, unfortunately, is that only a few of them actually fulfil such promise, either for lack of immediate need, motivation, or development of skills in creative thinking. We can educate those children with or without the cultivation of such talents; they will ordinarily not blossom to full extent on their own (p. 107).

Without educational opportunities and challenges, gifted children may hide their abilities or bury them in underachievement. Some become dropouts or deviants in a society that has ignored or even abused them. Whitmore (1979, 1980) has attributed these failures primarily to the social and academic environment of the classroom. The gifted child is "turned off" by conformity to precise directions, excessive repetition, memorization and drill, uniformity of assignments, and the lack of opportunity to pursue interests and work independently.

The education of the gifted and talented has received meagre support at best. Attempts to provide special education for these children have been sporadic and haphazard. As a result, many youngsters have failed to fulfil the potential of their outstanding ability.

Educational provisions in Canada

In the United States, Lyon (1976) estimated that less than four percent of gifted and talented children were receiving the educational services they needed for optimal development. Similarly, Dow (1981) discovered that less than 15 000 elementary school children in Canada were enrolled in special programs for the gifted. However, gifted education for Canadian children is gaining support, although progress is slow.

In the Maritime provinces, some school boards are providing programs for the gifted. Conferences, parent support groups, Saturday clubs, and university mentor programs bolster these educational provisions. New Brunswick intends to have legislation by 1987 requiring schools to make provision for the gifted (Willings, 1984).

In Quebec, the idea of education for the gifted is slowly but steadily making headway in various circles. Anglophone educators are taking the lead in this area. Dozens of Anglophone schools offer enrichment programs, notably within the Protestant School Board of Greater Montreal. Although eighty-five percent of Quebec's population is Francophone, only about half a dozen school boards have made enrichment programs a priority. Some enrichment services are offered at the elementary level, but there are virtually none in high schools or colleges (Gagne, 1984).

In Ontario, provisions have been made for gifted and talented children under the Education Amendment Act (1980). School boards are required to identify gifted children early and make special arrangements for their education. Recently, Ontario's programs for gifted pupils have been extended from elementary to high school levels. Ontario increasingly aims to provide enrichment programs throughout the elementary and secondary school system (Smyth, 1984).

In the Prairies, interest has grown dramatically in the past few years in the provision of enrichment educational programs. New government commitment to education for the gifted has been reinforced by the emergence of parent advocacy groups (Hengen, 1984; Yewchuk, 1984). In British Columbia, the number of enrichment programs has greatly increased in the past few years.

In the far north, providing special programs for gifted and talented children is particularly difficult. The major problem is the difficulty of delivering services to relatively few students of widely differing ethnic backgrounds scattered across a large geographical expanse. In this context, it is difficult to find appropriate assessment instruments for identifying gifted and talented children. It is also difficult to gain parental involvement and support, and to find program models, goals, and objectives meaningful to the local culture (Wilgosh and Mulcahy, 1984).

For example, Cambridge Bay is a community of approximately 850 people, of whom about eighty percent are Inuit. When an enrichment program was established there, parents were reluctant to lend it support. This was attributed mainly to their lack of initial involvement in program planning (Mulcahy, Wilgosh, Crawford, and Watters, 1984).

Technical aids

For most gifted children, technical aids, in the sense of hearing aids and wheelchairs, are not relevant. Gifted children should, however, be able to take advantage of new advances in information and communication technology, specifically as related to computers. Today's computers store, manipulate, and retrieve information far more efficiently than ever before. They help gifted students to overcome limitations and extend their abilities, much as prosthetic devices help the physically disabled (Kneedler, 1984).

The application of computers to the education of the gifted was pioneered in the Soviet Union during the 1950s. Computer activities give gifted children access to instant advanced instruction through complex, multilevel branching programs. Children also, through simulations and programming, gain access to phenomena outside the realm of their experience, but not beyond their level of understanding (Dover, 1983).

Gifted students bring a powerful store of talents to their interactions with computers. Because they possess above-average ability, creativity, and task commitment, they may well make significant contributions to computer technology through their involvement with computer activities in school (Dover, 1983).

Organizational models for program delivery

A variety of practices and programs have been devised to cater to gifted children over the years. The three most common types of educational provision are enrichment, ability grouping, and acceleration. All three models are used across the country. Research on the efficacy of each is somewhat inconclusive, although acceleration appears to have a slight edge. For a complete review of differential educational models, see Khatena (1982).

Enrichment

Often, in the regular classroom, a very bright child finishes work well ahead of the other students. The teacher may suggest that the child try, for example, another ten of the same type of math problem. This is not enrichment but more of the same. The child is soon likely to feel stifled, bored, and unchallenged.

Enrichment involves providing special activities in the regular class setting. These activities must involve a broader range of skills and deeper understanding than the regular curriculum. Enrichment activities are designed to challenge and interest children while focusing on their unique patterns of strength and weakness.

Curricula for gifted children should be:

- Subject-related and based on materials that encourage doing and thinking.
- Process-oriented, with an emphasis on process and skill development rather than knowledge acquisition.
- Student-selected, permitting students to choose and develop activities related to their own interests, abilities, and learning styles.
- Open-ended, allowing for a variety of methods and responses.
- Doing-centred, provoking active involvement, rather than passive attendance, from the learner (British Columbia, Ministry of Education, 1981).

Advocates of enrichment programs argue that they allow the child to remain in the regular classroom with age-level peers. Detractors point to the difficulty of meeting individual needs with a few extra activities in a generally inadequate learning-environment. Research on the results of the programs does not yield clear evidence that they adequately stimulate gifted children (Marland, 1972). However, these programs should not be abandoned. At present, they are often all that is available for gifted students.

Exhibit 5-4 presents an enrichment unit that examines "weather." The unit is based on Bloom's taxonomy of educational objectives (1956).

Exhibit 5-4 Enrichment unit on "weather."

Knowledge

- List all the weather terms you can discover.
- Define these weather terms: climate, temperature, humidity, precipitation, air masses, highs, and lows.
- Name as many different kinds of storms as you can.
- Find an old Farmer's Almanac. What are some old sayings about weather?

Comprehension

- Locate on a map the places where there are weather stations in Manitoba.
- Explain the difference between a tornado and a hurricane.
- Describe how meteorologists predict the weather.

Application

- Illustrate the different kinds of cloud.
- Use a thermometer and record the temperature outside twice a day for a week.
- Show how a tornado or a hurricane is formed.

Analysis

- Compare forecasts with the actual weather over the period of a week. How close do the forecasts come to predicting the weather?
- Contrast how forecasts were made before satellites and how they are made now. Which system is better?
- Conduct an experiment into how clouds are formed.

Synthesis

- Design a new weather station using all the newest equipment available for weather study.
- Collect weather information (temperature, winds, fronts, and so on), and prepare a forecast for three days.

Evaluation

- Decide whether our present system of weather forecasts is valuable. Be ready to defend your answer.
- Assess the value of forecasts and how they affect people's lives.
- Evaluate how much pollution is affecting the weather, and whether something should be done about it. Be ready to make suggestions.

(Adapted from Association of Gifted and Talented Children in B.C., 1983.)

Ability grouping

As the name suggests, ability grouping refers to removing gifted children from heterogeneous settings and placing them into special groups. In some cases, gifted children are removed to special classrooms. In others, independent groups of students work at different rates of progress within the same classroom.

Ability grouping may take several forms. Special groups may meet full-time or only part-time. They may be made up of students from a single school, or from several schools within a district. Special groups may meet during regular school hours, or on an extra-curricular basis.

Proponents of ability grouping argue that only when gifted children are grouped together can they be provided with truly effective instruction. The special classroom provides opportunities for acceleration and for horizontal expansion of the curriculum. Thus, if students complete material on the geography of a region ahead of their classmates, their teacher may help them expand their experiences horizontally by delving into the social customs, history, and traditions of the region.

Profile 5-2 describes a gifted boy, John, who was identified early and moved to an ability group part-time.

PROFILE 5-2

John was first tested in 1973 when he was in grade one. On the WISC-R he achieved a Full Scale IQ of 146. On the Woodcock Reading Mastery Tests he was reading at grade 7.5 level. On the Williams Test of Creativity, he was functioning at two standard deviations above the mean.

As John proceeded through school, he was helped to fulfil his potential by part-time studies in a special setting. The only problems his teachers found were his perfectionist tendencies, the great value he placed on high grades, and his constant frustration with time constraints when he was absorbed in an activity.

John was well-liked by his peers and considered himself "pretty good at soccer and hockey." In elementary school, he liked everything except printing from the board: "It makes my hand ache." By the time he reached grade eight, he still enjoyed school, though he continued to dislike "board work." He had developed a wide range of interests, including astronomy, chemistry, neurological studies, collecting fossils, and the Rod and Gun Club.

In high school, John had a community mentor and became very active in computers, sports, and the student council. In grade twelve, he earned sixteen As out of sixteen courses. He did not lose his interest in science, and he is currently achieving highly in this discipline at the university level.

Figure 5-3 shows a unit that John mapped in grade seven on an area of particular interest to him. No teacher input was involved in the mapping.

Opponents of ability grouping argue that it is undemocratic. They claim that it fosters intellectual elitism and limits contact between gifted and normal children. The research does not provide clear evidence for or against ability grouping. On the basis of her review of the literature, Hildreth (1966) concluded that ability grouping produces "slightly greater academic achievement in comparison with instruction of the bright in regular classes" (p. 320).

Figure 5-3 Example of webbing done by Grade 7 student in an IEP. The question was, How has the Theory of Relativity affected mankind?

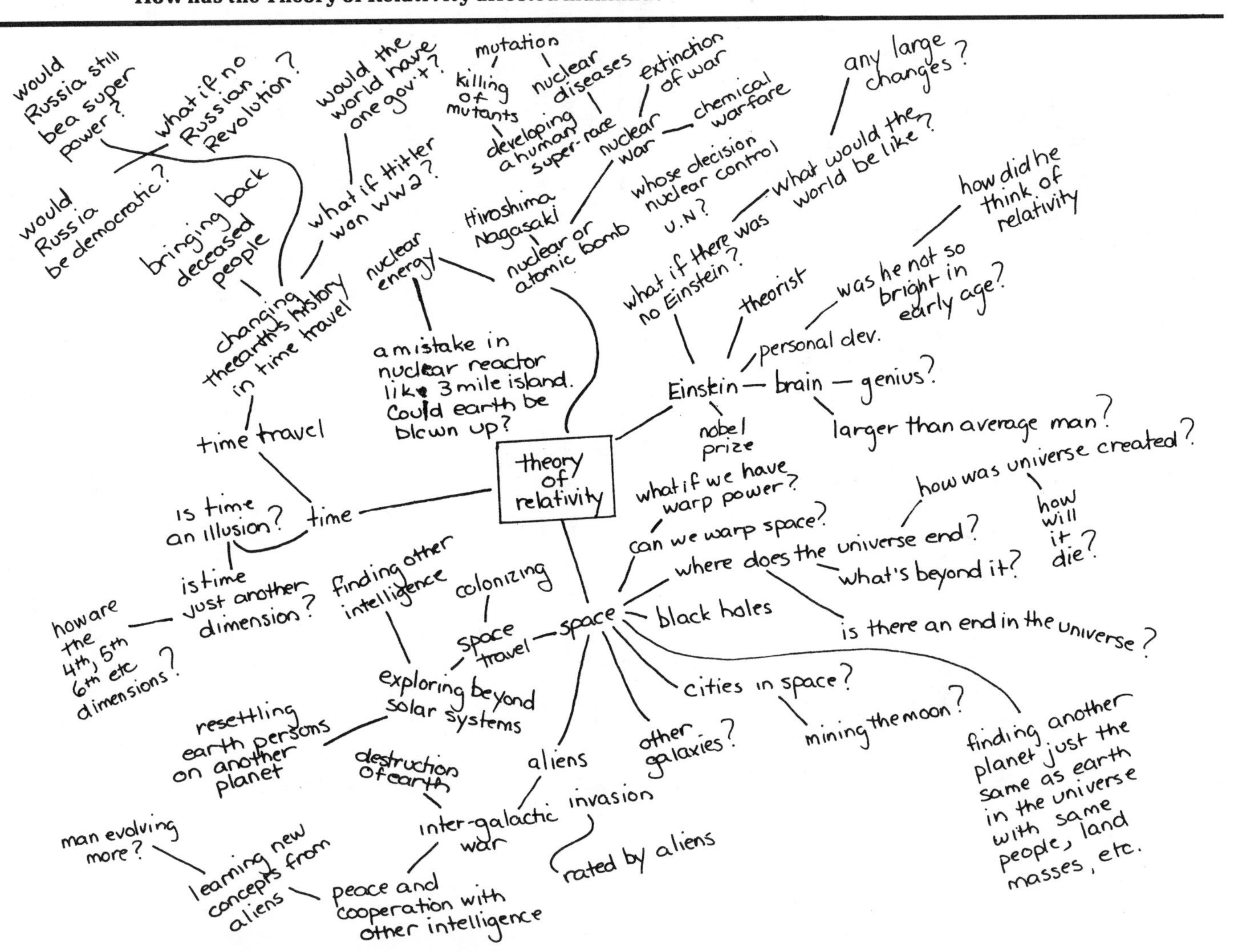

Acceleration

One way of using the established age-grade system to the advantage of the gifted is **acceleration**. This permits gifted children to progress through the educational system at their own rate. Several types of acceleration are possible: early admission to kindergarten; grade skipping; and rapid progress through a non-graded school system. Acceleration programs reduce the time that students need to complete the curriculum. By accelerating, students can maximize their intellectual potential and maintain their interest and motivation. They can enter high school, college, and graduate studies earlier, and get a faster start on their careers.

Opponents of acceleration fear the social and emotional consequences for a child who is grouped with considerably older classmates. However, a number of investigators have found no evidence of negative effects either intellectually, socially, or emotionally from moderate educational acceleration for the gifted (Gallagher, 1966; Gold, 1965; Terman and Oden, 1947).

Exhibit 5-5 outlines the major points of these and other organizational models for education of the gifted and talented. Not all these administrative arrangements, curriculum modifications, and training programs are available in every school district. Typically, more program options are available in urban and suburban areas and in the elementary schools. However, there is much variation across the country.

Exhibit 5-5 Organization models for the education of gifted and talented children.

- *Enrichment in the classroom.* A differentiated program of study offers gifted children experiences beyond the regular curriculum. This model is delivered by the regular classroom teacher, without assistance from a consultant or resource teacher.
- *Consultant teacher program.* Differentiated instruction is provided within the regular classroom by the classroom teacher with the assistance of an educational consultant or specialist.
- *Resource room program.* Gifted students leave the regular classroom for differentiated instruction provided by a specially trained teacher.
- *Community mentor program.* Gifted students interact on an individual basis with selected members of the community to study topics of special interest to them.
- *Independent study program.* Differentiated instruction consists of independent study projects supervised by a qualified adult.
- *Special class.* Gifted students are grouped together and receive instruction from a specially trained teacher.
- *Special school.* Gifted students receive differentiated instruction in a specialized school established for the purpose.
- *Acceleration.* Students speed up their progress through the existing curriculum to complete a prescribed program in a shorter time period. Acceleration includes grade skipping, early school beginning, and continuous progress.

(Adapted from Ontario Ministry of Education, 1978, p. 4.)

Models for educational enrichment

The Enrichment Triad Model (Renzulli, 1977) is one of the most widely used programming models for the education of gifted and talented children in North America. The Triad delineates three types of enrichment activities for students.

Type I is General Exploratory Activities. These are designed to expose pupils to exciting topics, ideas, and fields of knowledge not ordinarily covered by the regular curriculum. Type I activities are considered appropriate for all students. They include such items as visiting speakers, field trips, demonstrations, interest-development centres, and the use of many different kinds of audio-visual materials.

Type II involves Group Training Activities. These consist of methods, materials, and instructional techniques designed to develop thinking processes, research and reference skills, and personal and social skills. Type II activities are also appropriate for all children.

Type III activities are Individual or Small-Group Investigations. In these, students investigate real problems and topics using appropriate methods of inquiry. The success of Type III activities depends upon the interest and task commitment of the individual child. Although Type III enrichment is generally very rigorous and challenging, it is also highly motivating. Because student involvement is based on personal commitment to self-selected areas of study, outstanding products result (Reis and O'Shea, 1984).

Renzulli and Smith (1980) recently described a "revolving-door" plan to identify giftedness and provide enrichment activities. The Revolving Door Identification Model is designed to overcome many of the problems related to student selection, motivation, and interests. It represents a dramatic departure from traditional identification approaches.

The Revolving Door Model allows many students of above-average ability to participate in the program as their interests and motivation dictate. Students are not permanently in or out of the program, but can apply for special consideration to work on projects of their own choosing. Renzulli claims that this approach teaches students they must earn the right to participate. As well, it directly involves the classroom teacher in special projects. This leaves the resource-room teacher free to act as a consultant:

> The resource teacher helps the student to focus or frame the area of interest into a researchable problem; suggests where the student can find appropriate methodologies for pursuing the problem like a professional enquirer; helps the youngster to obtain appropriate resources (persons, equipment, reference materials, financial support); provides critical feedback, editorial assistance, encouragement, and a shoulder to cry on; and helps the child find appropriate outlets and audiences for his or her creative work (Renzulli, 1979, p. 34).

THE GIFTED AND TALENTED PRE-SCHOOLER

Good prenatal care, good early nutrition, a stimulating environment, and much one-to-one interaction with adults is likely to increase the child's potential for giftedness. As we have stated, early identification is very important to develop the child's abilities. Young gifted children can often be identified by their performance. An eighteen-month-old child may use language like most children who are thirty months. A three-year-old may tackle mathematical problems that are taught in the third grade. A four-year-old may be able to read and draw maps as well as most adults (Robinson, Roedell, and Jackson, 1979).

Hall and Skinner (1980) recommend that parents keep a journal in which they record specific features of their child's development. Hall and Skinner have also developed some interesting assessment approaches for parents interested in evaluating their children. The test items relate to the child's motor ability, fine motor ability, and language.

Even in the pre-school years, gifted youngsters require programs that are challenging, innovative, and allow them to explore their own abilities. Their environment should be rich with attractive learning materials, manipulative experiences, explorative activities, language stimulation, and social interaction. An atmosphere of inquiry and curiosity should prevail. Children should be encouraged to ask questions and seek solutions to problems that interest them.

Programming for pre-school gifted children may involve more advanced curricula. These children may be more ready to learn formal skills, such as reading, than are their age-mates. In specific skill areas, they may already perform like much older children.

THE GIFTED AND TALENTED ADOLESCENT

Interest is currently mounting in the gifted student at the secondary level. The educational needs of high-school students can be most effectively met by accelerated placement for specific academic subjects, enrolment in special schools, mentor programs, and directed study programs.

Particularly beneficial at the secondary level is school and career counselling. A sympathetic school counsellor can help gifted students and their parents cope with the social and emotional problems that so often arise in high school. In the case of new culturally-different students, the counsellor can help to de-mystify the unfamiliar educational environment (McMillan and Loveland, 1984).

When programs for the gifted have not been developed, counsellors can do a great deal to help individual students. The counsellor can plan appropriate timetables, collapse the time needed to meet core requirements, and arrange contacts in the community and post-secondary institutions. Counsellors can also arrange for counselling if social or emotional problems arise (McMillan and Loveland, 1984).

Effective counselling also plays an important role in developmental career planning for the gifted. Career plans for average learners change between seventeen and nineteen years of age. For the gifted, changes in career plans can occur between thirteen and fourteen years, sixteen and eighteen years, and twenty-one and twenty-three years. A radical change in careers for the gifted develops between twenty-eight and thirty-two years. Talented children, meanwhile, often have fixed career goals prior to adolescence.

By ages thirteen or fourteen, some gifted students are already conditioned to avoid failure at all costs. They are willing to pursue career choices far below their potential (Willings, 1983). Counselling is important to help these students make more appropriate career plans.

TEACHERS OF THE GIFTED AND TALENTED

Should gifted children be taught by gifted teachers? At present, surprisingly little research has been done to determine who should teach gifted children. There is some evidence that successful high-school teachers of the gifted are mature, experienced, emotionally well-adjusted, and highly intelligent (Newland, 1962; Ward, 1961).

A teacher of the gifted needs to have high task commitment, the ability to stimulate the children's curiosity, a high level of knowledge of course-contents, and the flexibility to provide individualized programming in a democratic atmosphere. These characteristics, of course, are the mark of any good teacher. However, the teacher of the gifted should also have knowledge, understanding, and sympathy for the gifted population. The teacher should have a high level of creativity and energy to meet the special demands of gifted children. They should also feel supportive toward special education for gifted students (Bishop, 1968).

Currently, only Ontario requires teachers to obtain a Special Education certificate to work with gifted and talented children. No special certification is necessary in the other provinces and territories (Dow, 1981). Across the country, however, eight Education faculties offer special courses on the gifted and talented.

SUMMARY

At present, developments in education of the gifted and talented can be viewed with cautious optimism. Across the country, programs are expanding and service delivery is becoming more sophisticated. Slowly, educators are formalizing definitions and procedures as they become more committed to this form of special education.

Many issues and problems continue to plague the field. Not the least is the lack of a universally accepted definition of the gifted and talented. This lack of definition distorts prevalence figures and renders identification procedures more difficult.

Problems in definition arise partly because of the heterogeneous nature of the gifted population. Gifted and talented children display a wide variety of traits that are not always easily quantified and measured. Better identification measures are needed to identify gifted children within minority groups, such as the gifted handicapped, gifted females, and gifted children from other cultures.

Gifted and talented children offer Canada one of its greatest resources. However, these children will not attain their full potential without some special help. Educators must find some way to help these children triumph within an egalitarian school system.

BIBLIOGRAPHY

Abraham, W. (1958). *Common sense about gifted children.* New York: Harper and Row.

Alberta. (1983). *Report of the Minister's Task Force on gifted and talented pupils: Educating gifted and talented pupils in Alberta.* Alberta: Planning Services Branch, Alberta Education.

Association of Educators of Gifted, Talented and Creative Children in B.C., 1983, 5, 224-225.

Bain, D.A. (1980). Gifted and enriched education in Canada. In M. Csapo and L. Goguen (Eds.), *Special education across Canada: Issues and concerns for the '80s.* Vancouver: Centre for Human Development and Research.

Banks, R. (1979). "How would you like it if you were gifted?" *Special Education in Canada, 53,* 12-14.

Barnette, W.L. (1957). Advanced credit for the superior high-school student. *Journal of Higher Education, 28,* 15-20.

Bishop, W. (1968). Successful teachers of the gifted. *Exceptional Children, 34,* 317-325.

Bloom, B.S. (Ed.) (1956). *Taxonomy of educational objectives, handbook 1: Cognitive domain.* New York: David McKay.

Borthwick, B., Dow, I., Levesque, D., and Banks, R. (1980). *The gifted and talented students in Canada: Results of a CEA study.* Toronto: The Canadian Education Association.

British Columbia, Ministry of Education. (1981). *Enrichment and gifted education resource book.* Victoria: Ministry of Education.

British Columbia. (1984). *Manual of policies, procedures and guidelines.* Victoria: Ministry of Education.

Burdikin, J. (1983-84, fall, winter). Do gifted pupils have special needs? *Newsletter,* School District #43, Coquitlam.

Burdikin, J. and Perry, J. (1975). *A report to the Board of School Trustees on provisions for gifted children in School District #43 (Coquitlam).* Coquitlam, B.C.: Coquitlam School Board.

Callahan, C.M. (1979). The gifted and talented woman. In A.H. Passow (Ed.), *The gifted and talented: Their education and development.* Chicago: University of Chicago Press.

Callahan, C.M. (1981). Superior abilities. In J.M. Kauffman and D.P. Hallahan (Eds.), *Handbook of special education.* Englewood Cliffs, N.J.: Prentice-Hall.

Canada, Council of Ministers of Education. (1983). *Survey of special education in Canada, 1982-1983.* Winnipeg: Candid Research and Council of Ministers of Education, Canada.

Ciha, T.E., Harris, R., Hoffman, C. and Potter, M. (1974). Parents as identifiers of giftedness: Ignored but accurate. *Gifted Child Quarterly, 18,* 191-195.

Clark, B. (1979). *Growing up gifted.* Columbus, OH.: Merrill.

Dishart, M. (1981). Special education and personal needs of gifted and talented children. *Association of Educators of Gifted, Talented and Creative Children in B.C., 3,* 6-12.

Dover, A. (1983). Computers and the gifted: Past, present and future. *Gifted Child Quarterly, 27,* 81-85.

Dow, I.I. (1981). The education of gifted students in Canada. *Association of Educators of Gifted, Talented and Creative Children in B.C., 3,* 13-19.

Eisenstadt, J.M. (1978). Parental loss and genius. *American Psychologist, 33,* 211-223.

Elkin, W.F. (1982). Rethinking Bill 82. *Ottawa Law Review, 14,* 317-336.

Eysenck, H.J. (1979). *The structure and measurement of intelligence.* New York: Springer-Verlag.

Feldman, D. (1979). The mysterious case of extreme giftedness. In A.H. Passow (Ed.), *The education of the gifted and talented: Seventy-eighth yearbook of the National Society for the Study of Education.* Chicago: University of Chicago Press.

Fisch, R.O., Bilek, M.K., Horrobin, J.M. and Chang, P.N. (1976). Children with superior intelligence at 7 years of age. *American Journal of Diseases of Children, 130,* 481-487.

Gagne, F. (1984). Gifted programs in Quebec: Slow but steady progress. *Special Education in Canada, 58,* 147-148.

Gallagher, J.J. (1966). *Research summary of gifted child education.* Illinois: State of Illinois, Office of Superintendent of Public Instruction.

Gallagher, J.J. (1975a). *The gifted child in the elementary school.* Washington, D.C.: American Educational Research Foundation.

Gallagher, J.J. (1975b). *Teaching the gifted child (2nd ed.).* Boston: Allyn and Bacon.

Gallagher, J.J. (1979). Issues in the education of the gifted. In K.J. Rehage (Ed.), *The gifted and talented: Their education and development.* Chicago, IL.: University of Chicago Press.

Galton, F. (1869). *Hereditary genius: An enquiry into its laws and consequences.* London, New York: Appleton, 1870.

Gold, M.J. (1965). *Education of the intellectually gifted.* Columbus, OH.: Merrill.

Gowan, J.C. (1968). How parents can foster creativity in their children. In W. Michael (Ed.), *Reaching for creative endeavor.* Bloomington, IN.: Indiana University Press.

Guilford, J.P. (1967). *Way beyond the IQ.* Buffalo, N.Y.: Creative Education Foundation.

Guilford, J.P. (1975). Varieties of creative giftedness, their measurement and development. *Gifted Child Quarterly, 19,* 107-121.

Gutteridge, D. (29 March 1980). Gifted children a threatened resource. *Financial Post,* 9.

Hackney, H. (1981). The gifted child, the family and the school. *Gifted Child Quarterly, 25,* 51-54.

Hall, E.G. and Skinner, N. (1980). *Somewhere to turn: Strategies for parents of gifted and talented children.* New York: Teacher's College Press.

Hallahan, D.P. and Kauffman, J.M. (1982). *Exceptional children: Introduction to special education (2nd ed.).* Englewood Cliffs, N.J.: Prentice-Hall.

Handel, R.D. (1983). Teachers of gifted girls: Are there differences in classroom management? *Journal for the Education of the Gifted, 6,* 86-97.

Haugen, L. (1981). The culturally different and gifted student with emphasis on the gifted Native. *Association of Educators of Gifted, Creative and Talented Children in* B.C., *3,* 70-74.

Hengen, T.J. (1984). Education of the gifted: The Saskatchewan scene. *Special Education in Canada, 58,* 144.

Hildreth, G.H. (1966). *Introduction to the gifted.* New York: McGraw-Hill.

Hollingsworth, L. (1942). *Children above 180 IQ, Stanford-Binet: Origin and development.* New York: World Books.

Karnes, M.B. and Strong, P.S. (1978). *Nurturing leadership talent in early childhood.* Urbana, IL.: Institute for Child Behavior and Development, University of Illinois.

Khatena, J. (1982). *Educational psychology of the gifted.* New York: Wiley.

Khoury, J.T. and Appel, M.A. (1979). Gifted children: Current trends and issues. In A. Lane (Ed.), *Readings in human growth and development of the exceptional individual.* CT.: Special Learning Corporation.

Kneedler, R.D., with D.P. Hallahan and J.M. Kauffman (1984). *Special education for today.* Englewood Cliffs, N.J.: Prentice-Hall.

Kruger, T.H. (1976). *Visual imagery in problem solving and scientific creativity.* Derby, CT.: Seal Press.

Laycock, F. (1979). *Gifted children.* Glenview, IL.: Scott, Foresman.

Lewis, L. (1984 November). President, B.C. Association for Gifted and Talented Children. Personal communication.

Lichtenstein, R. (1982). New instruments, old problems for early identification. *Exceptional Children, 49,* 170-72.

Lindsay, B. (1978). Leadership giftedness: Developing a profile. *Journal for the Education of the Gifted, 1,* 63-69.

Lyon, H. (1976). Education of the gifted and talented. *Exceptional Children, 43,* 166-168.

MacMillan, E. and Loveland, G. (1984). Counselling for the gifted. *Special Education in Canada, 58,* 125-126.

Maker, C.J. (1977). *Providing programs for the gifted handicapped.* Reston, VA.: Council for Exceptional Children.

Malone, C.E. (1975). *Kindergarten bliss: Not so — for gifted the beginning may be the end.* La Jolla, CA.: Western Behavioral Sciences Institute.

Marland, S.P., Jr. (1972). *Education of the gifted and talented: Report to the Congress of the United States by the Commissioner of Education*. Washington, D.C. U.S. Government Printing Office.

Meeker, M., Mestyanek, L., and Meeker, R. (1976). *SOI Learning Abilities Test — Examiner's manual.* El Segundo, CA.: SOI Institute.

Montagu, A. (1977). *Life before birth.* New York: Signet Books.

Mulcahy, R., Wilgosh, L., Crawford, B., and Watters, B. (1984). Gifted education for Inuit youngsters: Problems and issues. *Special Education in Canada, 58,* 127-129.

Newland, T.E. (1962). Some observations on essential qualifications of teachers of the mentally superior. *Exceptional Children, 29,* 111-114.

Newland, T.E. (1976). *The gifted in socio-cultural perspective.* Englewood Cliffs, N.J.: Prentice-Hall.

Nichols, R.C. (1965). *The inheritance of general and specific ability.* Research Report No. 1. Evanston, IL.: National Merit Scholarship Corporation.

Nolte, J. (1976). *Nearly . . . everything you've always wanted to know about the gifted and talented.* Wawatosa, WI.: Wisconsin Council for the Gifted and Talented.

O'Brien Carrelli, A. (1982). Sex equality and the gifted. *Gifted — Creative — Talented, 25,* 2-7.

Ontario, Ministry of Education. (1978). *Curriculum ideas for teachers: Gifted, talented children.* Ontario, Ministry of Education.

Ontario, Ministry of Education. (1981). *Special education handbook.* Ontario: Ministry of Education.

Parnell, T. (1976). *Disposable native.* Edmonton: Alberta Human Rights Association.

Passow, A.H. (1981). The nature of giftedness and talent. *Gifted Child Quarterly, 25,* 5-10.

Pearce, N. (1983). A comparison of the WISC-R, Raven's Standard Progressive Matrices, and Meeker's SOI Screening Form for Gifted. *Gifted Child Quarterly, 27,* 13-19.

Perks, B. (1984). Identification of gifted children. Ed.D. dissertation, University of British Columbia.

Peterson, D.C. (1977). The heterogeneously gifted family. *Gifted Child Quarterly, 21,* 396-411.

Pledgie, T.K. (1982). Giftedness among handicapped children: Identification and programming development. *The Journal of Special Education, 16,* 221-227.

Pyryt, M.C. (1979). Inner-city students' perceptions of the gifted. *Journal for the Education of the Gifted, 2,* 99-105.

Reis, S.M. and O'Shea, A.A. (1984). An innovative enrichment program: The Enrichment Triad Revolving Door Model. *Special Education in Canada, 58,* 135-138.

Renzulli, J.S. (1977). *The enrichment triad model: A guide for developing defensible programs for the gifted and talented.* Wethersfield, CT.: Creative Learning Press.

Renzulli, J.S. (1978). What makes giftedness? Re-examining a definition? *Phi Delta Kappan, 60,* 180-184, 261.

Renzulli, J.S. (1979). *What makes giftedness?* Los Angeles: National/State Leadership Training Institute on the Gifted and Talented, Brief no. 6.

Renzulli, J.S. (1980). What we don't know about programming for the gifted and talented. *Phi Delta Kappan, 61,* 601-602.

Renzulli, J.S., Hartman, R.K., and Callahan, C.M. (1975). Scale for rating the behavioral characteristics of superior students. In W.B. Barbe and J.S. Renzulli (Eds.), *Psychology and education of the gifted (2nd ed.).* New York: Irvington.

Renzulli, J.S. (1978). What makes giftedness? Re-examining a definition. *Phi Delta Kappan, 60,* 180-184, 261.

Robinson, H.B., Roedell, W.C. and Jackson, N.E. (1979). Early identification and intervention. In A.H. Passow (Ed.), *The gifted and talented: Seventy-eighth yearbook of the National Society for the Study of Education.* Chicago, IL.: University of Chicago Press.

Rodenstein, J., Pfleger, L.R., and Colangelo, N. (1977). Career development of gifted women. *Gifted Child Quarterly, 21,* 340-347.

Roedell, W.C., Jackson, N.E. and Robinson, H.B. (1980). *Gifted young children.* New York: Teachers College Press.

Ross, R. (1979). A program model for altering children's consciousness. *Gifted Child Quarterly, 23,* 109-117.

Scarr-Salapatek, S. (1975). Genetics and the development of intelligence. In F.D. Horowitz (Ed.), *Review of child development research (Vol. 4).* Chicago, IL.: University of Chicago Press.

Schwartz, L.L. (1980). Advocacy for the neglected gifted: Females. *Gifted Child Quarterly, 24,* 113-117.

Shannon, D.C. (1957). What research says about acceleration. *Phi Delta Kappan, 39,* 70-73.

Simpson, D.J. (1984). "Half a loaf can be worse than none!" *Special Education in Canada, 58,* 120-121.

Smyth, E. (1984). Educating Ontario's ablest: An overview of historic and emerging trends. *Special Education in Canada, 58,* 145-147.

Stanley, J.C. (1979). The study and facilitation of talent for mathematics. In A.H. Passow (Ed.), *The gifted and talented: Their education and development: Seventy-eighth yearbook of the National Society for the Study of Education.* Chicago: University of Chicago Press.

Tannenbaum, A.J. (1962). *Adolescent attitudes toward academic brilliance.* New York: Bureau of Publications, Teachers College, Columbia University.

Terman, L.M. (1926). *Genetic studies of genius: Mental and physical traits of a thousand gifted children (2nd ed.)*. Stanford, CA.: Stanford University Press.

Terman, L.M. and Oden, M.H. (1947). *The gifted child grows up: Genetic studies of genius (Vol. IV)*. Stanford, CA.: Stanford University Press.

Terman, L. and Oden, M. (1951). The Stanford studies of the gifted. In P. Witty (Ed.), *The gifted child*. Lexington, MA.: D.C. Heath.

Terman, L.M. and Oden, M.H. (1959). *The gifted group at mid-life*. Stanford, CA.: Stanford University Press.

Thiel, R. and Thiel, A.F. (1977). A structured analysis of family interaction patterns and the underachieving gifted child. *Gifted Child Quarterly, 21,* 267-275.

Torrance, E.P. (1960). Explorations in creative thinking. *Education, 81,* 216-220.

Torrance, E.P. (1965). *Gifted children in the classroom*. New York: MacMillan.

Torrance, E.P. (1966). *The Torrance Tests of Creative Thinking: Norms and technical manual*. Princeton, N.J.: Personnel Press.

Torrance, E.P. (1969). Creative positives of disadvantaged children and youth. *Gifted Child Quarterly, 13,* 71-81.

Torrance, E.P. and Mourad, S. (1979). Role of hemisphericity in performance on selected measures of creativity. *Gifted Child Quarterly, 13,* 44-55.

Torrance, E.P. and Reynolds, C.R. (1978). Images of the future of gifted adolescents: Effects of alienation and specialized cerebral functioning. *Gifted Child Quarterly, 22,* 40-54.

United States (1978). *Gifted and Talented Children Act: PL 95-561, section 902.*

Vernon, P.E., Adamson, G., and Vernon, D.F. (1977). *The psychology and education of gifted children*. London: Methuen.

Ward, V. (1961). *Educating the gifted: An axiomatic approach*. Columbus, OH.: Merrill.

Whitmore, J.R. (1979). The etiology of underachievement in highly gifted young children *Journal for the Education of the Gifted, 3,* 38-51.

Whitmore, J.R. (1980). *Giftedness, conflict and underachievement*. Boston: Allyn and Bacon.

Whitmore, J.R. (1981). Gifted children with handicapping conditions: A new frontier. *Exceptional Children, 48,* 106-114.

Wilgosh, L. and Mulcahy, R. (1984). Feasible enrichment programs for the gifted in remote and isolated Canadian areas. *Special Education in Canada, 58,* 130-132.

Willerman, L. and Fiedler, M.R. (1974). Infant performance and intellectual precocity. *Child Development, 45,* 483-486.

Williams, R. (1980). Creativity Assessment Packet. Buffalo, NY: D.D.K. Publishers.

Willings, D. (1983). Issues in career choice for gifted students. *Teaching Exceptional children, 15,* 226-233.

Willings, D. (1984). The gifted in the Maritime provinces. *Special Education in Canada, 58,* 148-149.

Winzer, M.A. and O'Conner, A. (1981). Eugenics: The threat of the feeble-minded. *B.C. Journal of Special Education, 6,* 217-229.

Wolf, J.S. and Stephens, T.M. (1982). Gifted and talented. In N. Haring (Ed.), *Exceptional children and youth: An introduction to special education.* Columbus, OH.: Merrill.

Yewchuk, C. (1984). Gifted education in Alberta: Current developments. *Special Education in Canada,* 58, 142-143.

Zilli, M.G. (1971). Reasons why the gifted adolescent underachieves and some of the implications of guidance and counselling to this problem. *Gifted Child Quarterly, 15,* 279-291.

3

Children with Communication Disorders

INTRODUCTION

Communication is the essence of human socialization. It is the link that provides reciprocal interaction between the individual and the milieu (Levine, 1981). Communication includes written language and speech, as well as a variety of non-verbal forms, such as gestures and facial expressions.

Language and speech are learned by exposure and experience. Human language is incredibly complex, bound by structured rules and characteristic patterns of usage that change in different settings — intrapersonal, interpersonal, group, and societal (Levine, 1981). Yet small children learn languages long before school age, and do so with vivacity and playfulness. For most children, the ready acquisition of their culture's language and speech is a natural part of early maturation.

Some children, however, meet serious problems in the acquisition and use of speech and language. Indeed, speech problems are the most common handicapping condition in elementary school-age children. Speech and language problems not only constitute a field of exceptionality by themselves, but they cut across other areas. Many children with other handicapping conditions have speech and language disorders that further slow down their educational and social development.

Many children diagnosed as learning-disabled also suffer from problems in the area of speech and language. A child who cannot recognize symbols, or associate sounds and symbols, has great difficulty learning to read. The following two chapters offer an overview of these two interconnected fields — speech and language disorders, and learning disabilities.

CHAPTER SIX

Children with speech and language problems

SALLY M. ROGOW

Ever since man first mused about his own nature, it has been the gift of language that has surprised him most.

(Lenneberg)

Human beings can lead fulfilling lives without sight, hearing, or mobility, but without a means to communicate with others, life becomes lonely and empty of meaning. Disorders of speech and language impoverish and socially isolate the lives of those who suffer them. Speech and language problems cut across other categories of exceptionality, but they also constitute a category of exceptionality by themselves.

Speech and language problems are communication disorders. Speech disorders are problems encountered in the oral production of language. Language disorders are problems in comprehension and expression of thought. Speech may be considered the motor aspect of language production. Although it is possible to possess language and lack the ability to speak, it is not possible to have speech without language (Lenneberg, 1967).

To appreciate the nature of communication disorders, it is important to understand the normal development of language and speech. Language functions as a tool of social interaction and gives form to thought and imagination. It liberates us from the here and now, enabling us to consider the past and project to the future. It forms an inherent part of most human activity, and allows human beings to communicate with one another.

Stripped to its bare essentials, language is a system of sound symbols organized into conventional patterns to communicate meanings. Yet language is so basic to human functions that it defies such simple definition.

AN OVERVIEW OF LANGUAGE

Most linguistic theories recognize three distinct aspects to the structure of language (Crystal, Fletcher, and Garman, 1976). These are phonology (phonetics or sound structure), morphology and syntax (grammar), and meaning (semantics).

Phonology

Phonology is the sound system of the language. The smallest sound units are called **phonemes**. These are combined in particular ways to form identifiable language units such as the *s* we add to make words plural.

The phonemes of language are built up into distinct patterns and sequences that form meaningful symbols of reference. Although the functional units of spoken languages are phonemes, the true units of language are the conventional groupings of phonemes into meaningful units. These units are called **morphemes**. Morphemes may be words or significant elements, such as prefixes or suffixes. Sound units that are not words by themselves are called **bound morphemes**, because they are units of meaning only when combined with words. For example, the suffix *ness* can be added to many words in English.

Phonetics is the description of the speech sounds of a language. There are only twenty-six vowels and consonants in the English alphabet, but they are pronounced in different ways. For example, *s* may be pronounced /sh/ as in *sugar*, or /z/ as in *rose*. In order to accurately describe the sounds of all languages, the International Phonetic Alphabet is used in phonetic transcriptions of oral speech.

The phonemes of a particular language are arranged in patterns of stress, rhythm, and pitch. These patterns are referred to as the **prosody** of language. The prosody of a language is the suprasegmental aspect of phonology, while the phonemes are the segmental aspects. We can often recognize the speech of non-native English-speakers by subtle differences in prosodic patterns and the pronunciation of English phonemes. In order to learn a language, we need the ability to remember the sounds we hear and to identify them at a later time (Elliott, 1981).

Grammar

Syntax is the network of organizational principles underlying linguistic expression. Without syntax, language would become an incoherent jumble of vocabulary and sound (Crystal, Fletcher, and Garman, 1976). Syntactic rules govern what we call the grammar of language.

Grammar may be defined as the sum total of conventions that govern the communication of meaning of a particular language. It comprises those procedures employed by a speaker to build up functionally satisfying symbol sequences.

Semantics

Semantics is concerned with meaning. Meaning is the essence of language and is encoded in vocabulary, syntax, and phonology. There are several aspects of semantic development. Children perceive the semantic relations that pertain to a string of words before they can grammatically encode those relations. The earliest sentences express such underlying semantic relations such as agent-action-object ("Johnny ride car"), locative ("Here ball") and possessor-possessed ("Mommy's shoe"). Meaning must be understood before it can be linguistically encoded (de Villiers and de Villiers, 1978).

Pragmatics is concerned with the ways in which we use language. From the earliest stages of language development, children use language to query, request, describe, deny, and declare. The context of their interactions often determines how they use language.

Most children quickly learn to use somewhat different vocabularies and syntax when speaking to their parents than when speaking to strangers.

Communication is the main pragmatic function of human language. However, some utterances are social rituals which function in social interactions. In Canada, for example, "How are you?" is used as a standard greeting and not an intentional question. One aspect of the study of pragmatics examines how children learn those cultural rules that determine the social appropriateness of language use.

Our society uses language to negotiate most social relations. We deal constantly with clerks in stores, bankers, waiters, and a host of other people. For us, language has become the only means of interacting with the many people we encounter. We speak with friends and relatives in a far more informal manner than we speak with strangers. In some cultures, it is considered rude to speak with strangers until one has eaten a meal with them.

Some definitions

- **Communication** is the transmission of information.
- **Communicative competence** is the ability to comprehend and encode meaning.
- **Receptive language** is the comprehension of language.
- **Expressive language** is the formulation and production of language.

SPEECH AND LANGUAGE DEVELOPMENT

Speech Development

In normal development, speech and language emerge together. Speech is the vocal/motor channel of language, which can also be expressed by signing and by writing. Although speech development is parallel to and interwoven with language, the two are not identical. Speech depends for its development on a steady growth of the physcial and physiological system that supports it.

Speech development begins with the birth cry and ends with full articulatory control. Infants begin to experiment with sounds in the early months of life. By their eighth week, they can usually produce various vowel and consonant sounds. This **babbling** is a form of vocal play. It continues until about the fifth or sixth month, when vocal play becomes more purposive.

At around six months, children begin to repeat the sounds they hear. This late stage of babbling has been called the "lalling" stage. Deaf children enter the babbling stage, but do not advance into the sound imitations characteristic of the lalling of older infants. This suggests that hearing becomes integrated with sound production at about six months of age.

The babbling stage may be considered a period of "tuning up" and establishing the necessary integrations between hearing/listening and sound production. Babbling helps to develop the musculature of the lips and the mouth necessary for the later articulation of speech sounds (Mysak, 1982). At first, children imitate sounds they make themselves. Later, they attempt to imitate adult sounds. At about nine or ten months, they begin to imitate adults consistently. During this time, they learn to produce most of the individual sounds (phonemes) and sound combinations that appear in the language they hear. Consonant sounds are more difficult than vowel sounds, because they require fine motor control of the tongue and lips.

Sounds emitted by young infants indicate that there are two distinct types of vocalizations. The first type includes all the sounds related to crying. The second type includes all the other sounds that merge into the acoustic production of speech (Lenneberg, 1967). Infants begin to produce speech sounds at about six to eight weeks.

Exhibit 6-1 shows the progression of speech sounds in early infancy.

Exhibit 6-1 Speech sounds in early infancy.

6 to 8 weeks	Brief cooing sounds. These may be associated with smiling.
10 to 13 weeks	More frequent cooing. Human face elicits cooing response. During cooing, some articulatory organs are moving.
15 to 24 weeks	Sounds become more differentiated into vocalic and consonantal components. New articulatory modulations appear.

(Adapted from Lenneberg, 1967.)

Language development

How does language develop? Does it develop independently of cognitive and social development? Or is it a part of cognition? These are the questions that psychologists, linguists, and educators have been musing over for centuries. There are still no clear-cut answers, but in recent years we have learned a great deal about how language develops.

A parallel has been drawn between the child learning a native language and the linguist studying an unfamiliar one. Both the child and the linguist need to know the sound structure of the language (the phonology), the rules that govern the ordering of words within sentences (the syntax or grammar), and the meaning of words, phrases, and sentences (semantics). However, a child learning a first language is also learning meaning (Halliday, 1975). This search for meaning may be the propelling force behind the child's effort to learn.

Language learning begins in infancy and continues throughout life. The first indication of comprehension can be seen in the six-month-old baby. At this age, the baby begins to associate certain sound patterns with people, objects, and events in the environment.

Lewis (1963) noted the following sequence in the comprehension of meaning.

- *Six months.* The child responds to intonational qualities of what is said.
- *Nine months.* The appearance of specific actions in response to specific words such as "Wave Bye Bye."
- *Twelve months.* The first utterance of meaningful words.

Comprehensive studies of early language development clearly demonstrate the importance of mothers' talk to infants (Stern, 1977). Infants acquire early language through social interaction. They express and experience early communication through a wide variety of vocal interchanges with their mothers (Stern, 1977).

To gain control over linguistic structures, children require a high degree of participatory activity. The adult role in the child's learning is one of encouragement and provision of resources for skills and information (Wells, 1981). The quality of adult-child interaction is the single most important influence on the child's language development.

The quality of adult-child interaction is the single most important influence on the child's language development.
(M.C. Emme)

Language behaviour of infants

Studies of infant behaviour reveal the strategies that very young infants employ to perceive and interpret language information. Some of these strategies appear to be inborn, while others are heavily dependent upon experience. Infants attend to speech from a very early age. Their ability to ignore recurring regularities in the environment, and to concentrate on novel experiences, may account for the interest babies display in language patterns.

The way parents speak to their babies is believed to help children to learn. By exaggerating the rise and fall of their voices, slowing down their normal speech rates, and prolonging syllables, adults direct the infant's attention to the expressive features of speech (Stern, 1977). Infants quickly learn to produce their own sounds, such as gurgles and cries. Mothers learn to discriminate happy from unhappy sounds and respond accordingly.

By the time babies are five months old, they are able to reproduce the intonation patterns or melodies of the language they hear. At about six months, their interest shifts from the contours of speech sounds to the individual segments of speech (phonemes) (Stern, 1977). There is a curious intensity about six-month-old infants who are immersed in a rehearsal of the sounds of language. They discover that, when they move their lips and tongue in a certain way, they can produce the same sound over and over again.

Stark (1979) divides the vocal productions of the first eighteen months into five stages as follows:

- Birth to eight weeks: reflexive crying, swallowing, sneezing.
- Eight to twenty weeks: cooing, laughter.
- Sixteen to thirty weeks: vocal play (including isolation of primitive segment types).
- Twenty-five to fifty weeks: reduplicated babbling (series of repeated consonant-vowel syllables).
- Nine to eighteen months: non-reduplicated babbling, expressive jargon (stress and intonation patterns imposed on babbling).

At the end of the first year, the infant's motor system for speech production has become co-ordinated with breath control and the movements of lips and tongue. The earliest associations between words and meanings are expressed in the child's first words. Long before their first words are spoken, however, infants have become capable communicators. They use gaze, arm movement, facial expression, as well as vocalization to attract and respond to adult attention.

Infant signals take on a relatively consistent form, and are produced in the expectation they will promote a consistent response (Stern, 1977). This early signal system contains all the elements out of which true language is fashioned: a sound system; the interpretation of meaning; a response; and a structure (Stern, 1977).

By the time infants have reached the end of their first year, they have assigned meaning to sounds and understand the meaning of many words. One-year-olds can follow simple directions and associate many environmental clues with speech they have heard. This is a time of rapid language learning. Children have a great many experiences with listening to language, and become adept at discerning meaning from contextual as well as voice cues.

First words

First words emerge when there is sufficient mastery of articulatory mechanisms to produce clusters of phonemes (Mysak, 1976). The child's first words mark a progression from using sounds as simple markers or indicators to more precise encoding of persons, objects, or events. Infants use single-word utterances to encode precisely those items that are of interest to them. They name those items of experience to which they have given importance (de Villiers and de Villiers, 1978).

The advent of single-word utterances represents a giant stride on the road to language acquisition. However, it is also an extension of the child's earlier signaling system. The more responsive adults have been, and the more accurately they have interpreted the child's intentions, the better the child will be able to perceive the relationships between sounds and their meanings (Stern, 1977).

Exhibit 6-2 Examples of single-word utterances used by young children.

Molly is playing with large round wooden beads. One falls to the floor and rolls under a chair.	*Gone.*
Molly sees her mother bringing her a glass of milk.	*Milk.*
Molly, seeing she will need both hands to hold the glass, puts the bead on the chair.	*Chair.*
Molly takes the bead and puts it in the box.	*Box.*

First words show a consistent use of an utterance as the label for an object, person, or action (Byrne and Shervanian, 1977). The age for first words ranges from nine to nineteen months for normal children.

The child's first single-word utterances have been called holophrastic, because a single word is used to express a more complex idea (McNeill, 1970). To interpret the child's intention, adults rely on the context in which the holophrase is uttered. The more cues the child provides, the easier it is to interpret the utterance. When a child places a book on mother's lap, opens it, and says "Book," the mother easily deduces that the child wants to be read the story (Brown, 1973).

Morphology

Between eighteen and twenty-four months of age, children begin to combine words. As children develop two- and three-word utterances, they begin to express the child's knowledge of syntax and morphology (Byrne and Shervanian, 1977). As children learn to combine phonemes to express words (morphemes), they also learn to use inflections (bound morphemes). Inflections signify plurality, possession, verb tense, subject-verb agreement, and comparative and superlative forms of adjectives.

English has one of the simplest inflectional systems. The plural is expressed by adding s, possession is indicated by a final s, and past tense is indicated by adding *ed*.

Two-and-a-half-year-olds are able to express word relationships with appropriate inflections, adding plural endings or verb suffixes. This early mastery of morphological forms follows a logical order — the simplest and most obvious principles are learned before the more complex (Brown, 1973).

When young children first begin to combine words, they are concerned with word order. In English, word-order rules seem to be the first rules acquired (de Villiers and de Villiers, 1978). For example, the child may group the following words:

- Me fall.
- Bump table.
- Cup in box.
- No more milk.

By two-and-a-half years, children begin to use function words such as *in* and *on*, and the articles *a*, *an*, and *the*.

Brown (1973) studied three children, Adam, Eve, and Sarah, and recorded their emerging speech in their homes over a period of months. As he observed the growing length of the children's utterances, he concluded that the number of morphemes and inflections reflected stages of development. As a result of this discovery, Brown established stages of development based on mean length of utterances (MLU) of morphemes and bound morphemes in an utterance. He assigned each root (word) and each inflection one point. For example, the phrase *Daddy's hat* has a value of three (MLU). There is one point for *Daddy*, one point for the possessive *s*, and one point for *hat*.

Exhibit 6-3 shows the Mean Length of Utterance MLU for Brown's Five Stages of Language Development.

Exhibit 6-3 Stages of language development.

Stage	MLU	*Number of Bound Morphemes*
I	1.75	5
II	2.25	7
III	2.75	9
IV	3.50	11
V	4.00	13

(Adapted from Brown, 1973.)

Meaning

Children move quickly through the early stages, gathering linguistic information about words and how to use them. They seem to draw causal links by several means, using social, physical, and even whimsical associations. To be sure, children imitate the speech of adults around them and try to learn the language they actually hear. But in so doing, they sometimes reach beyond the borders of word meaning and overextend their word usage. An example of overextension is the little boy who calls every animal a *doggie*.

Syntax

As children expand their vocabulary and increase their need for productive communication, they begin to use words in sequence. Children's early phrases are the precursors of sentences. Their first utterances may be incomplete or incorrect, but their listeners know what they mean.

Children show a wide range of variation in the number of pre-sentences they use. Some children use only a few, and others as many as a thousand (Byrne and Shervanian, 1977).

The sentence is a key landmark in language acquisition. By three years of age, most children demonstrate the construction of simple affirmative-declarative sentences. They put together a noun-phrase for a subject and a verb-phrase for a predicate (Elliott, 1981). These basic relationships can be seen in the following examples from the conversation of a three year old:

- That is my ball.
- That big ball is heavy.
- She want her supper.
- I put book here.
- It broked up.

The basic units of the sentence consist of the subject and the predicate. These units are expanded in several ways. Modifiers (adjectives) are used for the subject, and objects are included in the predicate.

The early stages of language development establish the foundation for the later acquisition of more complex linguistic structures, such as the use of embedded or subordinate clauses. Clauses begin to be used by some children at four to four-and-a-half years of age. The following are some examples of the sentences of four-year-olds:

- That's the one that's broke.
- Every time he called me, I had to drop my toys right there.
- I don't want that one 'cause it's too little.

Another indicator of syntactic expansion is the use of conjunctions in the noun phrase and between main clauses:

- Mary and Alice play together.
- I got one blue one and one green one.
- I go home and eat my supper.

As syntax develops, the child learns how to change word order or add to and replace words to express more complex grammatic relationships. These changes are called transformations. Exhibit 6-4 shows the transformations that appear early in the speech of children.

Exhibit 6-4 Transformations that appear in early speech.

Transformation	Example
negation	I no drink it.
question	Who has it?
contraction	That's mine.
verb auxiliary — got	He's got mine.
verb auxiliary — is	The cat is drinking the milk.
verb auxiliary — do	I do want it.
infinitive complement	He wants to eat.

Sentence types

Sentences may be declarative, interrogative, or imperative. The declarative sentence is a statement, the interrogative a question, and the imperative a command. Each type of sentence is prosodically marked by the way the voice rises and falls when it is intoned. It is also marked by special words and the order of the words within the sentence. The question is a transformation of the declarative statement, because it inverts the word order. For example, "John is a big boy" becomes "Is John a big boy?"

As children learn to express questions, a definite sequence of acquisition can be observed. In the first stage, the question is expressed by a slight rising of the voice. The second stage involves the use of an interrogative word, such as who, what, where, which, and why. These words are placed in front of a word, phrase, or complete sentence, resulting in such questions as "Who that?" "What this?" and "Why you cry?" (Byrne and Shervanian, 1977). The third stage involves the principle of inversion. The child places the verb before the subject of the sentence to ask "Is Daddy home?" and "Does it belong here?" Tag questions, such as "You have one, don't you?" appear a little later (de Villiers and de Villiers, 1978.)

As syntax becomes more complex, many transformations can be used within the same utterance. Every language has its own system of rules for word combinations and transformations. Many languages are highly inflected and depend less on transformation of word order to express specific meanings. In both English and French, however, word order rules are especially important.

Vocabulary

The linguistic environment makes vocabulary available to the child. This environment may provide rich and varied language experience, or it may be severely limited. Whatever the environment, however, children seem to be able to rapidly assimilate the vocabulary they hear. It seems to take very little language to activate language-learning in normally hearing children.

Conversation

The simple utterances of two-year-olds refer to objects and events within their immediate personal experience. Before long, however, children begin to refer to absent objects and past events (de Villiers and de Villiers, 1978). Increasingly, children grow aware of their listeners' needs for information. Soon children are able to communicate with people outside their immediate families. By the time they are six, they can not only talk better, but they have become aware of how language is used (de Villiers and de Villiers, 1978).

Some aspects of discourse, such as learning to take turns in dialogue, are independent of language content. To become a conversationalist, the child must also become aware of signals that indicate mutual reference, such as word repetition and question intonation. In the following dialogue, the contingent query is used as a device for clarification.

- Mother: "We're having beans for supper."
- Child: "Baked beans?"
- Mother: "Baked beans made just the way you like them."

Garvey (1975) studied pairs of children between two and four years of age. She kept a tally of the appropriateness of their responses to queries from peers. The children successfully answered most queries with specific information, repeating whole utterances on request. Only the youngest group was comparatively inattentive.

Six-year-old children can recognize the ambiguity of language, and begin to take delight in jokes and riddles that rely on ambiguity (de Villiers and de Villiers, 1978). Six-year-olds can appreciate both direct and indirect meanings, and can laugh at a joke such as this one:

"Can you tell me the time?"
"Yes, I can."

Characteristics of language acquisition.

Some general characteristics mark a child's progress in learning language:

- Language learning is both cumulative and hierarchical (Byrne and Shervanian, 1977).
- The child uses a minimal number of linguistic features at first. First words are short and may have multiple meanings that depend on context for interpretation. Among the first features demonstrated is order in the use of phonemes and words within utterances and sentences.
- The child learns all aspects of language simultaneously. There is gradual mastery of phonology, morphology, syntax, and semantics. The semantic component continues to develop throughout the child's life.

Between eighteen months and three-and-a-half years, language growth is rapid. Language acquisition overlaps and relies upon social and cognitive growth. These aspects of development are closely intertwined, and really cannot be considered separately. A linguistic environment, an intact cognitive/perceptual system, and normal social interaction all underlie the development of language. If the child does not hear language, or has some impairment of the cognitive/perceptual mechanism, or has a troubled family background, the child's development of language will reflect these problems.

Language must be understood to be produced. There is still controversy among language scientists about whether comprehension precedes, or grows along with, the use of language (Byrne and Shervanian, 1977).

SPEECH AND LANGUAGE PROBLEMS OF CHILDREN WITH OTHER EXCEPTIONALITIES

Language and speech problems may both cause and result from delayed development. Even when mental retardation causes delayed speech and language, the length of delay contributes in turn to the severity of the mental handicap. Language and speech problems cut across most categories of exceptionality. They also affect, and are affected by, the child's social, emotional, and cognitive development.

Exhibit 6-5 outlines some of the signs by which children reveal language problems.

Exhibit 6-5 Signs of speech and language problems.

- History of early language delay.
- Child performs better on visual matching tasks, drawings, and blockbuilding than on language tasks.
- Immature speech patterns.
- Frequent grammatical errors.
- Difficulty in comprehending or following oral directions.
- Difficulty in communicating descriptive information.
- Word finding and language recall problems.

Language difficulties may be experienced by children who have no organic, sensory, or psychological problems. Children who grow up in an environment where the language they hear is distinctly different from standard English or French may experience learning problems in school. These children benefit from well-planned language programs as part of the curriculum.

Few language and speech problems exist independently of emotional, social, and cognitive aspects of development. In addition, language and speech problems are frequently associated with other categories of exceptionality.

Cultural and social deprivation

As we have stressed in this chapter, the child does not learn to speak in isolation from other people. Language acquisition takes place in the context of rich interaction between child and parent. Severe language deficits can result from social isolation. In these situations, it is not easy to tease out the language problem from the child's severe emotional and social deprivation.

Impoverished language

Children in large institutions do not enjoy the rich and varied adult encounters experienced by children in family settings. Studies of children in institutions indicate that these children speak less frequently and use fewer words and simpler language structures than their peers (Curtiss, 1977).

Genie offers an example of the severe effects of social and emotional deprivation on language and speech development. When she was thirteen and a half, in November 1970, she was discovered by the California authorities. Weighing a mere sixty pounds, Genie could not chew solid food and was unable to stand erect. From the age of twenty months, she had been confined to a small, contained room, strapped in an infant's crib, or tied to a potty chair. Her father believed her to be hopelessly retarded, and beat her if she made any noise. Genie's mother could only visit her a few minutes each day to feed her. There was no radio or television in the house.

When tested at the hospital, Genie was found to have normal hearing, vision, and eye-hand co-ordination, but she was mute and could only understand a few simple commands. She appeared to have no comprehension of grammar. Genie was placed with a foster family, who treated her much like a normal child. She began to develop speech, following a normal course of language development, but with marked differences.

After seven years of language acquisition, Genie continued to have articulation problems. Her intellectual development was in advance of her language development.

Genie's story suggests that there are critical periods in the acquisition of language and speech. The evidence for critical periods in first-language acquisition is "maddeningly indirect" (de Villiers and de Villiers, 1978). This is because such evidence must be derived from cases of children raised in isolation. Fortunately, this rarely happens.

There are several accounts in the literature of "wolf-children" who grew up in the wild, isolated from human society. Unfortunately, in every case, it has been impossible to determine whether the child was normal before being found. The most famous of these accounts is the story of Victor and his brilliant teacher, Jean Marc Gaspard Itard. Itard tried to teach Victor to speak, but Victor only learned to say a few words. However, Victor did learn to read simple words (Lane, 1976).

The case of Genie stimulated widespread interest among language scientists and neurologists. They hoped that a careful study of Genie's emerging language would reveal whether a critical period exists in language acquisition. Shortly after her rescue, Genie was tested with a series of language comprehension tests. Although she had begun to imitate words and learn names, her comprehension of grammar appeared grossly impaired (de Villiers and de Villiers, 1978).

Genie exhibited many variations from normal language acquisition. For instance, she used two hundred words before she began making two-word combinations. She did not ask questions spontaneously, and she demonstrated inconsistencies in word order. After many years of working with her, language therapists concluded that failure to acquire language during the normal period (two to five years) makes "development laborious and incomplete, but the similarities between it and normal acquisition outweigh the differences" (de Villiers and de Villiers, 1978, p. 219).

Slowness of maturation, then, does seem to constrain the rate and pattern of vocal development. Such constraints may shed some light on the language and speech development of mentally handicapped children.

Mentally retarded children

General language delay commensurate with intellectual delay is expected among a mentally handicapped population. However, the extent to which hearing loss, retarded motor development, and specific disabilities contribute to language delay is not known. Language development reflects the social and interpersonal relationships of the handicapped child, as well as underlying physical and neurological conditions.

Some mentally handicapped children perform better in other areas of cognitive development than they do on language tests. This discrepancy in performance suggests that mental handicaps may place constraints on language acquisition that do not apply to other areas of cognition. Mentally handicapped children may also hear less language than other children (Kleffner, 1973). Adults tend to speak less to non-verbal or low-verbal children. This is unfortunate, as it is important for parents of mentally handicapped children to maintain a high level of verbal stimulation, even when the child does not appear attentive to language.

Studies of the speech and language of the mentally handicapped indicate that:

- Language is acquired more slowly than by other children.
- Some retarded children have difficulty generalizing the rules of grammar.
- Deficits in certain cognitive abilities, such as short-term memory, may explain the lag in comprehension and production.
- Expressive language tends to be less complex. (Cromer, 1974).

PROFILE 6-1

Arty is eight years old. He had Down's syndrome and did not begin to speak until he was four. Arty's mother felt he could comprehend simple instructions long before he could speak. A larger than normal tongue, characteristic of Down's syndrome, interfered with his efforts to articulate.

At eight years, Arty's speech is similar to that of a much younger child. Here are a few sample utterances.

- "Dook, dook — I see a budderfy (butterfly)."
- "I eat supper — but don't want eat "teak" (steak)."
- "My kite "poken" (broken)."

These examples illustrate Arty's difficulty with sound blends. He tends to omit articles, pronouns, auxiliary verbs, and adjectives. The more words in an utterance, the more ungrammatic Arty's speech becomes.

Intervention programs for mentally handicapped children should stress language input from adults (Kleffner, 1973). Mentally retarded children such as Arty can and do benefit from speech therapy.

Children with cerebral palsy

The speech and language problems of children with cerebral palsy reflect the complexity of the condition. One child may be unable to speak at all, while another may be able to speak perfectly. Estimates vary of the percentage of children with cerebral palsy who also have speech and language problems (Mysak, 1982).

Disorders of posture, listening, breathing, voice, articulation and language are all found in association with cerebral palsy. Damage to the central nervous system can impair those centres in the brain involved with the regulation of breathing. Reported breathing problems among different types of cerebral palsy range from forty to eighty percent (Mysak, 1981). These problems may impair the ability to shift from vegetative to speech breathing. Vegetative breathing is regulated by the autonomic nervous system, while speech breathing is a higher and more complex function.

Children with cerebral palsy may also have weak thoracic and abdominal muscles, or airstream obstruction due to irregular movements of the vocal folds (Mysak, 1981). Motor dysfunctions which affect the organs of speech may make intelligible speech impossible. Alternate methods of communication are required for such children to communicate and develop language skills (Mysak, 1982).

Many children with cerebral palsy can acquire language in the absence of speech. Lenneberg (1967) reported a case of a nine-year-old boy who had never babbled nor spoken. Nonetheless, he could match pictures to words and sentences, indicating a comprehension of language. This child had a relatively rare condition known as cogenital dysarthria. This extreme dissociation between perceptive and productive ability proves that knowing a language is not the same as speaking it (Lenneberg, 1967).

The speech characteristics of children with spastic forms of cerebral palsy may include:

- Articulatory deficits;
- Laboured speech with distortion of sound.
- Uncontrolled pitch changes.
- Husky voice quality.

Deaf children

Profoundly deaf infants begin to babble at about the same age as hearing children. However, deaf children stop babbling and experience difficulty in learning to talk. Bellugi and Klima (1972) studied deaf children as they learned sign language. The children learned to sign simple constructions before more complex ones, and constructed holophrases and two-and three-word phrases before making more complex statements. This pattern mirrors that of normal language acquisition.

Some educators of the deaf argue that, with sign language, deaf people are not handicapped in the acquisition of language. Severe language disorders can be prevented by intervention techniques, based on Total Communication, the use of auditory stimulation and verbal language, speech reading, and a school-based manual system. In Chapter Eight, the language problems of deaf children are discussed in greater detail.

Blind children

As noted in Chapter Nine, the speech and language difficulties of blind children are more closely related to social and emotional factors than to blindness itself. Blindness need not lead to deficits in language learning.

The assumption that blind children experience problems of sensory reference has little basis in truth (Landau, 1983). Studies of the language of blind children "force us to modify the radical empiricist view of concept and word learning" (Landau, 1983, p. 75). Although the blind child's knowledge is gained through experience, "relevant experience is far more complex than a direct reflex of the sensorium" (Landau, 1983). Blind children who have been encouraged to explore their environments and interact with other people do not suffer delays in language acquisition. However, blind children with additional disabilities are at risk for language delays and disorders.

Emotionally disturbed children

Severe disorders of emotional development produce unusual patterns of speech and language. Autistic and psychotic children often exhibit prolonged **echolalia** or repetition of other people's words and phrases, sometimes called "parrot speech." Other children achieve complete mastery of language, but fail to use their language to communicate with others. They may conduct long monologues with themselves and yet be unable to converse with another person.

Neologisms is the term given to "made-up" words and phrases constructed by the severely disturbed child. This non-communicating style of speech often serves to isolate the child even more in a private world (Lenneberg, 1967). Psychiatric disorders may also be concomitant with mental retardation and neurological dysfunction. These problems may further delay acquisition of language.

Neurological dysfunction

Neurological dysfunction underlies the most severe types of speech and language disorder. **Childhood aphasia** is the term used to describe disorders affecting both receptive and expressive language processes. Aphasic-like disorders may appear in children suffering from severe emotional disturbance, mental handicaps, impaired hearing, cerebral palsy, or seizure disorders. Childhood aphasia will be discussed in greater detail later in this chapter.

Children with learning disabilities

Children with learning disabilities demonstrate wide variation in language acquisition. Some have normal receptive and expressive language, while others show specific oral-language problems (Byrne and Shervanian, 1977). In general, the ability of learning-disabled children to process and comprehend complex sentences is significantly lower than other children of the same age and intelligence (Wiig and Semel, 1973).

Wiig, Semel, and Abele evaluated the ability of learning-disabled twelve-year-olds to resolve sentences that had two meanings. The learning-disabled students peformed significantly more poorly than did their academically achieving age-peers. Their performance compared to that of much younger children (Wiig, 1982).

Learning-disabled children may also have difficulties with sentence repetitions. This is especially true when the model sentences contain more complex syntactic structures, such as subordinate clauses (Wiig, 1982). For example, a learning-disabled child was asked to repeat the model stimulus sentence: "The robber that the police caught escaped easily." The child replied, "The robber escaped easily."

Children with learning disabilities may display striking lags in knowledge and use of vocabulary. Some children have problems interpreting and remembering terms for space and time relationships (Wiig, 1981). Verb forms, adverbs and prepositions are often omitted or misused. Failure to master complex linguistic rules may underlie reading problems.

Learning to read can be viewed as the process of learning to superimpose an already known spoken-language code on a new, secondary visual symbol code. Children can only acquire proficiency in reading when they have developed a knowledge of language. They must bring all their experience with language to bear on the process of reading (Goodman, 1969).

SPEECH DISORDERS

The anatomical structures involved in the comprehension and production of language include the nervous system, the respiratory system, the oral portion of the digestive tract, and the auditory sense receptors. These structures are all involved in biological adaptation through breathing, sucking, chewing, swallowing, and alertness to danger signals (Byrne and Shervanian, 1977). Speech and language production also requires the use of organs that are involved in other functions such as eating, breathing and crying. For example, in addition to voice production, the larynx functions in crying, in keeping foreign objects out of the lungs, in coughing, and as a regulator of the exchange of oxygen and carbon dioxide in breathing (Leonard, 1982).

The speech mechanism

The physical structures involved in the production of speech function in a highly organized and integrated fashion. Each part is synchronized with other parts to produce a meaningful sequence of accurate speech sounds, maintaining proper levels of loudness, pitch, and a pleasing voice quality (Byrne and Shervanian, 1977).

Speech is produced in an airstream that is shaped and resonated by the lips, tongue, teeth, jaw, nasal cavity, larynx, and pharynx. Figure 6-1 shows the organs and musculature of speech.

Respiration, phonation, resonance, and articulation are the main components of the speech process:

- *Respiration.* Speech breathing is characterized by a shift from a nasal inflow-outflow pattern to an oral inflow-outflow pattern (Mysak, 1982).

- *Phonation and resonance.* The larynx produces sound, and the pharynx modifies it. The pharynx changes its size, shape, and tension, and combines with the nose or mouth to form the resonating chambers for speech. As the larynx and resonating cavities

Figure 6-1 The sound-producing mechanism in humans.

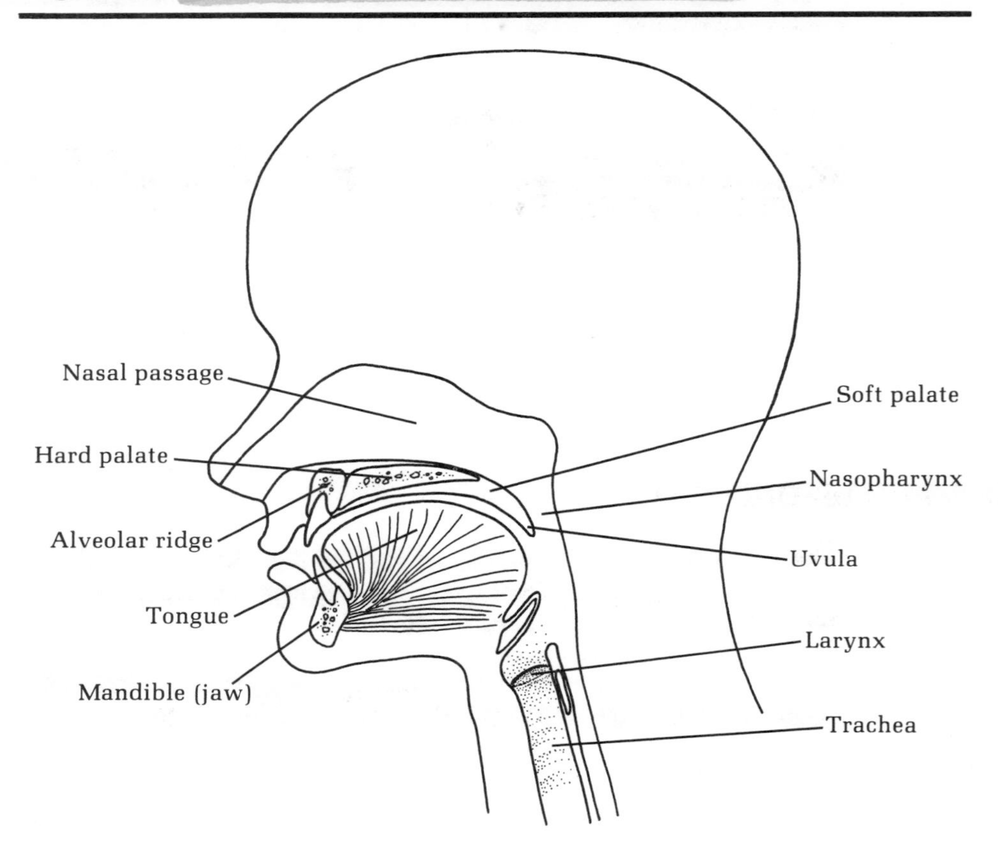

develop, the voice becomes louder, the pitch becomes lower, and the vocal tones increase in variety and range of inflectional patterns (Mysak, 1982).

- *Articulation.* The lips, tongue, teeth, mouth, and jaw articulate the sounds of speech. For example, /t/ and /d/ are produced by placing the tongue behind the teeth. In contrast, /p/ and /b/ are formed by closing the lips and then opening them to allow the air to escape. The only difference between /t/ and /d/ or /p/ and /b/ is that /d/ and /b/ are voiced, while /t/ and /p/ are voiceless.

Simply stated, the physiological process of speech involves three stages: vocalization (the ability to produce sound); articulation (the ability to form specific sounds); and modulation (the ability to control the loudness of the sounds produced (Byrne and Shervanian, 1977).

Children with a **speech defect** are those whose speech interferes with communication (Van Riper, 1978). Young children make many speech errors when learning how to talk. Mispronunciations and dysfluencies are common, but these errors are part of the developmental process. They only become disorders when they persist as characteristics in the speech of older children.

Classification of speech disorders

Speech disorders are defined as deficits in articulation, in voice quality, or as dysfluency of speech.

Articulatory disorders

Articulatory disorders are characterized by omissions, substitutions, distortions, and additions of speech sounds. By age seven, children should be able to produce all the speech sounds: vowels, consonants, dipthongs, and blends.

Omissions of speech sounds occur most frequently with blended sounds, such as /bl/, /pl/, /pr/, or /tr/. Omission errors refer to the leaving out of sounds in words, such as by substituting *pay* for *play*.

Substitutions of speech sounds occur when one consonant is replaced by another, such as *twick* for *trick*. Some children may substitute sounds in some words and not in others. A child may be able to say the word *yes* correctly, but substitute /l/ for /y/ in the word *yellow*.

Distortions involve deviation from normal speech sounds. For example, a lisp affects sibilant sounds such as /s/ and /z/. In a frontal lisp, a voiced or unvoiced /th/ may be substituted for /s/ and /z/ sounds. Distorted sounds are often caused by placing the tongue or lips in the wrong position for the production of a particular sound.

Addition of sounds refers to the adding of a sound to a word. The extra sound is usually added between blended sounds such as *terain* for *train*. Omissions, substitutions, distortions, and additions of speech sounds may occur in the initial, medial, or final position in a word. Articulation disorders may indicate that a child has not learned how to produce certain sounds correctly. Children who do not articulate some consonants may also not be able to discriminate those consonants (Winitz, 1975).

To treat articulation disorders, therapists teach children to listen, recognize, and discriminate consonant sounds, to produce articulated speech sounds, and to retain the memory of speech sounds (Winitz, 1975). Speech therapy must enable the child to produce accurate speech sounds outside the clinical environment.

Voice disorders

A voice that lacks power, is unpleasant, or abuses the vocal mechanism is likely to be considered defective (Perkins, 1978). Disorders of the voice include deviations of pitch, quality, and intensity. Disorders are characterized by hypernasality, breathiness, hoarseness, or huskiness. The child who "talks through the nose" has hypernasal speech. This may result from a cleft palate, or from partial paralysis of the soft palate, rendering the necessary closure of the nasal passage impossible.

In children, most voice disorders are functional, and are related to poor learning of voice control. Children who scream and talk loudly are in danger of abusing their vocal cords (Perkins, 1978).

The most common deviations in pitch seen by speech-language clinicians are levels that are too high or low, and levels that are monotonous with little variation of pitch (Moore, 1982). Children who do not speak loudly enough for their needs may suffer from hearing loss, an organic problem or reticence about speaking. Some children do not know how to use a "big" voice without abusing the vocal mechanism (Moore, 1982).

Major emphases in voice therapy include listening training, articulatory adjustment and breath control training. Breath control includes training to relax and reduce laryngeal tension, as well as other specialized techniques (Van Osdol and Shane, 1982).

Dysfluency

Stuttering Fluency is the smoothness with which sounds, syllables, words, and phrases flow together (Perkins, 1978). The most common dysfluency is **stuttering**, characterized by blocking, repetition, or prolongation of sounds, words, phrases, or syllables. The rate and rhythm of speech is affected, and facial tension or other types of body distortion may also appear (Van Osdol and Shane, 1982).

Wendell Johnson considered stuttering to be an anticipatory, apprehensive, and hypertonic avoidance reaction. In other words, stutterers are painfully aware of their stuttering, and become tense while speaking in dreaded anticipation of mistakes. Stuttering remains a baffling disturbance (Van Riper, 1978).

Stuttering is found among all ethnic and socioeconomic groups in Canada. It is the major subcategory of fluency disorder, and affects approximately one percent of the population (Shames and Florance, 1982). Two to ten times more males than females stutter.

The longer people stutter, the more likely they are to have associated emotional problems (Shames and Florance, 1981). Young stutterers become painfully aware of listeners' reactions, and often feel embarrassed, guilty, frustrated, and angry. They may feel helpless, lose confidence, and become confused. Many stutterers respond to their problem with aggression or by denying that they have a problem (Shames and Florance, 1981). Other may avoid situations where talking is expected. If stuttering continues unchecked, serious social and educational problems may result.

Stutterers often present a wide variety of secondary symptoms such as eye blinking, head jerking, or facial grimaces. Many demonstrate muscular tension and forcing when they try to speak. Stuttering problems should not be categorized as mild, moderate or severe based on overt behaviour alone (Shames and Florance, 1982).

The many studies of the symptoms and treatment of stuttering have not revealed all possible underlying causes. Fortunately, however, effective methods of therapy have been developed to treat the problem (Shames and Florance, 1982).

Cluttering Cluttered speech is sometimes confused with stuttering. Cluttering involves excessive speed of speech combined with disorganized sentence structure and articulation problems. Cluttered speech lacks appropriate phrasing or grouping of words within an utterance, and is difficult to understand.

Dysarthria Dysarthria refers to a partial or complete paralysis of the muscles associated with speech. When paralysis is complete, speech is impossible (Lenneberg, 1967). The term also refers to a group of related speech disorders resulting from disturbed muscular control over the speech mechanism (La Pointe, 1982).

Dysarthria is caused by a fundamental disturbance of movement or motoric function brought about by damage to the nervous system. Children with cerebral palsy often suffer from dysarthria. The motor impairment that affects their lips, tongue, jaw, and soft palate hinders the intelligibility of their speech (La Pointe, 1982).

When a child with dysarthria tries to talk, consonant sounds are distorted and efforts at speech may not be successful. Indeed, the harder the child tries to speak, the more difficult speech becomes.

Summary

Exhibit 6-6 outlines a summary of common speech disorders.

Exhibit 6-6 Summary of speech disorders.

Articulatory Disorders

- Substitutions — such errors as /w/ for /r/
- omissions — only parts of words are pronounced.
- distortions — words are mispronounced.
- sequencing — sounds or syllables are in the wrong order.

Voice Disorders

- pitch — too high, too low, or monotone
- loudness — too loud or too soft
- quality — nasal or hoarse
- speech flow — too slow or too fast
  — disturbed rhythm
  — Dysfluency, including cluttered speech, and stuttering, dysarthria.

Prevalence of speech disorders

Reliable figures of the prevalence of speech disorders among children are difficult to estimate. Criteria and definitions of communication disorders vary. The best estimates claim that five percent of the population between five and twenty-one have a speech disorder (Shames and Wiig, 1982). This figure does not include those with hearing handicaps, or language disorders that do not affect speech.

Speech disorders are the most prevalent childhood disorder (Byrne and Shervanian, 1977). A study published by the American Speech and Hearing Association (Shames and Wiig, 1982) suggested that speech disorders are broken down as follows:

■ articulation disorders	80%
■ stuttering	7%
■ voice disorders	2%
■ language disorders	3-5%
■ other	5-6%

Etiology of speech disorders

Structural inadequacies are a major cause of speech disorders in children. These may be structural inadequacies in the vocal folds (larynx), tongue, lips, teeth, palate, and resonating cavities. Most defects of this type are of a developmental nature, although they can result from physical injury and disease.

A second cause of speech disorder is damage or maldevelopment of the central and/or peripheral nervous system. Inadequacy of the hearing mechanism, causing hearing impairment, is the third major cause of speech disorders.

Cleft Palate

A cleft palate may involve both the lip and palate, or only the lip. A cleft may be unilateral or bilateral. If unilateral, the palate fuses to the vertical partition in the midline of the nose on only one side. A bilateral cleft fails to fuse to the nasal partition on both sides (Perkins, 1978). A complete cleft extends from the lip through to the hard and soft palate. An incomplete cleft may be limited to just the lip, the alvealor process, the hard palate, the soft palate, or a combination of these (Perkins, 1978).

Slow language development and delayed articulation are not uncommon in children with clefts. Those sounds that require the most pressure to produce, such as plosives, fricatives, and voiceless consonants, are the ones most often misarticulated. In addition, there may be malocclusion of the teeth in children with cleft palates.

Orthodontia and speech therapy play an important part in the treatment of children with cleft palates. In some cases, the condition can be surgically corrected. When other facial-skeletal anomalies accompany the cleft palate, prostheses designed to facilitate speech can be of great assistance.

Diagnosis and assessment of speech disorders

Assessment of articulatory, voice, and fluency disorders may be done by a speech/language clinician in the school or in a clinic setting. For children with relatively mild speech problems, and who function well at home and school, assessment may focus on speech alone (Byrne and Shervanian, 1977).

Children under age four are usually tested in their ability to echo or imitate the clinician's model. Children over four are usually asked to name either objects or pictures. Older children may be asked to read words or sentences or to describe objects (Byrne and Shervanian, 1977).

During the assessment, the clinician may test the child's production of phonemes in isolation, and in the initial, medial and final positions in words. The clinician also tries to determine whether there is a consistency in the child's error pattern.

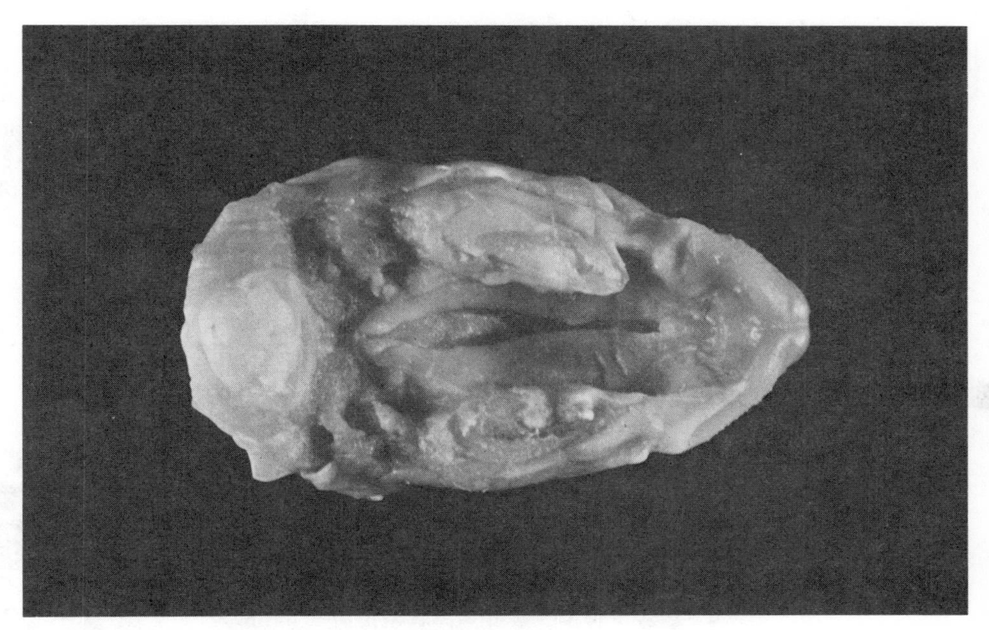

Photograph of a cleft palate in a hamster fetus.
(R.M. Shah)

PROFILE 6-2

Bennie is seven and a half, and has normal hearing. When he is nervous or in a hurry, his speech becomes difficult to understand. His speech is easier to understand when his sentences or replies are short.

The clinician asked Bennie to name the objects in a series of pictures. Bennie correctly produced all the phonemes in initial, medial, and final word positions up to approximately a five-year developmental level. He produced substitutions and distortions of certain sounds, such as /ts/, /s/, and /z/, in all positions. He could not correctly pronounce /th/, and usually substituted an /f/ sound. He also had problems with /r/ sounds, and sometimes substituted /w/ for /l/.

Bennie's clinician was not able to detect a clear /s/ in his conversational speech. The clinician tested Bennie more thoroughly for the sounds that were consistently missing or mispronounced. She used the Peabody Picture Vocabulary Test, the Illinois Test of Psycholinguistic Abilities, and an Articulation Test of Single Phonemes. She did not find any deviations in Benny's speech mechanism.

Bennie is the baby of the family, the youngest of four children. His parents both work and are away from home. Bennie knows he does not speak clearly. He has told the clinician that he tries hard, but he is bashful about speaking because the children at school make fun of him.

Bennie does not have enough chances to talk at home, and his self-consciousness at school further deprives him of necessary practice. Bennie's speech clinician and teacher have decided he needs individualized speech training. They have arranged an hour of speech therapy for him every day at school. Fortunately, Bennie's school has a full-time speech therapist to work with children with speech and language problems.

Benny's problems are caused by a combination of immaturity, lack of opportunities to practice speaking, and self-consciousness. His clinician has found that he consistently mispronounces the sounds /s/, /th/, /l/, and blended sounds such as /tr/, /pr/,/cl/. Now she must determine whether he fails to perceive those sounds, or simply mispronounces them. Then she can teach Bennie how to correctly produce misarticulated sounds and give him a great deal of speaking practice.

LANGUAGE DISORDERS

Language disorders are problems in the recognition and understanding of spoken language or in the ability to formulate well-organized grammatic sentences. Language disorders may be classified as receptive or expressive. **Receptive disorders** are those which interfere with the comprehension of spoken language. **Expressive disorders** are those which affect the formulation of grammatic utterances (Byrne and Shervanian, 1977). Language disorders in children frequently combine both receptive and expressive problems. They range in severity from mild language-learning difficulties to profoundly debilitating disorders.

In Canada, many terms are currently used to describe language disorders. These include *aphasia, dysphasia, communicatively impaired,* and *language-learning disabled.* Some Canadian clinicians prefer the terms *aphasia* or *dysphasia* because they suggest fairly specific conditions. Others prefer to use the general term language-disabled. In this chapter, we will use the term *aphasia* to refer to children whose primary impairment is an inability to communicate effectively with language (Byrne and Shervanian, 1977).

Language and speech are not synonymous terms. Language refers to the entire process of communication through symbolic codes, whether oral, pictorial, written, or signed. Speech is the motor aspect of language production. It is possible to have language without speech, but no-one can speak without knowing language.

Language disorders have long been recognized in children. However, not until the recent emergence of psycholinguistics were methods developed to study child language. Armed with new knowledge about how children acquire language, today's language clinicians and educators are developing new forms of treatment for children with language disorders (Leonard, 1981).

Classification of language disorders

The classification of language disorders often overlaps with other categories of exceptionality. However, some children with language difficulties have no identifiable physical, mental or sensory handicap. As stated earlier, **aphasia** and **dysphasia** can be used interchangeably to describe conditions in which a child's primary impairment is the inability to communicate effectively with verbal language (Byrne and Shervanian, 1977).

Aphasia

Aphasia in children may be developmental or acquired. Children with **developmental aphasia** have not fully acquired language. **Acquired aphasia** refers to conditions (trauma) that occurred after language had been developed (Byrne and Shervanian, 1977).

Receptive aphasia is usually accompanied by some expressive difficulty. Children with receptive aphasia may appear to talk in a free-flowing manner, but their words are incomprehensible. Children with severe global aphasia may also experience a variety of other perceptual problems, even though they have normal physical sight and hearing (Byrne and Shervanian, 1977; Mysak, 1976).

Children with expressive aphasia have difficulty formulating language. They may have trouble remembering words, or they may block on a word and hesitate often when speaking (Byrne and Shervanian, 1977).

Children with developmental aphasia or dysphasia, have been unable to develop adequate language. These children have shown severe delay in the development of receptive or expressive language, and do not suffer from any apparent additional handicapping conditions (Eisenson and Ingram, 1972). Children with severe communication problems may withdraw from social interaction, rendering diagnosis difficult. They may also show near-normal performance on non-verbal intelligence tests (Eisenson and Ingram, 1972).

Recent research has confirmed that dysphasic children have problems with rapid sound changes. This difficulty impairs their ability to identify and discriminate consonants (de Villiers and de Villiers, 1976). When the speech they hear is spoken at a slowed rate, their ability to comprehend is improved (Mysak, 1976). Menyuk (1971) has suggested that short-term memory deficit may account for the dysphasic child's language impairment.

Aphasia in children affects all aspects of language behaviour. It hinders comprehension and formulation of grammatic utterances, word usage, and the expression of meaning (Byrne and Shervanian, 1977). It is sometimes difficult to determine whether depressed cognitive functioning is the consequence or the cause of linguistic deficiency in dysphasic children.

Acquired aphasia

Acquired aphasia is a loss in linguistic ability that usually results from brain damage arising from serious illness or trauma to the head (Wiig and Shames, 1981). Lenneberg (1967) noted that if damage is confined to a single hemisphere of the brain and occurs before age nine, the child may be able to regain lost abilities and continue to develop normally. This means that age of onset is a critical factor in the child's progress.

Children who sustain injuries before the age of three may become temporarily mute and show a general inability to respond to the speech of others. However, very young children often make rapid improvement. They seem to relearn language in the same sequence as children acquiring language for the first time.

In children over three years, symptoms of aphasia are usually different. Verbal output and understanding are diminished but not altogether absent (Leonard, 1982). These children may find it hard to retrieve words they have used only moments earlier. Recovery is slower and residual problems are likely to remain.

Apraxia

Apraxia is the inability to program, position, and sequence the muscle movements involved in speech. The child with apraxia can produce the movements involved in articulation, but often fails to combine these movements with meaningful speech (Byrne and Shervanian, 1977). Some clinicians consider apraxia to be an aphasic disorder because it is an impairment in the processing of language (Mysak, 1976).

All forms of aphasia, dysphasia, and apraxia are caused by a disturbance of brain function. However, although children with these conditions are linguistically retarded, they are often near or within normal range in most other respects (Mysak, 1980). Prognosis for improvement depends on early identification of the problem, accurate assessment, and the development of individualized treatment programs (Mysak, 1980).

Delayed language development

A child with delayed language development learns language in an orderly progression but slower and less proficiently than normal age-peers (Kirk and Gallagher, 1979). Minor delays in language development may be caused by generalized immaturity rather than a language problem. Many young children who show minor delays catch up with their peers by the time they are five or six.

Language differences

Children who have grown up speaking regional dialects may experience difficulties when learning standard English or French. Studies of Black American and Native Canadian children have revealed considerable problems in English usage and comprehension. Although language differences cannot be considered language disorders, they do exacerbate problems where language disorders already exist. Assessment is particularly difficult in such cases, and clinicians must often seek assistance from speakers of the child's dialect.

Children who grow up in homes where English or French is not spoken need to be taught English or French as a second language. Children who speak other first languages may have difficulty with certain English or French phonemes. For example, many speakers of Japanese have trouble pronouncing the phoneme /r/. The problems of children from other language groups will be discussed further in Chapter Fourteen.

Mutism

Mutism refers to the total absence of language. It is a rare condition, related to severe emotional, neurological, or sensory disorder. The term **elective mutism** describes emotionally disturbed children who do not speak or speak only in certain circumstances. Elective mutism may be associated with a traumatic event, and is always symptomatic of a deep disturbance of psychological functioning.

Prevalence of language disorders

Because researchers disagree on the definition of language disorders, they often cite different prevalence figures. For example, Shames and Wiig (1982) define a language disorder as a form of speech disorder. Of the five percent of children with speech disorders, they claim that three to five percent have language disorders. De Villiers and de Villiers (1978) define language problems as separate from speech disorders. They estimate that twelve percent of children with communication problems have language delays or disorders.

To further confuse the issue, children in other categories of exceptionality often have language problems. This is particularly true of children with mental retardation, hearing handicaps, and neurological disorders.

Diagnosis and assessment of language disorders

Language disorders are generally assessed by a team comprising a psychologist, a speech clinician, a physician and possibly an educator or a neurologist. Before assessment can proceed, all physical and psychological disturbances to normal language development must first be ruled out.

A comprehensive assessment consists of:

- An interview of the family to gather all pertinent developmental and behavioural data.
- Formal tests to evaluate areas of the child's language abilities and disabilities.
- Informal assessments, including a sample of the child's language. Crystal, Fletcher, and Garman (1976) suggest this sample consist of a minimum of one hundred utterances.

Before a language disorder can be diagnosed, a thorough and comprehensive study of the child's linguistic skills must be made. Two types of test are used in the examination process — the norm-referenced standardized test and the criterion-referenced test (Leonard, 1982).

Screening

Standardized language tests are available for both screening and diagnosis. These tests usually include normative data which indicate how children of various ages might be expected to perform. Those children who perform below a certain score on a screening test are given further testing.

Screening for language proficiency in pre-school and kindergarten continues to be a controversial issue. Many children show minor delays in language development due to general immaturity. Some of these will catch up with their peers without special intervention, and others may not. Some educators emphasize enrichment of language experiences rather than specific remediation for pre-school and kindergarten children (de Villiers and de Villiers, 1976).

CHARACTERISTICS OF CHILDREN WITH SPEECH AND LANGUAGE DISORDERS

Social Adjustment

Any degree of disturbance in our communication with our fellows has an impact on social adjustment. Children who communicate poorly, whether due to speech or language disorders, are usually painfully aware of the fact. They may react by withdrawing from social contact, or by using physical means to gain others' attention.

Wendy is nine years old. She was physically abused by an alcoholic stepfather when she was four. Although she is physically normal, she has expressive aphasia. She speaks in short phrases and often mixes up words.

Wendy is sociable and enjoys being with other children. However, she is painfully shy and rarely speaks aloud in class, even when she knows she can answer the teacher's questions. When asked to speak, she vigorously shakes her head in refusal.

The more tense Wendy becomes, the more she feels confused. "The words get all mixed up," she once whispered to her teacher. "I afraid."

All types of speech and language disorders affect the ease with which children can communicate with their world. Many children find it so difficult to communicate that they become frustrated, withdrawn, and depressed. Others learn to rely on gesture and body language.

Academic achievement

As one would expect, children with language disorders perform poorly in those aspects of learning that rely on language. Children with problems in language acquisition invariably have difficulties learning to read. During grades three and four the demands on language proficiency increase. New content areas are introduced, such as Social Studies and Science. Abstract and symbolic materials make it increasingly difficult for children with language disorders to cope with academic subjects (Wiig, 1982).

Psychological correlates

Children with language disorders often perform within normal limits on non-verbal intelligence tests (Leonard, 1981). However, many cognitive abilities are clearly language dependent. For example, children with language problems tend to be more rigid and literal in their thinking. They lack the flexibility required for pretending, for playing word games, or for laughing at riddles and jokes.

Riddles and jokes are often based on a recognition that a word or phrase has multiple meanings. Solving a riddle involves the ability to recognize the ambiguity of the riddle question. For example, the riddle "When is the ocean friendly?" can be answered, "When it 'waves' at you." Riddles, puns, and a variety of other concepts depend on a child's ability to order and sequence words and sentences (Rogow, 1982).

Language disorders may be exacerbated by the child's interactions with the family. Research indicates that the parents of children with language disorders tend to talk more for their children (Leonard, 1982). Parents of children with language disorders engage in fewer play and language activities with their children. Mothers claim their children did not enjoy these games, but reluctance to interact seems reciprocal (Leonard, 1982).

Some difficulties experienced by children with language impairments may be a consequence of damage to the brain. Clearcut evidence of brain damage in such children is not easy to obtain. This may change with the use of new brain-scan equipment that permits more precise assessment of brain functioning (Leonard, 1982).

INTERVENTION

Medical intervention

Plastic surgery can largely prevent the wide-ranging speech problems associated with cleft palate and other oral-facial defects. Dental surgery may also be necessary for children with cleft palates. In cases of head-trauma injuries, immediate medical attention may help to reduce the extent of damage. Trauma medicine has made a great deal of progress in recent years, and new brain-scan techniques can pinpoint sites of injury in the brain.

Psychological intervention

Stuttering has long been treated with a variety of psychotherapeutic treatments. The main objective of treatment is to eliminate stuttering or to decrease its effect.

Therapy for stutterers includes psychotherapy, behaviour modification, and biofeedback (Shames and Florance, 1982). Some therapists combine a variety of techniques, including such new therapies as desensitization, parent-child verbal interaction, and fluency shaping (Shames and Florance, 1982).

Stuttering has long been regarded as a symptom of an underlying emotional problem. Many stutterers have benefited from intensive psychotherapeutic intervention.

Exhibit 6-7 Tips for teachers of children who stutter.

- Don't label the child a stutterer.
- Don't put pressure on the child through criticism or impatience.
- Don't engage the child in activities that increase non-fluency, such as the use of flashcards.
- Don't pity the child.
- Don't compare the child's speech with that of sisters, brothers, or classmates.
- Encourage the child to speak.

Educational intervention

Speech and language are crucial to academic success. Since the beginning of the twentieth century, speech and language habilitation programs have formed a part of our public school programs (Kirk and Gallagher, 1979).

Learning environments

Children with speech/language disorders may be placed in regular classes or in special classes within a school system. Children with minor disorders can often receive adequate assistance within the school from the learning-assistance teacher and a speech and language clinician. Some school systems employ specially trained language teachers.

Children with more severe problems require more intensive instruction. These children are limited in their ability to learn in regular classroom settings. Short-term immersion programs in a language centre or special class are often more appropriate for them.

A language centre/class provides a small group setting within a regular school. This environment allows for individualized programming and therapy, small-group experiences, and social interaction with students in regular classes (McDonald, 1984). The teacher's efforts are supported by a speech clinician, a school counsellor, and experienced aides and volunteers.

In a language centre/class, the major instructional emphasis is always on the remediation of the student's language problems. The curriculum includes a range of oral and written language activities. It also includes other academic subjects at the child's appropriate level to facilitate re-entry into the regular classroom (McDonald, 1985).

Educational Approaches

Several approaches may be used to teach children with language disorders. These approaches may be described as diagnostic-prescriptive, performance-oriented, interpersonal-interactive, or syntax-based. All these programs attempt to improve the child's linguistic competence. Some are designed for classroom use, while others require clinical settings.

Diagnostic-prescriptive approaches These approaches take into account the child's strengths and weaknesses in a given aspect of language. There are two forms of diagnostic-prescriptive approach — the process or ability model, and the task analysis model (Wiig, 1982).

In the process or ability model, intervention focuses on all the abilities involved in perceiving and discriminating speech, interpreting spoken language, and formulating language and speech. Intervention may also encompass short- and long-term memory, verbal reasoning, word retrieval, and the visual and motor processes involved in speaking, reading, and writing (Wiig, 1982).

In the task analysis model, every task involved in speech, language, and communication becomes the focus of intervention. The task analysis approach is often derived from the child's performance on criterion-referenced tests, such as the Clinical Evaluation of Language Functions (CELF) by Semel and Wiig (1980).

Performance-oriented approaches Performance-oriented approaches attempt to modify, decrease, or increase language behaviours (Wiig, 1982). Intervention is aimed at overt, measurable, disordered communication behaviours. Imitation and modeling of correct communication behaviours are stressed (Wiig, 1982).

Interpersonal-interactive approaches Interpersonal-interactive approaches aim to strengthen the child's ability to use language and to develop communicative competence. Specific objectives include helping the child to interpret contextual clues, strengthening role-taking and role-playing abilities, and increasing the range of verbal and nonverbal communication styles (Wiig, 1982).

Syntax-based programs Programs based on syntax teach the child specific language structures such as subject, verb, and object, and word-order relationships, such as question forms. Crystal, Fletcher, and Garman (1977) have developed the Language Assessment, Remediation, and Screening Procedure (LARSP) to provide a systematic methodology for the description and treatment of syntactical problems. The LARSP compares the syntactic patterns children use with those they should use (Crystal, Fletcher and Garman, 1976). Effective use of the LARSP requires that the clinician (or the teacher) be well-versed in techniques of language sampling and phonetic transcription. The Fokes Sentence Builder (1976) is another example of a syntax-based remedial language program in wide use.

Illebrun and Leong (1981) studied several different types of syntax-based program. They concluded that structural language programs are effective with linguistically delayed children. The various approaches are not mutually exclusive, and are often combined to encourage children to practice their language skills in a variety of situations. As Bloom and Lahey (1978) point out, however, it is also important to include content and usage, as well as form, in language instruction.

Delayed language programs Miller and Yoder (1974) emphasize that language teaching of delayed children should be based on the normal language acquisition process. Children must comprehend meaning before they can express it. Bricker and Bricker (1974) also stress the cognitive prerequisites for language acquisition. They organize their teaching program around the initial assessment and subsequent training of cognitive skills. They emphasize object permanence, classification, imitation, and representational play with objects (Bricker and Bricker, 1974). Other programs stress the transactional nature of early language development, and use play to develop communication skills (Rogow, 1981).

Teaching problems and techniques

A major problem in language-training concerns the transfer of learned language from the training setting to the natural environment. The generalization of language skills appears to be more restricted in children with language disorders (de Villiers and de Villiers, 1978). A great deal more research is needed before we know what approaches are most successful with what types of language disorder.

Recently there has been a growing interest on the part of educators, speech/language clinicians, psychologists, and others in the speech and language development of all exceptional children. In Canada, a wide variety of program models are in use. We are now realizing that many of the learning difficulties of children who are mentally handicapped are based on deficits in communication. The labels under which exceptional children are classified have become less important than their functional communication skills.

Exhibit 6-8 outlines some techniques used by clinicians and teachers in the classroom.

When working with children with speech and language disorders, it is important to follow these rules.

- Have the child face you. Sit with your face at the same level as the child's.
- Give directives as explicitly as possible. Avoid using unnecessary words.
- Speak clearly and at moderate speed to be more easily understood.

Exhibit 6-8 Techniques used by clinicians and teachers for students with language disorders.

- Simultaneous demonstration and talking.
- Story telling.
- Group discussion.
- Creative drama.
- Expansion.
- Modeling.
- Prompting.
- Echoing.
- Commands.
- Music and poetry.

(Adapted from Byrne and Shervanian, 1977.)

It is never too late to intervene with children who have speech and language problems. Older children, who may have already benefited from language intervention when they were younger, may experience new problems as the demands for language sophistication increase. The effects of communication problems on social interaction and school performance are so overwhelming that intervention should be available at all educational levels.

The speech/language clinician

The speech pathologist or speech clinician is trained in the evaluation and remedial treatment of speech and language problems in children and adults. In most provinces and states, a qualified clinician requires a master's degree in speech pathology and a year of closely supervised clinical work.

Speech pathologists work as consultants to schools and special education programs. They are also employed in hospitals and rehabilitation centres. In many programs across Canada, speech clinicians work as members of a diagnostic team in the evaluation and treatment of handicapped children. Some clinicians specialize in working with mentally handicapped and neurologically impaired children and adults. It is often the speech clinician who recommends alternate systems of communication for children who are not able to speak.

The role of the speech/language clinician includes the following:

- Supervision and administration of programs for children with communication disorders.
- Identification and diagnosis of speech/language problems.
- Consultation with teachers and others working with disordered children.

- Training and supervision of communication aides.
- Direct service to children and adults.
- Writing reports (Byrne and Shervanian, 1977).

The role of the teacher

Special educators have become increasingly aware of the important role of communicative competence in the child's ability to do academic work. Most preparation programs for special education teachers include one or more courses in language development and language disorders. Working closely with speech clinicians and psychologists, teachers have developed effective curricula for the teaching of language skills.

Alternate methods of communication: communication augmentation

Alternate methods of communication include those that depend on non-vocal means of expression and those that depend on technological devices.

Non-vocal communication

Non-speech or non-vocal, methods of communication employ signals, codes, symbols, and communication boards. These methods are used with severely impaired children. The mental abilities, motivation, and voluntary movement available to the child are important considerations in selecting a mode of communication.

Non-speech communication should not preclude speech therapy. A number of studies have shown an increase in speech attempts with the use of non-vocal methods of communication (Mysak, 1982).

Signal and code communication include the use of a simple Yes-No system, audiosignalling, and Morse Code. Yes or no signals may be indicated by movement of head, hand, face, or eye (Mysak, 1982). A portable audio-oscillator that emits a loud tone has been used to teach four simple signals (need, help, yes, no). The Morse Code has also been used as a method of communication.

Symbol systems involve the use of special symbols to represent sounds or words. Blissymbolics and rebus systems are widely used. Both these systems can be adapted for use as communication boards. Blissymbolics has been successful with children with severe motor disabilities. Depending on the child's ability, vocabularies of up to four hundred terms may be learned (Mysak, 1982).

Communication boards

Communication boards may be non-electric or electric. Boards should be developed on an individual basis in accordance with the child's needs. These boards may display Bliss symbols, numbers, letters, words, pictures, or sentences. An electronic communication board called the Audio-Monitoring Communication Board, or Auto-Com, has been successfully used with children who have no capacity for speech (Mysak, 1982).

The Pic-Board, developed in Canada, consists of pictures and symbols that represent objects and actions. The Pic Board is used to facilitate communication for children with cerebral palsy or those classified as mentally handicapped.

An electronic communication board called the Expressor was designed to facilitate the use of the Initial Teaching Alphabet (ITA). Each symbol in this system represents one sound. The child who learns all forty-four symbols is capable of producing any English word (Mysak, 1982).

Augmentative devices

Augmentative devices can be operated by the individual to communicate basic needs. They can be easily activated by movement of the hand or head, or even by an eye-blink. The Vocaid is an example of an augmentative device suitable for functional needs, such as a call for assistance. Some augmentative devices make use of speech synthesis.

Computer aids

Elaborate devices involving the computer enable disordered children to communicate more complex and subtle messages. These devices offer multiple outputs, such as print-out, screen, or speech-synthesized voice. They are easily activated by a variety of volitional movements, including eye control, ringer contact, or sipping and puffing on a blow-stick. Some of these devices also enable the individual to open windows and turn lights and televisions on or off.

Alternatives to Voice

Severe voice problems are encountered by persons who have developmental defects of the larynx or have had laryngectomies. New techniques of therapy have been developed to permit these persons to produce audible speech.

Several devices are now available that function as an **artificial larynx**. These are placed against the throat to produce electronic or pneumatic vibrations. These vibrations are then transmitted to the resonating cavities of the vocal tract (throat, mouth, and nose), where they are shaped into speech sounds (Perkins, 1978). The voice produced with an artificial larynx sounds hoarse and is lower in pitch, loudness, inflection, and intelligibility than a normal voice. Nonetheless, it does achieve effective intelligible speech (Perkins, 1978).

Esophageal speech involves the inflation of an air pocket near the top of the gullet. When this air is expelled, the neck of the esophagus is set into vibration (Perkins, 1978).

The field of communication augmentation is growing. The knowledge base of this new field of communication is derived mainly from clinical experience. Both assessment and selection of the type of augmentation to be used is highly individual and depends on such factors as the individual's level of linguistic competence, motor control and communication needs. Two main types of augmentation include unaided and aided approaches. Unaided approaches rely on gestural communication, while aided approaches depend on a system or device of some kind (Beukelman, Yurkston and Dowden, 1985).

SUMMARY

Speech and language disabilities interfere with the ease with which a child interacts with the world. Speech disorders are problems in the articulation of language sounds, voice production, and fluency. Language disorders are problems in the acquisition, comprehension, and formulation of language. Communication disorders can have painful consequences for all aspects of a child's development.

Children with hearing handicaps, learning disabilities, mental handicaps, and severe emotional disturbance often have manifest speech and language problems. Neurogenic language dysfunction accounts for a very small proportion of communication disorders. Some difficulties in language comprehension and expression are related to immaturity or to cultural differences.

Teachers and clinicians must always remember that a complex interaction of social, motor, cognitive, and linguistic factors underlie language disorders. They must also ensure that the language skills children acquire are transferred from the training session into the child's living environment.

BIBLIOGRAPHY

Bellugi, U. and Klima, E.S. (1972). The roots of language in the sign talk of the deaf. *Psychology Today* 6, 60-64.

Beukelman, D.R., Yurkston, K.M. and Dowden, P.A. (1985). *Communication Augmentation.* San Diego: College Hill Press.

Bloom, L. and Lahey, M. (1978). *Language development and disorders.* New York: John Wiley.

Bricker, W. and Bricker D. (1974). An early language training strategy. In R. Schiefelbusch and L. Lloyd, (Eds.) *Language perspectives: acquisition, retardation and intervention.* Baltimore, Maryland: University Park Press.

Brown, R. (1973). *A first language: The early stages.* Cambridge: Harvard University Press.

Byrne, M.E. and Shervanian, C.C. (1977). *Introduction to communication disorders.* New York: Harper and Row.

Carrow, E. (1974). *Carrow elicited language inventory.* Austin, Texas: Educational Concepts.

Cromer, R.F. (1974) Language in the mentally retarded: processes and diagnostic distinctions. In R. Schiefelbusch and L. Lloyd (eds.) *Language perspectives acquisition, retardation and intervention.* London: MacMillan.

Crystal, D., Fletcher, P., and Garman, M.G. (1976). *The grammatical analysis of language disability: A procedure for assessment and remediation.* London: Edward Arnold.

Curtiss, S. (1977). *Genie: A psycholinguistic study of a modern day "wild child."* New York: Academic Press.

de Villiers, J.G. and de Villiers, P.A. (1978). *Language acquisition.* Cambridge, MA.: Harvard University Press.

Eisenson, J. and Ingram, D. (1972) Childhood aphasia — an updated concept based on recent research. *Acta Symbolica 3,* 108-16.

Elliott, A.J. (1981). *Child language.* Cambridge, Eng.: Cambridge University Press.

Fokes, J. (1976). *Fokes sentence builder.* Boston, MA: Teaching Resource Corporation.

Garvey, C. (1975) Requests and responses in children's speech. *Journal of Child Language 2,* 41-63.

Goodman, K. (1969). Analysis of oral reading miscues. Applied psycholinguistics. *Reading Research Quarterly, 4,* 9-30.

Halliday, M.A.K. (1975). *Learning how to mean: Explorations in the development of language.* London: Edward Arnold.

Illerbrun, D. and Leong, C.K. (1981). Evaluating the effectiveness of structured language teaching with developmentally delayed children. *The Exceptional Child, 28(1),* 31-42.

Johnson, W. (1955) *Stuttering in children and adults: thirty years of research at the University of Iowa.* Minneapolis: University of Minnesota Press.

Kirk, S.A. and Gallagher, J.J. (1979). *Educating exceptional children.* Boston, MA.: Houghton-Mifflin.

Kleffner, F. (1973). *Language disorders in children.* Indianapolis: Bobbs Merrill.

Landau, B. (1983). Blind children's language is not 'meaningless.' In A. Mills (Ed.) Language acquisition in the blind child: Normal and deficient San Diego, CA.: College Hill Press.

Lane, H. (1976) *The wild boy of Aveyron.* Cambridge MA: Harvard University Press.

La Pointe, L. (1982). Neurogenic disorders of speech. In G. Shames and E.H. Wiig (Eds.) *Human communication disorders.* Toronto: Charles E. Merrill.

Lenneberg, E. (1967). *Biological foundations of language.* New York: Wiley and Sons.

Leonard, L.B. (1982). Early language development and language disorders. In G. Shames and E.H. Wiig (Eds.) *Human communication disorders.* Toronto: Charles E. Merrill.

Lewis, M.M. (1963). *Language, thought and personality in infancy and childhood.* New York: Basic Books.

McDonald, L. (1984). Personal communication.

McNeill, D. (1970). *The acquisition of language.* New York: Harper and Row.

Menyuk, P. (1971). *The acquisition and development of language.* Englewood Cliffs N.J.: Prentice-Hall.

Menyuk, P. (1977). *Language and maturation.* Cambridge, MA.: MIT Press.

Miller, J. and Yoder, (1974). An ontogenetic language teaching strategy for retarded children. In R.L. Schiefelbusch and L.L. Lloyd (Eds.), *Language perspectives: Acquisition retardation and intervention.* Baltimore, MD.: University Park Press.

Moore, P. (1982) Voice disorders. In G. Shames and E.H. Wiig (Eds.), *Human communication disorders.* Toronto: Charles E. Merrill.

Mysak, E. (1976) *Pathologies of speech systems.* Baltimore, Maryland: Williams and Wilkins Co.

Mysak, E. (1982). Cerebral palsy. In G. Shames and E.H. Wiig (Eds.), *Human communication disorders.* Toronto: Charles E. Merrill.

Newcomer, P. and Hammill, D.D. (1977). *Test of language development.* Austin, Texas: Pro-Ed.

Perkins, W.H. (1978). *Human perspectives in speech and language disorders.* St. Louis, Mo.: Moseby Press.

Rees, N. (1978). Pragmatics of language application to normal and disordered language development. In R.L. Schiefelbusch (Ed.), *Bases of language intervention.* Baltimore: University Park Press.

Rogow, S.M. (1981). Developing play skills and communicative competence in multiply handicapped young people. *Journal of Visual Impairment and Blindness 75 (5),* 197-202.

Rogow, S.M. (1982). Riddles and rhymes: The importance of speech play for blind and visually handicapped children. In C.E. Johnson and C. Thew (Eds.), *Proceedings of the 2nd International Congress for the Study of Child Language.*

Shames, G. and Florance, C. (1982). Disorders of fluency. In G. Shames and E.H. Wiig (Eds.) *Human communication disorders.* Toronto: Charles E. Merrill.

Stark, R.E. (1980) Stages of speech development in the first year of life. In G.H. Yeni-Komshian, C.A. Ferguson, and J. Kavanagh, (Eds.) *Child Phonology: Production vol. I.* New York: Academic Press.

Stern, D. (1977). *The first relationship: Infant and mother.* Cambridge, Eng.: Cambridge University Press.

Tallal, P. and Piercy, M. (1973) Defects of non-verbal auditory processing in children with developmental aphasia. *Nature. 242,* 468-469.

Templin, M.C. and Darley, F.L. (1969). *The Templin-Darley tests of articulation (2nd ed.).* Iowa City: University of Iowa.

Van Osdol, W.R. and Shane, J.H. (1977). *The exceptional individual, (3rd ed.).* Englewood Cliffs, N.J.: Prentice-Hall.

Van Riper, C. (1978). *Speech correction principals and methods (6th ed.).* Englewood Cliffs, N.J.: Prentice-Hall.

Wells, G. (1981). *Learning through interaction: The study of child language development.* Cambridge, Eng.: Cambridge University Press.

Wiig, E.H. (1982). Language disabilities in the school-aged child. In G. Shames and E.H. Wiig, (Eds.), *Human communication disorders.* Toronto: Charles E. Merrill.

Wiig, E.H. and Semel, E.M. (1976) *Language disabilities in children and adolescents.* Columbis, Ohio: Charles Merrill.

Wiig, E.H. and Semel, E.M. (1980). *Language assessment and intervention for the learning disabled.* Columbus, OH.: Charles E. Merrill.

Winitz, H. (1975). *From syllable to conversation.* Baltimore: University Park Press.

CHAPTER SEVEN

Children with learning disabilities

MARGRET WINZER

I just struggled to understand words that seemed to garble before my eyes, numbers that came out backwards, sentences that were hard to grasp.

(Rockefeller, 1976)

Some categories in special education can be easily identified by a common trait, such as hearing loss, visual impairment, or speech dysfunction. Learning disabilities, however, do not concern a single, easily identifiable handicap. Children with learning disabilities do not form a unified homogeneous group. They include vastly different populations and reveal a wide variety of behavioural and interpersonal problems.

Although learning-disabled children differ in many critical ways, they do share one common problem. All of these children are unable to learn through regular channels. Various problems prevent them from learning efficiently in the traditional classroom under traditional teaching techniques. If these problems go unchecked, the child's entire educational future may be threatened.

Exhibit 7-1 offers an overview of some of the problems faced by children with learning disabilities.

Exhibit 7-1 Who is the learning-disabled child?

- Usually ... this is an intelligent child who fails at school.
- Usually ... this is the child who at school-age reads *on* for *no*, writes *41* for *14*, *p* for *d*, or *q* for *b*, and cannot remember the sequence of letters that make up a word.
- Usually ... this is the child who hears the dog barking, the truck honking, but barely hears Mother calling, ... who hears the scratching of pencils, the sound of the air conditioner, and footsteps outside, but does not hear what the teacher says.
- Usually ... this is the child who forgets names of people, places, things, his own address and telephone number, but does remember the ads on television.

■ Usually . . . this is the child who loses homework, misplaces books, and does not know what day it is, or what year, or what season.

■ Usually . . . this is the child with the messy room, the shirt-tail hanging out, the shoelaces undone, the child who attracts dirt like a magnet.

■ Usually . . . this is the child who does not look before walking, who bumps into the door, who swings lunch boxes into the nearest legs, who trips easily, and who does not look at the person who is talking.

■ Usually . . . this is the child who has trouble lining up, who cannot help bothering the child ahead in line, . . . who does not stop talking, who giggles too much, and laughs the loudest.

■ Usually . . . this is the child who calls breakfast *lunch*, . . . who is confused by *yesterday*, *today*, and *tomorrow*, and whose timing is always off.

■ Usually . . . this is the child who cannot tolerate making the smallest mistake, . . . who tunes out in mid-conversation, . . . who is happy one moment and tearful the next.

■ Usually . . . this is the child who is reluctant to try anything new, who is frightened by change.

■ Usually . . . this is the child who says *I don't care* or *I won't* and really means *I can't*, . . . and who would rather be called bad than dumb.

■ Frequently . . . this is the child who cannot picture things mentally, who cannot visualize or remember what has been seen.

■ Frequently . . . this is the quiet child who bothers nobody in the classroom but does not learn.

■ Frequently . . . this is the older child whose language comes out jumbled, who stops and starts in the middle of a sentence or an idea, . . . who talks about hospitals, animals, and enemies.

■ Frequently . . . this is the child who hugs the cat too tightly but can't hold a pencil, . . . who gets frostbite in the snow, and does not feel the hot water until it burns.

■ Frequently . . . this is the good swimmer . . . who stumbles up the stairs.

■ Frequently . . . this is the child who draws the same thing over and over, . . . and who asks constant questions but does not seem interested in the answers.

■ Frequently . . . this is the child who cannot keep a friend, . . . and who prefers to play with younger children.

■ Frequently . . . this is the child who wants everything done in a certain way, . . . who tattle-tales, . . . picks on others for every little thing, and bosses everyone around.

■ Frequently . . . this is the expert strategist in checkers or chess who cannot understand a riddle or a joke.

■ Sometimes . . . this is the child who lopes through life, slow to get up, slow to move or to think, but quick to play.

- Sometimes . . . this is the child who rushes headlong into work, is the first one finished, and has done all the problems wrong.
- Sometimes . . . this is the child who can add and multiply but not subtract or divide, . . . who can do math mentally but cannot write it down.
- Sometimes . . . this is the child who skips words, omits them, or adds them when reading aloud.
- Sometimes . . . this is the child who smiles at everyone, greets strangers with open arms, says "hello" to anyone, . . . and whose good nature invites trouble as "the fall guy."
- Occasionally . . . this is the child who tends to feel that life is unfair, who carries a big chip on the shoulder, and refuses to try.
- Occasionally . . . this is the child who can understand the *Odyssey* of Homer, but cannot read the words *in, the,* or *if.*

Any of these children may well be a child with a learning disability.

(MacGregor, Rosenbaum, and Skoutajan, 1982.)

In the past, learning-disabled children have been described as hyperactive, distractible, inattentive, brain-damaged, slow-learning, dyslexic, perceptually disabled, aggressive, and emotionally labile. More unsavoury terms have included dull, lazy, inept, and disturbed. Because of difficulties in identification, learning-disabled youngsters have often been shunted into classes for the emotionally disturbed or the mentally retarded. Others have been placed in non-stimulating settings where their problems and progress have been improperly evaluated.

One classic example of misunderstood children are those who see words or groups of words backwards. Instead of "See the dog. See the dog run," they might read "See the god. See the run god." Teachers might encourage them to "try harder," but however hard they try, they still see the same words. When other children laugh at them, their confidence is undermined and they grow disheartened. This continues until one day they are diagnosed as emotionally disturbed. Meanwhile, their learning disability continues to be overlooked. (MacGregor, Rosenbaum and Skoutajan, 1982.

Profile 7-1 offers a particularly poignant example of a child whose learning disability was not identified. The letter was written many years after the person had left school.

PROFILE 7-1

Dear Teacher,

You will not, I am sure, remember me. I am the child you failed in the second grade many years ago. That failure had profound effects on my life. It was my first, but not my last, bitter taste of defeat. I never found out from my mother why I was failed that year. I was told only "that it was thought best."

The full implication of repeating a grade did not dawn on me until the day school started that next autumn. I had once felt like my younger sister's smart older brother, but now I felt like her slow, retarded brother. From that day onward, she and I were both in the same grade until we parted company in high school.

I hated school after that first day of my second-go-round in grade two. Teacher, I hated you. I hated being the same mental age as my younger sister. I hated authority. I had done my best to please you the year before, and my best was not good enough. I quit trying to please anyone in school.

You never asked me why I was hyperactive and could not sit still. You never wondered how it felt to be in the "blue birds" slow-reading group. You never asked how I felt about math, which I just could not do.

I wanted to be good at numbers, but I could not cope with the anger that math provoked in me. To some people, numbers are friendly little creatures that love you. To me, numbers were mean ugly biters that bullied me every chance they got. Hell, I thought, must be having to do numbers forever by working them out in your head. Spelling was also a painful subject. I used to avoid your eyes, and pray that you would not call on me.

As a young teenager, I thought I found the answer to all my problems in the power of alcohol. I relied on alcohol to change my fear into temporary courage, and to turn my feelings of low self-worth into superman-like confidence. At first my answer worked, but in time it became a one-way ticket to training school, jail, and personal defeat. Only by luck did I meet a counselor who understood my learning problems and helped to set me on the right path.

In closing, I'd just like to say that today you have other children like me in your classroom. They may be the shy wallflower types or the loud performers that get on your nerves and disturb the rest of the class. They may be the ones with hidden secrets who daydream all day long. One thing is certain — these children are deeply disturbed. They can't wake up from their nightmare — they are already awake and the nightmare will not go away.

Thank you for listening, teacher.

Brian.

Learning-disabled youngsters are neither emotionally disturbed nor mentally retarded. They stand in good company with similarly afflicted historical figures. Thomas Edison's teacher, for example, described him as "addled." Auguste Rodin's father complained that he had "an idiot for a son." Woodrow Wilson had severe problems with reading and writing (Thompson, 1971). Albert Einstein did not speak until age three; he found school so difficult that one teacher predicted that "nothing good" would come of him (Patten, 1973). Nelson Rockefeller, who became vice-president of the United States, encountered great difficulties with reading and supplied the quote that opens this chapter.

MAJOR ISSUES

The field of learning disabilities is the most recent category in special education. The term came into use in 1963 to describe students who experienced continual school failure yet did not fit into the traditional categories of exceptionality. Educational services for learning-disabled students were virtually non-existent in the early 1960s. Today, such sevices form the largest single program for exceptional children in many school districts.

Perhaps more than any other field of exceptionality, learning disabilities have generated controversy, confusion, and polarization among concerned professionals. The field is fraught with many misconceptions. Learning disabilities are ill-defined in the minds of many educators, psychologists, and parents. Their implications are neither understood nor adequately conceptualized by the majority of school administrators, (Cruickshank, 1979).

Of all the issues that currently plague the field of learning disabilities, the most challenging is the search for an appropriate definition. Perhaps in no other area of special education has so much effort been expended to define the field. Yet, so far, a universally acceptable definition has remained elusive. Indeed, some have likened learning disabilities to pornography: each is "impossible to define but you always know it when you see it" (Lerner, 1981).

Definitional problems may be the result of the field's recent evolution, its accelerated growth and its interdisciplinary nature. Problems also arise from the extremely heterogeneous nature of the learning-disabled population. Definitional problems create confusion in estimates of prevalence and considerations of etiology. They also present major difficulties in the design and use of tools and tests for assessment.

HISTORICAL PERSPECTIVES

To understand the field of learning disabilities, with all its confusion and controversy, it is important to have some knowledge of its beginnings. Many different disciplines have contributed to the field, each with its own professional orientation and focus. Physicians, neurologists, ophthalmologists, speech therapists, psychologists, and educators have all been involved in the diagnosis and treatment of children with learning disabilities.

Prior to 1963, children with learning disabilities were labelled in many different ways. These labels chiefly reflected a medical orientation, and attributed disabilities to various types of brain damage. Common labels included minimal brain dysfunction, brain-crippled, cerebral-disordered, neurologically impaired, dyslexic, and dysphasic.

Early research into learning disabilities focused primarily on three disorders — spoken language, written language, and motor and perceptual problems. This research was conducted by physicians and psychologists who emphasized clinical investigation rather than practical application in the schools. These researchers began by studying brain-injured adults and eventually studied children of normal intelligence (Mercer, 1979).

The development of the field of learning disabilities can be divided into three major phases. The foundations phase occurred between about 1800 and 1930. During this time, physicians investigated the etiology of specific learning disorders, classifying and categorizing them into different types. The transition phase took place from about 1930 to 1960. During this period, psychologists and educators used many of their predecessors' theories to develop diagnostic procedures and remedial programming. The integration phase began in 1960 and is still continuing. During this time, the field of learning disabilities was shaped into the form that we see today (Wiederholt, 1978).

Many inspired and dedicated individuals contributed to the development of the field of learning disabilities. In this section we can mention only a very few. Those interested in further reading are referred to Lerner (1981), Mann (1979), and Wiederholt (1978).

Much of the first, pioneering research in the field concerned children with reading problems. In the mid-1800s, three perceptive British physicians worked with public-school boys who had trouble learning to read. One physician, eye surgeon James Hinchelwood, believed that reading disabilities were due to the destruction or improper development of the memory centres of the left cerebral hemisphere of the brain (Park and Linden, 1968). In 1917, Hinchelwood published *Congenital word-blindess,* the first true monograph on the unique problems of children we now refer to as learning-disabled.

In the early 1920s, Samuel Orton, an American psychiatrist, refused to accept his colleagues' belief that learning problems were caused by emotional maladjustment. Orton noted that children with learning problems often displayed mixed laterality. He suggested that the failure of one hemisphere of the brain to become dominant caused the disorder. Today, ideas surrounding hemispheric dominance are still considered important in the field of learning disabilities.

The modern category of learning disabilities chiefly developed from concepts put forward by Alfred Strauss and Heinz Werner. Strauss, a neurologist, and Werner, a developmental psychologist, left Nazi Germany and joined the staff of the Wayne County Training School in Northville, Michigan. There they began a program of training and research for brain-damaged children.

Strauss and Werner studied the impact of brain injury on children's behavioural and psychological development. They drew a distinction between the exogenous (largely brain-damaged) and the endogenous (largely genetic) mentally retarded population. They outlined a behavioural syndrome that characterized the minimally brain-damaged child, later known as the **Strauss syndrome**. This outline has five principal components: hyperactivity; hyper-emotionalism; impulsiveness; distractibility; and perseveration. These components have been expanded, subdivided, and made more specific over the years, but they still describe the core behavioural characteristics of children with learning disabilities.

After Strauss and Werner, the focus of research gradually shifted to encompass seemingly normal children who were achieving poorly in school. A wide variety of confusing labels were used to describe these children. In 1963, at a Chicago parents' meeting, Samuel Kirk proposed the term "learning disabilities" as a standard description for children of normal intelligence with learning problems. Kirk defined his term carefully:

> Recently, I have used the term "learning disabilities" to describe a group of children who have disorders in development in language, speech, reading, and associated communication skills needed for social interaction. In this group, I do not include children who have sensory handicaps such as blindness or deafness, because we have methods of managing and training the deaf and the blind. I also exclude from this group children who have generalized mental retardation (Kirk, 1963, p. 3).

Kirk's speech had two major effects. First, it served as a catalyst to stimulate interest in the field. Second, it isolated the general characteristics of the population to be subsumed under the label of learning disabilities (Wiederholt, 1978). The new term implied an educational rather than medical orientation. Because it was also relatively nonstigmatizing, it appealed greatly to parents and educators.

Kirk's speech precipitated a vote to reorganize diverse groups into the Association for Children with Learning Disabilities (ACLD). Primarily a forum for parents of learning-disabled children, the ACLD expanded rapidly. The Canadian ACLD was formed in Toronto in 1970, and soon opened many chapters across the country.

NON-CATEGORICAL APPROACHES

The category of learning disabilities is certainly valuable in assisting children with elusive and complex learning problems. However, there are many similarities between these children and those described as mildly mentally retarded or emotionally disturbed. These similarities have prompted educators to examine non-categorical or cross-categorical approaches to special education. Because of its heterogeneous population and rapid growth rate, the field of learning disabilities has the potential to lead the movement against categorization (Lerner, 1981).

Briefly, **non-categorical approaches** encourage educators to emphasize the common characteristics among the categories of exceptionality. Children with mild problems — including those labelled as mildly retarded, mildly emotionally disturbed, behaviourally disordered, or learning disabled — are difficult to categorize through diagnostic methods. Moreover, their treatments often overlap, suggesting that diagnostic and intervention methods cut across the existing categories.

Advocates of non-categorical approaches argue that we should dispense with traditional labelling, categorization, and etiological considerations. Instead we should focus on the behaviours and most appropriate forms of intervention for each individual child. Hallahan and Kauffman (1976) propose a generic definition of mildly handicapped children that stresses education. Specifically, they suggest that "if the term learning disabilities is to continue to be used, . . . it be used to refer to learning problems found in children who have traditionally been classified as mildly handicapped, whether . . . emotionally disturbed, mildly retarded, or learning disabled" (p. 28).

DEFINITIONS OF LEARNING DISABILITIES

Parents and professionals often find it difficult to identify and define a child's learning disabilities. Because of the disparate characteristics of the learning-disabled population, a general definition of the category is extremely difficult. Nor can learning disabilities be measured by a numerical designation, such as an IQ score or a decibel loss.

Despite these problems, many definitions of learning disabilities have emerged. One recent study found more than forty-two definitional criteria in the literature (Ysseldyke, Thurlow, Graden, Wesson, Algozzine, and Deno, 1983). Most of the current definitions echo Kirk's original model, quoted earlier in this chapter.

Exhibit 7-2 outlines three definitions in current use. The first, proposed by the National Advisory Committee on Handicapped Children (1968), is the one from which many later definitions have branched. The second is that used by the Ontario Ministry of Education — its debt to the National Advisory Committee is obvious. The final definition is a relatively new attempt to overcome some of the shortcomings in earlier descriptions. It was formulated by a joint committee of the American Speech-Language-Hearing Association, the Association for Children with Learning Disabilities, the Division for Children with Communication Exceptionalities, the International Reading Association, and the Orton Dyslexia Society (1981).

Exhibit 7-2 Sample definitions of learning disabilities.

Children with special learning disabilities exhibit disorders in one or more of the basic psychological processes involved in understanding or using spoken or written language. These may be manifested in disorders of listening, thinking, talking, reading, writing, spelling, perceptual handicaps, brain injury, minimal brain dysfunction, dyslexia, developmental aphasia, etc. They do not include learning problems which are due primarily to visual, hearing, or motor handicaps, to mental retardation, emotional disturbance, or to environmental disadvantage (National Advisory Committee on Handicapped Children, 1968).

Learning disabilities are disorders in one or more of the processes involved in understanding or using symbols or spoken language. The disorders result in a significant discrepancy between academic achievement and assessed intellectual ability, with deficits in at least one of the following areas: receptive language — listening, reading; language processing — thinking, conceptualizing, integrating; expressive language — talking, spelling, writing, and mathematical computations. Such deficits become evident in both academic and social situations. The definition does not include children who have learning problems that are primarily the result of impairment of hearing, motor handicaps, mental retardation, primary emotional disturbance, or environmental, cultural, or economic disadvantage (Ontario, Ministry of Education, 1980).

Learning disabilities is a general term that refers to a heterogeneous group of disorders manifested by significant difficulties in the acquisition and use of listening, speaking, reading, writing, reasoning, or mathematical abilities. These disorders are intrinsic to the individual and presumed to be due to central nervous system dysfunction. Even though the learning disability may occur concomitantly with other handicapping conditions (e.g. sensory impairment, mental retardation, social and emotional disturbances) or environmental influences (e.g. cultural differences, insufficient/inappropriate instruction, psychogenic factors), it is not the direct result of these conditions or influences (Hammill, Leigh, McNutt, and Larsen, 1981, p. 336).

Although this plethora of definitions may appear very confusing, most of the commonly accepted definitions share common elements. The components generally found are:

- Neurological dysfunction.
- Uneven growth pattern.

- Difficulty in academic and learning tasks.
- Discrepancy between potential and performance.
- Exclusion of other causes.
- An unstated assumption that the learning-disabled student is of average or above-average intelligence.

Neurological dysfunctions

As stated earlier, much of the theoretical understanding of learning disabilities grew out of work with brain-damaged children in the 1930s and 1940s. Strauss argued that children with brain injuries are subject to major disorders in perception, thinking, and behaviour that reduce their ability to read, write, spell, or calculate. Many theorists still attribute learning disabilities to some type of brain impairment or central nervous system dysfunction. This pathological emphasis is particularly evident among medical professionals.

In educational circles, however, the tendency over the years has been to de-emphasize pathological aspects of the problem and stress behavioural ones. Many educators today would like to see the concept of presumed neurological impairment dropped entirely. These educators prefer to focus on each child's particular perceptual, cognitive, and motor problems and skills so that appropriate pscyho-educational programming can be developed.

Uneven growth pattern

According to many definitions, children with learning disabilities exhibit peaks and valleys in their performance. These children exhibit an irregular or uneven development of the various components of mental ability. While some of the components mature quickly, other areas of development lag behind. For example, some children are precocious verbally but far behind in motor and hand skills. These children may be verbally ahead of their age group, while finding it hard to hold a pencil or crayon, make shapes, or learn to print.

An uneven growth pattern is referred to in many definitions as "a disorder in one or more of the basic psychological processes." Uneven development may be either a cause or symptom of the child's overall learning problems.

Difficulty in academic or learning tasks

Academic problems are perhaps the clearest indicators of a learning disability. A child may encounter difficulties with a wide range of learning tasks. Specific problems may occur in the acquisition of speech and oral language, in reading, in written language, in handwriting, in spelling, in arithmetic, in motor skills, in perceptual skills, in thinking, or in psychosocial skills. These problems will be discussed in greater detail later in the chapter.

Discrepancy between potential and performance

The discrepancy between a child's potential and performance refers to the gap between what the child is capable of learning and what the child actually achieves. This

Learning-disabled children may have problems in visualizing their own body positions.
(M.C. Emme)

discrepancy allows educators to distinguish learning-disabled children from those who fail because of low intelligence, emotional disturbance, or other handicapping conditions.

The child's potential is judged by the mental age obtained on standardized tests of mental ability. This is compared to the child's performance on achievement tests. A difference of two years between the estimated potential and performance is frequently used as an indicator of academic retardation. To quantify the discrepancy, a number of formulae have been developed (e.g. Myklebust, 1968).

Many professionals have cautioned against undue reliance on the discrepancy criterion. Stephens (1977) warns that the practice of using discrepancy scores in the identification of learning disabilities has not yet been proven valid. Moreover, the commonly employed qualifying formulae have also come under criticism (e.g. McLeod, 1979).

Exclusion of other causes

Most definitions of learning disabilities exclude children whose exceptionality is primarily the result other causes. Learning-disabled children are not mentally retarded, emotionally disturbed, visually handicapped, hearing impaired, or culturally, socially, or economically disadvantaged. This is not to say that children with other handicaps cannot also be learning-disabled. However, by excluding other handicaps, the learning-disabled more easily obtain the funding and legislation they need (Kirk, 1974).

Average or above-average intelligence

Inherent in the whole concept of learning disabilities, and closely associated with the exclusionary clause, is the notion that the learning-disabled child is of average or above average intelligence. It should be noted that some educators question this concept, mainly in terms of diagnostic procedures and identification (Ames, 1968; Smith, Coleman, Dokecki, and Davis, 1977).

Changing terminology

As stated earlier, a wide variety of terms have evolved to describe the child now called learning-disabled. Much of this early terminology was drawn from the field of neurology. Some terms are still in general use, and warrant some explanation.

In the following terms, the prefix *a* means *an absence of* and *dys* means *disturbance of*:

- **Agnosia** implies a lack of knowledge, an inability to recognize the significance of sensory stimuli.
- **Dysgraphia** means a disturbance in the ability to express thoughts in writing.
- **Dyscalculia** is a disturbance in the ability to use numbers and do arithmetic.
- **Dyslexia** is a disturbance in the ability to read despite conventional instruction, adequate intelligence, and socio-cultural opportunity (Tansley and Panckhurst, 1981).

Of all these terms, dyslexia is the one that has become part of the common language. Precise definitions vary but, in North America, dyslexia means a reading disability. Reading problems are the major cause of poor school performance among all children, affecting ten to fifteen percent of the school-age population (Haring and Bateman, 1977; Harris and Sipay, 1980).

Nonetheless, dyslexia and learning disability should not be used synonymously.

Many children with mild reading problems have not been categorically identified as learning-disabled. And, while many learning-disabled children have reading difficulties, others suffer from a wide spectrum of problems.

Most educators are dispensing with the term *dyslexia* in favour of *reading disability*. In 1968, the National Advisory Committee on Dyslexia and Related Reading Disorders in the United States set out to examine their terminology. The next year, the Committee stated: "In view of . . . divergencies of opinion, the Committee believes that the use of the term *dyslexia* serves no useful purpose" (p. 38).

CLASSIFICATION OF LEARNING DISABILITIES

Learning disabilities encompass a complex constellation of behaviours and conditions. As a result, they are difficult to classify or subdivide into different types. Across Canada, several different classification schemes are to be found. In one province, children may be classified according to the severity of their learning disability. In another, they may be classed according to whether their disabilities are specific or general.

Exhibit 7-3 outlines some of the more common, informal classification systems.

Exhibit 7-3 Classification of learning disabilities.

Mild	This child can be served adequately in the regular classroom with some modification of approach.
Moderate	The learning disability will cause academic problems. The child will probably require part-time assistance outside the regular classroom.
Severe	The student will require special placement to cope with the learning disability.
General	The student's academic progress is mildly retarded in most areas.
Specific	The student has severe difficulties in specific areas but performs adequately in others.
Developmental	*Primary learning disabilities* include attention deficits, memory defects, perceptual and perceptual-motor defects. *Secondary learning disabilities* include thinking and language disorders.
Academic	Academic disabilities include problems in reading, spelling, writing, and arithmetic.

Minimal brain dysfunction and hyperactivity	Excessive, non-purposive hyperactive behaviour is accompanied by lack of attention, distractibility, emotional lability, and impulsiveness. These problems may or may not be the result of organic damage.
Perceptual-motor difficulties	These include problems in visual, auditory, haptic, and motor-processing areas.
Psycholinguistic and language difficulties.	These include problems in the interpretation and use of oral and written language.

PREVALENCE OF LEARNING DISABILITIES

Because definitions of learning disabilities are imprecise, prevalence figures are impossible to accurately determine. Estimates of the prevalence of learning-disabled children vary from one to thirty percent of the school-age population depending on the criteria used to determine the disability (Lerner, 1981). Exhibit 7-4 lists the estimates produced by a number of studies.

A recent Canadian study (McMurray, 1980) found that secondary-school principals estimated that from one to twenty-one percent of their schools' students were learning-disabled. These estimates varied according to the experience of the principal and the nature of the school. Generally, however, most Canadian estimates place the number of students with serious learning disabilities at from two to four percent of the school-age population.

Exhibit 7-4 Estimated prevalence of learning disabilities in the school-age population.

Study	*Estimated Prevalence of Learning Disabilities*
National Advisory Committee on Handicapped Children (1968)	1-3 percent
Kass and Myklebust (1969)	3-5 percent
Wallace and McLoughlin (1975)	20 percent
Hammill (1976)	3 percent
Little (1980)	2-4 percent
McMurray (1980)	1-21 percent

SOME GENERAL OBSERVATIONS

Although the actual number of learning-disabled children has yet to be determined, some general observations can be made. We can be fairly certain that, in every regular classroom in Canada, several children suffer from learning disabilities. Some of these children may simply be progressing at a slower rate in language, motor, cognitive, or socio-emotional development. They become penalized by procedures intended to find potential problems (Beers and Beers, 1980), and are labelled as learning disabled.

We also know that boys with learning disabilities outnumber girls about four to one (MacGregor, Rosenbaum, and Skoutajan, 1982). The reasons for this are somewhat unclear. It may be that boys tend to indulge in more overt, acting-out behaviour, and are therefore more likely to be referred for in-depth diagnosis.

In the chapter on gifted children, we mentioned the controversial theories concerning hemispheric dominance. Some authors (Critchley and Critchley, 1978; Pavlidis and Miles, 1981) view boys as more disposed than girls to reading problems. They see four predisposing factors: less developed right-hemisphere functions; greater specialization of right-hemisphere spatial skills; a lesser degree of left-hemisphere dominance; and slower maturation despite earlier lateralization of functions (Pavlidis and Miles, 1981).

ETIOLOGY OF LEARNING DISABILITIES

The causes of learning disabilities are as complex and varied as the disabilities themselves. Moreover, various suspected causes interact in subtle ways, rendering etiology even more difficult to determine. In most cases, the cause of a child's learning disability remains unknown.

Despite these problems, numerous etiological factors have been proposed. These can be grouped into three basic categories: organic and biological; genetic; and environmental. The reader is also urged to reread the discussion of etiology in the chapter on mental retardation, as some of that material is relevant here.

Organic and biological factors

Minimal brain dysfunction (MBD).

The term **minimal brain dysfunction** (MBD) is a widely used diagnostic classification for children who present a wide variety of mildly disabling symptoms. The term suggests that slight damage to the brain hinders its most efficient functioning. Some researchers believe that minimal brain dysfunction is the root cause of all learning disabilities. However, it is seldom possible to prove that a learning-disabled child has suffered actual damage to the brain (Sandoval and Haapmanen, 1981).

Because of this lack of evidence, some professionals are willing to diagnose minimal brain dysfunction on the basis of a variety of behavioural signs (Gaddes, 1981). These behavioural signs are called "soft" signs because, unlike the "hard" signs of classical neurology, they offer only borderline indication of brain dysfunction. Examples of soft signs include an awkward gait, clumsiness, and mixed hand-dominance (Kneedler, 1984).

Although the medical profession continues to diagnose minimal brain dysfunction, special educators have reacted strongly against use of the term. The label of brain injury carries a note of finality and suggests that behavioural consequences are irreversible. Hence, the term minimal brain dysfunction may generate an array of negative expectations and attitudes.

Biochemical disturbances

Some researchers believe learning-disabled children may suffer from physiological problems, or biochemical disturbances. One of the most commonly mentioned sources of these disturbances is vitamin deficiency (Brenner, 1982). Researchers also believe that many children develop both diet- and environment-related allergies that adversely affect learning.

Food allergies were theoretically linked to hyperactivity by Feingold (1975, 1976). Feingold noted that artificial flavours, artificial preservatives, and artificial dyes were consumed in increasing quantities by North American children. He argued that approximately fifty percent of hyperactive children can be helped by eliminating from their diet artificial food colourings, dyes, and foods, such as apples, oranges, tomatoes, and strawberries, that naturally contain salicylates.

Very little solid evidence exists to support the theory of vitamin deficiency as a cause of learning disabilities. Support for the food-allergy theory is stronger. However, the findings of a few well-conducted studies indicate that Feingold's diet may only help a small percentage of hyperactive children (Spring and Sandoval, 1976). A few studies also suggest that claims for the importance of food allergies in causing learning disabilities are exaggerated (Henker and Whalen, 1980).

Maturational lag

A **maturation lag** means that a child is slow to reach some developmental milestones. Professionals estimate that between five and forty percent of kindergarten children with average or above-average intelligence experience developmental lags or perceptual handicaps (Bradley, 1975).

Several investigators have suggested that the immaturity of some learning-disabled youngsters is related to a maturational lag (Bender, 1968; De Hirsch, Jansky, and Langford, 1966). A lag does not necessarily imply a structural deficiency or limited potential. Children whose learning disabilities are the result of developmental lags may partly overcome their behaviour and learning problems as they grow older (Byrant, 1972).

Genetic factors

Learning disabilities tend to run in families (Owen, Adams, Forrest, Stoltz, and Fisher, 1971). Whether this is due to hereditary factors or to similar learning environments is still a matter of speculation. However, Yule and Rutter (1976) reported that slow-reading children were three times more likely to reveal a family history of reading difficulties. A large-scale study (Decker and Defries, 1980, 1981) compared the families of 125 children with reading disorders to a control group of average readers. The researchers found common reading problems in the families of the poor readers, especially among male members. This led them to argue that learning problems were familial in nature.

Of course, writing, spelling and reading problems are not biological features that can be inherited. Rather they stem from some underlying cognitive or neurological deficit. Research can only indicate in general that reading problems seem to be inherited. They cannot pinpoint which aspect of the problem is due to heredity (Thomson, 1984).

Environmental factors

The two environmental problems that have been studied most are the lack of early psychological stimulation and the effects of severe malnutrition. These two etiological factors are not always independent; in many cases, malnutrition and lack of early stimulation operate on the same child.

In the chapter on mental retardation, we discussed the difficulty of pinpointing environment as a cause. This is even more true of learning disabilities. The vast majority of learning-disabled children do not come from impoverished homes (Kneedler, 1984).

Some researchers argue that poor school environments may be a primary cause of mild learning disabilities (Engelmann, 1977; Haring, 1978; Lovitt, 1978). Engelmann (1977) argues that "Perhaps ninety percent or more of the children who are labelled 'learning-disabled' exhibit a disability not because of anything wrong with their perception, synapses, or memory, but because they have been seriously mistaught. Learning disabilities are made, not born" (pp. 46-47). Lloyd (1975) describes this phenomenon as teaching failure, **dyspedagogia**, or maleducation. He suggests that children in this category do not have learning problems, but their schools do.

Proponents of Lloyd's point of view believe that if teachers were better prepared to handle the special learning problems of children in the early school years, many learning disabilities could be avoided. Dyspedagogia implies more than poor teaching, however. It also includes poor curricula, poor health in the child, and poor attendance at school. Poor parental or professional attitudes may also function to weaken the child's motivation.

PREVENTION OF LEARNING DISABILITIES

The prevention of many learning problems has already been outlined in the section on the prevention of mental retardation in Chapter Four. The reader should review that section, bearing in mind its partial relevance to the prevention of learning disabilities. More specifically, however, one way to prevent learning disabilities is through the prevention of neurological damage. In addition, dyspedagogia can be to some extent eliminated through efficient early identification, early intervention, and appropriate program delivery.

DIAGNOSIS AND MEASUREMENT OF LEARNING DISABILITIES

When diagnosing a learning disability, the primary goal is to gather and analyze enough pertinent information to teach the child effectively. The major clinicians and educators try to pinpoint the child's atypical behaviour, explain it, and differentiate it from similar problems of other handicapped children. They then use this information to develop the remedial program best suited to the child's disability.

Some learning disabilities can be identified on the basis of sensitive observations by a skilled teacher or through scores obtained on group achievement tests. Discrepancies in a child's level of achievement in different areas may also be an important indicator of an underlying learning disorder. At other times, however, behaviour difficulties or conduct problems may mask a learning disability that is unsuspected by school personnel.

The diagnosis and identification of learning-disabled children often suffers from lack of co-ordination. Many professionals, within and outside the school system, become involved in the process. Each of these may hold very different views regarding the nature of learning disabilities. The pediatrician may stress minimal brain dysfunction, the psychiatrist behavioural disorders, and the psychologist intellectual adequacy.

Even within the school system, diagnosis and identification are often rather hit-and-miss. There is currently no single procedure to identify learning disabilities. Clinicians use a variety of tests and rely heavily on personal diagnostic judgement. There is little consensus regarding when children should be tested, by whom, and to what purpose.

As a result of inconsistent diagnostic procedures, children may be identified as learning-disabled in one province, or even in one school district, and not in another. Quite different identification procedures are employed across the country. For example, a 1980 Ontario study (MacIntyre, Keeton and Agard) found that school boards had independently developed their own assessment systems. These varied widely in the testing instruments, types of professional, and committees that were used. Another study in British Columbia (Winzer and Malarczyk, 1985) found little consistency in instrumentation, personnel, time of testing, and types of program delivery.

Generally, identification involves two processes — screening and diagnosis. Screening procedures examine large age-groups to identify children who fall below specified levels in areas of behaviour and attainment. Diagnosis follows screening, and investigates selected children to determine the precise nature of their difficulties.

Figure 7-1 outlines the major areas involved in the diagnostic process.

Lerner (1981) notes that data for diagnosis can be obtained in five major ways. These methods are not discrete, but overlap and complement one another. Lerner's measures include: a case history and/or interview; observation; informal testing; criterion referenced testing; and formal standardized testing.

Case history

The case history offers information, insights, and clues concerning the child's background and development. Parents or other primary caregivers can provide firsthand information about the family setting, the learning problems of other family members, the child's health history, and the child's prenatal, birth, and perinatal history. They can also report the age at which the child reached various developmental milestones, and discuss

Figure 7-1 An overview of the diagnostic process.

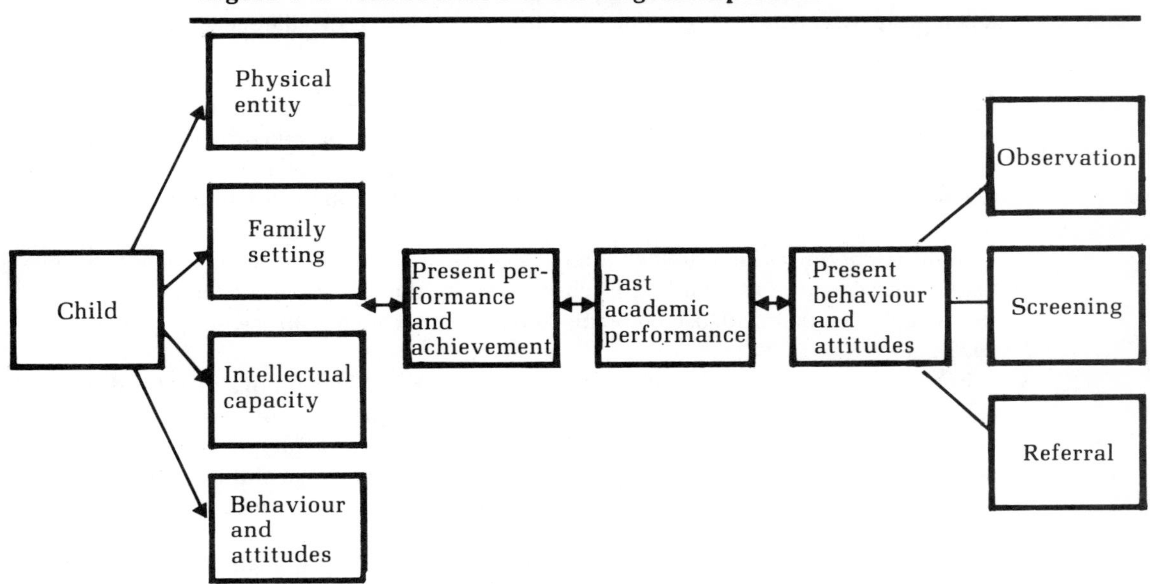

the child's behavioural and attitudinal responses within the family and community. The child's school history can also be obtained from parents, school files, and school personnel. Older children can be interviewed to supply additional information about their interests, aspirations, and concerns.

Observation

Parents, teachers, and others can observe the child's behavioural and attitudinal responses in a variety of settings. In the classroom, the observer might note such items as off-task and out-of-seat behaviour, ability to follow directions, ability to use spoken language, and motor control and mobility.

Pupil-behaviour rating scales and behavioural checklists are often used to quantify and document observations. Rating scales are usually completed by the classroom teacher. They are a quick and inexpensive instrument for measuring, recording, and communicating information about large numbers of children (Winzer and Malarczyk, 1984). Rating scales help to identify students at various levels of school adjustment and provide information about how well each child is functioning. They predict learning problems and allow a comparison of each child's behaviour and performance with the group norm (Kratochwill, 1980; Swift and Spivack, 1969). Because children are observed in a more or less standard classroom situation (Edelbrock, 1979), their behaviour is measured at the time and place of its natural occurrence.

Many rating scales are currently in use. The Referral Check List, for example, assesses levels of communication and socialization (Huberty, Quirk, and Swan, 1973; Morris and Arrant, 1978). The Conners' Teacher Rating Scale helps teachers to describe behaviour problems, especially those related to hyperactivity (Conners, 1969; Goyette, Conners, and Ulrich, 1978). The Myklebust Pupil Rating Scale was developed as one component of a comprehensive study of learning disabilities in children (Myklebust, 1971; 1973).

Informal testing

Recently, there has been a growing disenchantment with formal tests and a trend toward the use of informal measures. These measures are usually designed by the teacher to address the problems of individual children. As a result, informal measures encourage teachers to look closely at what specific skills are involved in the learning of academic tasks.

Informal measures include such things as check lists, inventories, and teacher-made tests. Assessment of reading can be carried out by the use of miscue (error) analysis (Burke and Goodman, 1970; Goodman, 1967) or through "cloze procedures" (Jongsma, 1971).

Inventories are simply lists of skills that the teacher can look for in students. **Miscue analysis** offers a more sophisticated measure to assess reading errors. A **miscue** occurs when the reader misinterprets semantic, syntactic, or graphophonic cues to predict events that do no occur in the text (Ewoldt, 1982). For example, a child might read the sentence "the boy sat on the step" as "the boy fell on the steps." In this case, "fell" would be a miscue, although "steps" would not.

Cloze procedures measure reading difficulty, serve as a diagnostic tool, and offer insight into a child's language competence. Every fifth word in a reading passage is omitted, until there are up to a hundred blanks. The child fills each blank with the "best," or most suitable, word. Children who score eighty percent or over are operating at an independent reading level. Children who score between forty and eighty percent are at a reading instructional level, and those who score below forty percent are at a frustration level for that reading selection.

Criterion-referenced testing

Like informal measures, criterion-referenced tests are usually designed by the individual teacher to assess the problems of the individual child. Unlike standardized tests, they do not compare the child's results to an age, grade or performance norm.

Criterion-referenced tests attempt to measure the child's specific degree of knowledge in a particular area of learning. The teacher sets instructional objectives, or criteria, for the child to work toward. For example, the teacher's objective may be to teach the child the letters of the alphabet. The child's performance is then assessed in relation to the criterion, the alphabet.

Criterion-referenced testing is particularly easy to integrate with a child's individual educational program. The testing is performed simply to determine what needs to be taught.

Formal testing

By definition, a learning disability involves a discrepancy between a child's potential and performance. Therefore, one of the first steps in the formal diagnosis of a learning disability is an assessment of the child's intellectual potential. Once this is judged to be normal, the child's academic performance must be assessed. Tests to determine the child's psychological processing are also given. In fact, there are literally hundreds of tests and measures that can be used to assess the child's various areas of functioning.

The efficacy of some of the measures in the assessment of learning-disabled children has come into question. A discussion of this issue would be too complex for this introductory text. For a Canadian perspective, the reader is referred to Bunch and Robertson (1979). A more detailed analysis can be found in Sattler (1982).

Exhibit 7-5 outlines some of the main tools employed in the identification of learning-disabled children in Canada. Of course, not all of these measures are used at any one time. The tester chooses those most suitable for the learning problems of the individual child.

Exhibit 7-5 Some measures used to identify children with learning disabilities.

Early identification tests	Boehm Test of Basic Concepts Denver Developmental Screening Test Medvedeff Assessment System Metropolitan Readiness Test (Slingerland) Pre-reading Screening Procedures
Tests of mental ability	McCarthy Scales of Children's Abilities Slosson Intelligence Test Wechsler Intelligence Scale for Children (WISC-R)
Achievement tests	Canadian Test of Basic Skills (CTBS) Durrell Analysis of Reading Difficulty Gates-McKillop Reading Test Peabody Individual Achievement Test Stanford Achievement Tests Wide Range Achievement Test (WRAT)
Language tests	Peabody Picture Vocabulary Test (PPVT) Test of Adolescent Language (TOAL) Test of Language Development (TOLD) Test of Written Language (TOWL)
Process-oriented tests:	
Visual tests	Beery Buklentica Test of Visual Motor Integration Bender Visual Motor Gestalt Test Frostig Developmental Test of Visual Perception
Auditory tests	Goldman-Friscoe-Woodcock Test of Auditory Discrimination Illinois Test of Psycholinguistic Abilities Wepman Test of Auditory Discrimination
Memory tests	Benton Visual Retention Test Graham-Kendall Memory for Designs Test
Motor tests	Purdue Perceptual Motor Survey
Behaviour tests	Myklebust Pupil Behaviour Rating Scale
Social tests	Vineland Social Maturity Scale

Tests of mental ability

The major purpose of intellectual assessment is to rule out the possibility of mental retardation. The most widely employed IQ test in the identification of learning disabilities is the Wechsler Intelligence Scale for Children — Revised (Wechsler, 1974). Most professionals agree that the WISC-R has proven both valid and reliable in the assessment of the intelligence of learning-disabled children.

Some psychologists look for a discrepancy between the child's scores on the Verbal and Performance scales of the WISC-R. They may also place considerable emphasis on the pattern of subtest scores. A wide scatter of scores may indicate peaks and valleys in the child's development, an indicator of a learning disability.

Achievement tests

Standardized achievement tests are commonly used to assess the child's performance in the school setting. These may be administered individually or to a group of children. Because learning-disabled children have a variety of academic problems, achievement tests measure a spectrum of academic tasks such as oral reading, reading comprehension, language, spelling, math, and general knowledge.

Process-oriented tests and measures

Psychological processing refers to how an individual interprets sensory information and puts it to meaningful intellectual use. Theories about learning disabilities have long taken into account the possibility of processing deficiencies. As Torgesen (1979) argues, when a child of normal intelligence receives essentially the same information as other children and yet responds very differently, we can assume that the child is processing the information in some different manner. In the absence of deep behavioural disturbances, the learning-disabled child is set apart by unique behaviours in the mind. These behaviours have typically been referred to as the psychological processes.

Psychological-process problems are not directly observable and must be inferred from the child's academic performance. These problems are thought to underly certain academic difficulties. For example, a child's reading problem may be the result of a process-problem in auditory discrimination or visual figure-ground. Tests are given to identify the specific psychological processes in which the child is deficient. The child's education program then focuses on the underlying deficits rather than on the reading problem directly.

The use of tests to diagnose underlying processing deficits has been introduced only since the introduction of learning disabilities as an exceptional category. These tests have caused much concern and controversy. Opponents argue that it is impossible to accurately assess underlying psychological processes. They maintain that some of the most widely used testing instruments are poor predictors of academic achievement.

A wide variety of psychological processing tests are available. These purport to assess such areas as auditory and visual processing, underlying motor sub-skills, and tactile and kinesthetic functions. Exhibit 7-6 shows the auditory and visual processing sub-skills upon which many of these tests focus.

Exhibit 7-6 Examples of visual and auditory processes.

Process	*Ability*	*Implications and Problems*
visual perception	The ability to make visual stimuli meaningful.	The child may have problems attending to and interpreting visual stimuli.
visual discrimination	The ability to perceive dominant features in different objects or symbols.	The child may confuse letters and words that look alike. The child may not see the internal detail, as in *rid/red,* or may fail to see the general configuration, as in *ship/snip.*
visual closure	The ability to identify a common object from an incomplete visual presentation.	The child may have difficulty assembling puzzles and objects, identifying missing parts, or completing words by closing spaces between letters, as in *rab-bit.*
visual figure-ground	The ability to focus on the foreground and ignore the background visual stimuli.	The child may not be able to distinguish words; for example, the child may be unable to point to the first word of a second paragraph.
visual memory	The ability to recall the dominant features of the stimulus item.	The child may not be able to copy patterns or arrange blocks in a series.
visual sequential memory	The ability to recollect the sequence of a number of items presented visually.	The child fails to recognize visually familiar words and forgets the arrangement of letters in a word.
auditory perception	The ability to recognize and interpret stimuli that are heard.	The child may have problems attending to and interpreting auditory stimuli.
auditory discrimination	The ability to recognize differences between sounds and to identify similarities and differences between words.	The child may not hear the similarities in initial or final sounds in words or be able to discriminate short vowels such as *pin, pan, pen.*

auditory closure	The ability to identify sounds and words from an incomplete auditory presentation.	The child may have problems in sound-symbol association and especially in blending sounds.
auditory figure-ground	The ability to focus on the foreground sound and ignore other sounds.	The child may not focus on the dominant sound; the fan on the overhead projector may be more important than the teacher's voice.
auditory memory	The ability to recognize and recall previously presented auditory stimuli.	The child may have problems retaining and recalling auditory experiences.
auditory sequential memory	The ability to reproduce from memory sequences presented auditorally.	The child may forget or confuse oral directions, the sequence of events, the sequence of letters in a word, or the sequence of words in a sentence.

Early identification of learning disabilities

There are obvious advantages in the early identification of potential learning disorders. Early identification may prevent the child from developing bad habits that have to be unlearned. Teachers are well aware, for example, of how difficult it is to change the way children form letters in cursive script once they have internalized incorrect formations. Most importantly, however, early identification may prevent the child from entering the frustration and failure cycle typical of intelligent children who fail to learn.

Early identification of learning difficulties requires considerable skill in prediction. Educators and clinicians must identify children likely to encounter school problems before they have been exposed to formal school programs. Early identification can:

- Locate children who are not developing at a satisfactory rate in psycho-motor or cognitive areas.
- Locate children who may be academically or socially at risk, and who may require more in-depth evaluation, remediation, or medical treatment.
- Locate children who are not developing language at a satisfactory rate and may require additional instruction.
- Enable school personnel to understand the child's problems and plan educational experiences that maximize the child's strengths.
- Enable the provision of services during the critical formative years of the child's education.
- Distinguish a learning disability from other childhood handicaps, such as mental retardation or emotional disturbance.

Early identification of learning disabilities must be used to plan appropriate programs rather than simply to label or categorize the child. Findings must be frequently monitored to reflect and encourage changes in the child's competency. As well, care must be taken not to label children "high risk" on the basis of minimal evidence or to justify over-zealous testing.

The optimal time for screening is still a matter of debate, but there is increasing evidence to support pre-school screening. Pre-school children are identified through developmental disabilities because they have not yet encountered academic subjects. Pre-school identification is directly related to behaviours observed by parents and pre-school teachers. Problem behaviours might include poor attention span or failure to respond to oral language and visual symbols. A child might also be out of touch with the environment, manifested by poor motor control, low body image, and poor visual and auditory discrimination.

In Canada, early identification techniques are often applied prior to or just at school entry (Davidson, Silverman and Hughes, 1981). In Ontario, for example, school boards must have established procedures to identify the learning abilities of all children at entry into kindergarten or grade one. British Columbia uses a three- to four-month observation period in kindergarten, and Quebec has initiated readiness-testing in kindergarten. New Brunswick carries out pre-school screening in the community prior to fall school entry. Nova Scotia experimented with pre-kindergarten identification procedures, but now uses kindergarten for early identification (Davidson, Silverman, and Hughes, 1981).

In kindergarten, as at the pre-school level, the observation of behaviour serves as a valuable indicator of potential learning problems. Tests at the kindergarten level attempt to assess a child's readiness for academic learning in specific areas of school achievement. These tests are also used as screening instruments in the early identification of academic difficulties.

A variety of screening methods and systems are used for early identification. Slingerland (1968), for example, has a pre-reading screening procedure that can be used with first-graders to assess potential reading disorders. A similar screening device, widely used in Canada (O'Connor, 1980), has been developed by Jansky and De Hirsch (1972).

Educators have enthusiastically endorsed the concept of early identification as a preventive strategy for children with potential learning disabilities. Unfortunately, however, despite this endorsement, early identification is often neglected. One Canadian study (Davidson, Silverman, and Hughes, 1981) attempted to gather data on early identification outside Ontario. The investigation produced scant data, and the comments of respondents in various ministries of education suggested that early identification programs were not a high priority. All the provinces did indicate that some form of identification for exceptional and at-risk children was in place. However, identification procedures showed little consistency across school districts (Davidson, Silverman and Hughes, 1981).

In Ontario, early identification is now enforced by the Education Amendment Act. Many Ontario school boards have developed their own assessment procedures. Others use the Windsor Early Identification procedures, or adaptations of it.

The Windsor Early Identification Project

The Windsor Early Identification Project was a research project initiated in 1970 and funded by the Ontario Ministry of Education. By 1975, all schools in the Windsor School Board were following its recommendations for early identification procedures.

The Project emphasizes teacher observations supported by medical and social data provided by the parents. It aims to predict a child's learning problems in grade one and prevent them from developing further. The Project stresses four interrelated steps in the identification process. These are parent involvement; determination of the child's health status; identification of the child's educational needs; and follow-up treatment of the child's identified learning problems.

Parent involvement first takes the form of pre-registration and registration interviews. Later, parents are informed of the teacher's observations. If they are interested, they are informed of steps they can take to assist their children in the home.

The child's health status is screened by public health nurses. Special attention is paid to hearing, vision, and speech.

In the senior kindergarten year, the teacher rates each child's global functioning as markedly problematic, mildly below average, average, or above average. The teacher uses a kit to assess such areas as colour recognition, math skills, and receptive and expressive language. Scores are converted to a five-point rating scale and compared to the child's age, pre-school experience, and attendance level. Behavioural characteristics are also taken into account, such as passivity, overactivity, level of self-esteem, attention span, and level of adjustment.

When the screening indicates, specific children can be more fully diagnosed using the School Readiness Test. This procedure was developed and first administered by board psychologists in Windsor. After testing, programming is then developed with the help of primary consultants.

The Windsor Early Identification procedures enable curricula to be adapted and individualized as soon as possible in a child's career. Throughout the next years, the child's progress and educational program are continually re-evaluated. The school also plays a key role in keeping parents informed of their children's progress (O'Bryan, 1976, 1979, 1981).

CHARACTERISTICS OF LEARNING-DISABLED CHILDREN

Many dozens of different characteristics have been attributed to the learning-disabled. Most of us have at least one of the various symptoms of learning disabilities. However, one symptom does not make a learning disability. Children with learning disabilities exhibit an entire syndrome, or collection, of symptoms. Their problems lie well outside the normal range for their age-level, and persist despite repeated efforts to correct them. They are handicapped by their disabilities, and prevented from realizing their full potential (Dow, O'Reilly, Hill, and Dostaler, 1981).

Clements (1966) listed ten major characteristics of learning disabilities, in order of frequency.

- Hyperactivity.
- Perceptual-motor impairments.
- Emotional lability.
- General co-ordination deficits.
- Disorders of attention.
- Impulsivity.
- Disorders of memory and thinking.
- Specific academic problems (reading, writing, spelling, arithmetic).
- Disorders of speech and hearing.
- Equivocal neurological signs and EEG irregularities.

Since Clements' report, very little systematic, experimental research has been done to determine the incidence, or even the nature, of these characteristics. Moreover, Clements' list is no longer considered accurate in its order of frequency. For example, academic problems are now considered the primary characteristic of learning disabilities, rather than placing eighth.

Very few, if any, learning-disabled children exhibit all the characteristics on Clements' list. However, the list provides a good starting point for discussion. In the following pages, Clements' characteristics have been regrouped for organization and clarity.

Perceptual, perceptual-motor, and co-ordination problems

Early researchers who studied brain damaged children often looked for perceptual disturbances in their subjects. Samuel Orton, Heinz Werner, and Alfred Strauss were pioneers in this area. They identified a number of perceptual abnormalities, sometimes in children with no evidence of brain damage. Associates of Strauss and Werner, such as Newell Kephart, later popularized the notion that learning-disabled children also have perceptual and perceptual-motor problems (Hallahan and Kauffman, 1982). Several leading authorities continue to stress that perception and neurological problems are key factors in learning disabilities (Cruickshank, 1976). However, in recent years, emphasis on perceptual problems has diminished.

Perception involves the use of the senses to recognize, discriminate, and interpret stimuli. Those unable to perform these functions are said to have perceptual disorders. Perceptual problems can also be classed as psychological processing deficits. Those ascribed to learning-disabled children include visual and auditory processing dysfunctions, as well as haptic disorders. Haptic perception concerns information transmitted through touch, body movement, and position.

Visual perception problems are most commonly associated with learning disabilities. Children with visual perceptual problems are prone to difficulties with oculomotor co-ordination, with spatial relations, with figure-ground perception, with the discrimination of differences, and with the recognition of likenesses. Many studies (e.g. Calfee, 1977; Coleman, 1968; Leton, 1962; Lyle, 1968; Satz, Taylor, Friel, and Fletcher, 1978; Whipple and Kodman, 1969) indicate that visual perceptual problems are common among reading-disabled children. Although some of these studies can be criticized on methodological grounds, the evidence strongly suggests that learning-disabled children, as a group, perform poorly on tasks designed to assess visual perceptual abilities (Hallahan, 1975).

Children with auditory processing dysfunctions are frequently not discovered until much later than visually impaired children. Children with auditory problems are often first recognized when they attempt to spell words. Their poor spelling results from their inability to discriminate sounds, to blend sounds, and to encode (spell) or decode (read) words.

Most perceptual research into reading problems has concentrated on visual rather than auditory functions. This has been based on the assumption that reading is primarily a visual task, an assumption that research into the reading process is currently revising. Certainly spelling and writing are not simply visual processes (Thomson, 1984). Several studies (Flynn and Byrne, 1970; Golden and Steiner, 1969; Harber, 1980; Henry, 1975; Lingren, 1969) have shown that auditory disorders occur with greater than normal frequency among learning-disabled children. In a classroom, the child with an auditory dysfunction may have difficulty synthesizing sounds into words, analyzing words into word parts, and associating sounds with symbols.

Haptic problems are thought to be relatively uncommon (Mercer, 1979). They may be important in handwriting, because tactile information dictates the grasp of a pen or pencil. However, many researchers have suggested a relationship between visual-motor and haptic abilities and body image and laterality (Hallahan, Kauffman, and Lloyd, 1985).

Body image refers to children's awareness of their bodies, the inter-relation of their body parts, and the relationship of their bodies to the environment. Children with body-image problems may not be able to organize themselves within their environment. They may have difficulty putting on a sweater, or walking across the classroom without knocking down chairs and desks.

Laterality implies an awareness within the body of the difference between left and right. **Directionality** refers to an awareness of left and right in the environment outside the body. At approximately five or six years of age, most children consistently prefer to use one side of their bodies in dealing with the world (Murray, 1981). Dominance can easily be evaluated by simply noting which hand, foot, or eye the child prefers to use. The preferred hand is established by asking the child to write or to throw a ball; the preferred foot by asking the child to hop or kick a ball. The dominant eye is determined by asking the child to look through a paper folded into a cone (Cheek, 1978; Murray, 1981).

The laterality theory maintains that learning is adversely affected if the child does not establish a tendency to perform most functions with one side of the body. Many children who use their left hand are considered at high-risk for learning disabilities. According to the theory, mixed dominance is not a problem in itself. Rather, problems arise when children confuse directionality or fail to discriminate right from left (Belmont and Birch, 1973). Difficulties may also arise when a child is forced to change hands to perform a task (Cheek, 1978; Eden, 1978). However, after a survey of the literature related to hemispheric dominance, Leong (1980) determined that support for the laterality theory was less than conclusive. Mercer (1982) observed that most researchers and professionals in medicine, psychology, and education place little practical value on the theory.

Children with perceptual-motor impairments have problems identifying or reproducing information they receive through their senses. These children have difficulty discriminating symbols, and may reverse letters and shapes in their printing and drawing. They have trouble accurately reproducing or copying information received visually or auditorily. Examples of perceptual-motor problems include difficulties in identifying the letters of the alphabet, reading the printed page from left to right, drawing basic shapes, and staying on the line when printing or writing.

General inco-ordination refers to a lack of muscular control. A student with gross motor control problems may walk with an awkward gait, have difficulty throwing or catching a ball, or have trouble skipping and hopping.

Hyperactivity and disorders of attention

The hyperactive syndrome was first described in the medical literature a century ago. Since that time, it has become one of the most deeply investigated and controversial disorders within the fields of pediatric medicine, clinical psychology, and education (Gadow, 1979). Strauss and Werner pinpointed hyperactivity as a major problem among the children they studied. As we have seen, Clements (1966) gave hyperactivity top billing in his list of characteristics of learning-disabled youngsters.

Hyperactive children display rates of motor activity that are too high for their age-groups. They indulge in excessive, non-purposeful movement. Their accelerated rates of activity disturb others, worry teachers, and cause their families discomfort and even despair. The hyperactive child, says Csapo (1976), slides down the banisters of school life with all the splinters pointing the wrong way.

The prevalence of hyperactivity is estimated at between five and ten percent of the school-age population (Gadow, 1979). Hyperactive boys outnumber girls four or five to one (Rutter, 1975).

PROFILE 7-2

John is seven years old and in a grade-two class. His teacher describes him as fidgety, as boundlessly energetic, as an excessive talker to the point of perseveration. According to his teacher, John only attends to tasks for a very short period, and often fails to complete work at all. He draws attention to himself in the classroom by being awkward and clumsy, and acts out his anger rather than verbalizing it. John also has trouble making and keeping friends. He seldom engages in constructive play, alone or with classmates.

John's mother found similar behaviour in the home. John could never seem to sit still. He talked from morning to night, wandering aimlessly from one topic to another. In the social domain, he showed extreme frustration when corrected, and often embarrassed his family in public. He was also very hard on his personal possessions.

Because John was an only child, his parents had no other children to compare his behaviour with. However, they were deeply concerned about his behaviour and reaching the point of exhaustion. They readily agreed when the school personnel suggested an in-depth diagnostic work-up.

A psychoeducational assessment confirmed the observations of John's teacher and parents. Although the psychologist found John inattentive, distractible, and unable to control his continuous activity, he did manage to complete a WISC-R and a number of other tests. The psychologist concluded that John displayed normal intelligence. His severe learning deficits, such as his inability to read, were due to his disturbing classroom behaviour. The psychologist found that John had not yet developed laterality and experienced left-right confusion. John performed poorly on auditory tasks involving discrimination, sequence, and memory. This may have accounted for his anomalies in articulation and syntax, as well as his failure to learn basic reading skills through a phonics approach. The psychologist suggested that further medical evaluation of John's hyperactive behaviour be undertaken. (Adapted from Darnforth, 1984).

Young hyperactive children are constantly on the move, pushing, poking, asking questions, but never waiting for answers. In the classroom, they are unable to sit still. When confined to a seat, they translate their need to be active into finger- and foot-tapping, as well as other disruptive activities.

Hyperactive teenagers may manifest their condition differently. These students drum their fingers, shuffle their feet, open and close their desks, and continually visit the pencil sharpener, other desks, and other areas of distraction. An estimated eighty percent of hyperactive children remain hyperactive as adults. Then they may experience difficulties in forming close relationships and display impulsive behaviour (Hyperactive children . . . , 1979).

Hyperactive children suffer from short attention spans, as do children with other attention disorders. Children who cannot sit still have great dificulty initiating and sustaining the thought processes needed for school work. Children with attention disorders find it hard to focus and hold their attention for appropriate lengths of time. They are repeatedly unable to concentrate on specific tasks long enough to complete them.

Children with attention disorders are easily distractible. They are unable to concentrate on a task because they have not learned to screen out irrelevant stimuli. They may also **perseverate**, in which they purposelessly, and sometimes disadvantageously, repeat an activity. For example, a child may finish addition problems on page one and continue them on page two, even though the instructions clearly indicate a switch to subtraction.

At the other extreme from hyperactivity are those children called hypoactive. **Hypoactivity** describes a state of unnatural non-activity. Hypoactive children may sit quietly for long periods in school but accomplish very little work. They do not disrupt the class or disturb the teacher. In fact, their very stillness may cause their problems to be overlooked.

Language problems

Perhaps as many as half of all learning-disabled children have speech and language problems (Marge, 1972). However, until recently, professionals have tended to overlook language in favour of perceptual problems. Systematic research into language problems has only been undertaken in the last few years. Only minimal research exists concerning the speech and language problems of adolescent learning-disabled students (Sitko and Gillespie, 1970).

Learning-disabled children exhibit a variety of language deficits. Although they have problems with both expressive and receptive language, they seem to have greater difficulty using expressive language (Hessler and Kitchen, 1980; Noel, 1980).

Learning-disabled children often have difficulties with articulation (Montgomery, 1981). They may show immature speech patterns, mild speech irregularities, and general unintelligibility. They may also show cluttering — a rapid, jerky, stumbling speech with marked omissions (Harris, 1970). They may substitute inappropriate words, repeat the same phrase over and over, or use a monotonous voice. Learning-disabled students may have problems organizing phrases and words into sentences. They are also more likely to make syntactical or grammatical errors (Bryan and Pflaum, 1978; Vogel, 1974).

When listening, learning-disabled children tend to misperceive spoken phonemes requiring very fine discriminations, such as /m/ and /n/. They also confuse voiced and unvoiced consonants, such as /f/ and /v/ (Wiig and Semel, 1976).

Learning-disabled children may have problems with semantics, the meaning of language (Denckla and Rudel, 1976; Wiig and Semel, 1974). They are also likely to have difficulties with pragmatics, the appropriate use of language in social settings (Bryan, Donahue and Pearl, 1981; Noel, 1980). Learning-disabled children tend to take things very literally, missing the subtle nuances of language. For example, one learning-disabled adolescent went to the laundromat for the first time with a small load of washing. On a towel, he had read the instruction, "Wash colors separately." He proceeded to do exactly that, using a separate washing machine for each shade of colour. He spent nine dollars and infuriated the other patrons. Another student was handed a tape by a frazzled teacher and asked to "Put it on the video." The boy set it neatly on top of the machine.

Disorders of memory and thinking

Children with memory and thinking disorders have difficulty remembering information over long or short periods of time. They have trouble recalling what things sounded like or looked like. These children forget basic personal information, such as their telephone numbers, and they forget words learned only the day before. Memory of past experiences must be retained and compared in order to organize and interpret information. Otherwise, each experience is unique, with no referrent to past learning.

Recently, there has been a growing interest in the memory problems of learning-disabled children. In general, these children demonstrate memory deficits for both auditory and visual stimuli (Aten and Davis, 1968; Bakker, 1967, 1971; Bryan, 1974, Cohen and Netley, 1981; Kail, Chi, Ingram and Danner, 1977; Kauffman, 1976; Torgesen and Goldman, 1977). Teachers frequently report that learning-disabled students forget spelling words, math facts, or directions.

Learning-disabled students may have deficits in **metacognition**, the awareness of basic learning strategies. Metacognition involves two major components: an awareness of the skills, strategies, and resources needed to perform a task effectively; and the ability to use self-regulating mechanisms to ensure the successful completion of the task. These self-regulating mechanisms may include planning one's moves, evaluating the effectiveness of one's ongoing activities, checking the outcomes of one's efforts, and remediating whatever difficulties arise (Baker, 1982; Kneedler, 1984).

Thinking requires the ability to conceptualize and solve problems. Because learning-disabled children are of normal intelligence, they are clearly able to think. However, many learning-disabled children are weak in concept development and problem-solving strategies (Braun, 1963; Hallahan, Kauffman, and Ball, 1973). Many also experience problems with abstraction, conceptualization, and generalization. Because words are the tools of thought, these difficulties may stem from limited vocabulary or the inability to absorb the full significance of words.

Students who organize information poorly tend to be impulsive when solving problems. They are likely to miss a logical train of thought and fail to consider appropriate alternatives before embarking on a course of action. In addition, they tend not to learn from experience. Their responses to problem situations indicate an inability to generalize and apply what they have learned in other situations.

DEVELOPMENTAL CONSEQUENCES OF LEARNING DISABILITIES

Our knowledge of the developmental consequences of learning disabilities remains sparse and hypothetical. We do know however, that learning-disabled children experience academic, social, and personality problems. These latter problems are often accompanied by an emotional overlay, manifested in emotional or behavioural problems.

Academic problems

Academic underachievement is the hallmark of the learning-disabled population. Some children suffer deficits in all areas; for others, only a few specific academic skills may be affected. Reading, writing, and mathematics are three of the major areas in which difficulties occur.

As we have already stated, attention disorders further compound academic problems. Learning-disabled children have been found less attentive in a variety of school subjects (Bryan, 1974). They demonstrate less task-oriented behaviour during instruction, and more non-constructive off-task behaviour. One study found a learning-disabled sample to be on task only fifty-seven percent of the time, as compared to seventy percent for the nondisabled sample (McKinney, McLure and Feagans, 1982). Learning-disabled children often displayed a maladaptive style of response during instructional activities, possibly as a result of their poor cognitive performance.

Reading disorders rank high on the list of the academic problems of learning-disabled children. Approximately ten to fifteen percent of the general school-age population have reading difficulties (Harris and Sipay, 1980). Among learning-disabled children, the figure could be as high as eighty-five percent (Kaluger and Kolson, 1978). At the secondary level, the primary reading disability of learning-disabled students is in the area of reading comprehension (Lindsay and Kerlin, 1979).

Students with hard-core reading difficulties might have a variety of problems. They may be unable to deal with symbols, unable to synthesize parts of a word into a whole, or unable to organize words into meaningful clusters. Reading-disabled students often miss or confuse important details, such as *and* or *but*, resulting in confused interpretations of meaning. When these students read aloud, their reading may be stilted and full of substitutions, omissions, and additions.

Someone once quipped that the ability to spell is a gift from God (Lerner, 1981). Spelling is one area of the curriculum where neither creativity nor divergent thinking is encouraged — only one pattern of letters is considered correct. Although many good readers spell badly, bad readers are nearly always terrible spellers (Lerner, 1981). The spelling achievement of many learning-disabled children lags behind their grade placement (Carpenter and Miller, 1982; Frauenheim, 1978). Many of these children also show marked impairment in all other forms of written expression.

Although much literature has been produced on disabilities, little research has concerned problems of written expression. Some learning-disabled children can speak well yet cannot write a simple sentence. At the secondary level, a student's linguistic age in writing may lag six to eight years behind the linguistic age in speaking (Weiner, 1979). Some children have serious spelling difficulties, and others are unable to classify and categorize information into coherent sentences (Wallace and McLoughlin, 1975). For other youngsters, problems in written expression stem from a lack of understanding of linguistic rules. These children are unable to produce sentences displaying correct syntactic and grammatical order (Wallace and McLoughlin, 1975). Their most frequent mistakes involve word omissions, distorted word order, incorrect verb and pronoun usage, and lack of punctuation (Johnson and Myklebust, 1967).

Students with a handwriting disability tend to write laboriously and as little as possible. They may produce clearly deviant writing, manifested by scrawling letter formation, reversals, transformations, uneven slant, and inability to keep to the lines on the paper. Sometimes, poor co-ordination or perceptual-motor difficulties may be at the root of handwriting problems. The left-handed child may also experience greater difficulty with handwriting.

Although reading difficulties represent the most common academic disability, math problems also affect many learning-disabled students. Disorders related to perception, directionality, abstract thinking, memory, and reading can all contribute to an arithmetic disabilitiy.

During the preschool and primary years, children with arithmetic disabilities cannot sort objects by size, match objects, understand the language of arithmetic, or grasp the concept of rational counting. During the elementary years, these children have trouble with computational skills (Otto, McMenemy, and Smith, 1973). At the secondary level, students with arithmetic disabilities continue to experience these basic problems (Mercer, 1979).

PROFILE 7-3

Danny is ten and a half, and attends a grade-five open-area classroom. This year, he has seen the learning-assistance teacher regularly because of his below-grade-level performance, especially in arithmetic.

Danny's learning difficulties were noted as early as junior kindergarten. At that time, he had difficulty with fine-motor activities, such as cutting, pasting, and pencil work. His learning problems have continued throughout his school years. He currently meets

Figure 7-2 Example of learning-disabled child's handwriting, showing problems with directionality, letter transposition, and repetition.

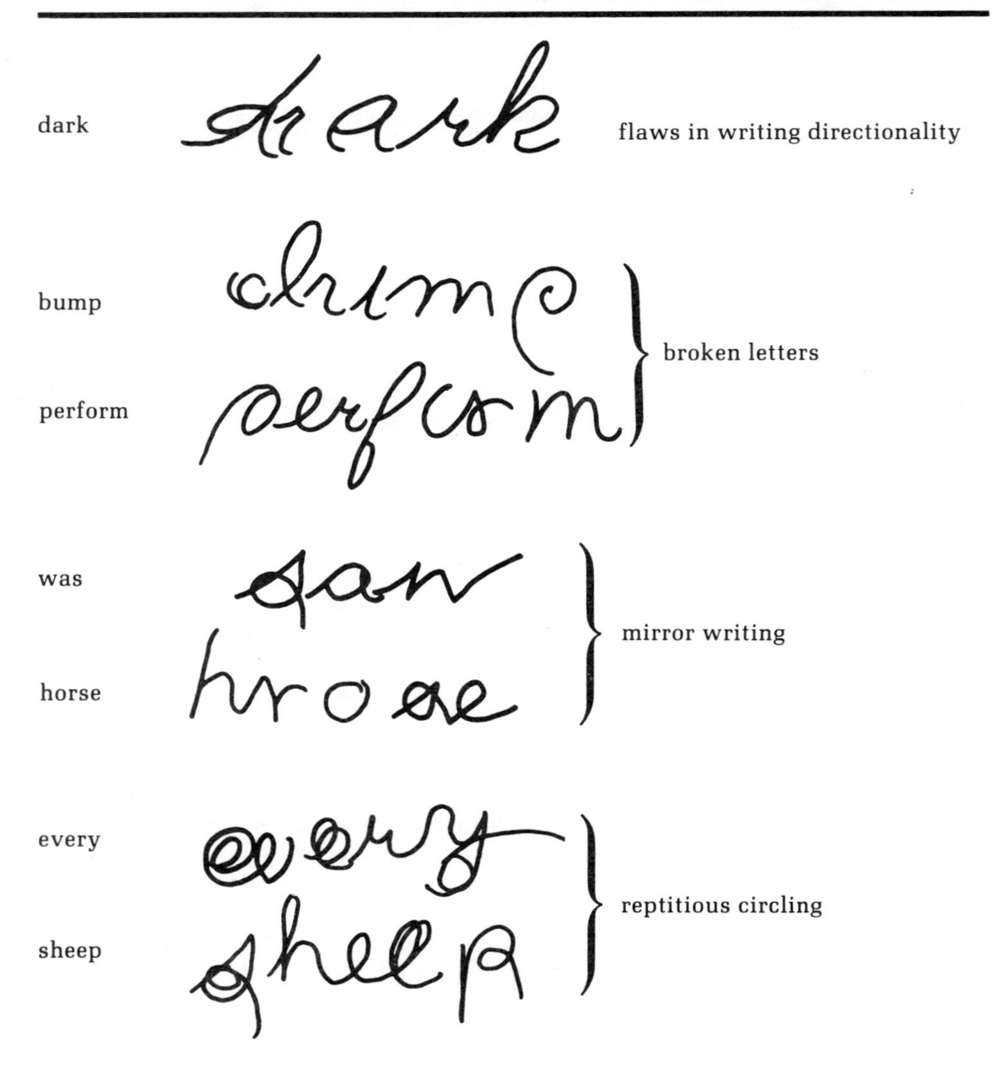

weekly with a child psychiatrist to find ways to cope with the frustration he feels at school. These sessions are intended to bolster Danny's poor self-concept, as some of his problems may result from poor motivation.

Danny received a complete psychoeducational assessment at the opening of this school year. On the WISC-R, he scored well within the normal range. His results showed no major discrepancy between the Verbal and Performance scales, and there was little sub-test scatter of scores. On the Peabody Picture Vocabulary Test, the Bender Visual-Motor Gestalt Test, the Beery Buktenica Developmental Test of Visual Motor Integration, and the Wepman Auditory Discrimination Test, Danny fell well into the normal range for his age.

On reading tests (Wide Range Achievement Test, reading subtest, and the Silvaroli Classroom Reading Inventory — Sight Words), Danny scored one to two years below his grade-level. The examiner noted that Danny found the entire reading process — both sight words and oral paragraphs — extremely distasteful. In math tests (Wide Range Achievement Test, arithmetic subtest, and the Key Math Diagnostic Test), Danny showed serious deficits that placed him two to three years below grade level.

Following the assessment, the psychologist observed that Danny was a child of normal ability who was functioning well below his potential in reading and arithmetic. In reading, Danny has an adequate sight-word vocabulary, but is unable to use phonetic analysis skills to supplement this. His arithmetic shows a failure to grasp basic concepts — number facts, the idea of "carrying" in addition, the method of subtraction and concepts related to time, money, and measurement. Without these basic skills, he has little foundation on which to build higher-level math skills. (Adapted from Haqq 1984.)

Social and emotional problems

Despite definitions that define learning-disabled children strictly in terms of intellect and achievement, these children face many emotional and social complications. Many students with learning disabilities get along brilliantly with their peers. However, a significant number have trouble establishing friendships. Some have little social awareness and poor social relationships, while others tend to be gullible and easily led.

Determining the social and psychological effects of a learning disability is extremely difficult. However, we know that some learning-disabled students experience significant problems in social adjustment, social perception, self-concept, and motivation. These behaviours may be associated with their inability to achieve, their lack of success and a general lack of support from parents and teachers. Lerner (1981) found that learning-disabled children lacked systematic and organized social judgement, and had trouble perceiving the moods of others. They had problems making friends and establishing supportive family relationships. They also suffered from poor self-concept.

Learning-disabled children tend to be rejected by their peers (Bryan, 1974, 1976). They receive more criticism from their peers, as well as from their teachers (Bryan, 1975). In one interesting study (Bryan, 1975), observers unfamiliar with the children's academic status viewed videotapes of learning-disabled and nondisabled children within a standardized experimental setting. The observers attributed more negative characteristics to the disabled than to the nondisabled children.

The reasons why learning-disabled children inspire negative responses are not clear. Perhaps they speak in a less pleasant manner, and tend to ignore interpersonal signals from their peers (Bryan and Bryan, 1979). Learning-disabled children are less accurate than non-disabled children in interpreting the non-verbal behaviour of others (Bryan, 1977).

Learning-disabled children are generally described as having poor self-esteem, an external locus of control, poor motivation, and learned helplessness. These children tend to view themselves as controlled by outer rather than inner forces. They are less likely than their peers to attribute success to their own ability and failure to their own lack of effort (Bryan, Donahue, and Pearl, 1981). Children who display **learned helplessness** have no faith that their efforts will result in desired outcomes. Because these children expect to fail, they lose their motivation.

The social and personality problems of learning-disabled children are at least as disabling as their academic problems. These children may develop an **emotional overlay** — emotional or behavioural problems that develop as a result of a learning disorder. **Emotional lability**, or frequent changes of mood, is one form of personal and social maladjustment.

By the time learning-disabled children reach adolescence, they may be deeply enmeshed in a web of failure and unhappiness. According to Siegel (1974), learning-disabled adolescents are prone to impulsiveness, a low frustration threshold, irritability, low self-esteem, and suggestibility. Siegel claims that, under certain conditions, these behaviours may result in anti-social or criminal acts.

Juvenile delinquency

Much research and discussion has explored the possibility of a link between learning disabilities and juvenile delinquency (e.g. Berman and Siegel, 1976; Hogenson, 1974; Lane, 1980; Mauser, 1974; Mulligan, 1969; Tarnopol, 1970; Weiss, Ninde and Werry, 1971; Winzer, 1981). The notion of such a link arises, in part, from the continual school failure that characterizes both conditions. The academic careers of juvenile delinquents follow a common pattern. Many experience school failure, frustration, acting-out behaviour, truancy, apprehension by the authorities, more frustration, the development of a poor self-image, and alienation. Eventually, they are expelled or drop out of school in response to an overwhelming sense of defeat (Winzer, 1981). As we have seen, the experiences of learning-disabled students show many parallels to this cycle.

Two major models have been presented to link delinquency and learning disabilities. The first, the School Failure Rationale, argues that children with learning disabilities tend to be grouped by adults and peers with other problem children. The labelling causes the children to form negative self-images, and to associate with peers who are hostile to school and prone to delinquent acts. The learning-disabled children embark on a career of absenteeism, truancy, suspension, and dropping out. With so much free time, they have many opportunities for delinquent behaviour, and perhaps also feel an economic pressure to commit crime.

The second model is the Susceptibility Rationale. This model argues that certain learning disabilities lead to general impulsiveness, poor perception of social clues and a lack of ability to learn from experience. As a result, learning-disabled children are less aware of the usual social sanctions and more likely to behave in a delinquent fashion (Lane, 1980).

Research has lent little support to either of these models. Indeed, recent findings have formulated a quite different hypothesis, the Different Treatment Rationale. Research has found that learning-disabled and non-disabled youth are apprehended by the authorities in approximately the same numbers for the same misdemeanours and offences. However, learning-disabled youth are more likely to be brought before the courts. These higher rates of adjudication could be due to the language and communication problems of learning disabled students, or to subtle personality problems. In addition, the courts may hold a somewhat negative predisposition toward learning-disabled students based on their poor school records (Lane, 1980).

PARENTING THE LEARNING-DISABLED CHILD

Parents of learning-disabled children may seem, at first glance, much more fortunate than parents of children with more severe handicaps. However, learning disabilities create much confusion within the family. In particular, a lack of clear diagnosis may cause great concern and anxiety, resulting in high levels of stress for parents.

The receptive and expressive language problems of learning-disabled children may cause them to appear slow, confused, impulsive, inattentive, or even obstinate. Parents may react to these problems with guilt, overprotection, rejection, or concern. Children may react in turn to negative parental responses by developing secondary emotional problems. These further exacerbate interpersonal problems, and compound the learning disorder (Wiig and Semel, 1976).

Meier (1971) examined the health histories of mothers of children identified as learning-disabled. He found these women had more chronic illness than average, and were more often over forty years of age. About twenty percent of their children had been born prematurely, as compared to five percent of the control group.

In a study of the family climate (Margalit and Heiman, 1984), the parents of learning-disabled children reported more rigidity, control, and order. These parents were more likely to demonstrate conflict-avoidance behaviour, resulting in less conflict resolution, overprotective relationships, and rigidity. Mothers seemed more prone to these traits than fathers.

Mothers of learning-disabled children react more negatively to their children's achievement experiences than mothers of nondisabled children. They also hold lower expectations for their children's future academic achievement (Chapman and Boersma, 1979). These mothers find their children more difficult to talk to, more impulsive, more anxious, and less able to structure the environment than their siblings (Owen, Adams, Forrest, Stoltz, and Fisher, 1971).

Parents of a learning-disabled child must provide a great deal of emotional and social support. Often they must explain the disability to the child. They must emphasize that they know the child is not stupid or lazy. They must communicate uncritical love to the child, regardless of school success. They must build up the child's self-esteem at every level, and never compare the disabled child unfavourably with other siblings. Parents must also alter their criteria for praise, rewarding small improvements in their child's development.

INTERVENTION WITH THE LEARNING-DISABLED CHILD

A wide variety of intervention approaches and techniques have been employed with learning-disabled children. None of these approaches has been proven effective for all children. For example, some studies support training for visual perceptual functions (Brod and Hamilton, 1973; Meikle and Kilpatrick, 1971). Other research suggests that such training is not in the least helpful (Camp, 1973; Chapman and Wedell, 1972; Mann, 1970). Similar controversy surrounds psycholinguistic training (Hammill and Larsen, 1974), stimulant drugs and diets, as well as various educational approaches and techniques.

Some of the controversy surrounding intervention results from the newness of the field. Much also results from the disparate characteristics of learning-disabled children. Because of the extremely heterogeneous nature of the population, no single approach, method, or technique can offer a solution to every problem.

Medical intervention

Historically, medicine and learning disabilities have been closely linked, particularly in the area of diagnosis. At present, the medical profession maintains an active interest in learning disabilities. The current focus of medical interest includes drug therapy, megavitamin therapy, diet management, and neurophysiological training. A great deal of medical research and experimentation is currently underway in these areas.

Drug therapy

Drugs were first used in the treatment of hyperactive children in 1937 (Lall, 1977). In recent years, the use of drugs with learning-disabled children has increased considerably. Indeed, in some classes of learning disabled students, medication is taken daily by forty percent of children (Cruickshank, 1979).

A variety of drugs have been prescribed to control hyperactive and inattentive behaviour. The two most commonly recommended are the psychostimulants, methylphendate (Ritalin) and dextroamphetamine (Dexedrine). Ritalin is used more often than Dexedrine because it seems to produce fewer side effects (Krager and Safer, 1974).

There is little question that drugs are often successful in reducing hyperactive behaviour and increasing attention skills. However, the use of drugs raises several major concerns. Some of these can be outlined as follows:

- Hyperactivity can be considered, in some cases at least, to be "in the eye of the beholder." Hyperactive behaviour cannot easily be medically determined. One parent's energetic child may well be another's hyperactive child.
- Typically, only about two-thirds of children react favourably to drug treatment. The remaining third are adversely affected when given stimulants at levels sufficient to affect behaviour (Kinsbourne, 1979).
- Short-term side effects of drugs are common, although not all children are affected in the same way. The most frequent side effects seem to be a decrease in appetite, and an increase in sleeplessness.
- Although relatively little empirical evidence on long-term side effects exists, several potentially serious findings have emerged. Stimulant drugs cause an increase to the heart rate (Aman and Werry, 1975). In addition, some children who took Ritalin for longer than three years experienced growth inhibition (Safer, Allen and Barr, 1972).
- The use of drugs as a treatment may suggest that hyperactivity is a specific disease.
- The drugs may stimulate mood elevation and create a psychological dependence.
- Medications are poor substitutes for good educational programming. Parents often resort to drugs when good programming is unavailable and when teachers are ill-prepared to deal with their child's problems. (Cruickshank, 1979).

■ Behaviour modification has been used successfully to work with distractible and hyperactive children (Hallahan and Kauffman, 1976). In the long run, this may be a more successful technique for permanent behaviour change.

■ Many teachers do not sufficiently understand the nature of drug therapy. When drugs are prescribed, physicians, teachers, and parents should be in close communication to understand the treatment and monitor the dosage.

Megavitamin therapy

Megavitamin therapy, or orthomolecular management, is based on the premise that large amounts of vitamins will enable the body to better fulfil its requirements. Cott (1971, 1972) used megavitamins with learning-disabled children. He noted decreased hyperactivity and improved concentration. Krippner (1975) argued that orthomolecular medicine is a viable alternative to drug treatment for hyperactive children. Nevertheless, this form of intervention remains highly controversial.

Diet management

One theoretical source of biochemical disturbance is allergy to foods, food dyes, artificial flavours, and preservatives. For example, Kittler (1970) reported studies in which the behaviour of some children improved when foods such as chocolate and milk were excluded from their diet.

Feingold (1975) popularized the notion that some substances in foods could be linked to hyperactivity. Feingold hypothesized that artificial colourings and flavourings were pharmacologically active substances that produced or aggravated hyperactive symptoms in children. He proposed a diet to restrict the intake of artificial food colours, flavours, preservatives, and foods with natural salicylates. After a stabilization period, foods would be gradually reintroduced to identify the particular items that adversely affected the child.

Informal clinical evaluations and parent testimony suggest that the Feingold diet relieved hyperactivity in thirty to forty percent of the children who tried it (Swanson and Kinsbourne, 1980). Results of controlled studies have shown equivocal results (Spring and Sandoval, 1976), and skepticism concerning Feingold's hypothesis persists.

Neurophysiological training

Treatments based on neurophysiological training attribute learning disabilities to some underlying neurological dysfunction. These approaches are extremely controversial.

The work of Glen Doman, a physical therapist, and Carl Delacato, an educational psychologist, is the most prominent in this area. Doman and Delacato argue that neurological organization can be achieved through specific and structured patterning techniques. The central principle of their theory can be encapsulated by the phrase "ontogeny recapitulates phylogeny." They believe that each human being matures through stages that parallel the evolution of living species. Any child who fails to pass through a certain sequence of developmental stages in mobility, language, and sensorimotor competence suffers from poor neurological organization, and possibly brain damage (Freeman, 1967). According to this theory, development of neurological organization begins in the womb and ends when the child is about eight years old.

Doman and Delecato believe that neurological organization can be attained through training. They designed a treatment procedure called patterning, which stresses motor activities. The treatment begins with teaching the child to roll over, and progresses through thirteen stages to cross-patterned walking.

Doman's and Delacato's treatment procedures have been embraced by the public and attacked by professional groups. In recent years, it has come to be thought of as a radical and unconventional intervention with learning-disabled children.

Technical intervention

Computer technology has much to offer the learning-disabled student. Already there are program learning packages, voice printers, programs to teach logic, and programs to develop self-concept. Moreover, the computer has infinite patience for daily review (Barnes, 1983).

Some programs have been designed to provide supplemental drill and practice in academic skills. These programs drill and evaluate skills at the student's own level, and provide skill review and practice. Other programs attempt to overcome passivity and help the child take an active part in the learning process. These programs develop active-learning styles and problem-solving strategies, focusing on discovery-learning rather than drill. Still other programs attempt to reduce the teacher's work-load. For example, Hasselbring and Crossland (1982) have developed a microcomputer version of spelling tests that reduce examiner time and scoring errors.

Educational intervention

Intervention in an educational setting occurs in a wide variety of ways. These are largely determined by how learning disabilities are defined and understood in a particular school. Disparities in approach, program delivery, and technique are also related to the heterogeneity of the learning-disabled population and to the relative newness of the field.

Administrative arrangements

Many educators believe that the learning-disabled suffer only mild learning problems and can be easily served within the regular classroom. However, children with learning disabilities have conditions that range from mild to severe. A range of settings has been developed to serve this extremely heterogeneous group. These include public schools, private schools, clinics, residential schools, college and university diagnostic centres, as well as other programs. Within the public school system, resources for learning-disabled children may include resource rooms, itinerant teachers, and self-contained classes.

The regular classroom. Nowhere is today's emphasis on mainstreaming more apparent than in the field of learning-disabilities. Most learning disabled children are taught in the regular classroom, supplemented by instruction in the resource room. This model allows the child to function primarily in the regular classroom, perhaps with some curricular adaptations. To succeed, this approach requires considerable collaboration among the classroom teacher, the resource-room teacher, and other specialists, such as speech therapists, available within the educational system.

The self-contained classroom. For children with more severe learning disabilities, the regular classroom may not be suitable. Many of these children need time in special self-contained classrooms in order to improve their academic and behavioural skills. Whenever possible, children in segregated classrooms should be encouraged to join their regular peer groups. They should also follow the regular program in subjects in which they are competent. The ultimate goal of segregated classes is to return the child to the regular classroom.

Stimulus-reduced classrooms. Some self-contained classrooms attempt to provide non-stimulating environments so that severely learning-disabled children will not be distracted by extraneous stimuli. In these rooms, as many visual and auditory stimuli as possible are removed. Walls, woodwork, and furniture are painted the same colour and left unadorned. Even the teacher is careful to wear nonstimulating colours and nondistracting jewellery.

Children in stimulus-reduced classes work mainly in individual cubicles on individualized programs with a great deal of teacher direction. Every minute is planned to avoid wasted or unproductive time. Precise rules and routines are strictly adhered to.

This structured-classroom approach is sometimes referred to as an "engineered classroom." It was originally recommended by Strauss and his colleagues, and later refined by Cruickshank and his associates (Cruickshank, Bentzen, Ratseburg and Tannhauser, 1961).

Today, blacked-out windows and completely bare walls are no longer thought necessary. However, many teachers have found nondistracting environments helpful, and have set up special cubicles in which learning-disabled children can concentrate on their work.

Residential schools. Despite the field's emphasis on mainstreaming, several residential schools for severely learning-disabled students have recently sprung up. However, residential placements are never considered permanent. Their goal is to help the student develop the skills to function in the regular classroom or the work force.

A number of residential schools are operated by private non-profit organizations. These include Cedar Lodge on Vancouver Island and the Edmonton Academy in Alberta. The Edmonton Academy opened in 1983, and is based on the philosophy that learning-disabled students can best be educated apart from the mainstream. Most students spend two or three years at the Academy before re-integration into the regular school system (Edmonton, 1983).

Other residential schools are operated within the public school system. In British Columbia, for example, Regional Educational Support Centres help children whose learning disabilities require services not available in their home districts (Chilliwack, Handbook, 1981). Residence at these centres is relatively brief, usually three or four months. In Ontario's two residential schools, average residence is about two years. Again, the schools try to help students develop compensatory strategies for re-entry into the regular school system or entry into the work force (Winzer and Vainio, 1981).

Educational approaches

A diverse range of approaches exists in educational intervention for learning-disabled children. Here we can only describe the three major approaches. For a more thorough understanding, the reader is referred to Hallahan, Kauffman, and Lloyd (1985), Lerner (1981) Canadian perspectives are provided by Dow, O'Reilly, Hill, and Dostaler (1981) and by Robertson and Bunch (1980). A particularly innovative approach has been devised by Feurstein, whose work began with intervention with children from post-war Israeli refugee camps (Cole, 1985; Feuerstein, Krasilowsky, and Rand, 1974; Feurstein, Miller, Hoffman, Rand, Mintzker, and Jenson, 1981; Feurstein, Rand, and Hoffman, 1980).

Three general approaches are taken in the remediation of learning disabilities. The ability- or process-training approach focuses on the remediation of a specific developmental disability. The task-training, or skill approach focuses on helping children to learn. A third approach combines both of these models into a single training program. Educators tend to draw from each approach the techniques they consider most suitable to the individual child.

Ability- or process-training approach

The ability-training model is based on the premise that learning disabilities are caused by impaired processes within the child. Proponents of ability training believe these impaired perceptual processes can be measured, reduced, or eliminated to create greater academic efficiency. Training procedures are designed to improve specific perceptual problems, such as attention, language, discrimination, thinking, memory, and so forth.

One of the difficulties with this approach is that a perceptual faculty, such as memory, cannot be trained in isolation. It has to be trained along with content, such as memory for words or math. Even when a child's perceptual level is markedly improved, the child still requires academic and conceptual skills to perform better at school. Moreover, for children older than nine, remediation is unlikely to be effective for perceptual problems of discrimination, memory, sequence, closure, and spatial organization. By this age, basic processing ability is as developed as it will ever be (Wepman, Cruickshank, Deutsch, Morency, and Strother, 1975).

Studies have indicated that ability training succeeds in only about twenty-four percent of cases. Apparently, the perceptual processes measured in differential diagnosis are highly resistant to training by existing procedures (Arter and Jenkins, 1979). More often than not, even when perceptual processes improve, academic performance and reading achievement do not.

The skill approach

The skill model assumes that the child's problems are external, and result from some gap in instruction. Rather than trying to remediate perceptual deficits, the skill model focuses on the student's ability to perform academic tasks. Teachers provide direct instruction in weak academic areas.

Within each subject area, a hierarchy of skills is defined. Instruction begins at the level of the simplest skill not mastered by the child. Earlier in the chapter, Danny's profile showed him functioning well below grade-level in math and reading. Exhibit 7-7 outlines a skill-level approach to remediation for Danny.

Exhibit 7-7 A skill approach to intervention.

In arithmetic, Danny exhibits a marked discrepancy between his potential and his performance. He functions more than two years below his grade level in this area. He is also retarded in his reading, though not as severely. By using his extensive sight-word vocabulary, he is able to partly camouflage his deficit in word-attack skills. Danny's academic problems seriously frustrate him, and he is increasingly resorting to overt, acting-out behaviour.

Danny requires an individual math program that will help him learn the basic skills in which he is deficient. He must master the number facts to nineteen and develop a concept of place value before he can learn the four arithmetic processes. To master the number facts he needs daily oral and written drill, as well as many opportunities to generalize these facts to other situations. Place value should be taught with many concrete materials, such as popsicle sticks, Cuisenaire rods, and a calculator. Danny will need much practice to translate concrete sums into numerical notations. To build his self-esteem, praise should be realistic and consistent. His progress should be charted with some type of graphic display.

Improvement in reading may be accomplished with a word-family approach. This will build on his strong sight-word vocabulary, while strengthening his weak phonic skills. Rather than focusing on sound-symbol association, Danny may benefit from much work in structural analysis of such items as prefixes, suffixes and compound words. Although Danny should try to remain in the same reading program as the rest of his class, his success and attitude to reading might improve with a special set of high-interest, low-vocabulary readers.

Danny's social problems appear to arise directly from his academic frustration. His learning tasks should be structured to allow him much success. He must demonstrate mastery of each step before progressing onward.

Task analysis — analyzing the behavioural components and prerequisite skills of a task — plays an integral role in the skills approach. Task analysis indentifies which elements of the task the child must master. For example, reading skills are broken down into the smallest possible steps and taught one step at a time.

As in any teaching approach, the skills model should be tailored to the needs of the individual child. The teacher may need to adjust the materials, change the timing, alter the lesson format, or adjust evaluation techniques to help the individual child achieve success.

Modality processing techniques. Modality processing is aligned to the skill model in that the child's strengths and weaknesses determine the program. Advocates of this approach believe that many learning-disabled children develop preferred learning styles, and come to depend on a specific modality. For example, a child with a visual dysfunction prefers the auditory modality, and learns to read more easily through a phonics method. Contrastingly, the child with a visual preference learns reading best through a sight-word method.

Combined ability- and task-training approach

In some cases, children require a combination of the above process- and task-oriented approaches. Instead, for example, of learning auditory discrimination of gross sounds, they learn auditory discrimination of the sounds and letters needed for reading. Because they are learning skills directly required for academic performance, generalization of training is not a major concern.

The combination approach encourages teachers to work with academic materials while still attempting to improve perceptual processes. Fernald's VAKT (visual-auditory-kinesthetic-tactile) method (Fernald, 1943), although certainly not new, still provides the prime example of this approach. Fernald was a psychologist interested in children who had difficulty learning to read or spell. Her method is a process-task approach, because it trains visual memory of words and phrases while incorporating auditory, touch, and movement components.

The Fernald technique takes a multi-sensory approach to the teaching of spelling and vocabulary. The procedure combines visual, auditory, tactile, and haptic modes of learning. The following steps illustrate the procedure:

- The teacher writes the word to be learned in large letters with the side of the chalk on the board, saying the word aloud.

- The child writes the word on an individual flash card with crayon, saying the word aloud.

- The child traces the letters three times with the forefinger of the dominant hand. Each time, the child pronounces the word and each of its letters aloud.

- The child stands up and traces the letters in the air, saying the word and its letters aloud.

- The child traces the word on a friend's back three times, saying the word and its letters aloud.

- The child traces the word on a hand three times, saying the word and its letters aloud.

- The child now re-writes the word, saying it aloud, and using the model word if necessary.

- With the model turned over, the child writes the word while saying it aloud. The child checks the word with the model.

- If unsuccessful, the child repeats the entire process. Upon success, the child continues to the next word.

Curricular modifications

The major characteristic of learning-disabled pupils is an inability to learn adequately in the regular classroom through traditional teaching techniques. Because of the heterogeneous nature of the learning-disabled population, schools must provide different administrative arrangements and varied approaches. In addition, they must be willing to permit modifications to the regular curriculum.

Language

A sizable proportion of learning-disabled children suffer language dysfunctions. Language ability is critical to learning in general, and particularly to the acquisition of adequate reading skills.

Students may require specialized help with speech production and oral language, especially syntax and pragmatics. They may also need special assessment and structured programming to develop written language and spelling.

Reading

Special educators have assumed that reading-disabled students need special programs to teach them to read. A large variety of reading methods have been developed. We have already discussed the Fernald techniques. Other programs for reading-disabled students include Alphaphonetic (Gillingham and Stillman, 1965), Distar (Englemann and Bruner, 1969), Colour Phonics System (Bannatyne, 1966), and Words in Color (Gattegno, 1962). Regular reading programs, such as basal series, phonics, phonic-linguistics, programmed series, and language experience, are also used with learning-disabled children. In Canada, the Basic Literacy for Adults Development (BLADE), produced by Canada Manpower, has been used successfully with reading-disabled adolescents and young adults (Winzer, 1981).

Handwriting

Some handwriting difficulties are due to basic problems such as poor co-ordination, perceptual-motor difficulties, and left-handedness. The left-handed child may need special help to orient paper and pencil while other children may need help to overcome letter reversals or misorientations. Still other children need help to keep between the lines, form letters, and maintain spacing.

Mathematics

As stated earlier, arithmetic problems occur with less frequency than reading disabilities, and have traditionally received less attention. However, children who are behind in arithmetic may well perform adequately in reading and spelling.

Remediation of arithmetic problems requires step-by-step instruction, beginning at the child's level of performance and advancing at the child's own rate. Whenever possible, concrete materials should be used. Organization games are also valuable teaching tools, especially those that provide multisensory experiences that sharpen visual-perceptual skills within a solid framework of mathematics (Swett, 1978).

Exhibit 7-8 offers some teaching tips for the education of learning-disabled children.

Exhibit 7-8 Tips for teachers of learning-disabled children.

- Be specific, consistent, and systematic in your expectations and actions. Make sure lessons are highly structured and stick closely to classroom routine.
- Maintain a warm and supportive emotional climate.
- Be honest but liberal with praise and rewards.
- Stress, at all times, areas of the language hierarchy. Offer children special help with problems in spoken language.
- Preface all remarks with the title or main idea of the lesson.
- Change the tone or volume of your voice to emphasize important points in the lesson.
- Give verbal cues, such as "listen carefully" or "this is crucial," before presenting important information.
- Immediately after teaching an important concept, check for recall by asking, "What did I say?"
- Vary presentations to include visual and audio-visual components.
- After you give directions, have the student repeat them aloud.
- Avoid calling on the child in class unless the child volunteers to contribute.
- Reduce the amount of printed or written work.
- If the child seems to be having visual and spatial problems, use unlined paper. In math, graph paper helps some children to organize their work.
- Homework may be important in your program, but remember that the learning-disabled child can be easily overwhelmed by too much of it.
- Modify grades and report cards to reflect the child's individual level of improvement.

THE LEARNING-DISABLED PRE-SCHOOLER

As stated earlier, the diagnosis of learning disabilities at the pre-school level is more a matter of prediction than identification. It is not possible, strictly speaking, to identify a child as learning-disabled before the child is involved in academic tasks. Traditional pre-schools do not teach academic tasks because of a strong belief in a pressure-free environment (Beers and Beers, 1980). Because of the tenuous nature of early identification and the non-academic nature of pre-school education, we find very little programming specifically designed for learning-disabled pre-schoolers.

THE LEARNING-DISABLED ADOLESCENT

Lately, interest has grown dramatically in secondary-level learning-disabled students. Until recently, however, relatively little programming was in place for these students. As a result, little data exists to describe these students and recommend appropriate programming.

Adolescents differ profoundly from children physically, mentally, and emotionally. Adolescent characteristics, such as puberty, the quest for independence, and peer-group pressure, interact with and complicate learning problems. Adolescents do not outgrow reading difficulties or hyperactivity but must continue to come to terms with them.

According to Deschler (1978), learning-disabled adolescents often display these characteristics:

- A deficit in basic academic areas, such as reading and mathematics.
- Weaknesses (but also strengths) in social, emotional, and learning areas.
- Reduced motivation and poor self-concept.
- Subtle manifestations of earlier learning-disabled traits, such as unco-ordination and hyperactivity.

One goal of adolescence is independence, both in and out of the classroom. Successful social adjustment and classroom performance depend, in part, on the degree to which a student can function autonomously. Typically, secondary students no longer have close interaction with and supervision by teachers (Deschler, 1978). Indeed, learning-disabled secondary students have been characterized as leading unstructured lives in structured environments (Brown, 1978).

Exhibit 7-9 outlines some of the ways that life for a learning-disabled adolescent changes in high school. Before adolescence, learning programs are developmental, but at the secondary level, they tend to be compensatory. Teachers try to teach basic skills in order to satisfy content-area requirements. Students are taught to concentrate on their best skills to meet academic requirements.

TEACHERS OF THE LEARNING-DISABLED

The success of learning-disabled students depends in large measure on the competence of their teachers. When learning disabilities were first recognized in the early 1970s, teachers had little or no preparation for their new roles. Today, however, many pre-service and in-service training programs are offered by universities, school districts, and other agencies.

Teachers of learning-disabled children often experience a great deal of frustration. The children's inconsistent performance can be bewildering, and their uninhibited behaviour can be exasperating. Teachers must be versed in many approaches to learning so they can match their students' strengths and needs with appropriate facets of the

Exhibit 7-9 The learning-disabled adolescent in the secondary school.

Characteristic	*Implications*
Increased behavioural independence.	Students are less amenable to rules.
Increased mobility.	Students are more likely to be absent and to disrupt their learning program.
Increased unsupervised time.	Students are more likely to be tardy.
Need for making life decisions.	Students are poorly prepared for these decisions.
Increase in social pressures and distractions.	Remedial classwork is not a high priority.
Lessening of parent-school involvement.	Parents become more concerned about achievement and post-secondary planning.
More pronounced emotional and behavioural problems accompany learning disabilities.	Secondary educators may be forced to address these emotional problems before attempting academic remediation.

(Adapted from Brown, 1978, pp. 76-77.)

curriculum. They must become aware of each child's experience, interests, feelings, environmental background, developmental level, strengths, needs, preferred learning style, and level of emotional adjustment. Teachers must learn to tailor expectations, time schedules, curriculum tasks, and learning approaches to the needs of each student. They must also help each learner achieve a feeling of success (Ontario, Ministry of Education, 1980).

SUMMARY

Many disciplines have helped develop the field of learning disabilities, each with a different concept of the problem. This, along with the heterogeneity of the learning-disabled population, accounts for varying approaches to etiology, diagnosis, and treatment.

Medical concepts of learning disabilities underlay early development in the field. These assumed that learning-disabled children suffered undetermined neurological problems that interfered with learning. These problems were typically understood to involve the syndrome of minimal brain dysfunction, with the focal symptoms of hyperactivity, distractibility, and impulsivity.

Numerous treatment approaches are still based on the medical model. However, educators currently take the view that the academic performance of the learning-disabled child is of most consequence. These educators have devised various techniques to remediate or compensate for learning deficits.

Learning disabilities hinder academic performance and may result in emotional overlays that disrupt social development. However, with early identification and appropriate intervention, learning-disabled children can overcome, or at least compensate for, some of their major problems. For children with learning disorders, special education is the vital intervening factor.

BIBLIOGRAPHY

Aman, M.G. and Werry, J.S. (1975). Methylphenidate in children: Effects upon cardiorespiratory functioning. *International Journal of Mental Health, 4,* 119-131.

Ames, L.B. (1968). A low intelligence quotient is often not recognized as the chief cause of many learning difficulties. *Journal of Learning Disabilities, 1,* 735-738.

Arter, J.A. and Jenkins, J.R. (1979). Differential diagnosis — prescriptive teaching: A critical appraisal. *Perceptual and Motor Skills, 49,* 517-554.

Aten, J. and Davis, J. (1968). Disturbances in the perception of auditory sequence in children with minimal cerebral dysfunction. *Journal of Speech and Hearing Research, 11,* 236-245.

Baker, L. (1982). An evaluation of the role of metacognitive deficits in learning disabilities. *Topics in Learning and Learning Disabilities, 2,* 27-35.

Bakker, D.J. (1967). Temporal order, meaningfulness and reading ability. *Perceptual and Motor Skills, 24,* 1027-1030.

Bakker, D.J. (1971). *Temporal order in disturbed reading.* Rotterdam: University of Rotterdam Press.

Bannatyne, A.D. (1966). The color phonics system. In J. Money (Ed.), *The disabled readers.* Baltimore: John Hopkins Press.

Barnes, D.B. (1983, Spring). Technology, education and the learning disabled. *National Canadian Association for Children and Adults with Learning Disabilities,* p. 10.

Beers, C.S. and Beers, J.W. (1980). Early identification of learning disabilities: Facts and fallacies. *Elementary School Journal, 81,* 67-76.

Belmont, L. and Birch, H.G. (1973). Lateral dominance, lateral awareness and reading disability. In H.A. Solan (Ed.) *The psychology of learning and reading difficulties.* New York: Simon and Schuster.

Bender, L.A. (1968). Neuropsychiatric disturbances. In A.H. Keeney and V.T. Keeney (Eds.). *Dyslexia: Diagnosis and treatment of reading disorders.* St. Louis: Mosby.

Berman, A. and Siegal, A.W. (1976). Adaptive and learning skills in juvenile delinquents: A neuropsychological analysis. *Journal of Learning Disabilities, 9,* 583-590.

Bradley, E. (1975). Screen them early! *Academic Therapy, 10,* 305-308.

Braun, J.D. (1963). Relations between concept formation ability and reading achievement at three developmental levels. *Child Development, 34,* 675-682.

Brenner, A. (1982). The effects of megadoses of selected B complex vitamins on children with hyperkinesis: Controlled studies with long-term follow-up. *Journal of Learning Disabilities, 15,* 258-264.

Brod, N. and Hamilton, D. (1973). Binocularity and reading. *Journal of Learning Disabilities, 6,* 574-576.

Brown, V.L. (1978). Curriculum development resources. In L. Mann, L. Goodman, and J.L. Wiederholt (Eds.), *Teaching the learning-disabled adolescent.* Boston: Houghton Mifflin.

Bryan, T.H. (1974). Peer popularity of learning disabled children. *Journal of Learning Disabilities,* 7, 621-625.

Bryan, T.H. (1975). Verbal communication of learning disabled children. Paper presented to the American Speech and Hearing Association, Washington, D.C.

Bryan, T.H. (1976). Peer popularity of learning disabled children: A replication. *Journal of Learning Disabilities, 9,* 307-311.

Bryan, T.H. (1977). Learning disabled children's comprehension of non-verbal communication. *Journal of Learning Disabilities, 10,* 501-506.

Bryan, T.H. and Bryan, J.H. (1979). Social interactions of learning disabled children. In A. Lane (Ed.), *Readings in human growth and development of the exceptional individual.* Connecticut: Special Learning Corporation.

Bryan, T.H., Donohue, M., and Pearl, R. (1981). Learning disabled children's peer interactions during a small-group problem-solving task. *Learning Disability Quarterly, 4,* 13-22.

Bryan, T.H. and Pflaum, S. (1978). Social interactions of learning disabled children: A linguistic, social, and cognitive analysis. *Learning Disability Quarterly, 1,* 70-79.

Bunch, G. and Robertson, G. (1979). *Selected psychoeducational tests: A layman's handbook.* Toronto: Pfarmigan Press.

Burke, C. and Goodman, K. (1970). What a child reads: A psycholinguistic analysis. *Elementary English, 47,* 12-130.

Byrant, N.D. (1972). Subject variables: Definition, incidence, characteristics and correlates. In N.D. Byrant and C. Kass (Eds.), *Final report: LTI in learning disabilities (Vol. 1).* Tucson, AZ: University of Arizona.

Calfee, R.C. (1977). Assessment of independent reading skills: Basic research and practical applications. In A.S. Reber and D.L. Scarborough (Eds.), *Toward a psychology of reading.* Hillside, N.J.: Lawrence Erlbaum.

Camp, B. (1973). Psychiatric tests and learning tests in severely disabled readers. *Journal of Learning Disabilities, 6,* 512-517.

Carpenter, D. and Miller, L.J. (1982). Spelling ability of reading disabled LD students and able readers. *Learning Disability Quarterly, 5,* 65-70.

Chapman, J.W. and Boersma, F.J. (1979). Learning disabilities, locus of control and mother attitudes. *Journal of Educational Psychology, 71,* 250-258.

Chapman, L.J. and Wedell, K. (1972). Perceptual-motor abilities and reversal errors in children's handwriting. *Journal of Learning Disabilities, 5,* 321-325.

Cheek, D.B. (1978, September). Were you originally left-handed? The hand clasp test and evidence from ideomotor questioning. *Swedish Journal of Hypnosis,* 17-25.

Chilliwack Regional Centre for Children with Severe Learning Disabilities. (1981). *Handbook.* Victoria: British Columbia Ministry of Education.

Clements, S.D. (1966). *Minimal brain dysfunction in children: Terminology and identification, phase 1 of a three phrase project.* Washington, D.C.: U.S. Department of Health, Education and Welfare, Public Health Service Bulletin, no. 1415.

Cohen, R.L. and Netley, C. (1981). Short term memory deficits in reading disabled children, in the absence of opportunity for rehearsal strategies. *Intelligence, 5,* 69-76.

Cole, J.L. (1985). Developing cognitive strategies in learning disabled adolescents. M.Ed. major paper, University of British Columbia.

Coleman, H.M. (1968). Visual perception and reading dysfunction. *Journal of Learning Disabilities, 1,* 116-123.

Conners, C.K. (1969). A teacher rating scale for use in drug studies with children. *American Journal of Psychiatry, 6,* 884-888.

Cott, A. (1971). Orthomolecular approach to the treatment of learning disabilities. *Schizophrenia, 3,* 95-12.

Cott, A. (1972). Megavitamins: The orthomolecular approach to behavioral disorders and learning disabilities. *Academic Therapy, 7,* 245-257.

Critchley, M. and Critchley, E.A. (1978). *Dyslexia defined.* London: William Heinmann.

Cruickshank, W.M. (1976). William M. Cruickshank. In J.M. Kaufmann and D.P. Hallahan (Eds.), *Teaching children with learning disabilities: Personal perspectives.* Columbus, OH.: Merrill.

Cruickshank, W.M. (1979). Myths and realities in learning disabilities. In A. Lane (Ed.), *Readings in human growth and development of the exceptional individual.* Connecticut: Special Learning Corporation.

Cruickshank, W.M., Bentzen, F.A., Ratseburg, F.H., and Tannhauser, M.T. (1961). *A teaching method for brain-injured and hyperactive children.* Syracuse: Syracuse University Press.

Csapo, M. (1976). *Glue him down: Teaching hyperactive children.* Vancouver: Centre for Human Development and Research.

Darnforth, M. (1984). Case files, personal correspondence. Davidson, I., Silverman, H., and Hughes, M. (1981). *Learning disabilities: Identification and intervention practices.* Toronto: Ontario Ministry of Education.

Decker, S.N. and DeFries, J.C. (1980). Cognitive abilities in families with reading disabled children. *Journal of Learning Disabilities, 13,* 517-522.

Decker, S.N. and DeFries, J.C. (1981). Cognitive ability profiles in families of reading disabled children. *Developmental Medicine and Child Neurology, 23,* 217-227.

De Hirsch, K., Jansky, J. and Langford, W.S. (1966). *The predicting of reading failure: A preliminary study of reading, writing and spelling in pre-school children.* New York: Columbia University.

Denckla, M.B. and Rudel, R.G. (1976). Naming of object drawings by dyslexic and other learning disabled children. *Brain and Language, 3,* 1-16.

Deschler, D.D. (1978). Psychoeducational aspects of learning-disabled adolescents. In L. Mann, L. Goodman, and J.L. Wiederholt (Eds.). *Teaching the learning disabled adolescent.* Boston: Houghton Mifflin.

Dow, I.I., O'Reilly, R.R., Hill, M.R., and Dostaler, A.M. (1981). *Manual for teachers of students with learning disabilities.* Ontario: Ministry of Education.

Edmonton gets its first "step-up" school (1983, Winter). *BCACLD Newsbrief.*

Edelbrock, C. (1979). Empirical classification of children's behavior disorders: Progress based on parent and teacher ratings. *School Psychology Digest, 8,* 355-369.

Eden, A. (1978). Switching babies' hands is an absolute no-no! *Family Weekly, 5.*

Englemann, S.E. (1977). Sequencing cognitive and academic tasks. In R.D. Kneedler and S.G. Tarner (Eds.) *Changing perspectives in special education.* Columbus, OH.: Merrill.

Englemann, S.E. and Bruner, E.C. (1969). *Distar reading: An instructional system.* Chicago: Science Research Associates.

Ewoldt, C. (1982). Diagnostic approaches and procedures and the reading process. *Volta Review, 84,* 83-94.

Feingold, B.F. (1975). Hyperkinesis and learning disabilities linked to artificial food flavors and dyes. *American Journal of Nursing, 75,* 797-803.

Feingold, B.F. (1976). Hyperkinesis and learning disabilities linked to the ingestion of artificial food colors and flavors. *Journal of Learning Disabilities, 9,* 551-559.

Fernald, G.M. (1943). *Remedial techniques in basic school subjects.* New York: McGraw-Hill.

Feurstein, R., Krasilowsky, D., and Rand, Y. (1974). Innovative educational strategies for the integration of high-risk adolescents in Israel. *Phi Delta Kappan, 55,* 556-558.

Feurstein, R., Miller, R., Hoffman, M., Rand, Y., Mintzker, Y., and Jenson, M. (1981). Cognitive modifiability in adolescence: Cognitive structure and the effects of intervention *Journal of Special Education, 15* 269-287.

Feurstein, R., Rand, Y., and Hoffman, M. (1980). *Instrumental enrichment: An intervention program for cognitive modifiability.* Baltimore, MD: University Park Press.

Flynn, P.T. and Byrne, M.C. (1970). Relationship between reading and selected auditory abilities of third grade children. *Journal of Speech and Hearing Research, 13,* 731-740.

Frauenheim, J.G. (1978). Academic achievement characteristics of adult males who were diagnosed as dyslexic in childhood. *Journal of Learning Disabilities, 11,* 476-483.

Freeman, R.D. (1967). Controversy over "patterning" as a treatment for brain damage in children. *Journal of the American Medical Association, 202,* 385-388.

Gaddes, W.H. (1981). Neuropsychology, fact or mythology, educational help or hindrance? *School Psychology Review, 10,* 322-330.

Gadow, K.D. (1979). *Children on medication: A primer for school personnel.* Reston, VA: Council for Exceptional Children.

Gattengo, C. (1962). *Words in color.* Chicago: Learning Materials.

Gillingham, A. and Stillman, B. (1965). *Remedial training for children with specific disability in reading, spelling and penmanship (5th ed.).* Cambridge, MA: Educators Publishing Service.

Golden, N.E., and Steiner, S.R. (1969). Auditory and visual functions in good and poor readers. *Journal of Learning Disabilities, 2,* 476-481.

Goodman, K. (1967). Reading: A psycholinguistic guessing game. *Journal of the Reading Specialist, 6,* 126-133.

Goyette, C.H., Conners, C.K. and Ulrich, R.F. (1978). Normative data on revised Conners' Parent and Teacher Rating Scales. *Journal of Abnormal Child Psychology, 6,* 221-236.

Hallahan, D.P. (1975). Comparative research studies on the psychological characteristics of learning disabled children. In W. Cruickshank and D.P. Hallahan (Eds.), *Perceptual and learning disabilities in children: Psychoeducational practices (Vol. 1).* Syracuse: Syracuse University Press.

Hallahan, D.P. and Kauffman, J.M. (1976). *Introduction to learning disabilities: A psycho-behavioral approach.* Englewood Cliffs, N.J.: Prentice-Hall.

Hallahan, D.P. and Kauffman, J.M. (1982). *Exceptional children: Introduction to special education (2nd ed.).* Englewood Cliffs, N.J.: Prentice-Hall.

Hallahan, D.P., Kauffman, J.M., and Ball, D.W. (1973). Selective attention and cognitive tempo of low achieving and high achieving sixth grade males. *Perceptual and Motor Skills, 36,* 579-583.

Hallahan, D.P., Kauffman, J.M. and Lloyd, J. (1985). *Introduction to learning disabilities (2nd ed.).* Englewood Cliffs, N.J.: Prentice-Hall.

Hammill, D.D. (1976). Defining "LD" for programmatic purposes. *Academic Therapy, 12,* 29-37.

Hammill, D.D. and Larsen, S.C. (1974). The effectiveness of psycholinguistic training. *Exceptional Children, 41,* 5-14.

Hammill, D.D., Leigh, L.E., McNutt, G., and Larsen, S.C. (1981). A new definition of learning disabilities. *Learning Disability Quarterly, 4,* 336-342.

Haqq, D. (1984). *Case files, personal correspondence.*

Harber, J.R. (1980). Auditory perception and reading: Another look. *Learning Disability Quarterly, 3,* 19-25.

Haring, N.G. (1978). Research in the classroom: Problems and procedures. In N.G. Haring, T.C. Lovitt, M.D. Eaton, and C.L. Harren (Eds.), *The fourth R: Research in the classroom.* Columbus, OH.: Merrill.

Haring, N.G. and Bateman, B. (1977). *Teaching the learning disabled child.* Englewood Cliffs, N.J.: Prentice-Hall.

Harris, A.J. (1970). *How to increase reading ability (5th. ed.),* New York: David McKay.

Harris, A.J. and Sipay, E.R. (1980). *How to increase reading ability: A guide to developmental and remedial methods (7th ed.).* New York: Longman.

Hasselbring, T.S. and Crossland, C.L. (1982). Application of microcomputer technology to spelling assessment of learning disabled students. *Learning Disability Quarterly, 5,* 80-82.

Henker, B. and Whalen, B. (1980). The changing faces of hyperactivity: Retrospect and prospect. In C.K. Whalen and B. Henker (Eds.), *Hyperactive children: The social ecology of identification and treatment.* New York: Academic Press.

Henry, A. (1975). Specific difficulties in reading. *Remedial Education, 10,* 81-85.

Hessler, G. and Kitchen, D. (1980). Language characteristics of a purposive sample of early elementary learning disabled students. *Learning Disability Quarterly, 3,* 36-41.

Hinchelwood, J. (1917). *Congenital word-blindness.* London: H.K. Lewis.

Hogenson, D.L. (1974). Reading failure and juvenile delinquency. *Bulletin of the Orton Society, 24,* 64-169.

Huberty, C.J., Quirk, J.P., and Swan, W. (1973). An evaluation system for a psycho-educational treatment program for emotionally disturbed children. *Educational Technology, 13,* 73-79.

Hyperactive children don't always outgrow symptoms. (1979, December 13). *Toronto Globe and Mail,* p. 14.

Jansky, J. and De Hirsch, K. (1972). *Preventing reading failure.* New York: Harper and Row.

Johnson, D.J. and Myklebust, H.R. (1967). *Learning disabilities: Educational principles and practices.* New York: Grune and Stratton.

Jongsma, E. (1971). *The cloze procedure as a teaching technique.* Newark, DE.: International Reading Association.

Kail, R.V., Chi, M.T., Ingram, A.L., and Danner, W.F. (1977). Constructive aspects of children's reading comprehension. *Child Development, 48,* 684-688.

Kaluger, G. and Kolson, C.J. (1978). *Reading and learning disabilities (2nd. ed.).* Columbus, OH.: Merrill.

Kass, C. and Myklebust, H. (1969). Learning disabilities: An educational definition. *Journal of Learning Disabilities, 2,* 377-379.

Kauffman, A.S. (1967). A new approach to interpretation of test scatter on WISC-R. *Journal of Learning Disabilities, 9,* 160-168.

Kinsbourne, M. (1979). Dangers attending the stimulant therapy of hyperactive children. *Special Education in Canada, 53,* 12-14.

Kirk, S.A. (1963, April 6). Behavioral diagnosis and remediation of learning disabilities. In *Proceedings of the conference on exploration into the problems of the perceptually handicapped child, first annual meeting (vol. 1).* Chicago.

Kirk, S.A. (1974). Introduction to *State of the art: Where are we in learning disabilities?* Los Angeles: Association for Children with Learning Disabilities and California Association for Neurologically Handicapped Children.

Kittler, F.J. (1970). The effect of allergy on children with minimal brain damage. In F. Speer (Ed.), *Allergy of the nervous system.* Springfield, IL.: Charles C. Thomas.

Kneedler, R.D., with D.P. Hallahan and J.M. Kauffman. (1984). *Special education for today.* Englewood Cliffs, N.J.: Prentice Hall.

Krager, J.M. and Safer, D.J. (1974). Type and prevalence of medication used in the treatment of hyperactive children. *New England Journal of Medicine, 291,* 1118-1120.

Kratochwill, T.R. (1980). Behavioral assessment of academic and social problems: Implications for the Individual Education Program. *School Psychology Review, 9,* 199-206.

Krippner, S. (1975). An alternative to drug treatment for hyperactive children. *Academic Therapy, 10,* 433-439.

Lall, G.R. (1977). Hyperkinetic children: A synopsis of possible causes, treatment, and educational aspects. *Special Education in Canada, 52,* 21-23.

Lane, B. (1980). The relationship of learning disabilities to juvenile delinquency: Current status. *Journal of Learning Disabilities, 13,* 425-435.

Leong, C.K. (1980). Laterality and reading proficiency in children. *Reading Research Quarterly, 15,* 185-202.

Lerner, J. (1981). *Learning disabilities: Theories, diagnosis and teaching strategies (3rd ed.).* Boston: Houghton Mifflin.

Leton, D.A. (1962). Visual-motor capacities and ocular efficiency in reading. *Perceptual and Motor Skills, 15,* 407-432.

Lindsay, J.D. and Kerlin M.A. (1979). Learning disabilities and reading disorders: A brief review of the secondary level literature. *Journal of Learning Disabilities, 12,* 408-415.

Lingren, R.H. (1969). Performance of disabled and normal readers on the Bender-Gestalt auditory discrimination test, and visual-motor matching. *Perceptual and Motor Skills, 29,* 152-154.

Little, D.M. (1980). Learning disabilities and the severely learning disabled — Status quo in B.C. *B.C. Journal of Special Education, 4,* 155-163.

Lloyd, J.W. (1975). The pedagogical orientation: An argument for improving instruction. *Journal of Learning Disabilities, 8,* 74-78.

Lovitt, T.C. (1978). The learning disabled. In N.G. Haring (Ed.), *Behavior of exceptional children (2nd ed.).* Columbus, OH.: Merrill.

Lyle, J.G. (1968). Reading retardation and reversal tendency: A factorial study. *Child Development, 40,* 833-843.

MacGregor, K., Rosenbaum, S., Skoutajan, K. (1982). *Putting the pieces together: A parent's guide to special education in Ontario.* Toronto: Ontario Association for Children with Learning Disabilities.

MacIntyre, R., Keeton, A., and Agard, R. (1980). *Identification of learning disabilities: A validity study.* Toronto: Ontario Ministry of Education.

Mann, L. (1970). Perceptual training: Misdirections and redirections. *American Journal of Orthopsychiatry, 40,* 30-38.

Mann, L. (1979). *On the trail of process.* New York: Grune and Stratton.

Margalit, M. and Heiman, T. (1984). Family climate and anxiety expressions of families with a learning disabled boy. Paper presented at the Sixth International Conference on Learning Disabilities, Dallas, Texas.

Marge, M. (1972). The general problem of language disabilities in children. In J.V. Irwin and M. Marge (Eds.), *Principles of childhood language disabilities.* Englewood Cliffs, N.J.: Prentice-Hall.

Mauser, A.J. (1974). Learning disabilities and delinquent youth. *Academic Therapy, 9,* 389-402.

McKinney, J.D., McLure, S., and Feagans, L. (1982). Classroom behavior of learning disabled children. *Learning Disability Quarterly, 5,* 45-51.

McLeod, J. (1979). Educational underachievement: Toward a defensible psychometric definition. *Journal of Learning Disabilities, 12,* 322-330.

McMurray, J.G. (1980). Learning disabled adolescents: Perspectives from Canadian principals. *Special Education in Canada, 55,* 10-14.

Meier, J.H. (1971). Prevalence and characteristics of learning disabilities found in second grade children. *Journal of Learning Disabilities, 4,* 6-21.

Meikle, S. and Kilpatrick, D. (1971). Changes in perceptual, motor, and reading test scores in a remedial reading group. *The Canadian Psychologist, 12,* 254-269.

Mercer, C.D. (1979). *Children and adolescents with learning disabilities.* Columbus, OH.: Merrill.

Mercer, C.D. (1982). Learning disabilities. In N.G. Haring (Ed.), *Exceptional children and youth, (3rd ed.).* Columbus, OH.: Merrill.

Montgomery, D. (1981). Do dyslexics have difficulty assessing auditory information? *Psychological Research, 43,* 235-245.

Morris, J.E. and Arrant, D. (1978). Behaviour ratings of emotionally disturbed children by teachers, parents, and school psychologists. *Psychology in the Schools, 15,* 450-455.

Mulligan, W. (1969). A study of dyslexia and delinquency. *Academic Therapy, 4,* 177-187.

Murray, M.E. (1981). Diagnostic psychological testing for reading/learning disorders in pre-school children. *Reading Psychology, 2,* 146-157.

Myklebust, H.R. (1968). Learning disabilities: Definition and overview. In H.R. Myklebust (Ed.), *Progress in learning disabilities (Vol. 1).* New York: Grune and Stratton.

Myklebust, H.R. (1971). *The Pupil Rating Scale: Screening for learning disabilities.* New York: Grune and Stratton.

Myklebust, H.R. (1973). Identification and diagnosis of children with learning disabilities: An interdisciplinary study of criteria. *Seminars in Psychiatry, 5,* 55-77.

National Advisory Committee on Dyslexia and Related Reading Disorders. (1969). *Reading disorders in the United States.* Washington, D.C.: United States Department of Health, Education and Welfare.

National Advisory Committee on Handicapped Children. (1968). *First annual report, special education for handicapped children.* Washington, D.C.: United States Department of Health, Education, and Welfare.

Noel, M. (1980). Referential communication abilities of learning disabled children. *Learning Disability Quarterly, 3,* 70-87.

O'Bryan, K.G. (1976). *The Windsor Early Identification Project.* Toronto: Ontario Ministry of Education.

O'Bryan, K.G. (1979). *Windsor Early Identification study of data and procedures.* Toronto: Ontario Ministry of Education.

O'Bryan, K.G. (1981). The Windsor Early Identification Project revisited. In *Review and Evaluation Bulletin, Early identification and intervention: Selected proceedings from the fourth international symposium on learning problems, Toronto, 1979 (Vol. 2).* Toronto: Ontario Ministry of Education.

O'Connor, A. (1980). Early screening: Some problems and practices. *B.C. Journal of Special Education, 4,* 271-282.

Ontario Ministry of Education. (1980). *Curriculum ideas for teachers: Children with learning disabilities.* Toronto: Ontario Ministry of Education.

Otto, W., McMenemy, R.A., and Smith, R.J. (1973). *Corrective and remedial teaching.* Boston: Houghton Mifflin.

Owen, F.W., Adams, P.A., Forrest, T., Stoltz, L.M., and Fisher, S. (1971). Learning disorders in children: Sibling studies. *Monographs of the Society for Research in Child Development, 36,* 4 (144).

Park, G.E. and Linden, J.D. (1968). The etiology of reading disabilities: An historical perspective. *Journal of Learning Disabilities, 1,* 318-331.

Patten, B.M. (1973). Visually mediated thinking: A report of the case of Albert Einstein. *Journal of Learning Disabilities, 6,* 415-420.

Pavlidis, G.T. and Miles, T.R. (1981). *Dyslexia research and its application to education.* New York: Wiley.

Robertson, G. and Bunch, G. (1980). *Selected educational programs; A layman's handbook.* Orillia, Ontario: Ptarmigan Press.

Rockefeller, N.A. (1976, October 16). Don't accept anyone's verdict that you are lazy, stupid or retarded! *TV Guide,* pp. 12-14.

Rutter, M. (1975). *Helping troubled children.* (Middlesex, England: Penguin Books.

Safer, D.J., Allen, R.P., and Barr, E. (1972). Depression of growth in hyperactive children on stimulant drugs. *New England Journal of Medicine, 287,* 217-220.

Sandoval, J. and Haapmanen, R.M. (1981). A critical commentary on neuropsychology in the school: Are we ready? *School Psychology and Review, 10,* 381-388.

Sattler, J.M. (1982). *Assessment of children's intelligence and special abilities (2nd ed.).* Boston: Allyn and Bacon.

Satz, P., Taylor, H.G., Friel, J., and Fletcher, J.M. (1978). Some developmental and predictive precursors of reading disabilities: A six year follow up. In A.L. Benton and D. Pearl (Eds.), *Dyslexia: An appraisal of current knowledge.* New York: Oxford University Press.

Siegel, E. (1974). *The exceptional child grows up.* New York; E.P. Dutton.

Sitko, M.C. and Gillespie, P.H. (1970). Language and speech difficulties. In L. Mann, L. Goodman, and J.L. Wiederholt (Eds.), *Teaching the learning disabled adolescent.* Boston: Houghton Mifflin.

Slingerland, B.H. (1968). *Pre-reading screening procedures.* Cambridge, MA.: Educators Publishing Service.

Smith, M.D., Coleman, J.M., Dokecki, P.R., and Davis, E.E. (1977). Intellectual characteristics of school-labelled learning-disabled children. *Exceptional Children, 43,* 352-357.

Spring, C. and Sandoval, J. (1976). Food additives and hyperkinesis: A critical evaluation of the evidence. *Journal of Learning Disabilities, 9,* 560-569.

Stephens, T.M. (1977). *Teaching skills to children with learning and behavior disorders.* Columbus, OH.: Charles Merrill.

Swanson, J.M. and Kinsbourne, M. (1980). Artificial food colours impair the learning of hyperactive children. Report to the Nutrition Foundation, Hospital for Sick Children, Toronto.

Swett, S.C. (1978). Math and LD: A new perspective. *Academic Therapy, 14,* 5-13.

Swift, M. and Spivack, G. (1969). Clarifying the relationship between academic success and overt classroom behaviour. *Exceptional children, 36,* 99-104.

Tansley, P. and Panckhurst, J. (1981). *Children with specific learning difficulties.* Windsor, Eng.: Nelson Publishing.

Tarnopol, L.T. (1970). Delinquency and minimal brain dysfunction. *Journal of Learning Disabilities, 3,* 200-207.

Thompson, L.J. (1971). Language disabilities in men of eminence. *Journal of Learning Disabilities, 4,* 34-44.

Thomson, M. (1984). *Developmental dyslexia.* London: Edward Arnold.

Torgesen, J.K. (1979). What shall we do with psychological processes? *Journal of Learning Disabilities, 12,* 514-521.

Torgesen, J.K. and Goldman, T. (1977). Verbal rehearsal and short-term memory in reading disabled children. *Child Development, 48,* 56-60.

Vogel, S.A. (1974). Syntactic abilities in normal and dyslexic children. *Journal of Learning Disabilities, 7,* 103-109.

Wallace, G. and McLoughlin, J. (1975). *Learning disabilities: Concepts and characteristics.* Columbus, OH: Merrill.

Wechsler, D. (1974). *The Wechsler Intelligence Scale for Children, Revised.* New York: Psychological Corporation.

Weiner, E.S. (1979). Improvement in reading through writing. *Academic Therapy, 14,* 589-595.

Weiss, G., Ninde, K., and Werry, J.S. (1971). Studies on the hyperactive child. *Archives of General Psychiatry, 24,* 409-414.

Wepman, J.M., Cruickshank, W.M., Deutsch, D.P., Morency, A., and Strother, C.R. (1975). Learning disabilities. In N. Hobbs (Ed.), *Issues in the classification of children (Vol. 1).* San Francisco: Jossey-Bass.

Whipple, C.I. and Kodman, F.A. (1969). A study of discrimination and perceptual learning with retarded readers. *Journal of Educational Psychology, 60,* 1-5.

Wiederholt, J.L. (1978). Adolescents with learning disabilities: The problem in perspective. In A. Mann, L. Goodman, and J.L. Wiederholt (Eds.), *Teaching the learning-disabled adolescent.* Boston: Houghton Mifflin.

Wiig, E.H. and Semel, E.H. (1974). Productive language abilities in learning-disabled adolescents. *Journal of Learning Disabilities, 8,* 578-588.

Wiig, E.H. and Semel, E.H. (1976). *Language disabilities in children and adolescents.* Columbus, OH: Merrill.

Winzer, M.A. (1981). Juvenile delinquency: Educational perspectives. *B.C. Journal of Special Education, 5,* 293-302.

Winzer, M. and Malarczyk, B. (1984, June). The unknown variable: Identifying learning disabilities with pupil behaviour rating scales. Paper presented at A.G. Bell Conference, Portland Oregon. ERIC ED 254-046.

Winzer, M. and Malarczyk, B. (1985). Identifying the learning disabled: A survey of procedures in British Columbia. Unpublished paper, University of British Columbia.

Winzer, M. and Vainio, C. (1981). The Trillium School. *Special Education in Canada, 56,* 23.

Ysseldyke, J.E., Thurlow, J., Graden, J., Wesson C., Algozzine, B., and Deno, S. (1983). Generalizations from five years of research on assessment and decision making: The University of Minnesota Institute. *Exceptional Education Quarterly, 4,* 75-93.

Yule, W. and Rutter, M. (1976). Epidemiology and social implications of specific retardation. In R.M. Knights and D.J. Bakker (Eds.), *The neuropsychology of learning disorders.* Baltimore, MD: University Park Press.

4

Children with Sensory Deficits

INTRODUCTION

Hearing and vision are known as the distant senses, because they connect us so profoundly with our environment. The loss of hearing or vision isolates the individual from family, friends, the community, and the physical environment. Hearing and visual handicaps can damage a person psychologically, socially, emotionally and educationally.

Few children of school age are completely blind or deaf. Far more common are children who see poorly or are hard-of-hearing. Many hearing and vision problems go undetected until children reach school-age. Some children's problems are never identified. These children may be mislabelled as learning-disabled, or dismissed as dull, stupid, or lazy.

In rural or remote areas, children with vision or hearing problems are especially likely to go undetected. These areas suffer from a lack of efficient identification procedures and appropriate services. Hearing and visual impairments are very widespread, for example, among the Native population. They are endemic throughout the Northwest Territories, and most prevalent in the Eastern and Central Arctic. Despite these wide-ranging problems, however, many hearing and visual disorders go undetected and untreated (Watters, 1980). Moreover, incidence and prevalence rates in these areas are extremely difficult to determine.

Like much special education, the teaching of blind and deaf children has moved from segregated institutions and schools to integrated programs within public schools. Today, hearing- and visually-impaired children in North America attend schools in their home communities. Resource-room and itinerant-teacher programs have been established, and residential schools have become more community-oriented.

CHAPTER EIGHT

Children with hearing impairments

MARGRET WINZER

The most effective "cure" for deafness is not medicine, not mechanical or electronic devices nor the surgical blade, but understanding. And ironically, understanding is free. Before we can develop understanding, we must create awareness.

(Gannon, 1979)

Hearing loss is silent, painless, and invisible. It is one of our least recognized and most misunderstood ailments. Most people think of deafness as simply a lack of sound. However, as Helen Keller (1933) has pointed out, deafness also "means the loss of the most vital stimulus — the sound of the voice that brings language, sets thoughts astir, and keeps us in the intellectual company of men" (p. 68).

More people suffer from hearing loss than from blindness, cancer, tuberculosis, venereal disease, multiple sclerosis, and kidney disease put together. Hearing loss can be acquired at any age, although the likelihood of developing it increases with age. Men are more likely to suffer hearing loss because of their disproportionate participation in war, high-risk occupations, and sports (McLoughlin, 1982).

In normal child development, speech and language are acquired spontaneously and almost effortlessly. Babies do not merely listen passively to the language around them. They communicate non-verbally long before they speak their first words. Infants take in, process, and organize the language they hear. Like miniature linguists, they recreate for themselves the language of their culture.

For deaf babies, life is a silent movie, devoid of sound effects and spoken script. Severe hearing loss stops children from hearing the sounds made by themselves and others. Inevitably this hinders or halts the acquisition of speech and language.

Many myths and prejudices have historically surrounded the deaf. Some are founded on the ancient notion that speech and hearing occupy a common site in the brain. This fallacy has led to such pejorative terminology as deaf mute, deaf and dumb, and dummy. Another myth holds that deaf persons lack abstract-thinking capacity, and can only function normally if restricted to concrete activities.

Many hearing people regard sign language as a sort of ghetto slang, a system employed by those unable to learn "real" language. Others believe that all hearing-impaired people are endowed with the ability to lip read. Still others believe in the myth of compensation, which holds that deaf people develop superior visual abilities (Bolton, 1976).

Myths and prejudices regarding deafness are so widespread that some deaf spokespersons have claimed that non-disabled people form their largest handicap (Carney, 1973). Others, such as Gannon, whose quote opens this chapter, have made fervent pleas for greater public awareness of their problems.

THE HUMAN EAR

The human ear is a truly marvellous instrument. It can detect sounds much softer than the dropping of a pin, and still filter sounds a million times louder. It is one of the most complex organs in the body, a triumph of miniaturization, fitting into a space not much larger than a hazelnut.

The ear collects sound, processes it, and transmits it to be decoded in the brain. Its anatomy is usually discussed in terms of the external, the middle, and the inner ear. Figure 8-1 illustrates the major parts of the hearing mechanism.

Figure 8-1 Anatomy of the human ear.

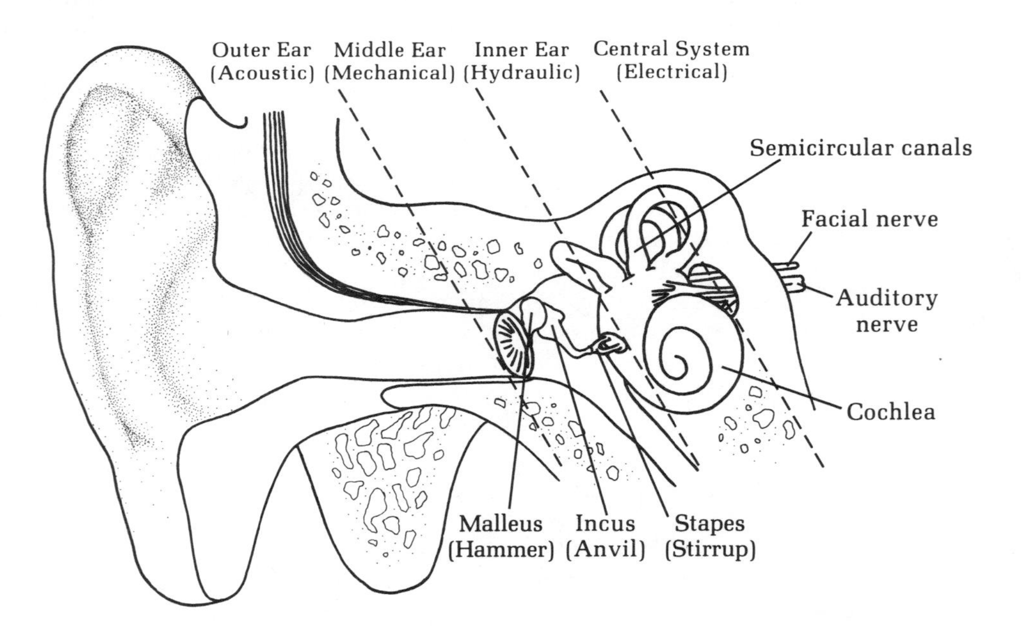

The external ear

The outer ear is the cartilage structure on the side of the head, referred to as the **auricle** or the **pinna**. This is the least complex part of the hearing mechanism, and the least important for hearing. An external canal, or **meatus**, runs obliquely from the pinna to the ear drum. The **ear drum** is a tough, tightly stretched **tympanic membrane** that separates the outer from the middle ear. At the ear drum, hearing really begins.

The auricle serves to collect sound waves and funnel them into the meatus. The external canal is lined with coarse hairs and four thousand wax glands that secrete ceremum. This wax traps insects, dust, and other irritants, guards against infection, and lubricates the canal and ear drum. The ear drum is a concave membrane that vibrates freely when struck by sound waves. Even the faint vibrations of a whisper cause it to vibrate, but perhaps only a billionth of a centimetre.

The middle ear

The inner surface of the ear drum is located in the air-filled cavity of the middle ear. The inner ear-drum surface consists of three small bones, the **malleus, incus,** and **stapes**, often called the hammer, anvil, and stirrup. These tiny bones, the smallest in the human body, form a bridge between the ear drum and the inner-ear entrance, or **oval window**. There are two muscles in the inner ear, one joined to the stapes and the other to the ear drum. The **Eustachian tube** connects the middle ear to the nasopharynx. In the middle ear, the transmission of sound becomes more sophisticated. When sound waves strike the ear drum, it vibrates and moves the three small bones. These bones transmit the vibrations across the middle-ear cavity to the inner ear through the oval window. The middle ear amplifies the sound about twenty-two times, and also protects the inner ear from very loud noise.

The Eustachian tube serves to equalize the pressure on both sides of the ear drum. You may have experienced the discomfort of unequal pressure in an airplane descent. To clear the Eustachian tube and make the ears "pop," passengers yawn deeply, suck on hard candy, blow their noses, or swallow.

The inner ear

The inner ear, the real organ of hearing, is located in a cavern of the skull and filled with a watery fluid. The inner ear is about the size of a pea, an intricate mechanism with thousands of moving parts. Because it looks like a complex maze of passages, the inner ear is called the labyrinth. It contains the **cochlea** and the **vestibular mechanism**, which are interdependent in their functioning.

The cochlea is a tiny, snail-shaped structure filled with a fluid similar to cerebral spinal fluid. Its twisting interior is studded with thousands of microscopic hair cells, each one tuned to a particular vibration. Within the cochlea are highly specialized structures, such as the Organ of Corti and Reissner's membrane. The auditory nerve, which is about the diameter of a pencil lead, relays messages to the brain.

Behind the cochlea lies the vestibular mechanism, composed of three fluid-filled semi-circular canals. These loops of tubing are the organs of balance.

The intricacy of the inner ear structure is matched by the complexity of its function. When the stapes vibrates on the oval window leading to the inner ear, the fluid in the

Exhibit 8-1 The sequence of hearing

- Sound waves enter the ear, travel through the auditory canal, and set up vibrations in the ear drum.
- The vibrations of the ear drum move the bones of the middle ear.
- The footplate of the stapes moves the oval window and sets the cochlear fluid in motion.
- The movement causes the hairs immersed in the cochlear fluid to move. This movement stimulates the attached cells to send a tiny electrical impulse along the fibres of the auditory nerve to the brain.
- In the brain, impulses are translated into meaningful sound.

cochlea begins to move. A low-pitched sound pushes at the top of the cochlea and a high-pitched sound at the base. For example, if middle-C is sounded, then the cochlea's middle-C hair cells vibrate, waving in the fluid. The waving produces a wisp of electricity that feeds into the auditory nerve and is transmitted to the brain. There the signal is unscrambled and converted into meaningful sound.

We hear our own voices by a different process, the bone conduction of sound. Sound travels directly through the jawbones to the inner ear fluid. Thus, we hear ourselves quite differently from how our listeners hear us, and often have trouble recognizing our own voices on a tape recorder.

Information regarding movement and balance is fed to the brain through the vestibular mechanism. Other nerve endings in the body also contribute to the sense of balance — those in the eyes, the feet, muscles, and joints.

DEFINITIONS OF HEARING IMPAIRMENT

A number of definitions and classification systems are used for the hearing-impaired. The Conference of Executives of American Schools for the Deaf (Ad Hoc Committee, 1975) has developed a widely accepted definition with an educational orientation. According to this definition:

> **Hearing impairment** is a generic term indicating a hearing disability that may range in severity from mild to profound. It includes the subsets of deaf and hard-of-hearing.
>
> A **hard-of-hearing person** is one who, generally with the use of a hearing aid, has residual hearing sufficient to enable successful processing of linguistic information through audition.
>
> A **deaf person** is one whose hearing disability precludes successful processing of linguistic information through audition, with or without a hearing aid.

CLASSIFICATION OF HEARING IMPAIRMENT

The distinction between deaf and hard-of-hearing is not as clear-cut as the above definition implies. Both groups are heterogeneous, and sub-categories of each are often used.

The classifier's orientation often determines the system of classification that is used. Those with a strictly physiological perspective are interested primarily in the measurable degree of hearing loss. Educators want to know how the hearing impairment will affect the child's functioning, especially in speech and language. Because hearing loss is closely linked to language delay, educators tend to categorize chiefly on the basis of language ability.

Classifications are usually based on the degree of hearing impairment, the cause and site of the deficit, and the age at which the impairment developed.

Measurement of hearing

Hearing acuity is measured by the subject's response to loudness across a range of frequencies. A **Bel**, named after Alexander Graham Bell, is a unit of loudness intensity. Each Bel is broken down into ten parts, known as **decibels** (dB).

A decibel represents the smallest difference in loudness intensity that can be perceived. Zero dB designates the point at which people with normal hearing can detect the faintest sound. Hearing loss is measured on a decibel scale, beginning with 0 dB. However, a loss of 60 dB is not merely six times greater than 10 dB. The figures are logarithmetic, not arithmetic, so that 60 dB is 10^6 louder than 10 dB.

Figure 8-2 shows the dB level of some common sounds on an audiogram, a chart on which hearing is recorded.

Sound waves are produced by the to-and-fro movement of molecules. One complete to-and-fro movement constitutes a cycle, and the number of cycles per second determines the frequency of a sound. Cycles per second are measured in **hertz** (Hz) — a frequency of 1000 Hz indicates 1000 cycles per second. As the frequency increases, the pitch of the sound becomes higher.

Although the human ear is sensitive to frequencies between 20 Hz and 20 000 Hz, most human speech falls between 500 Hz and 2000 Hz. This range of pitch is known as the speech range. Middle C on a piano is about 500 Hz.

Hearing impairment can be caused by interference with any part of the ear's transmission system. Impairment may take the form of restriction in the range of frequencies received, distortions along the frequency spectrum, or a failure to perceive sounds.

Classification by degree of hearing impairment

Hearing loss is classified according to the amount of hearing in a person's better ear. Decibels and hertz are used to measure loudness and frequency. Children are classed as deaf or hard-of-hearing, depending on whether they hear sounds at certain intensities of loudness. This classification is further structured by designations of mild, moderate, severe, and profound hearing loss.

Figure 8-2 Chart showing the hearing level of some common sounds.

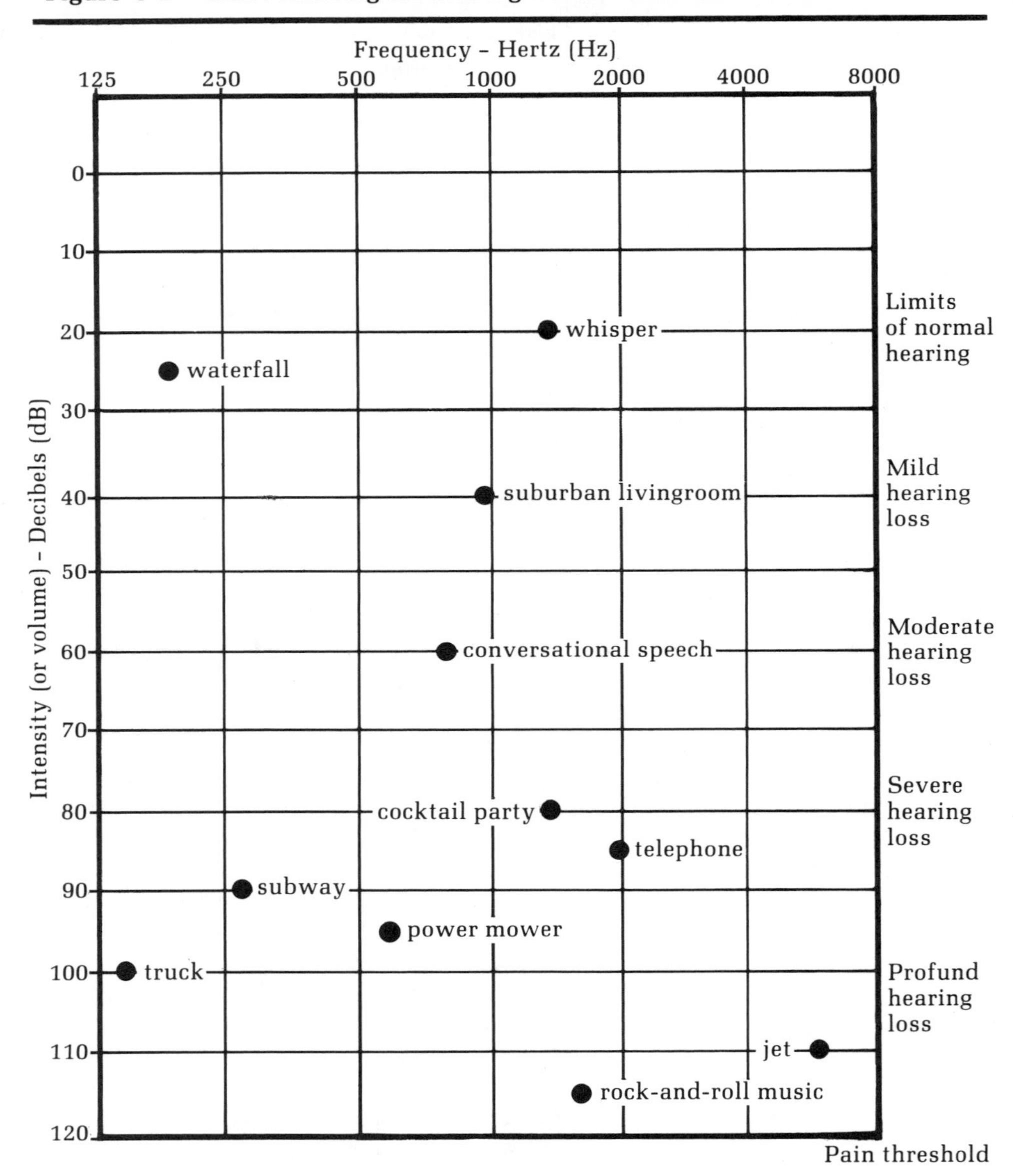

Exhibit 8-2 illustrates the levels of hearing impairment.

Exhibit 8-2 Levels of hearing impairment.

Range	Severity	Implications
■ 0-25 dB	Insignificant	
■ 25-40 db	mild hearing loss; hard-of-hearing.	May have difficulty with faint or distant sounds. May have problems in conversations, groups, or settings with much ambient noise.
■ 40-60 dB	moderate hearing loss; hard-of-hearing.	Frequent difficulty with normal speech, especially in conversations, groups, and class discussions.
■ 60-90 dB	severe hearing loss; hard-of-hearing to deaf.	Great difficulty with even loud or amplified speech, which seems faint and distorted. Requires amplification and intensive speech and language training.
■ 90 dB+	profound hearing loss; deaf.	May be aware of loud sounds and vibrations, but generally cannot understand even amplified speech.

Classification by site of the loss

Hearing impairment is also classified according to the part of the hearing mechanism that is affected. Problems in the mechanical transmission of sound waves through the outer and middle ear are called **conductive losses**. These types of hearing loss, affecting the outer or middle ear only, usually respond favourably to medical or surgical intervention.

Impairments in the inner ear may be caused by abnormal sense organs or a defective auditory nerve. These **sensori-neural** impairments interfere with the conversion of sound waves to neural impulses for the brain. Sensori-neural hearing losses may be partial or complete, and often affect higher frequencies more than others. Sensori-neural hearing loss is the most common among seriously impaired children, and cannot, at this time, be medically or surgically reversed.

Classification by age of onset

Because hearing impairment and language delay are closely connected, educators are concerned about the age of onset of the loss. A **congenital hearing impairment** is one that is present at birth. An **adventitious hearing impairment** is acquired some time after birth, through accident or disease.

Children with congenital hearing losses do not have the opportunity to practise the listening skills essential to develop speech and language. Inevitably, congenital hearing impairment affects every aspect of communication development from birth onward (Sanders, 1971). Children who acquire hearing impairments after they develop speech and language may find it easier to develop communication skills. The later in life an impairment occurs, the greater the child's linguistic capabilities are likely to be.

Because the age of onset is so critical to speech and language development, educators classify children according to this factor. Children with **pre-lingual deafness** are those who were deaf prior to the development of speech and language. Children with **post-lingual deafness** became deaf after the development of speech and language. The cut-off point is often set at two years of age (Meadow, 1980).

Additional classifications

A hearing loss in one ear only is known as a **unilateral hearing impairment**. Generally, persons with unilateral hearing loss function normally, although they may have problems locating the direction of sound. If an individual suffers a **bilateral hearing loss**, amplification may be used in the better ear.

Additional terms used to classify deaf adults include non-verbal, low-verbal, manual, or oral (Stewart, 1981). These terms must be used with caution, because they describe the manifestations of deafness, rather than the impairment itself.

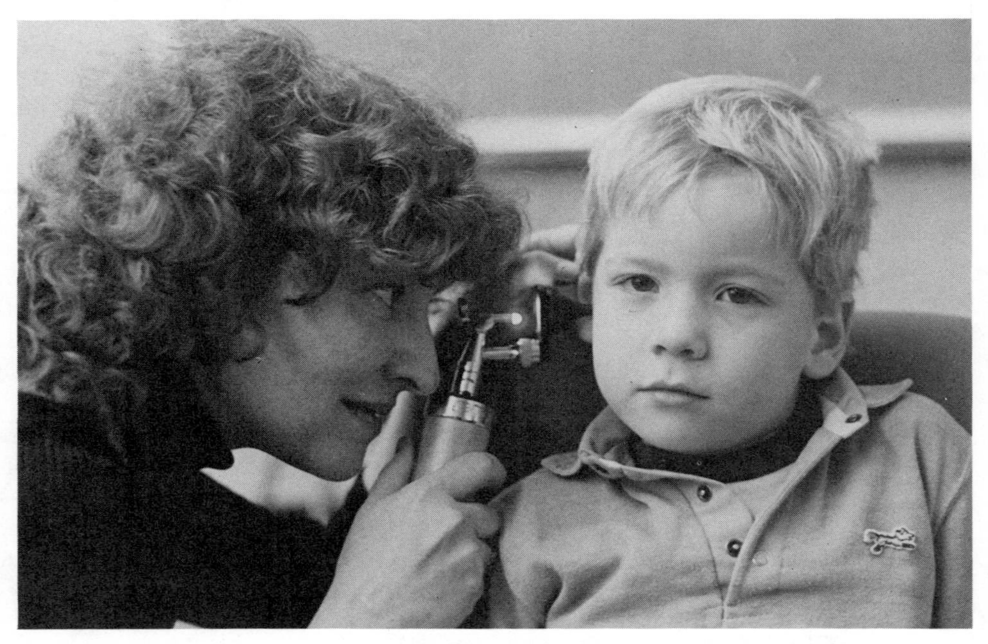

Children with congenital hearing loss do not have the opportunity to practise the listening skills essential to developing speech and language.
(T. Wilson)

PREVALENCE OF HEARING IMPAIRMENT

It is extremely difficult to arrive at a true determination of the prevalence of hearing impairments. The major factors that hinder accurate figures are as follows:

- Inconsistent definitional data.
- Confusion regarding identification and reporting.
- Methodological problems in surveys.
- Difficulties in accurate early identification.
- Increasing prevalence of hearing impairment with age.
- Difficulties of estimation among multi-handicapped individuals, who are often reported according to their primary disability.

Approximately one in ten Canadians, or about two million people, have some form of hearing impairment. Perhaps one in forty has an impairment serious enough to affect daily life or communication, and one in four hundred, or about fifty thousand has profound deafness. Hearing loss among the aged is especially common. Serious hearing problems affect one in ten people over sixty-five, and four out of ten over seventy-five (Ontario, Ministry of Health, 1978).

Hearing loss is most tragic when it strikes the very young. Its incidence at birth is quite low, however — in Canada, hearing loss affects 1 baby in every 1500 (Canadian Hearing Society, 1976). Hearing impairment occurs at similar rates within various ethnic, genetic, and socio-economic groups (Greenberg and Calderon, 1984). Approximately one-third of all hearing-impaired children suffer from additional handicapping conditions (Meadow, 1980).

In 1979, a total of 3971 Canadian children had been identified as hearing-impaired. Of these, 49.6 percent had profound hearing loss and 95.7 percent were pre-lingually hearing-impaired. More boys (54.6 percent) than girls (45.4 percent) suffered hearing impairments (Karchmer, Petersen, Allen, and Osborn, 1981).

In the United States, an estimated 2 out of every 1000 persons under nineteen suffer from a severe hearing disorder (Schein and Delk, 1974). American figures for 1979 show the ratio of hearing disabled males to females under nineteen as 54 to 46 percent (Moores, 1982).

ETIOLOGY OF HEARING IMPAIRMENT

Most of the available information on the causes of hearing impairment is concerned with deafness, as opposed to mild hearing loss. However, Howie (1975) reports that ninety-five percent of children will experience some ear infection in the first five years of life. Even mild losses can result in educational difficulties.

Impairments of the outer ear

As stated earlier, the auricle and the external canal are much less important to hearing than the middle and inner ears. Problems can occur, however, which require medical or surgical intervention before they impede the child's education.

External otitis, or swimmer's ear, is an infection of the skin of the external auditory canal. In the canal, an excessive build-up of wax can result in lessened hearing acuity. Infrequently, a child is born with missing or undeveloped pinnae or auditory canals. This condition, known as **atresia**, interferes with the air conduction of sound. Perforation of the ear drum, resulting from any number of causes, can also produce hearing impairment.

Impairments of the middle ear

Although middle-ear hearing impairments are generally more serious, most can be corrected.

In **Otitis media**, the mucosal lining of the middle ear becomes inflamed and the cavity filled with fluid. This condition often results from upper-respiratory-tract infection, and can be corrected medically. It is the most common form of middle-ear conductive hearing loss (Davis and Silverman, 1978).

Otitis media occurs frequently in children and is endemic in the Native school-age population (Watters, 1980). With repeated bouts of infection, children may get "glue ear" or secretory otis media. This can become chronic, cause a conductive hearing loss, and lead to serious damage to the middle ear bones that may require reconstructive surgery (*Hearing Loss*, 1982). The language abilities of children suffering from recurrent or untreated otitis media may become delayed or disordered (Zinkus, Gottlieb, and Shapiro, 1978). Although this problem is less severe than profound hearing loss, it is also more widespread.

Otosclerosis is characterized by the destruction of the capsular bone in the middle ear and the growth of a weblike bone that attaches to and restricts the stapes. Otosclerosis is a hereditary disease that affects 2 percent of the population, and is clinically active in more than 0.5 percent (Hearing loss, 1982). The condition is rare in children, and is not usually noticed until adolescence or the early twenties. Resultant hearing loss can be at the 50 or 60 dB level, necessitating the use of a hearing aid or corrective surgery. Otosclerosis is twice as common in females as in males.

Other middle-ear problems can be caused by blows to the head or a fall. They can also result from congenital defects.

Impairments of the inner ear

The most severe hearing impairments are caused by sensori-neural problems of the inner ear. A great many childhood sensori-neural impairments are attributed to "causes unknown." However, Moores (1982) has documented five major causes of sensori-neural deafness: heredity; maternal rubella; meningitis; mother-child blood incompatibility (e.g. Rh factor); and prematurity. The most devastating losses stem from meningitis, maternal rubella, and hereditary factors.

Estimates of the number of children with hearing loss due to hereditary factors range from thirty to sixty percent (Moores, 1982). There are about sixty types of hereditary deafness. Hearing problems may be inherited on a dominant trait (fourteen percent), a recessive trait (forty-four percent), or as a sex-linked disorder (two percent) (Lowenbraun and Thompson, 1982).

The high incidence of marriage between hearing-impaired people is a factor in the high incidence of hereditary hearing loss. Many schools for the deaf contain students whose parents and grandparents also attended there. One Canadian study traced a family with a genetic trait for deafness from 1865 to 1978. Of 154 descendants, nearly ten percent (15) were born deaf (Winzer, 1981).

Hearing loss can be inherited alone or in combination with other abnormalities in a syndrome. Hearing loss accompanies skeletal deformities in Treacher-Collins syndrome, abnormal skin pigmentation in Waardenburg's syndrome, and sometimes the multiple disabilities of Down's syndrome. Approximately four to five percent of the congenitally hearing-impaired have Usher's syndrome, which results in hearing impairment and a progressive deterioration of the visual field through retinitis pigmentosa (Bond, 1981). Pedred's syndrome and Jervell and Lang-Neilson syndrome are also associated with hearing impairment.

Maternal rubella is the most common identifiable cause of deafness from an external source. Rubella, or German measles, is usually acquired by pregnant mothers through an airborne virus. Often the virus leaves the mother symptom-free and concentrates on the embryo. The infection may cause the child to be born with hearing loss, defective vision, heart irregularities, and disorders of the nervous system. Recent information suggests that some rubella children may demonstrate progressively increasing hearing loss (Anvar, Mencher, and Keet, 1984; Bordley and Alford, 1970).

Meningitis occurs in many varieties, and is considered one of the major causes of acquired sensori-neural hearing loss (Childhood Hearing, 1984). The high fever that accompanies the disease is very dangerous to the inner ear. Even drugs used in the past to treat meningitis have been found to be toxic to the hearing system (see *Childhood Hearing*, 1984, p. 10).

Incompatibility of blood type between mother and infant may cause hearing impairment along with several other disorders. Rh-positive and Rh-negative blood are extremely incompatible. During second and subsequent pregnancies, an Rh-negative mother produces antibodies that attack the red cells of an Rh-positive fetus.

Prematurity by itself does not cause deafness. However, premature and low-birth-weight babies are at higher risk for hearing disorders. A problem such as undetected rubella may be the cause of early delivery. Deafness can also result from birth complications such as prolonged labour, abrupt birth, or the use of obstetric instruments. Failure to breathe immediately after birth, or **apnea**, is another commonly reported cause of hearing problems.

Among adults, progressive nerve deterioration, known as **prebycusis**, is the most common cause of auditory defect. The older one gets, the more one is prone to prebycusis. Meniere's disease is a particularly devasting problem for adults. This condition is characterized by nausea, vertigo, and **tinnitus**, a high-pitched throbbing or ringing in the ear. In its extreme form, tinnitus causes severe depression as the sound becomes unbearable, especially at night (Hearing loss, 1982). Surgical intervention or medication sometimes helps those with Meniere's Disease, but there is still no satisfactory treatment.

Intercranial tumours, cerebral hemorrhages, and prolonged exposure to tones of high intensity are also increasingly recognized causes of sensori-neural hearing loss.

PREVENTION OF HEARING IMPAIRMENT

In North America, we pay less attention to hearing loss than to almost any other medical problem (Hopper, 1975). Certainly, not all hearing loss can be prevented. However, increased awareness can serve to prevent many hearing problems.

High risk registers

A child at high risk is more likely than most children to develop some specific disability. High-risk factors include complications during the mother's pregnancy, certain postnatal conditions, the medical or genetic history of the family, and the socio-economic background of the family. Most hospitals keep high-risk registers to identify infants at risk for potential hearing loss. These registers list the various medical factors that render hearing impairments more likely. A high-risk register for hearing impairment might list these factors:

- Family history of childhood hearing impairment.
- Perinatal complications, such as prolonged labour, prematurity, complications during delivery, the use of obstetric instruments, or severe anoxia.
- Neonatal complications, such as low birth-weight or very high birth-weight.
- Anatomic malformations involving the head or neck.

Genetic Counselling

The genetics specialist is primarily concerned with prevention. In the past few decades, the fertility of the deaf has rapidly approached that of the general population. Moreover, a deaf person typically marries someone else with a hearing handicap. As a result, genetic transmission of deafness has become increasingly common (Welch, 1981). Empirical evidence indicates that the risk of deaf offspring for a deaf couple is approximately ten percent (Fay, 1898; Fraser, 1976). This average figure includes couples at very high risk and others for whom risk is minimal.

The genetics specialist offers counselling to couples and informs them of genetic risks. Once armed with this knowledge, the couple can plan their family accordingly.

Prevention of acquired deafness

Problems associated with mother-child blood incompatibility have apparently decreased since the 1968 advent of anti-Rh gamma globulin (Rho Gam). If injected into the mother within seventy-two hours of birth, she will not produce the harmful antibodies that can harm later babies.

A rubella vaccine was developed in 1968, and is now given to preschool children. Over the next two decades, this vaccine may reduce the numbers of children suffering rubella complications to a small trickle (Welch, 1981).

Industrial noise

Noise levels sufficient to cause hearing damage are a growing problem in industry. For example, a power mower emits 100 dB, a subway train 90, a riveting gun 130, and a jet takeoff 105 or more. Muscles in the middle ear protect the inner ear from excessively loud, low-pitched sounds. However, no such action protects the ear from the new, high-pitched industrial sounds.

The Ontario Workers' Compensation Board reported that between 1956 and 1974, cases of noise-induced deafness rose from 25 to 2317. Even people far removed from urban centres are not immune to noise-induced hearing damage. A study by Saskatchewan's Department of Agriculture found that one-third of all tractor-driving farmers over the age of fifty suffered a hearing impairment (Hopper, 1975).

Modern music may also be causing hearing impairments. Rock-and-roll bands often reach 115 dB. One expert argues that tickets to rock shows should be labelled: "Warning — this concert may be hazardous to your ears" (Hopper, 1975).

Foreign objects

Nature designed the ear to clean itself. An old saying claims that if the finger were intended to go in the ear, it would have been made small enough to fit. Unfortunately, many other things do fit — the ends of pencils, beads, carrots, peanuts, and bobby pins. Even cotton swabs can do enormous damage, either by puncturing the paper-thin ear drum, or pushing accumulations of wax further into the ear (Ontario, Ministry of Health, 1978).

DIAGNOSIS AND MEASUREMENT OF HEARING IMPAIRMENT

Audiology is the science of detecting and correcting hearing impairment. The major purposes of audiology are as follows:

- To assist in medical diagnosis.
- To provide an overall assessment of hearing to ascertain the need for supportive services.
- To screen large populations for individuals who require more in-depth assessment.
- To detect changes in hearing that might have resulted from exposure to hazard. (Davis, 1978a.)

Audiologists use many sophisticated methods to assess hearing. They use three general types of hearing test — pure tone audiometry, speech audiometry, and specialized tests for very young or difficult-to-assesss children.

Screening

Often the first step in an assessment procedure is the inital identification of a problem through some sort of screening test. Children with severe hearing losses are likely to be identified in the first years of life. Those with less severe problems may not be identified until they undergo a routine school screening.

The most common screening instrument is the **sweep test**. This uses a portable audiometer to present tones at 20 to 25 dB across a range of frequencies (Kneedler, 1984). Children who reveal problems at the screening level are then referred for in-depth audiological evaluations.

Pure-tone audiometry

A child's degree of hearing loss, measured in decibel and hertz units, can be ascertained with a pure-tone audiometer in an environment relatively free of external noise. Pure-tone audiometry is designed to establish an individual's threshold for hearing at a variety of different frequencies. A *threshold of hearing* is the level at which a person can first detect a sound.

The procedure for testing sensitivity to pure tones is relatively simple. The audiologist presents a variety of tones at decibel levels from 0 to 110 dB across a range of frequencies, usually 125 to 8000 Hz. As the individual responds, the data for each ear are plotted on a chart of hearing called an audiogram.

Figure 8-3 shows an audiogram on which is plotted the average loss (in both ears) of three different individuals.

Person A has a flat loss of about 70 dB. In other words, Person A only begins to detect sound at the level of 70 dB. Person A would be regarded as moderately hearing impaired. A hearing aid would help greatly, because of the amount of residual hearing, especially across the speech range.

Person B suffers a "ski-slope" hearing loss and is profoundly deaf. Person C displays a saucer-shaped audiological pattern, which a number of researchers (Anderson, Barr and

Figure 8-3 An audiogram or "hearing-profile" for three different people.

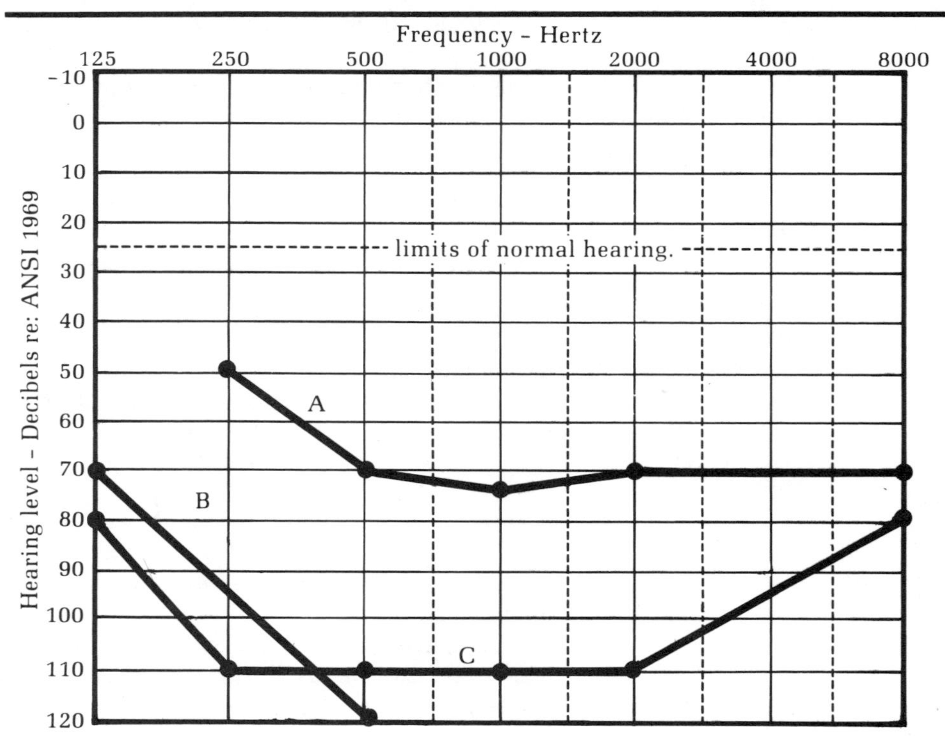

Wedenberg, 1970; Fitzgerald, Sitton and McConnell, 1970; Vernon, 1967a) have found common in children with hearing loss due to rubella. Because Person C has much residual hearing in the high and low frequencies, amplification will be very beneficial.

Speech audiometry

A technique called **speech audiometry** has been developed to assess a child's ability to detect and understand speech. **Speech detection** reflects the intensity level at which a person can hear, but not necessarily understand, speech. Much more important is the **speech reception threshold (SRT)**, which is the level at which the individual actually understands the speech.

One way to assess the speech reception threshold is to present a person with a list of **spondees**, or two-syllable words that have equal stress on each syllable. *Baseball* and *ice-cream* are two examples. Each ear is tested separately, and the level at which half the words are understood is considered the speech reception threshold.

Tests for young children

Pure-tone and speech audiometry can only be used with people who understand what is expected of them. The diagnostic process requires a person to discriminate among

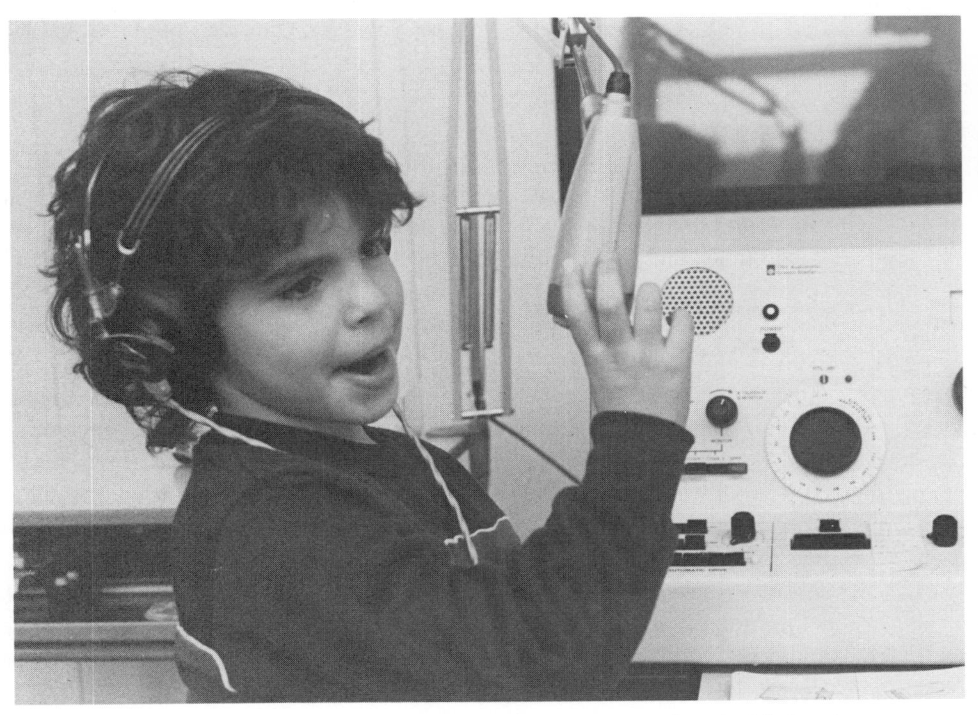

Speech audiometry is used to assess the speech reception threshold (SRT). (T. Wilson)

sounds of differing intensity and tone, and then communicate those discriminations.

The audiometric evaluation of any child under four is fraught with difficulties. So that hearing impairment can be identified as early as possible, a number of special tests have been devised for very young children. Special tests have also been developed for those whose handicaps do not suit standard pure-tone audiometric testing.

Play audiometry

This technique for children over two uses the audiometer but asks for different responses. A game is set up whereby the child performs an activity in response to a sound. The children respond by building stacking toys, dropping blocks into a box, or putting pieces into a puzzle.

Reflex audiometry

Up to the age of five or six months, infants display reflexive behaviours to loud sounds which are useful for the testing of hearing. Present at birth is the **Moro reflex**, a startle movement that affects face, arms, trunk, legs, and eyes (Davis, 1978b). Infants also show an orienting response, by turning their heads or bodies toward the source of a sound (Hallahan and Kauffman, 1982). These methods obviously give crude measures and do not permit assessment of each ear. However, they do supply valuable information regarding hearing status.

Crib-O-Gram

A new approach to evaluating the hearing status of newborns is a device called the Crib-O-Gram. This device is attached to the hospital crib and introduces periodic auditory signals. Resulting changes in the infant's behaviour are systematically recorded, (Jones and Simmons, 1977).

Electrophysiological assessment

This technique is one of the most important recent developments in the assessment of hearing loss in very young children. **Electrophysiological assessment** measures responses to auditory stimulation but requires no active participation on the part of the child. Electrodes are attached to the scalp and reveal changes in the brain's electrical activity when the subject hears a sound (Wiley, 1980).

Acoustic impedance audiometry

Another important recent development is **acoustic impedance audiometry**. This technique assesses conductive hearing loss by measuring the movement of the ear drum and middle-ear muscles and bones in response to auditory stimulation (Northern, 1980; Towne, 1979).

Early identification of hearing loss

The early identification of hearing loss is of paramount importance in helping the child to develop as normally as possible. The infant years are crucial to language acquisition, biologically and socially (Pollack, 1970). As the infant grows older, the handicapping effects of a hearing impairment can become cumulative and hinder the child from reaching developmental milestones. However, although educators are optimistic, early and accurate identification of hearing impairments remains an elusive dream.

Identification in infants

During infancy, children who are born deaf most closely resemble their hearing peers. Vision plays the leading role in an infant's first efforts to independently explore the environment (Gesell and Amatruda, 1947). As the infant's new world comes into sharper visual focus, the developing neuromuscular system sparks a push toward motor exploration. The infant reaches out to touch, feel, taste, and probe, accompanying all these actions by automatic vocalizations. Deaf infants follow this pattern of behaviour just as hearing infants do (Levine, 1981).

Hearing-impaired infants cry and coo, and vocalize much like other children during the first few months of life. Not until they reach the babbling stage at about six months do their sound patterns become differentiated from hearing infants (Telford and Sawrey, 1981). Deaf infants quickly abandon the babbling stage, and demonstrate a significant decrease in babbling behaviour by ten months of age (Lenneberg, 1967). Unlike hearing infants, deaf infants cannot hear their own babbling or receive reinforcement from the speech of adults.

Hearing loss is often suspected when children are about twelve months and expected to say their first words. Many hearing impairments, however, are not suspected until much later than this. In Canada, even when hearing loss is suspected early, an average delay of a year takes place between suspicion and diagnosis (Lyon and Lyon, 1982). At the earliest, then, the child is two years old, and often much older, before any sort of intervention, remediation, or rehabilitation is likely to begin.

Many delays in detection are caused by physicians. An Atlantic Canada study found that 71 percent of parents had suspected their child's hearing loss before the child was eighteen months of age. Of their doctors, 58.2 percent waited up to three months before confirming parents' suspicions, 20 percent delayed up to a year, and 21 percent did not diagnose hearing loss until one to six years later (Canning, 1980). In a Vancouver study, many physicians rejected parental suspicions and about one-third refused to refer the child to a specialist. The time lag between suspicion and diagnosis averaged 9.7 months for profoundly deaf children and 16.4 months for those who were severely deaf (Freeman, 1977).

Hard-of-hearing children

Despite delays, deaf children are likely to be identified during the pre-school years. However, the hearing problems of hard-of-hearing children may not be detected until they undergo a routine school screening.

Hard-of-hearing children can use spoken language adequately to transmit and receive information. They can use their residual hearing to develop speech and language skills although they may use speechreading to supplement auditory clues. However, even with adequate speech and language skills, hard-of-hearing children may be at risk educationally.

Exhibit 8-3 outlines some of the behaviours that suggest mild hearing loss. Teachers and parents should be alert for these behaviours, and send children with suspected problems for an in-depth audiological evaluation.

Exhibit 8-3 Possible signs of mild hearing loss in children.

- Does there appear to be a physical problem associated with the ears, such as earaches, buzzing, discharge, or frequent colds and sore throats?
- Does the child have poor articulation, particularly missing some of the consonant sounds?
- Does the child cock the head or turn the body toward the speaker in an obvious effort to hear more accurately?
- Does the child have more than usual trouble in following directions?
- Does the child frequently ask for information to be repeated?
- Does the child appear to be inattentive or unresponsive when spoken to in a normal voice?
- Does the child speak or sing too loudly or too softly?
- Does the child talk too much and appear not to want to relinquish control of the conversation?
- Is the child withdrawn and unwilling to mingle with classmates or neighbours?
- Does the child give incorrect answers to simple questions?
- Is the child functioning below potential ability in school?
- Is the child becoming a behaviour problem at school or at home?

Confusion in differential diagnosis

Undetected hard-of-hearing children are sometimes characterized by such unsavoury terms as lazy, inattentive, unmotivated, or even dull and stupid. For undetected deaf children, this problem may be much worse. Because childhood deafness has ambiguous symptoms and is medically quite rare, it may be misdiagnosed. The symptoms are sometimes confused with those of mental retardation, emotional disturbance, or perceptual difficulties (Meadow, 1980).

PROFILE 8-1

At seven-and-a-half, Albert already had a reputation as being disruptive in the classroom and difficult to manage. He was inattentive and restless in his behaviour, aggressive with other children, and poor in academic work. His speech was slurred, and he had a lisp.

In kindergarten and grade one, Albert's teachers had considered him immature and somewhat slow to learn. As he approached his eighth birthday, however, his learning problems were increasing. He was having particular trouble with language arts.

Although he had a small vocabulary of sight words, he was defeated by sound-symbol association and basic phonic skills for word attack.

After a teacher referral for in-depth diagnosis, Albert was labelled as learning-disabled. However, even one-to-one with a learning-assistance teacher, he made little progress. His parents blamed the school for his increasing frustration and unhappiness.

When Albert saw the speech-language pathologist the root of his problem was finally discovered. The pathologist found that Albert had trouble recognizing and enunciating higher-pitched speech sounds. This led the pathologist to suspect hearing impairment.

At last Albert was diagnosed as suffering a 55 dB hearing loss. Because this loss occurred in the high frequencies between 4000 Hz and 8000 Hz, it had been missed in regular school screening tests.

Albert's audiologist did not suggest amplification for him. However, Albert's classroom environment and curriculum have been modified. His seating has been changed to the front of the room. His teacher is concentrating on building a strong sight-word vocabulary and using a "word family" approach to improve his reading vocabulary. Most importantly, Albert now understands his problem and can begin to adjust to it.

CHARACTERISTICS OF THE HEARING IMPAIRED

The cognitive development of the hearing-impaired child is a provocative and challenging area for research. Studies have considered the relationship between language and thought, problems related to the attainment of concepts, perceptual-motor processes, attributes of memory function, performance on tests of intelligence, and academic achievement (Meadow, 1980).

Intelligence

Cognitive development is traditionally assessed through standardized tests purporting to evaluate intellectual ability. Between 1900 and 1950, studies of deaf school children showed them to be three or four years behind hearing children and about ten IQ points below the norm (Meadow, 1980). This led early researchers to conclude that educational programming should concentrate on motor and mechanical skills rather than intellectual abilities (Pintner, 1941).

By the 1950s, researchers realized that the general intellectual level of the hearing-impaired child was not inferior to that of hearing children. Rather, the perceptual and conceptual processes of congenitally deaf children failed to develop normally (Myklebust, 1953, 1960). Today, with testing procedures directed to linguistic capabilities, deaf children score within the normal range on the performance scales of tests of mental ability. Their mean scores, however, are somewhat lower than those of hearing children (Meadow, 1980).

Non-verbal IQ tests are the most appropriate for deaf children. The most widely used IQ test is the performance scale of the Wechsler Intelligence Scale for Children, Revised (WISC-R) (Wechsler, 1974). This is believed to yield fairly valid IQ scores for deaf children aged nine to sixteen. The Verbal Scale is usually omitted from the battery, and an IQ score is calculated on the basis of the Performance Scale alone.

The Performance Scale of the WISC-R was standardized using a hearing-impaired sample (Anderson and Sisco, 1977). It is now widely used in conjunction with the Hiskey-Nebraska Test of Learning Aptitude (Hiskey, 1966) to evaluate the cognitive abilities of the hearing-impaired population between six and seventeen (Sullivan and Vernon, 1979). Test instructions may be given orally, in pantomime, through Total Communication, or with the use of visual aids.

Other popular non-verbal scales include the Goodenough-Harris Drawing Test (Harris, 1963) and Raven's Progressive Matrices (Raven, 1948) for children nine years and older. The Leiter International Performance Scale (Leiter, 1948) has remained extremely popular because it is administered by pantomime and needs no verbal cues or responses. As well, the Non-verbal Test of Cognitive Skills is coming into wide use (Johnson and Boyd, 1981), as is the Test of Non-Verbal Intelligence (Brown, Sherbenou, and Dollar, 1982).

Conceptual abilities

Comparisons of concept formation and abstract-thinking skills between hearing-impaired and normally hearing children have yielded somewhat inconsistent results. When differences arise, the crucial factor appears to be language. Some researchers have found that deaf children consistently demonstrate the same thinking processes as hearing children when the tasks involved are not dependent on language (Furth, 1964, 1966, 1971; Vernon, 1967b). Others have found that deaf children who have acquired some language consistently outperform those with less language ability (Schlesinger and Meadow, 1972; Silverman, 1967). Deaf children with limited language appear markedly slower in mastering some abstract concepts. However, other researchers suggest this may be due to inadequate communication between the hearing-impaired and those around them (Liben, 1978).

Many educators and researchers currently accept that deaf children can think logically without a linguistic system. However, the mastery of a language system is of enormous benefit in problem-solving and academic performance.

Memory

Studies of the performance of deaf children on memory tasks show conflicting results, possibly related to different test materials. For example, deaf children are more likely to retain words that have a sign equivalent than words that do not. They are more likely than hearing children to remember geometric forms than digits. Deaf children use word association patterns similar to those of hearing children of a younger age (Meadow, 1980).

Speech and language

Speech and language are the areas of development most severely affected by a hearing impairment. Speech and language problems vary considerably due to many factors. These include the degree of hearing loss, the training and use of residual hearing, the child's age at the impairment's onset, the etiology of the impairment, the family climate, the early mode of communication, and the educational setting (Meadow, 1980).

For children with mild or moderate hearing loss, the effect on speech and language may be minimal. As long as the voice sounds of conversational speech remain audible, effective communication skills are possible. Although children with moderate hearing loss cannot hear unvoiced sounds or distant speech, language delays can be prevented if their impairment is diagnosed and treated early (Ling and Ling, 1978).

For deaf children, most loud speech is inaudible, even with the most sophisticated aids. These children have significant problems in learning language. They also develop significant articulation, voice quality and tone-discrimination problems (Oyers and Frankman, 1975). Because deaf children cannot hear the words of people around them, they have no language models. When deaf children enter school, they are usually unable to speak or understand any language. On average, they take three years to prepare for first grade, and from ten to twelve years to complete the eight elementary grades (Silverman, Lane, and Doehring, 1964). Even with optimal effective intervention, the language levels of most deaf children are seriously retarded.

Speech is another area of serious difficulty. In one study, teachers rated the intelligibility of the speech of their hearing-impaired students. More than forty-two percent of the children were rated as barely intelligible or unintelligible. According to the survey, approximately thirteen percent of the children would not even try to use their voices for speech (Jensema, Karchmer, and Trybus, 1978).

According to a common myth, deaf individuals have an ability to lip-read that compensates for the lack of hearing. This is patently false; the average deaf school-leaver can read lips no better than hearing peers (Conrad, 1979). Lip-reading, or **speech reading**, is the skill of understanding speech through watching not only lips, but also faces. Facial expressions give spoken words a whole spectrum of feelings, attitudes, and visual clues.

Speech reading is a difficult skill to acquire because only about thirty percent of English sounds are visible on the lips (Stewart, 1984). Speech readers must have enough language knowledge to anticipate and fill in missing words. Moreover, the average speaker makes about thirteen articulatory movements a second during normal conversation. The average observer can visually record only eight or nine movements a second (Sanders, 1971).

Academic achievement

The academic achievement of deaf children is closely aligned to their acquisition of language. Because of this, academic achievement contrasts poorly with documented potential. Deaf students appear to be uniformly educationally retarded by three to five years.

Numerous studies of reading achievement have shown that the mean reading scores of deaf children are well below those of hearing children. Deaf children lag two to eight years behind hearing children in reading skills. Typically, deaf students graduate from school reading at a grade four level. (Ling, 1981; Mindel and Vernon, 1971; Trybus and Karchmer, 1977). This is below or barely at a newspaper literacy level.

Deaf children are less educationally retarded in more mechanical skills, such as arithmetic computation and spelling. Surprisingly, the spelling ability of deaf children has hardly been studied at all. It does appear, however, that deaf children may be superior in spelling performance (Gates and Chase, 1926; Hoemann, Andrews, Florian,

Hoemann and Jensema, 1976; Templin, 1948), a puzzling finding in light of the complexity of the rules of English spelling.

Mathematics computation is an area in which deaf children often achieve well. They are less successful at mathematics problems, which are predicated on a language base.

Social and emotional development

Deaf children show a higher degree of emotional instability, neuroticism, and social maladjustment than hearing children (Schein, 1975). The barriers of deafness and limited language appear to increase a sense of frustration, loneliness, helplessness, and despair. The severity of social maladjustment patterns often depends on the severity of the hearing loss and the type of impairment. Severe hearing losses are more likely to result in extreme social isolation. Children with sensori-neural disorders need more help to adapt socially because of problems in processing and internalizing auditory information.

Estimates of the rate of emotional disturbance among hearing-impaired children range from 8 to 22 percent (Meadow, 1980). A Vancouver study looked at 120 hearing-impaired children between five and fifteen. According to parents and teachers, 22.6 percent of these children had psychiatric disorders ranging from moderate to severe. Mothers of deaf children were much more likely than other mothers to find their children restless, possessive, overly dependent, disobedient, fussy, distressing, destructive, and dishonest (Freeman, Malkin, and Hastings, 1975).

Abnormal social development in hearing-impaired children is often manifested by impulsive, irresponsible, and dependent behaviour. Frequently, deaf children seem to disregard the feelings and misunderstand the actions of others. They typically exhibit a high degree of egocentricity and a low frustration level. These traits cause them to make inordinate demands and to act out their frustrations if demands are not met (Harris, 1978; Meadow, 1980). In the Vancouver study, children with psychiatric disorders included those who shunned social relations, exhibited bizarre behaviour, were extremely anxious, or were persistently involved in major delinquency (Freeman, Malkin and Hastings, 1975).

The social immaturity of many hearing-impaired children inevitably causes personal and social difficulties. Therefore, the development of personal and social skills is considered an important element of education for the hearing-impaired (White, 1982).

PARENTING THE HEARING-IMPAIRED CHILD

The diagnostic process is frequently traumatic for parents, and may influence their feelings for their hearing-impaired child for many years. Yet diagnosis marks only the beginning of the family's struggle. After initial diagnosis, parents often pass through a psychological crisis that includes guilt, sorrow, shock, and denial (Spink, 1976).

While the child's parents pass through these disturbances, the child's own psychological structure is also being shaken. Although children are remarkably resilient, recent research indicates that deaf children suffer a range of negative effects. Of these consequences, we are still relatively unknowledgeable (Clarke, 1982). We do know, however, that the absence of meaningful, satisfying communication between young deaf children and their parents may result in disturbed and fragmented communication, isolation from the family, later poor school achievement, and higher rates of psychiatric disturbance (Greenberg and Calderon, 1984).

Parental attitudes can have a strong positive or negative effect on their child's educational progress. Parents who cannot accept their child's handicap cannot consolidate their efforts with schools and other support agencies. This may interfere substantially with the child's educational growth. It is vital that the parents of a hearing-impaired child appreciate their role in developing communication skills, offering psychological stability, and providing a nurturing environment.

Deaf children of deaf parents

Children deafened by genetic factors are often born into families who already have experience with deafness. Approximately ten percent of hearing-impaired babies are born to deaf parents. These children form a distinct sub-group within the hearing-impaired population. They consistently perform at a higher level on tests of academic achievement than do deaf children of hearing parents. Vernon (1969) found that deaf children with deaf parents achieved in school at about two-thirds the rate of hearing students. Children who became deaf because of blood incompatibility (Rh factor) achieved at a rate of one-half of hearing students. Children deafened by reason of prematurity, rubella, or meningitis achieved at a rate slightly lower than one-half of those with normal hearing.

Deaf children with deaf parents may have higher achievement levels as a direct result of close exposure to other deaf people. Because their parents are fluent in sign language they usually experience language acquisition and family interaction earlier and at a greater rate than other deaf children. This prevents much frustration for both parents and children, and assists the children's emotional development. Emotional-behavioural disturbance among deaf children with deaf parents is about half as prevalent as among deaf children with hearing parents (Stokoe and Battison, 1975).

Because deaf parents understand their child's condition, they seem better able to cope with the guilt, shame, and sorrow that accompany diagnosis. In addition, deaf children of deaf parents rarely suffer additional injuries to the nervous system before birth. As a result, their incidence of secondary handicaps is no greater than for the population at large.

Deaf children of hearing parents

Deaf children with hearing parents comprise more than ninety percent of the young deaf population. Hearing parents use spoken language as their primary mode of communication. Their children's first exposure to language is oral, whether comprehensible or not.

Hearing parents are much more likely than deaf parents to view their child's diagnosis as a tragic crisis. Hearing parents often express feelings of incompetence, self-doubt, and sorrow. In some cases, the birth of a hearing-impaired child threatens family integration and destroys the balance of family relationships (Meadow, 1980).

Hearing children of deaf parents

Although not actually hearing-impaired, the hearing children of deaf parents often develop problems. In Canada especially, little research has been done to discover the special needs of this group.

When research has been done, it has chiefly focused on the effects of early exposure to sign language in the home. One study (Schiff and Ventry, 1976) of fifty-two hearing children of deaf parents found that only twenty-three had developed normal language. The other twenty-nine developed speech and language problems, including defective articulation, deviant stress and intonation patterns, and fluency disorders. These problems did not disappear after the children entered school. In another study, Murphy and Slorach (1983) found that, of six pre-school hearing children of deaf parents, three showed delayed and deviant language development and three had other language problems.

Other researchers in this area have looked at family climate (Robinson and Weathers, 1974), cognitive development (Tendler, 1976), and the involvement of hearing children in the deaf community (Higgins, 1979). Results of this meagre work are inconclusive, and more investigation is needed into hearing children's relationships with deaf parents, deaf siblings, the deaf community, and the "hearing world." Research is also needed to examine how these children's childhoods are redefined as they become "hearing mediators" in their homes.

INTERVENTION WITH THE HEARING-IMPAIRED

Children who are deaf or hard-of-hearing require considerable intervention to provide health care, rehabilitation, therapy, and education. Generally, intervention involves two major components. The first is medical intervention to try to correct the physical causes of hearing loss. Medical intervention includes the amplification of sound through hearing aids. The second form of intervention focuses on minimizing the educational and phychological consequences of hearing impairment. Educational intervention takes the form of special education and related services.

Medical intervention

As stated earlier, many conductive hearing losses can be corrected medically. Chronic otitis media can be alleviated by antibiotics in the early stages and by a **myringotomy**, or puncture of the eardrum to drain off fluid. Microsurgery now permits an operation to free the stapes in the case of otosclerosis.

Today's otological surgeon can surgically reconstruct the middle ear (tympanoplasty), rebuild the bones of ossicular chain, and repair, shift, or rebuild a new ear drum. Surgeons can construct new membraneous windows into the inner ear. When infants are born with atresia, surgeons can make a bony canal into the middle ear (Hearing loss, 1982; Telford and Sawrey, 1981).

The cochlear implant is a relatively new surgical procedure of great promise. This electronic implant can stimulate the auditory nerve directly, delivering electrical stimuli to whatever auditory nerve fibres remain in a deaf ear. The cochlear implant can also provide selective stimulation, related to acoustic freqency, for different nerve fibres, through several electrodes (Paparella and Davis, 1978).

Technical aids

In recent years, there have been major advances in technological devices to aid the hearing-impaired. Hearing-aids have been reduced from bulky, uncomfortable body-aids to tiny, unobtrusive behind-the-ear models. New inventions, such as flashing doorbells, now help the deaf in communication and household management. In addition, computer technology holds great promise for the education of hearing-impaired children.

Amplification

Once a child's medical and audiological data have been gathered, the child should receive and wear a personal hearing aid as soon as possible. Hearing-aids can be worn by infants, as well as by children and adults. Most hearing-impaired children benefit from their use, especially when auditory training begins early.

Hearing aids differ in size, cost, and efficiency. With recent advances in the manufacture of miniature transistors, the efficiency of very small units has increased dramatically. Today's hearing aid is a compact device, made up of miniature parts working together to make sounds louder.

A hearing aid consists of the following parts:

- A microphone that receives sound waves and changes them into electrical impulses.
- An amplifier that increases the strength of the electrical signals.
- A battery that provides electrical energy to operate the hearing aid.
- A loudspeaker, called a receiver, that changes electrically amplified sounds back into sound waves. On a body aid, the receiver earphone is separated from the hearing-aid case by a cord. In an ear-level hearing aid, all four components are housed together.
- A custom-made ear mould that directs sounds into the ear.

Hearing aids are primarily sound amplifiers. They can help children to develop their residual hearing, to improve the audition of their own voices, to use speech in a purposeful way, and to expand their vocabulary and language ability. However, although hearing aids may alleviate the problems of hearing loss, they cannot eliminate problems altogether.

Many children resist wearing a hearing aid because the awkwardness of the strange appliance outweighs their awareness of any benefits. Parents must be patient and persistent to overcome this initial reluctance. After children are fitted with hearing aids, they still have much work to do before they can use or understand speech. They must learn to interpret sounds they hear and to duplicate the sounds of speech (Stassen, 1978).

Even a profoundly deaf child can benefit from a hearing aid. A few distorted fragments of sound can help immensely in speech and language acquisition. Almost every hearing-impaired child can derive some benefit from amplification.

Despite the proven effectiveness of hearing aids, only one hearing-impaired person in three actually owns and uses one (Schein and Delk, 1974). There are many reasons for this:

- There is a wide-spread belief that persons with sensori-neural hearing loss cannot benefit at all from an aid. One deaf adult, with a loss of 100 dB in both ears, demonstrated that this is not always true. With amplification in both ears, this adult enjoys reading the text of a story while listening to it on a tape recorder. By listening while reading, he can associate the vocalizations with the corresponding words and phrases in the text (Pottharst, 1983).
- Another belief holds that hearing aids are not appropriate for persons with mild hearing losses. However, many mild losses can be alleviated successfully with amplification.
- A particularly misleading fallacy claims that high-frequency losses cannot be corrected by a hearing aid. This is true of body aids, which rub against clothing and drown out high frequencies with low-frequency sound (Sanders, 1971). However, behind-the-ear models create no such problems. Hearing aids can also be programmed to amplify certain frequencies more than others.
- Some people cannot become used to the noise of the hearing aid. Because amplification is indiscriminate, it may flood the individual with disconcerting auditory stimulation. A hearing aid intensifies and, to some extent, distorts sound.
- Some people are restrained from wearing a hearing aid by vanity or self-consciousness.
- Economic factors may also prevent some people from wearing hearing aids. Not only are hearing aids expensive, but batteries, ear moulds and receivers may need to be replaced.

Like all mechanical instruments, hearing aids have a tendency to break down or malfunction. Small children are especially hard on hearing aids, exposing them to dirt, jello, the family dog, the toilet bowl, and the classroom aquarium. Teachers and parents should check frequently that the aid is working, is turned on, has batteries, fits snugly, and is free of wax and dirt.

In special classrooms, group amplification systems may be used. Currently, the FM (frequency modulation) system is the most popular. With a classroom FM system, the carrier wave is transmitted through the air via frequency modulation from a teacher-worn microphone to a student-worn receiver. FM transmission allows hearing-impaired students to hear the teacher clearly from any location in the classroom (Van Dyke, 1982).

Vibrotactile devices

To aid the hearing-impaired child in speech development, vibrotactile devices have been developed (Sheehy and Hansen, 1983). These vibrate to let children feel and imitate sound differences in duration, intensity, rhythmic pattern, pitch, and voice control. They also differentiate look-alike consonants, such as p/b/m, t/d/n/l, and sh/ch. Children can hold the device in their hands or strap it to their arms.

Telephone devices

The teletyper and printer (TTD) is a commercially available device that allows hearing-impaired people to use the telephone. Rather than listening to a message and responding orally, the TTD allows the deaf person to communicate by reading and typing. Typed messages are changed to electrical signals and then retranslated back to print on a TTD at the other end of the telephone connection.

Household devices

To aid deaf adults in the home, a number of tools have been developed. These devices visually signal when, for example, the baby is crying, the telephone or doorbell is ringing, or a wake-up alarm, smoke alarm, or fire alarm has sounded.

Captioned films

Captioned television shows have been a boon for the hearing-impaired population. The close-captioning process translates dialogue into captions or subtitles. These captions are then converted to electronic codes that can be inserted into the television picture on specially adapted sets.

Educators of hearing-impaired children make extensive use of captioned films in the classroom. Unfortunately, not all films are suitable for captioning. Some sound tracks cannot be duplicated through subtitles because of the rate or inflection of speech, the use of ambient noise or sound effects, or the speed of quick-cut editing and rapid scene changes (Parlatto, 1977).

Microcomputers

Micro-computers have quickly assumed a key role in the education of the hearing impaired. Stoker (1983) has claimed: "It is not an exaggeration to suggest that the microcomputer chip will be remembered as the technological product that changed the course of history for the hearing-impaired population" (p. 364).

Although computers cannot replace the classroom teacher, they are patient, consistent, and accurate teaching tools. If appropriate software is developed, computers will someday deliver a degree and quality of vocabulary and language development hitherto impossible for hearing-impaired children (Stoker, 1983).

In one study, hearing-impaired students were given computer programs to teach them elementary mathematics and language skills. These children achieved gains equal to the expected gains of normally hearing children (Bitzer, 1979). Other researchers report successful use of programs to develop the suprasegmental aspects of speech (Murray, 1979) and language constructions (Ward and Rostron, 1983; Withrow, 1979).

Educational intervention

Learning Environments

Due to the impact of mainstreaming, the delivery of educational services to the hearing-impaired is in a state of change. In Canada, there are six basic educational programs, ranging from residential schools to regular class placement with support services (Clarke and Leslie, 1980).

The most popular models for educational intervention are as follows:

- Residential schools are the most traditional setting for education of the deaf. Many children in these schools now return daily to their own homes. Canada has nine large residential schools, all of which offer day programs. Because deaf parents often send their children to residential schools those facilities have helped foster the concept of a deaf community and a deaf culture (Meadow, 1972).
- Day schools are similar to residential schools, except that all students reside at home.
- Self-contained special classes are located within regular elementary or secondary schools. These offer separate programs for hearing-impaired students.
- A part-time integration program encourages hearing-impaired students from special classes to spend part of their day with normally hearing students. Hearing-impaired students may attend regular classes for physical education and art, or for more academic subjects, such as mathematics and social studies. In the regular classroom, an interpreter may be available for hearing-impaired students.
- Resource rooms, or partial segregation programs, offer hearing-impaired students from regular classes a chance to obtain tutorial assistance in a special class from a trained teacher of the deaf. Again, an interpreter may also be available for the students when in the regular classroom.
- Itinerant programs provide specialist teachers to offer tutorial assistance to hearing-impaired students who are mainstreamed into regular classrooms. The itinerant teacher assists the child and the regular classroom teacher, as well as acting as facilitator or liaison with other support personnel, parents, and school administrators.

Communication modes

In 1578, a Spanish monk, Ponce de Leon, successfully taught the deaf children of some of Spain's wealthiest families. Since that first experiment, a continuous debate has raged regarding the most appropriate mode of communication for use in the education of the hearing-impaired. Today, this debate continues unabated. Moreover, advocates of particular methods "have been inclined to defend the efficacy of their preferred method rhetorically and emotionally rather than empirically" (White and Stevenson, 1975, p. 565).

Before describing the major communication philosophies, methods, and approaches, more should be said about this long-lasting controversy. Throughout the history of deaf education, educators have divided themselves into two irreconcilable camps. The **oralists** have viewed deafness as a human handicap to be overcome through the development of speech and lip-reading. The **manualists** have argued that deafness is a human difference that requires its own language, the language of signs. So divisive did the argument become in the late 1800s that it affected such areas as curriculum, industrial training, the sex of teachers, the value of deaf teachers, and the rights of the deaf to marry and procreate (Winzer, 1981).

The arguments continue today, although most educators attempt to suit the method to the child, rather than vice versa. Under the two major philosophies — manual and oral — a number of educational methods and approaches have developed. Appropriate methods are now usually determined by the severity of the loss, the age of onset, and the wishes of the parents.

The oral/aural method From 1817 to 1867, hearing-impaired students in Canada and the United States were instructed entirely through manual methods. Largely through the influence of Alexander Graham Bell, oral methods of instruction were slowly introduced. By about 1910, nearly all hearing-impaired children were instructed by oral methods, a situation that lasted until the mid-1960s.

The pure oral method placed stress on speech, lip-reading, and writing. It forbade the natural gestures that we all use as part of our communication. The pure oral method was followed by the oral method, which stressed speech and lip-reading along with amplification through newly invented hearing aids. The oral method downplayed the importance of writing, and permitted natural gestures.

The current oral method is more correctly called the **oral-aural** approach. It places stress on speech and speech-reading, and uses amplification as a vital part of education.

The **acoupedic method** is an oral approach in that it aims to develop intelligible speech through the maximum development of listening skills (Pollack, 1970). This method excludes all visual clues, such as speech reading, and encourages the child to use residual hearing to the greatest extent possible. The acoupedic approach requires early detection, early amplification, unisensory stimulation, a normal learning environment, the use of auditory feedback mechanisms, individual instruction, and the preparation of parents to act as first models of communication (Pollack, 1980). With recent advances in hearing-aid technology, acoupedic approaches have gained in popularity.

Cued speech is another primarily oral method of communication that is currently gaining favour in Canada and the United States. This system uses eight configurations and four hand positions to supplement the visible manifestations of speech (Cornett, 1984). The hand cues add information to the speech-reading process so that all single sounds can be identified by the hearing-impaired.

According to its originator, Orin Cornett, Cued speech can be learned in twelve to fifteen hours. Cornett claims that if parents learned and used Cued speech consistently, their hearing-impaired children would learn language easily in the home (Barres, 1978). A Vancouver study has demonstrated that deaf students learn language and other academic skills more effectively with Cued speech than with traditional oral teaching, (Cornett, 1975).

The **Rochester method** uses finger-spelling in conjunction with speech, speech-reading, and amplification. Finger spelling adds a visible supplement to oral-aural language to provide deaf children with more complete, visible language patterns. The Rochester method was adopted at Ontario's three schools for the hearing-impaired in 1974 (McLure, 1975). These schools have now adopted Total Communication teaching methods.

Total Communication Manual communication has traditionally been discouraged under the assumption that children who used signs would not be motivated to learn to speak, use their residual hearing, or speech-read. Recently, however, many educators have shifted from an oral emphasis to one that stresses a combination of methods. Accumulating research indicates that children taught by oral methods use sign language with their peers, even when punished for doing so. Only about seventeen percent of students taught by oral methods ever become orally fluent, but nearly seventy-five percent of deaf children become fluent manually. Moreover, it now seems that early manual communication helps, rather than hinders, later development of oral language. Deaf children of deaf parents outperform deaf children of hearing parents on measures of language skills, suggesting the beneficial effects of early experience with sign language (Charrow and Fletcher, 1974; Hoemann, 1974; Moores, Weiss, and Goodwin, 1975; Vernon, 1975).

By the early 1970s, the benefits of using some manual components in education for the hearing-impaired were apparent. Subsequently, programs for the deaf began adopting an approach that stressed all forms of communication, including signs and speech. **Total Communication** may be defined as the use of speech, speech reading, and amplification, along with the simultaneous use of a school-based manual system. In a school-based system, signs are taught in the same order as language. This teaches the child to communicate manually using correct syntax.

Since its first proposal in 1966, Total Communication has been adopted by schools across Canada and the United States. It is currently the most popular teaching method in Canadian schools and classes for the hearing-impaired.

American Sign Language (ASL) Unlike school-based manual systems, American Sign Language (ASL or Ameslan) does not follow the semantic and syntactic structure of spoken language. ASL is recognized by linguists as a true language in itself, quite different from spoken language. ASL has its own vocabulary, its own grammar, its own word order, and its own history.

ASL is founded on combinations of symbolic gestures produced by the shape, the location, and the movement of the hands. Many of the signs symbolize concepts rather than individual words. ASL has no signs for the grammatical markers, such as *ed* and *ing*, that express verb tense and condition. Rather, users depend on facial expression and body language to replace voice intonation and enhance meaning (Meadow, 1980; Odgen and Lipsett, 1982).

Many people consider ASL to be the natural language of the deaf. Some suggest that ASL be tested in the classroom to assess its value in the overall educational development of deaf children (Stewart, 1981).

Sign systems around the world evolved from the sign language devised by de l'Epée in France in the mid-1700s. However, these systems are no longer universal. Like spoken language, each country has its own unique version (Stewart, 1984).

Language programs

The primary aim of education for the hearing-impaired is to develop language skills. Two major strategies for the teaching of language have evolved — the formal or grammatical approach, and the informal or natural approach.

ASL has its own semantic and syntactic structure. This deaf sign-language user is talking about his work. Literally, the signs translate as: boring (A), work (B), alot (C).

The grammatical approach tries to focus the student's attention on the structural aspects of language. Armed with this structural information, students learn to generate language deductively. The natural approach attempts to parallel the way in which hearing children acquire language. The content and sequence of instruction are determined by the needs of individual children (Schmitt, 1966).

Curricular modifications

Education for hearing-impaired children differs chiefly in degree from that of hearing children. In both, the child's success is based on a mastery of verbal and written language. The public schools attempt to broaden students' comprehension to include reading and written language. Schools and classes for the hearing-impaired must teach an entire language system.

Exhibit 8-4 shows the many facets of language a deaf child must master in order to learn the single word *mother*.

The deaf child may require extensive curriculum modification to compensate for the educational handicaps that often accompany severe hearing impairment. Modification of educational objectives may also be necessary to address the child's actual functional level rather than chronological age or grade placement.

Traditionally, educators of the deaf have been more concerned about how to teach rather than what to teach. As a result, curriculum development has been a low priority. There is a manifest need for more curriculum materials to meet the special needs of deaf students. La Sasso (1978) found that almost half the educators she surveyed felt a strong need for the development of special curricula for the hearing-impaired.

Because only a few materials have been developed specifically for the hearing-

Exhibit 8-4 Language learning for hearing-impaired children.

To learn the word *mother*, a deaf child must:

- Learn the concept.
- Learn to say the word.
- Learn to lip-read the word.
- Learn the sound of the word through the hearing aid.
- Learn to recognize the printed word.
- Learn to recognize the written word.
- Learn to spell the word.
- Learn to print/write the word.
- Learn to sign the word.
- Learn to read the sign.
- Learn to fingerspell the word.
- Learn to read the fingerspelled word.
- Learn to use the word in context.
- Learn to recognize the word in different contexts.

(Adapted from Levine, 1981, p. 100.)

impaired, teachers are often forced to use standard teaching materials. The subject matter in these materials is usually presented in linguistic structures far too complex for most hearing-impaired students. Teachers must spend a great deal of time rewriting materials or working with students on specific language skills before they can introduce course content.

Mainstreaming

Before hearing-impaired children can be placed in mainstream programs, mainstream educators must first accept them into the regular schools. These educators must also be willing to provide adequately for the children's education (Leckie, 1978).

The advantages of mainstreaming for hearing-impaired children are many. They no longer suffer socially and educationally from long separations from their families while they attend residential schools (Leslie, 1976; Ross, 1978). In the regular classroom, they are exposed to excellent language models and must learn to use speech to compete for attention and assistance from teachers and peers. In the psycho-social domain, children in regular schools are not further handicapped by abnormal surroundings. Their perceptions of themselves are based on comparisons with hearing peers, preparing them to cope in an integrated society (Clarke and Leslie, 1980; Northcott, 1980).

There are also some disadvantages to mainstreaming, especially for children with severe disabilities. Hearing-impaired children may feel lonely or socially rejected. Their friendships may be limited to one or two best friends. They may be unable to bear the stress of daily competition with hearing peers, especially if their families are not supportive. In some cases, the child's mainstream placement may be unrealistically related to the ego needs of the parent, rather than to the child's ability to work in the regular classroom (Northcott, 1980).

Many regular classroom teachers have no formal training with the hearing-impaired. Often they are daunted by the task of integrating and educating such children in their classrooms. First and foremost, they must learn how to adapt the physical characteristics of the classroom to the child's needs. Here are some suggestions:

- Allow hearing-impaired children to make full use of the visual and auditory clues they rely on so heavily. Seat them near the front of the room and a little to one side. The second seat from the front allows an optimal distance of about two metres for speech-reading and the detecting of visual cues.
- Allow children to turn in their seats when other students are talking, or to move their seats when they need a better view.
- Point or move your head to cue children in to the person who is talking or the object under discussion.
- Keep your face in the light to enhance speech-reading. Natural light is better than fluorescent lighting.
- Speak naturally. Do not over-enunciate, as this makes speech-reading more difficult. Try not to smile or whisper while speaking, as this distorts the shape of the lips.
- Try to stand still while talking. Remember that children cannot speech-read if you talk to the chalkboard or speak in the dark during a movie or a film strip.
- Use many visual aids. These are helpful for hearing children as well.
- Keep your book low when reading orally to allow the children a good view of your face.
- Keep the auditory and visual distractions in the classroom to a minimum. Environmental noises are a problem for children with hearing aids because all sounds are amplified.
- Repeat and rephrase information and directions. Encourage children to ask questions if they are not sure.
- Check daily that hearing aids are working. Try to keep a supply of extra batteries.

THE HEARING-IMPAIRED PRE-SCHOOLER

As stated earlier, the diagnosis of a hearing impairment can be traumatic for parents. Professionals in the pre-school area must help parents adjust to the impairment and overcome their initial reactions of denial, fear, sadness, anger, and guilt. Therefore, for the infant and toddler (birth to three years), intervention largely focuses on parent counselling and training.

Parents need to be instructed as to the nature of the hearing impairment, the stages of normal language development, the use of the hearing aid, and the various available modes of communication. Parents can be taught to reinforce their child's early vocalizations by responding with pleasure and attention through smiling, talking and touching. In this way, the child will be encouraged to continue vocalization as a means of receiving positive reinforcement.

In Canada, especially in urban areas, pre-school programs for hearing-impaired three-to six-year-olds are available. Programs are operated by provincial schools, by school boards, by speech and hearing hospital clinics, by private organizations, and by parent co-operatives. All of these programs attempt to:

- Develop language and communication skills.
- Provide experience with other children through playing and sharing.
- Help the child take advantage of residual hearing through auditory training and amplification.
- Develop readiness for basic reading and arithmetic.

PROFILE 8-2

Diana is three years old and attends a pre-school for hearing-impaired children five mornings a week. Diana's profound sensori-neural hearing loss was diagnosed at twenty months. Since that time, she has been fitted with a hearing aid that she tolerates, but does not yet appreciate.

Diana was two months premature and spent her early weeks in an incubator. Her mother suspected a hearing impairment by about eight months when Diana seemed impervious to cleaning, vacuuming or telephone sounds. As Diana grew, she reached all the physical developmental milestones early and became a sociable, gregarious child.

At two years of age, Diana's expressive language was restricted to two sounds — *ma*, for all her wants, and *moo* for a special doll. Receptively, she responded consistently to her own name and *no*. Diana also began to develop her own unique set of gestures and actions to convey meaning to her listeners.

Diana's parents decided to enrol her in a Total Communication pre-school program. This decision had more to do with geography than to adherence to any one method of communication.

Diana's pre-school teachers have set her several major goals. These include the introduction of simple noun, verb, and colour signs; some awareness of gross sounds through play activities and listening exercises; increased vocalizations; and practice in the suprasegmentals (loud/soft variation) of speech. They have also structured many activities to expose Diana to language. Diana's teachers will show her parents how to stimulate home communication and use home-making activities to present language. Diana's parents will be encouraged to learn sign language so that they can communicate more effectively with their daughter.

THE HEARING-IMPAIRED ADOLESCENT

The needs of the hearing-impaired adolescent are quite different from those of the younger child. The teenage years are characterized by major biological, psychological, and social change. Adolescence is a period of identity crisis, a period of intense peer-group attachments, of rebellion against established order, of physical change and social anxiety (Bond, 1981).

Secondary teachers must help hearing-impaired adolescents make the best possible adjustment to these pressures. The teachers should encourage:

- Social counselling to improve relations between hearing impaired students and their peers.
- Participation in extra-curricular activities.
- Vocational training and counselling to help hearing-impaired students assess their strengths, weaknesses, and interests. Teachers can encourage students to consider a broad array of options and to take the major role in decision making.

Post-secondary education

For the deaf, access to continuing education is extremely restricted. They are seldom able to make use of public facilities and materials. Yet deaf students need greater-than-average education to compete in the job market with normally hearing peers.

Many deaf adults are underemployed because they cannot find jobs commensurate with their abilities. In a study of 337 deaf and hard-of-hearing adults in thirteen Canadian cities and towns, it was found that the average family incomes were markedly lower than those of hearing families (Darbyshire, 1981).

Gallaudet College in Washington, D.C., was founded in 1864. Until 1965, it remained the only degree-granting institution for the deaf in the world. Today it is still the only liberal arts college for the deaf (Moores, 1982). Recently a number of Canadian community colleges have begun programs especially designed for the technical and vocational training of the hearing-impaired.

The acceptance of Total Communication in the schools has opened a professional route to deaf teachers that was virtually closed during the period of oral dominance. Today, a number of Canadian training programs for educators of the hearing-impaired gladly accept deaf applicants.

The deaf community

Education of the deaf began in North America in 1817. Ever since that time, the deaf have formed their own communities in metropolitan areas. These communities are maintained through marriages, friendships, casual acquaintances, clubs, religious groups, and special magazines. Deaf communities are made possible by the use of sign language and the commonality of experiences stemming from deafness (Stewart, 1981). They permit the deaf to interact and share their experiences with one another.

Many deaf people view their community as more than just a social organization. They see themselves as a unique culture, a minority group. No other handicapped group has formed itself into such a cohesive unit.

TEACHERS OF THE HEARING-IMPAIRED

The education of hearing-impaired children is complex, difficult, and often frustrating. Teachers require specialized training in areas such as language development, linguistics, and audiology. Teachers who work in a Total Communication setting must also be fluent in school-based manual systems.

In Canada, five programs are in operation to train teachers of the hearing-impaired. These are located at the University of British Columbia; the University of Alberta; the Teacher Education Centre in Belleville, Ontario; McGill University in Montreal; and at the Atlantic Provinces Resource Centre in Amherst, Nova Scotia (Clarke and Bibby, 1984). In the United States, eighty-one programs are in operation (Grant, 1983).

SUMMARY

A profound hearing-impairment is not the deprivation of sound, but the deprivation of language. The hearing-impaired are generally deficient in the language of their culture, even when expert in the language of signs. Although they have the same intellectual potential as the rest of the population, their deprivation of language can cause problems in every aspect of their functioning. Academically, most deaf graduates can barely read the daily newspaper. Emotionally, they are prone to more psychological and personal problems. Socially, they turn for acceptance to the deaf community where sign language is used for communication.

Hearing impairments are most tragic when they strike the very young. Pre-lingually deafened children face the most serious difficulties in acquiring the rudiments of language and speech. Parents of hearing-impaired children need much support to accept their children and come to terms with their condition. Deaf children of deaf parents have fewer problems because their parents understand deafness and expose them to sign language at an early age.

In recent decades, education of the hearing-impaired has undergone major and promising changes. There has been a movement toward mainstreaming for many hearing-impaired children, and a widespread adoption of Total Communication. There has also been substantial growth in such allied disciplines as audiology, electronics, linguistics, psychology, and speech sciences. These developments may soon significantly improve the prospects of hearing-impaired children.

BIBLIOGRAPHY

Anderson, H., Barr, B., and Wedenberg, E. (1970). Genetic disposition: Prerequisite for maternal rubella deafness. *Archives of Otolaryngology, 91,* 141-147.

Anderson, R.J. and Sisco, F.H. (1977). *Standardization of the* WISC-R *Performance Scale for deaf children.* Washington, D.C.: Gallaudet College, Office of Demographic Studies.

Anvar, B., Mencher, G.T., and Keet, S.J. (1984). Hearing loss and congenital rubella in Atlantic Canada. *Ear and Hearing,* 5, 346-348.

Barres, B. (1978). Cued speech keeps deaf pupils ahead. *Children Today,* 7, 28-30.

Bitzer, D. (1979). Uses of CBE for the handicapped. *American Annals of the Deaf, 124,* 553-558.

Bolton, B. (1976). *Psychology of deafness for rehabilitation counselors.* Baltimore, MD: University Park Press.

Bond, D.E. (1981). Aspects of behaviour and management of adolescents who are hearing-impaired. *The Teacher of the Deaf, 5,* 41-48.

Bordley, J. and Alford, B. (1979). The pathology of Rubella deafness. *International Audiology, 9,* 58-67.

Brown, L., Sherbenou, R.J., and Dollar, S.J. (1982). *Test of Nonverbal Intelligence: A language-free measure of cognitive ability.* Austin, TX.: Pro-Ed.

Canadian Hearing Society. (1976). *Deafness; the silent epidemic.* Toronto: Canadian Hearing Society.

Canning, B. (1980). A survey of the interaction of parents of hearing impaired children with the medical profession during the diagnostic process. M.A. thesis, Université de Moncton.

Carney, E.C. (1973). Deaf people in the world of work. In D. Watson (Ed.), *Readings on deafness.* New York: Deafness Research and Training Center.

Charrow, V.R. and Fletcher, J.D. (1974). English as a second language of deaf children. *Developmental Psychology, 10,* 463-470.

Childhood hearing impairment: Report of a task force. (1984). Ottawa: Department of Health and Welfare.

Clarke, B.R. (1982). Keynote address. First Convention of the Association for Parents of the Hearing Impaired in British Columbia. Vancouver: APHIBC.

Clarke, B.R. and Bibby, M.A. (1984). Canadian teacher training programs in education of the hearing impaired. *The* ACEHI *Journal, 10,* 63-76.

Clarke, B.R. and Leslie, P.T. (1980). Environmental alternatives for the hearing handicapped. In J. Schifani, R. Anderson, and S. Odle (Eds.), *Implementing learning in the least restrictive environment.* Baltimore, MD: University Park Press.

Conrad, R. (1979). *The deaf school child: Language and cognitive function.* London: Harper and Row.

Cornett, R.O. (1975) Cued speech and oralism: An analysis. *Audiology and Hearing Education, 1,* 26-33.

Cornett, R.O. (1984, June). Cued speech: What and why? Paper available at the A.G. Bell Convention, Portland, Oregon.

Darbyshire, J.O. (1981). Communication needs of hearing-impaired Canadians and their relevance to education. *The ACEHI Journal, 7,* 94-96.

Davis, H. (1978a). Audiometry: Other auditory tests. In H. Davis and S.R. Silverman (Eds.), *Hearing and deafness (4th ed.).* New York: Holt, Rinehart and Winston.

Davis, H. (1978b). Audiometry: Pure-tone and simple speech tests. In H. Davis and S.R. Silverman (Eds.), *Hearing and deafness (4th ed.).* New York: Holt, Rinehart and Winston.

Davis, H. and Silverman, S.R. (Eds.). (1978). *Hearing and deafness (4th ed.).* New York: Holt, Rinehart and Winston.

Fay, E.A. (1898). *Marriages of the deaf in America.* Washington, D.C.: Volta Bureau.

Fitzgerald, M.D., Sitton, A.B., and McConnell, F. (1970). Audiometric, developmental and learning characteristics of a group of rubella deaf children. *Journal of Speech and Hearing Disorders, 35,* 218-228.

Fraser, G.R. (1976). *The causes of profound deafness in childhood.* Baltimore, MD: John Hopkins University Press.

Freeman, R.D. (1977). Psychiatric aspects of sensory disorders and intervention. In P.J. Graham (Ed.), *Epidemiological approaches in child psychiatry.* New York: Academic Press.

Freeman, R.D., Malkin, S.F., and Hastings, J.O. (1975). Psychosocial problems of deaf children and their families: A comparative study. *American Annals of the Deaf, 120,* 391-405.

Furth, H.G. (1964). Research with the deaf: Implications for language and cognition. *Psychological Bulletin, 62,* 145-164.

Furth, H.G. (1966). *Thinking without language: Psychological implications of deafness.* New York: The Free Press.

Furth, H.G. (1971). Linguistic deficiency and thinking: Research with deaf subjects, 1964-1969. *Psychological Bulletin, 76,* 58-72.

Gannon, J.R. (1979, July 16). Shattering silence throughout the world. Paper presented at the Sixth Annual Convention of Quota International, Philadelphia.

Gates, A.I. and Chase, E.H. (1926). Methods of theories of learning to spell tested by studies of deaf children. *Journal of Educational Psychology, 17,* 289-300.

Gesell, A. and Amatruda, C.S. (1947). *Developmental diagnosis (2nd ed.).* New York: Paul B. Hoeber.

Grant, J. (1983). Teacher preparation: Issues and trends. *Volta Review, 85,* 90-96, 101.

Greenberg, M.T. and Calderon, R. (1984). Early intervention: Outcomes and issues. *Topics in Early Childhood Special Education, 3,* 1-9.

Hallahan, D.P. and Kauffman, J.M. (1982). *Exceptional children: Introduction to special education (2nd. ed.).* Englewood Cliffs, N.J.: Prentice-Hall.

Harris, D.B. (1963). *Goodenough-Harris Drawing Test Manual.* New York: Harcourt, Brace and World.

Harris, R.I. (1978). Impulse control in deaf children. In L.S. Liben (Ed.), *Deaf children: Developmental perspectives.* New York: Academic Press.

Hearing loss and surgery. (1982). *Lifeline Magazine, 4,* 8-10.

Higgins, P.C. (1979). Outsiders in a hearing world: The deaf community. *Urban Life, 8,* 3-22.

Hiskey, M.S. (1966). *Hiskey-Nebraska Test of Learning Aptitude.* Lincoln, NA.: Union College Press.

Hoemann, H.W. (1974). Deaf children's use of finger spelling to label pictures of common objects: A follow-up study. *Exceptional Children, 40,* 519-520.

Hoemann, H.W., Andrews, C.E., Florian, V.A., Hoemann, S.A., and Jensema, C.J. (1976). The spelling proficiency of deaf children. *American Annals of the Deaf, 121,* 489-493.

Hopper, D. (1975, October). Deafness: The silent epidemic (rpt.). *Reader's Digest.*

Howie, V.M. (1975). Natural history of otitis media. *Annals of Otology, Rhinology and Laryngology (Supplement 19), 84* 67-72.

Jensema, C.J., Karchmer, M.A., and Trybus, R.J. (1978). *The rated speech intelligibility of hearing impaired children: Basic relationships and a detailed analysis. Series R, No. 6.* Washington, D.C.: Gallaudet College, Office of Demographic Studies.

Johnson, J.O. and Boyd, H.F. (1981). *Nonverbal test of cognitive skills.* Columbus, OH.: Merrill.

Jones, F.R. and Simmons, F.B. (1977). Early identification of significant hearing loss. *Hearing Instruments, 2,* 77-81.

Karchmer, M.A., Petersen, L.M., Allen, T.E., and Osborn, T.I. (1981). *Highlights of the Canadian survey of hearing impaired children and youth.* Washington, D.C.: Gallaudet College, Office of Demographic Studies.

Keller, H. (1933). *Helen Keller in Scotland.* London: Methuen.

Kneedler, R., with D.P. Hallahan and J.M. Kauffman (1984). *Special education for today* Englewood Cliffs, N.J.: Prentice-Hall.

La Sasso, C. (1978). National survey of materials and procedures used to teach reading to hearing impaired children. *American Annals of the Deaf, 123,* 22-30.

Leckie, D.J. (1978). Creating a receptive climate in the mainstreaming program. In W. Northcott (Ed.), *The hearing impaired child in a regular classroom: Preschool, elementary, and secondary years.* Washington, D.C.: Alexander Graham Bell Association for the Deaf.

Leiter, R. (1948). *The Leiter International Performance Scale* New York: Wiley.

Lenneberg, E.H. (1967). *The biological foundations of language.* New York: Wiley.

Leslie, P.T. (1976). A rationale for a mainstream education for the hearing impaired. In G. Nix (Ed.), *Mainstream education for hearing impaired children and youth.* San Francisco: Grune and Stratton.

Levine, E.S. (1981). *The ecology of early deafness: Guides to fashioning environments and psychological assessments.* New York: Columbia University Press.

Liben, L.S. (1978). Developmental perspectives on the experiential deficiencies of deaf children. In L.S. Liben (Ed.), *Deaf children: Developmental perspectives.* New York: Academic Press.

Ling, A.H. (1981). Preparation of professionals in aural habilitation and education of hearing impaired children. *The ACEHI Journal, 7,* 108-112.

Ling, D. and Ling, A.H. (1978). *Aural rehabilitation: Foundations of verbal learning in hearing impaired children.* Washington, D.C.: Alexander Graham Bell Association for the Deaf.

Lowenbraun, S. and Thompson, M.D. (1982). Hearing impairments. In N.G. Haring (Ed.), *Exceptional children and youth (3rd ed.).* Columbus, OH.: Merrill.

Lyon, D.J. and Lyon, M.E. (1982). The importance of early detection. *The ACEHI Journal, 8,* 15-37.

McClure, W.J. (1975). The Rochester Method and the Florida School. *American Annals of the Deaf, 120,* 331-340.

McLoughlin, W.P. (1982). The deaf, the law and higher education. *Volta Review, 84,* 275-283.

Meadow, K.P. (1972). Sociolinguistics, sign language and the deaf sub-culture. In T.J. O'Rourke (Ed.), *Psycholinguistics and total communication: The state of the art.* Washington, D.C.: American Annals of the Deaf.

Meadow, K.P. (1980). *Deafness and child development.* Berkeley: University of California Press.

Mindel, E.D. and Vernon, M. (1971). *They grow in silence.* Silver Spring, MD.: National Association of the Deaf.

Moores, D.F. (1982). *Educating the deaf: Psychology, principles and practices (2nd ed.).* Boston: Houghton Mifflin.

Moores, D.F., Weiss, K.L., and Goodwin, M.W. (1975). Receptive abilities of deaf children across five modes of communication. *Exceptional Children, 40,* 22-28.

Murphy, J. and Slorach, N. (1983). The language development of pre-school hearing children of deaf parents. *British Journal of Disorders of Communication, 18,* 118-126.

Murray, R. (1979). Reinforcement of speech through the balloon captioning of song lyrics. *American Annals of the Deaf, 124,* 656-661.

Myklebust, H.R. (1953). Towards a new understanding of the deaf child. *American Annals of the Deaf, 98,* 345-357.

Myklebust, H.R. (1960). *The psychology of deafness.* New York: Grune and Stratton.

Northcott, W.H. (1980). *Implications of mainstreaming for the education of hearing-impaired children in the 1980s.* Washington, D.C.: Alexander Graham Bell Association for the Deaf.

Northern, J.L. (1980). Acoustic impedance measures in the Down's population. *Seminars in Speech, Language and Hearing, 1,* 81-86.

Odgen, P.W. and Lipsett, S. (1982). *The silent garden: Understanding the hearing impaired child.* New York: St. Martin's Press.

Ontario Ministry of Health (1978). *You and your hearing.* Toronto: Ontario Ministry of Health.

Oyers, H.J. and Frankman, J.P. (1975). *The aural rehabilitation process: A conceptual framework analysis.* New York: Holt, Rinehart and Winston.

Paparella, M.M. and Davis, H. (1978). Medical and surgical treatment of hearing loss. In H. Davis and S.R. Silverman (Eds.), *Hearing and deafness (4th ed.).* New York: Holt, Rinehart and Winston.

Parlatto, S.J. (1977). Those other captioned films: Captioned educational films. *American Annals of the Deaf, 122,* 33-37.

Pintner, R. (1941). The deaf. In R. Pintner, J. Eisenson, and M. Stanton (Eds.), *The psychology of the physically handicapped.* New York: Appleton-Century Crofts.

Pollack, D. (1970). *Educational audiology for the limited hearing infant.* Springfield, IL.; Thomas.

Pollack, D. (1980). Acoupedics: An approach to early management. In G.T. Mencher and S.E. Gerber (Eds.), *Early management of hearing loss.* New York: Grune and Stratton.

Pottharst, E. (1983). Literature on tape and the hearing impaired: Listening while reading with Winnie-the-Pooh and Candide. *Volta Review, 85,* 285-288.

Raven, J. (1948). *Progressive matrices.* New York: Psychological Corporation.

Report of the Ad Hoc Committee to define deaf and hard-of-hearing. (1975). *American Annals of the Deaf, 120,* 509-512.

Robinson, L.D. and Weathers. O.D. (1974). Family therapy of deaf parents and hearing children: A new dimension in psychotherapeutic intervention. *American Annals of the Deaf, 119,* 325-330.

Ross, M. (1978). Mainstreaming; Some social considerations. *Volta Review, 80,* 21-30.

Sanders, D. (1971). *Aural rehabilitation.* Englewood Cliffs, N.J.: Prentice-Hall.

Schein, J.D. (1975). Deaf students with other disabilities. *American Annals of the Deaf, 120,* 92-99.

Schein, J.D. and Delk, M.T. (1974). *The deaf population in the United States.* Silver Spring, MD.: National Association of the Deaf.

Schiff, N.B. and Ventry, I.M. (1976). Communication problems in hearing children of deaf parents. *Journal of Speech and Hearing Disorders, 41,* 348-358.

Schlesinger, H.S. and Meadow K.P. (1972). *Sound and sign: Childhood deafness and mental health.* Berkeley: University of California Press.

Schmitt, P.J. (1966). Language instruction for the deaf. *Volta Review, 68,* 85-105.

Sheehy, P. and Hansen, S.A. (1983). The use of vibrotactile aids with pre-school hearing impaired children: Case studies. *Volta Review, 85,* 14-26.

Silverman, S.R. (1967). Education of the deaf. In L.E. Travis (Ed.), *Handbook of speech pathology.* New York: Appleton Century-Crofts.

Silverman, S.R., Lane, H.S., and Doehring, D.G. (1964). Deaf children. In H. Davis and S.R. Silverman (Eds.), *Hearing and deafness.* New York: Holt, Rinehart and Winston.

Spink, D. (1976). Crisis intervention for parents of the deaf child. *Health and Social Work, 1,* 140-160.

Stassen, R.A. (1978). "I have one in my class who's wearing hearing aids!" In W. Northcott (Ed.), *The hearing impaired child in a regular classroom: Preschool, elementary and secondary years.* Washington, D.C.: Alexander Graham Bell Association for the Deaf.

Stewart, D.A. (1981). The role of ASL in teaching the deaf. *B.C. Journal of Special Education, 5,* 325-331.

Stewart, D.A. (1984). Mainstreaming deaf children: A different perspective. *The ACHEI Journal, 10,* 91-104.

Stoker, R.G. (1983). On computers and the hearing impaired. *Volta Review, 85,* 364-365.

Stokoe, W.C. Jr. and Battison, R. (1975). Sign language, mental health and satisfactory interaction. Unpublished paper, Linguistic Research Laboratory, Gallaudet College, Washington, D.C.

Sullivan, P. and Vernon, M. (1979). Psychological assessment of hearing-impaired children. *School Psychology Digest, 8,* 271-290.

Telford, C.W. and Sawrey, J.M. (1981). *The exceptional individual (4th ed.).* Englewood Cliffs, N.J.: Prentice-Hall.

Templin, M.C. (1948). A comparison of the spelling achievement of normal and defective hearing subjects. *Journal of Educational Psychology, 39,* 337-346.

Tendler, R. (1976). Maternal correlates and differentiation in hearing children of deaf parents. *Dissertation Abstracts International, 36 (8-B),* 4183.

Towne, C.C. (1979). Disorders of hearing, speech and language. In V.C. Vaughan, R.J. McKay, and R.E. Behrman (Eds.), *Testbook of pediatrics.* Philadelphia: Saunders.

Trybus, R.J. and Karchmer, M.A. (1977). School achievement scores of hearing impaired children: National data on achievement status and growth patterns. *American Annals of the Deaf, 122,* 62-69.

Van Dyke, L. (1982). An inservice training model for using the classroom FM system. *Volta Review, 84,* 344-351.

Vernon, M. (1967a). Characteristics associated with post-rubella children: Psychological, educational and physical. *Volta Review, 60,* 176-185.

Vernon, M. (1967b). Relationship of language to the thinking process. *Archives of General Psychiatry, 16,* 325-333.

Vernon, M. (1969). *Multiply handicapped deaf children: Medical, educational and psychological implications.* Washington, D.C.: Council for Exceptional Children.

Vernon, M. (1975). Myths in the education of deaf children. *Hearing and Speech News, 39 (4),* 13-17.

Ward, R.D. and Rostron, A.B. (1983). Computer-assisted learning for the hearing impaired: An interactive written language environment. *Volta Review, 85,* 346-351.

Watters, B. (1980). Special education in the Northwest Territories. In M. Csapo and L. Goguen (Eds.), *Special education across Canada: Issues and concerns for the '80s.* Vancouver: Centre for Human Development and Research.

Wechsler, D. (1974). *Wechsler Intelligence Scale for Children (Revised).* New York: Psychological Corporation.

Welch, J.P. (1981). Causes and prevention of deafness. *The ACEHI Journal, 7,* 33-39.

White, A.H. and Stevenson, V.M. (1975). The effects of total communication, manual communication, oral communication and reading on the learning of factual information in residential school deaf children. *American Annals of the Deaf, 120,* 48-57.

White, K.R. (1982). Defining and prioritizing the personal and social competencies needed by hearing-impaired students. *Volta Review, 84,* 266-274.

Wiley, T.L. (1980). Hearing disorders and audiometry. In T.J. Hixon, L.D. Shribard, and J.H. Saxman. *Introduction to communication disorders.* Englewood Cliffs, N.J.: Prentice-Hall.

Winzer, M.A. (1981). An examination of some selected factors that affected the education and socialization of the deaf of Ontario, 1870-1900. Doctoral dissertation, University of Toronto.

Withrow, M. (1979). Illustrating language through computer generated animation. *American Annals of the Deaf, 124,* 549-552.

Zinkus, P.W., Gottlieb, M.I., and Shapiro, M. (1978). Developmental and psychoeducational sequelae of chronic otitis media. *American Journal of the Disadvantaged Child, 132,* 1100-1104.

CHAPTER NINE

Children with visual impairments

SALLY ROGOW

A person who is severely impaired never knows his hidden sources of strength until he is treated like a normal human being and encouraged to shape his own life.

(Helen Keller)

It is difficult for most of us to imagine life without sight. Vision and hearing are the senses that most connect us with our world. A world without images seems bleak, frightening, and virtually impossible to navigate. Yet most of us are familiar with the outstanding achievements of blind people in almost every profession and walk of life.

Although visual handicaps are not as daunting as they seem, they do interfere with the ease of learning, social growth, and adjustment. Visual impairments cause complex and subtle problems in the development of children. These problems can only be overcome through special education.

The myths and stereotypes that surrounded blind people for centuries persist only as pale shadows today. These myths express fear of blindness and interweave two contradictory themes. On one hand, blindness has been associated with darkness, despair, loneliness, and punishment. On the other, it has been associated with superhuman and spiritual powers, uncanny memory ability, and musicality. Blind persons were believed to be compensated for their lack of sight by both psychological and physical factors (Koestler, 1976).

Blind people do not learn automatically to compensate for lack of sight. Through effort, concentration, and education, they learn to use their auditory and touch senses more accurately. Blind people must learn to pay more attention to auditory and tactile clues that sighted people can afford to ignore. We all locate objects by sound, but we are rarely conscious of it when we do it (Koestler, 1976).

Much education for the blind has been pioneered by the blind themselves. Louis Braille was a blind teacher who made blind literacy possible by inventing an embossed system of writing. Sir Franklin Fraser was a pioneer in education for the blind in Canada. The Canadian National Institute for the Blind (CNIB) was formed by blinded veterans after World War I. Since its inception, it has championed the cause of gainful employment for blind persons in Canada.

In recent years, many changes have occurred in the education of the visually impaired. Among the most dramatic are the integration of most blind children into public school classes, a new emphasis on the development of residual vision, and attention to the functional rather than the legal definitions of sight handicaps. In addition, educators now realize that residual sight is enhanced, rather than diminished, with use. As a result, children who were formerly classified as blind are now classified as low-vision or visually impaired (Barraga, 1976).

New advances have also occurred in the diagnosis and treatment of visual disorders, particularly in the fields of ophthalmology and optometry. Vastly improved optical aids have been developed to enable children with severe sight impairments to read print materials. Educators have learned a great deal more about the effects of visual handicaps on learning. This new awareness has broadened the category of children who can benefit from special education beyond legal definitions. Children with borderline problems now qualify for special education services, as do visually impaired multihandicapped children.

While in Canada, and in the western world, blindness in children is a low incidence handicap, from a world perspective blindness affects millions of children and adults. In Asia, Africa, and South America, severe poverty and lack of sanitation create conditions in which severe visual impairments thrive. There are ten million blind people living in the world today.

THE VISUAL SYSTEM

The visual system consists of the eye, which receives the light image, the nerve pathways, which transmit the image to the optical centres of the brain, and the brain itself, which interprets the image. Visual impairments can result from any interference of the passage of light as it travels from the outer surface of the eye along the nerve pathways to the brain (Harley and Lawrence, 1977).

The eye

The human eye is composed of the eyeball and accessory structures, such as the eyelids and muscles, that protect and move it. The eyeball is held in place by connective tissue in the orbit and is protected in front by the upper and lower eyelids. Figure 9-1 shows the structure of the eyeball.

The eye is probably the most precious square inch in the human body. It is only 2.5 centimetres in diameter, but its functions are extraordinarily complex and precise. The human eye can perceive large objects and small objects, close up and very far away. It can also detect a very small amount of light.

The eyeball is a sphere wrapped in three layers of tissue. The outermost layer consists of the sclera and cornea. The middle layer contains the iris and the lens, the muscles that support them, and the fluids that fill the eye's two chambers. The inner layer is the retina, the actual seeing part of the eye (Havener, 1979).

The eye needs light in order to see. Light rays from the environment are gathered and brought to focus on the retina. When the light reaches the **cornea**, its rays are refracted (bent) to pass through the watery anterior chamber of the eye. The light rays then

Figure 9-1 Parts of the human eye.

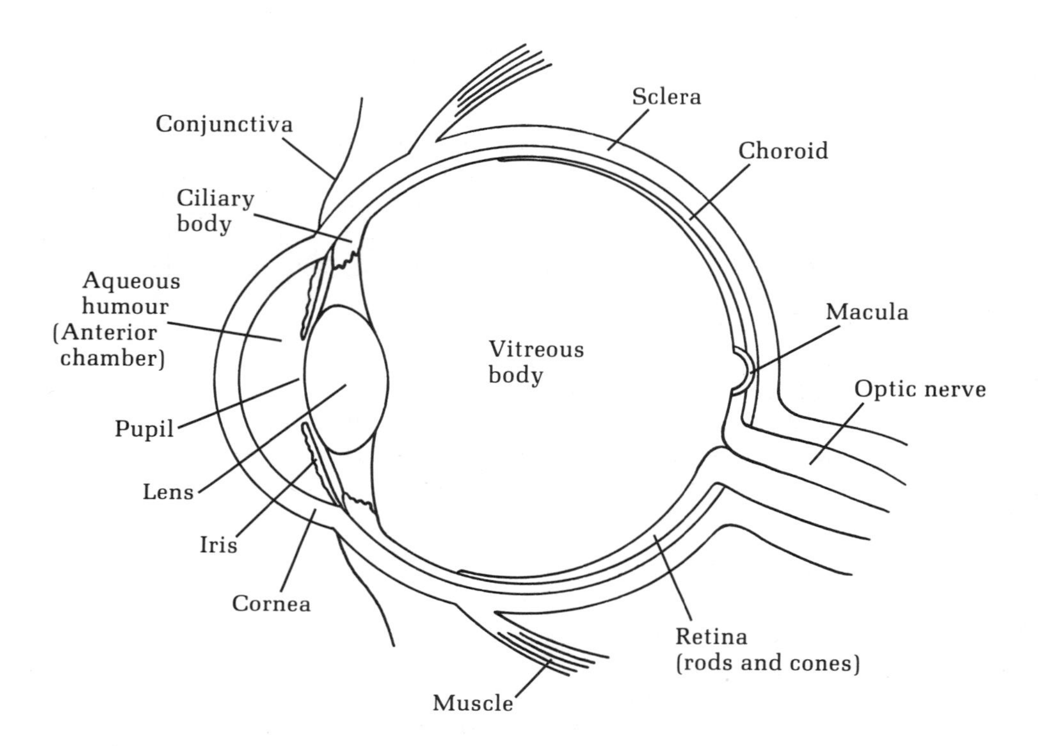

penetrate the *crystalline lens* where they are further refracted. The crystalline lens has the ability to change its shape to accommodate light from near and distant objects.

After the light penetrates the crystalline lens, it passes through the transparent, jelly-like substance of the vitreous humor. The light then comes to focus on the **fovea**, the most sensitive spot on the retina. The image received by the fovea is inverted — the bottom of an object appears as the top, and the top as the bottom.

The fovea possesses a rich supply of light sensitive nerve cells, the **rods** and **cones**. These nerve cells convert the light into electrochemical impulses that are transmitted to the brain. The electrochemical impulses leave through the back of the eye through the bundles of nerve fibres that form the optic nerve. Images are received and interpreted in the iccipital lobe of the brain. Vision is a function of the brain, not the eye.

Exhibit 9-1 outlines the important parts of the eye.

Exhibit 9-1 Parts of the eye.

Sclera	Tough, flexible white outer covering of the posterior portion of the eye. Its front part is commonly recognized as the white of the eye.
Cornea	A transparent window covering the front of the eye, continuous with the sclera.
Lacrimal Apparatus	Glands that provide the tear film essential to the health of the cornea.
Iris	Muscular circular shutter which gives the eye its colour and adapts the size of the pupil aperture in response to light intensity.
Lens	A crystalline lens held in suspension behind the iris.
Choroid	A vascular layer in which the blood supply to the retina is embedded.
Retina	The inner layer of the eye in which light receptor cells are embedded.
Ocular muscles	The muscles that allow the eye to focus on an object, follow a moving target, and rotate. Six muscles work in perfect synchrony to enable the two eyes to co-ordinate. Stereoscopic vision is the result of the synchrony of the two eyes (Harley and Lawrence, 1977).

Figure 9-2 Refraction and inversion of object.

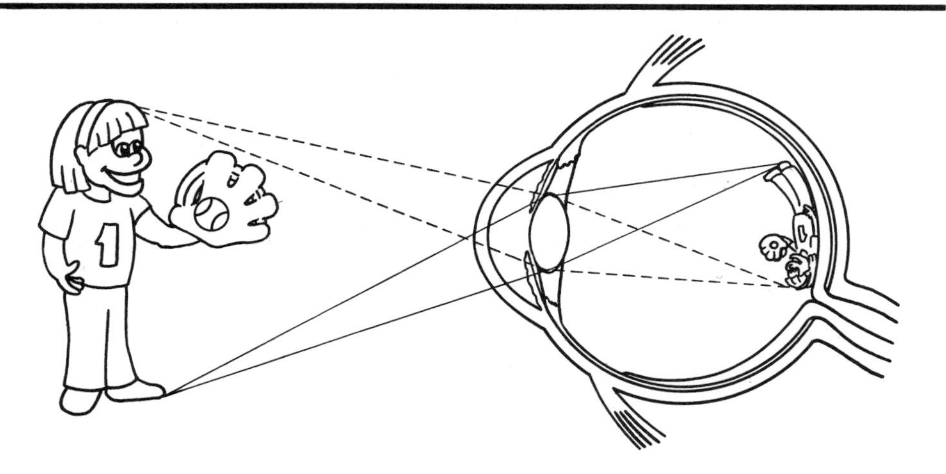

Vision takes place in the following sequence:

- Light rays reflected from the image are refracted by the cornea. (See Figure 9-2.)
- The refracted light rays pass through the aqueous humor.
- The light rays then pass through the lens and the vitreous humor.
- The rays are focused on the central part of the retina.
- The light receptor cells in the retina (rods and cones) are stimulated by the light rays and convert them to electrochemical energy.
- The energy is transmitted through the optic nerve to the visual centres of the brain.
- The brain receives and interprets the visual information.

The efficiency of the visual system is based on a range of personal and environmental variables that affect visual function. The functions of the visual system include:

- Visual acuity at near and distant points.
- Control of eye movements.
- Accommodative and adaptive capabilities of the eye.
- Speed and filtering capacities of the eye.
- Efficiency of the brain in processing and interpreting visual information (Barraga, 1976).

DEFINITIONS OF VISUAL IMPAIRMENT

The category of visually impaired includes both the blind and those with low vision. Two different types of definition are used for this category. The first are legal definitions, and the second are those that are more appropriate for educational purposes.

Legal definitions

In 1966, the World Health Organization found sixty-five different definitions in use by various countries to classify people as legally blind (Colenbrander, 1976). In Canada and the United States, the legal definition includes many people who in other countries would not be entitled to social, educational, or other services.

In Canada, **legal blindness** is defined as an acuity measure of 20/200 (6/60) or less in the better eye with the best correction; or visual acuity of more than 20/200 if the widest diameter of the field of vision subtends an angle no greater than 20 degrees (CNIB, 1980). The legal definition of partial sight includes those who have "a visual acuity greater than 20/200 but not greater than 20/70 in the better eye after correction" (CNIB, 1980).

Educational definitions

Legal definitions are based on visual acuity, which measures the smallest image distinguishable by the eye. Acuity measures may vary with age, lighting conditions, the effects of movement, and other factors. Acuity measures cannot predict how effectively children will utilize their remaining vision (Barraga, 1976). Nor can they predict how visually impaired children will vary in their experience of sight.

For these reasons, functional definitions have been found more useful than legal ones for educational purposes. Functional definitions indicate how well the child can use vision for learning. Barraga (1976) uses the following functional definition to describe the visually impaired child as one "whose visual impairment interferes with his optimal learning and achievement, unless adaptations are made in the methods of presenting learning experiences, the nature of the materials used and/or in the learning environment."

CLASSIFICATION OF VISUAL IMPAIRMENTS

Visual handicaps include a wide range in degree and type of visual disability. At one end of the spectrum are the totally blind, who have no sight at all. At the other are those with near-normal vision. Most visually handicapped persons, however, are low-vision — their corrected vision is lower than normal (Colenbrander, 1976).

Classification by degree

Faye (1976) classified individuals with visual impairments into five groups.

- Near-normal vision. Whatever the strength of corrective lenses or reading aids, these individuals are able to function without special training.
- Moderate functional impairment, a moderate reduction of acuity and no significant field loss. People in this group require specialized aids and lighting.
- Reduction in central vision, a moderate field loss, and a possible inability to cope physically or psychologically with impaired vision. These people may qualify for special services, as "legally blind" individuals.
- Poor functional vision and possible poor central vision, marked field loss, and psychological and physical adaptation problems. For these people, standard refraction is of little or no benefit. They usually require strong reading aids.
- Blind. These people are the most visually impaired. They require education, habilitation, or rehabilitation to function at an independent level.

When the term blind is prematurely applied, children are not expected to develop sight. As a result, they may fail to learn to use their residual vision, however limited it may be. Children who can use their residual vision should be called visually handicapped or visually impaired.

Classification by age of onset

Visually impaired children are often classified by age of onset. The importance of this classification increases with the child's age. Congenital low vision refers to conditions that are diagnosable at birth or shortly thereafter. Adventitious low vision refers to conditions caused by accident or disease some time after birth. Because many eye conditions change over time, age of onset can be an important factor. In general, children who acquire visual impairments after the age of five years have developed a visual memory.

Types of visual problems

Visual problems arise from any interference with the formation of images on the retina or the transmission of retinal images to the brain (Harley and Lawrence, 1977). Visual impairments may be classified as:

- *Refractive errors*, caused by irregularities in the shape or size of the eyeball, the cornea, or the lens.
- *Eye pathologies*, caused by damage or disease before or after birth to one or more structures of the eye.
- *Oculomotor problems*, caused by disturbances in eye movement.

The following terms play an important part in the discussion of ocular conditions.

- **Distance acuity** is measured with a letter chart. Normal vision is measured as 20/20. The numerator represents the distance at which the individual can read the chart. The denominator represents the distance at which a normal eye can read the chart (Havener, 1979).
- **Near acuity** is the ability to see close objects. Measurement of near vision is particularly important for children with reading problems.
- **Visual field** is that portion of space that can be seen with the fixated eye. The visual field can be divided into central and peripheral portions.
- **Accommodation** is the ability of the eye to bring an image to focus. When the normal eye looks at an object closer than five millimetres, it must accommodate in order to focus.
- **Refraction** is the clinical measure of the ability of the eye to focus an image (Havener, 1979). The curvatures of the cornea and lens give the eye its refractive power (Harley and Lawrence, 1977).
- **Colour vision** is the ability to accurately perceive colour. To test colour vision, test charts must be used in daylight or under the illumination of special light bulbs.

Refractive errors

There are four common types of refractive error that cause vision impairment.

- **Myopia**, or nearsightedness, is the greatest single cause of defective vision in children and young adults. The myopic eye is unable to achieve focus of the image on the retina. The length of the eye or the shape of the cornea cause light rays to focus in front of the retina. In most cases, myopia can be corrected with concave optical lenses (Harley and Lawrence, 1977).

■ **Hyperopia**, or farsightedness, is caused by too short an eye or too flat a corneal surface. The image is focused behind the retina. Corrective convex lenses effectively aid hyperoptic people.

■ **Astigmatism** is the result of an irregularity in the curvature of the cornea or lens of the eye. The rays of light are refracted unevenly so that horizontal and vertical rays are focused at different points on the retina. In most cases, astigmatism is correctable (Harley and Lawrence, 1977).

■ **Presbyopia** is a condition in which the lens of the eye loses its ability to accommodate to near objects. Most people at the age of forty or thereabout develop some degree of presbyopia and need glasses for close work. Presbyopia is a Greek word meaning "sight of age."

Errors of refraction may also occur in association with diseases of the eye or with oculomotor disturbances.

Disturbances of ocular motility

Normal vision requires the co-ordinated use of two eyes. Images from each eye are fused in the visual centres of the brain so that only one image is perceived. To achieve a synchronized image, each ocular muscle must work in perfect harmony with the other muscles of the two eyes. The most common oculomotor disorders prevent the eye from controlling its direction of focus.

Strabismus is a condition affecting one or both eyes. Convergent strabismus causes what is called "wall-eye". Strabismus may be evident at birth or may not appear until the child begins to look at objects close up. If untreated, strabismus may lead to a suppression of the image from one eye.

Nystagmus is a rhythmic involuntary movement of the eyes. Abnormalities of the central nervous system can also result in disruption of eye muscle co-ordination. Ocular motility problems are common in children with cerebral palsy and other neurological disorders.

Diseases of the eye

The most common eye diseases found in children cause clouding of the cornea and lens, and dysfunction of the retina and optic nerve. These diseases may be congenital or acquired some time after birth. Some conditions may be accompanied by other disorders. For example, diabetes is the leading cause of retinal disease in young North American adults (Harley and Lawrence, 1977).

A **cataract** is an opacity of the lens or its capsule, which restricts the eye's ability to receive light. Cataracts may be caused by maternal illness during pregnancy, genetic deficiency, penetrating injuries, severe blows to the eye, irradiation, electrical current, or explosive injuries. Cataracts in children may exist alone or be associated with another abnormality (Harley and Lawrence, 1977). Cataracts interfere with central and peripheral visual acuity (Jantzi, 1985). The vision of a child with cataracts can fluctuate under different lighting conditions.

Glaucoma is caused by increased intraocular pressure causing the slow death of nerve fibres. It is responsible for twelve percent of the blindess in Canada and the United States. Congenital glaucoma is a major cause of severe visual defects in children. Untreated, it can cause total blindness (Harley and Lawrence, 1977).

Retrolental fibroplasia (RLF) occurs most often in premature infants weighing two kilograms or less. High concentrations of oxygen in the incubator damage immature blood vessels in the infant's eyes and cause severe visual impairments or total blindness (Harley and Lawrence, 1977).

Retinitis pigmentosa is a hereditary disease that causes degeneration of retinal tissue and loss of peripheral vision. The age of onset of retinitis pigmentosa may vary from childhood to early adulthood. Other abnormalities, such as cataracts and glaucoma, may also be present. Familial nerve deafness associated with retinitis pigmentosa is known as Usher's syndrome, a leading cause of deaf-blindness.

Macular retinal degeneration results in extremely poor central vision and is often undetected in young children. Macular degeneration may be inherited, but is also associated with injuries such as contusions and concussions (Harley and Lawrence, 1977). Another type of retinal degeneration is associated with a high degree of myopia. Abnormal growth in eye length causes a thinning of the retina and destruction of retinal cells.

Diabetes is a major cause of retinal disease in young adults. Diabetic retinopathy is caused by damage to the blood vessels of the eyes.

Retinal detachment is a condition in which the outer layer of the retina is separated from the inner portion. Total blindness may result if the detached retina is not promptly reattached (Harley and Lawrence, 1977).

Optic nerve atrophy occurs when there has been damage to the fibres of the optic nerve. Degeneration of the nerve may be partial or complete, and its onset may be gradual or abrupt. Optic nerve atrophy may result from inadequate blood supply to the nerve, or from other optical diseases, such as glaucoma or retinal degeneration.

Other defects

Defects of colour vision arise from the absence or malfunctioning of the cone cells of the retina. Persons with colour defects are likely to confuse colours. Complete colour blindness is very rare.

Albinism is a condition in which light-absorbing pigment is absent from the retina. Children with albinism lack pigment in all parts of the body, causing very white skin and pale yellow hair. Albinism is associated with a severe loss of visual acuity.

PREVALENCE OF VISUAL IMPAIRMENTS

The number of children with visual impairments severe enough to warrant special educational services is estimated to be 0.14 percent (14/10 000) in both Canada and the United States. The incidence of total blindness is 0.01 percent (1 per 10 000). In 1981, there were 3023 children under nineteen years of age registered with the Canadian National Institute for the Blind (CNIB). These figures do not include Indian children living on reserves, children with borderline problems, and children who have not been registered.

Many children are identified as needing special educational services only after they are enrolled in schools where special education is offered. Increased availability of special education has produced higher estimates of visual impairment in the United States. The American Printing House for the Blind cites a figure of 4 children per 10 000 population, about four times the incidence figure usually cited. School districts in Canada have found a similar increase in the numbers of low-vision children identified when special services have been made available.

The Low Vision Association of Canada reports that 240 000 Canadians are low-visioned. Of that number, 70 000 are in the legal blindness category. Only about half of this number are registered with the CNIB (Carroll, 1983). Many people with low vision are reluctant to register for fear of being saddled with the stigma of blindness. Many children with visual problems are not identified until they enter school.

ETIOLOGY OF VISUAL IMPAIRMENTS

The leading cause of blindness in children under one year of age is hereditary (Harley and Lawrence, 1977). The second cause is infectious diseases, such as rubella, meningitis, encephalitis, and toxoplasmosis. Metabolic and vascular disease is the third major cause of visual impairments. These include diabetes in the mother and disturbances in the metabolism of the infant.

Prematurity has also been implicated in severe visual defects. Birth traumas, hydrocephaly, infections of the nervous system acquired after birth, oxygen deprivation, and brain hemorrhage are also common causes of visual impairment. In recent years, blindness from prenatal factors, such as ingestion of drugs by the mother, has been increasing. In seventy-seven percent of these cases, babies became blind at less than one year of age. A third of these lost all useful vision (Harley and Lawrence, 1977).

Abnormalities of the central nervous system may result in disruption of eye muscle co-ordination. Children with cerebral palsy secondary to brain damage often have impaired vision as a result of loss of control of ocular muscles. Encephalitis, meningitis, and brain tumours may also produce disturbances of ocular motor function. Children with these conditions frequently have impaired eye movements all their lives or may fail to develop stereoscopic vision. **Diplopia**, or double vision, may result from lack of co-ordination between the two eyes.

Diseases of the eye and uncorrectable refractive errors are the most common causes of visual impairment. The effects of any condition depend upon its severity and age of onset.

PREVENTION OF VISUAL IMPAIRMENT

In many instances, visual impairments are of unknown origin. However, genetic counselling and good pre-natal care, including proper nutrition and avoidance of alcohol and other drugs, may help to prevent severe visual impairments in infants. Total blindness in older children can often be prevented with immediate medical and surgical intervention in cases of retinal detachment, cataracts, and other forms of medically treatable eye disease.

DIAGNOSIS AND MEASUREMENT OF VISUAL IMPAIRMENTS

Two aspects of vision, the physical and the functional, need to be considered in diagnosing visually impaired children. The physical consists of measures of visual acuity, the scope of the visual field, and the effects of specific disease, injury, hereditary, and pre-natal factors. Functional aspects of vision include more subjective factors, such as a child's motivation and opportunity to use residual vision.

Even within the realm of physical diagnosis, a child's visual problems cannot be understood on the basis of acuity measures alone. The visual system operates at three levels (Barraga, 1976). The first is the level of sensation, which involves the recognition of light, form, and colour. Visual acuity is a measurable aspect of visual sensation. The second level is visuomotor. This concerns the brain's ability to focus the eye and co-ordinate sight with other body parts, such as hands. The third level is that of visual perception. This involves the ability of the brain to interpret and assign meaning to visual stimuli.

Ophthalmologists and optometrists are the eye care professionals trained to assess and diagnose the physical aspects of visual impairments. An **ophthalmologist** is a medical doctor who specializes in the treatment of the eye. The ophthalmologist may prescribe medication and perform surgery on the eye. The **optometrist** is not a physician, but is highly trained in the measuring and checking of visual functions and in the prescribing of corrective lenses.

Screening

The identification of visual problems in children requires the teamwork of educational, medical, and other personnel. An adequate screening program involves a carefully planned systematic effort (Harley and Lawrence, 1977). All children should be screened and observed in the classroom for behavioural and physical symptoms. Children who are suspected of having a visual problem should be referred for comprehensive eye examinations.

The screening test should be simple, short, inexpensive and easily administered. The most common screening procedure used for the measurement of central vision acuity is the Snellen Chart, shown in Figure 9-3. Hermann Snellen, a Dutch ophthalmologist, developed the chart in 1862. The standard-letter chart may be used for children, but the symbol-E chart is especially suitable for young children and those who cannot read.

Other screening tests may also be used to supplement the Snellen Chart. These include other measurements of visual fields and muscle-balance supplementary tests. In Canada, children are generally screened for vision problems in the schools. Children in whom a vision problem is suspected are referred for in-depth eye examinations.

Figure 9-3 Snellen Chart.

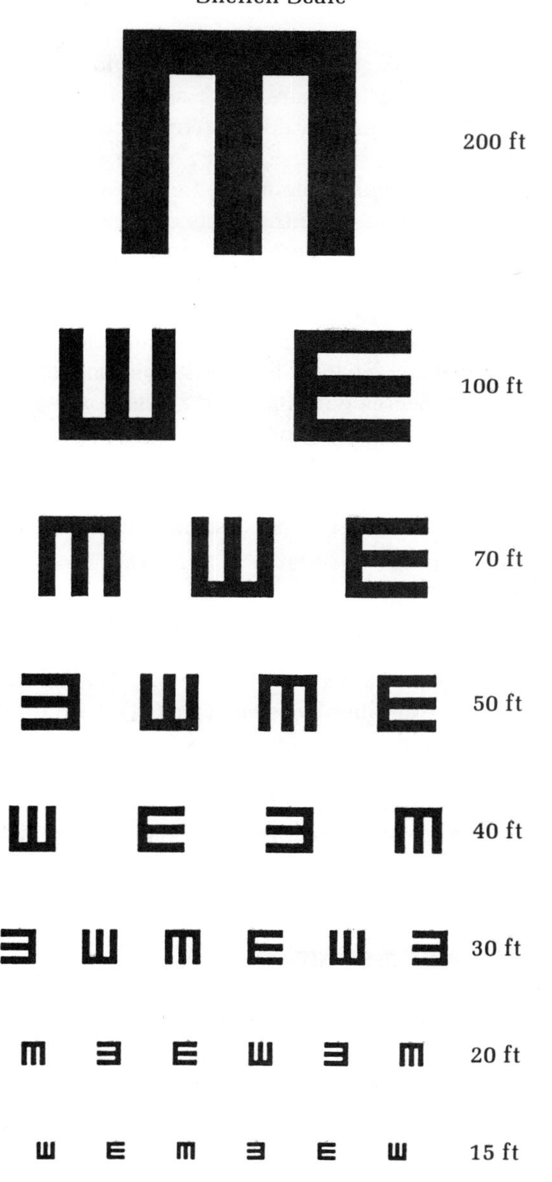

Eye examinations

In an eye examination, both visual acuity and visual perception are important. Visual acuity is a physical measurement of the eye's ability to see the details of objects or symbols at specified distances (Barraga, 1976). Visual perception is the brain's ability to give meaning to visual images.

Eye examiners must search carefully for a wide range of types and degrees of visual impairment. Near visual acuity, with and without distance correction, must always be determined in children with low vision. The measures of near visual acuity and the circumstances surrounding its measurement should always be explained to the child's teacher. Eye examination measurements show the child's maximum potential for achieved acuity. This may be very different from the level at which the child functions in school.

In addition to vision acuity, the visual fields are also measured. Measurements of visual fields are concerned with the angle of view. Examination of the central field indicates any obstructions in the central, most sensitive, portion of the retina. If the central field of vision is less than ten degrees, the child is not able to read comfortably. The field can be decreased by bringing the print closer to the child's eye (Jantzi, 1985).

Some children have good central vision, but very limited peripheral fields. The peripheral fields can be restricted by conditions such as retinitis pigmentosa. Lack of peripheral vision interferes with the child's ease of movement.

Light sensitivity is another complication of visual handicaps. In children who are sensitive to light, acuity increases with decreasing illumination. There is no rule governing the optimal amount of illumination suitable for all visually handicapped children. Careful assessment of sight also includes the testing of colour vision (Harley and Lawrence, 1977).

Testing vision in babies

Very young babies and visually handicapped children with additional disabilities can respond to field tests that use gross objects or lights. The child is held over the parent's shoulder facing the examiner, while a toy or other familiar object is moved into the temporal field. The child is tested for each eye separately and for both eyes together. The child's reaction is then observed (Faye, 1976). Visually evoked response (VER) is a sophisticated technique that measures the child's ability to see light and perceive change in visual stimuli. An optokinetic drum can also be used to evoke a visual response.

More detailed information on vision testing for multi-handicapped children is included in Chapter Thirteen.

Other assessment measures

The visual functioning of the low-vision child is determined by psychological as well as physical factors. The child's ability to interpret visual stimuli is indicated by the ability to discriminate three-dimensional objects, geometric shapes, and outline forms, and to interpret pictorial representations. (Barraga, 1964). Both formal and informal measures of assessment may be used. Informal methods include teacher and parent observations, and functional vision checklists.

Visual efficiency describes how well a child is able to use residual vision. Fluctuations of sight may be caused by light sensitivities, degenerative conditions, and interference in the visual field. Parents and teachers need to know how, when, and under what circumstances students can use their vision most effectively (Mangold and Roessing, 1982).

Students with central field defects may benefit from eccentric viewing techniques. Those who have nystagmus need to discover the best posture for reading. Those with poor peripheral vision can turn their heads, rather than move their eyes, for scanning (Mangold and Roessing, 1982). Some children with very low visual acuity make extremely good use of their remaining vision. Visual efficiency is influenced by such factors as age, motivation, experience, intelligence, and training.

Visual Efficiency Assessment materials are designed to evaluate the child's visual discrimination of forms and abstract symbols, visual closure, spatial perspectives, and abstract figure details (Barraga, 1976). Visual data should be collected over a period of years to accurately determine the child's progress in visual efficiency (Mangold and Roessing, 1982).

Profile 9-1 presents two children with very different levels of visual function.

PROFILE 9-1

Eight-year old Lynn has a progressive inherited eye condition, which has caused cataracts and retinal pathology in both eyes. She is a print reader and is classified as legally blind. Her mobility has not been as severely curtailed as her near vision. However, Lynn uses her remaining vision with high efficiency.

Lynn wears prescribed glasses, but she does her best close work in the morning. She is a lively, intelligent child and works hard at school. Large clear print and good illumination enhance her comfort while she is doing schoolwork. Lynn is not able to watch films or identify moving objects. She can identify colours and uses both flow-pens and crayons.

Lynn's teacher has found that Lynn is becoming more and more fatigued while reading. Due to her progressive condition, she can no longer work from the blackboard. As Lynn's vision deteriorates, she will increasingly depend on the use of auditory and tactile media.

Gerry is six years old and has nystagmus, a central vision problem. Although he can recognize many familiar objects, his visual skills are poor. Gerry has good language ability but is having many problems learning to read. He will need to develop basic visual tracking skills and to learn systematic ways of searching visual materials.

Identifying children with visual problems

Children with serious visual problems are likely to be identified in the pre-school years, often at birth.

Most children with visual impairments can use their vision for learning. As long as severely impaired children have some remaining vision, they are not blind and should not be called blind.

It is in parents' interest that teachers know:

- The child's medical diagnosis and prognosis, as related to instructional needs.
- The child's type of field defect.
- The nature of associated conditions, such as light sensitivity.
- The child's distance acuity, preferably at three metres.
- The child's reading acuity.
- Suggestions for optical aids the child might need. (Stokes, 1976.)

Intelligence testing and assessment

The intelligence testing of blind children is fraught with problems. The intelligence levels of blind and sighted children cannot be easily compared (Warren, 1984). No intelligence test has been devised that is equally meaningful for both groups. Tests for sighted children rely heavily on visual content and administration.

Much IQ testing of blind children has been conducted using the non-visual verbal portions of IQ tests. Various versions of the Binet tests (Interim Hayes-Binet and Perkins-Binet) and the verbal scales of the WISC are commonly used with blind children (Warren, 1984). However, many critics maintain that IQ tests for the blind do not evaluate them in a way comparable to the evaluation of sighted children (Warren, 1984). Moreover, because of the scarcity of predictive studies with blind children, extreme caution should be used when interpreting test results for predictive purposes (Coveny, 1976).

Today, most psychologists testing visually impaired children use a variety of tests. Often they combine the subtests of different instruments (Barraga, 1976). Several tests have been designed for visually impaired populations, using touch perception and specially developed form boards. However, these new tests are still in an experimental stage.

Barraga (1976) noted that the following issues should be considered prior to assessment:

- Purpose of assessment.
- Whether it is desirable to establish definitive norms or age-level equivalents.
- Whether a low level of functioning is due to lack of experience or opportunity to learn. Is a high level of functioning due to enriched background or greater learning capacity?
- Whether an inappropriate response is due to visual problems or learning problems.

The purpose of a comprehensive assessment is to help determine the most appropriate educational placement and educational plan for the individual visually impaired student. The assessment should include:

- Medical information on the nature and severity of the child's visual impairment, and a prognosis as to whether the condition is stable, fluctuating, or progressive. The eye-glass or contact-lens prescription and recommendations for special aids should also be included (Barraga, 1976).
- Family history and experience, including the parents' expectations and involvement in planning their child's education.

■ The Maxfield-Buchholz Social Maturity Scale may be used to supplement the accumulative record of observations.

Teachers and parents should be alert for signs that may indicate visual problems. Exhibit 9-2 outlines some of these indicators.

Exhibit 9-2 Signs of visual problems.

■ Does the child frequently fall or bump into objects?

■ Does the child hold objects very close to — or far from — the eyes?

■ Does the child appear to have abnormal eye movements?

■ Is the child slow or poor in reading?

■ Does the child have frequent eye infections, swollen eyelids, or watery eyes?

■ Does the child complain of fuzzy vision?

■ Does the child rub the eyes, squint, or shake the head, while looking at near or far objects?

■ Does the child tilt the head or close one eye?

■ Is the child fearful of walking down stairs or running freely?

■ Checklists or developmental scales are useful indicators of social, physical, and communication development. Checklists are useful as guides only, and cannot be used for predictive purposes.

■ Assessment of the child's readiness and life-adjustment skills.

■ Teacher observations and checklists should be derived from both formal and informal observation of mobility behaviour, use of hands in exploration, use of residual vision, and response to auditory stimuli. Teacher-made checklists can also be valuable in providing information about other areas.

■ Achievement tests should not be used earlier than the second grade, and probably not until third or fourth grade (Barraga, 1976).

CHARACTERISTICS OF THE VISUALLY IMPAIRED

Visually impaired children do not form a homogeneous population. Even children with the same visual acuity vary from one another in the use of their residual vision. Some children with restricted vision cannot see at a distance. Others are unable to see near images clearly. Some need special lighting and optical aids to learn visually. The early development of visually handicapped children is often more closely related to early experiences, family support, and stimulation than to their degree of visual impairment.

Children with severe visual-impairment can still use their remaining vision for learning.
(M. Campbell)

The developmental consequences of total blindness differ in some respects from those related to low vision. Blindness sharply reduces the range and variety of a child's experiences and restricts the child's ability to move freely within an environment (Lowenfeld, 1981).

Like other infants, visually handicapped children need to be stimulated and encouraged to develop curiosity and interest in the world outside their own bodies. Social, exploratory, and manipulative experiences lay the foundation for competence in communication, concept development, motor development, and self-reliance.

Early motor development

Congenitally blind children may be delayed in the area of motor development. They are less able to orient themselves to the external environment, through such skills as reaching, crawling, and walking (Warren, 1984). Delays in motor development are frequently attributed to restricted experiences. In the absence of vision, a child has little motivation to reach out into space.

The developmental lags of blind children are precisely those that affect successful mobility. In her study of blind infants, Fraiberg (1977) observed no delay in motor development until the onset of locomotor behaviour. Fraiberg concluded that auditory and tactile information do not adequately motivate movement. However, with adequate guidance, most blind children can "learn to travel safely, comfortably, gracefully, and independently (Warren, 1984).

Body image is important to the acquisition of mobility skills. Siegel and Murphy (1960) defined body image as a mental picture of one's own body. Cratty and Sams (1968) argued that body image is necessary for the development of spatial relations. Notions of body parts and how they may be used seem to bridge the areas of motor and concept development.

Without vision, infants find it more difficult to become aware of their bodies in space. Parents can place noise-making mobiles over the crib to encourage their child to move arms and legs in different ways. Items at the side of the crib encourage the child to move sideways. Through gross kinesthetic stimulation parents can heighten their infant's body awareness. They can also place the child in different positions to develop a feel for movement.

Play is one of the best ways for visually handicapped children to have the concrete experiences they require. Large and sturdy toys instruct them in manipulative skills and provide a sense of achievement. Play also teaches children how to be active in initiating interaction with adults.

People who can see take for granted their freedom of movement. For blind children, this freedom only exists to the extent that they can learn the skills and techniques for traveling without sight. To move freely within their environment, they must learn where, how, and in what direction to proceed. Without sufficient sight to guide them, they must be taught the special skills that permit independent travel.

Concept development

Blind children live in a world of smells, sounds, and textures. They build their knowledge out of their experience of their world. Out of their own perceptions, they form meaningful notions of the objects around them. However, the notions they form may differ from the notions of sighted children, relying far more on non-visual perceptions.

Visual information offers a rich variety of colour, shape, and size detail to permit object recognition. Congenitally blind children must build their concepts out of tactile, kinesthetic, and auditory experiences. Texture, weight, temperature, shape, and size merge into a sequence of touch sensations to permit identification of an object (Scott, 1969).

Blind children become quite efficient at recognizing objects through touch sensations. Gottesman (1971) found that the ability of blind children was comparable with the sighted on tasks of tactile perception. The learning problems of some blind children may be related to a failure to develop adaptive hand behaviour.

Blind children learn to gauge distance and direction from variations in sound. They perceive direction through sound localization, not visual angle of perspective.

Blind children are thought to lag significantly behind sighted children in the development of classification and conversation skills. Warren (1984) questions this belief on the basis that much traditional testing of classification and conversation is based on visual information. Even when traditional visual tasks are adapted into a tactual mode, they cannot be considered comparable.

The appreciation of humour is also a facet of cognitive development. Tait and Ward (1982) studied blind children's ability to recognize jokes. They concluded that blind children show no delay in humour appreciation.

Visually impaired children need a great deal of experience to develop accurate notions of the objects in their physical environment. No sensory modality is as rich in detail as vision. Neither the tactile (haptic) nor the auditory sense can offer the blind person the same range of perception as vision does the sighted (Rogow, 1975).

Social development

Attachment behaviours between infants and parents are facilitated by the infant's ability to elicit parental response. Severely visually impaired infants develop their own ways of engaging their parents' attention. Fraiberg (1975) noted how blind infants use their hands and bodies to contact their mothers and signal readiness for play. Instead of eye contact, blind babies use their hands, bodies, and sometimes their voices. When parents understand and respond to their signals, the process of mutually satisfying interpersonal relationships is established (Fraiberg, 1975).

Social adjustment

Many experiences contribute to children's feelings about themselves. Children develop a sense of worth by doing things for themselves, succeeding in a variety of activities, and feeling accepted and loved by those around them. If handicapped children are always treated as though they are not capable, they may begin to believe it and lose interest in trying (Alonso, Moor, and Raynor, 1978).

Blind students often need assistance to balance their interests and tackle new areas of learning. They may need more support and encouragement to take risks and overcome a fear of failure. Teachers should try to emphasize blind children's strengths without denying their special needs.

Severe visual impairments tend to interfere with spontaneous social activity and with social interaction and communication. Barriers may arise when blind children fail to make expected eye contact at first encounters with peers. Children born with visual deficits must learn what their culture expects in the way of behaviour and mannerisms. They must also accept that their visual impairment cannot be denied (Faye, 1976).

Visual functioning

Most visually handicapped children can improve their visual functioning (Barraga, 1964). The more children use their vision, particularly at close range, the more they stimulate the pathways to the brain. The brain accumulates a variety of visual images and stores them as memories. This process enables children with visual handicaps to function as visual learners (Barraga, 1976).

Visually efficient children know those conditions that enhance their visual functioning. These may include optimal classroom seating for best viewing, preferred field of view, compensation for field loss in mobility, and appropriate use of eccentric viewing techniques.

In the area of visual functioning, visually-impaired students have a number of special problems:

- Many children have had few or no normal visual experiences from which to build a visual memory.
- Children, especially when very young, are not aware they have a visual problem.
- Children tend to reject visual aids if they are not immediately helpful.
- Children make spontaneous use of residual vision only if other sensory systems are intact. Those children with perceptual disorders or psychomotor retardation may need a carefully planned sequenced program in order to learn to interpret visual stimuli (Faye, 1976).

Language development

Verbal language serves many important social and information-gathering functions for blind children. Even before they develop speech, blind children learn to use their voices to achieve and maintain social contact. They also learn a great deal about other people from voices. They learn to measure personal attention by the nearness of the speaker and by the touch gestures that accompany speech. These children become dependent on voice and adept at interpreting meaning from nuance or variations in tone.

Blind children show few differences from sighted children in the course of language acquisition. Anderson and Olson (1981) suggested that blind children's descriptions of tangible objects reflected their dependence on non-visual perception. Landau (1983), in a study of the vocabulary of very young blind children, could find no substantial differences from sighted children. Landau observed that blind children used the word "look" to describe the searching activities of their hands rather than eyes. Some other word meanings may differ for blind children as a result of experiential factors.

If blind children are spoken to and interacted with by adults, they begin to speak at the same time as sighted children. Language development is sometimes advanced among this population (Rogow, 1981).

Academic achievement

The educational achievements of visually impaired children are as variable as the population itself. Some visually impaired children are gifted and talented, while others are learning-disabled. Academic success is more closely related to social, cultural, and familial factors than to degree of visual impairment.

For some visually impaired children, scores on standard achievement tests may be depressed by slow responses due to fear of making errors. This is especially true of timed tests. In addition, research is needed into the educational achievements of visually impaired children in integrated public school classes.

Teaching methodologies also influence educational achievements of the visually impaired. When science and mathematics rely primarily on visual materials, they create difficulties for visually impaired children. According to Millar (1975), blind children code spatial information differently. Whereas the sighted person relies on visual representations, the blind rely on movement factors. For example, to grasp the notion of a balloon going up in the air, the blind child must feel its movement tugging upward on a handheld string. When science and mathematics rely primarily on visual materials, blind children have difficulty grasping them.

Some visually handicapped children may have learning problems related to poor visual imagery or visual memory. Poor control of eye movement and inability to focus may interfere with accuracy of perception, rate of visual perception, directionality, and figure/ground perception (Barraga, 1976). These visual problems can be overcome with careful attention and sequenced programs of instruction.

Multiply/visually handicapped children

Blindness combined with mental, neurological, or emotional handicaps results in a complex multiple handicap with profound effects on all aspects of cognitive and affective development. Often the developmental delays of these children baffle physicians, psychologists and educators. It is difficult to determine which handicaps are causes or consequences of the child's condition. Multiple handicaps will be further discussed in Chapter Thirteen.

PARENTING THE VISUALLY IMPAIRED CHILD

Many parents of blind infants feel anxious and apprehensive, and even grief-stricken, when they learn their child is blind. The first hours and days after diagnosis are critical for coming to terms with their child's handicap. Most families benefit from sensitive and well-informed support services at this time (Ferrell, 1985).

Parents require accurate information and strong support to help them stimulate and interact with their visually handicapped infants. The Canadian National Institute for the Blind attempts to reach all families of children registered as legally blind. The CNIB sends family- and child-service workers to offer counsel and support to parents. Public health agencies also offer parent support services, as do several other public and private agencies in Canada.

PROFILE 9-2

Linda Jones wept when the doctor told her and her husband that their newborn baby, Jenny, was blind. She had never considered this tragic possibility, and was terrified of the consequences. However, Linda loved Jenny just as much, and was moved by the baby's beauty and fragility. She realized she'd have to pull herself together and learn all she could, so that her baby would have a good start in life.

Linda felt estranged from the other mothers in the maternity ward, who fell silent whenever she approached. None of the other mothers seemed to know what to say. However, one of the nurses took the time to talk to Linda. "I know how you must feel," she said. "I also have a handicapped child, and know what you are going through now. It's normal to feel hurt and to grieve for your baby. Just remember that she's going to need you to be strong and hopeful. And she is such a beautiful little girl."

Linda began to notice her baby's perfect little features. Gradually her thoughts turned from her own feelings to concern for her child. The nurse came often and talked about her own experiences, helping Linda to sort out her sorrow and disappointment. By the time Linda left the hospital, she was ready to accept her daughter's handicap and face the problems it would bring.

INTERVENTION WITH THE VISUALLY IMPAIRED

Medical intervention

Medical intervention takes the form of medication, surgery, technical aids, and prescriptive lenses to control and maximize visual function. In recent years, laser-beam techniques have been used to reattach damaged retinas. Surgical techniques for the removal of cataracts, corneal transplants, and control of glaucoma have been greatly improved. Drug therapies have reduced the risk of blindness from glaucoma and diabetes. Artificial lens implants are in the developmental stage.

Medical interventions have been more successful in the treatment of eye disease for adults than for children.

Optical aids

Great strides have been made in the development of optic aids. Light-weight portable optical aids now permit many visually impaired persons to continue their professional and vocational lives with little disruption.

There are three main types of magnification and telescopic aids:

- Handheld magnifiers and telescopes.
- Stand magnifiers, such as fixed-focus magnifiers and focusable magnifiers.
- Head-borne aids, which include spectacles, clip-on aids, telescopes, and head-band aids.

Because strong lens magnification shortens the depth of field, low-vision aids must be held at a given distance from an object in order to see it clearly. With strong magnifications, the user can only see a small area through the lens at any given time (Carroll, 1983).

At low-vision centres, patients are taught to use a wide variety of modern optical aids. The Quebec government and the English-speaking Montreal Association of the Blind have co-operated in the development of low-vision rehabilitation services for French Canadians. In Ontario, the University of Waterloo provides rehabilitation in the out-patient clinic of the School of Optometry. In most other provinces, the Canadian National Institute for the Blind sponsors low-vision clinics in co-operation with the ophthalmology departments of provincial universities. Low-vision centres provide loans of optical aids, periods of training, referrals to other rehabilitation services, and a system of regular follow-up (Carroll, 1983).

LEARNING ENVIRONMENTS

Educational intervention

With the recent emphasis on mainstreaming, there has been a shift from segregated residential school education for severely visually handicapped students to education in neighbourhood schools. Although residential schools still exist in some parts of Canada, school districts are making available a continuum of placement options. Generally, these are the regular classroom with itinerant-teacher support, the resource room, and the special classroom (British Columbia Guidelines, 1978).

Integrated education is not a brand new concept for visually handicapped pupils. In the 1930s, "sight-saving" classes were established in Canada's western provinces for students with low vision who were able to read print. In these special classes, children with poor sight were encouraged to "save," or reduce demands on, their vision. When physicians and educators recognized that residual sight should be used rather than saved, these students were the first to be integrated into regular classes (Carlson, 1980).

Today, totally blind and other visually impaired students are enrolled along with sighted peers in all grades from kindergarten through secondary school. In order to offer these students support within the mainstream of education, three different types of program have been organized.

- The resource room functions as a part-time classroom and is staffed by a specialist teacher. Children attend for individual instruction when needed. The resource teacher also helps regular teachers administer special tests and adapt classroom materials. Resource rooms have been established in both elementary and secondary schools.

- In itinerant programs, the specialist teacher travels from school to school within the district. Itinerant teachers offer special instruction to children from kindergarten through secondary school, including those in special programs. Itinerant programs make it possible for most visually handicapped children to be integrated into regular grades. Specialist teachers work closely with all school personnel who are involved with the visually handicapped child.

- Self-contained special classrooms are designed mainly for younger children or students with special learning difficulties. The special class permits intensive individualized instruction and concentrated attention on a child's problems.

Successful mainstreaming of visually impaired students depends on four components. These are the availability of specialist teachers; access to special equipment and optical aids; a braille transcription service; and access to alternate programs for students who need them. The success of each student also depends on co-operation among principals, regular teachers, and special teachers.

As for the hearing-impaired, the education of children with visual handicaps is shared between provincial departments of education and local school districts. Provincial departments of education supply expensive instructional materials, braille books, braillers, typewriters, tape recorders, large print textbooks, and other specialized materials. School boards plan special programs and administer them directly.

Curricular modifications

Curriculum content for the visually impaired combines the general curriculum goals of the child's grade level along with specialized instruction. For blind students, specialized curricula offer lessons in braille-reading and writing, physical orientation and mobility, and basic living skills. Specialized curricula for low-vision students may include visual perceptual training (sight enhancement), orientation and mobility, use of optical aids, print-reading, and writing.

All visually impaired children have problems with reading speed. Teachers must allot extra time for the completion of reading tasks. Teachers might also consider cutting down the number of reading assignments for this group.

Visually impaired students can participate in practically all aspects of school activities. Physical education and creative activities are of particular importance to a well-rounded curriculum. In the elementary years, teachers should bear in mind three important needs of visually impaired youngsters. These are the need for concrete experience, the need for unifying experience, and the need to learn by doing (Lowenfeld, 1971). Residential schools in Nova Scotia, Ontario and Quebec are cooperating with school districts to provide resources to children in their home communities.

In addition to the regular curriculum, a number of special subjects are taught to visually impaired students. These include instruction in braille reading, orientation and mobility, use of maps, and use of technical and learning aids. Students able to use print materials may also receive instruction in the use of optical aids.

Braille The first embossed-dot system was developed by Captain Barbier as a military code that could be read at night. In 1829, Louis Braille used this idea to invent writing for the blind.

Before the braille alphabet books for the blind were awkward and clumsy. Although printed letters were embossed by hand, they were still very difficult to discern. Braille's alphabet was ideally suited for reading by touch. However, many decades passed before braille was used in schools to help blind children read. Not until the 1900s did braille win international acceptance as a reading medium for the blind.

The braille alphabet employs six dots arranged in two rows of three dots each. Each dot is numbered. Figure 9-4 shows the braille alphabet. Although Braille based his code on the French alphabet, the letter "w" was later added for English braille.

Braille is the medium of literacy for blind students. Both English and French braille have evolved into well-established systems that employ highly abbreviated signs and symbols. The complex rules underlying braille structure make the teaching of reading more complex and time-consuming than teaching print reading.

Braille can be adapted to all written languages, including those that do not use Roman letters. Chinese, Japanese, Russian, Greek, and Hebrew braille have all been developed in phonetic versions. French braille has its own system of signs and abbreviations based on the letter groups that occur most frequently in French.

Figure 9-4 The Braille alphabet in English. By placing dots in some of the open spots in the matrix, numbers and simple punctuation can be indicated.

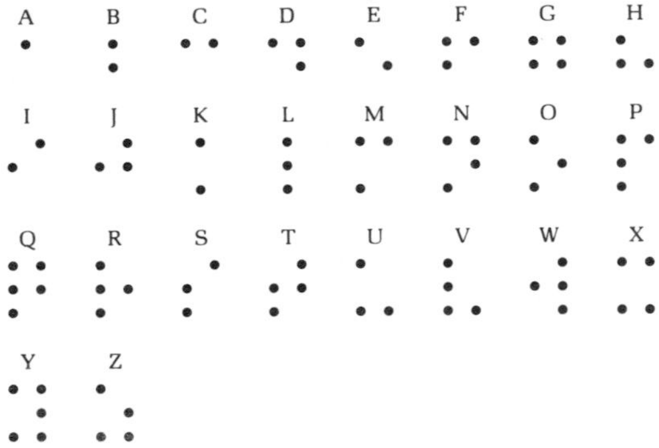

A B C D E F G H

I J K L M N O P

Q R S T U V W X

Y Z

A scientific and mathematical code has also been developed by Dr. Abraham Nemeth.

A skilled two-handed reader begins to read by placing both hands at the beginning of a line. When the middle of the line is reached, the right hand continues across the line while the left hand locates the beginning of the next line. The left hand begins to read the first several words of the new line while the right hand moves to its new reading position (Mangold, 1982).

Because the reading range of the fingers is much narrower than that of the eye, the unit of perception is the single letter, rather than word. Reading efficiency is more difficult, and readers must develop tactile tracking skills, a light touch, good reading posture, and smooth co-ordination of both hands (Mangold, 1976). Beginning braille readers should use the same kind of consumable workbook as sighted students. Children learn more quickly when they can work right in the pages of the book. They also require immediate feedback from their work (Mangold, 1982).

Some borderline students can benefit from knowing both braille and print. These students often use braille for long assignments and print for subjects like spelling and math. The use of braille should not label the student as "blind."

Math. Visually impaired children need to explore the dimensions of shape and build up a vocabulary of meaningful mathematical terms, such as sets, groups, and numbers. Such operations as addition and subtraction should be taught using concrete objects that can be manipulated. Children also need experience with size, shape, capacity, and volume.

Visually impaired children should be permitted to record simple mathematical data with pegboards or blocks. They should be encouraged to physically manipulate objects to learn about their qualities and relations to one another.

Creative arts. Visually handicapped children benefit from experience with a variety of art media. Experience with unstructured materials encourages personal expression and the development of a sense of achievement. Special emphasis should be placed on the creative use of hearing, touch, and smell.

Orientation and Mobility. Mobility is a daily issue in the lives of visually impaired children. Free choice of movement is taken for granted by people who can see. For the blind, this choice only exists to the extent that techniques for traveling without sight have been mastered.

To move freely within the environment, visually impaired children must know where they want to go, how, and in what direction. Without their sight to guide them, they must make maximum use of their other senses. They must also learn to correctly use a travel aid, usually a cane or a dog guide.

Orientation is the knowledge of one's own location in space. **Mobility** is the knowledge of how to get from one place to another. Orientation and mobility training teaches children to co-ordinate their sensory impressions and engage all their remaining senses. Children learn to find their way through touch, hearing, smell, equilibrium, proprioception and kinesthesis.

Children who are born blind or who become blind before they develop a visual memory must learn to rely on their sense of hearing. The sound environment can be used to identify direction, distance, and surrounding buildings. Sounds are intensified near tall concrete structures and are quietened in the snow. One aspect of sound localization is the phenomenon called **object perception**, the ability to perceive objects at close range (Hill and Ponder, 1976).

The sense of touch can provide important travel information, such as the texture and surface of objects. Touch can also be used to detect differences in temperature and air currents. The sense of smell is helpful for identifying landmarks such as restaurants and bakeries. Kinesthesis reveals changes in the tilt of surfaces and helps in the estimation of distances. Through kinesthesis, blind travelers also remain aware of their position, movement, and posture.

Blind children should begin orientation and mobility training as early in life as possible. As one child, Lila, observed to her mobility teacher, "Before I started to train, I didn't really know what a city street was. I used to be afraid to go outside because I thought the cars drove right beside the houses. I guess I didn't bother to think about where the people walked. My mother drove me everywhere."

Orientation and mobility training enable blind children to move with confidence and independence in their environment. Children learn to use a travel aid, such as the prescription cane, often referred to as the white or long cane.

The following is a sample of important concepts taught in mobility training:

- Landmarks are known objects in specific places that inform a child about the location. A ticking clock, a rosebush, or a particular building may all be used as landmarks.
- Shorelines are the edges formed where two surfaces meet, such as the lawn and the sidewalk, the curb and the road, or the walls and the floor.
- Trailing involves the use of the hand or the cane to follow a shoreline. Trailing is used to find landmarks, determine a sense of direction, and move in a parallel line. A child trails with the back of the hand to prevent injury to the fingers.
- When squaring off, the child lines the body up with a particular object to ascertain direction or location.

■ Protective techniques are hand and arm postures used to protect the body from bumping into things, such as partially opened doors (Hill and Ponder, 1976).

Orientation and mobility training are increasingly being included in the educational programs of the visually impaired. More and more special teachers are becoming qualified mobility specialists to provide direct services to their students. Some school districts employ mobility specialists who teach only orientation and mobility.

The prescription cane. The prescription cane was developed by Hoover (1947), for the rehabilitation of blinded war veterans. The cane is made of aluminum or fibreglass, its length determined by the user's height and comfort. The blind traveler holds the cane in front, swinging it in a small arc to detect obstacles.

Dog guides. Dog guides provide protection and companionship. They are usually German shepherds, golden or Labrador retrievers, and collies, breeds noted for their intelligence and stable disposition. The blind person and the dog guide are trained together to become an effective team.

Canada's first dog-guide centre is currently being established in Ontario. Only about one percent of the blind population actually use a dog guide. To qualify, one must be older than sixteen years, emotionally mature, and responsible.

Technical and educational aids

Technological assistance in the education of visually handicapped children is expanding at a rapid rate. Three types of technological aid are in current use. These are computers and calculators, reading devices, and mobility aids.

Computers and calculators

Most of the programs adapted for blind users were written for Apple computers, but other models are being adapted. Information input is through the regular computer keyboard or through a special braille keyboard. Computers for the blind have special speech or braille output devices. Students can use these computers to prepare assignments, keep files, learn to write computer programs, and perform any computer function.

Most school microcomputers can be used by visually impaired students with the addition of speech or tactile feedback devices. Transcription programs have been developed to permit direct braille transcription of computer material (Mellor, 1981). Large screen printout can also be used by low-vision students.

Paperless braillers are microcomputers with braille read-outs consisting of cells with movable pins. As soon as the cells are read, the pins form the next line of braille material. The user can also write in braille, store material, and correct or change as on a standard microcomputer (Mellor, 1981).

Calculators with synthetic voices that "talk" to the users are also in use. These calculators spell out operations as they are entered, and read the answers aloud.

Reading devices

The Optacon (Optic to Tactile Converter) is the most widely used reading device. The reader moves a small cylindrical camera over the lines of print. The camera scans the print letters, which are then converted to a tactile array. The reader reads by placing the left index finger over an array of 144 vibrating pins. The Optacon is portable, about the size of a large tape recorder. Recognition of letter shapes requires a great deal of skill and practice. However, young children as well as adults can use this device to gain immediate access to print materials.

The Kurzweil Reading Machine converts printed material to an audio output. Its camera picks up printed letters, which are then converted into synthesized speech.

Variable-speed tape recorders are the most commonly used speech compressors. Because most visually impaired persons do most of their reading by means of recordings, the variable-speed recorder permits faster reading.

Closed-circuit television reading aids resemble television sets. They have a camera that scans reading material and conveys it to a monitor for enlargement. Users can regulate the size of the image to their own needs. Some CCTV machines are powerful enough for use with microfiche.

Mobility aids

Travel aids work on a radar principle. They send out beams of ultrasound, which cannot be heard by the human ear. If the beam hits an object, some of the ultrasound is reflected back to the device and converted into audible tones.

The Sonicguide supplies three kinds of information aobut an object — direction, distance, and general surface characteristics. The Sonicguide may be used with a long cane or a dog guide, and can be fitted into eyeglass frames. The infant's Sonicguide uses a headband mounting and permits obstacle detection as close as fifty centimetres. With help from the Sonicguide, blind babies have learned to locate and reach for objects (Mellor, 1981).

The laser cane transmits invisible infrared light. When it detects an obstacle, some of the light beam is reflected back to the cane, vibrating a pin beneath the users index finger.

The Mowat Sensor is a small handheld device, light enough to be carried in a pocket or purse. It can be used to locate fallen objects, doorways, and even mailboxes (Mellor, 1981).

Other Educational Aids

In addition to the highly technical aids described above, the following materials and equipment are useful in the education of the visually impaired.

- Proper lighting.
- Movable and adjustable desks.

- Braillers.
- Typewriters.
- Tape recorders.
- Three-dimensional maps.
- Audio-books. These are tape recordings of texts and other important materials.
- Math aids, including embossed rulers and tape measures.
- Optical aids.

A variety of technical aids have been developed to assist visually-handicapped students.
(M. Campbell)

THE VISUALLY IMPAIRED PRE-SCHOOLER

Young children with visual impairments do not always react to their parents in the same way that sighted children do (Ferrell, 1985). Because visually impaired children may not look at adults, it is easy to misinterpret their lack of eye contact as disinterest. This makes it all the more important for parents to take the initiative in interaction and play.

To avoid the development of passivity and disinterest, parents should take active steps to interest children in the world around them. Children should be encouraged to develop their own learning techniques and to use all their non-visual senses (Ferrell, 1985). Without consistent intervention, children may perceive only fragments of sensory data. For example, a child may hear the refrigerator door open and close, the sound of Mother's footsteps on the floor, and the clatter of pots and pans. However, without assistance, the child may not associate these sounds with a sequence of food preparation.

Pre-school education helps children to establish the foundations for later learning. It is never too early to teach basic movement and communication skills. The following areas may need particular attention: hand development (prehension), locomotion, self-feeding, self-dressing, and object use (Fraiberg, 1977).

Early experiences in integrated settings with sighted children establish a sense of belonging and self-reliance. To a large degree, children learn to trust themselves as others trust them. In the pre-school, visually-impaired children can contribute to the building of co-operative relationships within the group. "Early mainstreaming experiences help children learn from each other, make and be friends, and recognize their strengths and abilities in comparison with others" (Alonso, Moor, and Raynor, 1978, p. 29).

Parents, teachers, and others were asked to consider the special needs of blind pre-school children. From their responses, the following list was compiled:

- Early awareness of their environment.
- Accurate medical diagnosis, including low-vision assessment.
- Socialization with other children.
- Pre-school experience away from home, but in a "home-like" setting.
- Structured learning experiences, because much of what must be learned will not happen incidentally.
- Parents who understand how to continually promote development and learning.
- Exposure to, and exploration of, stimulating environments.
- Stimulation for the whole being.
- Love and understanding.
- Time set aside for the child alone.
- Total involvement with the family.
- Story time.
- Tactile, verbal, and motor stimulation.

- Chances to learn from interacting with other children.
- Predictability in the day.
- Sense of success to promote further development.
- New experiences, such as field trips out into the public. (International Institute for Visually Impaired Children, 1981.)

Increased recognition of the importance of pre-school years has created parental demand for information and guidebooks of suggested activities (Ferrell, 1985). Various excellent handbooks for parents have been produced in recent years. Interesting toys are needed to encourage blind children to play at their age-level potential (Alonso, Moor, and Raynor, 1982).

PROFILE 9-3

We first met Jenny as a newborn in Profile 9-2. Her parents were told she was blind a few days after her birth. They never suspected she had any sight until her third birthday. At that time, Jenny exclaimed, "lights, lights," and pointed to the candles on her birthday cake.

At three years old, Jenny loves to play and is very sociable. Her language skills are advanced. She loves to be read to, and asks many questions. Jenny is very cautious about walking alone, however, and is somewhat delayed in gross-motor development.

Jenny is skilful with her hands and has several favourite toys. Her constant companion is a stuffed doll with long woolly hair and a satin face. Jenny talks a lot to her doll, who is called Little Jenny.

Jenny's mother worries that her daughter is too involved in her own fantasy world and has no friends nearby. She has decided to enrol Jenny in a pre-school program. Exhibit 9-3 outlines Jenny's educational plan.

Exhibit 9-3 Jenny's pre-school educational plan.

Instructional Objectives	*Educational Methods*	*Facilitator*
Jenny will make maximum use of her vision.	Allow and encourage Jenny to look at objects. Give her practice at looking by sitting with her and pointing out colours and shapes. Play a looking game with all children and encourage Jenny's participation.	Pre-school teacher and other children.
Encouragement will continue at home.	Perceptual/touch program.	Mother, with help from special teacher.

Jenny will participate in all activities with other children.	Make a place for Jenny to play. Mark her seat and let her find it. Ask her to help when appropriate. Let her know she is one of a group of children. Give clear directions. Include Jenny in all activities. Notice activities that seem most interesting to Jenny. Remark on her likes and dislikes. Encourage her to try different activities. Modify some activities to allow her full participation.	Pre-school teacher.
Jenny will develop realistic concepts about objects and experiences.	Provide concrete materials and encourage Jenny to describe and use a variety of objects.	Pre-school teacher.
	Ask Jenny to help set the table at home and learn where items are stored.	Mother.
	Describe sequences involved in object use.	Pre-school teacher and mother.
Jenny will develop notions of down, across, here, over.	Demonstrate concepts by using Jenny's own body.	Pre-school teacher.
Jenny will use correct posture for seated work.	Tell Jenny when she is sitting in a good position. Let her know how the better position will be helpful.	Pre-school teacher and mother
Jenny will become curious.	Let Jenny handle new toys and objects. Have "mystery" object games with all the children.	Pre-school teacher, mother, and other children.
Jenny will develop positive feelings about herself in the pre-school setting.	Compliment Jenny when she participates. Encourage her own initiative. Encourage and reward spontaneity. Discourage passivity and dependence on other children.	Pre-school teacher and other children.

THE VISUALLY IMPAIRED ADOLESCENT

PROFILE 9-4

Dave is a handsome fourteen-year-old. One afternoon, he stayed late at school to complete some of his assignments. During a short break, Dave confided to his teacher that he had always wanted to play basketball like his father. "That's the worst part of a visual handicap, he said. "You can't do the things you really want to."

Dave was born with a severe visual problem caused by damage to the optic nerve. He learned to read print with the aid of magnifiers and a closed-circuit electronic aid. In the fourth grade, he learned braille to supplement the slow, fatiguing process of reading print. With braille, he made much more efficient progress and became a determined and able student.

Throughout Dave's school career, he has been co-operative and eager to participate in classroom activities. His teachers have responded to his warmth, and the other children have never resented the special attention he has received. However, looking back, Dave's teacher now realizes that Dave probably never felt fully accepted.

Dave was always viewed by other children as the "blind boy." No one ever invited him to join a sports team or to go to the movies. He never made any close friends in his classes. As an adolescent, he is more aware than ever of the differences that separate him from his classmates.

Dave's teacher tried to talk to him about his problems. "Do you honestly feel that your handicap keeps you from being part of a group?" he asked. Dave nodded. "It's not that the other kids aren't friendly, but I can't do the things they admire. I can't be good in sports or drive a car and go downtown on my own."

Dave's teacher agreed that these activities are important to teenagers. He realized how alone Dave must often feel. He wished he could help Dave solve his social problems as easily as he could help with academic ones.

Unfortunately, as Dave knew, handicapped teenagers are only truly accepted to the degree that they can participate in activities popular with their peers. Dave's teacher sympathized and said, "Maybe we've been concentrating too hard on the academic side of your life here in school." However, the teacher knew that Dave himself would have to cope with his social problems. Dave's own shyness and feelings of inadequacy were what kept him from taking initiatives with his friends. As a result, his life had become too narrow and too concerned with his handicap.

Dave's experience highlights the confusions, uncertainties, and anxieties experienced by visually handicapped adolescents. Adolescence is a time of rapid physiological change and acute self-awareness. Erickson (1963) described adolescents as "primarily concerned with what they appear to be in the eyes of others as compared with what they feel they are, and with the question of how to connect the roles and skills cultivated earlier with the occupational prototypes of the day" (Erickson, 1963, p. 261).

Adolescence can be an exceptionally painful period for the over-dependent child. During adolescence, many visually handicapped children are unable to establish relationships with their peers. Even in integrated settings, visually impaired children often do not interact with sighted peers (Hoben, Lindstrom, Bish, Shapiro and Chalberg, 1979). Opportunities often need to be created for interaction between blind and sighted children. Projects that integrate these students should be encouraged.

Blind students often need to be made more aware of dress codes and the use of cosmetics. Personal counselling services and sex education may help those visually impaired students who need to develop greater social awareness. Without sight, or with very poor sight, children often miss out on the incidental learning and imitation of social role models.

Career and vocational education are particularly important for visually impaired adolescents. Volunteer experience in community agencies, career clubs, career days and counselling courses can help visually handicapped develop realistic career goals. Guidance, counselling, and instruction also help visually impaired adolescents to determine their own interests and become aware of their abilities.

Visually handicapped adolescents often confront the following problems:

- Difficulty in learning how to dress and use make-up to improve personal appearance. This problem is intensified when the appearance of the eyes is abnormal.
- Adolescents may have internalized the role of handicapped person from the attitude of parents or teachers.
- Parents and teachers may have blamed slow academic progress on visual problems, overlooking learning problems.
- Unattractive appearance of optical aids may cause adolescents to reject them.
- Competition with sighted peers is difficult, even with training and education.
- Realistic career choices are also difficult, especially when based on minimal experience.

In general, visually handicapped students need to do things for themselves and become responsible for their own possessions. Parents and teachers must convey realistic and positive expectations. At home or school, visually impaired students should be expected to observe the same standards of personal behaviour as sighted peers.

TEACHERS OF THE VISUALLY IMPAIRED

Teachers of visually impaired children have a demanding and far-reaching role. They require flexibility, versatility, and a wide range of knowledge and skills. These teachers must:

- Assess children in areas of braille-reading readiness, visual perception, mobility, and social development.
- Design and provide instructional programs in braille reading, braille math, and other academic subjects.
- Design and provide instruction in self-help skills.
- Understand the causes of visual impairments and interpret their medical, educational, and social implications.
- Adapt learning materials.
- Develop effective itinerant or resource-room programs.
- Consult and liase with parents and other teachers.
- Teach the use of visual aids and electronic reading devices.
- Assess and develop instructional programs for visually impaired children with additional handicaps.

In 1978, the University of British Columbia established Canada's first university-based professional development program for teachers of the visually impaired. This program consists of a full academic year of study combined with student-teaching experiences. It is designed for teachers working in itinerant and resource-room programs for blind and visually impaired children (including those with additional handicaps). In Ontario, Brantford's Ross McDonald Regional Centre for the Visually Handicapped provides teacher training and in-service teacher training in co-operation with the University of Western Ontario.

SUMMARY

Visual impairments cover a broad spectrum of type and degree of severity. The academic functioning of visually impaired children often has little relationship to degree of impairment.

For children with residual vision, the term blind should be avoided. These children should be encouraged as much as possible to use their vision for learning. Children who have had few or no visual experiences fail to develop visual memory. These children may demonstrate learning difficulties related to visual perceptual development. Other young children with visual handicaps may not even be aware they do not see well.

Educational intervention for the visually impaired is directed at the creation of optimal learning conditions. Today, specialized instruction is provided within the framework of integrated education.

In recent years, self-help groups, low-vision services, special educational services, parent and professional associations, and advocacy groups have improved the quality of life for visually impaired Canadians. Although much remains to be done, the barriers against normal participation for the visually impaired are gradually disappearing. Today, many visually handicapped Canadians are taking their rightful places as full participants in Canadian society.

BIBLIOGRAPHY

Alonso, L., Moor, P.M., and Raynor, S. (1978). *Mainstreaming preschoolers: Children with visual handicaps. A guide for teachers, parents and others who work with visually handicapped preschoolers.* Washington, D.C.: Department of Health, Education and Welfare.

Anderson, D. and Olson, M. (1981). Word meaning among congenitally blind children. *Journal of Visual Impairment and Blindness, 75,* 165-168.

Barraga, N.C. (1964). *Increased visual behavior in low vision children.* New York: American Foundation for the Blind.

Barraga, N.C. (1976). *Visual handicaps and learning: A developmental approach.* Belmont, CA.: Wadsworth.

Carlson, L. (1980). Special education in Saskatchewan. In M. Csapo and L. Goguen (Eds.), *Special education across Canada: Issues and concerns for the '80s.* Vancouver: Centre for Human Development and Research.

Carroll, B. (1983). *Eye trumpets: A consumer guide to low vision and low vision aids.* Toronto: Low Vision Association of Ontario.

Colenbrander, A. (1976). Low vision: Definition and classification. In E. Faye (Ed.), *Clinical Low Vision.* New York: Little, Brown.

Coveny, T.E. (1976). Standardized tests for visually handicapped children: A review of research. *New Outlook for the Blind, 70,* 232-236.

Cratty, B.J. and Sams, T.A. (1968). *The body-image of blind children.* New York: American Foundation for the Blind.

Erickson, E. (1963). *Childhood and society.* New York: W.W. Norton.

Faye, E. (1976). Clinical definition and classification of the low vision patient. In E. Faye (Ed.), *Clinical low vision.* New York: Little, Brown.

Ferrell, K.A. (1985). *Reach out and teach. Meeting the training needs of parents of visually impaired and multihandicapped children.* New York: American Foundation for the Blind.

Fraiberg, S. (1975). The development of human attachments in infants blind from birth. *Merrill-Palmer Quarterly, 21,* 315-334.

Fraiberg, S. (1977). *Insights from the blind.* N.Y.: Basic Books.

Gottesman, M. (1971). A comparative study of Piaget's developmental schema of sighted children with that of a group of blind children. *Child Development, 42,* 573-580.

Harley R.K. and Lawrence, G.A. (1977). *Visual impairment in the schools.* Springfield, IL.: Charles C. Thomas.

Havener, W.H. (1979). *Synopsis of ophthalmology.* St. Louis, MO.: Moseby.

Hill, E. and Ponder, P. (1976). *Orientation and mobility techniques: A Guide for the practitioner.* New York: American Foundation for the Blind.

Hoben, M., Lindstrom, V., Gish, S., Shapiro, S., and Chalberg, C. (1982). *Integration of vision impaired students and hearing impaired students in regular classrooms: A report of research.* Minneapolis, MN.: Hennepin Technical Center.

Jantzi, J. (1985). Personal communication.

Landau, B. (1983). Blind children's language is not 'meaningless.' In A.E. Mills (Ed.), *Language acquisition in the blind child.* San Diego: College Hill Press, pp. 62-76.

Lowenfeld, B. (1971). *Our blind children.* Springfield, IL.: Charles C. Thomas.

Mangold, S.S. (1982). Teaching reading via braille. In S. Mangold (Ed.), *A Teacher's guide to the special educational needs of blind and visually handicapped children.* New York: American Foundation for the Blind.

Mangold, S.S. and Roessing, L.J. (1982). Instructional needs of students with low vision. In S. Mangold (Ed.), *A teacher's guide to the special educational needs of blind and visually handicapped children.* New York: American Foundation for the Blind.

Maxfield, R.E. and Buchholz, S. (1957). *A social maturity scale for blind preschool children: A guide to its use.* New York: American Foundation for the Blind.

Mellor, M.C. (1981). *Aids for the 80s: What they are and what they do.* New York: American Foundation for the Blind.

Millar, S. (1975). Visual experience or translation rules? Drawing the human figure, by blind and sighted children. *Perceptions, 4,* 363-371.

Reynell, J. and Zinkin, P. (1975). New procedures for the developmental assessment of young children with severe visual handicaps. *Child: Care, Health and Development, 1,* 61-69.

Rogow, S.M. (1970). Retardation among blind children. *Education of the Visually Handicapped, 2,* 107-111.

Rogow, S.M. (1975). Perceptual organization in blind children. *New Outlook for the Blind, 69,* 226-233.

Rogow, S.M. (1981). The appreciation of riddles by blind and visually handicapped children. *Education of the Visually Handicapped, 13,* 4-10.

Scott, R. (1969). The socialization of blind children. In D. Joslin (Ed.), *Handbook of socialization theory and research.* New York: Rand McNally.

Siegel, A.W. and Murphy, T.J. (1970). *Postural determinants in the blind.* Final project report, Carlson (1980).

Stokes, L. (1976). Educational considerations for the child with low vision. In E. Faye (Ed.), *Clinical low vision.* N.Y.: Little, Brown.

Tait, P.E. and Ward, M. (1982). The comprehension of verbal humor by visually impaired children. *Journal of Visual Impairment and Blindness, 76,* 144-147.

Warren, D. (1984). Blindness and early child development. New York: American Foundation for the Blind.

Welsh, R.L. and Blasch, R.B. (1980). *Foundations of orientation and mobility.* New York: American Foundation for the Blind.

5

Children with Emotional Disturbance

INTRODUCTION

Many adults remember childhood as a time of joy and freedom, forgetting the many stresses and frustrations they encountered. Like adults, children suffer from fatigue, pain, conflict, fear, and anxiety. They react to these stresses in many different ways, depending on a complex matrix of biological, social, and psychological factors. Many children react by exhibiting problematic behaviours, but most outgrow these behaviours and learn more pleasant responses.

Some children remain in conflict with themselves and exhibit behaviour that is personally distressing and disturbing to those around them. These children are generally classified as emotionally disturbed. They are poor at making friends, and rarely succeed in establishing close and satisfying emotional ties with other people. Some withdraw, but most strike out at others with hostility and aggression. Emotionally disturbed children are constantly in conflict with those around them. They are frequently abusive, bossy, destructive, unpredictable, quarrelsome, and irresponsible.

Many professionals differentiate between two levels of severity when speaking of emotional disturbance. The most severe difficulties are subsumed under the general category of psychosis. Psychotic children suffer a complete breakdown in communication with those around them. Milder cases of emotional disturbance most commonly reveal a cluster of behaviour disorders. Mildly and moderately emotionally disturbed children may function well in some areas but demonstrate bizarre and problematic patterns of behaviour in others.

No category in special education is as difficult to define as emotional disturbance. Mildly or moderately emotionally disturbed children are particularly hard to identify and assess because professionals have been unable to agree on a comprehensive definition. The identification, classification, and defining of children with severe and profound behaviour disorders is somewhat easier, though still fraught with problems. However, although nearly every aspect of emotional disturbance is subject to debate, there is general agreement that emotionally disturbed children suffer very special problems.

Most of the controversy surrounding emotional disturbance concerns causes and treatments. This controversy arises because emotionally disturbed children are the concern of many different professionals: psychiatrists, psychologists, medical personnel, educators, various therapists, social workers, police and legal officers. Each of these professionals views the problem differently. The social worker, for example, views emotional disturbance within the context of family problems. A medical professional may view the problem as a manifestation of disease.

Only recently has the educational sector added its own perspective on emotional disturbance. Educators have had to deal with the school-related effects of problematic behaviour. As a result, they have attempted to devise intervention strategies for children whose barriers to learning appear to be primarily psychosocial. These attempts have led to a broadened conceptualization of emotional disturbance.

CHAPTER TEN

Children with mild and moderate emotional disturbance

MARGRET WINZER

Sometimes he sat mute and unmoving all morning or crawled about the schoolroom floor oblivious to the other children or to his teacher. At times he had violent temper tantrums. No one knew whether he was retarded or had suffered brain damage at birth.

(Axline, 1964)

Most of us have some experience with children with behaviour disorders. These troubled children create problems for almost everyone they interact with. They exhibit, to a marked and prolonged extent, behaviour that is clearly undesirable, inappropriate, and maladaptive in its social context.

Difficulties in the precise definition of emotional disturbance have created problems in estimating prevalence, identifying characteristics, assessment, etiology, treatments, and educational approaches. Professionals cannot even agree on whether to call these children emotionally disturbed, behaviourally disordered, socially maladjusted, deviant, psychologically impaired, educationally handicapped, character-disordered, or delinquent. Emotionally disturbed and behaviourally disordered are the most common terms, although the others are used almost interchangeably. In this chapter, we will use emotionally disturbed and behaviourally disordered.

Special education for emotionally disturbed students is a fairly modern development. In Canada, special institutions, such as reformatories, industrial schools, and refuges, were founded in the middle decades of the last century. These institutions were intended to serve delinquent, neglected, and vagrant children. However, many other "problem" children were also institutionalized, especially in the period before schooling was required for all children.

Even in the public school system, children who exhibited inappropriate behaviour were generally suspended or excluded. As time passed, more of these children were placed in classes for the mentally retarded, the brain injured, or the severely and profoundly disturbed. Not until the 1950s did special education for mildly and moderately disturbed children really emerge.

In the late 1960s and early 1970s, a number of provincial and national reports on education further stressed the need for educational services for emotionally disturbed children. Some of these reports — the Commission of Emotional and Learning Disorders in Children (Roberts and Lazure, 1970); the Standards for Education of Exceptional Children in Canada (Hardy, McLeod, Minto, Perkins, and Quance, 1971); and Children in Canada Residential Care (Csapo, 1981a) — urged the federal and provincial governments to assume responsibility for the education of all emotionally disturbed children. They also asked local education authorities to provide educational services for all children within their jurisdictions (Csapo, 1981a).

In the past decade, provision of services for emotionally disturbed children has rapidly developed. In 1969, for example, a survey of British Columbia schools (Laycock and Findlay, 1969) found that sixty-five percent of school districts had no definite policy concerning the education of emotionally disturbed children. By 1981, seventeen percent of districts provided classes for autistic children, seventy-five percent had rehabilitation classes, forty-nine percent had classes for the severely handicapped, and fourteen percent had classes for mildly disturbed children (Csapo, 1981a). Although the intensity and breadth of services for the emotionally disturbed varies, (Csapo, 1981b), each province is clearly attempting to arrive at its own individual solutions.

Exhibit 10-1 shows the growth in Quebec of special education, including that for the emotionally disturbed. This growth can be generalized to other parts of the country.

Exhibit 10-1 Special education services in Quebec.

Learning Disabilities	*1967-1968*	*1969-1970*	*1971-1972*	*1973-1974*	*1975-1976*	*1977-1978*
slight		10 131	18 050	28 098	42 193	41 147
severe			443	7 600	13 843	23 148
Mental Deficiency						
slight	18 906	22 312	23 068	24 612	19 876	16 608
severe	1 424	3 206	4 641	4 733	4 204	3 842
Handicaps						
sensory	138	184	615	706	728	1 251
physical	1 614	1 301	1 152	660	716	985
multiple				1 817	3 541	6 249
Socio-emotional Maladjustment						
severe	1 514	2 499	6 456	5 894	7 814	9 888
Total	23 596	39 933	54 425	74 120	92 915	103 118

(Csapo and Goguen, 1980, p. 96.)

DEFINITIONS OF EMOTIONAL DISTURBANCE

There is no universally accepted definition of emotional disturbance. Deviant behaviour has been defined and conceptualized in many ways, and definitions proposed from a variety of perspectives and disciplines (Cullinan, Epstein, and Lloyd, 1983). Many researchers have attempted to define disturbed child populations, while others have focused on disturbed behaviour. To still others, emotional disturbance is not a condition but a label, a subjective appraisal of the beholder.

The purpose of most definitions of emotional disturbance is to determine the locus of disturbance. Once this is determined, the definition can be extended to apply to the identification, measurement, and treatment of the condition. However, behavioural manifestations are often considered more important than a definitional construct. In a 1981 survey of British Columbia, for example, about half the schools surveyed had no working definition of emotional disturbance (Csapo, 1981a).

Many factors make it difficult to define mild and moderate emotional disturbance. These include:

- Lack of an adequate definition of mental health. Behavioural deviance necessarily has a referent in normative behaviour. However, because human emotions and behaviour are so varied, a precise notion of normalcy is difficult to derive. Mental health encompasses a wide spectrum of behaviours and cannot be measured quantitatively. We have no instruments to determine a mental health quotient analogous to the IQ.

- Varying behaviours exhibited by all children. Deviant and unusual behaviour may exist in the repertoires of normal children, usually as transient outlets for tension. At the same time, disturbed children may sometimes behave normally. Distinctions between normal and disturbed behaviour are generally in amount or degree rather than in kind. Emotionally disturbed children perform certain behaviours too often or intensely, or not often or intensely enough. Of course, some emotionally disturbed behaviours may be in themselves abnormal.

- Varying behaviours exhibited by disturbed children. Emotionally disturbed children are likely to display a wide variety of inappropriate behaviours which may or may not be consistent to particular situations. Their patterns of behaviour are often unpredictable and subtle, rendering their conditions even harder to define.

- Varying professional perspectives. Many disciplines work with behaviourally disordered children, each with its own theories concerning the causes, definition, and treatment of emotional disturbance. Even among educators, definitions vary. Some reflect administrative arrangements and others reflect observed in-class behaviour. Some educational definitions describe the child as disabled, others specify deficiencies in certain areas of behaviour, and still others focus on the interaction between pupil and teacher (Csapo, 1981a).

- The relationship between emotional disturbance and other disabling conditions. Emotional disturbance is very often associated with other handicapping conditions. Many children, for example, are both emotionally disturbed and mentally retarded (Balthazar and Stevens, 1975). In their study of hearing-impaired children, Schlesinger and Meadow (1972) found five times as many children with severe emotional disturbance and three times as many with moderate disturbance as they found among hearing students. Many learning-disabled students develop an overlay of emotional problems that compound their learning difficulties and conceal their primary disorder.

■ Social and cultural expectations. Emotional disturbances occur among the rich, the poor, the gifted, the retarded, and members of all racial and ethnic groups. However, those who are poor, multiply handicapped, or the victims of social discrimination are more likely to develop behaviour patterns classified as deviant (Goulder and Trybus, 1977; Jones, 1976; Kauffman, 1977; Morse, 1975). Minority-group children may bring to school different skills, expectations, and competencies than those valued by the dominant culture. Behaviour considered normal and adaptive in a subculture may be looked upon as deviant or inadequate by members of the dominant group (Hallahan and Kauffman, 1982).

Common elements in definitions

Many current definitions of emotional disturbance use language that is vague, general, and open to different interpretations. However, most definitions share some common elements. The mildly and moderately emotionally disturbed child exhibits behaviour that:

■ Deviates in an extreme manner from the norm.

■ Recurs chronically.

■ Violates social or cultural expectations.

■ Affects the child's self esteem, interpersonal relationships, and probably school achievement.

Of the many definitions currently available, Kauffman's (1977) is the most relevant from an educational point of view:

> Children with behaviour disorders are those who chronically and markedly respond to their environment in socially unacceptable and/or personally unsatisfying ways but who can be taught more socially acceptable and personally gratifying behaviour. Children with mild and moderate behaviour disorders can be taught effectively with their normal peers (if their teachers receive appropriate consultative help) or in special resource or self-contained classes with reasonable hope of quick reintegration with their normal peers. Children with severe and profound behaviour disorders require intensive and prolonged intervention and must be taught at home or in special classes, special schools, or residential institutions (p. 23).

Kauffman's (1977) definition takes into account levels of severity, and focuses on behaviours that are inconsistent with current societal standards and personally unsatisfactory. In addition, Kauffman recommends specific educational settings and maintains a positive outlook for the children's success through appropriate educational intervention.

CLASSIFICATION OF EMOTIONAL DISTURBANCE

Closely related to definitional problems are difficulties in classifying emotional disturbance into types and degrees of deviance. The controversy surrounding the issue does not only concern how and what to classify. Some professionals also challenge the value of any classification system at all.

Although a number of classification systems have been developed, few professionals in the field are happy with them. Critics argue that present classification systems do not include enough relevant data about a child's personality components for the selection of appropriate treatment strategies. Current systems also fail to offer comparable information about different patients on a common set of components (Cummings and Finger, 1980).

Classification by severity

Emotionally disturbed children are often classified in terms of the severity of their condition — mild, moderate, severe, or profound. Degrees of severity are useful in arranging an appropriate educational program. Children with mild emotional disturbance can be effectively managed by parents and teachers, if provided with support. Moderately disturbed children may remain in the regular school environment if given access to special therapies. Severe and profoundly emotionally disturbed children are usually placed in special classes or special schools.

Clinical classification

The principal modern classification system is the clinical classification provided by the American Psychiatric Association in the *Diagnostic and statistical manual of mental disorders* (*DSM III*) (1980). This classification system presents five dimensions of behaviour that include both personality and environmental factors. Exhibit 10-2 outlines the major dimensions.

Exhibit 10-2 Classification of mental disorders.

intellectual	— mental retardation
behavioural (overt)	— attention deficit disorders — conduct disorders
emotional	— anxiety disorders of childhood and adolescence — other disorders of childhood and adolescence
physical	— eating disorders — stereotyped movement disorders — other disorders with physical manifestations
developmental	— pervasive developmental disorders — specific developmental disorders

(American Psychiatric Association, 1980.)

Dimensional classification

The dimensional or statistical classification system of emotional disorders is more limited than the system propounded in DSM III. However, some educators prefer it because it has been empirically derived and describes behaviours typically seen in the classroom (Von Issor, Quay, and Love, 1980). Quay and his colleagues (1972, 1975, 1979) used behaviour ratings by teachers and parents, children's life-history characteristics, and children's questionnaire responses to derive four behavioural dimensions — conduct disorders; anxiety and withdrawal; socialized aggression; and immaturity.

Dimensions similar to those discovered by Quay have been found with remarkable consistency in many samples of children. For example, McDermott (1980, 1981) analyzed data in which more than 900 teachers observed and rated the behaviour of 2,527 Canadian school children using the Bristol Social Adjustment Guides (Stott, 1979); the Bristol scale provides ratings on a hundred statements about children's behaviour. Statistical analysis of the data found major dimensions similar to those discovered by Quay and other researchers.

The dimensional classification provides a relatively reliable basis for description (Achenbach and Edelbrock, 1978; Quay, 1975). We shall discuss the behavioural components of this classification when we look at the characteristics of emotionally disturbed children.

PREVALENCE OF EMOTIONAL DISTURBANCE

Children in ever-increasing numbers are currently being identified as emotionally disturbed. However, estimates of the prevalence of emotional disturbance vary tremendously, chiefly because of the lack of a clear and precise definitional construct. In Canada, we have made no systematic survey of disturbed individuals in the population. Such a survey would be extremely difficult, because notions of emotional disturbance are continually changing.

Parents and teachers tend to describe twenty to thirty percent of children at any given age as "having problems." They see ten to fifteen percent of children as in need of professional assistance for behavioural problems (Wood, 1982). However, in a longitudinal study of a large sample of school children, Rubin and Balow (1978) found that the individuals identified as "having problems" varied from year to year. After six years of schooling, almost sixty percent of the sampled children had been identified as a problem by at least one teacher.

Other surveys have indicated that anywhere from 0.01 to 40 percent of children may be considered disturbed, depending on the age of the children, the criteria used (Balow, 1979; Morse, 1975), and the level of severity focused upon. The best available research data indicates that 6 to 10 percent of school-age children exhibit serious and persistent behaviour problems (Kauffman, 1981).

The vast majority of children identified as emotionally disturbed fall into the mild and moderate categories. Boys outnumber girls by at least two to one in every classification, from mild through profound (Kelly, Bullock, and Dykes, 1977). Overall, boys exhibit more aggression and conduct disorders than girls (Quay, 1979; Shultz, Salvia, and Feinn, 1974); boys with the more serious forms of these disorders may outnumber girls by as high a ratio as twelve to one (Cummings and Finger, 1980). First-born males are more likely than later-borns to exhibit behaviour disorders and to be rated by teachers as anxious and aggressive toward their peers (Lahey, Hammer, Crumrine, and Forehand, 1980).

Most emotionally disturbed children come to the attention of professionals in the middle childhood or early teen years (Kneedler, 1984). The prevalence of behaviour disorders is low in the beginning grades, reaches a peak in the middle grades, and begins to fall off in junior high until the last years of high school (Morse, Cutler, and Fink, 1964).

As stated earlier, students from minority groups and those with other handicapping conditions are more likely to be identified as disturbed or maladjusted. Children from lower socioeconomic levels are also more likely to be regarded as problems.

ETIOLOGY OF EMOTIONAL DISTURBANCE

Historically, severe social deviance was attributed to demonic possession and treated through exorcism and other religious rituals. In the early 1900s, Freud and others promoted the idea that deviant behaviour could be explained in terms of subconscious phenomena and inner turmoil. More recently, some theorists have attributed disturbed behaviour to inappropriate learning. Other researchers focused on poor interactions between the child and the environment. Still others have suggested that aberrant behaviour is the result of such biological causes as brain damage, genetic factors, or biochemical differences.

Psychiatrists have traditionally placed great emphasis on identifying the causes of emotional disturbance in children. They hoped that an understanding of the origin of the disorder would lead directly to its treatment and cure. However, despite a vast amount of research, there is still no empirical evidence linking emotional disturbance to its causes (Kauffman, 1981; Kauffman and Kneedler, 1981). Of the many variables contributing to human experience, none has been conclusively shown to underlie emotional problems. Fortunately, however, it is not usually necessary to pinpoint the precise etiology of a behaviour disorder in order to provide effective intervention (Kauffman, 1977).

Biophysical model

Supporters of a biophysical approach believe that behaviour disorders can be traced to biological causes. The disorders may be inherited, may be acquired prenatally or perinatally, or may result from accidents, disease, or malnutrition later in life. However, even when a biophysical problem does exist, environmental factors probably combine with it to trigger behavioural disorders.

Traditionally, information about the relationship between biological factors and behaviour disorders has been scarce. Some evidence does suggest that certain biological factors do increase the risk of an emotional disturbance. These biological factors include genetic conditions, constitutional conditions, prenatal and birth factors, and environmental hazards. However, as in the case of mental retardation, biological causes are generally more evident among severely and profoundly disturbed children.

Geneticists maintain that no genes directly determine behaviour. However, some genes do determine enzymatic and biochemical functions that, in turn, can have both major and subtle behavioural effects. Some very specific genetic defects may cause dramatically disturbed behavioural functioning.

The relationship between brain damage and behaviour disorders continues to baffle researchers. Although severe and profound emotional disturbances may well be attributed to brain dysfunction (Werry, 1979), the same cannot be said for mild and moderate disorders. Indeed, most behaviour disorders are not caused by brain dysfunction, and many children with brain disorders do not show behavioural disturbances (Werry, 1979).

In the post-natal period, research indicates that severe, chronic deprivation of either general nutritional needs or certain special-diet substances can cause behaviour disorders along with physical disorders and mental retardation (Lahey and Ciminero, 1980). Malnutrition is not a widespread problem in Canada. Indeed, obesity is currently the major nutritional problem of the child population (Bateson, 1979).

Although behaviour may well be influenced by genetic, neurological, and biochemical factors, there is no real evidence that biological factors alone are at the root of the problem. Biology is hardly destiny, for social influences combine with biological predispositions to shape behaviour. A child's behaviour is profoundly influenced by the environment.

Psychosocial factors

The family is universally recognized as a fundamental influence on child behaviour. The family structure establishes the norms of behaviour and teaches, explicitly and implicitly, social, moral, and psychological lessons to the developing child. Therefore, much research and theory has focused on family patterns as possible sources of behaviour disorders.

A number of variables in the family environment appear to be related to behaviour disorders. These include:

- Divorce and separation.
- The absence of one or both parents.
- Parental conflict (Anthony, 1970; Parke and Collmer, 1975).
- Parent hostility, neglect, or abuse.
- Inconsistent or very lax discipline (Anthony, 1970; Hetherington and Martin, 1979).
- Chronic illness of one or both parents (Jenkins, 1966).

Deviant behaviour usually involves the interaction of several factors rather than a single cause. Each additional variable increases the risk of behaviour disorders, and the risk is greatest when several factors combine (Kauffman, 1977). Family conditions may predispose a child to develop behaviour disorders or may precipitate maladaptive behaviours through an immediate stress or incident.

Extrafamilial influences

Extrafamilial influences are those social agencies outside the family that influence a child's cognitive, social, and emotional development. Three important extrafamilial agents of socialization are schools, peer groups, and television.

Some researchers (Liebert, Sprafkin, and Davidson, 1982) believe that television has changed our daily lives more than any other technological innovation of the twentieth century. In most homes, youngsters begin watching television at approximately one and a half to two years of age (Hapkewicz, 1979). Between the ages of three and eleven, Canadian children watch about three to four hours of television a day. The time increases gradually until about age twelve, then declines somewhat during adolescence (Murray, 1980).

Research has shown that certain television programs have undesirable effects on social behaviour (Huston-Stein, Fox, Greer, Watkins, and Whitaker, 1981). Eighty percent of all prime-time television programs contain at least one incident of physical violence. On average, prime-time programs portray 7.5 violent acts an hour (Gerbner, Gross, Morgan, and Signorelli, 1980). By the time children are five years of age, they have viewed an estimated 30 000 violently aggressive acts on television (Eron, 1982). By the time they are sixteen, they have spent more time watching television than in school and have viewed over 13 000 television killings (Waters and Malamud, 1975).

Observation of aggression results in aggressive behaviour (Bandura, 1977). Not only is television a likely cause of aggressive behaviours in children but the effects are long-standing (Eron, 1982). Moreover, continued exposure to television violence encourages a child to become more aggressive and to choose more aggressive programs.

An interesting longitudinal study in the remote Canadian North (Grangberg and Steinbring, 1980) looked at three communities. Two of the communities were comprised of Manitoba Cree Indians and the third of Euro-Canadians. In one of the Cree communities, measures of aggression were taken before and after the introduction of television. The results were compared to the two control groups — the other Cree community, which had no television, and the Euro-Canadians, who had watched television for up to twenty years. In the experimental community, children who had a great deal of exposure to television showed an increase in aggressive behaviour. This increase was not found in children who watched less television, or in the community as a whole.

Eron (1982) suggests that children increase their viewing of violence up to the third grade, and then start to decrease it. However, the strongest relations between television violence and both simultaneous and later aggression have been reported for children in the eight- to twelve-year-old age range (Eron, 1982). Eron (1982) speculates that, because aggressive children tend to be unpopular, they spend more time watching television. The violence they see there serves to reassure them of the appropriateness of their behaviour while teaching them new coercive techniques.

A steady diet of violent programming may convince a child that the outside world is a violent place inhabited by people who rely on aggressive strategies to resolve conflicts. One research team (Eron, Heusmann, Brice, Fischer, and Mermalstein, 1983) looked at seven- to nine-year-old boys and girls who were judged to be highly aggressive by their peers. These children not only preferred violent programming but believed that violent shows were an accurate portrayal of everyday life.

Conceptual models of emotional disturbance

A number of conceptual models that attempt to explain emotional disturbance have emerged. These models tend to represent the different orientations of different disciplines. The models differ considerably in the importance they attach to finding the causes of disturbance. The psychodynamic model, for example, focuses rather exclusively on causation while the behavioural model is concerned with the outward manifestations of disturbance. The following models are the most relevant to educational intervention.

Psychodynamic approach

The psychodynamic approach continues to exert a strong and persuasive influence on the terminology, definitions, and taxonomies of emotional disturbance. The psychodynamic approach originated with Sigmund Freud in the early 1900s. It is a complex theory that attempts to locate the origins of behaviour disorders within the context of psychological development.

Proponents of the psychodynamic approach maintain that traditional psychoanalytic concepts can be used to find the underlying causes of emotional disturbance. Psychodynamic psychology is concerned with the development of and interaction among the intrapsychic (mental) processes believed to underlie human behaviour. According to this approach, behaviour disorders are observable symptoms reflecting the inner turmoil created by abnormal intrapsychic processes.

Advocates of psychodynamic approaches see little value in changing a person's behaviour. Instead, they concentrate on altering the underlying psychopathology by helping the person remember unfortunate experiences from infancy and early childhood. These memories provide insight, allowing the person to come to grips with the causes of disturbed behaviour.

Psychodynamic psychology has influenced the treatment of emotionally disturbed children in two major ways. First, it has been used to treat children in clinics, institutions, and schools, giving rise to such recent approaches as play therapy (Axline, 1969) and transactional analysis (Berne, 1964). Second, psychodynamic approaches have been used in educational settings and have played a large role in education for emotionally disturbed children. In the 1950s and 1960s, psychodynamic psychology was the dominant approach to educating the behaviourally disordered. Today, however, special education includes a broader range of intervention practices (Cullinan and Epstein, 1982).

Behavioural approaches

Early twentieth-century investigations of reflexive and voluntary behaviour laid the groundwork for modern behavioural psychology. Bolstered by Skinner's principles of operant conditioning, the behavioural model has exerted a profound influence upon psychotherapy, counselling, education, and special education (Cullinan and Epstein, 1982).

Behaviourists believe that all behaviour is learned, and that emotional disturbance represents inappropriate learning. In general, they do not define and classify emotional disturbance. Instead, they try to understand its origins by observing the relationship among the complex environmental factors that elicit and support deviant behaviour. They describe and measure deviant behaviour, and note the conditions under which it occurs. By changing these conditions, they attempt to extinguish undesirable behaviour.

Ecological approach

Educators of the emotionally disturbed have recently begun to examine the ecological concepts used in anthropology, ethnology, psychology, sociology, and other disciplines (Cullinan, Epstein and Lloyd, 1983). The ecological approach to emotional disturbance emphasizes the need to look at the total interaction of the child with the social environment. This approach assumes that aberrant behaviour results from a variety of interactions and transactions between the child and others in the environment.

The ecological approach reduces the danger of assuming that behavioural problems reside wholly within the child. The environment may not be providing the necessary supports to enable the child to progress in adaptive development. In order to overcome the disturbance in the interaction between child and environment, changes may need to be made in both.

Psychoeducational approach

Teachers are trained to focus on their students' positive learning goals rather than on their defects and problems. This philosophical framework is typical of the psychoeducational approach to behaviour disorders. It is a more positive, learning-directed approach than other forms of mental health treatment.

Advocates of the psychoeducational approach agree that children with behaviour disorders may have dealt unsuccessfully with developmental problems. While the approach attempts to discover why children display problem behaviour, it also lays stress on the acquisition of academic and daily-living skills.

Holistic approach

The holistic approach attempts to encompass many of the others. This approach recognizes that the etiology of inappropriate behaviour may be illness, childhood trauma, poor relations with others, inappropriate learning, problems in socialization, or any combination of these. Holistic professionals attempt to co-ordinate the many disciplines involved with the emotionally disturbed child (Hewett, 1974).

PREVENTION OF EMOTIONAL DISTURBANCE

If the specific causes of emotional disturbance were known, then prevention would be greatly simplified. However, with no empirical data on etiology, prevention measures can only focus on such general areas as nutrition, the family climate, and the prevention of child abuse and neglect. Of course, as for all exceptional conditions, early identification and intervention are vitally important.

Recently there has been increased interest in prevention manoeuvres in child mental health programs in Canada (McConville, 1982). The Mental Health Division of the Department of National Health and Welfare, for example, has appointed a Task Force on Child Mental Health to study clinical research endeavours in this area. The Task Force emphasizes early intervention to minimize the number of child and adolescent mental health disorders. In addition, the Clearing House Resource Services Project of the

Canadian Mental Health Association is well underway. This project collects information on mental health resources under the categories of promotion, prevention, treatment, care, and rehabilitation.

In Canada, such factors as ethnic variation, long distances, and marked regional variations in the nature and availability of services, pose particular challenges to the provision of mental health care for children. However, in many areas, integrated children's services have been developed to link up departments and jurisdictions and provide more efficient care (McConville, 1982).

DIAGNOSIS AND ASSESSMENT OF EMOTIONAL DISTURBANCE

Emotional disturbance is easier to identify than to define or classify. Problem behaviours are easily observed and seldom escape notice. Children with conduct disorders attract attention with their overtly disruptive behaviours. Immature and withdrawn children are a little harder to identify, but still fairly recognizable.

However, it is often difficult to determine whether problem behaviour is serious enough to warrant further diagnosis. Many temporary behaviour disorders occur in normally developing children. We do not want to identify a child incorrectly any more than we want to overlook a child who needs help.

A number of screening procedures have been devised to identify youngsters who deviate significantly in inter- and intra-personal learning and social behaviours. These procedures take into account a variety of settings and circumstances. Screening is used to:

- Locate children who are disturbed.
- Determine educational placement.
- Determine and assess teaching and management approaches (Kneedler, 1984).

The identification of children with behaviour disorders often begins with a feeling in the mind of a parent or teacher that something is wrong. The informal judgement of teachers has served as a fairly reliable means of screening children for emotional problems (Fremont, Klingsporn, and Wilson, 1976; Harris, King, and Drummond, 1978; Nelson, 1971). Other informal measures have included children's ratings of their peers and children's ratings of their own behaviour (Bower, 1969).

To help quantify and document subjective judgements, teachers commonly use behavioural checklists or teacher rating scales. The Devereux Child Behaviour Rating Scale (Spivack and Spotts, 1966), for example, is widely employed. The Bristol Social Adjustment Guides (Stott, 1979), which we mentioned earlier, contain a hundred statements about behaviour to be rated by teachers or others who know the child. The Bristol scales have separate editions for children in school, the family, or a residential institution. They also contain an optional delinquency prediction score for boys.

Teachers may also employ such behavioural analysis techniques as direct observation. A well-trained teacher can count and record a variety of problematic behaviours. For example, a teacher may be particularly worried about the physically aggressive behaviour shown by a young boy, James. In the course of a schoolday, James slaps, punches, and generally aggravates the other children in the room. The teacher begins by measuring James' behaviour and comparing it to that of three other children in the class. Over a period of at least five days, the teacher records a checkmark on a tally sheet each time James and the other three children exhibit physical aggression. The average number of aggressive behaviours in a day constitutes a baseline. The teacher can profile James' baseline, compare it to those of the other children, and decide whether to refer him for intensive assessment. In addition, when a program is begun to improve James' behaviour, the teacher can quickly measure James' progress by comparing his current status to the baseline.

Figure 10-1 shows the baseline for James and the other three children.

Figure 10-1 Baseline graph for charting physical aggression in children.

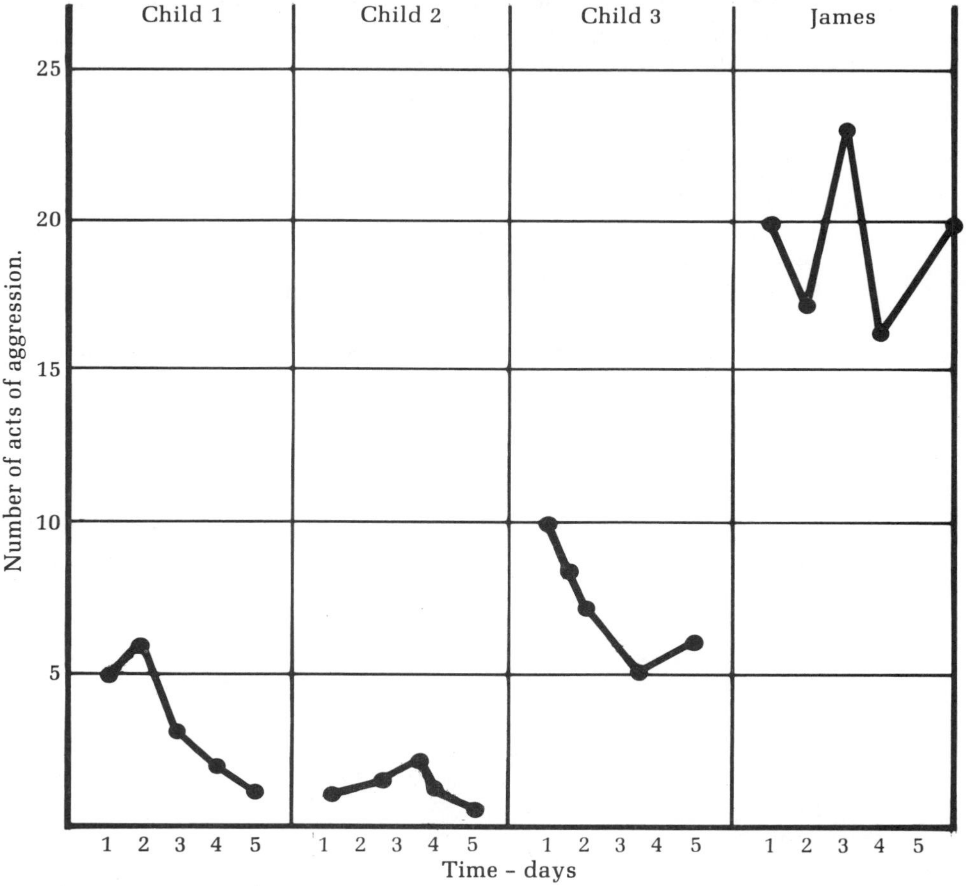

After screening, a child may be referred for diagnosis to a variety of personnel — psychologist, psychiatrist, social worker, special educator, or counsellor. Although a formal diagnosis may contain components that assess the child's potential and performance, the overall assessment remains subjective. No measure of emotional disturbance parallels the IQ test; emotions are simply not defined by subjective parameters.

The diagnostic process includes interviews with the child and the parents, behavioural observation, reports by the child, and peer reports. Also included may be measures of personality and self-concept such as the Piers-Harris Children's Self Concept Scale (Piers, 1969). However, these require a considerable degree of skill and experience to administer.

CHARACTERISTICS OF THE EMOTIONALLY DISTURBED

Children with behaviour disorders are difficult, cantankerous, and disruptive. Over a hundred characteristics have been attributed to them. Mildly and moderately emotionally disturbed children lack social skills and have unfortunate personality traits that elicit dislike and rejection from others. Frequently, they suffer from low self-esteem and poor self-concept.

Exhibit 10-3 lists the most common characteristics and behaviours of emotionally disturbed children. These traits only become problems when they occur chronically, acutely, and in tandem.

Exhibit 10-3 Characteristics and behaviours attributed to mildly and moderately emotionally disturbed children.

Socialized aggression	*Immaturity*
assaultive	clumsy
delinquent activity	frustrated easily
destructive	lacking initiative
disobedient	low tolerance levels
fighting	messy
gang vandalism	passive
hostility	short attention span
lying	slow worker
physically abusive	socially inadequate
sexually precocious	
socially maladjusted	
stealing	
substance abuse	
truancy	
vandalism	
verbally abusive	

Conduct disorders	*Anxiety and withdrawal*
assaultive	anxious
bossy	apathetic
cantankerous	apprehensive
defiant	clinging
destructive	cold
difficult	crying
disobedient	daydreaming
disruptive	dependent
distractible	depressed
fighting	detached
hostile	fantasizing
hyperaggressive	fearful
hyperactive	flat
impertinent	hand wringing
impulsive	headaches
insulting	hostile
irresponsible	inhibited
jealous	isolated
lacking self control	mute
lacking social skills	nauseated
lacking responsiveness	nervous
low self esteem	nightmares
lying	neurotic
physically aggressive	obsessive
poor interpersonal relations	over-controlled
poor self concept	pains
quarrelsome	perfectionist
short attention span	phobic
teasing	regressive behaviour
threatening	resistant to change
unpredictable	restless
verbally aggressive	secretive
	self-conscious
	self-reproachful
	short attention span
	shy
	suspicious
	timid
	threatened
	withdrawn

Despite these problems, the outlook for emotionally disturbed children is far from hopeless. Profile 10-1 presents the case of one child who managed to find himself and gain a footing on the road to success.

PROFILE 10-1

When Dick was twelve, he was involved in a loud dispute with his classroom teacher, and later with the school principal. This was the latest in a long series of disputes related to fights with other students, classroom arguments over the teacher's "fairness," and other noisy, disruptive behaviour. Dick had been in serious trouble with the principal on several earlier occasions. As a result of this final dispute, he was suspended from school. He was sent home on Friday afternoon with instructions not to return until a plan was worked out with his parents.

Dick did return, however. On Sunday afternoon, he went back to the school with a wagon full of rocks. Beginning at the back of the school building, he systematically broke window after window. By the time the police arrived, he had broken more than seventy windows and had circled half the building.

Dick's behaviour lent him a notoriety many other twelve-year-olds might have covertly envied. He was placed in a special program under the guidance of a special-class teacher. This teacher quickly saw the unhappiness beneath the wild outbursts of temper.

At first, Dick was fearful and apprehensive about being placed in a school for "crazies." However, within a few weeks, he had shed his hard shell and was pouring his energy into awkward but well-intentioned efforts to help some of his less able peers. Although there were some outbursts of the famous temper, these were limited to a few fights and more frequent kicking of walls, desks, and waste baskets.

During Dick's two years in a special program, his aggressive behaviours diminished. When his parents moved to another school district, he entered a regular school program. He progressed through his high-school years in a relatively unexceptional manner. (Adapted from Wood, 1982.)

Kauffman (1977) has outlined some general characteristics of behaviourally disordered children, as follows.

- The behaviours they exhibit do not compare favourably with those manifested by normal children.
- The problem behaviours are generally unacceptable to the child, to normal peers, and to adults.
- The number of problem behaviours exhibited is comparatively high.
- The problem behaviours interfere with the child's expected performance relative to chronological age.
- The intellectual capacity and academic achievement of behaviourally disturbed students are generally below average.

There is not room here to examine all the myriad problem behaviours that youngsters may display. In this section, we will look at the behavioural categories outlined by the dimensional classification system. Bear in mind, however, that many behaviours in these categories overlap.

Conduct disorders

All children have bad days, as do their teachers and parents. However, instead of articulating their distress, children reveal it in their behaviour. Most children do this at some time, but emotionally disturbed children exhibit problem behaviours that are both acute and chronic.

Hyperaggressive and highly disruptive children form the major portion of those identified in the schools as emotionally disturbed or behaviourally disordered (Kauffman, 1985). Aggression is of more concern to teachers than any other behaviour disorder (Bullock and Brown, 1972). Although aggression in moderation is a useful survival tool, it becomes a problem when it is prolonged, frequent and severe.

Conduct-disordered children are far from ideal students. They generally take part in verbal and physical aggression, and are poor at building interpersonal relationships. Children with conduct disorders are disobedient, destructive, defiant, disruptive, assaultive, impertinent, and jealous. They refuse to comply with requests, school rules, and the conventional limits of behaviour. Typically, they do not respond to adults who try to help them (Hallahan and Kauffman, 1982).

Children with conduct disorders have failed to develop reliable internal controls. Their behaviour is impulsive, distractible, hyperactive, and disruptive. They have short attention spans, and sometimes seem not to know right from wrong. Their behaviour is resistant to change through the usual forms of discipline. They have been in trouble so often that they are inured to scolding and punishment.

The behaviour of conduct-disordered children is not age-appropriate. For example, temper tantrums are common among two- and three-year-olds as these very young children strive toward independence. In a twelve-year-old, however, a temper tantrum is clearly inappropriate behaviour.

Aggression can be defined as any form of behaviour designed to harm or injure another living being who is motivated to avoid such treatment (Baron and Bryne, 1981). Children learn aggressive behaviour in many ways — by observing parents, siblings, friends, and characters from television and films. Children are more likely to be aggressive if they have opportunities to practice aggression, especially if no unpleasant consequences follow.

One of the most reliable findings in child-rearing literature maintains that cold and rejecting parents who apply physical punishment erratically and who permit their child to express frequent aggressive impulses are likely to raise hostile, aggressive children (Eron, 1982; Olweus, 1980). When parents ignore a child's aggressive outbursts, they legitimize combative activities and fail to encourage control over aggressive urges. This unchecked aggression then escalates until the parents spank their child. Unfortunately, the spanking serves as a model of the very aggressive behaviour that the parents are trying to suppress. Parents who rely on physical punishment to discipline aggression have children who are highly aggressive outside the home setting in which punishment normally occurs (Eron, 1982).

Although parental attitudes and child-rearing techniques are often crucial in the development of aggressive behaviour, many other forces may also be at work. When children find their aggression rewarded, for example, then the behaviour is reinforced. A young child who slaps another to obtain a special toy will consider the toy a reward for poor behaviour if no-one intervenes. As stated earlier, television has been cited as another factor in forming or aggravating aggressive tendencies.

The problems created by the aggressive behaviour of disturbed children should not be underestimated. Highly aggressive three-year-olds are likely to become aggressive five-year-olds (Emmerich, 1966). Children's levels of physical and verbal aggression at ages six through ten are fairly good predictors of their tendency to threaten, insult, tease, and compete with peers at ages ten to fourteen (Kagan and Moss, 1962; Olweus, 1979). Highly aggressive children are more likely to make fewer friends, be attacked by peers, and fail in school.

Children do not grow out of conduct disorders. Antisocial behaviour in childhood generally leads to poor social adjustment and mental health in later years, especially for boys. Conduct-disordered children are also at a high risk for delinquency (Robins, 1979). Children who are neurotic and withdrawn are apparently much more likely to later find and hold a job, overcome their emotional problems, and stay out of jails and mental hospitals than are children with conduct problems (Hallahan and Kauffman, 1982).

Withdrawal, anxiety, and isolation are characteristic of some emotionally disturbed children.
(C. Cox)

Anxiety and withdrawal

Conduct-disordered children externalize their behaviour through such acts as disobedience, lying, stealing, fighting, truancy, sexual delinquency, and destructiveness. In contrast, anxious and withdrawn children internalize their behaviour (Achenback, 1966). They may suffer from nausea, pains, headaches, phobias, fears, obsessions, shyness, nightmares, crying, depression, self-consciousness, and withdrawal. Withdrawn children are fearful, secretive, and apathetic. They tend to spend large amounts of time fantasizing and day-dreaming instead of interacting with those around them. Younger children may show regressive behaviours such as thumb-sucking, clinging, and toilet accidents.

Anxiety can be described as a fear with a future reference. Many people, for example, are anxious about entering new situations and meeting new people. In fact, in a survey of high-school-age and college students (Zimbordo, Pilkonis, and Norwood, 1975), forty percent reported that extreme shyness accompanied their interpersonal relations throughout their growing-up period. However, withdrawn and anxious children are so shy they find it painful to even go to school.

A **phobia** is an anxiety reaction that is specific to one stimulus, an intense fear with no rational basis. Some of the most common phobias are fears of the dark, of animals, of vehicles, and of school. However, any object or event can become the occasion for a phobic reaction. Rachman and Seligman (1976) have reported cases in which people developed powerful fears of chocolates and vegetables.

School phobias may be accompanied by physical illness associated with tension and extreme emotion. If forced to go to school, children with school phobias may spend most of the time either mute or crying. Hersov (1960) saw three distinctive patterns of school phobia based on the child's experience at home and at school. In the first, the child was timid at school and demanding at home, with an overindulgent mother and a passive father. In the second, the child was obedient at home and timid at school, with an overcontrolling mother and a passive father. In the third, the child was willful at home and friendly at school, with an overindulgent mother and a firm father. These findings point explicitly to the importance of the family factors in the development of school phobias.

Children who suffer from personality disorders do not suffer phobias. Instead they develop a pattern of adjustment to cope with anxiety. In doing so, they forego assertive, independent behaviour and tend to become excessively withdrawn. These children have low self-concept and little self-esteem. They are self-conscious, hypersensitive, and sad much of the time.

Unlike conduct-disordered children, whose disruptive behaviours call attention to them, anxious or withdrawn children may be overlooked in the classroom. Also unlike conduct-disordered children, anxious and withdrawn children are greater threats to themselves than to those around them. These children have limited or ineffectual social relationships. The most extreme manifestation of their low self-image is suicide, a phenomenon among young people that is currently drawing increased attention (e.g. Cohen-Sandler, Berman, and King, 1982).

Children whose anxiety disorders diminish in adolescence are not particularly likely to show serious maladjustment in adulthood. However, anxiety disorders in later adolescence do appear to predict adult maladjustment (Gersten, Langner, Eisenberg, Simcha-Fagen, and McCarthy, 1976). Anxiety-ridden older adolescents are more likely to be female, although the sex ratio is equal until that age (Cullinan and Epstein, 1982).

Immature children

Not much is known about the special nature of immature children. Although similar to withdrawn children, immature children seem less able to function in the regular classroom. They appear to be very clumsy, socially inadequate, passive, easily frustrated, messy, and lacking in initiative. They have a short attention span and frequently fail to finish assignments. Often they show a preference for younger playmates.

Socialized aggression

Children characterized as unsocialized and aggressive are quickly spotted by teachers and families. These children are hostile, disobedient, destructive, and often verbally and physically abusive. They tend to lie, steal, and vandalize, sometimes assaulting people as well as property. Unlike conduct-disordered children they are active in delinquent groups and loyal to delinquent friends. They are chronic violators of broad cultural mores and social values.

Socialized aggressive children are sometimes classed as socially maladjusted rather than emotionally disturbed. According to this distinction, emotional disturbance is persistently distressing to the child while social maladjustment may not be. Within their gangs, unsocialized, aggressive children may enjoy considerable prestige as a result of their aggressive and norm-violating behaviours. The United States federal definition of severe emotional disturbance (behavioural disorders) specifically excludes youngsters who are socially maladjusted but not emotionally disturbed (Cullinan and Epstein, 1982).

Socially maladjusted children, as well as those labelled unsocialized and aggressive, may take part in behaviours that include gang vandalism, stealing, fighting, truancy, sexual precocity, and substance abuse. These behaviours can rapidly lead to troubles with the law. Children who come to the attention of the courts gain a new label — juvenile delinquent.

Juvenile delinquency

Few human behaviours have been subject to as many varied and contradictory explanations as criminal activity. All the possible etiologies we have presented for emotional disturbance, plus quite a few more, have been proposed to account for juvenile delinquency. Leyton (1979) views unfortunate family relationships as paramount in delinquency. Ayers (1978) sees low self-confidence and fear of failure as characteristic of young offenders. Others attribute at least some responsibility for delinquency to poor self-concept and school failure (Jacobson, 1974; Mann, Goodman, and Wiederholt, 1978).

Some researchers believe that delinquent youth have a behaviour trait known as **social anomie**, a lack of entrenched societal norms and values. In other words, delinquent youths do not appear to internalize a coherent set of values and standards for regulating their own behaviour.

Others researchers adhere to the appealing theory of an innate criminal personality type. A survey of teachers in Canadian federal correctional facilities indicated that eighty percent attributed criminal personalities to offenders (Doig, 1979). Similarly, over half the police officers in a mid-sized Canadian city agreed that most criminals have criminal personalities (Hylton and Matonovitch, 1979).

The average inmate in Canada's prisons was once an adolescent with a behaviour problem. Typically, the problem first showed up in elementary school, causing the child to fail once or twice. Often the child was passed into high school because the elementary school lacked the resources to devote any more attention to such a troublesome, cantankerous, and potentially dangerous youngster (*Report to the Solicitor General*, 1979).

Offences by juveniles are on the rise (Bennett and Winzer, 1980; Leyton, 1979). This presents a grave concern to parents, the juvenile justice system, law enforcement agencies, and educators. Delinquency peaks during adolescence, although the age of children committing delinquent acts is decreasing. Traditionally the great majority of offenders have been boys, but delinquent behaviour is currently increasing among females.

Certain groups are disproportionately represented in the delinquent population. In British Columbia, for example, Native and Métis youth comprise almost twenty-five percent of the population in youth containment (Markwart, 1981).

Along with accelerated rates of juvenile crime, there has been a striking increase in the rate of recidivism. A **recidivist** is anyone incarcerated for new charges within two years of release from prison. Current estimates of Canadian recidivism rates range from forty-eight to sixty percent. Seventy percent of recidivists return to jail within the first year. Twice as many fifteen-year-olds as twenty-year-olds return to some form of confinement (Bennett and Winzer, 1980; Gendreau, Madden, and Leipeiger, 1977).

Due to increased rates of juvenile offences, incarceration, and recidivism concern is growing about the effectiveness of correctional programs. In addition, more research is badly needed into the causes and prevention of delinquent behaviour.

DEVELOPMENTAL CONSEQUENCES OF EMOTIONAL DISTURBANCE

Behaviourally disordered children deviate significantly from their peers in the quantity, quality, and modes of their emotional expression. Emotional disturbance may take one of many specific forms, or it may be manifested in pervasive adjustment difficulties. The severity of disturbance may range from mild to serious and debilitating.

Academic progress

In general, emotionally disturbed children do not achieve academically at the expected level for either their mental or chronological age. Only rarely is a disturbed child academically advanced. The few disturbed children who seem competent academically are seldom able to apply their skills to everyday problems (Hallahan and Kauffman, 1982).

Emotionally disturbed children are usually behind in reading, arithmetic, and spelling (Rose, Epstein, Cullinan, and Lloyd, 1981). Many also display special problems commonly associated with learning disabilities. These include distractibility, impulsivity, and hyperactivity.

Behaviour problems are often the cause of academic failure. Children with conduct disorders display problems early in their school careers. Children who are busy being aggressive and disruptive are not participating in the instructional process. They enter a pattern of severe academic failure that quickly becomes cyclical. Because these children do not learn the skills to cope with academic pressures they react by withdrawing or lashing out in angry frustration. This draws them deeper into frustration and failure.

Profile 10-2 presents a conduct-disordered child and one intervention used by his teacher.

PROFILE 10-2

As a pre-schooler in nursery school, Gary aggressively bit, fought, and scratched his way through the program. He threw terrible temper tantrums, and did not stop until he was about ten years old. He spent much of his time in elementary school ejected from the classroom or in the principal's office.

During Gary's first year in junior high school, his disruptive behaviour, fighting, and irrational conduct led to a number of suspensions. His achievement was at a very low level, hardly surprising given his behaviour problems, his apparent lack of academic interests, and his resentment of school and authority. Gary had large gaps in reading skills, both for word attack and comprehension. His spelling was poor and creative writing exercises were beyond him. Only in math did he show any interest or potential. Throughout his early school years, Gary worked at math and achieved at level. During math periods, his behaviour was also relatively serene.

By the middle of Gary's first year in junior high school, his behaviour had resulted in severe penalties. After he lit a fire on the school bus, he was transferred to a special class for children with problems. Even among this smaller group, Gary's behaviour continued to be outlandish. His achievement and academic interest were minimal, and he developed a more pronounced pattern of physical assault, swearing, truancy, and smoking.

Gary's teacher could see that his behaviour during math was calm while his behaviour during reading or language was at its most violent. In light of this, the teacher mounted a two-pronged program to alter Gary's behaviour and improve his academic functioning.

Gary's classroom environment was changed so that students worked in cubicles on individual programs for the first half of the morning. At the same time, a token economy system was established with the co-operation and input of all students in the class. Token economies are described later in this chapter.

The teacher also decided to stress Gary's strengths in order to help his weaknesses. Reading, as a specific subject area, was eliminated from his timetable. Math became the fulcrum of Gary's education, and the starting point for integrated programming. For example, as Gary tackled math word problems, his reading comprehension improved; he later enjoyed writing math problems for the class. Math concepts, such as distance and scale, were extended to other areas, such as social studies.

By the end of the school year, Gary's reading tests showed an advance of almost two years in vocabulary, word attack skills, and comprehension. As Gary found success in reading, his other subject areas also showed progress. Most important, however, his behaviour improved dramatically. While aggressive episodes continued, they were more often directed toward inanimate objects. Verbal abuse decreased and truancy was eliminated as Gary, for probably the first time in his life, began to see value in the learning experience.

Despite this progress, Gary is not yet ready to be integrated back into a regular program. He still requires structured and consistent behavioural intervention in a supportive environment that offers much success. However, Gary's self-esteem is definitely on the rise. He is beginning to be accepted and even admired by other students.

Conduct-disordered children are unwilling to submit to teacher authority. They create problems in classroom management, often alienating teachers and other students in the process. They soon learn to dislike the learning process and resent the school experience, and often resort to truancy. Withdrawn and anxious children have a different set of learning problems. Timid, passive behaviour, dependency, isolation, and withdrawal interfere with these children's development of their potential (Conger and Keane, 1981).

Research shows that mildly and moderately emotionally disturbed children are likely to perform less well on tests of mental ability. Research shows that most students identified as emotionally disturbed or behaviourally disordered are lower in IQ and achievement than the mean for their normal classmates (Kauffman, 1985).

Communication

Behaviourally disturbed children cannot be said to have communication disorders as such. Indeed, they often communicate too well. They interrupt in class, swear, use aggressive language, speak defiantly to adults, and indiscriminately vent their emotions. They often use language to disrupt and control social situations. This excessive use of language may not be a communication problem, but it is certainly a social problem.

Social development

Children with excessive feelings of aggression and defiance inevitably develop intense and far-ranging interpersonal problems. Emotionally disturbed children fail to interact appropriately with their teachers and are disliked by most of their peers (Drabman and Patterson, 1981; Newman and Simpson, 1983).

Aggressive children provoke a large number of fights and are more likely to become the targets of aggression. In fact, nonaggressive children who are harmed under ambiguous circumstances are much more likely to retaliate if the harmdoer has a reputation as an aggressive child (Dodge and Frame, 1982). Anxious children develop a defeatist attitude, along with feelings of worthlessness and excessive self-criticism. These children are also seriously hampered in social relationships. There is evidence that these and other emotionally disturbed children view themselves as alienated from the social mainstream (Keuthe, 1962; Weinstein, 1965).

PARENTING THE EMOTIONALLY DISTURBED CHILD

Early investigators into the development of childhood aggression assumed that parents' attitudes and child-rearing strategies played an important role. Certainly, there is some truth to this assumption. Children who live in very lax environments, where punishment is erratic and harsh, may never learn to control their aggressive impulses. As well, children who live in highly coercive family settings eventually become resistant to punishment. They learn to fight coercion with coercion, often defying their parents by repeating the very acts for which they are punished (Shaffer, 1985).

However, although parents may contribute to their child's aggression, the child may also influence the parents. Olweus (1980) notes that a child's temperament during the early years influences the mother's reactions to aggression. An impetuous and active boy may exhaust his mother, causing her to become more permissive of aggression. This increases the likelihood of further aggressive behaviour.

Many parents of emotionally disturbed children are indeed exhausted. The abusive, destructive, cantankerous behaviour of their youngsters causes disruption and disharmony in the home. Parents often blame themselves for problem behaviours, and are often held at least partly to blame by friends and neighbours. The behaviour of their children in public serves to embarrass and deflate the self-esteem of the entire family.

INTERVENTION WITH THE EMOTIONALLY DISTURBED

To understand emotionally disturbed children, it is essential to recognize that, among the diversity of symptoms, runs an undercurrent of anxiety, inhibition, apprehension, depression, and overcontrol (Edelbrock, 1979). Methods of intervention for these children have been largely developed according to various theoretical perspectives. No one method has proven effective for all emotionally disturbed children. Indeed, a consensus on intervention is as elusive as a universal definition of the problem.

Medical intervention

Natural sources of behaviour-changing drugs have long been known. However only in the last few decades have synthetic compounds rendered the effects of drugs more predictable. Stimulants and other drugs are often used in the management of behaviour problems.

Methylphenidate (Ritalin) and dextroamphetamine (Deanol) are the most common stimulants used to control the behaviour of disturbed children. Thioridazine (Mellaril), reserpine, and imipramine may also be prescribed for children with behaviour disorders (Guetzloe and Cline, 1979). Antidepressants, such as tricyclicimines, have been administered for such behaviour problems as enuresis and childhood depression. However, there has been little controlled clinical research into the effects of the antidepressants (Connors, 1972).

Researchers have reported a number of positive effects from the use of stimulant drugs. Many children exhibit signs of increased happiness, friendliness, and cooperation. Stimulants may also help the child to focus attention, to think more clearly, to inhibit problem behaviours, to perform in a more controlled manner, and to engage in more goal-directed pursuits (Guetzloe and Cline, 1979).

Connors and Werry (1979) reviewed the literature regarding the relative effects of different types of drug upon children with learning and behaviour problems. They concluded that stimulants produce positive effects when used in carefully controlled dosages along with educational programs. However, drug therapy has also produced many problems, some of which have been discussed in Chapters Two and Seven.

Educational intervention

Traditionally, emotionally disturbed children have chiefly been the concern of psychiatrists and psychologists. Until the 1960s, the preferred treatment for them was psychiatric in nature. However, as behaviourally disordered children have increasingly moved into the orbit of public schools, educators have had to find ways to cope with problem behaviours.

In many cases, special education for disturbed children requires changes in the child's total living environment. For these children, education must involve the family as well as a team of professionals from several fields. In all cases, the teacher must bear in mind that each child is unique. Children must be treated as individuals regardless of similarities in their behaviour patterns.

As we have seen, a number of conceptual models from various disciplines have been used to explain and treat emotional disturbance. Historically, all these models have played important roles in the field of education. Today, educational programs are based mainly upon psychoeducational or behavioural approaches. However, some educators draw ideas from a number of other approaches, arguing that no single model has proven adequate in the management of behaviourally disordered children.

Exhibit 10-4 outlines the main treatments and techniques of each of the major approaches used in education. The biological approach has already been discussed under Medical Intervention.

Psychodynamic approach

The psychodynamic approach was formulated chiefly by psychiatrists and clinical psychologists. These theorists believed that the guiding principles of pychoanalysis should be employed in educational intervention with emotionally disturbed children.

Psychodynamic intervention is aimed at the removal of the internal conflict that is presumed to cause the child's symptoms. Disturbed behaviour is viewed as a pathological imbalance among the dynamic parts of the mind. Educational intervention focuses on uncovering this underlying pathology to improve the child's psychological functioning.

The psychodynamic approach emphasizes the creation of a warm, supportive, nonthreatening atmosphere in which the child can consciously come to terms with repressed anxiety, conflict, and fear. Educational practices are designed to reveal and relieve the child's unconscious emotions and inner psychic conflicts. The teacher's major concern is to help the child overcome inner turmoil rather than to alter behaviour or teach academic skills. Individual, group, and family therapy are important dimensions of this approach.

Exhibit 10-4 Approaches to intervention with emotionally disturbed youngsters.

Approach	*Treatment*	*Sample of Methods*
Biological approach	Alter the child's physiology.	Drug therapy, change in diet.
Psychodynamic approach	Discover the underlying conflicts that cause problem behaviour.	Various therapies, such as play, art, and music. Includes individual, group, and family therapy.
Ecological approach	Change the nature of the interaction between the child and the environment.	Counselling and a team approach.
Psychoeducational approach	Create trust while helping the child to fulfil academic goals.	Therapies, crisis intervention, emphasizing success in academic pursuits.
Behavioural approach	Rearrange environmental events. Focus on behaviour, not underlying causes.	Reinforcers, punishment, time out, contracts, and the like.

Although psychodynamic theories have had considerable influence on educational intervention, the question of its effectiveness remains open. Even with the extension of psychodynamic theory beyond its Freudian psychoanalytic base, adherents are unable to put forward hard evidence of the usefulness of the approach with emotionally disturbed children (Wyne and O'Connor, 1979).

Ecological approach

Advocates of an ecological approach do not treat emotional disturbance as a condition in and of itself. Rather they view problem behaviours as arising from a disturbance or mismatch between the child and the ecosystem. The child acts upon the environment and is in turn acted upon by environmental influences. Problems develop when the child's relationship to a constellation of surrounding influences — family, school, and community — is somehow disturbed.

According to this approach, interventions must be directed at social norms, expectations, and circumstances, as well as at the child. Treatment consists of modifying elements in the child and the environment so that more constructive interactions can take place. In addition to altering the child's behaviour, intervention attempts to render the environment more supportive of desirable behaviour. To accomplish this, treatment must involve the family and the community.

Psychoeducational approach

The psychoeducational approach combines psychodynamic concepts with educational concerns. Educators are interested in finding the source of a student's poor behaviour, but are more involved in helping the student improve academic performance. Educators tend to make use of whatever treatments and techniques seem best for the child, regardless of theoretical orientation. They place a practical emphasis upon the child's performance in the classroom.

Teachers try to help disturbed children to see themselves in a more positive light. Children tend to improve their self-evaluations when they experience success and positive feedback from others (Herndon, 1971). Therefore, teachers try to provide children with rewarding and successful classroom and extra-curricular experiences.

Behavioural approach

Around 1960, behavioural psychology began to be used systematically to help students with behaviour problems. Today it is the preferred approach of many educators. Behavioural methods have proven very effective with emotionally disturbed children. They have been widely used, especially at the elementary school level (e.g. O'Leary and Becker, 1967).

Behaviourists do not concern themselves with the deep-rooted psychic problems that psychodynamic theorists claim underlie behaviour problems. Behaviourists do not categorize child's behaviour as abnormal, evil, mysterious, or deviant, nor do they relate it to any underlying abnormalities. Rather, behaviourists assume that the same principles that guide the development of normal behaviour are also involved in the development of inappropriate behaviour. They attempt to use those principles to alter the inappropriate behaviour.

There are three basic forms of treatment in the behavioural approach. The first uses teaching and training techniques to create behaviours that do not already exist. The second uses a number of techniques to maintain and generalize behaviours that are already established. The third uses others techniques to confine, reduce, or eliminate problem behaviour. Typically, all three forms of treatment are undertaken simultaneously.

Behavioural techniques try to change the events (antecedents) that precede problem behaviour, as well as the events (consequences) that follow. Reinforcers or rewards are used to increase desirable behaviour, and aversion techniques are used to decrease or extinguish undesirable behaviour. Reinforcement can be provided by anything that a child finds pleasurable. Primary reinforcers include candy and food, while secondary reinforcers include tokens and stars. Social reinforcers include a smile, a hug, and a pat on the back.

In Chapter Two, we outlined a number of the techniques used in behaviour therapy or behaviour modification. Some methods for behaviour change are widely employed in regular classrooms and in special self-contained settings. The most popular of these are token economies, contingency contracting, and daily report cards. The following discussions of these methods are guidelines only. Interested students should refer to the research literature. Gardner (1974) is especially recommended.

Token economies. Perhaps the most widespread technique used with emotionally disturbed children in schools today is a behavioural method known as the **token economy**. Token reinforcement programs have been implemented successfully in the classroom to achieve a variety of goals, including academic output, assignment completion (Ayllon and Roberts, 1974; McLaughlin and Malaby, 1972, 1974) and the management of specific behaviours.

In a token economy, children learn that certain desirable behaviours will earn certain tokens. The tokens can be any tangible object — stars, poker chips, check marks, and so on. These tokens have no value in themselves, but can be traded in for special reinforcers. The reinforcer may be free time, an art period, time in the library, or some other school-based activity that the children value. However, even the accumulation of tokens alone can help to establish more appropriate behaviours.

Some token-economy programs apply to the whole class, while others focus on individuals with behaviour problems (McLaughlin and Malaby, 1974). When establishing a token program, the following steps are important:

- Determine the behaviours that require change. Do this by counting the incidents of unacceptable behaviour over at least five observational periods.

- Focus on how to establish appropriate behaviour. For example, if children are constantly out of their seats, the target behaviour will be their on-task behaviour. When children are working, they cannot be out of their seats.

- Discuss the program with the class, clearly explaining the behaviours that will gain tokens, the nature of the reinforcers, and the number of tokens necessary to earn a reinforcer.

- Make sure the children clearly understand which behaviours will earn tokens. Behavioural expectations must be clear so that children will be properly motivated.

- Decide on the type of tokens, when they will be awarded, and how they will be awarded. Keep the tokens simple. Reward appropriate behaviour immediately and keep a master list of who has earned what.

- Decide on the nature of the reinforcer, the number of tokens necessary to earn it, and the best time to schedule it.

- As the program progresses, help the children develop more appropriate behaviour for more extended periods by expecting more for each token and by raising the token price of the reinforcer.

- The token should always be accompanied by a social reward — a smile, a pat on the back, or a compliment on good work. This encourages children to behave appropriately for social rewards rather than tokens and reinforcers. Ultimately they must learn to function independently of the token system in order to gain full control of their own behaviour.

The following profile outlines a token economy program that worked very successfully with a grade-seven class of behaviourally disordered children.

PROFILE 10-3

The grade-seven class at the end of the hall was well known to all the students and teachers in the school. Any trouble, vandalism, or disruptive behaviour could generally be traced to that group of nine children. Although each child in the class was unique, they all behaved in ways that were unacceptable to the school and the community.

The children in this class had been punished so often that disciplinary measures such as detentions, time out, and suspensions, had little meaning for them. Indeed, such punishments usually resulted in increased resentment toward school personnel and an even more active dislike of learning. Rather than using further aversive measures, the grade-seven teacher decided to institute a token-economy behavioural, program.

Because of her students' advanced age, the teacher invited and incorporated their suggestions for every step of the program. From some students, she won immediate co-operation. She decided to focus only on on-task behaviour, because the students' problem behaviours were so diverse.

During the first weeks of the program, the children were told exactly how much seat work would earn a token. For example, three math problems earned a poker chip. On Friday afternoon, students with ten chips could trade them in for a reinforcer, the viewing of a special film.

As the program continued, the teacher shaped her students' behaviour by making them work longer to earn tokens and by raising the token price of reinforcers. Wisely, she changed tokens and reinforcers often. She soon saw positive changes in behaviour, more on-task behaviour, increased learning, and a new sense of pride and achievement in the class.

Contingency contracting. Contingency contracting has also been used, especially with adolescents, to bring about positive changes in behaviour. The **contingency contract** is an arrangement between the teacher and the student. The contract contains explicit statements regarding privileges and responsibilities, reciprocal obligations, and accountability procedures for both parties (Stuart and Lott, 1972).

Exhibit 10-5 outlines a contingency contract.

Exhibit 10-5 A contingency contract.

Task:	*Contract:*
What the student will do	I will read five pages of my social studies text and answer questions at the end of the period.
When this must be done	During social studies class.
How must the student do the task	I will answer at least seventy-five percent of the questions correctly.
What the teacher will do	I will receive ten minutes of free time in exchange for this work.

The school program for emotionally disturbed children should be structured within a warm, supportive environment.
(C. Cox)

When arranging a contingency contract, teachers should bear in mind the following guidelines:

- The contract must be fair, honest, positive, and within the range of capabilities of the student.
- To be of long-term usefulness, contingency contracting should be employed systematically and consistently.
- Before signing, all involved should discuss the student's rights and responsibilities, the form of progress evaluation, and the type of reinforcer to be used.
- Student rewards should be both immediate and frequent.

Daily report card. Another effective intervention technique, used in conjunction with home-based reinforcement, is the daily report card (Barth, 1979). A **daily report card** is a report or note prepared by the teacher and sent home to the parents. The parents reward the child when they read on the card that specific, desirable behaviours have occurred (Smith, Williams, and McLaughlin, 1983). Daily report card systems have been effectively used to decrease such school problems as hyperactivity, disruptive behaviours, talking out, rule violations, and inappropriate classroom behaviours (e.g. Ayllon, Garber, and Pisor, 1975; Daugherty and Daugherty, 1977; Fairchild, 1976, O'Leary, Pelham, Rosenbaum, and Price, 1976). The daily report card offers parents increased communication and involvement in the learning process of their children (Martin and McLaughlin, 1981). It also stresses that parents and teachers are partners in the educational process.

Learning environments

Provision for children with behavioural problems can be made in a range of learning environments. Most children with mild and moderate emotional problems are taught in the regular classroom or the special self-contained class. Most special programs for behaviourally disordered children are designed for elementary schools. Few provisions have been made for disturbed children at the secondary level (Nelson and Kauffman, 1977).

Although many disturbed children can indeed be taught in the regular classroom, the integration of these children requires careful consideration of the consequences. As Kauffman, McCullough, and Sabornie (1984) point out, non-handicapped students as well as disturbed students must be shown that aggression and disruption carry serious social penalties. Some disturbed behaviours must result in a child's segregation from classmates, and other students must not be encouraged to tolerate them. However, once the child has learned to behave non-aggressively and non-disruptively in a segregated environment, reintegration should be the goal.

Curriculum adaptations

Academic curricula for emotionally disturbed children must come to terms with the students' affective needs. Besides academic success, disturbed children need a warm, supportive atmosphere that promotes an increase in self-esteem and self-concept. Exhibit 10-6 offers some general tips for teachers of emotionally disturbed children.

To enhance affective instruction, teachers can use art, drama, music, plays, and dance. These activities encourage students to discuss or act out in positive ways their unpleasant feelings. Affective lessons that focus on role-playing can have similar results. **Bibliotherapy**, or the reading of stories with positive role models, can also be useful.

Social intervention

Social intervention encompasses a variety of services to help emotionally disturbed children and their families. Children's Mental Health Centres provide a spectrum of treatment programs, including outpatient care, home care, day treatment, and residential treatment (Dubois, 1982). Foster care may also be used to remove the child from the home for a period of time. This may be done if the family is unable to cope with the child's behaviour, or if the home atmosphere is considered damaging for the child.

Exhibit 10-6 Tips for teachers of behaviourally disordered students.

Creating the environment:

- Establish supportive interpersonal relationships with the children. Try to create a warm atmosphere, characterized by acceptance without permissiveness.
- Establish routines and clear limits to behaviour.
- Be consistent.
- Focus on academic skills.
- Provide children with experiences in which they can succeed.
- Use appropriate procedures for behaviour management.
- Make school work meaningful and relevant to the children.
- Forgive and forget the past. Do not allow past misdeeds to form the basis for present interactions.
- Most importantly, help the children feel good about themselves. Convey the idea that you like them, but dislike problem behaviour.

Managing the environment:

- Remove objects or toys that cause problems.
- Consider your timetable. If problem behaviour emerges during a certain period such as just before lunch, try to schedule an activity like physical education for that time. If a certain subject causes problems, get it over with early and reward the children by letting them do something they enjoy.
- Keep a careful watch on scissors, pencils, and other potentially dangerous objects. Keep them stowed safely away until needed.
- Adhere closely to routines.
- Immediately remove the results of poor behaviour.
- Break up long lessons, listening times, or stories by changing the pace and allowing some physical movement.
- Be consistent in your expectations and demands of students.
- Make certain that children understand all your directions and expectations. They may interpret the command "share the paint," for example, quite differently than you.
- Be aware of the importance of classroom seating arrangements. Some combinations of children simply provoke trouble.
- Avert crisis situations whenever possible. If, for example, a child appears ready to tantrum, divert the child's attention with a new toy or activity.
- When crisis situations do occur, ask for help if you need it.

Historically, juvenile delinquency has been viewed as a social and legal concern. The federal government enacts legislation outlining juvenile offences, age limits, court procedures, and penalties. However, provincial governments administer the legislation, supply containment facilities, provide probation officers, and carry out court judgements.

Delinquent youth are provided for through a large network of child welfare and correctional resources. These programs may be open, residential, community-based, and are located wherever there are substantial populations of young people. A number of programs have been shown highly effective in preventing crime or reducing recidivism (Gendreau and Ross, 1979). However, no one program has been found to work for all clients (Ross, 1982).

Canadian correctional programs extend along a continuum of levels of intervention, beginning with diversion. At the extreme end is containment. A decision to contain a youth depends on the extent and seriousness of delinquent behaviour and on the youth's previous responsiveness to alternate measures (Markwart, 1981). For the "incorrigible" youngster, prison can be the last step on a dreary journey from the principal's office to the streets to the courts. Containment only takes place after repeated delinquent activity. For example, a 1979 study of seventy-three youths in British Columbian containment facilities (Markwart, 1981) found that males had an average of 15.6 offences prior to committal, and females an average of 8.8 offences.

At last count, Canada's prisons housed some 24 000 people, at a cost to taxpayers of $80 per inmate per day. In 1981, the most recent year for which figures are available, Canadian juvenile courts considered nearly 123 000 charges. Most involved property offences such as shoplifting and breaking and entering. Of all the charges, an overwhelming seventy-five percent led to findings of guilt (Maynard, 1984).

The typical Canadian prisoner is a young man who has failed one or more grades in school (Maynard, 1984). For example, a 1978 survey was taken of a hundred randomly selected inmates at the Maplehurst Correctional Complex in Milton, Ontario. The survey found that eight-three percent scored below grade-eight level in math, and thirty-nine percent below grade-eight level in English. Many inmates cannot write a letter or read a newspaper until they enter a literacy class in prison (Maynard, 1984).

In the past, delinquent children and adolescents in Canada have been subjected to treatments that if applied to adults would constitute clear violations of their rights. Canada's new Young Offender's Act (April 1984) has replaced the Juvenile Delinquent's Act that was first promulgated in 1908. The new Act establishes a system of courts, procedures, and dispositions for youth separate from those for adults.

In many ways, the new Act will provide for more protection under the law for juvenile offenders. For example, an arresting officer must now inform accused youngsters of their rights to contact a lawyer and their parents. Before juveniles are questioned by police, their rights and the nature of the charge must be explained in language they can understand. Under the Act, the maximum sentence a juvenile can receive is two years. In addition, more emphasis is now placed on community work and helping the victim as methods of atonement.

THE EMOTIONALLY DISTURBED PRE-SCHOOLER

As for all exceptional conditions, early identification and intervention are very important. However, it is extremely difficult to identify emotionally disturbed children at a very young age. All pre-school children display rapid and uneven development and wide variations in behaviour.

There is some evidence that mothers perceive mildly handicapped infants as lower in positive mood than do mothers of normal infants (Van Tassel, 1984). These mothers also find their children somewhat more fussy and irritable than normal. Behaviourally disordered pre-schoolers may exhibit patterns of irregular sleeping, eating, and aggressive behaviour. For example, Hartup (1974) found that, among normal children, unfocused temper tantrums diminish during the pre-school period and are uncommon after age four. In the behaviourally disordered child, tantrums are more likely to continue.

Emotionally disturbed behaviour is also difficult to identify at an early age because parents have highly subjective expectations, values, and reactions to their children. One parent may view behaviour as too aggressive or active that another dismisses as normal. Parents bring their own temperaments and personal styles to bear on child-rearing attitudes. They may unwittingly neglect or exacerbate their child's developmental difficulties.

Because identification is so difficult at the pre-school level, few programs have been designed specifically for emotionally disturbed pre-school children.

THE EMOTIONALLY DISTURBED ADOLESCENT

Adolescents and young adults are so varied in their behaviour disorders that programming for them is extremely difficult. By the time they reach adolescence, behaviourally disturbed students show increases in:

- Antisocial and law-breaking behaviour.
- Truancy.
- The need for vocational and career guidance.
- The need for instruction in matters such as drug abuse.
- The need for clear information regarding human sexuality (Kneedler, 1984).

Special education for emotionally disturbed adolescents is hampered by the fact that secondary education is more oriented toward subjects than students. Most current intervention practices, administrative arrangements, and teacher-training programs have been developed with younger children in mind. The few adolescent programs that do exist focus upon the psychoeducational or behavioural approach. However, there is little evidence that any of these programs have been effective (Nelson and Kauffman, 1977).

TEACHERS OF THE EMOTIONALLY DISTURBED

Teaching is stressful under the best of circumstances, and the effort of working with emotionally disturbed children contributes additional stress (Wood, 1982). Disturbed children present difficulties through the very nature of their inconsistent and disruptive behaviour. They require different management procedures than other students.

Teachers of emotionally disturbed children must be able to tolerate unpleasantness and rejection without being counteraggressive or reciprocally unpleasant. They must be secure in their own values, confident in their teaching and living skills and capable of drawing on private personality resources. In a revealing study of the literature, Roy (1981) found that many Canadian teachers suffer mental health problems of their own. Clearly, these teachers would not be appropriate for working with emotionally disturbed children.

SUMMARY

Special education for emotionally disturbed children is a comparatively recent field. Its objectives and methods have been shaped by diverse disciplines, including education, medicine, and psychodynamic and behavioural psychology. However, specialists from these disciplines disagree deeply about definitions, classifications, prevalence estimates, etiology, and terminology as they apply to behaviour disorders. Debate continues, despite an increasing educational perspective and recent progress in the conceptualization of emotional disturbance.

Much of the problem of defining emotional disturbance lies in the diverse nature of the exceptionality. Problem behaviours vary dramatically among the population, and generally differ from normal behaviours in length and intensity, rather than kind. Although emotional disturbance is viewed as a distinct category of exceptionality, it is often displayed by children with other handicaps. To further confuse the issue, it may be virtually impossible on the basis of learning characteristics, to distinguish mildly disturbed children from those labelled learning-disabled or mildly mentally retarded.

A number of conceptual approaches have evolved to explain and treat behaviour disorders. None of these, however, has yet offered a solution for the management of all emotionally disturbed children. Educators must ensure that the use of any particular treatment model is directed toward the specific needs of the child. A child's treatment should not be used as a means of demonstrating the efficacy of a preferred therapeutic approach.

BIBLIOGRAPHY

Achenbach, T.M. (1966). The classification of children's psychiatric symptoms: A factor-analytic study. *Psychological Monographs, 80,* 1-37.

Achenbach, T.M. and Edelbrock, C.S. (1978). The classification of child psychopathology: A review and analysis of empirical efforts. *Psychological Bulletin, 85,* 1275-1301.

American Psychiatric Association. (1980). *Diagnostic and statistical manual of mental disorders (3rd ed.).* Washington, D.C.: American Psychiatric Association.

Anthony, E.J. (1970). Behavior disorders. In P.H. Mussen (Ed.), *Carmichael's manual of child psychology, (3rd ed., Vol. 2).* New York: Wiley.

Axline, V.M. (1964): *Dibs: In search of self.* New York: Ballantine Books.

Axline, V.M. (1969). *Play therapy (2nd ed.).* New York: Ballantine Books.

Ayers, D. (October 26, 1978). Perspectives on education in prison. Paper presented to members of the OISE review in Penitentiary Education and Training, Kingston, Ontario.

Ayllon, T., Garber, S., and Pisor, K. (1975). The elimination of discipline problems through a combined school-home motivational system. *Behavior Therapy, 6,* 616-626.

Ayllon, T. and Roberts, M. (1974). Eliminating discipline problems by strengthening academic performance. *Journal of Applied Behavior Analysis, 7,* 71-76.

Balow, B. (1979). Definitional and prevalence problems in behavior disorders of children. *School Psychology Digest, 8,* 348-354.

Balthazar, E. and Stevens, H. (1975). *The emotionally disturbed mentally retarded.* Englewood Cliffs, N.J.: Pentice-Hall.

Bandura, A. (1977). *Social learning theory.* Englewood Cliffs, N.J.: Prentice-Hall.

Baron, R.A. and Byrne, D. (1981). *Social psychology: Understanding human interaction.* Boston: Allyn and Bacon.

Barth, R. (1979). Home-based reinforcement of school behavior: A review and analysis. *Review of Educational Research, 49,* 436-458.

Bateson, H. (October 30, 1979). Violence leads in childhood deaths. *Vancouver Province,* p. 3.

Bennett, J. and Winzer, M. (1980). *Education in correctional institutions: A preliminary survey.* Toronto: Federation of Provincial Schools Authority Teachers.

Berne, E. (1964). *Games people play.* New York: Grove Press.

Bower, E.M. (1969). *Early identification of emotionally handicapped children in school (2nd ed.).* Springfield, IL.: Thomas.

Bullock, L.M. and Brown, R.K. (1972). Behavioural dimensions of emotionally disturbed children. *Exceptional Children, 38,* 740-742.

Cohen-Sandler, R., Berman, A., and King, R. (1982). Life stress and symptomatology: Determinants of suicidal behaviour in children. *Journal of Child Psychiatry, 21,* 178-186.

Conger, J.C. and Keane, S.P. (1981). Social skills intervention in the treatment of isolated or withdrawn children. *Psychological Bulletin, 90,* 478-495.

Connors, C.K. (1972). Psychological effects of stimulant drugs in children with minimal brain dysfunction. *Pediatrics, 49,* 702-708.

Connors, C. and Werry, J.S. (1979). Pharmacotherapy. In H.C. Quay and J.S. Werry (Eds.), *Psychopathological disorders of childhood (2nd ed.).* New York: Wiley.

Csapo, M. (1981a). Educational provisions for emotionally disturbed children in British Columbia: A status report. *B.C. Journal of Special Education, 5,* 357-367.

Csapo, M. (1981b). The emotionally disturbed child in Canada's schools. *Behavioural Disorders, 6,* 139-149.

Csapo, M. and Goguen, L. (1980). *Special education in Canada: Issues and trends in the '80s.* Vancouver: Centre for Human Development and Research.

Cullinan, D. and Epstein, M.H. (1982). Behavior disorders. In N. Haring (Ed.), *Exceptional children and youth (3rd ed.).* Columbus, OH: Merrill.

Cullinan, D., Epstein, M.H., and Lloyd, J. (1982). *Behavior disorders.* Englewood Cliffs, N.J.: Prentice-Hall.

Cullinan, D., Epstein, M.H., and Lloyd, J.W. (1983). *Behavior disorders of children and adolescents.* Englewood Cliffs, N.J.: Prentice-Hall.

Cummings, S.T. and Finger, D.C. (1980). Emotional disorders. In H.E. Rie and E.D. Rie (Eds.), *Handbook of minimal brain dysfunction: A critical view.* New York: Wiley.

Daugherty, E. and Daugherty, A. (1977). The daily report card: A simplified and flexible package for classroom behavior and management. *Psychology in the Schools, 14,* 191-195.

Dodge, K.A. and Frame, C.L. (1982). Social cognitive biases and deficits in aggressive boys. *Child Development, 53,* 620-635.

Doig, J. (January 6, 1979). From the inside out. *The Canadian,* pp. 9-13.

Drabman, R.S. and Patterson, J. (1981). Disruptive behaviour and the social standing of exceptional children. *Exceptional Education Quarterly, 1,* 45-55.

Dubois, J. (1982). Ontario Association of Children's Mental Health Centres: Tenth Anniversary. *Canada's Mental Health, 30,* 20-21.

Edelbrock, C.S. (1979). Empirical classification of children's behavior disorders: Prognosis based on parent and teacher ratings. *School Psychology Digest, 8,* 355-369.

Emmerich, W. (1966). Continuity and stability in early social development: 11-Teacher's ratings. *Child Development, 37,* 17-27.

Eron, L. (1982). Parent-child interaction, television violence and aggression of children. *American Psychologist, 37,* 197-211.

Eron, L., Heusmann, L.R., Brice, P., Fischer, P., and Mermalstein, R. (1983). Age trend in the development of aggression, sex-typing, and related television habits. *Developmental Psychology, 19,* 71-77.

Fairchild, T. (1976). Home-school token economies: Bridging the communication gap. *Psychology in the Schools, 13,* 463-467.

Fremont, T., Klingsporn, M., and Wilson, J. (1976). Identifying emotionally disturbed children: The professionals differ. *Journal of School Psychology, 14,* 275-381.

Gardner, W.I. (1974). *Children with learning and behavior problems: A behavior management approach.* Boston: Allyn and Bacon.

Gendreau, P., Madden P., and Leipeiger, M. (1977). *Norms and recidivism for first incarcerates: Implications for programming.* Toronto: Ontario Ministry of Correctional Services.

Gendreau, P. and Ross, R.R. (October, 1979). Effective correctional treatment: Bibliotherapy for cynics. *Crime and Delinquency,* pp. 463-489.

Gerbner, G., Gross, L., Morgan, M., and Signorelli, N. (1980). The "mainstreaming" of America: Violence profile no. 11. *Journal of Communication, 30,* 10-29.

Gersten, J.C., Langner, T.S., Eisenberg, J.B., Simcha-Fagen, O., and McCarthy, E.D. (1976). Stability and change in types of behavioral disturbance of children and adolescents. *Journal of Abnormal Child Psychology, 4* 111-127.

Goulder, R.J. and Trybus, R.J. (1977). *The classroom behavior of emotionally disturbed hearing impaired children.* Washington, D.C.: Gallaudet College, Office of Demographic Studies.

Grangberg, G. and Steinbring, J. (1980). Television and the Canadian Indian. Winnipeg: University of Winnipeg, Department of Anthropology.

Guetzloe, E. and Cline, K. (1979). The medication of children with learning and behavior disorders. In A. Lane (Ed.), *Readings in human growth and development of the exceptional individual.* Connecticut: Special Learning Corporation.

Hallahan, D.P. and Kauffman, J.M. (1982). *Exceptional children: Introduction to special education (2nd ed.).* Englewood cliffs, N.J.: Prentice-Hall.

Hapkewicz, W.G. (1979). Children's reactions to cartoon violence. *Journal of Clinical Psychology, 8,* 30-34.

Hardy, M., McLeod, J., Minto, H., Perkins, S., and Quance, W. (1971). *Standards for educators of exceptional children.* Toronto: Crainford.

Harris, W., King, D., and Drummond, R. (1978). Personality variables of children nominated as emotionally handicapped by classroom teachers. *Psychology in the Schools, 15,* 361-363.

Hartup, W.W. (1974). Aggression in childhood: Developmental prespectives. *American Psychologist, 29,* 336-341.

Herndon, J. (1971). *How to survive in your native land.* New York: Simon and Schuster.

Hersov, L.A. (1960). Persistent nonattendance at school. *Journal of Child Psychology and Psychiatry, 1,* 130-136.

Hetherington, E.M. and Martin, B. (1979). Family interaction. In H.C. Quay and J.S. Werry (Eds.), *Psychopathological disorders of childhood (2nd ed.).* New York: Wiley.

Hewett, F.M. (1974). In J.M. Kauffman and C. Lewis (Eds.), *Teaching children with behavior disorders: Personal perspectives.* Columbus, OH: Charles E. Merrill.

Huston-Stein, A., Fox, S., Greer, D., Watkins, B.A., and Whitaker, J. (1981). The effects of TV action and violence on children's social behavior. *Journal of Genetic Psychology, 138,* 183-191.

Hylton, J.H. and Matonovitch, R. (1979). *Job satisfaction in the Regina Police Department.* Regina: Regina Police Department.

Jacobson, T. (1974). Learning disabilities and juvenile delinquency: A demonstrated relationship. In R.E. Weber (Ed.), *Handbook on learning disabilities: A prognosis for the child, the adolescent, the adult.* Englewood Cliffs, N.J.: Prentice-Hall.

Jenkins, R. (1966). Psychiatric syndrome in children and their relation to family background. *American Journal of Orthopsychiatry, 36,* 450-457.

Jones, R.L. (1976). (Ed.). *Mainstreaming and the minority child.* Reston, VA.: Council for Exceptional Children.

Kagan, J. and Moss, H.A. (1962). *Birth of maturity.* New York: Wiley.

Kauffman, J.M. (1977). *Characteristics of children's behavior disorders.* Columbus, OH: Merrill.

Kauffman, J.M. (1981). *Characteristics of children's behavior disorders (2nd ed.).* Columbus, OH: Merrill.

Kauffman, J.M. (1985). *Characteristics of children's behavior disorders (3rd ed.).* Columbus, OH: Merrill.

Kauffman, J.M. and Kneedler, R.D. (1981). Behavior disorders. In J.M. Kauffman and D.P. Hallahan (Eds.), *Handbook of Special Education.* Englewood Cliffs, N.J.: Prentice-Hall.

Kauffman, J.M., McCullough, L.L., and Sabornie, E.J. (1984). Integrating exceptional students: Special problems involving the emotionally disturbed/behaviourally disordered. *B.C. Journal of Special Education, 8,* 201-210.

Kelly, T.K., Bullock, L.M., and Dykes, M.K. (1977). Behavioural disorders: Teacher's perceptions. *Exceptional Children, 43,* 316-318.

Keuthe, J.L. (1962). Social schemes. *Journal of Abnormal and School Psychology, 64,* 31-38.

Kneedler, R.D., and D.P. Hallahan and J.M. Kauffman (1984). *Special education for today.* Englewood Cliffs, N.J.: Prentice-Hall.

Lahey, B.C. and Ciminero, A.R. (1980). *Maladaptive behavior: An introduction to abnormal psychology.* Glenview, IL.: Scott Foresman.

Lahey, B.B., Hammer, D., Crumrine, P.L., and Forehand, R.L. (1980). Birth order x sex interactions in child behavior problems. *Developmental Psychology, 16,* 608-615

Laycock, S. and Findlay, J. (1969). *Educational needs of emotionally disturbed children in the schools of British Columbia. Report No. 5.,* Vancouver: Educational Research Institute of British Columbia.

Leyton, E. (1979). *The myth of delinquency: An anatomy of juvenile nihilism.* Toronto: McClelland and Stewart.

Liebert, R.M., Sprafkin, J.N., and Davidson, E.S. (1982). *The early window: Effects of television on children and youth.* New York: Pergamon Press.

Mann, L., Goodman, L. and Wiederholt, J. (1978). *Teaching the learning-disabled adolescent.* Boston: Houghton Mifflin.

Markwart, A. (1981). Youth containment in British Columbia. *B.C. Journal of Special Education, 5,* 279-292.

Martin, R. and McLaughlin, T. (1981). A comparison between the effect of free time and daily report cards on the academic behaviour of junior high school students. *B.C. Journal of Special Education, 5,* 301-313.

Maynard, (November, 1984). The invisible problem. *Homemakers,* pp. 8-20.

McConville, B.J. (1982). Secondary prevention in child psychiatry: An overview with ideas for action. *Canada's Mental Health, 30,* 4-7.

McDermott, P.A. (1980). Prevalence and constituency of behavioral disturbance taxonomies in the regular school population. *Journal of Abnormal Child Psychology, 8,* 523-536.

McDermott, P.A. (1981). The manifestation of problem behaviour in ten age groups of Canadian school children. *Canadian Journal of Behavioural Science, 13,* 310-319.

McLaughlin, T. and Malaby, J. (1972). Intrinsic reinforcers in a classroom token economy. *Journal of Applied Behavior Analysis, 5,* 263-270.

McLaughlin, T. and Malaby, J. (1974). The utilization of an individual contingency program to control assignment completion in a token classroom: A case study. *Psychology in the Schools, 11,* 191-194.

Morse, W.C. (1975). The education of socially maladjusted and emotionally disturbed children. In W.H. Cruickshank and G.O. Johnson (Eds.), *Education of exceptional children and youth (3rd ed.).* Englewood Cliffs, N.J.: Prentice-Hall.

Morse, W.C., Cutler, R.L. and Fink, A.H. (1984). *Public school classes for the emotionally handicapped: A research analysis.* Washington, D.C.: Council for Exceptional Children.

Murray, J.P. (1980). *Television and youth: 25 years of research and controversy.* Boys Town, NE.: Boys Town Center for the Study of Youth Development.

Nelson, C.M. (1971). Techniques for screening conduct disturbed children. *Exceptional Children, 37,* 501-507.

Nelson, C.M. and Kauffman, J.M. (1977). Educational programming for secondary school age delinquent and maladjusted pupils. *Behavioural Disorders, 2,* 102-113.

Newman, R. and Simpson, R. (1983). Modifying the least restrictive environment to facilitate the integration of severely emotionally disturbed children and youth. *Behavioral Disorders, 8* 103-112.

O'Leary, K.D. and Becker, W.C. (1967). Behavior modification in an adjustment class: A token reinforcement program. *Exceptional Children, 33,* 627-642.

O'Leary, D., Pelham, W., Rosenbaum, A., and Price, G. (1976). Behavioral treatment of hyperkinetic children: An experimental evaluation of its usefulness. *Clinical Pediatrics, 15,* 510-515.

Olweus, D. (1979). Stability of aggressive reaction patterns in males: A review. *Psychological Bulletin, 86,* 852-875.

Olweus, D. (1980). Familial and temperamental determinants of aggressive behavior in adolescent boys: A causal analysis. *Developmental Psychology, 16,* 644-660.

Parke, R.D. and Collmer, C.W. (1975). Child abuse: An interdisciplinary analysis. In E. Hetherington (Ed.), *Review of child development research (Vol. 5).* Chicago: University of Chicago Press.

Piers, E.V. (1969). *Manual for the Piers-Harris Children's Self-Concept Scale.* Nashville: Counselor Recordings and Tests.

Quay, H.C. (1972). Patterns of aggression, withdrawal, and immaturity. In H.C. Quay and J.S. Werry, (Eds.), *Psychopathological disorders of childhood.* New York: Wiley.

Quay, H.C. (1975). Classification in the treatment of delinquency and antisocial behavior. In N. Hobbs (Ed.), *Issues in the classification of children (Vol. 1).* San Francisco: Jossey-Bass.

Quay, H.C. (1979). Classification. In H.C. Quay and J.S. Werry (Eds.), *Psychopathological disorders of childhood* (2nd ed.). New York: Wiley.

Rachman, S. and Seligman, M.E. (1976). Unprepared phobias: Be prepared. *Behavior Research and Therapy, 14,* 333-338.

Report to the Solicitor General of Canada concerning the educational programs of the Canadian correctional system. (1979). Toronto. OISE Press.

Roberts, C.A. and Lazure, M.D. (1970). *One million children: A national study of Canadian children with emotional and learning disorders.* Toronto: Crainford.

Robins, L.N. (1979). Follow-up studies. In H.C. Quay and J.S. Werry (Eds.), *Psychopathological disorders of childhood (2nd ed.).* New York: Wiley.

Rose, T.L., Epstein, M.H., Cullinan, D., and Lloyd, J. (1981). Academic programming for behaviorally disordered adolescents: An approach to remediation. In G. Brown, R.L. McDowell, and J. Smith (Eds.), *Educating adolescents with behavior disorders.* Columbus, OH: Merrill.

Ross, R.R. (1982). From therapy to teaching: Some reflections on effective correctional programming. *Canada's Mental Health, 30,* 2-3, 13.

Roy, M. (1981). Trained in stability to live in instability. *Canada's Mental Health, 29,* 16-18.

Rubin, R.A. and Balow, B. (1978). Prevalence of teacher identified behavior problems: A longitudinal study. *Exceptional Children, 45,* 102-111.

Schlesinger, H.S. and Meadow, K.P. (1972). *Sound and sign: Childhood deafness and mental health.* Los Angeles: University of California Press.

Schultz, E.W., Salvia, J.A., and Feinn, J. (1974). Prevalence of behavior symptoms in rural elementary school children. *Journal of Abnormal Child Psychology, 2,* 17-24.

Shaffer, D.R. (1985). *Developmental psychology: Theory, research, and applications.* Monterey, CA: Brooks/Cole.

Smith, M.A., Williams, R.L. and McLaughlin, T.F. (1983). The daily report card as an intervention technique for classroom academic and social behaviour: A review. *B.C. Journal of Special Education, 7,* 369-380.

Spivack, G. and Spotts, J. (1966). *Devereux Child Behavior (DCB) Rating Scale.* Devon, PA.: Devereux Foundation.

Stott, D.H. (1979). The Bristol Social Adjustment Guides. *Therapeutic Education, 7,* 34-44.

Stuart, R.A. and Lott, L.B. (1972). Behavioral contracting with delinquents: A cautionary note. *Journal of Behavior Therapy and Experimental Psychiatry, 3,* 161-169.

Van Tassel, E. (1984). Temperament characteristics of mildly developmentally delayed infants. *Journal of Developmental and Behavioral Pediatrics, 5,* 11-14.

Von Issor, A., Quay, H.C., and Love, C.T. (1980). Interrelationships among three measures of deviant behavior. *Exceptional Children, 46,* 272-276.

Waters, H.F. and Malamud, P. (March 10, 1975). Drop that gun, Captain Video. *Newsweek,* pp. 81-82.

Weinstein, L. (1965). Social schemata of emotionally disturbed boys. *Journal of Abnormal Psychology, 70,* 457-461.

Werry, J.S. (1979). The child psychoses. In H.C. Quay and J.S. Werry (Eds.), *Psychopathological disorders of childhood (2nd ed.).* New York: Wiley.

Wood, F.H. (1982). Living with the emotionally disturbed: Burden or opportunity? *B.C. Journal of Special Education, 6,* 1-10.

Wyne, M.D. and O'Conner, P.D. (1979). *Exceptional children: A developmental view.* Lexington, MA: D.C. Heath.

Zimbordo, P., Pilkonis, P., and Norwood, R. (1975). The social disease called shyness. *Psychology Today,* 69-72.

CHAPTER ELEVEN

Children with severe and profound emotional disturbance

MARGRET WINZER

It's rather trite to say public awareness and understanding [are] needed when it comes to an affliction like autism. [We] ... constantly must battle a public largely misinformed about a disorder that strikes about five children in every ten thousand and boys four times more frequently than girls.

(Mullin, 1985)

Profound emotional disturbances, or childhood psychoses, represent the most extreme forms of behavioural and emotional disorder. They have a devastating impact upon the child and upon everyone involved in the child's life. No other condition is so hard to understand and so far removed from the range of normal experience.

Psychotic children frequently exhibit bizarre and inappropriate behaviour. They may indulge in repetitive motor activity, self-stimulation, and self-mutilation. Many psychotic children are completely withdrawn. Some never speak at all, but pirouette in a silent, internal dance, impervious to all around them. Their world may consist of touch sensations, of familiar routines and rigidly obsessive behaviour. Nonetheless, these children may notice the smallest change in their surroundings, from a parent's new hairstyle to a door left slightly ajar.

Psychotic disorders have long baffled investigators and observers. Recorded cases of schizophrenia date from as far back as 1400 B.C. However, not until the early 1900s were psychotic children sufficiently distinguished from the mentally retarded to permit research into their condition. In 1905, Sante de Sanctus studied schizophrenic children for the first time. In 1911, the term autism came into use to refer to patients characterized by social withdrawal (Bleuler, 1911).

In the past, the majority of psychotic children were either taught in residential institutions or received no schooling at all (Cottle, 1976). Often these children were abandoned to languish in institutional settings that only heightened their personal isolation.

During the 1960s, the educational system began to assume responsibility for the education of psychotic children. Special education for psychotic children has drawn on developments in education, medicine, and psychology, and been strongly influenced by broad social and educational trends. Most severely and profoundly disturbed children are currently taught in special day schools or residential settings. However, many are urging that psychotic children be mainstreamed into more normal surroundings.

Because childhood psychoses are so spectacular and bizarre, they have probably attracted more attention than any other childhood disorders (Kanner, 1962). However, as for behaviour disorders, much controversy surrounds the treatment of psychotic children. This has arisen because the etiology of psychosis is vague, the symptoms severe and complex, the diagnosis difficult, the treatments unclear, and the prognosis uncertain at best.

The major debates concerning psychoses revolve around terminology and etiology. Lack of agreement on appropriate terminology has interfered with attempts to classify and understand psychotic conditions. A plethora of terms have been used interchangeably in the literature — childhood psychoses, childhood schizophrenia, infantile autism, atypical child syndrome, symbiotic psychosis, dementia praecocissima, dementia infantiles, and pervasive developmental disorder (Cummings and Finger, 1980).

Accompanying the problems in terminology are difficulties in classification. Some authorities view childhood psychoses as one inclusive category, ignoring distinctions among specific syndromes (Bomberg, Szurek, and Etemad, 1973). Some view autism and childhood schizophrenia as one and the same, while some claim they are different (Miller, 1974). Other researchers classify these disorders together, but distinguish them from other organic disorders (Ornitz, 1973). Still others distinguish infantile autism from childhood schizophrenia, and maintain that these two disorders constitute the major diagnostic divisions of childhood psychosis (Rimland, 1974; Rutter, 1974).

There is some evidence that infantile autism and childhood schizophrenia are sufficiently distinct to warrant separate treatment. This is especially true with regard to prevalence and etiology. In the following pages, therefore, we will discuss childhood psychosis under the two subcategories of infantile autism and childhood schizophrenia.

DEFINITIONS OF PROFOUND EMOTIONAL DISTURBANCE

Childhood psychosis is a general term used to refer to any number of maladaptive behaviours or clusters of behaviours. **Psychoses** are a heterogeneous group of clinical syndromes characterized by a severe disturbance in ego functioning. This disturbance affects various aspects of adaptive behaviour, including the perception and ordering of experience, the assessment of reality, the control and channelling of impulses, and the success of interpersonal relations (Cummings and Finger, 1980). Psychotic children show a pattern of behaviour characterized by a failure to recognize, understand, or respond appropriately to people in their environment. They demonstrate extreme withdrawal and a high frequency of problematic and bizarre behaviour.

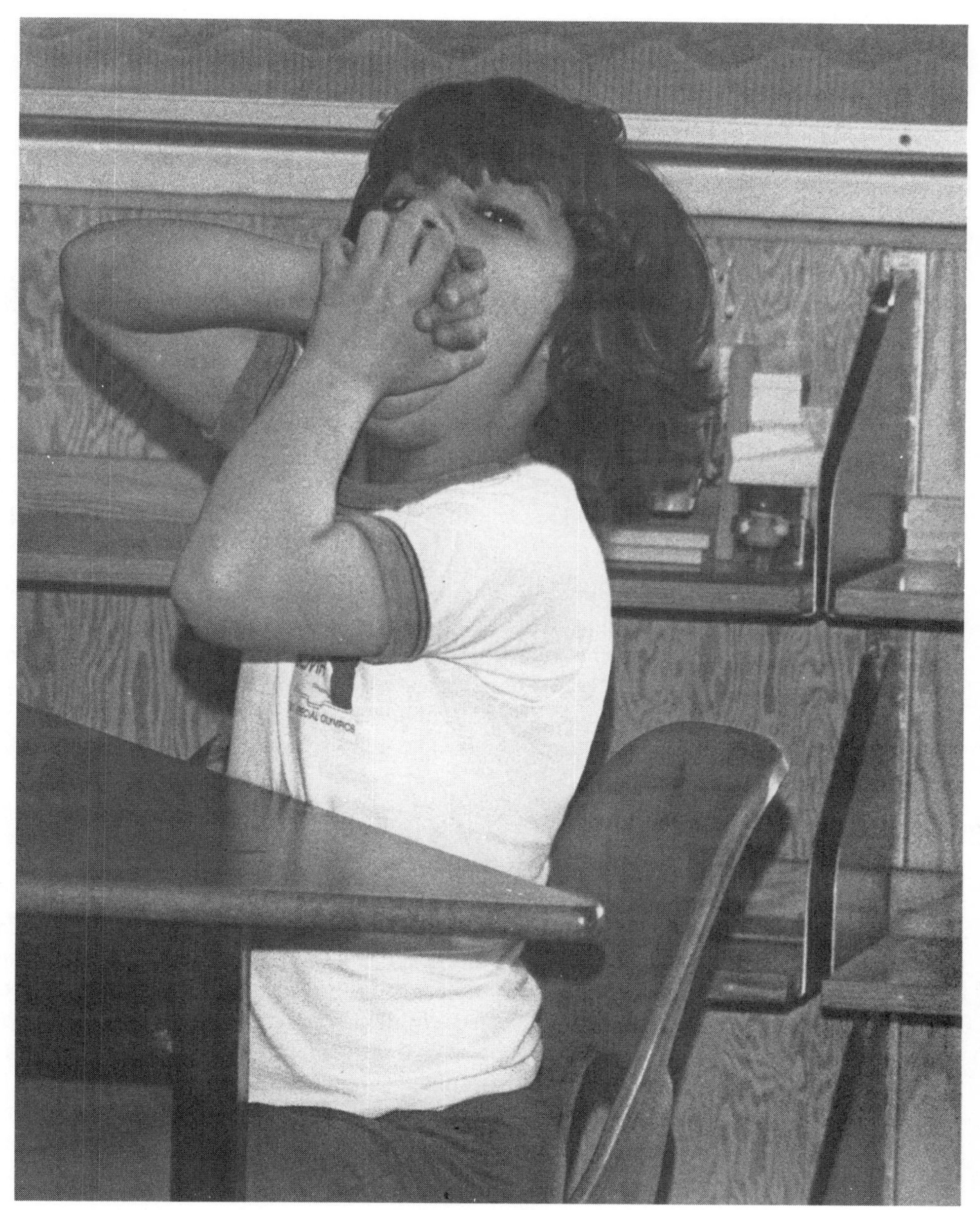

Children with severe emotional disorders are often characterized by bizarre behaviour.
(C. Cox)

Infantile autism

The word **autism** comes from the Greek *autos*, meaning self. Fittingly, then, the most prominent feature of autistic children is their apparent self-absorption and socially withdrawn behaviour (Wing, 1972). The boundaries of autism are often vague and undifferentiated, and much remains to be known about the condition. For these reasons, a precise definition is impossible. However, we can describe infantile autism as a syndrome consisting of a basic disturbance of cognitive development and abnormalities of language and communication, together with a variety of secondary behavioural and emotional problems. Autistic features may appear in different varieties and grades in children with the actual syndrome, as well as in children with other disorders.

Childhood schizophrenia

Infantile autism is differentiated from other childhood psychoses on the basis of its profound pervasiveness and the earliness of its onset — before thirty months of age. Childhood schizophrenia occurs later in childhood, often around the beginning of puberty. Before its onset, the child has usually developed according to normal patterns (Margolies, 1977; Newsom and Rincover, 1981). Childhood schizophrenia, then, may be defined as

> ... a pervasive psychotic disorder involving a decline or arrest of ego development following a period of relatively normal development, occurring in children who demonstrate some degree of useful language and relatedness to others. Among children characterized as schizophrenic, there are wide variations in personality organization, clinical course, intellectual functioning, and identifiable etiological conditions (Cummings and Finger, 1980, p. 510).

CLASSIFICATION OF PROFOUND EMOTIONAL DISTURBANCE

The *Diagnostic and statistical manual of mental disorders* (DSM III) (American Psychiatric Association, 1980) identifies several categories of adult, adolescent, and childhood psychotic disorders. The category of pervasive developmental disorders refers directly to childhood conditions and includes four classifications — infantile autism, disintegrative psychosis, other specific early childhood psychoses, and unspecified psychoses.

DSM III (1980) employs the term *pervasive developmental disorders* because childhood psychoses affect many basic areas of psychological development at the same time and to a severe degree. Psychotic children display severe qualitative abnormalities that are not normal for any stage of development. These disturbances are seen as distortions in development.

PREVALENCE OF PROFOUND EMOTIONAL DISTURBANCE

The importance of the study of childhood psychoses is not related to the incidence and prevalence of the disorder. Childhood psychoses are rare, although they have elicited an enormous amount of interest, concern, and research. Treffert (1970) estimated an incidence rate of 5 cases of childhood psychosis per 10 000 children, including 3.1 cases of childhood schizophrenia per 10 000 children.

Infantile autism occurs much less frequently than childhood schizophrenia, but the prognosis is more severe. Prevalence figures for autistic children vary widely, ranging from 0.7 per 10 000 to 4.8 per 10 000 school-aged children. In 1977, the Board of Directors of the Canadian Society for Autistic Children calculated the rate as 5 for every 10 000 live births (Csapo, 1981).

Among the autistic population, boys are estimated to outnumber girls by ratios that range from 2 to 1 to up to 5 to 1 (Csapo, 1979; Hingtgen and Bryson, 1972; Morse, 1975). DSM III (American Psychiatric Association, 1980) reports that the prevalence of infantile autism is fifty times as great in siblings of children with the disorder than in the general population.

Autistic children commonly suffer from accompanying handicapping conditions. A great many autistic children are also mentally retarded (Werry, 1971). In a British Columbia survey of 152 autistic children, Csapo (1979) found 85 percent to have additional handicapping conditions. These included mental retardation (51.1 percent), speech dysfunction and retardation (14 percent), and epilepsy and retardation (9.6 percent).

ETIOLOGY OF PROFOUND EMOTIONAL DISTURBANCE

The etiology of childhood psychoses is a broadly researched and widely disputed area. Etiological data can at best be described as inconclusive. Early theories focused upon the psychosocial origins of psychosis. Recent research, however, though not altogether compelling, leans strongly toward biological causes. Although this research is intriguing we can touch only briefly on it here.

Most of the many theories concerning the causes of childhood psychosis can be categorized as either nature or nurture. Nature theories stress biological dysfunction, while adherents of the nurture approach view the environment as the vital developmental factor. Although biological problems are more prominent among severely disturbed children than among children with milder disorders, the evidence is as yet inconclusive. The best approach may be multifactorial, attributing psychotic disorders to a combination of biological and environmental factors.

Infantile autism

In 1906, Eugene Blueler, a Swiss psychiatrist, used the term autistic to describe the withdrawn behaviours he observed among adult schizophrenics. Autism as a distinctive syndrome in children was first identified by Kanner in 1943.

Kanner described a number of symptoms that he observed among a group of eleven children. In particular, he stressed their profound withdrawal from human contact and their obsessive desire for sameness in their environment. Kanner also identified similarities in the families of the eleven children. He found the parents to be highly intelligent and unusually high achievers, but he also found them to be emotionally cold, aloof, and reserved in their interactions with their children.

Kanner himself did not reject biological factors as contributive causes of infantile autism. However, the researchers that followed him chose to focus almost exclusively on his psychogenic suppositions. They speculated that lack of adequate parenting was the primary factor in the onset of autism. Autistic infants were seen as withdrawing into isolation to escape a hostile world, deeply lacking in warmth, love, and nurturance.

Bettelheim (1967) adopted this same line of thought, interpreting autistic behaviour as a defence against a world perceived as hostile and rejecting. Bettelheim argued that children became autistic when their parents rejected them or failed to respond to their attempts to influence their environment. Because the children feel unable to exert any control over the external world, they withdraw into a private fantasy world and try to impose some order and consistency through an obsessive insistence on sameness. Bettelheim used the term "refrigerator mother" to characterize the mothers of autistic children (Csapo, 1981). An even more devastating term, "the schizophrenogenic mother," lays direct responsibility for the child's condition on the mother's failure to provide love and nurturance.

Bettelheim did not deny the possibility that genetic or organic causes might also contribute to infantile autism. Although Mahler (1952), Ward (1970), and others agreed that parents created a climate that encouraged autism, few investigators attributed the condition exclusively to parental behaviour. Evidence began to show that children from deprived settings were not at higher risk for autism, and that mothers of autistic children also had non-handicapped offspring. Gradually, the environmental theories were abandoned.

Researchers turned their attention to a range of biochemical, sensori-motor, neurological, and cognitive defects thought possibly to account for infantile autism. New evidence began to indicate that genetics, fetal complications, and central-nervous-system damage might be precursors of the disorder.

Increasing evidence is pointing to heredity as a contributing factor in some severe behaviour disorders (Lahey and Ciminero, 1980). A number of researchers (e.g. Links, Stockwell, Abichandani, and Simeon, 1980; Meryash, Szymanski, and Gerald, 1982; Tsai, Stewart, and August, 1981) have suggested the possibility of a genetic factor in infantile autism, while others have suggested the possibility of a genetic predisposition to autism (Furneaux and Roberts, 1977). Autism is often accompanied by minor physical anomalies, such as fine hair, large head circumference, and malformed ears (Links, Stockwell, Abichandani and Simeon, 1980). This fact has lent credence to the notion of a genetic factor.

The Manitoba Society for Autistic Children (1985) reports that a research study of autistic children and their families is currently underway in the Children's Hospital of Winnipeg. The study will examine up to forty children with autism, and will include a search for abnormal physical findings and chromosomal markers. As the society's newsletter explains, one such marker would be a fragile site on the end of the x chromosome in affected males. If autism were linked to this marker, more genetic counselling could be offered to families and affected boys might benefit from folic acid treatment (Manitoba Society [1985]).

There is solid evidence to connect obstetrical problems and subsequent emotional disturbance in children (Anthony, 1970; Goldstein, Caputo, and Taub, 1976). On average, autistic children experience more pre- and perinatal complications than their siblings (Links, Stockwell, Abichandani, and Simeon 1980). For example, in one study (Kolvin, Ounsted, and Roth, 1971), fifty-four percent of children with infantile psychosis had demonstrable neonatal and perinatal abnormalities when given neurological examinations.

Children with psychotic disorders often reveal signs of neurological defects (Werry, 1979). Among autistic children, eighty-three percent have been found to have brain lesions or pathological enlargements of the left temporal horn (Hauser, De Long, and Rosman, 1975). Twenty-one percent of children showing autistic symptoms before age six have been found to develop seizure disorders by age eighteen (Deykin and MacMahon, 1979). Psychiatric disorders subsequent to brain injuries in older children have also been reported (Brink, Imbus, and Woo-Sam, 1980). However, these psychiatric disorders may not be a direct result of the brain injury. More likely, they are a secondary reaction to the stresses accompanying the loss of perceptual and cognitive abilities (Fuld and Fisher, 1977).

Ornitz (1978) has attempted to account for autism on the basis of dysfunction in the vestibular area of the brain. This area is thought to modulate the interaction of sensory and motor functions. Ornitz argues that faulty modulation of sensory input is an intrinsic feature of the pattern of autistic behaviour. This faulty modulation results in disturbances of mobility and perception.

Research data are fairly conclusive that autistic children have incurred some damage to the brain. This brain damage may particularly affect the language centres. A recently advanced theory (De Myer, 1975a, 1975b, 1977) holds that autistic children have a neurologically based language dysfunction that seriously interferes with their learning of expressive speech and abstract language. In addition, autistic children are thought to have a visual-motor imitation deficiency akin to dyspraxia. This interferes with the learning of normal body language and the understanding of nonverbal communication, so important during the preverbal stage of development (Cummings and Fingers, 1980).

Ongoing research in genetics, neurochemistry, and neurology may lead to a more precise understanding of infantile autism. Some researchers are already beginning to view the condition in a new light. Depending on the etiological precursors, they see autism either as a health impairment or as a developmental disability (Valletutti and Sims-Tucker, 1984).

Schizophrenia

In view of the problems inherent in defining childhood schizophrenia, it is hardly surprising that its causes are the subject of considerable debate. Although many environmental factors have been forwarded, the weight of accumulating evidence points toward biological factors as the primary cause of the condition. Exhaustive reviews by Bender (1971a, 1971b), Goldfarb (1970), Werry (1971), and White (1974) describe research efforts that may be leading to much clearer understanding of both childhood and adult schizophrenia (Suran and Rizzo, 1983).

In the past, several environmental factors have been put forward as possible causes of childhood schizophrenia. For example, Despert (1968, 1970) observed that contemporary society reveals a weakening of family structure, frequent role reversals of husband and wife, and an unconscious rejection of the child. These factors combine to place tremendous anxiety on the developing youngster. As parents are beset by ambivalence and conflicts, family linkages are weakened, and the child's ego development and emotional well-being are undermined.

Further experiential factors thought to cause childhood schizophrenia have included maternal overprotection, maternal rejection, stimulus deprivation during infancy, inconsistent parenting, and severe and repeated emotional trauma (Cummings and Finger, 1980). However, many children exposed to these factors do not develop schizophrenia, and it is moot whether family forces alone are enough to produce such a devastating condition. Schizophrenic children display such a wide variety of symptom patterns and respond to so many different treatment modes that no one etiology seems sufficient to account for the disorder (Cummings and Finger, 1980).

One consistent finding in support of biological factors is the high frequency of prenatal and perinatal complications among infants later diagnosed as schizophrenic (Hingtgen and Bryson, 1972; White, 1974). A number of studies (Gittelman and Birch, 1967; Pollack and Woerner, 1966) have found a higher incidence of pregnancy and birth complications among schizophrenic children, including toxemias, vaginal bleeding, and maternal illness during pregnancy.

Investigators have also found a higher incidence of neurological symptoms in schizophrenic children. Childhood schizophrenia may be a manifestation of subtle neurological damage, similar in origin to such disorders as minimal brain dysfunction (Hingtgen and Bryson, 1972; White, 1974). Moreover, neurological dysfunction is highly correlated with birth and pregnancy complication. This offers further evidence that biological factors are responsible for childhood schizophrenia (Suran and Rizzo, 1983).

A number of intriguing studies suggest that genetic factors may also play a part in childhood schizophrenia (Heston, 1970). Studies of monozygotic twins (e.g. Gottesman and Shields, 1972, 1976) have found that if one twin is affected, the other, regardless of environmental variables, is more prone to the condition. Because fraternal twins do not correlate nearly as highly, a genetic determinant is indicated.

DIAGNOSIS AND ASSESSMENT OF PROFOUND EMOTIONAL DISTURBANCE

Many currents of research and investigation are interwoven in the diagnosis of childhood psychoses. Unfortunately, even when psychoses can be readily diagnosed, their cures and causes often remain a mystery. Nonetheless, diagnosis is crucial if causes and cures are to be found.

The initial diagnosis of infantile autism is often difficult. Autistic children display a wide range of behaviours, many of them similar to those found in children with other disorders. Before they are correctly diagnosed, autistic children may be falsely labelled as blind, deaf, or mentally retarded.

In the past, psychotic children, especially those with infantile autism, have been considered untestable by standardized intelligence tests. As a result, standardized tests were seldom administered to them. When tests were given, incomplete results were often interpreted on the basis of the examiner's intuitive sense of the child's peak skills.

There is now a growing recognition that broad and thorough assessment of autistic children is both possible and essential for fruitful treatment (Baker, 1983; Freeman, 1976; Rutter, 1973). Rutter (1973) has discussed the importance of multidisciplinary evaluation procedures and of a developmental perspective in assessment. Other investigators (Freeman and Ritvo, 1976; Marcus, 1978) have described how cognitive and behavioural assessment data can provide the basis for educational and behavioural programming.

Although traditional intelligence tests still play a role in assessment, several instruments have been designed specifically for autistic children (e.g. Flaharty, 1976; Schopler and Reichler, 1979). These tests take the special characteristics of the autistic syndrome into account. They examine a wide range of skill levels to accommodate the scattered development typical of autistic children. They also limit the use of language to tasks that measure language skills, using non-verbal techniques to examine other skills (Baker, 1983).

Despite new testing instruments, the testing of autistic children is extremely difficult. Because of their complex and varied handicaps, autistic children are exceptions to many of the rules by which psychoeducational tests have been designed and administered.

In addition to general cognitive tests, specialized instruments are often needed to explore particular diagnostic and treatment questions. Tests used to determine receptive and expressive language skills include language questionnaires that are completed by parents and clinicians. Tests that measure behavioural and social skills are also vital components of the diagnostic battery.

CHARACTERISTICS OF THE PROFOUNDLY EMOTIONALLY DISTURBED

To many people, psychotic children are beyond comprehension. Their behaviour is bizarre, their emotions intense, and their isolation total. Psychotic children have difficulty developing language skills, learning to communicate, and learning to relate to others. They display unusual bodily movements, inordinate fears, and extreme resistance to change.

The behaviour of psychotic children has traditionally placed them in the category of the uneducable. Even with structured intervention procedures, the prognosis for them is poor. Many psychotic children continue to exhibit disordered behaviour as adults. Instead of becoming self-sufficient, they require institutionalization or continuous care.

Although autistic and schizophrenic children share some common characteristics, there are several differences between them. A primary distinguishing feature is the age of onset. Infantile autism occurs before thirty months of age, and is usually preceded by markedly abnormal behaviour patterns. Childhood schizophrenia is of later onset. These children show a normal early pattern of development, followed by severe regression as the condition takes hold.

Exhibit 11-1 presents some of the major behavioural symptoms of infantile autism and childhood schizophrenia.

Exhibit 11-1 Behavioural characteristics of profoundly disturbed children.

Behavioural symptoms	*Infantile Autism*	*Childhood Schizophrenia*
Social development		
emotional responsiveness	–	×
lack of anticipatory response	+	–
social imitation	–	+
looks and walks through people	+	–
extreme aloneness	+	–
talks to, not with	+	–
strong attachment to inanimate objects	+	–
insistence on sameness	+	–
delusions and hallucinations	–	+
Motor and sensory functions		
not physically pliable	+	–
overly sensitive to stimuli	+	–
often graceful motor performance	+	×
unusual motor behaviours, such as repetitive movements	+	+

self-stimulation	+	+
self-mutilation	+	×
odd movements and grimaces	+	+
Language and communication		
delayed acquisition	+	–
deficient, deviant babble	+	–
sometimes thought to be deaf	+	–
overly sensitive to sound	+	–
non-verbal communication	–	+
echolalia	+	–
pronominal reversal	+	–
spontaneous speech	–	+
expressive-intonational features	–	+

– seldom occurs
× may occur
+ commonly occurs

Infantile autism

Autistic children never begin to establish normal human attachments. They are extremely alone from earliest infancy, and are unresponsive to other people. As infants, autistic children show far less mutual gaze and facial responsiveness than other children. Parents report that their autistic children do not respond in the normal way to being held. These children may be indifferent to physical contact, or may even show aversion to it.

In his review of the literature, Rimland (1964) gave the following description of young autistic children:

> The first awareness of any problem is often the observation that the child fails to make the usual anticipatory movements prior to being picked up. He also fails to make the usual adjustment to his body to adapt to the person carrying or holding him. Between the fourteenth and eighteenth months, several disturbing symptoms will have begun to appear. These include prolonged rocking and headbanging in the crib, apathy and disinterest in the surroundings, unusual fear of strangers, obsessive interest in certain toys or mechanical appliances, highly repetitive and ritualistic play, insistence on being left alone and that the physical environment remains unchanged, and very unusual language behaviour (p. 7).

Rimland has focused on some of the most prominent behaviours seen in young autistic children. These and other behaviours are presented in Exhibit 11-2.

Exhibit 11-2 Symptoms of infantile autism in the pre-school child.

Birth to eighteen months:

No mutual gazing.

Feeding problems, such as poor sucking.

Lack of smile response.

Apathy and unresponsiveness.

Rigidity and stiffness or limpness and hypotonia when held.

Constant crying, or an unusual absence of crying.

Repetitive motor movements.

Obsessive interest in certain objects.

Great resistance to change.

Eighteen months to two years:

Continued poor eye contact.

Withdrawal and isolation.

Difficulties in toilet training.

Odd eating habits and food preferences.

Feeding problems, such as refusal to hold food in the mouth, refusal to chew or swallow, or gagging.

Little or no development of speech.

Little or no receptive language skills.

Disinterest in toys, but obsessive play with some items.

After two years:

Continued withdrawal and isolation.

No development of co-operative play.

Continued problems with feeding, sleeping, and toileting.

Slow or precocious motor development.

Obsessive desire for sameness.

Development of repetitive habits, gestures, and mannerisms.

Tantrums at change or restriction of activities.

In older children autism reveals itself in fleeting eye contact and the failure to develop any relationships. These children fail to form attachments to other people. They seldom initiate contact, and sometimes seem to look or walk through others. They appear distant, aloof, or in a shell, and are extremely alone. Their only strong attachments are toward inanimate objects.

Autistic children are fascinated by things that spin. They can sit for hours with a toy car upside down, endlessly spinning the wheels. Unlike other children, they are virtually impossible to distract from this behaviour. Autistic children may become frustrated very easily and launch into a screaming tantrum. This screaming can continue for so long that parents and other bystanders may feel like joining in the cacophony.

The self-absorption of autistic children may be manifested in self-mutilation, such as hand biting or head banging. It may also take the form of self-stimulation, such as finger tapping and body rocking. These children are sometimes so withdrawn and self-absorbed that they are thought to be deaf or blind (Lovaas and Newson, 1976). Autistic children also develop impaired communication skills and an obsessive insistence on sameness.

Childhood schizophrenia

Although infantile autism is generally considered the most devastating of childhood psychoses, childhood schizophrenia is also extremely incapacitating. Because childhood schizophrenia does not typically take hold until early puberty, its victims escape early impairments of development in the realms of cognition, perception, and sensation. However, when the condition does take hold, affected children regress dramatically in their behaviour and social relations.

Schizophrenia implies extreme withdrawal from the real world. Childhood schizophrenia is characterized by a wide variety of disturbances in mood, thought, and behaviour. Affected children appear to be in a fantasy world, and display emotional apathy, indifference, and withdrawal. Apathy can quickly give way, however, to uncontrollable excitement or an enraged temper trantrum.

Schizophrenic children show a marked reduction in interests and human attachments. Their close relationships are severely disrupted. They experience an overall deterioration in work, social relations, and self-care. Their speech becomes limited and may reveal incoherent thinking. They may also develop delusions and experience hallucinations.

DEVELOPMENTAL CONSEQUENCES OF PROFOUND EMOTIONAL DISTURBANCE

Childhood psychoses affect nearly every area of a child's development and seriously hinder all aspects of progress. Psychotic children exhibit a range of disordered behaviours, and may appear to be severely retarded. They lack daily living skills, including such basic self-care skills as grooming, dressing, toileting, and feeding. Their language development is often so poor as to render verbal communication impossible. Unable to communicate with others, many psychotic children seem as helpless and vulnerable as infants (Hallahan and Kauffman, 1982).

Cognitive development

Many psychotic children function at pre-academic levels. Autistic children often display an extremely low level of cognitive functioning. Schizophrenic youngsters, however, show greater variability of intellectual functioning. Poor cognitive development affects children's ability to learn. Behaviour problems interfere with attention and motivation.

Severely and profoundly disturbed children are often untestable. Among those who can be tested most have IQs in the retarded range (Kauffman, 1981). Koegel, Rincover, and Egel (1982) estimate that seventy-five percent of autistic children are retarded, most in the severe or profound range. According to Csapo (1981), sixty percent of autistic children have IQs below 50, twenty percent between 50 and 70, and only twenty have IQs above 70. According to Kauffman (1981), the average IQ of an autistic child is around 50.

Some autistic children show extreme variability in intellectual functioning. These children may perform poorly on tasks requiring abstract thought, symbolism, and sequential logic. However, they perform well on tasks that demand manual and visual-spatial skills (Cummings and Finger, 1980).

Language development

Among psychotic children, language problems are endemic. Language is intimately related to cognition and to social development. Through language, human beings make their impact upon the world and establish and maintain relationships (Konstantareas, 1982; Oxman and Konstantareas, 1981).

Typically, psychotic children withdraw into their own isolated worlds. Their communication and language is either non-existent or bizarre in nature. Many severely disturbed children do not speak at all, nor do they appear to comprehend language. Other children show echolation, parroting, meaningless jargon, and the incessant repetition of questions and statements.

Severe abnormalities of language development are among the most striking features of infantile autism (Kanner, 1943). Ricks and Wing (1975) have summarized much of the current literature on communication among autistic children. They concluded that the children's primary language difficulty was in the handling of symbols.

Exhibit 11-3 presents a schematic representation of the autistic child's basic deficits in language and communication.

From infancy, autistic children show little or no ability to analyze or make sense of sounds, particularly the strings of words that make up language. Among autistic children, language comprehension and the understanding of gestures are considerably worse than among children with other language delays. For autistic children, language deficits seem different in quality, as well as more profound (Rutter, 1975).

Autistic children are almost invariably delayed in their use of speech. As they mature, their language and communication skills remain impaired. Fully half these children never develop speech at all (Cummings and Finger, 1980). Among those who do, speech frequently consists only of meaningless, repetitive, and stereotyped utterances. Attempts to communicate are characterized by immaturity and abnormalities in grammatical construction. Autistic children often use unusual words, with curious meta-

Exhibit 11-3 A schematic representation of the basic deficits in the language and communication of the autistic child.

Qualitative Defects	*Quantitative Defects*	*Deficits in Use of Pragmatics*
Lack of speech — with lack of gesture — with elementary gesture	Echolalia — immediate — delayed	Inability to take turns. Lack of adult-directed communication.
Delay in speech — brief (months) — extensive (years)	Pronominal reversal. Neologisms.	Lack of peer-directed communication.
Limited speech — S-R chains only — more advanced, but limited usage	Metaphorical use of language. Inappropriate remarks. Stereotypical language. Defects in articulation.	Inability to use objects symbolically. Poor use of prosody for expressing intent. Poor use of visual-facial features for metacommunication.

(Konstantareas, 1982.)

phors and odd expressions. They also display a lack of expressive-intonational features, such as stress or pitch.

Autistic children have great difficulty following the conventions of conversation and interpreting linguistic and non-linguistic contextual clues. They typically perseverate on topics, fail to recognize turn-taking rules, and fail to interpret such gestural clues as eye-contact, body posture, tone of voice, and facial expression. In addition, they fail to use gestures appropriately (Light, 1983).

Autistic children display poor language development in many other areas, such as play and imaginative skills. In later life, their language problems weaken their capacity for symbolic thought and abstract reasoning (Rutter, 1978b). Language development is also related to general prognosis (Csapo, 1981). Unless children achieve some use of spontaneous language by age five or six, their outlook is likely to be poor, even in those with a relatively high level of non-verbal skills (Eisenberg, 1956; Lotter, 1974).

Perceptual development and sensory response

Autistic children are often thought to be blind or deaf. They are often oblivious to what happens around them, they ignore other people, and they do not respond to communication. They may exhibit a generalized over- or under-responsiveness to incoming stimuli. For example, they may respond to sound with indifference, distress, or intense fascination.

Autistic children may display abnormal responses to visual stimuli. While fixating on an object or on lights, they may flutter their hands, cross their eyes, glance to the side, or unfocus their eyes. They may try to smell new objects, or run their hands and tongues over rough and smooth surfaces.

Motor development and developmental discrepancies

Autistic children may show grace and dexterity in motor development, while schizophrenic youngsters tend to lag in this area. However, autistic children may possess well-developed motor skills and still not be toilet-trained or capable of dressing themselves. For autistic children, toilet training is difficult and prolonged. It is not unusual to find autistic ten-year-olds who are not yet trained.

Motility patterns

As stated earlier, language deviations are a central problem in childhood psychoses. Instead of language, children turn to less problematic, more predictable, inanimate objects. They may sit for hours spinning or twirling an object, such as a shiny ashtray. Autistic children also commonly take part in stereotyped behaviour, ranging from repetitive body movements to ritualistic actions (Rutter, 1978a). These self-stimulating behaviours include such activities as finger playing, twirling, flapping the hands, jumping, rocking, swishing saliva, patting the cheeks, staring at lights, and humming for hours on end.

The play of autistic children is repetitive, ritualistic, and solitary. Often they exhibit self-abusive behaviour, and seem impervious to self-inflicted pain. Many autistic children bite, scratch, poke, and gouge themselves, repeatedly bang heads and bodies against walls, and hit themselves in the face or body. Some children hurt themselves so often they must be kept in restraints for their own safety.

Social and emotional development

In psychotic children, social development is minimal. Even at their most developed, social interactions are limited in their quality and scope.

Among schizophrenic youngsters, social relationships are invariably disturbed. Autistic children have severely impaired relationships with parents, family members, and others in the environment. Young autistic children do not attempt to gratify their needs through meaningful relationships with others. Rather, they behave toward people as if they were inanimate objects (Kyes and Hofling, 1980).

Autistic children often resent parents and others who try to show affection. They respond with aloofness and indifference, often becoming upset when interaction is demanded. Some severely disturbed children throw massive temper tantrums, during which they bite, kick, scratch, and strike out at others. Profile 11-1 describes a schizophrenic youngster who is showing a marked increase in tantruming behavior.

PROFILE 11-1

Mark had always been a difficult child. As a baby, he cried incessantly and was so afraid of strangers he would not let his mother out of his sight. During his pre-school years, he was a whining, clinging child. By the time he was twelve, he had become totally withdrawn and seemed to survive in a fantasy world of his own making.

When Mark ventured out of his fantasy world, it was to kick, bite, scream, and throw tantrums. In Mark's special class in a large Toronto school, an incident occurred that illustrates his aberrant behaviour. Another child borrowed Mark's bottle of white-out fluid. Mark reacted by grabbing a nearby baseball bat, swinging wildly, and threatening to kill the child. When the teacher tried to restrain him by holding his arms, she was badly kicked, punched, and bitten.

Following his tirade, Mark sat for the rest of the day in his cubby. With his thumb in his mouth, he slowly rocked back and forth. All efforts to draw him out failed.

Mark has been diagnosed as suffering from childhood schizophrenia. He is in therapy and a special class, but he continues to withdraw more and more. His outbursts are becoming more violent and prolonged, and he treats other children with calculated cruelty. His parents find him almost impossible to handle in the home. They are seriously considering institutionalization.

Psychotic children show a wide range of inappropriate emotional reactions. Some show almost no emotion, while others may laugh, cry, or tantrum for no apparent reason. Autistic children may be extremely fearful of non-existent dangers, but show no fear of genuine dangers. A few have a tendency to wander, and are frequently found miles from their homes.

Prognosis

Researchers in the area of childhood psychoses agree on one thing only — the dismal prognosis for psychotic children. There is virtually no likelihood of these children attaining normal intellectual functioning within the context of available treatments and educational techniques (Suran and Rizzo, 1983). Even after years of the most effective treatment, psychotic children are likely to remain at the retarded level, requiring close supervision and care.

The educational prognosis for young autistic children improves as they learn social skills. Children must first learn basic social behaviours, such as communication, and be trained to refrain from socially unacceptable actions. After these lessons have been learned, they can proceed to further education. Unfortunately, due to their unresponsiveness and lack of communication skills, autistic children are very hard to train. Very few receive academic training beyond basic levels.

The social prognosis for autistic children is equally poor. Even the most successful autistic youngsters show impoverished human relationships and a lack of social confidence (Kugelmas, 1970). One child in six makes an adequate social adjustment to perform some kind of regular work in adulthood. Another one in six develops a modest degree of self-sufficiency. The other two-thirds remain severely handicapped and unable to live independent lives (American Psychiatric Association, 1980).

For most autistic children, then, the prognosis is incredibly bleak. When they become adults, they are likely to spend much of their lives in institutions (Lovaas, Koegel, Simmons, and Stevens-Long, 1973). For one in three autistic children, problems worsen with the onset of puberty. These children never recover to their previous already low level of functioning.

PARENTING THE PROFOUNDLY DISTURBED CHILD

Until quite recently, parental affective behaviour was viewed as a major contributing factor to childhood psychoses. Parents of autistic children were blamed for their children's condition; parental detachment and inability to relate were thought to foster the more severe isolation of autism (Friedman, 1974). Today, investigators have largely abandoned the notion that parental behaviour is the sole cause of childhood psychoses. The onus of parental guilt has been lifted.

Raising and training a psychotic child can nevertheless cause enormous stress for parents and family. Caregivers must contend with the bizarre, withdrawn attitudes of autistism or the clinging behaviours of schizophrenia. Profile 11-2 relates the experiences of one mother of an autistic child.

PROFILE 11-2

"David is our third child. Although the pregnancy was uneventful, he was born nearly a month early with a prolonged and arduous labour. When we brought David home, he was fussy and distractible, and he cried almost constantly. He had feeding problems with breast and bottle, and could not be comforted by holding or rocking. rocking.

Even with his feeding problems, David gained weight and developed into a beautiful child. However, his crying continued and worried the entire family. By the time David was a year old, we were sure he had some problem or disorder.

Most of the time, David lay in his crib. He never seemed to notice when anyone walked into the room. He never smiled, and never liked to be picked up and held. Except for crying, he made almost no sounds, especially not the babbling sounds his two older sisters had made.

At first, we suspected David was deaf. For nearly a year, we went from doctor to doctor seeking help. One doctor said David might be hearing-impaired, and told us to come back in six months. Another suggested he was severely mentally retarded, and another said he was simply slow in developing.

One evening, a friend who taught special children was visiting the house. He tried to play with David, but could garner no responses. We discussed our frustration and growing sense of hopelessness. The teacher suggested we get in touch with a local society that helped the parents of troubled children. At this time, the word autism had still never been mentioned.

Within a month of being directed to the right facilities, David had been diagnosed as autistic. In a way, the diagnosis was a relief. Although we had hoped that David was only slow to mature, we knew in our hearts that something was truly amiss. Professionals may rail against labels, but we badly needed a starting point, a direction in which to find help.

As soon as David was diagnosed, we contacted a local facility for autistic children. A therapist from the centre immediately began working with David in our home. When David was old enough, he attended a special pre-school on a daily basis.

At nine years old, David still attends a special school. As a family, we now understand his problems, although we sometimes find it very difficult to cope with them. David has

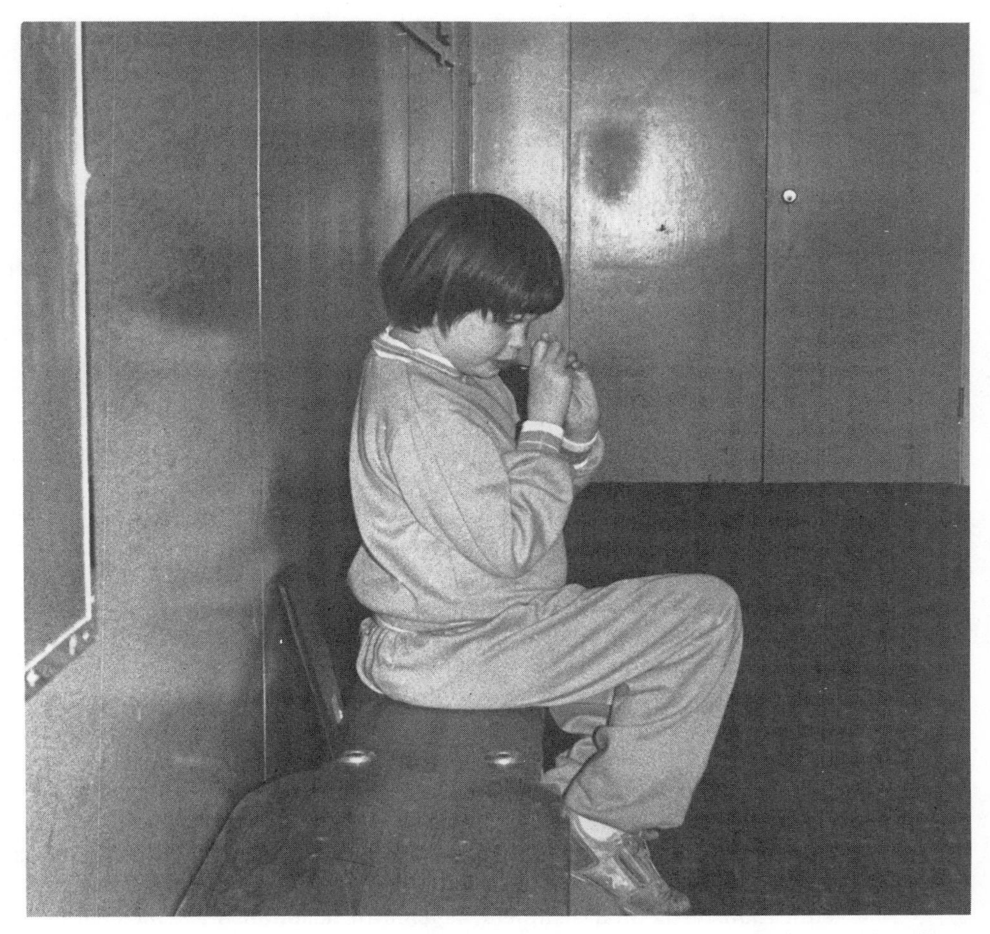

Autistic children may fail to communicate effectively with even the closest family members.
(R. Cox)

developed only a few words of speech. His baby crying has given way to a high-pitched whine, that goes on and on. David is extremely rigid in his attitudes. He has massive temper tantrums that frighten his sisters at home and embarrass us all in public. He is just beginning to be toilet-trained, and still has eating problems. He has great difficulty dressing himself, although he is better at taking his clothes off.

David's teachers and therapists have been tactful but honest in their assessment of David's potential and progress. We no longer hope that David might one day attend a regular school. Now we pray that David can learn enough skills to be self-sufficient.

Another worry is the continuing effect of David's behaviour on his older sisters. Teenagers have their own wants and needs. We cannot let David disrupt their lives too seriously. Nor can we impose too heavily on them for babysitting."

Parents of autistic children are continually faced with their children's failure to respond to interaction. Autistic children are likely to ignore the presence of their mother or other family members. They show little response to their mother's voice, do not anticipate being picked up, and do not adopt their body postures to the people holding them. Their early communication acts are generally disruptive. These behaviours inevitably have a profound effect on patterns of parental interaction. This effect is compounded in later years by these children's lack of verbal responsiveness and bizarre and inappropriate behaviours.

Early in their child's life, parents must be taught appropriate ways of handling the infant or toddler. In this way, parents can play a key role in their child's therapy. Most training programs for young autistic children are based on the development of a therapeutic one-to-one relationship. Clearly, parents are the most appropriate people to fill this position.

As Howlin (1981) points out, parental involvement in therapy ensures individual treatment for each child. Therapy can take place throughout as much of the day as possible, and does not have to be generalized from a clinic setting to the home. With parents as principal therapists, children are trained by the people who care most about their welfare and progress.

INTERVENTION WITH THE PROFOUNDLY DISTURBED

At present, there is no specific treatment to help psychotic children reduce their anxiety and cope more effectively with reality. Although much research is underway, the outlook remains discouraging. No one treatment method has yet proven notably effective with psychotic children. As a result, the prognosis for these children remains very poor (Suran and Rizzo, 1983).

Over the past years, many different approaches to therapy for psychotic children have been tried. These include psychotherapy, family therapy, speech therapy, special education, residential treatment, psychiatric hospitalization, medication, megavitamin therapy, sensory stimulation, and sensory isolation. However, despite strong claims by individual researchers, no one method has been conclusively shown to substantially alleviate childhood psychosis.

In this section, we will touch only briefly on the approaches most relevant to education. For background to this outline, the reader is urged to review the various conceptual models and educational approaches discussed in the previous chapter.

Medical intervention

A wide variety of medications have proven useful in the treatment of schizophrenic youngsters. Of these, stimulants and tranquilizers are the most commonly administered. In the treatment of autism, however, drug therapy has shown inconclusive but unpromising results (Steucher, 1972). There is little evidence that tranquilizers or stimulants significantly enhance the treatment of autistic children (Cantwell, 1975; Weiner, 1979).

Educational intervention

Although the causes of childhood psychoses are unknown, various conceptual models have been used to treat them. Treatments are unlikely to cure psychosis, but they can alleviate the symptoms. Psychotic children can learn to make small gains and develop basic skills.

Administrative arrangements

In the years following Kanner's identification of the syndrome, most autistic children were institutionalized with minimal custodial care (Light, 1983). In the 1950s, advocates began to argue that autistic children could and should be educated. However, many psychiatrists and other professionals believed that autistic children could most effectively be treated away from their homes. Treatment was based on the development of a therapeutic relationship between therapist and child. Typically, this took place in a residential setting.

By the 1970s, the education of autistic children was firmly entrenched. Moreover, professionals began to encourage parents to keep their children at home. Today, many autistic children live in their own homes. If the strain on the family becomes too great, children may be placed in foster homes, group homes, residential training centres, or institutions. Children are only enrolled in residential programs when they are seriously delayed in feeding, toileting, or self-help skills, when their families badly need relief, or when they must be placed under extensive observation and assessment.

Community programs have developed to help parents in the management and training of their autistic children. Across Canada, these programs are highly flexible and provide one-to-one therapy for each child. Community therapists work in schools, daycare, and residential treatment centres, or in the child own home. They help parents and teachers to establish and maintain appropriate behaviour and daily living skills. Community programs attempt to provide the support and training an autistic child needs to become integrated into the community.

Much controversy surrounds the placement of psychotic children in regular schools. Advocates argue that regular school placement is a vital element in normalization for all children, exceptionality notwithstanding. Opponents feel that some psychotic behaviours, such as resistance to change and inability to generalize from one situation to another, preclude regular school placement for many psychotic children. Despite this controversy, the trend in Canada today appears to be toward normalization in all areas, including the school environment.

Regardless of setting, three major approaches are used in the education and training of psychotic children. The psychodynamic and behavioural approaches are the most popular of these. A psychoeducational approach is also in use.

Psychodynamic approaches

Before the 1960s, almost all intervention with psychotic children was founded on psychodynamic principles; today, this approach is still widely used. Psychodynamic treatment is usually conducted in a residential setting away from the parents. Typically, treatment lasts several years. Children are given individual therapy within a therapeutic environment designed to promote and sustain emotional growth. Treatment may also be given through outpatient clinics or day treatment centres.

The psychodynamic approach tries to help the child understand the inner forces that guide their behaviour. By responding to the child in a way that is consistent, positive, and accepting, the therapist builds the child's confidence and trust. At the same time, the therapist helps the child to understand the sources of conflicting, ambivalent emotions.

Behavioural approaches

Autistic children have proven very resistant to psychotherapy. However, some improvement does seem to occur with the use of operant conditioning and educational techniques (Csapo, 1981). In recent years, the research literature has been flooded with positive reports of the use of behaviour therapy in the treatment of psychotic children (Margolies, 1977; Schopler, 1976).

Behavioural therapists do not claim to cure autism. Rather, they attempt to modify "deficits" and "excesses" in behaviour patterns. The basic assumptions and techniques of behaviourism were discussed in Chapter 10. Essentially, behavioural techniques attempt to establish appropriate behaviours and extinguish inappropriate ones.

Behavioural approaches have been used to teach autistic children to focus attention, to imitate actions, and to label objects and pictures (Block, Gersten and Kromblum, 1980). Children have also been taught basic speech skills, such as vocalizing and word imitation (Howlin, 1981; Lovaas, Schreibman and Koegel, 1974). Others have been helped to extinguish temper tantrums (Forehand and Atkeson, 1981).

Behaviourists claim that behaviour modification trains autistic children to lead a more useful existence. Critics respond that behavioural techniques program children to perform like robots, unable to generalize their learning to other situations. These critics claim that the child's trained responses are much too closely linked to the original training situation. Light (1983) found that a child trained to answer, "Fine, thank you" to one trainer's "How are you?" does not necessarily respond the same way to another trainer.

Despite these criticisms, the general evaluation of behaviour therapy has been cautiously optimistic. However, behaviour modification holds no promise of normalization or intellectual improvement for the autistic child. Even with behaviour modification, most autistic children still need supervision. Many will eventually be institutionalized (Csapo, 1981).

THE PROFOUNDLY DISTURBED PRE-SCHOOLER

By definition, infantile autism affects the child before thirty months of age. Autistic behaviours are clearly manifested in infancy, although not always correctly diagnosed. Ideally, the treatment for autistic infants involves the parents as well as a variety of professionals.

With proper training and support, parents can learn how to manage their child and how to stimulate social and communication development. The training of infants and toddlers begins with establishing their self-concept. Children must learn who, what, and where they are in order to realize they are separate from others. Once they are aware of themselves as separate beings, they are ready to establish basic relationships. Their prognosis improves and they are ready to learn new tasks.

Parents can be highly effective in the role of therapist, developing and maintaining many skills in their child. Howlin (1981), for example, trained parents to use behavioural techniques to stimulate language at home and to deal with obsessions, rituals, phobias, temper tantrums, and hyperactivity. The parents also learned to teach constructive play and social skills. After a six-month period, their children spoke much more than previously, and used appropriate, communicative language.

THE PROFOUNDLY DISTURBED ADOLESCENT

The prognosis for the psychotic adolescent is not nearly as promising as for the pre-school child, who is at an optimal age to develop social and communication skills. The education of a psychotic adolescent depends on the progress and abilities of each individual. In general, adolescents are primarily taught living and self-help skills to encourage them to become self-sufficient adults.

TEACHERS OF THE PROFOUNDLY EMOTIONALLY DISTURBED

The teaching and training of psychotic children is a very specialized area. Teachers require well-honed skills, great patience, and much flexibility. They must be able to work and communicate effectively with a wide variety of professionals, and be aware of new and changing techniques for stimulating psychotic children to learn. Teachers must also be comfortable in the difficult settings in which psychotic children are often educated.

SUMMARY

Childhood psychoses have a devastating effect on child development. Moreover, the prognosis for psychotic children is extremely bleak. Although many treatment approaches have been attempted in a range of settings, no one method has proven notably effective in the education and training of profoundly disturbed children.

While educators try to find ways to teach psychotic youngsters, researchers are probing into the causes of infantile autism and childhood schizophrenia. Until quite recently, the child's home environment, and especially interaction with the primary caregiver, was viewed as the major underlying cause of childhood psychosis. This environmental emphasis has now largely ceded to a stress on biological factors.

At present, investigators are avidly exploring such possible causes of psychosis as biochemical disturbance, subtle genetic aberration, and neurophysiological dysfunction. When the causes of childhood psychoses at last become known, we will be able to mount intervention approaches much more effectively.

BIBLIOGRAPHY

American Psychiatric Association. (1980). *Diagnostic and statistical manual of mental disorders. (3rd ed.)*, Washington, D.C.: American Psychiatric Association.

Anthony, E.J. (1968). Developmental antecedents of schizophrenia. In S. Katz and D. Rosenthal (Eds.), *Transmission of schizophrenia.* London: Pergamon Press.

Baker, A.F. (1983). Psychological assessment of autistic children. *Clinical Psychology Review, 3,* 44-59.

Bender, L. (1971a). Alpha and omega of childhood schizophrenia. *Journal of Autism and Childhood Schizophrenia, 1,* 115-118.

Bender, L. (1971b). The nature of childhood psychosis. In J. G. Howell (Ed.), *Modern perspectives in international child psychiatry.* New York: Brunner/Mazel.

Bettelheim, B. (1967). *The empty fortress: Infantile autism and the birth of self.* New York: Free Press.

Block, J.H., Gersten, E., and Kromblum, S. (1980). Evaluation of a language program for young autistic children. *Journal of Speech and Hearing Disorders,* 45, 76-89.

Blueler, E. (1911). *Dementia praecox or the group of schizophrenias.* New York: International University Press, 1950.

Bomberg, D., Szurek, S., and Etemad, J. (1973). A statistical study of a group of psychotic children. In S. Szurek and I.N. Berlin (Eds.), *Clinical studies in childhood psychoses.* New York: Brunner/Mazel.

Brink, J.D., Imbus, C., and Woo-Sam, J. (1980). Physical recovery after closed head trauma in children and adolescents. *Journal of Pediatrics, 97,* 721-727.

Cantwell, D.P. (1975). Clinical picture, epidemiology, and classifications of the hyperactive child syndrome. In D.P. Cantwell (Ed.), *The hyperactive child: Diagnosis, management, current research.* New York: Spectrum.

Cottle, T.J. (1976). *Barred from school: 2 million children.* Washington, D.C.: New Republic Book Company.

Csapo, M. (1979). Prevalence and needs assessment study of autistic children in British Columbia. *B.C. Journal of Special Education, 3,* 159-191.

Csapo, M. (1981). *Children with behaviour and social disorders: A Canadian focus.* Vancouver: Centre for Human Development and Research.

Cummings, S.T. and Finger, D.C. (1980). Emotional disorders. In H.E. Rie and E.D. Rie (Eds.), *Handbook of minimal brain dysfunction: A critical view.* New York: Wiley.

De Myer, M.K. (1975a). Motor, perceptual motor, and intellectual abilities in autistic children. In L. Wing (Ed.), *Early childhood autism (2nd ed.).* London: Pergamon.

De Myer, M.K. (1975b). The nature of neurophysiological disability in autistic children *Journal of Autism and Childhood Schizophrenia, 5,* 109-128.

De Myer, M.K. (1977). Research in infantile autism: A strategy and its results. In S. Chess and A. Thomas (Eds.), *Annual progress in child psychiatry and child development.* New York: Brunner/Mazel.

Despert, J.L. (1968). *Schizophrenia in children.* New York: Brunner.

Despert, J.L. (1970). *The emotionally disturbed child: An inquiry into family patterns.* New York: Anchor Books.

Deykin, E.Y. and MacMahon, B. (1979). The incidence of seizures among children with autistic symptoms. *American Journal of Psychiatry, 116,* 1310-1312.

Eisenberg, L. (1956). The autistic child in adolescence. *American Journal of Psychiatry, 112,* 607-612.

Flaharty, R. (1976). Evaluation and prescription for exceptional children. In E.R. Ritvo, B.J. Freeman, E.M. Ornitz, and P.E. Tanguay (Eds.), *Autism: Diagnosis, current research and management.* New York: Spectrum.

Forehand, R. and Atkeson, B.M. (1981). Behavior modification with severely disturbed children. In W.E. Craighead, A.E. Kazdin, and M.J. Mahoney (Eds.), *Behavior modification: Principles, issues, and applications.* Boston: Houghton Mifflin.

Freeman, B.J. (1976). Evaluating autistic children. *Journal of Pediatric Psychology, 1,* 18-21.

Freeman, B.J. and Ritvo, E.R. (1976). Cognitive assessment. In E.R. Ritvo, B.J. Freeman, E.M. Ornitz, and P.E. Tanguay (Eds.), *Autism: Diagnosis, current research and management.* New York: Spectrum.

Friedman, E. (1974). Early infantile autism. *Journal of Child Clinical Psychology, 3,* 4-10.

Fuld, P.A. and Fisher, P. (1977). Recovery of intellectual ability after closed head surgery. *Developmental Medicine and Child Neurology, 19,* 495-502.

Furneaux, B. and Roberts, B. (Eds.) (1977). *Autistic children.* London: Routledge and Paul.

Gittlelman, M. and Birch, H.G. (1967). Childhood schizophrenia: Intellectual, neurologic status, perinatal risk, prognosis, and family pathology. *Archives of General Psychiatry, 17,* 16-25.

Goldfarb, W. (1970). Childhood psychosis. In P.H. Mussen (Ed.), *Manual of child psychology*. New York: Wiley.

Goldstein, K.M., Caputo, D.V., and Taub, H.B. (1976). The effect of prenatal and perinatal complications on development at one year of age. *Child Development, 47,* 613-621.

Gottesman, I.I. and Shields, J. (1972). *Schizophrenia and genetics.* New York: Academic Press.

Gottesman, I.I. and Shields, J. (1976). A critical review of recent adoption, twin, and family studies of schizophrenics: Behavioural genetic perspectives. *Schizophrenia Bulletin, 2,* 360-401.

Hauser, S.L., De Long, G.R., and Rosman, N.P. (1975). Pneumographic findings in infantile autism syndrome: A correlation with temporal lobe disease. *Brain, 98,* 667-688.

Hallahan, D.P. and Kauffman, J.M. (1982). *Exceptional children: Introduction to special education. (2nd ed.).* Englewood Cliffs, N.J.: Prentice-Hall.

Heston, L.L. (1970). The genetics of schizophrenic and schizoid disease. *Science, 167,* 249-256.

Hingtgen, J.M. and Bryson, C.Q. (1972). Recent developments in the study of early childhood psychoses: Infantile autism, childhood schizophrenia, and related disorders. *Schizophrenia Bulletin, 5,* 8-54.

Howlin, P. (1981). The results of a home-bound language training program with autistic children. *British Journal of Disorders of Communication, 16,* 73-87.

Kanner, L. (1943). Autistic disturbances of affective contact. *Nervous Child, 2,* 217-250.

Kanner, L. (1962). Emotionally disturbed children: A historical review. *Child Development, 33,* 97-102.

Kauffman, J.M. (1981). *Characteristics of children's behavior disorders (2nd ed.).* Columbus, OH: Merrill.

Koegel, R.L., Rincover, A., and Egel, A.L. (1982). *Educating and understanding autistic children.* San Diego, CA: College-Hill Press.

Kolvin, I., Ounsted, C., and Roth, M. (1971). Cerebral dysfunction and childhood psychoses. *British Journal of Psychiatry, 118,* 407-414.

Konstantareas, M.M. (1982). Variability of linguistic impairment in autism: Its relevance to intervention. *B.C. Journal of Special Education, 6,* 231-247.

Kugelmas, I.N. (1970). *The autistic child.* Springfield, IL: Thomas.

Kyes, J. and Hofling, C.K. (1980). *Basic psychiatric concepts in nursing (4th ed.).* Toronto: Lippincott.

Lahey, B.B. and Ciminero, A.R. (1980). *Maladaptive behavior: An introduction to abnormal psychology.* Glenview, IL: Scott Foresman.

Light, J.C. (1983). Language intervention programs for autistic children. *Special Education in Canada, 57,* 11-14.

Links, P.S., Stockwell, M., Abichandani, F., and Simeon, E. (1980). Minor physical anomalies in childhood autism. Part II: Their relationship to maternal age. *Journal of Autism and Developmental disorders, 10,* 287-292.

Lotter, V. (1974). Factors relating to outcome in autistic children. *Journal of Autism and Childhood Schizophrenia, 4,* 263-277.

Lovaas, O.I. and Newsom, C.D. (1976). Behaviour modification with psychotic children. In H. Leitenberg (Ed.), *Handbook of behavior modification and behavior therapy.* Englewood Cliffs, N.J.: Prentice-Hall.

Lovaas, O.I., Koegel, R.L., Simmons, J.Q., and Stevens-Long, J.S. (1973). Some generalization and follow-up measures on autistic children in behavior therapy. *Journal of Applied Behavior Analysis, 6,* 131-166.

Lovaas, O.I., Schreibman, L., and Koegel, R.L. (1974). A behavior modification approach to the treatment of autistic children. *Journal of Autism and Childhood Schizophrenia, 4,* 111-129.

Mahler, M.S. (1952). On child psychosis and schizophrenia: Autistic and symbiotic infantile psychoses. In R.S. Eissler, (Ed.), *Psychoanalytic study of the child (Vol. 7).* New York: International University Press, pp. 286-305.

Manitoba Society for Autistic Children (1985). *Newletter.* Manitoba: Manitoba Society for Autistic Children.

Marcus, L.M. (1978). Developmental assessment as a basis for planning educational programs for autistic children. *Behavioral Disorders, 3,* 219-226.

Margolies, P.J. (1977). Behavioral approaches to the treatment of early infantile autism: A review. *Psychological Bulletin, 84* 249-264.

Meryash, D., Szymanski, L., and Gerald, P. (1982). Infantile autism associated with the fragile-X syndrome. *Journal of Autism and Developmental Disorders, 12,* 295-300.

Miller, R.T. (1974). Childhood schizophrenia: A review of selected literature. *International Journal of Mental health, 3,* 3-46.

Morse, W.C. (1975). The education of socially maladjusted and emotionally disturbed children. In W.H. Cruickshank and G.O. Johnson (Eds.), *Education of exceptional children and youth (3rd ed.).* Englewood Cliffs, N.J.: Prentice-Hall.

Mullin, B. (May 18, 1985). Group has uphill battle. *Winnipeg Free Press.*

Newsom, C. and Rincover, A. (1981). Autism. In E.J. Mash and L.G. Terdal (Eds.), *Behavioral assessment of childhood disorders.* New York: Guildford.

Ornitz, E.M. (1973). Childhood autism: A review of the clinical and experimental literature. *California Medicine, 118,* 21-47.

Ornitz, E.M. (1978). Neurophysiologic studies. In M. Rutter and E. Schopler (Eds.), *Autism: A reappraisal of concepts and treatment.* New York: Plenum.

Oxman, J. and Konstantareas, M. (1981). On the nature and variability of linguistic impairment in autism. *Clinical Psychology Review, 1,* 337-352.

Pollack, M. and Woerner, M.G. (1966). Pre- and peri-natal complications and "childhood schizophrenia": A comparison of five controlled studies. *Journal of Child Psychology and Psychiatry, 7,* 235-242.

Ricks, D.M. and Wing, L. (1975). Language, communication, and the use of symbols in normal and autistic children. *Journal of Autism and Childhood Schizophrenia, 5,* 191-221.

Rimland, B. (1964). Infantile autism. New York: Appleton-Century-Crofts.

Rimland, B. (1974). Infantile autism: Status and research. In A. Davids (Ed.), *Child personality and psychopathology: Current topics.* New York: Wiley.

Rutter, M. (1973). The assessment and treatment of preschool autistic children. *Early Child Development and Care, 3,* 13-29.

Rutter, M. (1974). The development of infantile autism. *Psychological Medicine, 4,* 147-163.

Rutter, M. (1975). The development of infantile autism. In S. Chess and A. Thomas (Eds.), *Annual progress in child psychiatry and child development.* New York: Brunner/-Mazel.

Rutter, M. (1978a). Diagnosis and definition. In M. Rutter and E. Schopler (Eds.), *Autism: A reappraisal of concepts and treatment.* New York: Plenum.

Rutter, M. (1978b). Language disorder and infantile autism. In M. Rutter and E. Schopler (Eds.), *Autism: A reappraisal of concepts and treatment.* New York: Plenum.

Schopler, E. (1976). Toward reducing behavior problems in autistic children. *Journal of Autism and Childhood Schizophrenia, 6,* 1-13.

Schopler, E. and Reichler, R.J. (1979). *Individualized assessment and treatment for autistic and developmentally disabled children (Vol. 1): Psychoeducational profile.* Baltimore, MD: University Park Press.

Stuecher, U. (1972). *Tommy: A treatment study of an autistic child.* Reston, VA: Council for Exceptional Children.

Suran, G.B. and Rizzo, J.V. (1983). *Special children: An integrative approach (2nd ed.).* Glenview, IL: Scott Foresman.

Treffert, D.A. (1970). Epidemiology of infantile autism. *Archives of General Psychiatry, 23,* 431-438.

Tsai, L., Stewart, M., and August, G. (1981). Implication of sex differences in the familial transmission of infantile autism. *Journal of Autism and Developmental Disorders, 11,* 165-173.

Valletutti, P.J. and Sims-Tucker, B.M. (Eds.). (1984). *Severely and profoundly handicapped students: Their nature and needs.* Baltimore, MD: Paul H. Brookes.

Ward, A.J. (1970). Early infantile autism: Diagnosis, etiology and treatment. *Psychological Bulletin, 73,* 350-362.

Weiner, M. (1979). *Clinical pharmacology and therapeutics in nursing.* New York: McGraw Hill.

Werry, J.S. (1971). Childhood psychosis. In H.C. Quay and J.S. Werry (Eds.), *Psychopathological disorders of childhood.* New York: Wiley.

Werry, J.S. (1979). The childhood psychoses. In H.C. Quay and J.S. Werry (Eds.), *Psychopathological disorders in childhood (2nd ed).* New York: Wiley.

White, L. (1974). Organic factors and psychophysiology in childhood schizophrenia. *Psychological Bulletin, 81,* 238-255.

Wing, L. (1972). *Autistic children.* Secaucus, N.J.: Citadel.

6

Other Exceptional Children

INTRODUCTION

The scene: The reception hall of a rehabilitation centre for children.

Enter: Barry, age thirteen, very handsome, well co-ordinated, highly intelligent, and clearly depressed. He has a slight limp in one leg. G.B., a recreation worker, follows Barry into the room.

G.B. Hi Barry! Can I help you with anything?
Barry: Nah!
G.B.: Something's bugging you!
Barry: It's this dumb, gimpy leg!
G.B.: I know it bothers you, but look at Joe who can't even sit up without being tied and George who lost an arm and a leg.
Barry: I don't care about them!
G.B. But Barry, you have so much going for you — you're smart and the other kids like you and look up to you. You can do almost anything. So why is the limp so terrible?
Barry: You don't know what this limp does to me!
G.B.: What does it do?
Barry: (with anguish) I've spent my whole life planning to be a major league pitcher!

Children with physical impairments, health problems, and multihandicaps are the subjects of the next two chapters. Chapter Twelve addresses the nature of physical and neurological disabilities and the management of children with serious health problems. Chapter Thirteen focuses on the deaf/blind, the blind and deaf mentally handicapped, and the blind and deaf physically handicapped.

Although physical, neurological, and multiple handicaps have complex, widespread, and interactive consequences, they do not conquer the indomitable human spirit. Serious handicaps often inspire great creativity and ingenious invention. The teaching of severely handicapped children presents special education with its greatest challenge, and brings into clearer focus many of the issues that face special educators today.

Chapter Fourteen deals with the problems of children from minority cultural backgrounds. Many culturally different children have special educational needs, especially when they speak little English or French. Culturally different children with handicaps often have considerable difficulty finding the help they need to overcome their problems.

CHAPTER TWELVE

Children with physical and health problems

CHARLOTTE DAVID

Physical and health problems have been with us always. Some are transient, others life-long; some occur more frequently in children, others in adults; some are associated with impairments of the nervous system, and others are not. Because of the number and diversity of health and physical problems, we cannot present very many of these conditions in this text. However, we will describe several long-term disabilities and discuss their impact on the lives of children and adolescents.

Advances in bio-medical knowledge and technology have virtually eliminated many infectious diseases, such as polio, measles, diphtheria, scarlet fever, and whooping cough. Before the advent of vaccines, such childhood illnesses were considered inevitable. Although most children survived the infections without major consequences, some children suffered lifelong effects, including sensory loss and neurological damage. Even today, despite the availability of vaccines, some children contract these diseases because they are not innoculated against them.

Many physical and health problems arise from conditions other than childhood infections. These include impairments associated with prenatal problems, prematurity, and problems of gestation. Physical and health problems may also arise from a variety of genetic and environmental causes.

Physically disabled students are those who have a physical impairment, other than a visual or a hearing loss. Children with **chronic health problems** are those with diseases or medical conditions that interfere with their ability to lead a normal life.

PREVALENCE OF PHYSICAL AND HEALTH PROBLEMS

The prevalence of chronic health and physical problems is very difficult to determine in view of the variety of conditions that give rise to such problems. Many inconsistencies occur in the definitions of various disorders. Different provinces use different methods for gathering data producing very different results. Nation-wide health statistics tend to rely on a limited number of categories, which means that many health problems go uncounted. In both provincial and national surveys, individuals with multiple handicaps may be counted several times.

Schiffer and Hunt (1963) studied data collected by the U.S. National Health Survey between 1954 and 1961. They found that about one child in every five under the age of seventeen had at least one chronic disorder. Approximately one half of all the reported chronic conditions were allergic and respiratory disorders. Another 11 to 12 percent involved paralysis and orthopedic disorders. The remaining 40.5 percent reflected a wide range of other chronic conditions. Canadian figures are probably similar to these.

One of the paradoxes in the advance of medicine is that the prevalence of certain conditions has actually increased. This is because children now survive with physical or health problems that would have claimed their lives a decade or more ago. For example, premature babies born as early as twenty-four weeks and weighing little more than fifteen hundred grams can now be successfully cared for in neonatal intensive care units. These infants, who would not have lived a few decades ago, now have about a thirty-percent chance to survive. The survival rate increases to sixty percent after twenty-eight weeks, and to eighty-five or ninety percent at twenty-eight weeks (Musgrove, 1984). However, from fifteen to twenty percent of these premature infants suffer handicapping conditions (Musgrove, 1984) a much higher ratio than occurs in children born at full term.

Of course, medical advances have also lowered the prevalence rates of some conditions. The development of anti-polio and other vaccines has resulted in a marked decline in the incidence of certain diseases.

CHILDREN'S CONCEPTS OF ILLNESS AND DISABILITY

A child's concept of illness or disability is clearly age-related. The child too young to understand abstractions and causal relationships tends to assume that someone must be to blame for an illness. For example, a young child in hospital with a respiratory illness might explain this condition with the statement: "My brother took my umbrella away and I got wet."

Vernon, Foley, Sipowicz, and Schulman (1965) concluded that children's conceptions of illness are associated with punishment and abandonment. Children "do not experience an illness or disability as an objective, comprehensive event that occurs to the body. Instead, they experience the illness subjectively and bring their own experience to bear in making sense of the illness" (Suran and Rizzo, 1979, p. 181). Gradually, however, children learn to understand such concepts as bacteria, germs, and accidents. They then begin to define illness in adult terms.

Simeonsson, Buckley, and Monson (1979) studied sixty hospitalized children, aged five, seven, and nine years of age. They concluded that, with advancing age, children tend to shift their concepts of illness causality from concrete to abstract notions.

THE CENTRAL NERVOUS SYSTEM

The spinal cord and the brain are the two major components of the central nervous system. Each is composed of neurons and glial cells. **Neurons** (nerve cells) are the basic units of neurological function, while the **glial cells** support and nourish the neurons.

In common with all cells, neurons have a cell body, a cell membrane, a nucleus, and a cytoplasm. However, unlike other cells, mature neurons do not reproduce. When they are destroyed, their loss is permanent.

Neurons vary in size, shape, and location, but share two distinguishing physical features — the dendrites and the axons. The **dendrites** and the cell body receive incoming electrical signals. The **axons** contain molecules of chemical transmitters to send the nervous impulse from one nerve cell to another. The impulse travels across a gap, which is called the synapse.

The network of neurons includes **receptor cells**, which provide us with sensory information. It also includes **motor cells**, which activate responses to the outside world. Between receptor and motor cells lie neurons that process such functions as emotions, memory, learning, and thought.

All neural tissue can be described as either grey or white. The grey matter is composed of cell bodies and their dendrites. The white matter is composed of axons, which are covered in a white fatty sheath of **myelin**. Although the central nervous system of newborn children contains the full component of neurons, comparatively few of the axons are covered with myelin. As the central nervous system develops, dendrites and axons grow and myelin is laid down. This is essential for the smooth transmission of neural signals.

The spinal cord

The spinal cord is a pencil-thin, segmented collection of neurons that are related to specific parts of the body. Each segment contains both sensory and motor neurons. The axons of sensory cells transmit information from each side of the body to the opposite side of the brain. Bodily sensation is limited to touch, temperature, pressure, pain, and proprioception, which is the awareness of body movement. The motor cells on each side of the spinal cord receive messages from the motor cells on the opposite side of the brain.

The spinal cord also acts as a reflex centre. If you touch a very hot object you pull your hand away quickly. The pain receptors in your skin cause sensory nerves to send a message to the motor cells in the spinal cord. The spinal cord quickly sends back a message that causes the hand to move. This reflex occurs before the brain even has time to assess the situation.

Damage to sensory cells in the spinal cord results in loss of sensation to the parts of the body affected by those cells. Damage to motor cells in the spinal cord results in **flaccid paralysis**. This is an inability to move the muscles because the neural impulses needed for muscle contraction are lacking.

Figure 12-1 Human Brain: Lateral view of left hemisphere.

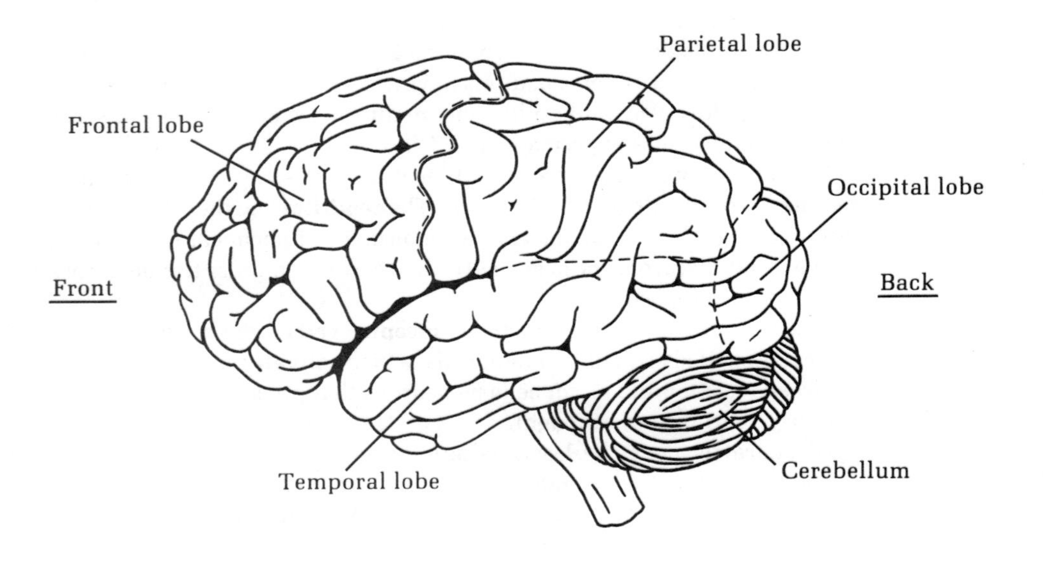

Figure 12-2 Medial view of right hemisphere.

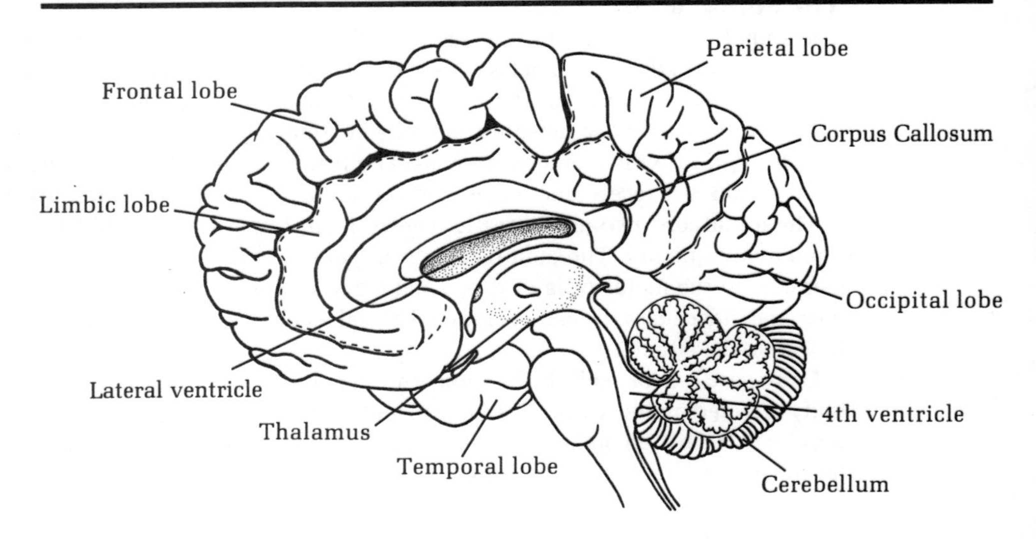

The brain

The brain is a densely packed, incredibly complex organ that weights about 1.4 kilograms and contains billions of neurons. The brain is so complex that many scientists believe it is beyond its own ability to comprehend.

For the sake of brevity, our discussion of the human brain will be limited to the cerebrum, the thalamus, the hypothalamus, and the basal ganglia.

The **cerebrum** consists of the left and the right hemispheres of the brain. Although these hemispheres look much alike, they are not functionally the same. The left hemisphere is sometimes referred to as the analytic brain, while the right hemisphere is referred to as the aesthetic brain. The capacity for speech, for example, is usually located in the left hemisphere.

The two hemispheres are interconnected by a great many myelin-covered axons that convey information from one side to the other. These axons are so densely packed that in the medial section of the cerebrum they appear to form a single white body, called the **corpus callosum**. The outer section of the cerebrum consists of the grey cell bodies of the **cerebral cortex**, believed to be the most highly evolved portion of the central nervous system. The cerebral cortex enables a broad spectrum of highly complex human cognitive functions.

In early studies of the cerebral cortex, researchers found that its neurons differed in shape, size, and distribution. Using that information, researchers produced numerical maps of the cortex that we still refer to today when speaking of its parts. Another, less specific way to identify the parts of the cortex is by its lobes. The occipital lobe is associated with vision, and the parietal lobe is involved in spatial orientation. The frontal lobe appears to be necessary in anticipatory activity, and the temporal lobe has an auditory function. A fifth lobe, which is apparent only in a medial view of the brain, appears to be associated with sexual and emotional functions. The lobes may also perform other functions besides these primary ones. Indeed, researchers are finding that many parts of the brain contribute to functions hitherto only associated with one specific area.

Among the many substructures within each hemisphere of the brain are the thalamus, the hypothalamus, and the basal ganglia. In addition to its other functions, the **thalamus** acts as a relay station between sensory systems and the cerebral cortex. The **hypothalamus** is important in the control of the internal environment of the body. The **cerebellum** and the **basal ganglia** share control in the co-ordination of both fine and gross motor activity. They also control the maintenance of posture and equilibrium.

The brain also contains four ventricles. At these sites, cerebrospinal fluid is manufactured. Cerebrospinal fluid circulates within and around the brain and spinal cord.

NEUROLOGICAL IMPAIRMENTS

Neurological impairments result from damage or dysfunction of the brain and/or spinal cord. Such damage may occur before, during, or after birth. The effects of such damage vary greatly. Wide variations occur in the onset of symptoms, the parts of the body involved, the nature of symptoms, the degree of severity, and the possible multiplicity of impairments.

Injury to the spinal cord alone tends to result in motor and sensory disabilities, without affecting such areas as intellectual function and special sensory functions (vision, hearing, and speech). Injury to the brain may result in a relatively limited specific disorder. However, such an injury may also cause very wide-ranging effects, including motor disturbance, sensory loss, intellectual deficit, speech and language disorders, and emotional and behavioural difficulties.

Most spinal cord damage is caused by congenital malformations, infections, or accidents. Damage to the brain, however, may result from many other causes besides these.

Exhibit 12-1 outlines some of the causes of damage to the central nervous system.

Exhibit 12-1

Some causes of damage to the central nervous system, with examples.

Cause	*Example*
neoplasms	brain tumour
oxygen deprivation (anoxia)	carbon monoxide poisoning
maternal infection	rubella, syphilis
maternal intoxication	fetal alcohol syndrome
child intoxication	lead poisoning
child infection	encephalitis
malnutrition	inadequate protein before or shortly after birth
vascular accidents	brain hemorrhage
radiation	excessive x-rays
genetic defects	errors of metabolism
developmental errors	absence of brain substance
trauma	automobile accident resulting in direct brain injury
chromosomal abnormalities	Down's syndrome
gestational problems	prematurity

Because so many factors have been associated with neural and physical damage, a science has been established to study them. **Teratology** is the study of agents that interfere with normal embryological or fetal development. Such agents, called **teratogens**, include drugs, viral and bacterial infections, heavy metals, pollutants, irradiation, and the like.

Cerebral palsy

Cerebral palsy is a condition caused by damage to the brain before, during, or after birth. It is chiefly characterized by motor disorder and often accompanied by other disabilities. The diagnosis of cerebral palsy is age-related. A child who suffers damage to the motor systems of the brain after about age six is not diagnosed as having cerebral palsy, even when the same motor disorders are present.

Although cerebral palsy is neither progressive nor curable, therapeutic programs are nonetheless important. Physical therapy can prevent such physical problems as **contracture**, a shortening of the muscles, tendons, and ligaments that results in postural distortion.

Prevalence of cerebral palsy

Cerebral palsy is one of the most common crippling disorders in children. The incidence and prevalence figures for this condition vary according to the perspectives of various authors. Friedman and MacQueen (1971) estimated the prevalence of cerebral palsy at 1.7 per 1000 live children. However, they included only those children in need of special education. Kurland, Kurtzke, and Goldberg (1973) suggest an incidence rate of 1 child per 1000 live births, and a prevalence rate of .6 per 1000 live children. The most commonly estimated incidence figures range from 3 to 6 cerebral-palsied children per 1000 live births (Apgar and Beck, 1974).

Classification of cerebral palsy

Cerebral palsy may be classified by topography or by type. The topographical classification system refers to the parts of the body, and is not limited to cerebral palsy alone. Exhibit 12-2 outlines the topographical system. Note that the suffix *plegia* refers to paralysis.

Exhibit 12-2

Topographical classification of cerebral palsy.

Monoplegia	One limb impaired.
Diplegia	Four limbs involved, with legs most impaired.
Hemiplegia	One side of the body impaired.
Paraplegia	Lower limbs of the body impaired.
Triplegia	Three limbs impaired.
Double hemiplegia	Both sides of the body impaired, with each side affected differently.
Quadriplegia	All four limbs impaired.

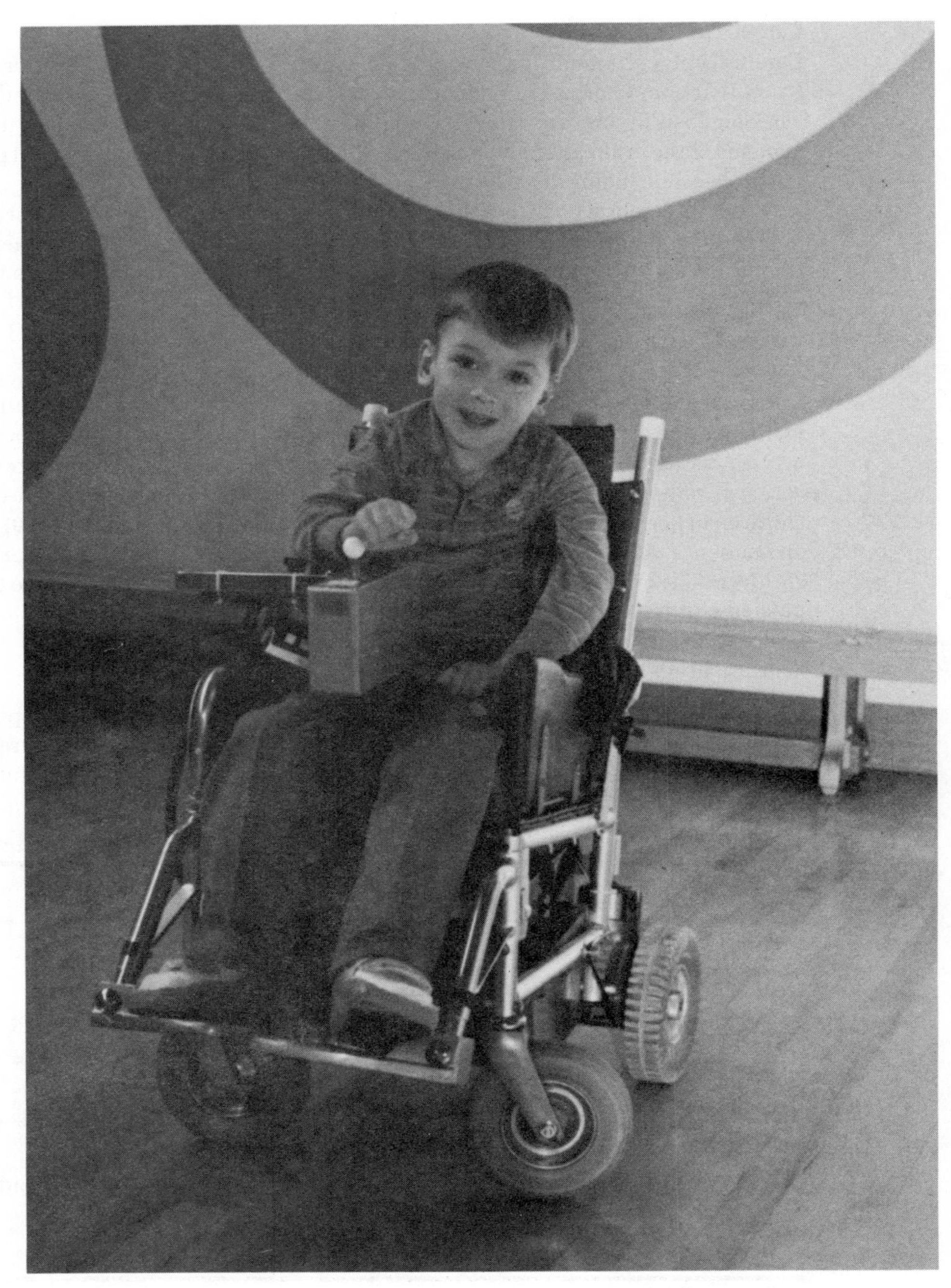

In this electric wheel-chair, controls are positioned in the midline to eliminate extraneous reflex activity. Ball-grip accommodates the spastic hand grasp. (L. Snider)

When classified by type, cerebral palsy can be differentiated according to five specific motor patterns. **Spastic cerebral palsy** affects approximately fifty percent of the cerebral palsied population. **Spasticity** is characterized by slow, laborious, poorly co-ordinated voluntary movement. It results from the continued presence of a primitive reflex called the **stretch reflex**. The stretch reflex is one of several primitive reflexes present in all newborns. If these reflexes persist beyond infancy, they act as impediments to the development of smooth, co-ordinated movement.

Virtually all muscles exist in pairs that are antagonistic in action. For example, to bend the arm at the elbow, the biceps muscle contracts and the opposing muscle, the triceps, relaxes. In the presence of the stretch reflex, however, a muscle contracts involuntarily when suddenly stretched. Thus, when the arm is bent suddenly the biceps contracts, but the reflex causes contraction in the opposing triceps as well. A "mini-war" results, rendering movement impossible to control. Children with spastic cerebral palsy, then, cannot move when and how they choose.

Athetoid cerebral palsy is found in approximately twenty-five percent of the cerebral-palsied population. **Athetosis** is characterized by constant, involuntary, writhing movements, especially in the hands and wrists. Contractions occur in successive groups of muscles, creating extraneous movement that interferes with purposive action. Children with athetoid cerebral palsy are unable to stop moving when they want to. However, athetosis does stop during sleep.

Ataxic cerebral palsy occurs in approximately fifteen percent of sufferers. **Ataxia** is characterized by poor co-ordination of the movements associated with balance, posture, and spatial orientation. Children with ataxia tend to walk with a wide gait, their legs well apart to compensate for poor equilibrium. They also exhibit generalized inco-ordination of both fine and gross movements.

Rigidity is a rare form of cerebral palsy. It is characterized by continuous diffuse muscle tension resulting in stiffness. **Tremors** are also rare. This type of cerebral palsy is characterized by involuntary, rhythmic movements of certain muscles. Some classifications include the category of mixed cerebral palsy. This denotes the presence of two or more types in the same person.

The brain damage that results in cerebral palsy is not always limited to motor areas alone. Indeed, cerebral palsy can generally be seen as a multi-handicapping condition (Cruickshank, 1976). Most children with cerebral palsy, whether mild, moderate, or severe, are likely to exhibit one or more additional impairments. These impairments include mental retardation, learning disabilities, sensory loss, epilepsy, speech difficulties, and emotional and behavioural disorders.

Associated disabilities

Mental retardation Many people assume from the external appearance of the condition that children with cerebral palsy are mentally retarded. In fact, children with cerebral palsy display a full range of intellectual ability, from severe impairment to giftedness. However, the hypothetical intelligence curve for these children indicates that the incidence of mental retardation is significantly higher than average. Little evidence exists to link the severity of intellectual impairment with any particular type of cerebral palsy.

The intelligence testing of cerebral-palsied children is often very difficult. Intelligence tests are largely standardized on a physically normal population. Many of the tasks that are used in such tests must be eliminated because of motor difficulties, sensory impairment and special problems. If standard tests are used at all, they must be used with a high degree of sophistication.

Speech and language problems Speech difficulties in cerebral-palsied children are essentially an aspect of motor disorder. Adequate speech requires control of breathing, movement of mouth and lips, and manipulation of the tongue. As a result of poor muscle co-ordination, children with cerebral palsy enunciate their words poorly and are sometimes unintelligible.

The errors of articulation that accompany cerebral palsy are known by a separate label. **Dysarthria** is defined as a disorder of articulation, resulting from brain damage, associated with poor control of the muscles of speech. As in the case of intellectual functioning, estimates of the prevalence of speech disorders vary. According to these estimates, from fifty to eighty-three percent of cerebral-palsied children have speech problems (Cruickshank, 1976; Stephen, 1958).

Language impairments are quite different from speech disorders. Language includes symbols in many forms: speech, writing, gestures (movement), and so on. Language impairments are much less common than speech disorders. However, damage to certain parts of the cerebral hemisphere — usually the left hemisphere — can result in language disorders for some children with cerebral palsy.

Sensory loss Visual, auditory, and other sensory impairments are relatively common among cerebral-palsied children. Sensory impairments have been reported in half the cases of hemiplegic cerebral palsy (Tizzard, Paine, and Carothers, 1954). For discussion of the effects of sensory problems, see Chapters Eight, Nine, and Thirteen.

Other related problems An estimated one-half of children with cerebral palsy suffer one or more epileptic seizures. In addition, from fifteen to twenty percent of cerebral-palsied youngsters are likely to have some type of specific learning disability (Telford and Sawrey, 1981).

Developmental consequences of cerebral palsy

As the number of accompanying disorders indicates, cerebral palsy is a very complex multihandicapping condition. However, not every child with cerebral palsy faces all or even most of these disorders. Usually children with limited and localized brain injuries face fewer limitations than children with diffuse, extensive brain damage.

The developmental consequences of cerebral palsy vary in relation to many factors. These include:

- The type of cerebral palsy.
- The degree of severity.

- The presence or absence of other disabilities in addition to motor disorders.
- The time of diagnosis and intervention.
- The availability of appropriate services for both child and parents.
- The attitudes and rearing practices of the family.

It is reasonable to assume then, that no two children with cerebral palsy develop in the same way. Nevertheless, the presence of extensive motor disorder alone does, to a greater or lesser degree, interfere with normal development.

Each stage of motor development causes a shift in a child's interaction with the environment. Within twelve to fourteen weeks of birth, normal children achieve control of head movements. Within six months, they pull to a sitting position. At about twelve to fourteen months, they begin to walk unaided. These milestones offer children increased opportunities to make better use of sensory experience, to gain greater perceptual awareness, and to learn to manipulate objects and the self.

Damage to the motor systems impedes this course of normal development. Cerebral-palsied children have little control of the musculature necessary to reach developmental milestones. Intervention must take place as early as possible to create the opportunities and experiences necessary for a child's development. When other problems, such as sensory loss or speech disorders, are also present, early intervention is even more important.

Technical and educational aids

Cerebral-palsied children often require technical aids to improve ambulation, such as wheelchairs, crutches, braces, and standing tables. Children with articulation difficulties may require devices that act as substitutes for speech. Children who cannot speak intelligibly or manipulate objects by hand may have enough head control to use a head wand. This wand, attached to a headband or helmet, can be used for pointing, manipulating switches, painting, calculating, and communicating via an electric typewriter or computer.

Children who can point with hands or head wands can use Blissymbolics and other pictographic systems to substitute for speech. Blissymbolics were invented by Charles Bliss to serve as the basis of an international language. Although Bliss never achieved this goal, his symbols have allowed many severely disabled persons to communicate with those around them. Bliss symbols include nouns, actions, emotions, concepts, and combinations.

Daily living aids include special devices to assist such functions as eating, dressing, and brushing teeth. For example, the **spork** (combined spoon and fork) acts as both a spearing and scooping device. A child unable to grasp properly can hold the spork with help from a band around the hand. The child may also use this band to hold a toothbrush, a crayon, and many other objects.

Many other ingenious orthotics have been developed by inventive people. An **orthotic** is an instrument that replaces a relatively non-functional part of the body.

Adapted pencil grip makes use of existing hand function to develop more complex prehensile activity. *(L. Snider)*

PROFILE 12-1

In the first years of her life, Rhonda was diagnosed as having quadraplegic cerebral palsy. She showed the pattern of uncontrolled extraneous movement characterized by athetosis. As she progressed through the pre-school years, the severity of her motor impairment became clear. She was unable to walk or even sit without support, and her speech was virtually unintelligible. However, despite her speech problems, Rhonda was perfectly capable of understanding the speech and language of others.

As Rhonda approached school age, she was enrolled in a rehabilitation day centre. There she received physical and occupational therapy, speech training, and schooling. Rhonda's teachers soon realized that, despite her severe motor handicaps, Rhonda was intellectually gifted.

Throughout the elementary grades, Rhonda was provided with special devices that permitted her to communicate her knowledge. For example, she used an electric typewriter with a plate covering the spaces between the keys. Because Rhonda had insufficient control of her fingers, she typed with a wand attached to her head band. Although her head had to be supported, she managed to produce much of her school work through this device.

Rhonda's intellectual capacity opened the doors for her entry into a regular secondary school. There were, of course, many limitations in Rhonda's school life. Because of her motor disability, she could not type at a normal rate. Although a few teachers and students learned to understand her speech, she took longer to communicate with others. She was also unable to participate in many social activities.

Despite Rhonda's limitations, she made many friends at school. She was particularly interested in literature, and successfully graduated from secondary school. After graduation, she left home to share an apartment with two friends.

As an adult, Rhonda still partly depends on others to assist her in many physical ways. However, she is very capable in her profession as free-lance journalist and poet. In her writing, Rhonda explores many issues that involve the handicapped community. In particular, she is concerned about the attitudes of non-handicapped society. Rhonda wants to persuade society that handicapped adults can make their own decisions and take full responsibility for their own lives.

Epilepsy

Epilepsy is one of the oldest recorded disorders of humanity. Early Greek literature records that Hippocrates ascribed epilepsy to a disorder of the brain. In the Gospel according to St. Mark, clear references are made to epileptic seizures (Robb, 1981). Despite this early awareness, however, there was little known of the causes of epilepsy. Early theories of its origin largely concerned magic and the visitations of good or evil spirits.

During the 1800s the great neurologist, Hughlings Jackson, defined epilepsy as a condition produced by a sudden, violent, electrical discharge of brain cells. The International League Against Epilepsy, a world-wide organization of scientists, defines epilepsy as a chronic condition of various origins characterized by recurrent epileptic seizures, no matter what other clinical or laboratory signs and symptoms appear (Epilepsy Foundation of America, 1973).

The word *epilepsy* is derived from the Greek meaning "to be seized" and we still describe epilepsy in terms of seizures. A seizure may sometimes be called a convulsion or fit. A single seizure may occur in a person who does not have epilepsy. Such a symptom might reflect some transitory event, such as high fever, heat exhaustion, ingestion of certain chemicals, or interference with the normal supply of oxygen to the brain.

Etiology of epilepsy

Epilepsy is not a disease, but a symptom of brain disorder. It may be caused by any condition that results in damage to the brain or its functions. However, this does not imply that brain damage necessarily results in epileptic seizures.

Sometimes the causes of epilepsy cannot be found. In that case, we refer to the condition as **idiopathic epilepsy**, or epilepsy of unknown origin. If the individual shows strong evidence of brain damage, we refer to the condition as **symptomatic epilepsy**.

Prevalence of epilepsy

Estimates of the prevalence of epilepsy vary from 0.5 to 1.0 percent of the population. Variations depend on the definition of injury and on whether transient, episodic convulsions are included in the figures (Hallahan and Kauffman, 1982). When Guerin (1979) investigated the populations of more than twenty schools, he found that 3.65 per 1000 children had epilepsy.

Classification of epilepsy

Many kinds of seizures fall under the general classification of epilepsy. The type of seizure depends on the region of the brain in which it originates. The type of seizure also depends, to some extent, on the brain's maturation and its ability to spread the electric discharge to other parts of the body (Robb, 1981).

Although the International Classification of Epileptic Seizures (Gastaut, 1970) is somewhat complex for our purposes, it does make a useful distinction between generalized and partial seizures. **Generalized seizures** are bilateral and symmetrical without local onset in the brain. They are often accompanied by loss of consciousness. **Partial seizures** begin locally and may or may not cause alterations in consciousness.

The most common forms of generalized seizure are **grand mal** and **petit mal** seizures. Many individuals experience both these forms.

The grand mal seizure proceeds through relatively distinct stages. Some epileptics consistently experience an aura just before the seizure's onset. This aura may be a subjective sensory or memory experience, such as an odour that is not present in reality. It may take the form of an odd internal sensation, or even a memory phenomenon in which the person actually experiences a scene from the past (Krupp and Chatton, 1983).

Shortly after the aura appears, the individual loses consciousness, falls, and develops generalized stiffness of the body. During this tonic phase, the arms are flexed (bent) and the legs extended (straight). The trunk muscles are also in spasm, so that breathing ceases.

After a varying period of tonic activity, the clonic stage follows. In this phase, the person exhibits alternate relaxations and contractions of the skeletal musculature. These produce what are often referred to as thrashing movements. In the throes of the clonic state, the person may lose bladder and bowel control, bite the tongue, and froth at the mouth.

After two to five minutes, convulsive movements diminish and finally stop. This is followed by the gradual regaining of consciousness. During this time, the person may experience confusion, headache, or other symptoms. A period of deep sleep marks the end of the seizure.

Exhibit 12-3 presents some tips and procedures for teachers of epileptic children. If a child has a seizure in the classroom, teachers should do all they can to prevent injury.

Exhibit 12-3

How to cope with an epileptic seizure in the classroom.

- Keep calm. Children are less likely to panic if you appear in control.
- Loosen the convulsing child's collar and other tight clothing.
- Put something soft under the child's head.
- Do not try to restrain the child — you cannot stop the seizure.
- Remove dangerous obstacles, such as furniture and sharp objects.
- Do not force anything between the child's teeth.
- After the seizure, turn the child to one side to allow saliva to drain from the mouth.
- Do not offer anything to drink until the child is fully awake.
- Let the child rest afterward.
- If the seizure lasts beyond five minutes, or if the child seems to pass from one seizure to another without regaining consciousness, call the school nurse or physician and notify the child's parents. This is a rare occurrence and should be treated as an emergency.
- After the seizure, offer the child emotional reassurance.

The petit mal seizure is considerably less dramatic than the grand mal. The petit mal is often referred to as an "absence seizure." It most frequently occurs in children.

The classic absence seizure takes only fifteen to thirty seconds. It is so brief that it is often overlooked or misinterpreted. The child ceases all activity and appears to stare vacantly, as though daydreaming. During this period, there is a loss or clouding of consciousness. The return to consciousness is abrupt, and the child immediately resumes interrupted activities.

During other forms of petit mal seizure, the child's eyes may blink or shift and the hands may move aimlessly. On some occasions, the seizure may be prolonged, lasting for minutes or hours. During these long seizures, the child may simply appear confused and dazed.

Petit mal seizures are likely to occur several times a day. They often occur when the child is sedentary, and infrequently during exercise (Berkow, 1982). Both grand mal and petit mal seizures may be either idiopathic or symptomatic.

Partial seizures occur in many forms, but the common feature in each is the localized origin of brain irritability. One form of partial seizure is the **Jacksonian seizure**, which is characterized by motor symptoms without impaired consciousness. For example, spasmodic (clonic) movements might start in the peripheral portion of a limb, such as the left thumb. These movements might then progress in an orderly fashion toward the central portion of the body down into the left leg.

The Jacksonian seizure only occurs in cases of symptomatic epilepsy. Sometimes the violent electrical discharge that begins in one hemisphere of the brain spreads to the other. If this happens, the individual loses consciousness and undergoes a grand mal convulsion.

Another type of partial seizure is the **psychomotor seizure**, sometimes called the psychomotor equivalent. Psychomotor seizures often include a clouding of consciousness and amnesia (loss of memory of the event). These symptoms are accompanied by relatively complex, well-organized movements, such as plucking at clothing or any other patterned activity.

Treatment of epilepsy

Medical treatment of epilepsy focuses primarily on control of the seizures. Drug therapy can control about fifty percent of grand mal seizures, forty percent of petit mals, and thirty-five percent of psychomotor seizures. Drugs can also reduce the frequency of grand mal and petit mal seizures in thirty-five percent of cases, and of psychomotor attacks in fifty percent of cases (Berkow, 1982). The choice of drugs is related to the type of seizure pattern and the presence of side effects from the drugs.

Developmental consequences of epilepsy

The developmental consequences of epilepsy are apt to be extremely varied. Children with idiopathic epilepsy are likely to develop normally whereas those with symptomatic epilepsy are not.

Children who experience seizures before age two are usually suffering the effects of developmental defects, birth injuries, or a metabolic disease affecting the brain (Berkow, 1982). These children are more likely to exhibit multiple disorders, such as mental retardation, sensory loss or motor disability. For these children, developmental consequences are determined by the number and types of additional disorders.

Idiopathic epilepsy generally begins between two and fourteen years of age. Most children with idiopathic epilepsy function normally between attacks, and approximately seventy percent have normal or higher intelligence (Dikmen, Matthews, and Harley, 1975). The seizures themselves do not seem to cause mental retardation (Suran and Rizzo, 1983).

The stigma of epilepsy

The major handicap of epilepsy is not the condition itself, but society's attitude toward it. Confusion and misunderstanding continue to surround the condition, despite the success of modern treatment. As a result, epileptics face discrimination in employment, in social relations, driving automobiles and so on (Telford and Sawrey, 1981).

Even though many well known, distinguished people with epilepsy have made important contributions to society, negative myths about the condition remain. Some people continue to equate epilepsy with mental retardation or mental illness. Although some persons with symptomatic epilepsy may exhibit mental retardation, they are in the minority of the epileptic population. Among persons with idiopathic epilepsy, mental illness does not occur more frequently than in the larger population.

Our culture greatly values beauty, health, and perfection. Seizures, particularly of the grand mal variety, are not consonant with those values. The observer of a grand mal seizure may become frightened by the victim's loss of self-control, and conclude that epilepsy is a major imperfection. Although children with epilepsy are usually as healthy as other children, they are generally perceived as suffering from an illness. All these factors help to account for society's negative response to epilepsy (Epilepsy Foundation of America, 1973).

Fetal Alcohol Syndrome

The connection between maternal alcohol consumption and faulty development of offspring has been recognized since ancient times (Benson, Bobak, and Jensen, 1981). In the Old Testament, for example, an angel warns the mother of Samson: "Thou shalt conceive and bear a son. Now therefore beware, I pray thee, and drink not wine or strong drink" (Judges 13:3-4). However, only in the last decade has a relationship been truly established between chronic maternal drinking and a specific pattern of anomalies in their infants.

Fetal Alcohol Syndrome (FAS) is a unique disorder characterized by a pattern of anomalies in the children of drinking mothers. It is usually recognized as a major cause of birth defects and mental retardation today (Edwards, 1981).

Etiology of Fetal Alcohol Syndrome

Ethanol is the kind of alcohol used in beer, wine, whiskey, and other alcoholic beverages. Ethanol crosses the placental barrier and enters the bloodstream of the fetus. Like all alcohol, ethanol has an affinity for the brain and an enormous capacity to absorb water. Enloe (1980) suggests that alcohol absorbs fluid from the developing brain of the fetus, resulting in the death of brain cells. A concomitant reduction in brain size due to fluid loss may result in mental retardation.

Much is still unknown about Fetal Alcohol Syndrome. The medical profession has not yet determined a safe level of alcohol for pregnant mothers. However, heavy drinking during pregnancy has been defined as an intake of ninety millilitres or about three ounces of absolute alcohol (Landesman-Dwyer, Martin, Smith, and Streissguth, 1980).

Because of metabolic variations in individuals, little is definitively known about the relationship between quantity and frequency of maternal alcohol ingestion and the number of child defects. Future research may provide data on the effects of alcohol with regard to critical periods of fetal development (Graham-Clay, 1983).

Prevalence of Fetal Alcohol Syndrome

General estimates of the incidence of full-blown Fetal Alcohol Syndrome are one to two per thousand live births. Children who exhibit only partial FAS are thought to number three to five live births per thousand (Sandor, 1981). For many reasons, these figures are probably underestimations. The syndrome may sometimes go undiagnosed, particularly if the condition is not full blown. Symptoms may be mistaken for another condition, particularly if the doctor is not aware that the mother drinks.

Developmental consequences of Fetal Alcohol Syndrome

In its full form, Fetal Alcohol Syndrome may affect the child's entire body. Abnormalities may be present in the nervous system, the musculo-skeletal structure, the cranio-facial structure, and the internal organs, especially the heart and genito-urinary tract. Exhibit 12-4 outlines some of the problems that may be associated with FAS.

Exhibit 12-4

Specific symptoms associated with Fetal Alcohol Syndrome.

Neurological	*Craniofacial*
mental retardation	low set ears
microcephaly (small head)	short low-bridged nose
seizures	epicanthic folds
tremors	short lower jaw
irritability	long upper lip
poor fine co-ordination	droopy eyelids
hyperactivity	high palate
speech delay	
Skeletal	*Other*
club foot	cardiac defects
spinal fusion	kidney defects
growth deficiency	genital defects
abnormal palmar creases	low weight gain

Absante (1981) studied a group of seventy-four children with FAS. The children exhibited seizures, irritability, speech delay, skeletal malformations, signs of cerebral palsy, general developmental delay, behavioural problems, mental retardation, and other learning deficits. These disorders occurred in numerous combinations. The incidence of each sign was variable, ranging from three to thirty-two percent of the studied population.

The educational consequences of FAS vary according to each child's symptoms. Some children with average IQs may exhibit learning difficulties as a result of behaviour disorders. Other children might have severe mental retardation and motor disorders. Although some symptoms may be relatively subtle in cases of partial FAS, the full-blown syndrome must be considered a multihandicapping condition.

Perhaps the most appalling aspect of FAS is that it is entirely preventable. A major public awareness campaign is required, directed at educating prospective mothers about the potentially harmful effects of alcohol on their unborn children (Graham-Clay, 1983).

Spina bifida

Midline defects, often referred to as **clefts**, result from the failure of parts of the embryo to fuse completely. Such defects may occur in many parts of the body, including the lip, the palate, the eye, and the spine.

Spina bifida is a congenital midline defect of the spinal column, in which one or more vertebrae fail to close during embryological development. This spinal defect may be found anywhere between the skull and the lowest segments of the vertebrae. The severity of the problem is apparent at birth (Myers, Cerone, and Olson, 1981), and the cause is unknown. The condition sometimes occurs in combination with hydrocephalus.

Prevalence of spina bifida

The prevalence of spina bifida varies widely from country to country. For example, the incidence in Ireland is about 4 to 5 children per 1000 live births, while in parts of Nigeria it is .2 per 1000 live births. Between 1964 and 1970, the incidence of spina bifida in British Columbia was .76 per 1000 live births. Variations of number occur also from area to area within a country, or even within a city (Freeman, 1974).

Classification of spina bifida

Spina bifida refers to a group of defects, ranging from those with few or no adverse effects to those with severely disabling consequences. Spina bifida is divided into three main forms: spina bifida occulta, spina bifida with meningocele, and spina bifida with myelomeningocele.

Spina bifida occulta is the mildest form of spina bifida, and has few or no negative consequences. The only visible sign of this condition, if any, is a clump of hair on the skin covering the area of the cleft.

In **Spina bifida with meningocele**, the membranes surrounding the spinal cord (meninges) protrude from the plane of the spine and form a sac containing cerebrospinal fluid. It is most often treated surgically to replace the sac within the bony column. Following treatment, this condition does not usually create any major difficulties.

Spina bifida with myelomeningocele is the most severe type of spina bifida. In this condition, the protruding sac contains parts of the spinal cord as well as cerebrospinal fluid. The spinal cord not only enters the sac but is itself abnormal. Although surgical treatment is necessary to deal with the sac, the neurological damage is irreversible.

The effects of myelomeningocele vary considerably, depending on the location of the cleft. The higher the cleft, the greater the damage. Clefts in the lowest area of the spine may result in incontinence without paralysis. Clefts in the higher spinal regions produce paralysis and loss of sensation in the lower limbs, incontinence, and kidney problems. They also produce associated musculo-skeletal deviations, such as abnormality of the rib cage and curvature of the spine.

Developmental consequences of spina bifida

Children with spina bifida occulta or with meningocele are likely to develop normally. However, children with myelomeningocele suffer neurological damage that interferes with some aspects of growth and development. The most obvious neurological damage is the flaccid paralysis of the lower parts of the body. This necessitates the use of braces, crutches, or wheelchairs.

In the absence of other conditions, spina bifida does not preclude adequate learning ability. However, many children with spina bifida have difficulty moving from one place to another in the school. They are also subject to frequent absences from school because of their need for hospitalization and medical treatment. They may find it more difficult to maintain positive relationships with their peers, thus hindering their social and psychological growth.

Children with myelomeningocele lack sensation and control of their bladders and bowel sphincters. Although incontinence in itself does not create learning difficulties, it is likely to create social and psychological barriers for children in school. Non-handicapped children usually view incontinence as a sign of immaturity or infantile behaviour, and react accordingly. As incontinent children mature enough to learn the techniques necessary to cope with their condition, the social barriers may disappear.

Early intervention is vital for children with spinal bifida and their families. Parents must be educated to promote their children's independence. This involves an acceptance of the disability as well as a recognition of their child's individual strengths and abilities. Parental acceptance and caring are key elements in every child's sense of self-worth.

Hydrocephalus

Hydrocephalus is a condition characterized by an excessive accumulation of cerebrospinal fluid in the brain due to an obstruction of its flow. Since fluids are largely non-compressible, the accumulation of cerebrospinal fluid in an enclosed area places pressure on the brain and the skull. The pressure against the skull creates thinning of the bone and separation of the sutures (the seams between the plates of the skull). At the same time, the fluid also impinges upon the brain tissue, causing distortion of brain substance and damage and death to neurons.

In some instances, hydrocephalus arrests itself spontaneously. In other instances, the condition progresses and creates increasing pressure on the skull. The progressive accumulation of CSF may result in mental retardation, motor disorders, seizures, and even death. Because the conditions resulting from hydrocephalus are secondary to the blockage of cerebrospinal fluid, the treatment is directed toward the reduction of the fluid pressure.

Treatment of hydrocephalus

Before the 1950s, no treatment existed for hydrocephalus. Children whose hydrocephalus was not arrested were likely to develop marked symptoms. By the age of about three months, their heads became too large and heavy for them to lift. All too frequently, their condition ended in death.

In 1952, an engineer named Holter developed an effective shunt (tube) to drain off excess cerebrospinal fluid and reduce the pressure on the brain. Since the invention of this shunt, many children with hydrocephalus have been spared extensive impairments.

Developmental consequences of combined spina bifida and hydrocephalus

Both hydrocephalus and spina bifida may occur as solitary conditions. However, they are frequently found together. Hydrocephalus without spina bifida may result in a range of mild to severe physical and mental disabilities. With spina bifida, the number of disabilities increases dramatically. The damage to the brain in hydrocephalus and to the spinal cord in spina bifida is likely to produce a multihandicapped child.

Developmental consequences vary with the degree of severity of the two conditions and with the success or failure of treatment. Developmental variations have been clearly shown in a study by Lorber (1976). Lorber followed the progress of 848 children with spina bifida with or without hydrocephalus. All the children were treated from their day of birth and studied from 1959 to 1968. Of 848 children, only 50 percent survived this nine-year period. Physical handicaps were found in 81.5 percent (345 children), moderate physical impairments in 17.2 percent (73 children), and a complete absence of physical disability in 1.4 percent (6 children). Of the 345 children with severe physical problems, 59 percent had IQs of 80 and above, 27 percent had IQs between 60 and 79, and 14 percent had IQs below 60.

Hydrocephalus is included among the clinical forms of mental retardation. Nevertheless, some individuals with even gross hydrocephalus may attain average and above-average intelligence scores. Soare and Raimondi (1977) found no correlation between degrees of severity of hydrocephalus and IQs.

Multiple sclerosis

Multiple sclerosis is a neurological disorder of unknown cause that presents itself in late adolescence and early adulthood. Multiple sclerosis is a slowly progressive disease of the central nervous system, characterized by patchy scarring or hardening of the myelin coat of the nerve cells in the brain and spinal cord. This demyelinization results in varied neurological symptoms. There are periods of remission of various lengths, followed by recurrence of symptoms.

Prevalence of multiple sclerosis

Multiple sclerosis affects females more frequently than males, and is more common in temperate climates than in the tropics. The incidence in temperate zones is approximately one per thousand people, while the rate of occurrence in the tropics is one per ten thousand (Berkow, 1982). Because of Canada's climate, we can assume a relatively high incidence of multiple sclerosis.

Characteristics of multiple sclerosis

The symptoms of multiple sclerosis include a variety of sensory problems (especially visual), tremors, muscle weakness, spasticity, speech difficulties, dizziness, mild emotional disturbance, difficulty in walking, and other problems (Hallahan and Kauffman, 1982). There is no specific treatment for the disease. Individuals should be encouraged to live as normal and active a life as possible, but should avoid overwork and fatigue. School-age adolescents should remain in regular classroom unless the symptoms render school attendance impossible. If this is the case, hospital or home instruction is warranted.

MUSCULOSKELETAL IMPAIRMENTS

For purposes of this discussion, **musculoskeletal impairments** are those conditions that impede bodily movement in the absence of damage to the central nervous system. In this section we will discuss a few specific disorders in which bones or muscles are involved. The causes of such conditions range from inherited diseases and congenital malformations to infections and accidents.

This scooter board is useful for mobility in classroom. It promotes open hand position, and diminishes the effects of spasticity.
(L. Snider)

Muscular dystrophy

Muscular dystrophy is a group of inherited conditions characterized by degeneration of muscle fibres without neurological deficit. Muscular dystrophy might more accurately be called muscular dystrophies, in that it occurs in different forms. Although all forms are characterized by progressive muscle weakness, they differ with regard to age of onset, the site of initial muscular involvement, and the kinds of hereditary transmission.

Classification of muscular dystrophy

The most common type of the disorder is **Duchenne's muscular dystrophy**, often called pseudohypertrophic muscular dystrophy. This form typically occurs in boys and is inherited through a sex-linked recessive gene. Onset is early and may be evident when the child is learning to walk. By the age of four to seven years, the child exhibits a waddling gait, frequent falls, difficulty in climbing stairs, and difficulty when standing up from a sitting position (Berkow, 1982). The child's pelvic area is affected first, and then the shoulder girdle.

The term *pseudohypertrophic* means "false growth," and describes an enlargement of the calves and sometimes other muscles. This enlargement occurs as a result of fatty deposits in the muscle along with degeneration of true muscle fibres. The child grows steadily weaker, and by ten to twelve years of age is likely to be confined to a wheelchair.

The life span of a child with Duchenne's muscular dystrophy is short. As of now, no treatment has been found to stop muscle decline. However, life span may be extended by encouraging the child to maintain normal activity as long as possible.

Landouzy-Dejerine muscular dystrophy is also known as facioscapulohumeral muscular dystrophy. The latter name refers to the facial and shoulder girdle muscles, which are the areas first affected. This type of muscular dystrophy occurs in both sexes and commonly starts in adolescence, although onset may occur any time between childhood and late adulthood. The progression of the disease alternates with prolonged periods of apparent arrest. The facial features of affected children including drooping of eyelids and thickening of the lip. The shoulder girdle is weakened, but the forearms are spared. Inheritance is through dominant genes, but is not sex-linked (Berkow, 1982).

Although these are the most common forms of muscular dystrophy, several others exist. All types are characterized by progressive muscular weakness and tissue change. However, the types do vary in the life span they permit. Before the advent of antibiotics, the life expectancy for children with Duchenne's was even shorter than it is now. Death usually occurred in adolescence as a result of exhaustion, respiratory infection, or heart failure, with pneumonia as the most frequent killer. In Landouzy-Dejerine, on the other hand, life expectancy is normal (Krupp and Chatton, 1983). In all instances, people with muscular dystrophy should be encouraged to continue normal activity as long as possible.

Although muscular dystrophy results in decreased mobility over time, there is little evidence to indicate a decrease in intellectual function. However, Karagan and Zellweger (1978) found that children with Duchenne's muscular dystrophy tended to have lower than average verbal IQs. Apparently, about fifty percent of patients with Duchenne's have a lower IQ than genetic expectations would suggest (Berkow, 1982).

Arthritis

Arthritis is a common term for a variety of chronic systemic conditions involving inflammation of the joints. Arthritis may lead to the destruction of joints. Its cause is unknown, and a cure is non-existent. The most common form is rheumatoid arthritis.

Many people assume that arthritis is a condition common to adults, especially the aged. In reality it is no respecter of age, and occurs frequently in children. **Juvenile arthritis** (called Still's Disease) is similar in some respects to the adult type. Joint pain is a common feature. The disease affects the large joints, sometimes to the extent of interfering with growth in the bony structures. Other complications of juvenile arthritis include eye and respiratory infections, enlarged spleen, and inflammation of the tissue covering the heart.

Fortunately, about seventy-five percent of children with arthritis experience remission of the disease. The prognosis is more favourable for children than for adults (Berkow, 1982).

Limb deficiencies and other bony malformations

Limb deficiencies include the loss or absence of entire limbs or parts of limbs. A child born with such a condition is said to have a **congenital amputation**. Although congenital amputations have occurred throughout history, only recently have we begun to understand their causes.

A most dramatic occurrence of congenital amputations of unusually large proportions occurred in the late 1950s and early 1960s. The culprit was found to be Thalidomide, an antinausea drug prescribed for morning sickness in pregnant women. In Canada, the United States, and Europe, thousands of children were born with missing or deformed limbs. This specific condition is called **phocomelia**, a congenital deformity in which parts of limbs or entire limbs are missing or very short.

Congenital amputations are much less prevalent than acquired amputations. Many children lose limbs in mishaps involving vehicles, contact with high voltage lines, burns, and other accidents. In some instances, surgical amputations may be performed to prevent the spread of bone cancer or massive infections. Defective limbs or parts of limbs may also be amputated to permit the use of **prostheses**, functional devices that substitute for missing body parts.

Abnormalities of the bony structures include a number of conditions other than limb deficiencies. Some are congenital, such as spina bifida, cleft palate, clubfoot, hip dislocation, and osteogenesis imperfecta. Others may result from a bacterial infection such as tuberculosis. Still others, such as curvature of the spine, may exist as secondary abnormalities associated with such primary disorders as **atrophy**, a form of muscle weakness caused by nerve degeneration.

Exhibit 12-5 outlines some of the orthopedic conditions that affect children.

CHRONIC HEALTH PROBLEMS

The classification of chronic health problems excludes neurological and musculoskeletal disorders. Despite these exclusions, however, the number of health problems involving other body systems is staggering. As many as one child in every five may suffer from a chronic health disorder (Schiffer and Hunt, 1963). In this section, however, we must restrict discussion to a few very specific and sometimes life-threatening conditions.

Exhibit 12-6 outlines some chronic health problems of children.

Exhibit 12-5 Other orthopedic conditions that affect children.

Club foot	Congenital malpositioning of one or both feet.
Osteomyelitis	Bacterial infection of the bones.
Osteogenesis imperfecta	Congenital abnormality of the bony cells resulting in frequent fractures causing deformities.
Scoliosis	Congenital or acquired curvature of the spine, often caused by muscle weakness, dystrophy, or atrophy.
Hip dislocation	Congenital misplacement of the thigh bone in the hip socket.
Legg-Calve-Perthes	Flattening of the head of a long bone, usually the thigh.
Muscular atrophy	Degeneration of muscle tissue due to neural damage.

Exhibit 12-6 Some chronic health conditions.

Nephritis and nephrosis	Disease or disorder of the kidneys caused by infection, trauma, poisoning, and other diseases. May be either acquired or congenital.
Hemophilia	An inherited disorder in which a blood clotting factor is lacking to some degree. The two major types are sex-linked, and a third type is not.
Rheumatic fever	Inflammation of joints, which may spread to the brain or heart. (Usually associated with streptococcal infection.)
Tuberculosis	Infection by the tubercule bacillus, which may invade any part of the body.
Sickle cell anemia	An inherited blood disorder characterized by distortion of red blood cells, essentially occurring among Blacks. Symptoms are recurrent attacks of fever and pain in limbs and abdomen.
Asthma	Chronic episodic respiratory condition characterized by difficulty in breathing due to narrowing of airways.

Cystic fibrosis

Cystic fibrosis is a genetically determined inborn error of metabolism, involving the exocrine glands (glands with ducts). The disorder primarily affects the respiratory and digestive systems. Symptoms include high salt concentration in the sweat glands and the production of thick, sticky mucus that clogs breathing and digestion. The mucus obstruction in the lungs creates pockets of infection and pulmonary dysfunction. These frequently result in chronic episodes of pneumonia and bronchitis.

Cystic fibrosis affects virtually all parts of the digestive system. The pancreas, gall bladder, liver, and intestines often function abnormally and exhibit changes in the tissues. Children with this often fail to gain weight despite increased appetite. They grow very slowly and never appear to thrive (Holsclaw, 1978).

Etiology and prevalence of cystic fibrosis

Cystic fibrosis is the most lethal hereditary disorder among the Caucasian population. One of every 20 Caucasians is a carrier, and 1 child in 2500 live births is affected. Cystic fibrosis is transmitted by an autosomal, recessive gene. Therefore, both parents must be carriers to pass on the disease.

In a family with an affected child, 2 out of 3 siblings are likely to be carriers, and 1 out of 5 is likely to have the disease (Baird, 1984). The only preventive measure lies in genetic counselling, which allows the parents to decide whether or not to produce more children. Siblings without cystic fibrosis should be informed, at an appropriate age, that they may be carriers of the disease.

Treatment of cystic fibrosis

The medical management of children with cystic fibrosis is intensive. Physiotherapy is a major tool in the prevention of lung disorders. Parents must learn the techniques of therapy to assist in their child's treatment. This usually consists of twice-daily, half-hour sessions involving chest percussion and postural drainage. The purpose of pounding the chest is to elicit coughing, which encourages the elimination of mucus. The changes in posture also aid in the draining process.

Antibiotics are prescribed for cystic fibrosis when lung infections are present. Diet can be quite effective in the management of disorders of the digestive system. The special diet is high in protein, high in calories, and low in fats. This is combined with dosages of an enzyme needed to compensate for an insufficiency of the pancreas. Children with cystic fibrosis are also encouraged to exercise and participate in motor activity of all kinds.

Before antibiotics were available, approximately seventy-five percent of children with cystic fibrosis died before age ten (Schwachman and Kulczycki, 1958). At present, many patients in their twenties and thirties are being treated for the disease. Some persons with cystic fibrosis are still alive in their forties (Schwachman, Kowalski, and Khaw, 1977).

Developmental consequences of cystic fibrosis

Children with cystic fibrosis do not suffer intellectual impairment. They should be educated in regular classrooms. However, they will probably be frequently absent from school because of respiratory or intestinal disorders.

A major problem of cystic fibrosis concerns parents' reactions to the short life expectancy of their child. Parents often transmit their anxiety to the child. They may also create conflict and jealousy among normal siblings by spending a disproportionate amount of time with their cystic fibrotic child. As children with the disease become adolescents and adults, they face a number of problems. The transition to independent living may be very difficult, following their necessarily dependent relationships with parents (Boyle, di Sant'Agnase, Sack, Millican, and Kulczycki, 1976). In addition, cystic fibrotic males are sterile, and females have reduced fertility. However, despite these and other problems, most cystic fibrotic adults cope reasonably well (Schwachman, Kowalski, and Khaw, 1977).

Diabetes mellitus

Diabetes mellitus is defined as a disorder of sugar metabolism resulting from the failure of the pancreas to manufacture sufficient insulin. Diabetes is divided into two major types. Type I is called insulin-dependent diabetes (IDDM), and Type II called non-insulin dependent (NIDDM). Type I is usually associated with early onset (under twenty-five years of age), and includes juvenile diabetes. Type II ordinarily occurs after about forty years of age (Krupp and Chatton, 1983).

Etiology and prevalence of diabetes mellitus

The assumed prevalence of diabetes in Canada is slightly more than a million cases, or approximately one in twenty Canadians (Shee, 1985, personal communication). The causes of diabetes are not clearly understood. Type II diabetes is often associated with overweight, and susceptibility may be genetically transmitted. Type I diabetes, however, which affects children, does not appear to be genetically linked. Juvenile diabetes probably results from a variable interaction of hereditary and environmental factors (Berkow, 1983).

Developmental consequences of diabetes mellitus

Before manufactured insulin was available, children with juvenile diabetes could expect to live only about two years after the onset of the condition. Such is obviously no longer the case. Although many complications may arise, diabetic children who maintain their proper regime of diet, insulin, and exercise are likely to attain a relatively normal life span.

The onset of juvenile diabetes is usually very abrupt. Symptoms include thirst, hunger, weight loss, fatigue or weakness, extensive urination, and sometimes blurred vision. Onset may occur several months after an outbreak of specific viruses, including mumps and German measles (Rodger and Hunt, 1980).

Treatment of diabetes mellitus

The treatment of diabetes involves a diet low in carbohydrates and fats, accompanied by regular injections of insulin. Food intake, insulin, and exercise must be carefully balanced and monitored throughout the diabetic's life. For children, the balance of these three factors is often difficult to maintain, particularly in the presence of illness or infection. Too little food or too much activity cause levels of sugar in the blood to drop, resulting in an insulin reaction. Too little activity, too much food, or too little insulin may, over a prolonged period of time, result in a condition called **acidosis**. Both insulin coma and acidosis are potentially dangerous states.

School personnel must always be informed when a student is diabetic. Teachers should understand the child's condition and recognize signs of imbalance. Health personnel should provide appropriate guidelines regarding the timing of school meals and the timing and types of school exercise.

Teachers of diabetic children should always have a supply of sugar in some form on hand. When teachers see signs of insulin reaction, they should immediately give the child food such as fruit juice, candy bars, non-diet carbonated drinks, or sugar (five small cubes, two packets, or two teaspoons). Children old enough to recognize the symptoms should carry a sugar supply and be permitted to treat the reaction themselves.

If the child does not improve within fifteen to twenty minutes, the teacher should administer more sugar. If no improvement follows the second feeding, the child's parents or physician should be called. No serious harm results from mistakenly treating an insulin reaction, but insulin coma may result if treatment is not given when needed.

Exhibit 12-7 Information for teachers about diabetes.

Hypoglycemia, or insulin reaction, is a state of abnormally low levels of glucose in the blood. Hypoglycemia is an emergency condition and could result in convulsions or coma. It must be treated immediately by giving the child some form of sugar. The signs of hypoglycemia are:

- Tiredness.
- Malaise, nausea.
- Headache.
- Drowsiness.
- Pallor or flushing.
- Sweating and dizziness.
- Trembling, nervousness.
- Blurred vision.
- Unusual behaviour.

Hyperglycemia is a state of abnormally high blood-glucose levels. This is not an emergency situation, but does need to be corrected. It may be caused by inadequate amounts of insulin, by infections, or by excessive food intake. If any child shows the following symptoms, you should contact the child's parents or doctor.

- Increased thirst.
- Nausea and vomiting.
- Stomach cramps.
- Blurred vision.
- Frequent and excessive urination.

The onset of acidosis is more gradual. Symptoms include confusion, lethargy, extreme thirst, nausea, and a fruity odour on the breath. Teachers who recognize these symptoms should seek prompt medical treatment.

Diabetic children can participate in all school activities unless otherwise advised by a physician. Diabetes causes no impediment to intellectual function, and diabetic children should not be considered different from other students. However, in addition to regular education, diabetic children must be taught to manage their condition. Parents and medical personnel must teach older diabetic children to inject their own insulin, monitor their blood sugar or urine sugar levels, and maintain a balance among nutrition, exercise, and insulin levels. Children who can manage these tasks achieve a high level of independence.

Exhibit 12-7 offers information about diabetes that might be useful to teachers.

Cancer

Cancer is a general term for about a hundred diseases characterized by the abnormal and uncontrolled growth of cells. Cancers occur in many forms, attacking many parts of the body. Cancers vary in their symptoms, their prognoses, and the speed of cancerous growths (tumours). Among children, the most common types of cancer are leukemia and cancerous tumours of the eye, brain, bone, and kidney (Meyen, 1978).

The treatment of cancer depends upon the type and location of the disease. The major forms of treatment are surgery, chemotherapy, and radiation. Much of the treatment may result in visible short-term or long-term effects. Children with bone cancer may experience the amputation of a limb. Children who undergo chemotherapy may lose their hair, although it will probably grow back (National Cancer Institute, 1980).

Although treatment for cancer can be extremely unpleasant, survival rates have dramatically increased over the past twenty years. This is particularly true for some forms of leukemia and for tumours of the kidney.

Developmental consequences of cancer

The consequences of cancer are associated with the type, extent, and location of cancerous growths. The most immediate effect on children is their fear concerning treatment. Children must be informed about their illness and treatment to whatever extent their age and understanding permits. Children who know what to expect experience less stress than those who must face the unknown. Even armed with knowledge, however, children will not find it easy to suffer the effects of cancer and its treatment. Symptoms and side-effects may include nausea, fatigue, weakness, loss of hair, and, in some instances, loss of body parts.

Children with cancer are likely to spend some time in hospital. They may make several visits to hospital, some as day patients and some in residence. Children have two major occupations — schooling and play. They should be able to pursue both these activities in the hospital. The hospital teacher should work in close contact with the child's school. The child should also stay in touch with the regular school teacher.

Before the child returns to school, the teacher must be prepared to see changes. The child may be less energetic than before, and may be preoccupied with the serious nature of the illness. The other students should be prepared to see physical changes in their classmate, such as hair loss or weight change. The teacher should tell the students that cancer is not contagious, and that their classmate is still basically the same person they knew before.

Despite increased survival rates, cancer is often fatal. Parents, teachers, and other caretakers must make every attempt to forego pity and embarrassment and treat children with cancer as individuals. Many youngsters with cancer resent being treated differently from other children in school or at home. They prefer to be challenged to learn, to play, to socialize, and to grow as people. Parents and teachers must work to provide opportunities for these children to function as normally as possible.

TERMINAL ILLNESS

Although death comes to all of us, the death of a child is difficult to bear. Ours is a society that attempts to deny death, particularly in the young. Kübler-Ross (1969) stands out as someone who has learned to deal with death and dying as aspects of the continuum of life. Kübler-Ross recognizes the inevitability of death and our society's need to come to terms with the termination of life as we know it.

Although Kübler-Ross has dealt largely with adults, much of what she has discovered also applies to the families of dying children. Through her research, she has identified five stages of reaction to dying — denial, grief, bargaining, depression, and acceptance. She has also been instrumental in establishing hospices in which the dying are dealt with as living people. These hospices permit people to spend their last days in an environment of comfort and understanding.

Nagy (1948) identified the concepts that healthy children have about death. She found that children under five see death as a departure, in the sense that the dying person moves somewhere else. Children between five and nine years tend to personify death in the guise of ghosts, skeletons, or other fantasy figures external to themselves. Children of this age feel they can escape death. However, children over nine recognize death as an inevitable cessation of life.

Spinetta, Rigler, and Karon (1974) studied a number of children who were facing death. They found an increased sense of isolation among these children, and a tendency to withdraw from others around them. Bluebond-Langner (1978) studied terminally-ill leukemic children to find out how they learned they were dying and how they hid their knowledge from parents and medical personnel. She found that information about their condition is available to children from many sources. However, children's understanding of this information depends on their individual experience with their disease, and is not related to age (Embleton, 1979).

The parents of dying children undergo a great deal of stress. When conventional medical treatments fails, they sometimes hunt for miracle drugs and faith healers. They may focus normal feelings of anger upon medical personnel, other family members or any other available target. They may experience feelings of guilt, believing they should have noticed symptoms sooner or been more lenient in their discipline.

As the child's death becomes more of a reality, the family tends to draw together. After the death, a period of mourning and adjustment takes place. Teams of professionals are sometimes available to help the family come to terms with the loss of a child.

ALLERGIES AND ASTHMA

Allergy

Allergy is the term used interchangeably with hypersensitivity, and can be defined as "an abnormal and varied reaction which occurs following a contact with substances or agents which normally do not cause symptoms in other individuals." (Kuzemko, 1978).

Etiology and prevalence of allergies

Allergies constitute the most common chronic disease in pediatrics. Allergic diseases are estimated to range from 6.6% to 28.5% in children and adolescents. Crawford (1982) stated that a survey of all children suffering from chronic diseases indicates that 32.8% were afflicted with allergies — 10.8% with hay fever, 11.4% with asthma and 10.67% with other allergies.

The etiology of allergies is divided into two groups. An atopic allergy is associated with hereditary and/or familial factors, while a non-atopic allergy results from antibodies produced in response to allergens in the environment. The risk of children with both parents who have a positive history of allergy is 30 to 40%, while the risk of children with one parent with a positive history is 20 to 30% (Kuzemko, 1978).

Substances that cause reactive allergic responses are divided into four categories: inhalants, contactants, ingestants and injectants. Inhalants include dust, pollens, molds, aerosol sprays and strong odours. Contactants are substances which come into contact with the skin, including fabrics, metals, cosmetics and chemicals. Ingestants are foods and drugs, and injectants are agents or substances that enter the body through the skin, including mosquito bites, bee stings and some drugs (Voignier and Bridgewater, 1980).

Types of Allergic Reactions

Berkow (1982) lists a number of types of reactions. Allergic rhinitis may be either seasonal or perennial. The seasonal type is called hay fever, which is induced by windborne pollens, while the perennial form is present throughout the year. Both forms involve nasal congestion, itching of the nose or repetitive sneezing.

Allergic pulmonary disease is usually referred to as bronchial asthma. The major symptom is a narrowing of the bronchial tubes resulting in diminished air flow.

Urticaria and eczema are skin reactions resulting in rashes, itching, swelling and seeping of bodily fluids through the skin.

Physical allergy is a response to cold, heat and sunlight. Allergic conjunctivitis is a description of itching of the eyes and excessive tears. Gastro-intestinal allergy is a response to specific foods or drugs.

Food Allergies

Over the past decade there has been considerable argument about food allergies in relation to hyperactivity and emotional, behavioural and learning problems in children. Crook (1980) and Rapp (1979) are among several physicians who have used elimination diets to determine the possibility that food allergies might be responsible for inapprop-

Exhibit 12-8 Some substances or agents which precipitate allergic reactions.

■ molds	■ smoke
■ pollens	■ chemicals
■ foods	■ strong odours
■ feathers	■ fabrics
■ house dust	■ metals
■ insects	■ pets
■ chalk dust	■ excessive heat, cold or sunlight

Exhibit 12-9 Symptoms of allergies.

■ wheezing	
■ itching	■ irritability
■ rashes	■ complaints of headache, stomach pain or earache
■ sniffling	■ sore throat
■ dry, hacking cough	■ decreased attention span
■ rubbing nose and eyes	■ decreased appetite
■ repeated colds	■ fatigue
■ mouth breathing	■ slow growth
■ frequent nose bleeds	■ impaired hearing
■ pallor	■ restlessness
■ dark circles under eyes	■ red puffy eyes

riate behaviours and physical complaints such as headache and abdominal pain. In a study of 136 hyperactive children, Crook noted eleven foods that appeared to precipitate hyperactivity. Such foods included sugar, milk, corn, wheat and eggs. Parental observations indicated that 41 children showed an excellent response to elimination diets, 60 children showed a good response, 16 showed poor response and the parents of 17 children were not certain. A study such as the above is basically clinical; the purpose is to treat the children. The conflict lies between the clinician and the scientist. Bock and May (1983) suggest that there is a need for greater scientific rigor and analysis before an orderly approach to diagnosis and treatment is possible.

Asthma

Childhood bronchial asthma presents a significant public health problem, with major impact on health outcomes as well as with disruption of the living patterns of the patient and their families" (Freudenberg, Feldman, Clark, Millman, Valle, and Waslewski, 1980, p. 522). Asthma may be acute or chronic, and may be severe, moderate or intermittent.

Asthma is a variable, reversible obstruction of the airways, characterized by the narrowing of bronchial tubes, swelling of tissue and clogging of mucus (Smith, 1978). Flenley (1981) suggests simply that bronchial asthma is a condition of recurrent episodes of acute limitation of air flow.

Etiology and prevalence of asthma

Asthma and hay fever are extremely common in most developed nations. The estimated prevalence of asthma alone ranges from five to fifteen percent of children under fifteen years (Pituch, and Bruggeman, 1982). Asthma may occur at any age, but it is found most frequently in children. Boys are twice as likely as girls to exhibit the condition. Many asthmatic children improve or go into remission in adolescence (Flenley, 1981).

Symptoms and Stimuli of Asthmatic Attacks

The symptoms of asthmatic attacks are wheezing, paroxysmal coughing and shortness of breath. The stimuli associated with bronchospasms are infection, physical exertion, climatic change and endocrine or emotional factors (McGovern, 1973).

Medical treatment

Various medications are used in the treatment of asthma. Bronchodilators are used to relieve obstruction of airflow. In severe states of asthma corticosteroids are useful. Both types of medication, however, have side effects. Bronchodilators may over-stimulate the child and cause hyperactive behaviour. Excessive use of corticosteroids may result in abnormal hair growth, excessive appetite and slowed growth. Common sense factors in treatment, other than medications, include rest, sufficient fluids, and play and work to tolerance (Smith, 1978).

Developmental consequences of asthma

Asthmatic children are often faced with various school difficulties. Absenteeism is a common problem, especially in the first three years of school. Pituch and Bruggeman (1982) indicate that 20 to 25 percent of all school absences occur as a result of asthma.

Despite the fact that the population of asthmatic children have slightly higher I.Q. scores than average, they are likely to be underachievers and were found to be one to three years behind in their school work (Freudenberg, Feldman, Clark, Millman, Valle, and Waslewski 1980).

In earlier times asthmatic children were restricted to limited physical activity. Research has indicated that such children can participate in physical activities most of the time if they are under proper medical management. A full program of activity is advised with a minimum of restriction. Schneider, Melton, and Reisch (1980) conducted a study indicating that a proper curriculum of physical education resulted in reduced absenteeism, and fewer severe asthmatic attacks. The curriculum included progressive exercise of abdominal and back muscles, breathing exercises and general conditioning. Students progressed from mild to moderate to strenuous exercise. Some children were given medication prior to the physical education classes. Results of the study showed increased self confidence in students' ability to control breathing problems and their recognition that they could participate in activities with their peers.

Teachers should seek informed medical opinion and listen to parents' concerns. Children with asthma should be encouraged to be active; as they develop a healthy self concept they learn to take control of their condition (Smith, 1978).

In the past, asthma was thought to be an emotional or psychological disorder. The fear of attacks and the interference with breathing may make it difficult for affected children and their families to live normally. Some parents are concerned about damage to heart and lungs, and are fearful of death. The consequence of such anxiety may result in overprotection of the child and neglect of siblings (Pituch and Bruggeman, 1980).

ABUSED AND NEGLECTED CHILDREN

The history of humanity is rife with examples of cruelty to children. From ancient times, severe physical punishment was justified as a means to maintain discipline, to transmit educational ideas, to please certain gods, or to expel evil spirits (Radbill, 1974). Newborns were killed or abandoned as a measure of population control, and young children were mutilated in the cause of beauty. Youngsters were indentured or forced into slavery, or deliberately maimed so they would arouse pity as beggars. The list of horrors grew through many centuries and most cultures.

In the 1800s, the Industrial Revolution resulted in the subjugation of children of lower socioeconomic class as factory and mine labourers. In Canada and other nations, children eight years of age worked up to sixteen hours a day. They were subject to beatings and starvation, and many succumbed to occupational hazards and diseases.

In Canada, child protection legislation was first formulated in the 1880s. In 1893, the Children's Protection Act provided a legal basis for the formation of Children's Aid Societies. In the 1940s and 1950s, physicians began to recognize the non-accidental nature of injuries in children (Caffey, 1946).

In the early 1960s, the American Academy of Pediatrics sponsored a seminar to present the problem of child abuse. A group of physicians from the University of Colorado's School of Medicine identified the problem of abuse as a medical syndrome, and called it the **Battered Child Syndrome** (Kempe, Silverman, Steele, Droegemueller, and Silver, 1962). By the 1970s, policies were established and laws enacted to recognize and protect abused and neglected children.

Definitions of abuse and neglect

Definitions of child abuse and neglect vary only slightly from place to place. **Child abuse and neglect** is the physical or mental injury, sexual abuse, negligent treatment, or maltreatment of a child by caretakers.

Definitions have also been developed to describe specific aspects of abuse and neglect. "**Physical abuse** is non-accidental physical injury to the child. **Sexual abuse** is sexual involvement imposed upon a child by an adult" (Tower, 1984, p. 24). Finkelhor (1979) also points out the child's inability to consent to abuse. Consent is based upon knowledge and authority, neither of which is at the child's command.

Physical neglect refers to the failure of caretakers to meet a child's basic physical needs. **Emotional neglect** refers to the failure of caretakers to provide the loving, positive emotional atmosphere necessary to the development of self-esteem in the child.

Child abuse and neglect cannot be attributed to any single cause. Neither can we attribute such behaviour to any particular class of people. Child abuse occurs among rich and poor families in urban and rural areas, regardless of race, religion, ethnicity, or family configuration. Child abuse and neglect may occur at any point between conception (fetal alcohol syndrome) and late adolescence. In some families, only one of several children is abused.

Although abuse cannot be attributed to any one factor, it is associated with at least three characteristics. Abusive parents have little knowledge of good parenting, and hold unrealistic expectations of their children. They are unable to cope with the complex problems of life, and are in urgent need of help. In many cases, abusive parents have been abused children themselves (Kline, 1977).

Prevalence of abuse and neglect

Child abuse appears to be on the increase (Fontana and Besharov, 1979). However, it is impossible to know the dimensions of the problem because of widespread underreporting. Young children usually do not disclose the source of their injuries, and physicians may not recognize that abuse is involved. Many children may never receive medical attention. As a result, the prevalence of physical abuse and neglect is largely unknown.

More is known about the prevalence of sexual child abuse in Canada, thanks to a national committee that has studied the problem. The Committee on Sexual Offences against Children and Youths (1984) found sexual abuse to be an "endemic" problem. Moreover, although public awareness of the problem has increased, the Committee indicated that widespread sexual abuse has been a problem for some time.

The Committee estimated that, "at sometime during their lives, about one in two females and one in three males have been victims of unwanted sexual acts. About four in five of these incidents first happened to those persons when they were children or youths" (p. 175). According to the Committee, only a few of these victims were very young children under seven. Most were children between twelve and eighteen years of age. Most of the victims did not seek assistance. Those who did were most likely to approach either the police or their physicians.

Characteristics of abused and neglected children

Child abuse and neglect may have both physical and behavioural manifestations. Physical abuse may be detected by obvious signs, such as extensive bruises. Other signs include bald spots indicative of hair pulling, burns from cigarettes, and burns in the shape of such objects as irons, pokers, or circular stove elements. Children may also have glove-like burns, indicating immersion of the hand in a hot liquid. Various marks may indicate blows from a hand, a strap, an electric cord, or a rope. Abused children may also have unexplained lacerations, particularly about the face and head.

Behavioural indicators of physical abuse may include intolerance of physical contact and the inappropriate wearing of clothing that covers the body. Abused children may have a tendency to arrive at school very early and stay late, suggesting a fear of going home. They may complain of soreness or demonstrate extreme aggression, withdrawal, or overcompliant behaviour.

Physically neglected children show quite different signs from those who are abused. Neglected children tend to be ill-clothed and ill-fed. They may have untreated physical or medical problems, and appear to be tired and listless. Their possible, behavioural responses include stealing food, falling asleep, frequent school absence, and pugnacious and destructive activity.

Many people believe sexual abuse is perpetrated by strangers. On the contrary, between seventy and eight-five percent of sexual child abuse is committed by people known — and often loved — by the victims (Tower, 1984). Most incidents of sexual abuse are veiled in an aura of secrecy. Physical and behavioural indicators of sexual abuse are generally subtle and difficult to perceive.

Nonetheless, victims of sexual abuse may display a number of symptoms. Children may have difficulty walking or sitting, or may cry without provocation. They may manifest fear of males or act seductively toward them. Victims may show sudden drops in school performance or sudden non-participation in school activities, accompanied by unusually infantile or withdrawn behaviour (Broadhurst, Edmunds, and MacDicker, 1979). Medical examination may reveal bleeding or bruising in the genital area, frequent urinary tract infections (normally rare in children) and occasionally, venereal disease. Sexual abuse, it should be noted, affects both boys and girls.

Indicators of emotional maltreatment are varied. Many children develop emotional or behavioural disorders for no apparent reason. Many of these cases probably result from the failure of parents and caregivers to meet their children's basic emotional needs. Emotionally abused children exhibit a variety of disorders, including delayed development, neurotic traits, and infantile or antisocial behaviour.

Developmental consequences of abuse and neglect

The consequences of abuse and neglect are too numerous to count. They include physical disorders, emotional problems, mental illness, drug addiction, personality disorders, criminal behaviours, school problems, lack of empathy, overcompliance, intense anger, and strong feelings of worthlessness. Battered children who are too young or frightened to talk about their experiences are at great risk for permanent physical and mental damage. Many of these children die of their injuries. Van Stolk (1978), for example, presented several case studies of children up to six years of age who died of injuries caused by parents, older siblings, foster parents, and other caregivers.

Children who survive the stresses of abuse or neglect grow up to feel unloved, uncared for, and abandoned. Many are likely to inflict on their own children the damage inflicted upon themselves.

Characteristics of child abusers

Caretakers who abuse or neglect children do so for a variety of reasons. In some instances, their behaviour may be associated with mental illness. In other cases, alcohol and drug addiction appear to be causative factors.

Some parents expect children to be good, loving, and obedient at all times. They cannot understand that youngsters have limited control, capabilities, and comprehension. These parents ascribe adult functions to children, expecting them to fulfil parental needs. Some adults use excessive discipline because they see it as their duty to make children behave. Their children's disobedience or inattention threatens their perceptions of themselves as good parents (Van Stolk, 1978).

Children learn parenting techniques from their own experiences in the family. A loved, cared-for child learns to become a good parent. A child who is unloved, neglected, and abused learns bad parenting behaviours. If a parent who was abused has a healthy, docile child, abusive tendencies may be held in check. However, if the child is ill or difficult to manage, or if other stresses occur, the parent may well harm the child.

Many abusive parents express remorse and ask for help. Others explain self-righteously that their behaviour is necessary to teach their children to be good.

Prevention of abuse and neglect

In Canada, awareness of child neglect and abuse has greatly increased and strong child protection laws have been enacted. This has led to the development of many policies and programs for intervention, education, and prevention. Laws now require the reporting of possible instances of abuse to appropriate authorities. Teachers, neighbours, physicians, and anyone else who suspects child abuse are required by law to seek assistance for the child.

INTERVENTION FOR CHILDREN WITH PHYSICAL AND HEALTH PROBLEMS

The varied group of exceptional children addressed in this chapter collectively require a variety of medical, social, and educational services. Medical interventions may include surgical procedures, prosthetic devices, and ongoing medical treatment. Physical, occupational, and speech therapies may also be indicated. Social services agencies frequently become involved with these children and their families. As they grow older, they may need counselling and other support for independent living.

Educational intervention

Children with physical and health problems have the same educational needs as all other children. Special education only becomes necessary if the children are also developmentally delayed, emotionally disturbed, or forced to frequently be absent from school. In these cases, children may receive help in special classes, learning assistance centres, or itinerant-teacher programs. Some children may be taught in their homes. Others may be taught in acute-care or extended-care hospitals.

Physically disabled children may need special adaptive or access devices in order to function in the regular classroom. However, they require little adjustment in curriculum or instructional practice. Educational intervention for children with multiple impairments is discussed in Chapter Thirteen.

The most important element in educational intervention is an awareness of the individual needs of each child. All disabled children are complex individuals — they cannot be defined by their braces, wheelchairs, and physical limitations. They have their own strengths and weaknesses, their own interests, and their unique brand of dignity. Although they may require special tools, they can benefit from educational experiences just as non-disabled children can.

THE PHYSICALLY IMPAIRED OR HEALTH-DISABLED PRE-SCHOOLER

The early identification of a child's condition is essential to permit the earliest possible intervention. Active intervention techniques include whatever therapies, treatments, and experiences contribute to the optimal healthy development of the physically impaired child. As Conner, Williamson, and Siepp (1978) point out, handicapped infants particularly need "specialized interventions that will assist them in closing the gap between their levels of functioning and those of their chronological age peers and help prevent their developing secondary and tertiary disabilities" (p. 26). Such interventions include infant stimulation as well as treatment (Connor, Williamson, and Siepp, 1978).

For infants and preschoolers, parent-support services are an essential aspect of intervention. A number of social service agencies, such as the Canadian Cerebral Palsy Association, the Epilepsy Association, the Cystic Fibrosis Association, and many others, provide special assistance to parents. They may offer direct treatment services, provide parent counselling and support, or publish information. Parents of physically disabled and health impaired children are encouraged to contact these organizations.

THE PHYSICALLY IMPAIRED OR HEALTH-DISABLED ADOLESCENT

Adolescents with physical or health problems are often concerned about getting married, having children, and participating in the workforce. The normal social and psychological stresses of adolescence are exaggerated in the presence of physical and health disabilities. For this reason, disabled teenagers often benefit from counselling.

Adolescents must be assisted in planning careers and finding vocational placements. Problems of physical access may restrict the teenager's independent life style. Current efforts to make public places and public transportation more accessible promise to enhance the quality of life for all disabled persons.

Adolescents need to become aware of the spectrum of support services available to them. They may suffer needless problems of personal adjustment because of lack of access to information and services.

SUMMARY

Children with physical impairments and health problems constitute a varied population. They differ markedly in behavioural, intellectual, and psychological characteristics. Depending on the type and severity of their impairments, they may require extensive or frequent hospitalization, special technological aids, and drug therapy. They may also require special education and social and psychological counselling.

Although neurological damage is essentially permanent, its effects depend upon the severity and location of the injury. Spinal cord damage may result in sensory and motor impairment, but does not affect intellectual capacity. Brain injury or dysfunction may result in multiple impairments, including intellectual deficits, learning difficulties, seizures, sensory loss, speech and language problems, and spastic paralysis. These impairments give rise to a variety of special education needs.

Musculoskeletal conditions result in physical handicaps associated with defects and infections of muscle and bone. Some conditions, such as muscular dystrophy, are degenerative and progressive while others remain static. In the absence of brain damage, most children with physical handicaps can attend regular classes.

Chronic health problems include many specific conditions such as diabetes, cystic fibrosis, asthma, and hemophilia. Children and parents must be educated in the appropriate techniques for coping with the problem condition.

Children's concepts of illness or disability are age-related. Younger children are more likely to believe that illness is associated with punishment or abandonment. Older children tend to define illness in adult terms.

Cancer is a general term for the abnormal and uncontrolled growth of cells. Although survival rates have greatly increased in the past twenty years, cancer is often a fatal illness. Terminal illness in children is particularly difficult to bear. The families of dying children go through various stages of reaction, including denial, grief, and acceptance. Dying children often feel a deep sense of isolation.

Child abuse and neglect has only recently been recognized as an extremely widespread problem. Children may be abused physically, emotionally, or sexually. Teachers should learn to recognize the signs of abuse and neglect. All citizens, lay or professional, are legally required to report suspected cases of abuse.

No single profession is capable of assuming responsibility for the development of these children. Parents, teachers, physicians, psychologists, therapists, nurses and social workers all play some role in intervention. Together they can help physically impaired children to achieve lives that are as independent and fulfilling as possible.

BIBLIOGRAPHY

Absante, K.O. (1981). Fetal alcohol syndrome in Northwest B.C. and the Yukon. *B.C. Medical Journal, 23,* 331-335.

Apgar, V. and Beck, J. (1974). *Is my baby all right?* New York: Pocket Books.

Benson, R.C., Bobak, I.M., and Jensen, M.D. (1981). *Maternity care: The nurse and the family*. St. Louis: C.V. Mosky.

Berkow, R. (Ed.). (1982). *The Merck manual of diagnosis and therapy*. Rahway, N.J.: Merck, Sharp and Dohme.

Bluebond-Langner, M. (1978). *The private world of dying children.* Princeton, N.J.: Princeton University Press.

Bock, S.A. and May, C.D. (1983). Adverse reactions to food caused by sensitivity. In E. Middleton, C.E. Reed, and E.F. Ellis (Eds.) (2nd Edition), *Allergy: Principles and practice.* Toronto: C.V. Mosby.

Boyle, I.R., di Sant'Agnese, P.A., Sack, S., Millican, F., and Kulczycki, L.L. (1976). Emotional adjustment of adolescents and young adults with cystic fibrosis. *Journal of Pediatrics, 88,* 318-326.

Broadhurst, D.D., Edmunds, M., and MacDicker, R.A. (1979). *Early childhood programs and the prevention and treatment of child abuse and neglect: The user manual series.* Washington D.C.: U.S. Department of Health, Education and Welfare.

Caffey, J. (1946). Multiple fractures in the long bones of infants suffering from chronic subdural hematoma. *American Journal of Roentgenology, 56,* 163-173.

Committee on Sexual Offences against Children and Youths. (1984). *Report (Vol. 1).* Ottawa: Canadian Government Publication Centre.

Conner, F.P., Williamson, G.G., and Siepp, J.M. (1978). *Program guide for infants and toddlers with neuromotor and other developmental disabilities.* New York: Teacher's College, Columbia University.

Crawford, L.V. (Ed.) (1982). *Pediatric allergic diseases.* Garden City, N.Y.: Medical Examination Publishing Company.

Crook, W.G. (1980). Can what a child eats make him dull, stupid or hyperactive? *Journal of Learning Disabilities, 13,* 281-286.

Cruickshank, W.M. (Ed.). (1976). *Cerebral Palsy: A developmental disability.* New York: Syracuse University Press.

Dikmen, S., Matthews, C.G., and Harley, J.P. (1975). The effect of early versus late onset of major motor epilepsy upon cognition-intellectual performance. *Epilepsia, 76,* 73-81.

Edwards, M.S. (1981). Fetal Alcohol Syndrome. *Journal of Nursing, 14,* 6-8.

Embleton, L. (1979). Children, cancer and death. *Canada's Mental Health, 27,* 12-15.

Enloe, C.F. (1980). How alcohol affects the developing fetus. *Nutrition Today, 15,* 12-15.

Epilepsy Foundation of America. (1973). *Answers to the most frequent questions people ask about epilepsy.* Washington, D.C.: American Epilepsy Association.

Finkelhor, D. (1979). *Sexually victimized children.* New York: MacMillan.

Flenley, D.C. (1981). *Respiratory medicine.* London: Bailliere Tindall.

Fontana, V.J. and Besharov, D.R. (1979). *The maltreated child (4th ed.).* Springfield, IL.: Charles C. Thomas.

Freeman, J.M. (1974). *Practical management of meningomyelocele.* Baltimore: University Park Press.

Freudenberg, N., Feldman, C.H., Clark, N.M., Millman, E.J., Valle, I. and Waslewski, Y. (1980). The impact of bronchial asthma on school attendance and performance. *Journal of School Health, 50,* 522-526.

Friedman, R.J. and MacQueen, J.C. (1971). Psychoeducational considerations of physically handicapped conditions in children. *Exceptional Children, 3(7),* 538-539.

Gastaut, H. (1970). Clinical and electroencephalographical classification of epileptic seizures. *Epilepsia, 11,* 102-113.

Graham-Clay, S. (1983). Fetal Alcohol Syndrome: A review of the current human research. *Canada's Mental Health, 31,* 2-5.

Guerin, G.R. (1979). School achievement and behaviour of children with mild or moderate health conditions. *Journal of Special Education, 13,* 179-186.

Hallahan, D.P. and Kauffman, J.M. (1982). *Exceptional children: Introduction to special education (2nd ed.).* Englewood Cliffs, N.J.: Prentice-Hall.

Holsclaw, D.S. (1978). Recognition and management of patients with cystic fibrosis. *Pediatric Annals, 7,* 9-10.

Karagan, N. and Zellweger, H. (1978). Early verbal disability in children with Duchenne muscular dystrophy. *Developmental Medicine and Child Neurology, 20,* 435-441.

Kempe, C., Silverman, F., Steele, B., Droegemueller, W., and Silver, H. (1962). The battered child syndrome. *Journal of the American Medical Association, 181,* 17-24.

Kline, D.F. (1977). *Child abuse and neglect: A primer for school personnel.* Reston, VA.: Council for Exceptional Children.

Krupp, M.A. and Chatton, M.J. (Eds.). (1983). *Current medical diagnosis and treatment.* Los Altos, CA.: Lange Medical Publications.

Kübler-Ross, E. (1969). *On death and dying.* New York: MacMillan.

Kurland, L.T., Kurtzke, J.F., and Goldberg, I.D. (1973). *Epimediology of neurologic and sense organ disorders.* Cambridge, MA.: Harvard University Press.

Kuzemko, J.A. (1978). *Allergy in children.* Kent, England: Pittman Medical.

Lorber, J. (1976). Selection for treatment. *Nursing Times, 72,* 9-11.

Meyen, E.L. (1978). *Exceptional children and youth: An introduction*. Denver: Love.

McGovern, J.P. (1973). Chronic respiratory diseases of school age children. *Journal of School Health, 46,* 344-354.

Pituch, M. and Bruggeman, J. (1982). Lungs unlimited. *Children Today, 11,* 6-10.

Musgrove, P. (1984, November 21). Struggling to survive. *The Vancouver Sun*, pp. 1-2.

Myers, G., Cerone, S., and Olson, A. (1981). *A guide for helping the child with spina bifida.* Springfield, IL.: Charles C. Thomas.

Nagy, M.H. (1948). The child's view of death. *Journal of Genetic Psychology, 73,* 3-27.

National Cancer Institute. (1980). *Students with cancer: A resource for the educator.* Washington, D.C.: U.S. Department of Health, Education and Welfare.

Radbill, S.X. (1974). A history of child abuse and infanticide. In C.H. Kempe and R.E. Helfer (Eds.), *The battered child.* Chicago: University of Chicago Press.

Rapp, D.J. (1979). Food allergy and hyperactivity. *Journal of Learning Disabilities, 12,* 608-616.

Robb, P. (1981). *Epilepsy: A manual for health workers.* Bethesda, MD.: U.S. Department of Health and Human Services.

Rodger, N.W. and Hunt, J.A. (1980). *Research horizons.* Toronto: Canadian Diabetic Association.

Sandor, G. (1981). Fetal Alcohol Syndrome: Cardiac malformations. *B.C. Medical Journal, 23,* 326-327.

Schiffer, C.G. and Hunt, E.P. (1963). *Illness among children: Data from U.S. National Survey.* Washington, D.C.: U.S. Department of Health, Education and Welfare.

Schneider, M.R., Melton, B.H. and Reisch, J.S. (1980). Effects of a progressive exercise program on absenteeism among school children with asthma. *Journal of School Health, 48,* 311.

Schwachman, H. and Kulczycki, L.L. (1958). Long term study of 105 patients with cystic fibrosis. *American Journal of Diseases in Children, 96,* 6-15.

Schwachman, H., Kowalski, M., and Khaw, K.T. (1977). Cystic fibrosis: A new outlook. *Medicine, 56,* 129-149.

Simeonsson, R.J., Buckley, L., and Monson, L. (1979). Conception of illness causality in hospitalized children. *Journal of Pediatric Psychology, 4,* 77-84.

Smith, S.P. (1978). Some (not all) facts about asthma. *Journal of School Health, 48,* 311.

Soare, P.L. and Raimondi, A. (1977). Intellectual and perceptual-motor characteristics of treated myelomeningocele children. *American Journal of Diseases in Children, 131,* 199-204.

Spinetta, J.J., Rigler, D., and Karon, M. (1974). Personal space as a measure of the dying child's sense of isolation, *Journal of Consulting and Clinical Psychology, 42,* 751-756.

Stephen, E. (1958). Cerebral palsy and mental defects. In A.M. Clarke and A.D. Clarke (Eds.), *Mental deficiency: The changing outlook.* New York: Free Press.

Streissguth, A.P., Landesman-Dwyer, S., Martin, J.C., and Smith, D.W. (1980). Teratogenic effects of alcohol in human and laboratory animals. *Science, 209,* 353-361.

Suran, B.G. and Rizzo, J.V. (1979). *Special children: An integrative approach.* Glenview, IL.: Scott Foresman.

Suran, B.G. and Rizzo, J.V. (1983). *Special children: An integrative approach (2nd ed.).* Glenview, IL.: Scott Foresman.

Telford, C.W. and Sawrey, J.M. (1981). *The exceptional individual (4th ed.).* Englewood Cliffs, N.J.: Prentice-Hall.

Tizzard, J.P., Paine, R.J., and Carothers, B. (1954). Disturbance of sensation in children with hemiplegia. *Journal of The American Medical Association, 155,* 628-632.

Tower, C.C. (1984). *Child abuse and neglect: A teacher's handbook for detection, reporting and classroom management.* Washington, D.C.: National Education Association.

Van Stolk, M. (1978). *The battered child in Canada.* Toronto: McClelland and Stewart.

Vernon, D., Foley, J.M., Sipowicz, R.R., and Shulman, J.L. (1965). *The psychological responses of children to hospitalization and illness.* Springfield, Ill.: Charles C. Thomas.

Voignier, R.R. and Bridgewater, S.C. (1980). Allergies in young children. *Young Children, 35,* 67-70.

CHAPTER THIRTEEN

Children with Multiple Handicaps

SALLY M. ROGOW

Courage can be such quiet, nameless things —
the patient things that strive when hope seems lost:
a first frail flower that dares the last sharp frost,
the bird that seeks the sky on crippled wings,
a valiant heart that smiles, though each day brings
some fresh defect, some sorrow unforeseen —
all things that toil against despair, yet glean
something of joy from life's deep, hidden springs.
A flame burns brighter when strong winds are blowing:
it leaps into the shadows, and its fire
gathers more light to push the darkness out.
So courage is: intensely glowing,
kindled from hope, and fanned by the desire
to put the darkness of the soul to rout.
(Robert Smithdas, deaf and blind poet and rehabilitation leader, 1966.)

In recent years, there has been a dramatic shift in attitude and approach toward children with multiple handicaps. These children are no longer regarded as hopeless, tragic, and beyond the reach of therapeutic and educational intervention. Several important events have brought about this shift in attitude and approach. Parents' associations have spearheaded a social movement to extend educational and treatment services to the most severely afflicted children. As a result of new medical technology, intensive-care nurseries, and life-saving techniques, many infants are surviving who would have perished just a few years ago.

Recent research into infant development has led to an increased sophistication of educational and therapeutic interventions. As multihandicapped children gain access to educational and treatment services, they are increasingly demonstrating their capacity for learning. Researchers are currently compiling startling and dramatic evidence that shows even the most severely disabled can become productive members of society.

This chapter will discuss the specific and general issues that pertain to children with multiple handicaps. Particular attention will be paid to children who combine visual and hearing handicaps, and to those who combine sensory losses with physical and neurological handicaps. As stated throughout the text, children within any one category of exceptionality form an extremely heterogeneous group. This is even more true of multihandicapped children.

Several myths continue to surround multiply handicapped children. The most pervasive of these are outlined in the following examples.

- "Multihandicapped children are all severely retarded." This myth is particularly vicious because it suggests that multihandicapped children cannot learn. Multihandicapped children need a responsive environment capable of providing appropriate stimulation and opportunities for interaction. Parents and teachers must believe in the children's ability to learn and adapt, and must understand how to facilitate responsiveness and learning. Under these conditions, multihandicapped children can learn adaptive behaviours.

- "All learning is sequential, and follows upon a basic development of motor behaviour." This myth also discourages education intervention with multihandicapped children. These children require stimulation of all their senses. They need help in order to integrate their sensory experiences, and they need meaningful stimulation that motivates them to respond. Some children can never acquire skilled motor patterns. They reveal their intelligence only after they develop language.

- "Children must respond to a single stimulus before they respond to more complex ones." This myth denies the complex nature of the stimuli that exist in the real world. Sound is accompanied by image, and smell by taste. Children must be able to integrate sensory impressions in order to make sense of their environment. Multisensory approaches provide rich and realistic impressions, while a single-stimulus approach may hinder concept development.

- "Multihandicapped children are not able to learn language." Children who are unable to physically manipulate their world may still be able to perceive and interpret far more language than their motor responses indicate. Severely multiply handicapped children who are unable to speak can be helped to express their knowledge through alternate forms of communication.

- "It is important to identify the most severe or 'primary' handicap." This myth may prevent children from receiving the services they require. Primary handicaps are often impossible to identify. For example, blind and retarded children may be visually inattentive because they do not see or because they are intellectually unaware of the visual environment. Single-problem approaches also ignore the fact that blind or deaf children who are also retarded require very different interventions than mentally handicapped children with no visual or hearing impairments.

DEFINITIONS OF MULTIPLE HANDICAPS

Multiple handicaps affect all body/mind systems in different ways and to different degrees. To an even greater degree than for children with single handicaps, each child must be considered individually.

PROFILE 13-1

"My favourite things to do are to eat chocolate, talk to my friends, read with my teacher, and tell jokes."

Eddy is a severely multihandicapped ten-year-old boy. His spastic quadriplegia restricts him to limited movement in one arm and hand, and the ability to turn his head. He is also totally blind.

Eddy is known to have suffered a cerebral infection right after his birth. He had severe symptoms and a high fever, but he recovered quickly and was sent home with his adoptive parents at the age of ten days. Eddy's mother began to suspect something was terribly wrong soon after she brought him home. His head was floppy and he never "looked" at anything. He was also very upset and cried a great deal.

Eddy's mother found it hard to accept the doctors' diagnosis. "Looking back, I still feel the frustration that a whole year went by and we didn't know what to do for him. When the doctors told us that Eddy was blind, mentally retarded, and probably deaf, and that we should put him in an institution, my husband and I started to cry. They were sentencing Eddy. They talked about him as if he weren't human at all. One thing I did know about Eddy was that he knew me. He loved to cuddle. Physical contact was important to him, especially before he could talk."

When Eddy was about three years old, he tried to speak. Although his parents knew he was trying, his words didn't become intelligible until he was about five. When he was seven, he spoke in whole sentences, corrected his own pronunciation, and became interested in word meanings.

Eddy is now enrolled in a second-grade class. Had he not had parents and teachers who sensed his intelligence and provided stimulating experiences, this little boy would have been lost.

The profile of Eddy warns us of the dangers of stereotyping multihandicapped children and of making precipitate diagnoses and predictions about their capacities. The profile also demonstrates that when children are defined by handicaps alone, the dimension of individuality is lost.

Although individual differences must be borne in mind, certain parameters are useful in defining multiple handicaps. Some definitions attempt to offer comprehensive generic descriptions of multiple handicaps. Others describe the parameters of types of handicapping conditions.

Generic definitions

Thompson (1976) provides a comprehensive generic definition of the multiply handicapped. According to Thompson, this category includes:

> those children who, because of the intensity of their physical, mental, or emotional problems, or a combination of such problems, need educational, social, psychological, and medical services which will make it possible for them to maximize their full potential for meaningful participation in society and for self-fulfilment (p. 41).

Thompson's definition includes the severely and profoundly retarded children, deaf-blind children, mentally retarded deaf-blind children, and physically disabled and severely emotionally disturbed children (Van Osdol and Shane, 1982).

Multisensory impaired is a generic term used to define children with sight and hearing handicaps. This definition includes children who may also be developmentally delayed or have neurological impairments (Kysela, 1985).

A third generic definition is offered by the term **multiple dependent handicapped**. This refers to severely mentally handicapped children who also have sensory and/or physical handicaps (Kysela, 1985). Children described as multiple dependent display a wide variety of visual, auditory, and physical/neurological handicaps.

Generic definitions tend to use very broad parameters. They tend to obscure the effects of visual and hearing handicaps, making it harder to clinically interpret the needs of individual children. Generic definitions do not give rise to specialized programs. Children with visual or hearing impairments who are enrolled in generic programs may not have access to specialist services, such as orientation and mobility training, low-vision services, or communication training. Another problem is that inclusive generic definitions also tend to combine multihandicapped children with severely or profoundly retarded children, despite the fact that not all multihandicapped children are retarded.

Because of these problems, some educators avoid generic definitions. They prefer specific definitions for each group of multi-impaired children. Many define the multi-impaired population in terms of the types of program they require (Sontag, Smith, and Sailor, 1977).

Specific definitions

Specific definitions are categorical, considering one multi-handicapping condition only. Definitions have been developed for such conditions as deaf/blindess, visual/physical/mental handicaps, and hearing/physical/mental handicaps.

Deaf-blind children

In the United States, the deaf-blind child is defined as:

> a child who has both auditory and visual impairments, the combination of which cause such severe communication and other developmental and educational problems that he cannot properly be accommodated in special education programs either for the hearing handicapped child or for the visually handicapped child (Kirk and Gallagher, 1979, p. 437).

The same definition is used in Canada.

For deaf-blind children, severity of sensory impairment is a major factor in determining their level of educational functioning. The severity of the impairments also determines the types of services these children will require (Jensema, 1980).

Visually/multihandicapped children

This category refers to those visually/multi-impaired children who cannot appropriately be accommodated in programs for mentally handicapped children without sight problems. Visually/multi-impaired children require specialized services for the visually impaired in order to realize their developmental potential.

Visually/multihandicapped children have a range of additional impairments that run the entire diagnostic gamut. Many have these problems from birth, while others have conditions that result from a lack of sensory stimulation and experience. Some developmental slowness can often be attributed to parental attitudes. No child is more at risk to become the victim of emotional, environmental and experiential deprivation than the visually/multihandicapped child (Moor, 1968). Problem behaviours that result from emotional disturbance are often confused with the behavioural characteristics of mental retardation, childhood autism, and related problems.

Deaf mentally handicapped children

This category includes children "who have hearing impairments, subaverage general intellectual functioning and deficits in adaptive behaviour. The combination of these three factors requires services beyond those traditionally needed by persons with either mental retardation or hearing impairments". (Healey and Karp-Nortman, 1975, p. 9).

Multiply/physically handicapped children

When combined with cerebral palsy, visual and hearing impairments tend to intensify the condition's multiple effects on the child's total functioning. Visually or hearing impaired children with cerebral palsy are those children with the disorder who have a visual or hearing loss severe enough as to require special services (Kirk and Gallagher, 1979).

Some children with brain damage have severe visual impairments but are not treated as visually impaired. For these children, "damage to the motor area seems to be more visible and the child's response to light seems to be so minimal, that professionals often forget the need to intervene visually to increase use of residual vision . . ." (Hammer, 1984, p. 10).

Problems with Definitions

At their best, definitions can become "passports," opening the door to special services (Ysseldyke and Algozzine, 1982). However, definitions that are applied without reference to treatment programs simply become "labels" that isolate the child. Definitions that focus on the individual problems rather than addressing complex social and environmental problems become ". . . deleterious to the future of the child" (Gallagher, cited in Ysseldyke and Algozzine, 1982).

In the absence of active intervention and educational programs, the potential abilities of multiply handicapped children are very difficult to identify. Intelligence is most often judged on the basis of learned behaviours, such as language, that result from interaction with other people. Sensory impaired children who function at severe or profound levels of retardation have very few opportunities to discover the important connections between themselves and the world around them. This makes their actual learning potential difficult to assess.

CLASSIFICATION OF MULTIPLY HANDICAPPED CHILDREN

The tendency to administer services on the basis of labels and categories has resulted in the creation of a number of overlapping and restrictive systems of classification. The multiply handicapped population in Canada is presently classified in three ways:

- According to the single handicap considered to be primary.
- According to the agency providing services.
- According to the type of educational program in which the child is enrolled.

Classification by primary handicap

Regardless of how children with multiple handicaps are classified, they continue to require a broad spectrum of medical, educational, and therapeutic services. However, because of the rigidity of the single-handicap classification system, those children whose handicaps cut across several categories of impairments have tended to fall between the cracks. Special services for the visually impaired, the hearing-impaired, and the physically handicapped have not in the past been extended to children served by agencies, schools, and institutions for the mentally retarded (Hammer, 1984). Fortunately, this situation is changing. Teachers and other professionals are becoming more aware of the vision and hearing needs of the multihandicapped population.

Many professionals now recognize that multiply handicapped children cannot be appropriately classified under the category of a single handicap. They require access to special services for all the impairments they suffer, whether sensory, physical, mental, or behavioural.

Classification by agency

Children who combine sensory handicaps with cerebral palsy may be registered for service with agencies for the blind, the deaf, or the cerebral-palsied. The same multiply handicapped child might be identified within the service delivery systems of any of these generic agencies.

Classification by type of program

In some provinces, classification by type of program has facilitated the entry of deaf/blind children into educational programs specifically designed for them. In provinces where no deaf-blind programs exist, these children tend not to be identified until they are much older. Many are served by school programs designed for the mentally retarded, the hearing impaired, or the visually impaired.

Both blindness and deafness, when combined with even mild retardation, tend to depress and repress levels of cognitive and adaptive functioning. Only in recent years have the unique needs of visually/multiply handicapped children been recognized. Many of these children were previously placed in wards for the profoundly retarded, with few educational programs available to them. The same was true for deaf children who functioned on a retarded level. Bereft of any system of communication, most of these children appeared far more mentally handicapped than they were.

PREVALENCE OF MULTIPLE HANDICAPS

Because Canada does not have a national registry of handicapped children, obtaining accurate prevalence figures is almost impossible. In addition, prevalence figures for multiple handicaps tend to be affected by changes in technology, demographic trends, and social factors (Hayden and Beck, 1981). However, those prevalence figures that are available indicate that the numbers are greater than has been assumed. Recently, the British Columbia Health Surveillance Registry began to increase the sources of their information, using a combination of birth forms and reports from Public Health units, special treatment centres, voluntary health agencies, and private physicians. As a result, the Registry found an increase of fifteen percent in reported cases of multiple handicaps (Hayden and Beck, 1981).

Blue (1983) conducted a survey and identified ninety-four deaf-blind children in Canada. This minimal figure included only those children registered with the CNIB. In order to identify more deaf-blind children in Canada, a task force was established. The mandate of the Task Force was to:

- Assess the current service needs of the deaf-blind population, particularly with respect to intervention services.
- Analyze currently available services.
- Identify current and anticipated gaps in the service network for the deaf-blind.
- Estimate the costs involved for each of the major service agencies, as well as any alternative service programs.
- Prepare a statement of the resource commitment that can be expected from various service sectors, with special reference to the proposal of a separate national agency for the deaf-blind (Blue, 1983).

The Canadian task force reported that 623 deaf-blind persons were registered with the CNIB. Of these, 90 were children under sixteen years of age (Blue, 1983). In 1977 alone, 406 multihandicapped, legally blind children were reported to the CNIB, but it is thought that a much larger number exists (Reesor, 1977).

In a study conducted by the American Foundation for the Blind, fifty percent of blind children were found to have additional disabilities (Graham, 1975). Meadow (1982) found that thirty-three percent of hearing-impaired children have additional handicaps. The most common of these additional disorders are mental retardation and emotional disturbance.

An estimated forty-four percent of children with cerebral palsy have uncorrectable visual anomalies (Kirk and Gallagher, 1979). Warburg (1976) estimates that at least five percent of mentally handicapped children are severely visually impaired. Projecting from the recent American figures quoted by Suran and Rizzo (1979), we can estimate approximately 4000 multi-impaired children in Canada, or 1 in 2500 children.

ETIOLOGY OF MULTIPLE HANDICAPS

With the exception of rubella, the etiology of multiple handicaps parallels that of physical handicaps. This is especially true of nervous system damage that results in severe motor impairment. To review the etiology of physical handicaps, see Chapter Twelve, on physical and health problems. Nervous system disorders resulting in multiple handicaps may also be the result of trauma or accident. Child abuse is a major cause of multiple handicaps in young children.

Rubella

Rubella has been mentioned previously in this text as a cause of a variety of conditions. At its most devastating, its consequences include deaf/blindness and severe multiple disabilities. Rubella is a virus which, when contracted in pregnancy, can cause gross impairments in the affected fetus. When rubella is contracted in the first trimester of pregnancy, the affected infant may have combined sight and hearing disabilities, heart defects, a damaged nervous system, and other body system problems.

When maternal rubella occurs within the first three months of pregnancy, there is a fifteen to twenty percent risk that some fetal organs will be affected (Van Dijk, 1982). Studies have also shown that many children who appear normal at birth later prove to be "hidden victims" of the disease. A recent Canadian study (Feldman 1977) suggests that some children with psychiatric and delayed-language problems were possibly victims of the rubella virus.

The fetal organs likely to be affected by rubella are those whose development is underway when the mother contracts the virus. The eye, ear, nervous system, and heart are especially vulnerable at early periods of fetal development (Van Dijk, 1982). Hearing impairment is the most common manifestation of congenital rubella, acquired during the later stages of pregnancy. The rubella virus may stay alive for many months after birth (Van Dijk, 1982).

A variety of eye diseases are associated with rubella. These include cataracts, nystagmus, glaucoma, and retinal disorders. The hearing impairments associated with rubella range from mild to severe.

Most rubella children who have combined sight and hearing problems are neither totally blind nor profoundly deaf. However, the combination of these sensory impairments with central nervous system defects creates severe learning handicaps for these children (Van Dijk, 1982).

Other infections

Meningitis and encephalitis in the newborn infant are probably the result of infection in the birth canal. Meningitis contracted immediately after birth is a major cause of multiple handicaps. Fifty percent of the infants who survive the disease have significant neurological impairments. These include cerebral palsy, hydrocephalus, convulsive disorders, and hearing and visual handicaps (Fenichel, 1980).

Usher's Syndrome

Familial nerve deafness associated with pigment degeneration of the retina is known as Usher's Syndrome (Harley and Lawrence, 1977). The child with Usher's may have a diagnosable hearing handicap at birth or soon after. The age of onset of the associated visual disability ranges from early childhood to early adulthood (Harley and Lawrence, 1977). See the discussion of retinitis pigmentosa in Chapter Nine.

Birth disorders

Hydrocephaly is frequently associated with multiple impairments. If treatment is unsuccessful or only partially successful, the child may have damage to the optic nerve as well as motor handicaps (Harley and Lawrence, 1977).

Injuries to the central nervous system incurred during the birth process account for a significant number of multihandicapped children. Most birth injuries result in deprivation of oxygen to the immature brain. This leads to abridgement of nervous system function (Fenichel, 1980).

Pathologically and clinically, deprivation of oxygen to the infant brain is similar to cases of stroke in the adult brain. In a direct sense, the hypoxic infant suffers stroke (Fenichel, 1980). The factors that influence recovery include the size and severity of the injury (Fenichel, 1980).

Children who are born prematurely, especially those whose birth weight is less than 1500 grams, are particularly vulnerable to insults of the central nervous system (Fenichel, 1980).

Chromosomal disorders

There are many different chromosomal disorders that affect children. Many of these disorders reveal themselves in newborns through intra-uterine growth retardation, **hypotonia**, and anomalies of the face and hands. Hypotonia is present at birth, even when normal tone or spasticity develops later (Fenichel, 1981).

Children born with genetic defects often have complex multiple disorders affecting several different body systems. Fortunately, chromosomal disorders account for the least number of multi-impaired children.

Nervous system disorders

Sight and hearing handicaps in multi-impaired children are frequently related to disorders of the central nervous system (Warburg, 1976). In a study of blind mentally handicapped children, spastic palsy was observed in fifty-eight percent of the children. Epilepsy was observed in sixty-eight percent (Warburg, 1976).

Cortical blindness

Cortical blindness sometimes refers to blindness caused by swelling in the brain tissue, due to trauma, infection, or congenital malformations (Hammer, 1984). At other times, the term describes blindness that cannot be medically explained. Most often, children who are congenitally cortically blind have other problems that are serious enough to affect several body systems.

Some central nervous system disorders may be manifest by a lack of response to light stimulus in the cortex. Drug use by pregnant mothers may also cause cortical blindness in their infants.

DIAGNOSIS AND ASSESSMENT OF MULTIPLE HANDICAPS

Medical diagnosis

Several diagnostic procedures are used to determine the exact nature, and sometimes the underlying cause, of multiple handicaps. These include:

- A careful medical history.
- Psychological and psychiatric assessment.
- Laboratory tests to detect metabolic disorders.
- Cytogenetic studies.
- Clinical neurophysiological investigation, through electroencephalograms (EEG), tests of auditory and visual potential, and electromyograms to test nerve conduction.
- Neuroradiology, which involves skull x-rays, echoencephalography, radio-isotope brain scans, and PET and CAT scans. The CAT scan, or computerized axial tomography, can pinpoint the presence of brain lesions.

Thorough medical reports for individual children can often prevent misdiagnosis or the overlooking of areas of function. For example, children diagnosed as cortically blind often have residual vision. When residual vision is found in a child's visually evoked response test, early visual stimulation can be realistically included in the child's intervention program.

Ivanainen (1981) maintains that a thorough neurological examination, using all available developmental-neurological techniques, often reveals the cause of the condition. Ivanainen's own studies in Finland revealed the etiology in ninety percent of his subjects. Ivanainen also observed that, in the physical examination, "it is extremely important that the physician has good contact with the patient" (p. 72).

Medical assessment should be undertaken for the multihandicapped child as early as possible. When the nature of the condition is understood, it is easier to begin appropriate treatment and to advise the child's family. Medical investigators should hold the same presumption of treatment for the multihandicapped as for other patients suffering cerebral symptoms (Ivanainen, 1982).

Hearing testing

The two most common forms of hearing testing are electrophysiological methods and behavioural methods (Murphy and Shallop, 1979). Electrophysiological procedures include electroencephalograph-evoked (EEG) response audiometry and impedance audiometry. For more information about the latter, see Chapter Eight on hearing disorders.

Behavioural testing includes observation of behaviour, play audiometry, and visually-reinforced audiometry (Murphy and Shallop, 1979). In **behaviour observation**

audiometry (BOA), a sound is presented to a child in a soundproof room. The tester observes the child for any behaviour response, such as an eyeblink or turning of the head. **Play audiometry** involves teaching a child to respond when a sound is presented. **Visually reinforced audiometry** refers to the technique of combining visual stimulation with an auditory stimulus. A common form of visual stimulation is the use of large lighted plastic toys. These toys are illuminated when sound is presented to provide reinforcement for the correct response. Visually reinforced audiometry relies on the child's ability to see visual cues, which cannot be assumed with multi-impaired children.

It is often difficult to distinguish whether children are inattentive to an auditory stimulus because they do not hear it or because they are simply inattentive. This is particularly true of children who ae mentally retarded or behaviour-disordered. Various methods have been devised to train children to respond to audiometric testing. **Tangible-reinforcer operant-conditioning audiometry (TROCA)** is a technique that has been successful with very young and multi-impaired children (Murphy and Shallop, 1978). This technique uses tactile rather than visual cues.

Electrodiagnostic instruments often provide the most reliable information about a child's ability to receive sound stimuli. **Instrumental response recordings** are techniques that do not rely on the child's behaviour. **Electrical response audiometry** (ERA) refers to the measurement of various evoked electrical potentials that are responses to auditory stimuli (Murphy and Shallop, 1980). These tests help to detect hearing responses, but do not provide information about the child's ability to interpret auditory stimuli. Behavioural and ERA measures provide diagnosticians with the specific assessments and comparative results they need to determine a prognosis (Murphy and Shallop, 1980). A medical follow-up should be a routine part of the diagnostic process. For example, an ophthalmologist might discover that a rubella-deafened child also suffers from retinitis pigmentosa. A medical follow-up over an extended period is needed to monitor and prevent possible visual deterioration (Murphy and Shallop, 1980).

Vision testing

It is often difficult to determine whether multi-impaired children have usable vision. This is particularly true of children with neurological handicaps who seem unable to establish normal visual contact. Although these children often seem visually inattentive, the normal appearance of their eyes may cause visual problems to go unnoticed.

Because vision is so important to learning, visual potential must be assessed as early as possible. New electro-diagnostic procedures have been developed to assess the electrical activity of the visual pathway and occipital cortex of the brain. The presence of electrical activity indicates that an active pathway exists (Ikeda, 1976).

Three electrophysiological techniques are in current diagnostic use:

- The **electro-oculogram** (EOG) can be performed on infants and multihandicapped children under general anesthetic. This test measures the ability of visual nerve cells to respond to light (Ikeda, 1976).

- The **electro-retinogram** (ERG) measures the chain of electrical nerve responses created by a flashing light. This allows the examiner to assess the functional state of the retina (Ikeda, 1976).

- The **visually evoked responses** (VER) technique records the reception of light images by the visual cortex. This permits the examiner to test visual responses behind the retina of the eye. The VER is a valuable test for infants and multihandicapped children (Ikeda, 1976).

In addition to electro-diagnostic testing, children should receive a thorough eye examination. This should determine:

- The presence or absence of ocular pathology.
- Ocular motor function.
- Response to moving targets. The ability to track moving objects indicates that the child has vision.
- Assessment of pupillary light reflexes. If the visual pathway of the brain is intact, the pupil contracts in the presence of light. However, the pupillary reflex is present in cases where damage is in the occipital cortex, rather than the eye itself (Harley and Lawrence, 1977).

When visual stimulation occurs, the child usually shows an observable response (Barraga, 1980). Assessment of the type of visual response is needed to provide appropriate visual stimulation to the multihandicapped visually impaired child (Barraga, 1980). Efron and Duboff (1975) have developed a visual guide to assess and improve the visual functioning of multihandicapped children.

Psychological and educational assessment

Psychological and educational assessments of multiply handicapped children are best made in familiar surroundings, using familiar tasks and materials. The testing of multiply handicapped children challenges the ingenuity of even the most experienced psychologists. Observational data and parent interviews are often the best indicators of the child's level of skill and awareness.

Psychological assessment

The psychological assessment of multiply-impaired children has two separate but equally important goals. These are:

- Measurement of the overall level of intellectual function.
- Exploration of the individual child's impairments and abilities (Gould, 1981).

A number of different methods may be used to achieve these goals. These include:

- Psychometric tests.
- Learning tests.
- Direct observation.
- Informant interviews.

Psychometric tests are not suitable for a large proportion of multiply impaired children (Liepman, 1981). Because the value of IQ scores for diagnosis is relatively limited for the multiply impaired, other types of instrument have been developed. These instruments measure the child's ability to perform in areas of motor skills, language and communication, social behaviour, and self-help skills. The instruments permit comparison of each child's performance at different points in time, rather than trying to establish the child's relative standing on a normative scale (Liepman, 1981).

Direct observation techniques permit assessment of children's behaviour and achievements in their normal daily routine (Liepman, 1981). Televised recordings of children's behaviour in familiar, unfamiliar, structured, and unstructured settings provide invaluable information. Videotapes made at various intervals allow teachers and clinicians to establish a learning program for a child over time (Donlon and Curtis, 1972).

A number of questionnaires and interview schedules have been constructed for use with parents, teachers, and other key informants (Liepman, 1981). These provide important information about every aspect of the child's progress.

The aim of psychological assessment is to clearly indicate areas of ability and function, as well as disabilities and gaps in development (Gould, 1981). It is now common practice to use a combination of developmental scales, observational checklists, and formal intelligence tests. No one assessment tool can meet the needs of a population as diverse as the multihandicapped.

Assessment materials should be chosen to supplement each other, and specific instruments should vary according to the needs of the individual. A simple, standardized assessment might be administered to an entire class to make initial evaluations and to determine class placement. This would then be followed by a second assessment tool, which would elicit as much detailed information as possible about the individual child. This second assessment would be chosen to accommodate the child's individual level of functioning, sensory handicaps, and so on.

All assessments should be administered on a regular basis, usually once or twice a year. Individualized teaching programs should be reviewed and revised frequently. When several different tests are used, discrepancies and inconsistencies in each child's profile become more apparent. These discrepancies are often helpful in planning an individualized educational program.

No psychological assessment is complete without the careful collection of data from parent interviews. Parents are often able to give information about their child's abilities that are not obvious in testing or teaching situations.

Educational assessment

The primary goal of educational assessment is to establish an individual educational plan (IEP) for the multiply impaired student. Educational assessment focuses on functional areas of competence in such areas as communication, social behaviour, and self-help and independence skills. For many children, educational assessment also measures areas of academic competence, such as reading, writing, and mathematics. Educational assessments should be made over a long period of time and at regular intervals.

The assessment of a multiply-handicapped child must attempt to answer the following questions:

- Is the child attentive to auditory language and symbolic code systems?
- How are the child's hands used? Are they limp like wet sponges or are they actively employed for exploration and manipulation?
- How does the child respond to training?
- Does the child refuse to learn because of poor motivation? Or is the material too complex and confusing?
- Does the child use vision and hearing to their fullest potential? (Hammer, 1984.)

A number of developmental scales and assessment tools are helpful in the psychological and educational assessment of children with multiple handicaps. Two of the most useful are Assessment Tools for Use with the Severely Multiply Handicapped (Kansas State Department of Education, revised 1979), and the Progress Assessment Chart of Social and Personal Development.

PREVENTION OF MULTIPLE HANDICAPS

Adequate pre-natal care, good nutrition, and avoidance of alcohol and drugs have improved the health of mothers and babies. Maternal rubella can be effectively prevented by the rubella vaccine. Research is underway for ways to prevent and cure other congenital birth defects.

The extreme consequences of severe physical, sensory, and mental handicaps can often be prevented by early infant intervention programs followed by ongoing medical care and treatment. Some conditions of the eye and ear can be treated medically or surgically. Cosmetic or plastic surgery can in some cases correct skeletal anomalies that cause visual or hearing problems. Cosmetic surgery may also help the child to win social acceptance.

Recent advances in genetics have increased our understanding of genetically-linked disorders. Genetic counselling is available to help prevent the frequency of genetic conditions.

DEVELOPMENTAL CONSEQUENCES OF MULTIPLE HANDICAPS

In non-handicapped children, normal physiological development produces steady, organized patterns of behaviour (Van Dijk, 1982). Where a pathology of the central nervous system exists, the organization of behaviour is disturbed. The child's early development is often uneven. For example, a developmentally-delayed multisensory handicapped child may walk at a relatively early age, but be severely delayed in the acquisition of language.

Many domains of learning depend on a child's ability to interact with the environment. As a result, multiply handicapped children may need more time to reach developmental milestones. Children with visual and motor problems, for example, take longer to learn hand/eye co-ordination. However, because of the variety of developmental disabilities presented by multiply handicapped children, generalization is virtually impossible (Rogow, Hass, and Humphries, 1984).

Academic Achievement

Deaf-blind children

The first deaf-blind child to be educated was Laura Bridgman. Her teacher was Dr. Samuel Gridley Howe, the founder and director of the Perkins School for the Blind. Dr. Howe taught Laura to read and write. Her achievements were noted by Charles Dickens, who was visiting North America at the time (Guldager, 1969).

Almost everyone is familiar with the extraordinary accomplishments of Helen Keller. She was taught by Ann Sullivan Macy, a highly creative and intuitive teacher who provided as much stimulation and motivation as possible. A play by William Gibson, *The Miracle Worker*, tells the dramatic story of Helen's early education. Helen's early accomplishments proved to be but a foretaste of her extraordinary achievements in adult life.

Canada has also produced dramatic accounts of the education of deaf-blind children. Ludivine Lachance was a wild and undisciplined deaf-blind girl from a remote village in Quebec. In 1911, at the age of 16, she was brought to Montreal's convent school for the deaf. There, the Sisters of Providence successfully taught Ludivine the rudiments of language and manual skill (Koestler, 1978).

The learning and educational attainments of deaf-blind children depend on several factors. These include the quality of education, the age at which education begins, the age of onset of both deafness and blindness, and the nature of additional handicaps (Van Dijk, 1982).

Studies of deaf-blind rubella children reveal great differences between this group and other deaf-blind children (Van Dijk, 1982). These differences are primarily due to the gross effects of the rubella virus on other body systems. However, studies of learning patterns in all deaf-blind children indicate that early intervention is crucial to later educational success (Van Dijk, 1982). At least one-third of deaf-blind children go on to succeed in academic programs.

Brain-damaged multiply-handicapped children are too often dismissed as hopelessly damaged. Sensory impairments have a masking effect and depress levels of function. As a result of misdiagnosis, blind or deaf multihandicapped children are denied the stimulation and educational interventions they require for optimal development.

Communication

Most multihandicapped infants are deprived of orienting movements of the head and body, as well as purposive gaze. This leaves them with no available modality through which to communicate. They are unable to clearly co-ordinate actions of looking, searching, reaching, and touching, which operate as functional units of communication.

Multi-impaired children find it very difficult to acquire the complex symbol system of language without enough sensory data to make that language meaningful. Because their perception of events is impaired, they also find it hard to develop awareness, attention, anticipation, and purpose. Multihandicapped children must often learn techniques for acquiring knowledge as well as the knowledge itself.

Social adjustment

Little research has been directed toward the social development of multiply handicapped children. Studies and assessment tools are badly needed to examine personality and emotional functioning among this group. Such studies may provide information that helps the multihandicapped to develop independence strategies and coping behaviours (Rosen, Clark, and Kivitz, 1977).

Studies of "helplessness" among disabled populations suggest that helplessness and passivity are encouraged by overly sheltered experiences at home or within an institution (Rosen, Clark, and Kivitz, 1977). Behaviours such as rocking, eye-poking, limb posturing, twirling, thumb-sucking, and complex hand movements have been found to occur in the absence of interactions with the physical and social environment. These stereotypic behaviours are far more common in restricted environments than in integrated ones (Rosen, Clark, and Kivitz, 1977).

Studies of the social adjustment of severely handicapped persons to community facilities paint a fairly optimistic picture. These studies suggest that environment plays a critical role in the acquisition of adaptive behaviours (Cegelka and Prehm, 1982). Personality variables, such as responsiveness and motivation are often good predictors of an individual's adjustment and adaptability (Rosen, Clark and Kivitz, 1977).

The onset of attachment behaviours and social interaction may be severely delayed in multihandicapped infants. The baby's first months may be dominated by periods of hospitalization, feeding problems, and an inability to maintain a wakeful state. The problems can cause serious delays in infant/adult interaction. Later, when educational intervention begins, these children may appear self-absorbed and difficult to reach (Van Dijk, 1982).

Multi-impaired children often demonstrate a wide range of associated handicaps, such as motor dysfunction, convulsive disorders, and delayed speech development. These problems contribute to difficulties in social interaction. Emotional problems may develop, manifested by any or all of the following personality traits:

- Frequent panic reactions.
- Hyperkinesis.
- Autism.
- Withdrawal.
- Frequent tantrum behaviour (Van Dijk, 1982).

Problem behaviours are often associated with inconsistent treatment in the home. They may also reflect the intense frustration caused by the child's inability to communicate. In some cases, the cause of problem behaviours is unknown. Such behaviours often seem related to the type of brain damage the child has sustained.

Teachers of multi-impaired children must be careful not to focus only on maladaptive behaviours. Multiple treatment modalities should be employed. These might include:

- Supportive play therapy.
- Medication.
- Family counselling.
- Correction or amelioration of associated somatic handicaps.
- Aid in seeking community resources.
- Sequential follow-up to assure continuity of needed services (Menolascino, 1974).

PROFILE 13-2

Donna is five years old. She is a deaf-blind child whose mother had rubella before she even realized she was pregnant. Donna and her family live in a northern town in British Columbia.

Soon after birth, Donna was diagnosed as having bilateral cataracts and a moderate hearing loss. Her mother noticed how fascinated Donna was with lights. Even as a baby, she flicked her fingers in front of her eyes.

Donna seemed not to notice familiar adults and was often cranky and fussy. She had many feeding problems from a very early age. She could not suck on a bottle and had to be fed with a spoon. Her family found it easier to pacify her than to insist on a regular feeding and sleeping schedule.

By the time Donna was two years old, she had developed a strong will and could be very stubborn. When her mother did not give her what she wanted, she would throw herself down on the floor, kicking and screaming. Donna's mother realized that she was encouraging Donna's behaviour by anticipating her every need. She began to look for a pre-school program where Donna would be accepted.

Concept development

Children with multi-sensory handicaps have difficulty making sense of the confusion of sounds and textures that surround them. Sensory handicaps distort, delay, and interfere with the accuracy of perception, making it hard for children to establish the identities and relationships of people and objects. For example, deaf-blind children or visually-impaired retarded children may perceive only fragments of information. In their world, objects appear or disappear without any indicator of where they've come from or gone to. These children do not see their mother place an object in their hand, or watch the ball roll away. They do not know how others use the object or for what purpose it has been designed. They perceive the world as unpredictable and irregular, full of confusion. As a result, they do not learn to anticipate or predict (Rogow, 1982).

Stereotypic behaviour

Many multiply handicapped children demonstrate a single behaviour over and over again. Some of these stereotypic behaviours seem to interfere with learning. Children who engage in stereotypic mannerisms often seem self-absorbed and locked in a private world.

Stereotypic behaviours can provide important information to the teacher or clinician.

They may serve as an important indicator of ability. For example, light gazing or hand-flapping in front of a light indicates that the child has some vision (Ficociello, 1977). These behaviours should be observed. They may serve as an important indicator of ability. Stereotypic behaviours can often be modified and adapted. They often disappear altogether when children become more interested in doing things with other people.

PARENTING THE MULTIPLY HANDICAPPED CHILD

PROFILE 13-3

'Why?' is a word that all parents of handicapped children are familiar with, a word most ask when they first find out about their child's handicapping condition. As a parent of a severely multihandicapped child, I remember, over a decade ago, repeating 'Why? Why? Why?' many times. Finally, my husband said, "If you knew why, would it change things? Would we put our son aside and forget we ever had him?" Obviously not.

In retrospect, the best advice given to us by a doctor at the time was 'Wait and see how your son will develop.' No promises came with those words, but the hope was not taken away. However, five months later a neurologist casually said to me during an office visit, 'Can't this child see?' 'I think so,' I replied. I was cruelly told 'No, he can't,' and I shall never forget that day or the term 'cortically blind' the rest of my life. I learned though that life goes on no matter what happens.

During the next two years, I was to deal with five different specialists while I searched independently for an early intervention program. I had to cope with an irritable crying child twenty hours a day, often left alone while my husband travelled with his job.

Finally I was able to hook up with a parent group. I'll never forget a mom stating, loud and clear, 'My son is *only* blind.' From that day on, I've always wondered where this son of mine belongs — this sweet little boy who happens to have cerebral palsy, mental retardation and cortical blindness. He's in a day program in a residential school for the blind, he lives in a middle-class neighbourhood in a large metropolitan city, and he has parents who love him and give him quality care. Yet where does he belong? Medical technology saved his life, and I will be forever grateful. But it has been up to me — the "pioneer" parent — to help find a place for him in this world (Corey, 1984).

For the child with multiple handicaps, early intervention is even more crucial than for other handicapped children. The goals of early intervention include:

- Teaching parents to provide sensory stimulation and to encourage adaptive behaviour (Haynes, 1978).
- Preventing secondary handicaps, such as behavioural problems and developmental handicaps produced by experience deprivation and understimulation.
- Early acquisition of communication and language skills.

Intervention during infancy and early childhood is a powerful variable in the prevention of secondary handicaps. Many of the behaviour problems observed among multihandicapped children result from a lack of programs during developmental periods (Grunewald, 1974). The process of aiding these children's development should begin from the moment of birth. Parents can learn to coax and nurture adaptive behaviour. They can also be helped to develop mutually satisfying relationships with their handicapped babies (Haynes, 1978).

The National Collaborative Infant Project has made the following recommendations for early intervention services for multihandicapped infants (Haynes, 1978).

- The expertise of the different types of agency serving multihandicapped children should be shared so that services are enriched, expanded, and made more comprehensive.
- A learning plan should be developed for handicapped children in their first two years of life.
- The family should be supported in the role of primary teacher and caregiver for children under two years of age.
- The effectiveness of service programs should be increased through the merging of medical and educational programs.
- Both scientific and lay communities should be informed about early intervention programs for infants and their families (Haynes, 1978).

In families with handicapped children, several stress periods have been identified:

- Birth.
- Diagnosis.
- Developmental delay.
- School entrance.
- Adolescence.
- Vocational planning.
- Death of a parent.
- Institutional placement.

During each of these periods, parents must be able to make informed, independent decisions about how to proceed with their child's treatment. No matter what decision they make, however, families should continue their involvement in their child's life. Making arrangements for the child to live outside the home should not terminate family relationships.

INTERVENTION WITH THE MULTIPLY HANDICAPPED

Medical and therapeutic intervention

Health-care professionals have long recognized the need for an interdisciplinary approach to therapeutic services. However, traditional interdisciplinary approaches are often costly and create needless duplication of effort. Often there is poor follow-through and an absence of effective interaction with clients.

In a transdisciplinary system, which cuts across traditional disciplinary boundaries, each team member must be willing to relinquish certain roles and share specialized skills (Haynes, 1978). In a transdisciplinary model, traditional disciplinary boundaries no longer restrict the sharing of information and knowledge among team members (Haynes, 1978).

The role of the physician

The physician, usually a pediatrician, has the primary responsibility for guiding parents through the early diagnostic phase. The physician also helps parents cope with the numerous medical problems that tend to arise with severely handicapped children (Howard, 1982). The physician provides ongoing review of the child's medical problems, medication, etiology, prognosis, and the effects of medication on behaviour and learning.

Many hospitals have developed clinics or child evaluation centres for handicapped and at-risk children. These centres provide assessment, diagnostic, and management services. They provide a team of specialists that may include a psychologist, a psychiatrist, a speech and hearing therapist, a physical therapist, an occupational therapist, a pediatric neurologist, a social worker, a nutritionist, a learning consultant, and a pediatric nurse.

Professionals should bear in mind that parents know their child best. Parents should be actively involved throughout the evaluation, program development, and placement of their handicapped child (Haynes, 1978).

The following factors should be considered when planning a program for the multiply handicapped child.

- Special arrangements may be needed to accommodate seizure activity, medications, allergies, susceptibility to illness, poor muscle strength, and special feeding problems.
- Heart defects may require monitoring or curtailment of certain activities.
- Physical deformities may require special equipment.
- Alterations may be needed in work, play, and rest schedules.
- Prosthetic devices may be needed.
- Special positioning or handling techniques may be needed.
- Special feeding techniques may be prescribed.

Physical and occupational therapy

The goals of physical and occupational therapy are gross motor development, muscle relaxation, and fine motor control. These are essential treatments for most multiply handicapped children.

Speech and language therapy

Speech-language therapy assists the child's development of speech and language. This form of therapy may also be used with children who have difficulty controlling the fine motor muscles needed for eating (Tucker and Jensema, 1984). Speech/language pathologists may also develop alternate systems of communication for children who cannot talk.

Educational Intervention

Learning environments

Multiply handicapped children may be educated in a variety of settings. Some may attend regular or special classrooms in public schools. Others may learn in special schools, residential schools, or school programs in hospitals and institutions.

Regular Schools. Children with mild sensory or physical impairments may learn well in the regular classroom, provided they receive additional support from specialist teachers. These children are able to participate in academic programs, and benefit from interaction with non-handicapped peers. In addition to regular teaching, they may require the services of speech/language pathologists, physical therapists, audiologists, mobility specialists, and specialist teachers of the visually or hearing impaired.

To accommodate multihandicapped children, the physical environment of the school often needs to be modified. Ramps for wheelchairs, guardrails in toilets, and non-skid surfaces help multi-impaired children to become more independent. Children become less frustrated and fatigued in classrooms that provide comfortable seating, adjustable lighting, quiet corners, and easily accessible shelves and cupboards. The special equipment needs for the physically and sensorily handicapped have been discussed in other chapters.

The attitudes and expectations of the teacher are of the utmost importance to the multi-handicapped student. The teacher must be knowledgeable about the child's physical problems and requirements. The teacher must also know how to plan learning experiences that encourage motivation and promote personal and social adjustment (Kirk and Gallagher, 1979). Multi-handicapped children form an extremely heterogeneous group and require a wide range of curricular adaptations. As a result, much classroom work must be individualized (Kirk and Gallagher, 1979).

Residential Settings. Many multiply disabled children live in residential institutions. These children need an extensive network of services to enable them to survive. Oswin (1978) has made the following recommendations to the staffs of large institutions to improve the living environments for these children.

- Continuity of staff should be maintained so that children can form stable relationships with adults.
- Staff should be aware that multihandicapped children are especially vulnerable to lack of attention.
- Staff should avoid encouraging behaviours that will not help the children to develop to their potential. They should especially avoid encouraging stereotyped responses.
- Furniture should not imprison children, and should encourage social interaction. Children should not be isolated in "bean chairs," wheelchairs, or armchairs. Children

should be grouped in clusters rather than rows, and should be within touching distance of other children and adults (Oswin, 1978).

- Toys should be purchased that encourage group interaction.
- Regular staff meetings should be held to discuss the development and maintenance of good child-care practice.
- All staff members should receive training to provide insight into child development, the effects of institutional care, and children's play and mothering needs (Oswin, 1978).

Group homes are a recent development in residential living for the multiply handicapped. Three to six young people live together, sharing responsibilities and mutually assisting one another. To help individuals who cannot be completely independent, the group home is managed by a residential counselor.

PROFILE 13-4

Teddy is blind and physically handicapped. He has recently moved from a large residential institution to a small group home in a suburban community. Teddy's new home is a three-bedroom ranch-style bungalow. For the first time, he has his own room and his own possessions.

Teddy's new home has created many new opportunities for him to learn the skills of community living. He has learned how to purchase food in the neighbourhood supermarket and how to make his own bed. He has also learned how to set the table and prepare his own toast for breakfast.

"This is my room. This is the house I live in now," Teddy proudly tells his visitor. "I am not as dumb as I used to think I was," he grins. "All I needed was someone to teach me. My counselors, Jim and Elaine — they know how to teach guys like me. All I used to do was listen to my radio. But now I can be an active man."

Some multihandicapped adolescents in group homes continue to require active medical treatment and therapy. These can be provided within the community when services are well-co-ordinated. The Community Living Boards in British Columbia and other provinces arrange for the provision of a wide variety of services. These agencies are proving that comprehensive co-ordinated services can be developed for severely multihandicapped persons within the community (B.C. MHP, 1983).

Other school settings. Hearing/visually impaired children who see well enough to learn through deaf-education techniques may be enrolled in special classes or schools for the hearing-impaired. These children require additional help from specialist teachers of the visually impaired to develop maximum use of their remaining vision.

Children with moderate to severe sensory impairments may require programs specifically designed for deaf-blind children. In Canada, special programs have been established in residential schools for the blind as well as in schools for the deaf.

Hospital-based day schools have been established to avoid the difficulties and expense involved in transporting multihandicapped physically-disabled children to school programs. Children attend school in hospital classrooms, where medical treatment and physiotherapy are readily available. Critics of these specialized segregated classrooms argue that the children who attend them have few opportunities to associate with non-handicapped peers.

Educational programs have also been established in mental retardation facilities. With the current emphasis on stimulation of the developing child, fewer Canadian deaf-blind children are being misdiagnosed as severely or profoundly retarded. However, a number of multisensorily impaired children continue to be served by schools and institutions for the mentally handicapped.

Educational approaches

Multihandicapped students present a range of special educational and psychosocial needs (Hammer, 1984). Curricula designed for the multi-impaired must reflect both areas of development. Educational needs include language development, visual and auditory training, mobility training, and self-care skills. Psychosocial needs include adaptive behaviour, group activities, life skills, and a range of socialization experiences (Hammer, 1984).

Educational programs are based on the course of normal child development. They are intended to build foundation skills that enable children to gain increasing mastery of their environments (Suran and Rizzo, 1979). Because different models of child development emphasize different dimensions of growth, considerable variation can be found in programs designed for multiply handicapped students.

Three important developmental models are the sensory-integration model, the co-active model, and the cognitive model.

Sensory integration models. Sensory integration is the ability to perceive and connect sensory information from the environment. Multihandicapped children have difficulty integrating sensory information because their sensory impairments prevent the reception of clear sensory information.

Children with both seeing and hearing handicaps receive reduced information from two primary sensory channels. Physically impaired children with sensory impairments have trouble using one sense to compensate for another. Emphasis on multi-sensory experiences helps these children to combine information from the eyes, ears, hands, body, and so on.

Sensory integration programs also stress the importance of body image, providing activities to develop children's awareness of themselves (Guldager, 1970). **Motor planning** is the ability to plan a new motor task. Motor planning is involved in the learning of all purposive movement activities, including walking, talking, feeding oneself, and dressing. Sensory integration lays the foundation for all perceptual motor skills, such as eye-hand co-ordination, posture, and balance. These sensory motor skills are fundamental to learning.

Severely afflicted multi-impaired children are unable to reach out beyond their own bodies. Children may appear not to recognize other family members, or they may be obsessively engaged in such self-stimulating behaviours as light-gazing or hand-flapping. They experience little body image awareness.

Guldager (1970) defined body image as the ability to perceive oneself and other objects as permanent entities. A developing body image can be seen through control of body movement, skill in manipulating the environment, and imitation (Guldager, 1970). This development can be encouraged by activities and games that require movement, knowledge of body parts, and increasing competence in self-care skills.

Most deaf/blind children do have some sight. Visual stimulation programs attempt to develop visual perceptual skills as a basis for cognition and academic tasks (Ficociello, 1977). The work of Barraga (1964) and others has shown that children with serious visual impairments can be taught to look. Looking is a learned ability (Barraga, 1964).

Exhibit 13-1 outlines the goals of vision stimulation for visually/multi-impaired children including the deaf/blind.

Vision training for multiply impaired children is similar to that for other visually impaired children. However, modifications are required at all levels. More time should be allotted for activities, and objects should be used that do not require verbal instruction.

Visual training should be incorporated into all areas of the instructional program. Multiply-impaired children develop eye contact as they learn to look (Rogow, Hass, and Humphries, 1983). Children should be encouraged to use their vision in all aspects of their development, including self-feeding and self-dressing (Ficociello, 1977).

Children with multiple handicaps, even those classified as deaf/blind, do have some hearing. However, as in the case of residual vision, they often do not attach meaning to the sounds they hear. It is crucial that these children develop auditory sensitivity at an early age.

Formal auditory training begins with the development of sound awareness. To achieve this, music is often used in combination with gross motor activities. The next step is discrimination of sounds, which teaches children to respond differently to different sounds. To teach sound localization, teachers often combine sound with a visual or tactile stimulus (Murphy and Shallop, 1979).

Sensory experiences should be developed that teach children to interpret and use auditory, visual, tactile and kinesthetic information. If children cannot interpret sensory information, they do not build a logical interpretation of the environment. Without sensory information, language has little meaning. Sensory experiences are the building blocks of concept development (Rogow, 1982).

Exploratory and manipulative play helps children to learn about objects and events. Children use their experience in handling, manipulating, and exploring objects to develop skills with which to explore the environment. Reach-and-grasp, finger, and hand development are especially important to learning.

Children whose ability to move is restricted may require mechanical and electronic support to enable them to learn by their own efforts. Physical and occupational therapy can help children to develop hand skills, body co-ordination, and other physical skills. Children should be as physically comfortable as possible in the teaching situation.

Co-active models. Co-active models of intervention place emphasis on the child's interactions with the environment. Van Dijk (1982), who developed co-active movement theory, argues that the problems of the multisensory impaired child are of foremost concern in the area of motor functioning (Van Dijk, 1982). Although sensory integration is an important aspect of the Van Dijk program, the program's primary goal is to enable the child to enter satisfying relationships with other people.

Exhibit 13-1 Goals of visual stimulation.

Visual skills
- attention to light and objects
- tracking and scanning
- figure-ground discrimination

Motor skills involving vision
- eye/hand co-ordination
- eye/foot co-ordination
- gross and fine motor skills

Mobility
- indoor mobility
- outdoor mobility

Body image
- identification of body parts

Visual perception
- object discrimination
- use of pictures
- sorting and classification
- sequencing

In order to overcome barriers to information access and personal interaction, multiply handicapped children must be taught *how* to learn, as well as what to learn. One of the teachers' most important roles is to teach learning strategies to the children. Teachers must establish a clear goal, model the desired behaviour, and respond to children's efforts to communicate (Rogow, 1982).

PROFILE 13-5

Joey was eight years old, congenitally blind, with a history of psychomotor convulsions. He appeared to have few interests, and he frequently had tantrums at home and at school. Although Joey had a vocabulary of food words such as "apple," "orange," "milk," "juice," "bread," and "butter," he did not use these words to ask for food. Instead, he simply cried when he didn't get the food he wanted.

At school, Joey often threw down the toys his teacher gave him to play with. The teacher always responded by patting Joey and saying, "Oh, I guess you don't want that toy." Then the teacher would take Joey's hand and lead him to a toy box. Saying "Let's find something you do like," she would help him find another toy.

By responding to Joey in this manner, his teacher showed him that she interpreted his rejection of the toy as a signal for "I don't want this." By treating Joey's own actions as communication, the teacher was modelling a communicative response. Joey learned that he did have some control over his environment. This was an important breakthrough.

Before long, Joey was signalling his needs on his own initiative. He learned how to make choices for himself. Joey's parents also learned to understand his signals. Instead of trying to make Joey conform to a desirable mode of behaviour, they could relax with the knowledge that he was learning adaptive skills.

Joey's natural signals were used as a basis for a systematic vocabulary of natural gestures. With this basis for systematic communication, Joey was motivated to learn more signs and symbols. He now uses a communication board in combination with his system of gestural signs.

In the earliest stages of building communication, the child's emotional and cognitive development cannot be treated separately. Progress in both areas appears when the child initiates more frequent and more satisfying movement toward objects and other people (Rogow, 1982).

Co-active methodology is based on the notion that children must become aware of themselves before they can successfully attach meaning to objects and events. The goals of co-active educational programs are:

- To develop self-awareness.
- To attach meaning to things and events.
- To encourage imitation and the use of signals.

Van Dijk (1982) believes that early movement patterns underlie cognitive and language development. In co-active movement programs, the following instructional sequence is employed:

- The teacher imitates the child's movements, however primitive and unorganized. During this stage, the teacher develops a trusting and affectionate relationship with the child.
- The teacher moves "co-actively" with the child, rolling with the child, crawling alongside the child, and so on.
- The child learns to imitate the teacher's actions. Pantomime and pretend games may be introduced at this stage.
- Through imitation, the child learns to replicate the teacher's actions with objects, the teacher's actions depicted in a picture, a stranger's actions depicted in a picture, and so on.
- The child learns to use natural gestures as signals to make requests and communicate needs and wants.
- The child learns the names of persons and objects. At this stage, vocabulary is developed.

Cognitive models. Developmental models based on the principles of cognitive development stress Piaget's theory of development. Cognitive models do not ignore sensory integration or the importance of social interaction. However, they place a strong emphasis on the child's ability to handle objects and initiate activities.

Cognitive-based interventions attempt to develop the child's motivation through a variety of planned learning experiences. They also help the child to develop concepts by forming realistic associations between objects and their use. Multihandicapped children are often excluded from such everyday sensations as the feeling of grass or pavement beneath the feet, the sight of clouds and colours in the sky, or the sound of birds and airplanes. They may feel anxious or frustrated when confronted with unfamiliar experiences and variations in their routines.

PROFILE 13-6

Flora had never been in the pool before she was taken by her teacher. She was frightened by the sounds of the pool room and held her body stiffly, whimpering while her teacher held her in the water. Only after repeated experience in the water did she begin to relax. She began to understand that her body felt strange and buoyant because of the water. Before long, she started looking forward to her time in the school's swimming pool.

Flora's years of understimulation had taken a heavy toll. Her response to every new situation was to grow fearful and become rigid and resistant. However, through the persistence of her teachers, Flora slowly learned to become familiar with a variety of new and strange experiences. Gradually Flora's fears are subsiding. She is gaining new confidence in herself and her ability to cope with an unfamiliar world.

Curricular modifications

According to Haring and Bricker (1976) a number of essential components are needed to provide a comprehensive system of education for most multiply handicapped children. These components are as follows:

- *A developmental framework.* Three basic ideas underlie the developmental approach. First, children follow a sequence of development, learning to vocalize before they talk, and so on. Second, children must be able to perform simple tasks before they can perform complex ones. Third, to perform complex behaviour, children must learn to co-ordinate and modify components of simpler behaviour.
- *Early and continuous intervention.* Early intervention can prevent the consequences of sensory deprivation and emotional withdrawal.
- *Systematic instructional procedures.* Because so many multihandicapped children miss so much incidental learning, they must be helped to develop a foundation for later and more complex learning.
- *Appropriate curricula.* Curriculum materials must be developed to meet the individualized educational goals of each child.
- *Adjunctive services.* These include the provision of medical and therapeutic treatments to individual children. Associated professionals may also provide specific training and instruction to parents (Kirk and Gallagher, 1976).
- *Objective evaluation.* Each child's educational plan should include a regular assessment of the child's progress and a detailed evaluation of the educational program. Evaluation of the program is essential to ensure that inappropriate programs do not impede children's progress.

Children who have physical/neurological handicaps in addition to sensory or mental handicaps have further educational needs. Stainback and Stainback (1977) offer the following teaching suggestions for working with severely handicapped children:

- Begin instruction only after the child is properly relaxed.
- Make sure the child is properly positioned for good body alignment, optimal movement, and good visual range. Seating equipment should support proper body alignment. Never leave the child in a reclining position throughout the day.
- Actively involve the child in the instruction. Develop short- and long-range goals that emphasize the child's self-help capabilities. Use prosthetic aids to enhance active involvement.
- Talk to the child. Meaningful language stimulation is important, even when the child does not appear to understand. Keep sentences short, and use an expressive voice. Often, multi-impaired children are able to comprehend far more than they are able to indicate.

Communication training. "Of all the problems faced by the multiply handicapped child, perhaps the most serious is the interference with communication" (Kirk and Gallagher, 1979, p. 455). Multiply handicapped children require training in all aspects of understanding and expression.

Children who are unable to acquire oral language may learn to use manual signing systems (Kirk and Gallagher, 1979). Communication boards may be used by physically handicapped children who cannot use their hands to sign or gesture. Communication boards employing printed words, pictures, or Bliss symbols have been used successfully with a range of multiply handicapped children (Guess, Sailor, and Baer 1977).

A primary goal in working with deaf/blind children is to teach them to communicate in the easiest way possible. Several systems may be used in place of speech (Watson and Nicholas, 1978), including the following alternatives.

- *Natural gestures.* These are simple movements of one or both hands to convey meaning to the child. For example, the word "eat" is indicated by tapping the lips with the fingertips of one hand. Natural gestures may vary from child to child. If a child consistently points to the mouth to indicate hunger, then everyone working with that child should use the same gesture.
- *Finger spelling.* This involves spelling every word letter by letter using a manual alphabet.
- *Sign language.* A number of sign languages have been developed by the deaf community.

For most deaf/blind children with other impairments, natural gesturing offers the best foundation for communication. Natural gestures can be easily individualized. When children can consistently use a variety of gestures, they can begin to move on to more complex communication systems (Watson and Nicholas, 1978).

"With the acquisition of speech, I moved from the baby phase of my mental growth to my identity as a separate, conscious and, to a degree, self-determining ego" (Helen Keller, 1957, p. 21). All children who are capable of speech should undergo intensive speech training. Many deaf/blind children have learned to perceive speech through the vibration method. According to this method, the deaf/blind person places a thumb on the speaker's lip, an index finger on the speaker's jaw, and three fingers on the speaker's neck. This allows the person to manually perceive the vibration of the speaker's voice, the tension of the speaker's facial muscles, and the shape of the speaker's lips.

The vibration method was first adapted for use by deaf/blind children by Hall (Stenquist, 1974). It was later refined into the Tadoma method of speech reading by Kate and Sophia Alcorn (Alcorn, 1956).

Communication training for multiply handicapped children who are not hearing impaired may also employ natural gestures. Techniques that combine touch and sound are helpful in teaching communication to blind multi-impaired children.

Exhibit 13-2 Tips for teaching communication to multihandicapped children.

- Reinforce vocalizations as frequently and consistently as possible.
- Provide vocal reinforcement a short time after the child stops vocalizing. This offers a model dialogue and ensures that the child is not interrupted. It also reinforces turn-taking patterns.
- Vocal reinforcement should include the imitation of the child's sounds, whether verbal or pre-verbal.
- Cue the child to the appropriate moments for vocalization by emphasizing the difference between periods of adult vocalization and adult silence. Place your mouth on the child's cheek or hand when speaking, so that the child can "feel" your speech. Continue to hold your mouth against the child's cheek or hand between vocalizations, so that the child can "feel" silence.
- Improve the quality of language stimulation by interspersing short bursts of speech with short periods of silence.
- Do not treat blind children as if they were totally blind. However, make sure to accompany communication with rhythmic body actions, touch sensations, or actions that engage a number of senses simultaneously.
- It does not take long to establish faulty interaction patterns in the first few months of a blind/multihandicapped infant's life. However, it takes a great deal of time to undo ineffective interaction patterns and shape new effective ones.
- Use playful social routines, rhyming verses, and other communication games that are enjoyable for you and the child. For older students, try using rock and roll and other rhythmic patterns.
- Encourage spontaneity by rewarding spontaneous behaviour. Let the child sometimes determine the lesson structure. Allow the child to develop lessons based on a special interest.
- Co-actively imitate and play with child.
- Treat the child's signals as meaningful and respond accordingly. Make it clear that you enjoy the child's responsiveness.
- Model the behaviours you want the child to learn.

Communication aids. In addition to amplification devices, a number of electronic aids are now employed to teach language and speech to multisensory-impaired children. These include electronic communication boards, talking disc, devices, telebraille, and tell-a-touch devices.

The talking disc, primarily used in Great Britain, is made of plastic and has a handle by which it can be rotated. An opening in the handle reveals specific letters, in print or braille characters (Kates and Schein, 1980). In this way, deaf-blind persons can read the words spelled on the disc.

Telebraille enables deaf/blind people to communicate in braille over the telephone. To send a message, the deaf-blind person presses the keys on a keyboard. The typed letters or braille contractions are converted into a signal and transmitted through the telephone wires. When the signal is received it is typed out as a braille message (Kates and Schein, 1980).

Orientation and mobility training. Orientation and mobility training is important for multihandicapped children with sight problems. Although training goals are the same as for other visually handicapped children, some of the teaching techniques may differ. Non-verbal children must often be encouraged to move freely and without fear before they are ready to learn proper cane techniques. Some specialists introduce cane travel before the child is technically ready in the hope of developing greater confidence (Wurzberger, 1984). This has proved very successful with low-functioning blind children.

Orientation and mobility training teaches multiply handicapped blind children a basic knowledge of the environment. It also teaches them how to find their way to specific locations, such as the schoolroom or the workshop.

Life skills training. The ultimate goal of education for multi-impaired children is to enable them to live as independently as possible. Even for children who can never achieve full independence, life-skills training contributes to feelings of confidence, self-reliance, and personal satisfaction. **Life skills** are those skills that promote self-care. These include basic hygiene, grooming, and self-dressing, as well as mobility, money-handling, shopping, housekeeping, leisure skills, and so on.

By the time multiply-impaired children reach adolescence, they should have mastered the rudiments of independent living. Ideally, they should be able to live away from their families for short or long periods of time (Hammer, 1974).

Recreation and leisure activities. Recreation and leisure services for the multi-impaired form an important part of the child's total education program. Recreation activities teach a variety of skills and offer the reward of immediate enjoyment. Children willingly take part in recreation activities on a voluntary basis (Neal, 1975). Perhaps the most important contribution of a leisure-activity program is to provide a setting for multi-impaired children to learn they have some control over their environment (Hammer, 1984).

Social isolation is always a problem for the severely handicapped. Children who are both deaf and blind find it difficult to establish spontaneous social contacts. Sighted persons are often needed to act as social mediators (Salmon, 1970).

Special efforts are often required to enable deaf-blind children to participate in recreational activities. However, a staff of reliable and skilful volunteers make it possible for even the most severely handicapped child to participate in leisure activities.

THE MULTIPLY HANDICAPPED PRE-SCHOOLER

Multihandicapped children often experience their first interactions with other children in pre-school programs. In the pre-school setting, an emphasis on communication and language training can be formalized and structured. Children can be taught to master a system of communication that works for them.

PROFILE 13-7

We met Donna earlier in this chapter. When she first entered a pre-school setting, she had no adequate means of communicating. Her teachers wisely concluded that her frequent tantrums and destructive behaviour were expressions of frustration. They decided to make communication of basic needs the first priority in Donna's education.

The teachers held a meeting with Donna's parents to find out as much as they could about her behaviour at home. Her mother told them about Donna's fascination with candy wrappers and coloured pictures of foods. The teachers decided to make a communication game for Donna using colourful pictures of food. Pictures of a chocolate cookie, a vanilla cookie, an apple, and a banana were posted on large plastic chips and placed in a little basket.

Every day, Donna was offered a choice of the foods shown in the pictures. If she showed her teacher the chocolate-cookie picture, she received the chocolate cookie. Donna quickly made the association and was fascinated by the game. Her teachers began to use other pictures to communicate requests such as "Put on your coat" and "Let's go outdoors."

Within a month Donna had a collection of plastic chips that she could use to express her needs and wants. Her teachers had established a foundation for her communication training.

Pre-school programs offer multi-handicapped children the socialization experiences and activities they need. Multi-handicapped children have an intense need for frequent and sustained human contact. They need to be touched, moved, cuddled, spoken to, and held by the hand (Oswin, 1978). Pre-school programs should teach these children how to take turns, how to share, and how to behave in a socially responsible way. These are the adaptive behaviours that enable multihandicapped children to function in school settings.

During the pre-school years, the major components of a functional educational curriculum should be introduced. These components include sensory training, language training, orientation and mobility training, and preparation for community living.

TEACHERS OF THE MULTIPLY HANDICAPPED

In North America, teachers of the multiply handicapped tend to receive inadequate training. Teachers need to be prepared both philosophically and educationally to construct the broadly-based instructional programs required by multiply handicapped children. They need university preparation programs that better reflect the work they are called upon to do in the classroom.

Without solid preparation, teachers often feel inadequate when faced with the compelling needs of non-verbal and non-communicating children. As Hammer (1984) points out, "A long-term training commitment [is needed] to upgrade teachers with new information, new techniques, action research, and changes in practices" (p. 14). For example, teachers receive little training in the use of technology for the multiply impaired. As a result, important new equipment is too often ignored or misused (Hammer, 1984).

Teachers also require training to work more effectively with parents. They must know how to listen to parents, how to identify family problems, and how to co-operate with parents in seeking solutions to problems (Hammer, 1984).

In Canada, teachers of the multihandicapped have often been trained as teachers of the mentally handicapped or as primary school teachers. Many of these teachers are keenly aware of their undertraining. They constantly seek workshops and seminars to provide them with the teaching skills they need.

Bain and Csapo (1984) surveyed special-education teacher-training programs in Canada. They found only seven universities that currently provide coursework and experience in the teaching of multihandicapped children. The W. Ross MacDonald School in Ontario provides a practical training course for teachers of the deaf-blind. The University of Alberta offers teacher preparation for the dependent multiply handicapped. The University of British Columbia includes teacher preparation for the visually/multihandicapped in its postgraduate program for teachers of the visually impaired.

SUMMARY

Multiply handicapped children are those who have multisensory impairments or those who combine sensory disorders with physical, neurological, and mental handicaps. These children require careful educational and habilitative planning from birth through adulthood. Some of these children are mentally handicapped, some have normal intelligence, and some are even gifted.

Multi-handicapped children require the services of many disciplines — education, physiotherapy, occupational therapy, speech language pathology, audiology, and medicine. As a result, a transdisciplinary approach to their treatment and education is recommended.

Despite their severe impairments, these children can be helped to develop to their fullest potential as individuals. This development can be achieved through alteration of the physical environment, sensory stimulation, and well-planned, consistent, habilitative and educational programs.

A great deal of hope for the multiply impaired lies in the area of technological research and development. Improved aids and devices are currently being developed to enrich education and improve the quality of life for multihandicapped children everywhere.

BIBLIOGRAPHY

Alcorn, S. (1956). *Tadoma method.* Watertown, MA.: Perkins School for the Blind.

Barraga, N. (1964). *Increased visual behavior in low vision children.* New York: American Foundation for the Blind.

Barraga, N. (1980). *Program to develop visual efficiency in visual functioning.* Louisville, Kentucky: American Printing House for the Blind.

Blue, M.T. (1983). A study of services for the deaf-blind in Canada. Unpublished paper.

Cegelka, P.T. and Prehm, H.J. (1982). *Mental retardation: From categories to people.* Columbus, OH: Merrill.

Corey, Fay. (1984). Awareness. In *Newsletter* of the National Association of Parents of Visually Impaired Children, USA.

Csapo, M. and Bain, D. (1985). Teacher education for the severely and profoundly handicapped. Unpublished.

Donlon, E.T. and Curtis, W.S. (1972). *The development and evaluation of a videotape protocol for the examination of multihandicapped deaf-blind children.* Athens, Georgia: University of Georgia.

Efron, M. and Duboff, B. (1975). *A vision guide for teachers of deaf-blind children.* Raleigh, N.C.: Special Education Instructional Materials Development Center.

Feldman, R.B., Mendelson, J., Poteck, M., Rothman, S.J., Portnoy, J., and Eaton, W.W. *A search for congenital rubella by response to MPV-77 vaccine in children attending language, learning or psychiatric clinics.* Unpublished survey, Montreal.

Fenichel, G.H. (1980). *Neonatal neurology*. New York: Churchill Livingstone.

Ficociello, C. (1977). Vision stimulation for low functioning deaf-blind rubella children. In M.A. Thomas (Ed.), *Developing skills in severely and profoundly handicapped children*. Reston, VA: Council for Exceptional Children.

Gould, J. (1981). Psychometric tests: Their uses and limitations. In B. Cooper (Ed.), *Assessing the handicaps and needs of mentally retarded children*. New York: Academic Press.

Graham, M.D. (1970). *The deaf-blind: Some studies and suggestions for a national program*. New York: American Foundation for the Blind.

Greenland, C. (1976). *Vision Canada: The unmet needs of blind Canadians*. Toronto, Ont.: MacDonald-Downie.

Grunewald, K. (1974). International trends in the care of the severely and profoundly retarded and multiple handicapped. In F.J. Menaloscino and P.M. Pearson (Eds.), *Beyond the limits: Innovations in services for the severely and profoundly retarded*. Seattle, WA: Special Child Publications.

Guess, D., Sailor, W., and Baer, D.M. (1977). A behavioral-remedial approach to language training for the severely handicapped. In E. Sontag (Ed.), *Educational programming for the severely and profoundly handicapped*. Reston, VA: Council for Exceptional Children.

Guldager, L.C. (1969). The deaf-blind: Their education and their needs. *Exceptional Children, 36 (3)*, 203-205.

Guldager, V. (1970). *Body image and the severely handicapped rubella child*. Boston: Perkins School for the Blind.

Hammer, E. (October, 1984). Quality of life for the multiply handicapped child. Paper prepared for Helen Keller seminar on the multiply handicapped, New York City.

Haring, N. and Bricker, D. (1976). Overview of comprehensive services for the severely and profoundly handicapped. In N. Haring and L. Brown (Eds.), *Teaching the severely handicapped (Vol. I)*. New York: Grune and Stratton.

Harley, R.K. and Lawrence, G.A. (1977). *Visual impairment in the schools*. Springfield, IL.: Charles C. Thomas.

Hayden, A.M. and Beck. (1981). The epidemiology of high risk and handicapped infants. In C.T. Ramey and P.L. Trohanis (Eds.), *Finding and educating high-risk and handicapped infants*. Baltimore: University of Park Press.

Haynes, U.B. (1976). The national collaborative infant project. In T.D. Tjossem (Ed.), *Intervention strategies for high-risk infants and young children*. Baltimore: University Park Press.

Healy, W. and Karp-Nortman, D. (1975). *The hearing impaired, mentally retarded: Recommendations for action*. Washington, D.C.: American Speech and Hearing Association.

Hewitt, H. (1978). An educational schema for children with the dual disability of deafness and blindness. *The Australian Journal of Mental Retardation, 5(3),* 81-85.

Howard, J. (1982). The role of the pediatrician with young exceptional children. *Exceptional Children, 48,* 316-322.

Ikeda, M. (1976). Electrophysiology of the retina and visual pathway. In F.C. Ross (Ed.), *Medical ophthalmology.* London: Chapman and Hall.

Ivanainen, M. (1981). Neurological examination of the mentally retarded child: Evidence of central nervous system abnormality. In B. Cooper (Ed.), *Assessing the handicaps and needs of mentally retarded children.* New York: Academic Press.

Jensema, C.J. and Mullins, J. (1974). Onset and additional handicaps in hearing impaired children. *The American Annals of the Deaf,* 701-705.

Kates, L. and Schein, J.D. (1980). A complete guide to communication with deaf-blind persons. Silver Springs, MD: National Association for the Deaf.

Keller, H. (1957). *Teacher: Ann Sullivan Macy.* New York: Doubleday.

Kirk, S.A. and Gallagher, J.J. (1979). *Educating exceptional children.* Boston: Houghton and Mifflin.

Kluckhohn, C. (1964). *Mirror for man: A survey of human behavior and social attitudes.* New York: Fawcett Publications (McGraw-Hill).

Koestler, F.A. (1976). *The unseen minority: A social history of blindness in the United States.* New York: American Foundation for the Blind.

Kysela, G. (1985). Personal communication.

Liepman, M.C. (1981). Test procedures and other techniques for the assessment of handicaps: Problems of method. In B. Cooper (Ed.), *Assessing the handicaps and needs of mentally retarded children.* New York: Academic Press.

McInnes, J.M. and Treffry, J.A. (1982). *Deaf-blind infants and children: A developmental guide.* Toronto: University of Toronto Press.

Meadow, K.P. (1980). *Deafness and child development.* Berkeley, CA: University of California Press.

Menaloscino, F.J. and Pearson, P.M. (1974). *Beyond the limits: Innovations in services for the severely and profoundly retarded.* Seattle, WA: Special Child Publications.

Moor, P.M. (1968). *No time to lose.* New York: American Foundation for the Blind.

Murphy, K.P. and Shallop, J.K. (1978). Identification of hearing loss in young children: Prenatal to age six. In S. Singh and J. Lynch (Eds.), *Diagnostic procedures in hearing, speech and language.* Baltimore: University Park Press.

Neal, L. (1975). Positive perspectives of leisure potential for the deaf-blind. In S.A. Brannan (Ed.), *Our new challenge: Recreation for the deaf-blind.* Portland: Portland State University.

Oswin, M. (1978). *Children living in long-stay hospitals.* London: William Heinemann Medical Books.

Reesor, B. (1977). The Community isn't ready — why? In S. Rogow and M. Rodriguez (Eds.) *Perspectives and prospects in the education of the world's blind children.* Toronto: Ministry of Community and Social Services.

Robinson, M. and Robinson, N.M. (1976). *The mentally retarded child.* New York: McGraw-Hill.

Rogow, S.M. (1982). A communication curriculum for blind multi-handicapped children. In S. Mangold (Ed.), *A teacher's guide to the special educational needs of blind and visually handicapped children.* New York: American Foundation for the Blind.

Rogow, S., Hass, J., and Humphries, C. (1984). Learning to look: Cognitive aspects of visual attention. *Canadian Journal of Optometry, 46(1),* 31-235.

Rosen, M., Clark, J.R., and Kivitz, M.S. (1977). *Habilitation of the handicapped: New dimensions in programs for the developmentally disabled.* Baltimore: University Park Press.

Rowland, C. (1984). "Preverbal communication of blind infants and their mothers." *Journal of Visual Impairment and Blindness* 78:7, 297-302.

Salmon, P.J. (1970). *Out of the shadows.* New York: Normal Center for Deaf-Blind Youths and Adults.

Smithdas, Robert J. (1966). "Courage." In P.J. Salmon, *Out of the Shadows.* New York: National Centre for Deaf-Blind Youths and Adults, 1970.

Sontag, E., Smith, F., and Sailor, W. (1977). The severely/profoundly handicapped: Who are they? Where are they? Where are we? *Journal of Special Education, 11,* 5-11.

Stainback, W. and Stainback, S. (1977). Teaching the profoundly handicapped in the public school setting. In M.A. Thomas (Ed.), *Developing skills in severely and profoundly handicapped children.* Reston, VA: Council for Exceptional Children.

Suran, B.G. and Rizzo, J.V. (1979). *Special children: An integrative approach.* Glenview, IL: Scott Foresman.

Thompson, R. (1976). The severely handicapped: A new horizon. *Exceptional Children, 43(3),* 141-143.

Valletutti, P.J. and Christophos, F. (1977). Interdisciplinary approaches to human services: An introduction and overview. In P.J. Valletutti and F. Christophos (Eds.), *Interdisciplinary approaches to human services.* Baltimore: University Park Press.

Van Dijk, J. (1982). *Rubella handicapped children: The effects of bi-lateral cataract and/or hearing impairment on behavior and learning.* The Netherlands: Swets and Zeitlinger.

Van Osdol, W.R. and Shane, D.B. (1982). *An introduction to exceptional children.* Dubuque, Iowa: Wiliam C. Brown.

Warburg, M. (1977). *Blindness among 7600 mentally retarded children in Denmark.* Conference proceedings: Study group on infants and children with visual defects. Nottingham, Eng.: University of Nottingham.

Watson, M.J. and Nicholas, J.L. (1978). *A practical guide to the training of low functioning deaf-blind children.* Connecticut: Oak Hill School.

Wurzberger, B. (1985) Personal communication.

Ysseldyke, J.E. and Algozzine, B. (1982). *Critical issues in special and remedial education.* Boston: Houghton-Mifflin.

CHAPTER FOURTEEN

Children who are culturally different

SALLY M. ROGOW

The characteristics of the human animal which make culture possible are the ability to learn, to communicate by a system of learned symbols, and to transmit learned behavior from generation to generation. But what is learned varies widely from society to society and even in different sectors of the same society.

(Clyde Kluckhohn, 1964)

Cultural diversity has long been a Canadian reality. Many different Native peoples inhabited the land long before it was first settled by the French. In the late 1700s, immigrants began to arrive from England, Ireland, Scotland, Wales, and the United States. By the late 1800s, immigrants came from the West Indies, parts of Asia, and all of Europe. Throughout the 1900s, new Canadians continued to arrive from all over the world. Each wave of immigrants brought with it a set of cultural traditions, lifestyles, and beliefs (Burnett, 1984).

With the 1967 liberalization of Canada's immigration laws, many more immigrants have arrived from Asia, Latin America, the West Indies, and Europe (Newman, 1978). As a result, Canadian schools have experienced an influx of children who speak neither English nor French. This new focus on cultural plurality has helped shape educational policies that not only tolerate, but actively encourage, cultural differences. At the same time, educators have become increasingly aware of the problems of the culturally different child. This awareness has extended to children from non-immigrant minority groups, such as Native children, who have experienced prejudice and discrimination in the past.

The term "culturally different" is used in some books to refer to children who are disadvantaged or culturally deprived (Suran and Rizzo, 1983). However, although many culturally different children do live in conditions of poverty, many others come from economically stable and even wealthy families.

Some "culturally different" children do not speak English (or French) when they first attend school. These are the children of recent immigrants to Canada from countries in Europe, Asia, Africa, and Latin America. Other children belong to minority groups who may speak a non-standard form of English, and whose strong sense of cultural identity sets them apart from traditional Canadian culture. These include Native and West Indian children. Still other culturally different children speak standard English but live according to a set of cultural mores and practices that depart from middle-class Canadian norms.

ETHNIC GROUPS IN CANADA

Isajiw (1974) noted two forms of ethnicity in Canada. "The first type of ethnic group is a people who share a distinct culture; people who have gone through the primary process of socialization in their culture and no other" (Isajiw, p. 29). The second type concerns those who carry on only some of the traditions of their ethnic culture. These people have been socialized in both the culture of their group and the culture of the dominant society. The tie that binds them to other ethnic-group members is "not the sharing of culture; rather, it is a feeling of identity with them" (Isajiw, 1974, p. 30).

In a national sample of Canadians, O'Bryan, Reitz, and Kuplowska (1975) found that over forty percent of second-generation Canadians and over thirty percent of third-generation Canadians identified themselves as "ethnic" or "ethnic-Canadian". The cultural traditions of ethnic minorities are powerful factors in the socialization of children. In the past, Canada has tended to encourage the assimilation of culturally different groups. However, since the 1960s, a considerable effort has been made to establish a policy of cultural pluralism, in recognition of the value of cultural differences to the Canadian mosaic (Newman, 1978).

Distribution of new immigrants

Almost a quarter of a million people emigrated to Canada in 1971 and 1972. Approximately half these came from non-English-speaking (or French-speaking) countries (World Almanac, 1974). Exhibit 14-1 shows the largest ethnic groups in Canada in 1976.

Ninety-one percent of all immigrants to Canada have settled in Quebec, Ontario, Alberta, and British Columbia (Ashworth, 1975). In 1978, Ontario absorbed forty-nine percent of new arrivals, by far the highest proportion. Quebec was second, and British Columbia third (World Almanac, 1979). Exhibit 14-3 lists the number of new immigrants who settled in each of Canada's provinces in 1979.

Exhibit 14-1 Largest ethnic groups in Canada, 1976.

	1976	*Percentage of Canadian population*
Chinese	132 560	0.6
German	476 715	2.1
Greek	92 530	0.4
Indo-Pakistani	58 420	0.4
Italian	484 045	2.1
Canadian Indian	117 110	0.6
Inuit	15 900	0.1
Portuguese	126 535	0.5
Ukrainian	144 760	1.2

(Statistics Canada, 1976.)

Exhibit 14-2 lists the continents from which immigrants arrived in 1979.

Exhibit 14-2 Place of origin of immigrants to Canada, 1979.

Europe	28 752
North and Central America	18 263
Asia	24 541
South America	6 480
Australasia	1 349
Africa	3 910
Oceania	796
Total	84 091

(Canada Year Book, 1981.)

Exhibit 14-3 Immigration by province, 1979.

Ontario	40 914
Quebec	14 501
British Columbia	12 999
Alberta	9 066
Manitoba	3 397
Saskatchewan	1 532
Nova Scotia	957
New Brunswick	636
Newfoundland	379
Yukon and Northwest Territories	156
Prince Edward Island	154
Total	84 691

(Canada Year Book, 1981.)

Within each province, the countries or groups of countries that have provided the largest number of immigrant children are as follows:

- *Quebec:* West Indies, Bermuda, Portugal, Greece, France, Italy.
- *Ontario:* Portugal, West Indies, Italy, Africa, South America.
- *Alberta:* China, Africa, Portugal, India, Hong Kong.
- *British Columbia:* Africa, China, India, Portugal, Hong Kong. (Ashworth, 1975.)

Immigration from China and from India and Pakistan increased from 2 045 in 1963 to 27 582 in 1973 (Ashworth, 1975). The largest number of Asian immigrants settled in Western Canada. Many of the immigrants from Africa at this time were East Indians who were expelled from Uganda.

The North

The Northlands include the Yukon, the Northwest Territories, and roughly the northern two-thirds of British Columbia, Alberta, Saskatchewan, Manitoba, Ontario, and Quebec. Although this area includes four-fifths of Canada's land mass, it contains a relatively small proportion of the Canadian population. Sixty-nine percent of the Northlands population is made up of Indians, Inuit, and Métis. More than half these Native peoples speak in their own languages (Driedger, 1978).

The West

The West includes the southern portion of British Columbia, Alberta, Saskatchewan, and Manitoba. Although British Canadians form the largest population group, they do not form a majority in this region (Driedger, 1978). The West is predominantly rural and agricultural, with substantial numbers of British, German, Ukrainian, French, and others. Eighty-five percent of Western people speak English.

Southern Ontario

This urban industrial area has recently attracted many new immigrants from Northern and Southern Europe, Asia, and the West Indies. Seventy-five percent of people in Ontario speak English as a first language. Five percent speak French and twenty percent speak other languages (Driedger, 1978).

Quebec

In Quebec, French is spoken by the large majority. The five million French Canadians living in Quebec represent the largest minority regional group in Canada (Driedger, 1978).

The Atlantic provinces

Newfoundland, Nova Scotia, and Prince Edward Island approach a condition of British-Canadian uniculturism. Ninety-five percent of the residents in this area speak English. The Native population is small, and other ethnic groups are barely represented.

New Brunswick is one of the most bilingual and bicultural regions of Canada. About twenty-five percent of the residents speak French and about sixty-six percent speak English. Ten percent of the population speak a language other than English or French (Driedger, 1978).

DEVELOPMENTAL CONSEQUENCES OF CULTURAL DIFFERENCE

The term *developmental consequences* is somewhat inappropriate to a discussion of culturally different children. All children, regardless of ethnicity, become socialized within a cultural context. Moreover, culturally different children are, by definition, an extremely heterogeneous population. Cultural factors vary widely from ethnic group to ethnic group. Economic backgrounds, parental education levels, and residential settings also vary widely, just as they do among non-immigrant children.

Some developmental problems do tend to arise, however, as culturally different children interact with the dominant society. Many children first encounter the dominant culture at school. For these children, school is often a frightening and alienating experience. They must struggle with a strange language and somehow make sense of the confusing attitudes and expectations of their peers.

Social and emotional development

Culture conflict is the clash between the family's cultural values and those of the dominant society. This conflict often makes it difficult for culturally different children to adjust to Canadian schools. For example, a child who is rewarded for maintaining silence at home may find it very difficult to speak aloud in the classroom.

Cultural conflicts are caused by disparities in social conventions, values, and expectations. The more disparate the culture from the Canadian norm, the greater the likelihood of conflict.

Children who suffer the effects of culture conflict often become anxious and defensive (Head, 1984). Their sense of alienation and isolation may lead "to frustration, anger, anti-social behaviour, and difficulties at home and at school" (Head, 1984, p. 269). Sociocultural factors also play "an extremely important role in the adaptation problems of the culturally different child" (Head, 1984, p. 269).

Culture conflict may occur between the child and the family, or between the family and the school. Many immigrant parents do not approve of what they perceive as the "permissiveness" of Canadian schools. Some believe their children are neglected or not sufficiently encouraged to intermingle with school peers. Within the family, different attitudes toward discipline may lead to value conflicts. When discipline problems do arise, they tend to derive from the same sources as disciplinary problems among Canadian-born children (Ashworth, 1975).

Ashworth (1975) circulated a questionnaire to teachers of New Canadians across Canada. The groups that were perceived as having the most social adjustment difficulties were those "whose language and culture differ most from the English language and Canadian culture" (Ashworth, 1975, p. 159). Teachers also reported that lack of prior education contributes to school adjustment problems, especially for children from developing countries. Dropouts tended to be most frequent among those groups who are economically disadvantaged. Some education sociologists see similarities between the problems of "culturally deprived" children from poor homes and the problems of immigrant children in Canadian cities (Ramcharan, 1979).

Most anti-social behaviour among minority adolescents is directed against the home community. Poverty, alienation, and family breakdown create conditions that breed anger, hopelessness, and crime. Discrimination and rejection cruelly damage the self-esteem of culturally different children. However, cultural differences may fuel the fires of conflict, but they do not alone account for social maladjustment.

PROFILE 14-1

Fear, by Maria

I remember how strange I felt when I first came to school. I couldn't understand English very well. I was afraid of the other children.

One big girl came over and started to shout at me. I did not know why she was so angry, and I ran away from her crying. A teacher came over but I couldn't tell her what was wrong.

Most of the kids didn't pay attention. But this one girl liked to make fun of me. She pretended she could speak Chinese and followed me around the playground shouting strange sounds.

It took me a long time to feel comfortable in that school. I never forgot the fear that big girl made me feel.

Speech and Language

The perception of cultural difference is enhanced by linguistic difference. Speaking a language other than English reinforces the loneliness of the culturally different child. At the same time, however, linguistic distinctiveness is a basic component of personal identity for many of Canada's ethnic minorities (McLeod, 1975).

Thirty percent of the students enrolled in Toronto schools have been born outside Canada, and almost fifty percent have a first language other than English. As of 1976, children born in Portugal made up the largest group of foreign-born students. The second largest was West Indian students, whose numbers more than tripled since 1971. Students born in Italy ranked third, Chinese students fourth, Greek students fifth, and British students sixth (Murray, 1977). In Vancouver, thirty-eight percent of elementary-school students spoke a first language other than English when they first entered school (Ashworth, 1979).

As discussed in Chapter Six, cultural differences have a profound effect on how children learn. For example, many immigrant children are taught to restrain their expressive behaviour in the presence of adults and strangers (Alleyne, 1976). In Canadian schools, however, children are continually required to express themselves in front of adults and strangers, despite cultural norms to the contrary.

Many West Indian children learn to speak a dialect form of English in their homes. English-language speech in Jamaica, Guyana, Trinidad, and Barbados varies widely in syntax, grammar, and phonology. It ranges from the speech of uneducated rural dwellers to that of upper-middle-class intellectuals and professionals. Many West Indian children are likely to understand much more standard English than they are at first able to produce. Language teachers should try to discover the precise dialect variations of English that their students have already learned (Alleyne, 1976). The same is true for Haitian immigrants to Quebec, who speak non-standard dialects of French.

Teachers have observed that most culturally different younger children speak their native tongues at home. Many receive little reinforcement for English (or French) language skills outside the school. At the high-school level, many students become self-conscious about their limited English and hesitate before initiating conversation (Ashworth, 1975). On the basis of English-language test scores, many culturally different children have been mislabelled as "slow learners" or "learning disabled."

Most immigrant children acquire fairly fluent, peer-appropriate, face-to-face communication skills within less than two years of their arrival in Canada (Cummins, 1984). However, these face-to-face communication skills develop much more quickly than academic language skills. Cummins (1984) questions the validity of English-language IQ tests that are given before children attain full English-language competence.

The speech and language issue is complex and not easily resolved. Language problems are often difficult to determine without a careful assessment in the child's native language as well as in English. Children whose languages are very different in phonology and syntax have the most difficulty mastering English. When English is not used in the home, children find it harder to acquire the level of proficiency necessary for academic success. On the other hand, when children focus only on learning English, they often lose proficiency in their native tongues.

Academic Achievement

Academic achievement is related both to family educational background and to mastery of the language of instruction. Culturally different children with university-educated parents have far fewer educational problems than those with poorly educated parents.

Because of language and adjustment problems, many culturally different children find themselves in remedial classes. Others enter the non-academic stream in secondary school. Teachers often find it impossible to determine whether students' learning problems are related to cultural differences or to learning disabilities. When school values clash with a child's cultural values, the child may become hostile toward school (Bowen, 1976). A great many culturally different children "drop out" of high school (D'Oyley, 1976).

The educational placement of immigrant children is often complicated by lack of proper educational documentation. Without documentation, the academic achievements of immigrant children often go unrecognized.

Language arts, reading, and mathematics present the greatest academic difficulties to culturally different children. An estimated fifty percent of West Indian children in Toronto have severe difficulties in the language arts (D'Oyley, 1976).

The age of immigrant children on entering the Canadian school system may determine their future success. Older children have missed more school work. The time they must spend learning English or French causes them to fall further behind their English-speaking (or French-speaking) peers. They may grow discouraged and eventually become early school-leavers (Caccia, 1975).

During the late 1960s and early 1970s, several studies examined academic achievement among different ethnic groups. These studies indicated that, given equal conditions, culturally different students would perform academically as well as their classmates. Other studies have shown that disadvantaged children are more likely to underachieve at school, whether or not they are culturally different (Cohen and Manion, 1983).

The educational attainments of Native students have improved considerably over the past decade, but "results are still far below the goals and needs of the Indian communities" (More, 1985, p. 83). Among Native students, the high-school completion rate is about a third of the rate for non-Native students. The average Native student fails about half of all school courses (More, 1985).

The causes of underachievement among Native students are complex. Factors include dialect differences, lack of home support for education, poor home-school relations, lack of motivation, and insufficient school financing. Recent improvements are attributed to more appropriate curricula, more Native-run schools, and the use of Native people as teachers and teachers' aides (More, 1985).

EDUCATION OF CULTURALLY DIFFERENT CHILDREN

Historical background

Educational policies reflect the social attitudes of the nation. Canada has played a leading role in welcoming immigrants from diverse cultural backgrounds. However, its educational policies have in the past been based on the assumption that all immigrant groups want to assimilate as quickly and completely as possible (McLeod, 1975).

For more than a century, assimilation and "Canadianization" governed the education of culturally different children. Even French Canadians and immigrants from Ireland were pressured to conform to "Anglo-Saxon" or "Anglo-Canadian" ideals. In 1918, J.T.M. Anderson summed up the national attitude when he presented immigrant resistance to assimilation as an urgent national problem. Ethnic groups who refused to assimilate were a "threat to Canadian unity and progress" (cited in McLeod, 1975, p. 23). According to Anderson, education alone could inject "Canadian language and values into these communities" McLeod, 1975, p. 23).

Anderson's attitude was typical of the Anglo-Canadian paternalism which prevailed in the early 1900s (McLeod, 1975). Culturally different groups were acceptable as long as they attempted to conform to Anglo-Canadian culture. Immigrant groups, such as German and Russian religious groups, who resisted assimilation provoked antagonism. Many Canadians demanded that immigration be stopped altogether.

The policy of rapid assimilation created a social climate in which cultural differences were considered unacceptable. Children of immigrants often felt they belonged nowhere — they were neither Canadian nor members of their parents' ethnic group. Culture conflict alienated culturally different children, causing deep feelings of inferiority and even shame (Ashworth, 1979).

Culture conflict long characterized the education of Native Canadians. For many decades, Native children were removed from their families and enrolled in residential schools. There they were forbidden to speak Native languages or adhere to Native customs and beliefs. Only recently has the destructive impact of residential schools on Native culture been recognized. However, although some Native groups are beginning to govern their own schools, Native education continues to be plagued by a lack of funds and resources (Ashworth, 1979).

Immigration after World War II radically changed the demography of Canada. As culturally different citizens began to participate in the political life of the country, their needs began to claim greater attention. As a result Canadians have become more sensitive to minority causes (McLeod, 1975). In addition, strong Quebecois demands for a greater role in Canadian affairs have produced a new tolerance of minority language and cultural groups. As a result, many changes have taken place in educational policies for the culturally different.

Multicultural education

In 1971, Prime Minister Trudeau declared to the House of Commons that "A policy of multiculturalism within a bilingual framework commends itself to the Government of Canada as the most suitable means of assuring the cultural freedom of Canadians." Since that declaration, many schools have introduced multicultural programs in which "every child has the chance to benefit from the cultural heritage of others, as well as from his or her own" (Murray, 1977, p. 92).

Before multiculturalism, Canadian schools were facing a serious crisis. Studies showed that the school children who fared most poorly were recent non-British immigrants from low-income homes. Clearly, something had to be done for the thousands of non-English-speaking children who enrolled in school each year. In Toronto alone, roughly fifteen percent of school-children began school with no knowledge of English (Murray, 1977).

Many teachers and school administrators rejected the "Canadianism" approach with its philosophy of cultural immersion. Some objected that Canadianism lacked the financial resources to make it work, while others criticized the policy for neglecting students' ethnic backgrounds and promoting assimilation. Ethnic community groups also challenged the Canadianism approach. They began to demand courses in their children's first languages.

In 1974, the Toronto School Board formed a committee to study the problems of the immigrant child. The committee's report, entitled "The Bias of Culture," proposed new attitudes and policies concerning immigrant children. The following issues were identified as areas of major concern.

- The need for English-(or French)-as-a-Second-Language (ESL) programs.
- Educational opportunity deficiencies.
- Maintenance of original cultures and languages.
- Multiculturalism and the curriculum.
- System sensitivity.
- Community-school relations.
- Responsibilities of senior governments (Murray, 1977).

Other cities soon began similar studies and established multicultural programs of their own. The Vancouver School Board appointed a Task Force in 1974 to study the problems of bilingual immigrant children. The Task Force found an increasing number of children in both elementary and secondary schools who spoke a language other than English in their homes. The Task Force recommended that teachers with special training be assigned to English-as-a-Second-Language classes. It further recommended limiting these classes to twelve students each (Ashworth, 1975).

Multicultural approaches to education recognize an equal status for all cultural groups in Canada. Multicultural education accepts individual cultural differences and recognizes individual needs. Its purpose is to provide all students with the skills they need to function as equal participants in society. A multicultural program also teaches students to relate well to members of other cultures and to appreciate cultural diversity (Burke, 1984).

It is not easy to translate the ideal of multiculturalism into actual school programs. Many educators believe that a multicultural perspective should permeate the curriculum for all students (Wilson, 1983). However most provincial education departments consider some or all of the following to be multicultural programs:

- English-(or French)-as-a-second language (ESL) classes. These classes teach English or French to New Canadian children.
- Classes in languages other than English or French. These programs are designed to preserve minority languages in Canada. They may be offered during or after school, and are sometimes sponsored by particular ethnic groups.
- Anti-discrimination programs. These are designed to prevent or counter ethnic discrimination. An example is the Alternatives to Racism project in British Columbia.
- Programs that stress cultural diversity. These are often part of the Social Studies curriculum (Wilson, 1984).

The aim of Canadian schools has become integration rather than assimilation. Children's own cultural traditions are acknowledged and shared, rather than ignored. Culturally different children are no longer made to feel ashamed of their language or customs. Ideally, integration permits a blending of new and old cultures within the child's personality.

The problems posed by immigrant children to Canadian schools are considerable. In larger urban centres, a great many children come to school with no knowledge of English or French. However, the education of culturally different children is a cultural issue, and not simply a language problem. Immigrant children need opportunities to combine their own cultures with the new culture as they learn (Murray, 1977).

Learning environments

The school placement of culturally different children varies according to the numbers of children who require help. In large urban centres, many schools offer special classes to provide English (or French) instruction. These English-as-a-Second-Language (ESL) classes often function as reception classes for new immigrants.

A **reception class** is made up entirely of students who require intensive English (or French) language training. In the reception class, "the expertise of a trained teacher and equipment which can speed language-learning come together; efficiency in language teaching is at a maximum" (Ashworth, 1975, p. 19). The effectiveness of the reception class may be reduced if children are permitted to speak their native language to one another. Children may not understand the necessity of learning English. Because the class is isolated from other students, the child has few opportunities to hear and speak acceptable English.

Children often have difficulty leaving reception classes, especially when they must go to a different school. In secondary schools, it is difficult to integrate children in the middle of the school year.

Educators who stress cultural integration recommend placing immigrant children directly into the regular classroom. However, if children are placed at the level of their English-language development, older children may find themselves with much younger classmates. Ten-year-olds who are placed in grade-one classes are likely to become very discouraged.

Cultural integration also threatens the child's cultural identity. As Ashworth (1975) has noted, "Many people feel that to put a young immigrant into a good school solves the problem because 'in a couple of years he'll just disappear.' We feel that this is a definition of the problem rather than its solution" (p. 14).

Withdrawal classes attempt to provide immigrant children with the opportunity to learn English and still be part of the school. There are three types of withdrawal programs: half-day classes; itinerant ESL instruction; and school-based ESL instruction (Ashworth, 1975).

In the withdrawal system, children spend part of their day in integrated settings and the rest receiving intensive language training from an ESL teacher. They may learn English in half-day classes or in the resource room, either individually or in small groups. The half-day withdrawal program works well in elementary schools.

According to Cummins (1984), children who arrive in Canada at age six or older take from five to seven years to develop a knowledge of English vocabulary that approaches grade norms. Children acquire sufficient communication skills for interacting with their peers long before they develop the language proficiency they need to ensure academic success (Cummins, 1984).

Some schools offer **bilingual education programs**. Children learn English or French, and receive basic instruction in their first languages to keep them from falling behind. The children are placed in regular school programs as soon as possible.

Transition programs may take many forms. Most offer ESL classes, either during or after school. Most also offer instruction in first languages, and work to develop good home-school relations.

In 1973, children entering a Toronto kindergarten class were greeted with familiar Italian words of greeting. These children were taking part in an experimental Italian-transition program. At first the teacher spoke only in Italian. English was gradually introduced until the students became fluent in it. They were then ready to enter a regular program, and to read and write in English (Murray, 1977).

In reporting on this program, Mary Purbhoo and Stan Shapson (1974) observed that the teacher's use of language depended very much on individual children and situations. Sometimes the teacher asked questions of the whole class in Italian, and sometimes in English. At other times, the teacher switched back and forth between the two languages.

At the end of the two-year pilot project, researchers noted that "The most important effects may have been those of the first few months when the children were not suddenly faced with a novel environment combined with an unfamiliar language" (Murray, 1977, p. 97). The school principal was convinced that the program contributed to effective home-school relationships. The experiment effectively demonstrated that transition programs can work for kindergarten students.

In some school districts, **after-school language classes** are offered to children in their first languages. Programs have been approved for language instruction in Italian, Greek, Chinese, Portuguese, and other languages. Many school boards now offer a variety of languages as optional credit courses for students.

For Native children, the learning environment is often quite different. Native children may attend federal, provincial, territorial, parochial, or band-controlled schools. (More, 1985). More and more Native communities are developing on-reserve schools that are controlled by band councils. These schools incorporate Native culture and learning styles into the education of Native children (More, 1985).

Curricular adaptations

Children are motivated most to do the things they do best. Programs for culturally different children should emphasize the children's creative abilities. Creative strengths include those abilities that "can be observed with a high degree of frequency among culturally different students." (Torrance, 1977, p. 25). According to Torrance, these abilities include:

- Ability to express feelings and emotions.
- Ability to improvise with commonplace materials.
- Articulateness in role playing and storytelling.
- Ability in the visual arts.
- Musical ability.
- Humour.
- Richness of imagery in informal language.
- Problem-solving.

In a multicultural program, all students should have access to resource materials that provide accurate information about different cultural groups (Banks, 1981). Ethnic diversity should permeate the total school environment, and should be reflected in assemblies, wall decorations, extracurricular activities, and classroom events. School policies and procedures should foster understanding among all groups of students.

The multicultural curriculum should promote values, attitudes, and behaviours that support ethnic pluralism. The multicultural curriculum should provide many opportunities to develop appreciation of ethnic differences. It should also encourage sharing of aesthetic traditions among children from various ethnic groups (Cohen and Manion, 1983). More (1985) noted a tendency among both non-Natives and Natives to emphasize traditional Native culture to the exclusion of contemporary Native culture. To be culturally relevant curricula that concern Native culture must be related to contemporary as well as traditional cultural practices (More, 1985).

Elliston (1977 a, 1978) found that the needs of Canadian newcomers fell into six main categories:

- Information.
- Upgrading or learning opportunities.
- Escort or support services.
- Conflict-management skills.
- Problem-solving skills.
- Confidence-building strategies.

To respond to these needs, multicultural centres have been established in several Canadian cities. These centres are designed to encourage "effective intercultural communication" and to provide "opportunities for people to acquire knowledge and skills consonant with citizenship expectations" (Elliston, 1984, p. 319).

New immigrant groups, as well as some Native communities, have found it difficult to effectively communicate with the larger society. A lack of communication is often at the heart of cultural difficulties. Education must play an important role in bringing culturally different children together with their peers. This is a major goal of comprehensive multicultural education programs.

CULTURALLY DIFFERENT HANDICAPPED CHILDREN

Definitions

Conventional definitions of exceptionalities do not always apply to the culturally different exceptional child. This is particularly true of children for whom English or French is not a first language. Mercer (1971) cautions that some children may be clinically labelled as abnormal, although they are functioning quite normally within their own cultural group. Many special factors must be considered when defining a culturally different exceptional child. These include the role of language, the family's expectations, cultural attitudes towards handicapping conditions, and the relationship between the child's cultural community and the larger society.

Three major problems must be considered when defining or classifying culturally different exceptional children. These are:

- The means of assessment.
- The interpretation and use of test results.
- Knowledge of familial expectations.

Fortunately, most educators now realize the "endemic cultural bias of commercially produced tests" (Samuda, 1984, p. 359). For example, we now understand that definitions of mental retardation based on academic performance or IQ tests do not apply in the case of children whose first language is not English or French.

PROFILE 14-2

Tomasino was a Portuguese ten-year-old boy. His teacher noticed that he appeared to be of average intelligence, but was not able to perform at grade level. Tomas was well-behaved and polite, but seemed to have great difficulty with schoolwork.

Tomas' teacher referred him for testing. On his tests, Tomas registered an extreme discrepancy between his verbal and performance scores. This discrepancy was attributed to a poor ability to form generalizations or make abstractions, and poor problem-solving abilities.

Tomas's parents were called to the school to discuss his problems. Tomas's mother, a widow, explained that Tomas was often tired because he got up at five each morning to complete his newspaper route before school. She also explained that her own English was so poor that she always spoke with her children in Portuguese.

According to his mother, Tomas was very smart indeed. He not only delivered newspapers, but he kept the family accounts and helped to take care of the younger children.

Canadian educators are just beginning to be aware of the impact of cultural and linguistic differences on test performance. Cummins (1984) observed that the assessment, identification, and placement of minority-language children is often carried out by educators and psychologists whose "knowledge about the process of second-language acquisition" is inadequate (Cummins, 1984, p. 248).

Culturally different exceptional children do not include those whose ethnic backgrounds hinder their mastery of English or French. Culturally different exceptional children can more appropriately be defined as children who have diagnosable handicapping conditions recognized as such by their cultural community.

Cultural Attitudes

The responses of culturally different families to their handicapped children have much in common with those of families in the dominant culture. Special difficulties arise, however, when insufficient communication exists between these families and the professionals who serve them. Problems may also arise as a result of culturally determined attitudes toward the handicapped.

Attitudes toward handicapped persons vary among cultural minorities. Native peoples are generally accepting of physical and mental handicaps. Many Native parents teach their children not to point, stare, or laugh at handicapped persons. Families are expected to care for those who cannot care for themselves, without shame, scorn, or derision. Family ties are deep and strong, and handicapped family members are never abandoned:

> Physical and mental handicaps are accepted by Native people as a birth consequence or God's plan. There are not feelings of scorn or shame displayed toward a person with a physical or mental handicap. Life is considered sacred and is not to be mocked in any way. Staring, pointing, laughing, or hurting a handicapped person is not to be tolerated by parents or relatives. Caring for the severely handicapped child is not considered to be an extraordinary effort (Paul, 1985).

Among other cultural groups with strong family ties, handicapped children are also cared for and protected. In some cases, strong family loyalty may result in over-protection.

Teachers have observed that parents from cultural minority groups are often reluctant to place their severely handicapped children in regular classes. Many culturally different parents perceive their child as needing total care. Parents worry that their child may be hurt, rejected, or even feared. They often try to keep their child safe at home. In some cases, religious beliefs cause parents to isolate handicapped children (Advani, 1979).

Cultural differences present Canadian schools with many difficult communication problems. School counselors should be aware of different cultural traditions and attitudes, as well as the importance of making educational services as available as possible to minority families. A well-informed counselor can prove invaluable in bridging the gap between home and school.

PREVALENCE OF CULTURALLY DIFFERENT HANDICAPPED CHILDREN

Determining the prevalence of handicaps among the culturally different is particularly difficult. There has been little recognition or understanding of the cultural and linguistic variables that occur among culturally different populations (Erickson and Walker, 1983).

It has been estimated that the incidence of exceptionality among cultural minorities is at least as high as that for the general population, if not higher. Among the general population, eight to twelve percent of school-aged children are considered exceptional. However, these figures may be higher for the culturally different population due to the role of health and nutrition.

The incidence of physical handicaps in some minority groups is related to conditions associated with poverty (Erickson and Walker, 1983). Among Native children, hearing handicaps may be markedly more common than among the population as a whole (Stewart, 1983). The schools serving Native Canadians rarely have any special education facilities. This fact alone obscures the identification of Native children with special needs.

CLASSIFICATION OF CULTURALLY DIFFERENT HANDICAPPED CHILDREN

Culturally different children are represented in all categories of exceptionality: mental retardation, emotional disturbance, visual impairment, hearing impairment, and speech and language disorders. The identification of mental retardation and learning disabilities is particularly problematic for culturally different children (Erickson and Walker, 1983). Tucker (1980) noted that "learning-disabled" provided a convenient label for a disproportionate number of culturally different children with learning problems at school.

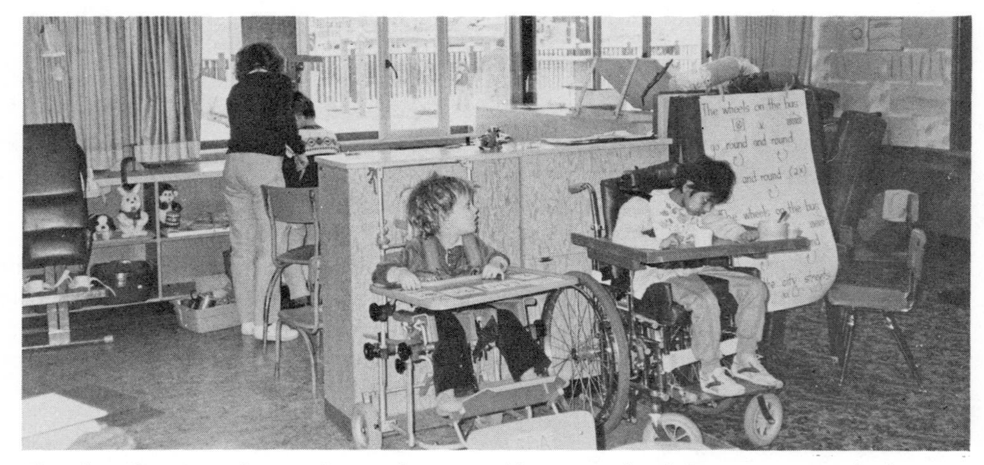

The identification of mental retardation and learning disabilities is particularly problematic with culturally different children. *(origin unknown)*

Emotional and Behaviour Disorders

Emotionally disturbed children fail to get along well with others, and often achieve poorly at school (De Blassie and Franco, 1983). According to Cohen and Manion (1983), culturally different children who fare poorly in the dominant society may share the following characteristics:

- An experiential background that does not fit the expectations of a middle-class-oriented curriculum.
- Economic impoverishment.
- Poor self-concept.
- A feeling of rejection by society.
- Poor attention span in school.

De Blassie and Franco (1983) maintain that the academic success of ethnic-minority children is heavily influenced by their family's socioeconomic status. They argue that emotional disturbance among these children is more often related to culture conflict than to personality disorder. Acculturation pressures, lack of communication skills, and social prejudice can all function to make children feel insecure within the school setting (De Blassie and Franco, 1983). High levels of anxiety are often present among emotionally disturbed culturally different children.

Some culturally different children may be rebelling against the values of their families. They may blame their families for being different and unacceptable to their peers. These children may try to find acceptance among their peers outside the home or school setting. They may find a home-away-from-home on the city streets.

Health problems of Native children

The leading communication disorder affecting Native children is conductive hearing loss. The United States Indian Health Service began to report cases of otitis media in 1961. Since that time, it has become the second-most reported health condition among the Native population (Stewart, 1983). Among Native children, the acute state of otitis media is seen most often before the age of two years. For a discussion of the condition, see Chapter Eight.

Cambon, Galbraith, and Kong (1965) and Ling, McCoy, and Levinson (1969) reported that approximately fifteen percent of Inuit and Indian children in Canada have hearing loss due to repeated ear infection. Ophthalmology clinics that travel to Indian reserves find similarly a higher-than-average incidence of eye infections that can affect sight. However, precise figures are difficult to obtain.

DIAGNOSIS AND ASSESSMENT OF CULTURALLY DIFFERENT HANDICAPPED CHILDREN

Many parents of culturally different children have complained that their children are over-represented in special education programs. Studies have shown that group intelligence testing does tend to discriminate against minority children.

When minority children are placed in special classes, they are indelibly branded and rarely transferred (de Blassie and Franco, 1983). Examiners should not attempt to compare culturally different children with national norms. Instead they should explore how the children compare with their own cultural population (Omark and Watson, 1983).

Psychological testing

As late as the 1950s, most psychological testing was culturally biased, testing all children according to dominant cultural standards. Since that time, examiners have realized that behaviour and the measurement of behaviour are cultural phenomena (Berry, 1975).

Behaviour does not develop in a cultural vacuum, nor can it be sampled without culturally based assumptions. As Berry (1975) has stated:

> Cultural goals and values influence not only behavioural development but also psychological theory and testing procedures. Where these differ between the population being sampled and the psychological tester, culturally based discontinuities usually render the test results uninterpretable, or, if interpreted, hopelessly ethnocentric (pp. 151-152).

Many minority children have had no opportunity to develop test-taking skills. Some have never seen the games and puzzles that many tests use. Often these children must be trained in how to take tests (Omark and Watson, 1983). They must understand the purpose of the procedure and be motivated to perform at their best.

The assessment of culturally different children should:

- Provide an accurate appraisal of the child's level and mode of functioning within the context of the child's cultural experience.
- Identify the child's specific educational needs.
- Focus on the child's strengths and abilities as the basis for the development of new skills.
- Be an ongoing process, rather than a single event.

Culture-fair testing

Experience has shown that culture-fair testing is extremely difficult to achieve. Conventional intelligence tests discriminate against children for whom English or French is not a first language. On most IQ tests, language proficiency is the basis of successful performance (Cummins, 1984).

An eclectic approach is recommended to the testing of culturally different children (De Blassie and Franco, 1983). To achieve cultural fairness, teachers should know how to construct tests and how to use such non-test assessment tools as rating scales, interviews, observation, and case studies. The use of test and non-test data should emphasize diagnosis rather than prediction. The predictive validity of most standardized test scores is poor. However, the diagnostic validity is excellent if the tests are used along with non-test data and demographic information (De Blassie and Franco, 1983).

A Comprehensive Individual Assessment of a culturally different child should include historical-etiological information, current assessable characteristics, specific treatments or interventions, and the particular diagnosis. An unpublished study by Tucker suggests that cultural bias particularly affects the categories of mental retardation, emotional disturbance, learning disabilities, and minimal brain dysfunction.

In order to make a comprehensive diagnosis, it is necessary to use a combination of different assessment instruments. The involvement of parents should also be emphasized. Examiners should make use of all the following sources of information:

- Observational data.
- Data from medical examinations.
- Language dominance data.
- Educational assessment data.
- Sensory/motor functioning data.
- Adaptive behaviour data.
- Developmental and medical data.
- Personality assessment data.
- Intellectual assessment data.

Some test instruments have been developed specifically for use with ethnically different children (Toronto and Sherrill, 1983). However, these are not always available. Exercise caution when using tests that have merely been adapted for use. Simple translation from one language to another does not eliminate cultural bias. For example, the Wechsler Intelligence Scale for Children (WISC) (Wechsler, 1949) was translated into Spanish for use in Puerto Rico. Test results showed an average intelligence score of eighty-eight and a standard deviation of twenty-two points (Toronto and Sherrill, 1983).

Culturally different children are less homogeneous as a group than children of the dominant Anglo-Canadian culture. There are wide linguistic, educational, and social differences within ethnic minority groups (Toronto and Sherrill, 1983). As a result, there seems to be more variance in test scores among minority-group members.

Standardized language tests serve the function of identifying language-disordered children. Language samples permit an indepth assessment of the individual's communication ability, including pragmatic, semantic, synctactic, and phonologic skills (Prutting, 1983). However, when eliciting a language sample, the examiner must be familiar with the cultural style of the child's language. When possible, a familiar adult should be involved in collecting the language sample.

When interpreting the sample, the examiner must determine whether problems arise in the child's native language as well as in English or French. Children who function adequately in their native languages are less restricted by their lack of English-speaking skills than children who are delayed in both their languages. However, the examiner must be sensitive to the child's native linguistic rules and cultural values in order to evaluate that child's communicative performance (Prutting, 1983).

Some testing instruments have adaptations for culturally different handicapped persons. Some of these may take a long time to administer, but the results often justify the extra time expenditures (Torrance, 1974).

Exhibit 14-4 Some tests for culturally different children.

- Arthur Point Scale of Performance Tests: Forms I and II. These tests are individually administered for the age-range of 4.5 to superior adult.
- Chicago Non-Verbal Examination. This test is designed specifically for children with English-language problems, such as deaf or culturally different children.
- IPAT Culture-Fair Intelligence Test: Scales, I, II, and III. These scales were specially designed for culturally different persons.
- Leiter International Performance Scale. This scale presents norms for a variety of culturally different groups.
- Raven's Progressive Matrices Test. This test has no time limit, and may be administered to a group of children. It has been used by examiners engaged in cross-cultural research.
- Test of General Ability. This test was designed to measure general intelligence and learning ability, independent of such academic skills as arithmetic and reading.
- The Torrance Tests of Creative Thinking, Figural and Verbal: Forms A and B. These tests permit students to respond in terms of their own experiences (Torrance, 1974). They are useful for a wide range of ages, and have been translated into twenty-five different languages.

Some testing procedures have been devised specifically to discover giftedness among the culturally different. These tests have been developed because traditional and "culture free" tests have been unable to identify gifted children (Torrance, 1974). Torrance (1974) argued that the use of traditional tests used with minority populations violates the three basic testing principles of validity, reliability, and standardization.

Bernal (1974) has developed a set of criteria for recognizing giftedness among culturally different children. According to these criteria, gifted children display several of the following traits:

- Mature and responsible for their age.
- Great imitators and elaborators of adult behaviour.
- Regarded as leaders, and quiet but influential.
- Ideas and suggestions are valued by their peers.
- Often called upon to mediate disputes, plan strategies, and so on.
- Quick to grasp new ideas.
- Pursue ideas with persistence.

- Initiate and maintain meaningful transactions with adults.
- Facile in acquiring other languages.

Education of culturally different handicapped children

In large cities, culturally different exceptional children have access to a range of special education services. They may receive instruction in regular classes, resource rooms, itinerant programs, or special classes. However, practical multicultural approaches to the education of exceptional children have not yet been clearly defined. Special educators have been slow to develop awareness of the role of cultural differences (Cummins, 1984).

In Canada, governments have begun to address the special problems created by cultural attitudes, assessment difficulties, and the delivery of services to isolated communities. Several provinces have devised outreach programs for handicapped children in rural communities. Although these developments are promising, it is still too early to report on their effectiveness.

In most ways, the problems of identification, parent-support services, early intervention, educational placement, and treatment services are the same for all exceptional children, regardless of ethnic origin. In other ways, however, problems for culturally different exceptional children are unique and differ from group to group. As we have seen, some special problems are created by cultural attitudes toward the handicapped. There are also unique problems in assessment and placement, especially for children whose parents do not speak English in the home.

In practically every special education program, members of culturally different populations may be found. The school provides these children with their main access to specialized services for handicapped school-aged children.

Minority-group children are generally placed in special education classes alongside other children with similar handicaps. Until recently few adjustments have been made to accommodate their presence in these programs. However, special educators are well aware of the effects that cultural attitudes and language problems have on the adjustment of handicapped children.

Many cultural groups have established their own services for handicapped children. Some of these agencies are religious in nature, and are likely to appeal most to parents who belong to that religious denomination.

Paraprofessionals, or teachers' aides, have been trained and used for many years in a variety of settings. Trained aides who speak the child's language play a valuable role in the child's medical and educational intervention. However, paraprofessionals should only be assigned to work with close supervision and frequent consultations with teachers and therapists (Linares, 1983).

Some culturally different parents find it difficult to understand the goals of the school for their child. These parents need a forum to openly discuss their concerns without fear that they are being judged. Like all parents, they need information about how best to help their children. Cultural conflicts are often caused by simple misunderstandings and a lack of communication. By speaking to parents in their own languages, bringing them into schools, and putting them in touch with other parents of handicapped children, educators can do much to improve cultural relations.

Families of culturally different children should be kept well-informed of all assessments and interventions. Clinics and schools must ensure that families understand and approve all aspects of treatment. In larger cities, such as Toronto and Vancouver, the school boards employ interpreters for this purpose. Even in rural areas, interpreter services should be available for immigrant children and their families.

Exhibit 14-5 Tips for dealing with parents of culturally different handicapped children.

- Explain to parents the opportunities that exist for handicapped people in Canada.
- Invite parents to the school to see for themselves what their children are doing.
- Explain to parents the objectives of their children's programs.
- Enlist the support of parents for particular problems.
- Listen carefully and patiently to parents' explanations of their children's behaviour.
- Offer concrete and practical teaching suggestions that can also be used in the home.
- Encourage parents to participate during school hours. Invite them to come and tell the students stories, myths, and legends from their home countries. Encourage them to bring samples of art work or crafts, and to share their cultural traditions.
- Ask parents to help you incorporate aspects of their child's cultural background into the child's educational program. The parents might provide songs, stories, customs, and so on, that form the child's cultural heritage.

Speech and language

To provide language intervention to a culturally different child, the clinician must first determine which language to work in. Children with language disorders require a complete language system through which they can effectively communicate. Rather than struggling with two languages, they should receive assistance in the language in which they already have the most skills.

To provide adequate language therapy, the speech/language clinician must be able to use the child's own language fluently and correctly (Linares, 1983). In some cases, teacher aides who speak the child's language may be employed to carry out language therapy.

Native students

Some Native peoples control their local schools in matters of curriculum, teacher appointments, and funding for maintenance. Some Native schools have rejected special services provided by off-reserve professionals. They are concerned that interference from outside will cause misunderstandings and erode their hard-won control of education.

Some Native parents also reject special services because they fear their handicapped child will be taken away from them. These parents may feel that medical or professional help is too often used to separate children from their families. As a result, they resist efforts to have their children placed in treatment centres, residential facilities, and group homes away from the reserve.

Federal, provincial, and Native agencies share responsibility for providing special education to the Native population. Because of this multiple delivery system, responsibility for special education problems is difficult to allocate. Anderson and Anderson (1983) have made the following suggestions to improve Native special education programs.

- Child-find programs should be introduced.
- Individualized education plans should be developed for each exceptional child.
- Native personnel should be developed.
- Appropriate materials and procedures should be employed in evaluation.
- Children should be placed in the most appropriate environment.
- Confidentiality should be safeguarded.
- Advocacy programs should be developed to safeguard children's and parents' rights.

Lack of access to a full range of special education services continues to be a problem in isolated and rural areas. In isolated communities, the problems of culturally different handicapped children are frequently exacerbated by prejudice, inadequate educational financing, and lack of communication with provincial ministries of education.

THE CULTURALLY DIFFERENT HANDICAPPED PRE-SCHOOLER

Very young minority children with handicaps require the same level of services as other handicapped infants and pre-schoolers. Teachers who serve children in their homes have a unique opportunity to involve minority families in the educational process. To do this effectively, teachers must establish good working relationships with family members. Homebound teachers should also be sure to provide useful, creditable information about the education process (Wilson, Mulligan, and Turner, 1985).

Teachers who enter their students' homes must become aware of differences in cultural practices. They must consider the parents' point of view, and be sensitive to the situation of individual families. For example, a single Native mother may be distrustful of government services, and prefer to seek assistance from a church group. Teachers must also understand that basic family needs must be met before education can become a focus of family concern (Wilson, Mulligan, and Turner, 1985).

The homebound teacher should demonstrate the care of the handicapped child, rather than simply giving verbal advice. Whenever possible, the teacher should take advantage of the child's natural setting to build educational experiences out of normal activities. For example, the teacher can use the bathroom to teach self-help skills, body parts, and basic health concepts. By using common objects, teachers show parents that children do not need a great many toys to learn (Wilson, Mulligan, and Turner, 1985).

Teachers should try to verbally agree with parents upon identified instructional goals. However, problems may arise through misunderstanding of cultural practices. For example, all may verbally agree that the child needs to develop more respect for authority. However, in practice, some cultural groups do not discipline or place any restrictions on handicapped children in the home. Without an awareness of this cultural practice, the teacher may enter into unspoken conflict with the parents. Unless cultural differences are made explicit and reconciled, teachers and parents become subject to unspoken feelings of frustration and hostility (Wilson, Mulligan, and Turner, 1985). This is especially true when the parent who meets with the teacher is not the one who works with the child.

PROFILE 14-3

Mr. Christophos often attended school meetings. He was very anxious that his severely handicapped son become more active and responsive. His eyes lit up as he described how he could get his four-year-old son to laugh. He had even persuaded the boy to reach for a toy.

Mrs. Christophos was so busy caring for her new baby and other family members that she had little free time for play with her handicapped son. Mr. Christophos, on the other hand, enjoyed playing with the boy. He set a special time aside for teaching his son in the evening after work. In this case, the father was best able to carry out a teaching program in the home.

THE CULTURALLY DIFFERENT HANDICAPPED ADOLESCENT

Many handicapped adolescents who arrive from other countries have had little or no school experience. Their parents often find it difficult, after years of caring for their children at home, to realize that some measure of independence is possible for them. Unfortunately, the schools are ill-equipped to help these adolescents. Although there are many special education programs in secondary schools, few can accommodate children who do not speak English or French.

The profile of Laura illustrates some of the complex problems faced by disabled culturally different adolescents.

PROFILE 14-4

Laura was a beautiful fourteen-year-old girl with a severe physical handicap. She came with her family from a small village in southern Italy, where her grandmother had taken care of her. Laura had learned to sew and knit, but she had never been enrolled in school.

When Laura's parents were told that she could attend school in Toronto, they did not want to send her. "She cannot speak English," her father protested. "And she is not a strong girl. It would be too much," Laura's father did not understand the purpose of education for Laura. "She will never be made to work," he told the school counselor. "My wife and I will take care of Laura for her whole life. We love this girl very much, and we want her life to be easy and comfortable."

Laura herself, however, wanted to go to school. "I want to have friends in the new country and be able to read books and write. I know I can learn the language, Papa," she pleaded. Laura's older brothers agreed with her and argued on her behalf. "Just because she is crippled, Papa, is no reason to keep her from having friends."

After many hours of family discussion, Laura's parents agreed to let her attend classes. However, they continued to have misgivings. They worried that the school would fill Laura's head with false hopes for the future. They did not dream that Laura might someday be able to lead an independent life.

When Laura told her parents about her work program at the school, they worried even more. Only after several months did they begin to understand that a rewarding life was possible for a handicapped girl.

For the first time in her life, Laura had friends among her peers. She felt alive and happy and looked forward each day to her time at school. She faced many hardships and frustrations, and had to struggle to learn her new language. She overcame these problems, however, because she knew she was building a future.

Although Laura was fortunate, many other newly arrived adolescents do not fare as well. Language problems and family attitudes often prevent culturally different handicapped teenagers from participating fully in Canadian life.

SUMMARY

In recent years, Canadian educational policies have become more responsive to the needs of culturally different children. A philosophy of multiculturalism currently expresses a national recognition of cultural plurality in Canadian schools. Multicultural policies are at least partly a response to a recent crisis in urban schools. This was caused by a large influx of children with little or no knowledge of English or French. Multicultural school programs and multicultural centres have been developed to combat prejudice and to help cultural minorities adjust to Canadian life.

Culturally different children, even from a single ethnic group, are an extremely heterogeneous population. Their learning styles, aptitudes, motivation levels, and family backgrounds differ just as greatly as those of their Anglo-Canadian peers. Educators must be sure to focus on the needs of each individual child, and to resist cultural stereotypes. Only this way can educational planning be sufficiently flexible and suited to the child.

Culturally different handicapped children face a number of special problems, especially in the area of assessment and placement. The effects of disabilities are often compounded by language problems, cultural attitudes, and poor communication between home and school. Educators should make a strong attempt to enlist the help of the family and community in meeting the child's individual and cultural needs.

BIBLIOGRAPHY

Advani, L. (1979). Attitudes towards the blind in Asian countries. In M. Rodriguez and S. Rogow (Eds.), *Perspectives and prospects in the education of the world's blind children.* Toronto: Ministry of Community and Social Services.

Alleyne, M. (1976). Dimensions and varieties of West Indian English and the implications for teaching. In V. D'Oyley and H. Silverman (Eds.), *Black student in urban Canada.* Special issue, TESL *Talk* 7:1 (Jan., 1976), 35-60.

Anderson, G.R. and Anderson, S.K. (1983). The exceptional Native American. In D.R. Omark and J.G. Enckson (Eds.) *The bilingual exceptional child.* San Diego, CA.: College Hill Press.

Anderson, J.T.M. (1918). The education of the New Canadian. Cited in K.W. McLeod, (1975). A short history of the immigrant as New Canadian. In A. Wolfgang (Ed.), *Education of immigrant students.* Toronto: McClelland and Stewart.

Ashworth, M. (1975). *Immigrant children and Canadian schools.* Toronto: McClelland and Stewart.

Ashworth, M. (1979). *The forces which shaped them: A history of the education of minority group children in British Columbia.* Vancouver: New Star Books.

Banks, J.A. (1981). *Multiethnic Education: Theory and Practice.* Boston: Allyn and Bacon.

Benavides, A. (1985). Planning effective special education for exceptional language minorities. *Teaching Exceptional Children 17:2,* 127-132.

Bernal, E.M. (1975). Specific suggestions for identification. In E.G. Fitzgerald (Ed.), *The first national conference on the disadvantaged gifted.* Ventura, CA.: Ventura County Superintendent of Schools.

Berry, J.W. (1975). Psychological testing across cultures. In A. Wolfgang (Ed.), *Education of immigrant students: Issues and answers.* Toronto: OISE Press.

Bowen, N.V. (1976). Children's cognitive development: The black child in a different culture. In V. D'Oyley and M. Silverman (Eds.), *Black students in urban Canada.* Toronto: Ontario Ministry of Culture and Recreation.

Burke, M.E. (1984). Educational implications of cultural diversity. In R.J. Samuda, J.W. Berry, and M. Laferriere (Eds.), *Multiculturalism in Canada.* Toronto: Allyn and Bacon.

Burnet, J. (1984). Myths and multiculturalism. In R.J. Samuda, J.W. Berry, and M. Laferriere (Eds.), *Multiculturalism in Canada.* Toronto: Allyn and Bacon.

Caccia, C.L. (1975). Immigrant education and multiculturalism. In A. Wolfgang (Ed.), *Education of immigrant students.* Toronto: OISE Press.

Cambon, K., Galbraith, J.D., and Kong, G. (1965). Middle ear disease in the Indians of Mount Currie Reserve, British Columbia. *Canadian Medical Association Journal, 93,* 1201.

Canada Year Book. (1981). Ottawa: Statistics Canada.

Cohen, L. and Manion, L. (1983). *Multicultural classrooms: Perspectives for teachers.* London: Crook Helm.

Cummins, J.P. (1984). Psychological assessment of minority language students. In R.J. Samuda, J.W. Berry, and M. Laferriere (Eds.), *Multiculturalism in Canada.* Toronto: Allyn and Bacon.

De Blassie, R.R. and Franco, J.N. (1983). Psychological and educational assessment of bilingual children. In D.R. Omark and J.G. Erickson (Eds.), *The Bilingual exceptional child.* San Diego, CA.: College Hill Press.

D'Oyley, V. (1976). Entering urban education: The case of the black student. In V. D'Oyley and M. Silverman (Eds.), *Black students in Urban Canada.* Toronto: Ontario Ministry of Culture and Recreation.

Driedger, L. (1978). Introduction: Ethnic identity in the Canadian mosaic. In L. Driedger (Ed.), *The Canadian ethnic mosaic: A quest for identity.* Toronto: McClelland and Stewart.

Edwards, J. (1984). The social and political context of bilingual education. In R.J. Samuda, J.W. Berry, and M. Laferriere (Eds.), *Multiculturalism in Canada.* Toronto: Allyn and Bacon.

Erickson, J.G. and Walker, C.L. (1983) Bilingual exceptional children: What are the issues? In D.R. Omark and J.G. Erickson (Eds.), *The Bilingual exceptional child.* San Diego: CA: College Hill Press.

Elliston, I.N. (1984). Multicultural centres: A focus for intercultural education. In R.J. Samuda, J.W. Berry, and M. Laferriere (Eds.), *Multiculturalism in Canada.* Toronto: Allyn and Bacon.

Graham, M.D. (1975). Prevalence of middle ear disease among the Indian population of coastal British Columbia. *Hearing Instruments, 26,* 26.

Head, W.A. (1984). Historical, social and cultural factors in the adaptation of nonwhite students in Toronto schools. In R.J. Samuda, J.W. Berry, and M. Laferriere (Eds.), *Multiculturalism in Canada.* Toronto: Allyn and Bacon.

Isajiw, W.W. (1978). Olga in wonderland: Ethnicity in a technological society. In L. Driedger (Ed.), *The Canadian ethnic mosaic: A quest for identity.* Toronto: McClelland and Stewart.

Jenness, E. (1966). *The Indian tribes of Canada.* Toronto: Ryerson Press.

La Farge, O. (1957). *A pictorial history of the American Indian.* New York: Crown Publishers.

Linares, N. (1983). Management of communicatively handicapped Hispanic American children. In D.R. Omark and J.G. Erickson (Eds.), *The bilingual exceptional child.* San Diego, CA: College Hill Press.

Ling, D., McCoy, R.M., and Levinson, E.D. (1969). The incidence of middle ear disease and its educational implications among Baffin Island Eskimo children. *Canadian Journal of Public Health, 60,* 385.

McLeod, K.W. (1975). A short history of immigrant students as New Canadians. In A. Wolfgang (Ed.), *Education of immigrant students.* Toronto: McClelland and Stewart.

More, A.T. (November 1984). *Okanagan-Nicola Indian Quality of Education Study.* Penticton, B.C.: Okanagan Indian Learning Institute.

Murray, J. (1977). *Toronto educational governance: Multiculturalism case studies.* Toronto: Ministry of Education.

Newman, W.M. (1978). Theoretical perspectives for the analysis of social pluralism. In L. Driedger (Ed.), *The Canadian ethnic mosaic: A quest for identity.* Toronto: McClelland and Stewart.

Nuru, N. (1983). Educational issues, ideology and the role of national organizations. In D.R. Omark and J.G. Erickson (Eds.), *The Bilingual Exceptional Child.* San Diego, CA.: College Hill Press.

O'Bryan, K.G., Reitz, J.G., and Kuplowska, O.M. (1976). *Non-official languages: a study in Canadian multiculturalism.* Ottawa: Document S42-7/1976.

Omark, D.R. and Watson, D.L. (1983). Psychological testing and bilingual education: The need for reconceptualization. In D.R. Omark and J.G. Erickson (Eds.), *The bilingual exceptional child.* San Diego, CA.: College Hill Press.

Paul, S. (1985). Personal Communication.

Prutting, C.A. (1983). "Assessing communicative behavior using a language sample." In Omark, D.R. and Erickson, J.G. (eds.) *The bilingual exceptional child.* San Diego, CA.: College Hill Press.

Ramcharan, S. (1975). Special problems of immigrant children in the Toronto school system. In A. Wolfgang (Ed.), *Education of immigrant students: Issues and answers.* Toronto: OISE Press.

Samuda, R.J. (1984). Assessing the abilities of minority students within a multiethnic milieu. In R.J. Samuda, J.W. Berry, and M. Laferriere (Eds.), Multiculturalism in Canada. Toronto: Allyn and Bacon.

Samuda, R.J., Berry, J.W., and Laferriere, M. (1984). *Multiculturalism in Canada.* Toronto: Allyn and Bacon.

Shapson, S.M. and Prubhoo, M. (1974). *Second language programs for young children.* Toronto: Toronto Board of Education.

Stewart, J.L. (1983). Communication disorders in the American Indian population. In D.R. Omark and J.G. Erickson (Eds.), *The bilingual exceptional child.* San Diego, CA: College Hill Press.

Sung, B.L. (1967). *Mountain of gold: The study of the Chinese in America.* New York: MacMillan.

Suran, B.G. and Rizzo, J.V. (1983). *Special children: an integrative approach.* Glenview, IL: Scott Foresman.

Torrance, P. (1977). *Discovery and nurturance of giftedness in the culturally different.* Reston, VA.: Council for Exceptional Children.

Tucker, J.A. (undated). Operationalizing the diagnostic-intervention process. In *Non-biased assessment of minority group children with bias toward none.* Lexington: University of Kentucky.

Weiss, M.S. (1974). *Valley City: A Chinese community in America.* Cambridge, MA.: Schenkman Publishing Company.

Wilson, J.D. (1984). Multicultural programs in Canadian education. In R.J. Samuda, J.W. Berry, and M. Laferriere (Eds.), *Multiculturalism in Canada.* Toronto: Allyn and Bacon.

Wilson, R.C., Mulligan, M., and Turner, R.M. (1985). Early childhood intervention in an urban setting. *Teaching Exceptional Children, 17:2,* 134-139.

GLOSSARY

acceleration: allowing gifted children to progress through the education system at their own rate

accommodation: the ability of the eye to change for incoming light

achievement tests: tests that indicate the extent of a child's school learning

acidosis: a condition in diabetes in which blood sugar levels drop, causing an insulin reaction

acoupedic method: an oral approach to educating learning-impaired pupils that stresses the maximum development of residual hearing

acoustic impedence audiometry: procedure that assesses conductive hearing loss by measuring the movement of the ear drum, the middle-ear muscles, the bones in response to auditory stimulation

acquired aphasia: a loss of linguistic ability that results from brain damage caused by serious illness or head trauma

adaptive behaviour: how well a person is able to adapt to environmental demands

additions: refers to speech disorders in which extra sounds are added

adventitious hearing impairment: hearing loss acquired some time after birth, through accident or disease

after-school language classes: designed to help children study their native language

aggression: any form of behaviour designed to harm or injure another person

agnosia: a lack of knowledge; an inability to recognize the significance of sensory stimuli

albinism: a condition in which the body lacks pigment

allergy: hypersensitivity to a substance (such as a food, dust) which is harmless to most people; manifested in a physiological disorder

American Sign Language (ASL or AMSLAN): a language with its own semantic and syntactic structures, used by the majority of adult deaf individuals

anoxia: prolonged oxygen deprivation that can lead to irreversible brain damage

anxiety: a fear with a future reference

aphasia: a language disorder affecting both receptive and expressive language processes

apnea: failure to breath

apraxia: the inability to program, position, and sequence the muscle movements involved in speech

arthritis: a term for a variety of chronic systemic conditions involving inflammation of the joints

articulatory disorders: speech disorders characterized by omissions, distortions, and additions of speech sounds

artificial larynx: device that allows individuals with larynx problems to produce audible speech

assessment: the process of determining whether a child exhibits a problem, what the problem is, its causes, its potential course, its developmental consequences, and the best approaches to intervention and remediation

asthma: a chronic disorder characterized by difficulty in breathing, usually caused by an allergy to ingested substances

astigmatism: a refractive visual error which results from an irregularity in the curvature of the cornea or lens of the eye

ataxia: a condition characterized by poor coordination of the movements associated with balance, posture, and spatial orientation

athetosis: a type of cerebral palsy characterized by constant, involuntary, writhing movements

atrophy: a form of muscle weakness caused by nerve degeneration

atypical abilities: outstanding strengths or abilities in a specific or narrow field

auditory atresia: missing or undeveloped pinnae or auditory canals

augmentative devices: aids that allow a non-verbal individual to communicate basic needs

auricle: the cartilage structure on the side of the head which forms the outer ear

axons: part of the neurons in the brain which contain molecules and chemical transmitters. Axons send nervous impulses from one nerve cell to another.

babbling: a form of vocal play seen in infants as they develop language

basal ganglia: the part of the brain that, with the cerebellum, controls the coordination of fine and gross motor activity, and maintains posture and equilibrium

battered child syndrome: child abuse

behaviour observation audiometry: an audiometric method in which the child's behaviour, in response to certain sounds, is observed

Bel: a unit of loudness, usually broken into ten decibels (dB)

bibliotherapy: an approach used with emotionally disturbed youngsters which consists of reading stories with positive role models

bilateral hearing loss: hearing impairment in both ears

bilingual education: children study a second language while still receiving basic instruction in their first language

body image: awareness of body, the interrelation of body parts, and the relationship of the whole body to the environment

bound morphemes: sound units which are not words by themselves, but gain meaning when they are combined with words

cancer: a general term for about a hundred diseases characterized by the abnormal and uncontrolled growth of cells

cataract: an eye pathology in which there is an opacity of the lens or its capsule, which restricts the eye's ability to receive light

cerebellum: the part of the brain that, with the basal ganglia, controls the coordination of fine and gross motor activity, and maintains posture and equilibrium

cerebral cortex: part of the brain, the "grey matter"

cerebral palsy: a condition caused by damage to the brain, characterized by motor disorder, and often accompanied by other disabilities

cerebrum: consists of the left and right hemisphere of the brain; the part of the brain controlling conscious, intellectual activity

child abuse and neglect: the physical or mental injury, sexual abuse, negligent treatment, or maltreatment of a child by caretakers

child advocate: a person who pleads for, or defends, a particular child-related cause

child advocacy: any social, political, or legal action that is intended to achieve a better life for children from infancy to late adolescence

child development: a series of patterned and predictable changes that foster the child's ability to cope with and master the external environment

chronic health problems: permanent, or frequently recurring diseases or medical conditions that interfere with an individual's ability to lead a normal life

clefts: midline defects which result from failue of parts of the embryo to fuse completely

cloze procedures: assessment measures for reading difficulty and language competence

cluttered speech: involves excessive speech speed, combined with disorganized sentence structure and articulation problems

co-active model: an educational approach for multiply handicapped youngsters which stresses interaction with persons in the child's environment

cochlea: a tiny, snail-shaped structure in the inner ear which contains highly specialized structures for hearing

colour vision: the eye's ability to distinguish and comprehend colours

communication: the transmission of information

communication boards: boards to which symbols are attached, used to facilitate communication for non-verbal individuals

communicative competence: the ability to comprehend and encode meaning

conductive losses: hearing losses affecting only the outer and middle ear which usually respond favourably to medical or surgical interventions

cones: light sensitive nerve cells found in the retina of the eye

congenital amputation: a condition in which the child is born lacking entire limbs or parts of limbs

congenital condition: present at birth

consultants: educational personnel who assist classroom teachers to maintain exceptional children in regular school programs

contents: term used by J.P. Guilford to indicate how a learner classifies processed information

contingency contract: a behaviour intervention technique in which a contract is drawn up and signed by the student and other involved parties

contracture: a shortening of the muscles, tendons, and ligaments that results in postural distortion

cornea: a transparent window covering the front of the eye, continuous with the sclera

corpus collosum: a densely packed, myelin covered mass of axons which connect the cerebral hemispheres

cortical blindness: blindness caused by swelling in the brain tissue, due to trauma, infection, or congenital malformations

creativity: the process of bringing unusual and unexpected responses to bear on a given situation or problem

crystalline lens: a structure held in suspension behind the iris of the eye

Cued speech: an oral approach to educating hearing-impaired pupils that uses eight hand configurations in order to aid speech reading

culture conflict: the clash between a family's cultural values and those of the dominant society

cystic fibrosis: a genetically determined inborn error of metabolism, involving the exocrine glands

daily report card: a behaviour-intervention technique in which a report is sent home daily

deaf: individuals whose hearing disability precludes successful processing of linguistic information through audition, with or without a hearing aid

decibels (dB): units of intensity or loudness of sound

delayed language problem: language problems that affect the normal language acquisition process

dendrites: part of the neurons in the brain that receive incoming electrical signals

developmental aphasia: a childhood language disorder in which youngsters do not fully acquire language

developmental milestones: various critical behaviours that children typically perform at certain ages

diabetes mellitus: a disorder of sugar metabolism resulting from the failure of the pancreas to manufacture sufficient insulin

diagnosis: the art of identifying disease from its symptoms

diagnostic — prescriptive approach: an approach to teaching language delayed students which includes the ability model and the task analysis model

differential diagnosis: the precise specification that a given set of symptoms is indicative of one disorder rather than another

diplopia: double vision

directionality: an awareness of left and right in the environment outside the body

disabled: refers to any person whose functioning is reduced as a result of a significant physical, learning, or social problem

distance acuity: the ability to perceive distant objects

distortions: refers to speech disorders in which a deviation from normal speech sounds is apparent

dizygotic twins: fraternal twins

dog guides: specially trained dogs used to assist blind people in travelling

Duchenne's muscular dystrophy: the most common type of muscular dystrophy which characterized by the formation of fatty deposits, accompanied by muscular degeneration

dysarthria: an articulation disorder, resulting from brain damage, and associated with poor control of the speech muscles

dyscalculia: disturbance in the ability to use numbers and do arithmetic

dysgraphia: a disturbance in the ability to express thoughts in writing

dyslexia: disturbance in the ability to read, despite conventional instruction

dyspedagogia: poor teaching methods which may themselves be the cause of learning disabilities

dysphasia: a language disorder

ear drum: a tough, tightly stretched membrane that separates the outer ear from the middle ear

echolalia: meaningless repetition of words and phrases

elective mutism: mutism found among emotionally disturbed children who refuse speak, or speak only in certain circumstances

electrical response audiometry: measurement of various evoked electrical potentials that are responses to auditory stimuli

electro-oculogram: a test that measures the ability of visual nerve cells to respond to light

electrophysiological assessment: procedures that measure responses to sensory stimulation but require no active participation on the part of the child being tested

electro-retinogram: measures the chain of electrical nerve responses created by a flashing light

emotional lability: frequent mood changes

emotional neglect: the failure of caretakers to provide the loving, positive environment necessary to the development of a child's self-esteem

emotional overlay: emotional or behavioural problems that develop as a result of a learning disorder

epilepsy: a condition characterized by a burst of electrical energy in the brain, and physical convulsions

esophageal speech: speech produced by the inflation of an air pocket near the top of the gullet

eugenics: the notion that only certain groups in society are worthy to marry and procreate

Eustachian tube: connects the middle ear to the nasopharynx and serves to equalize air pressure

exceptional children: those who have difficulty in realizing their full human potential. Their intellectual, emotional, physical, or social performance falls below or rises above that of other children.

expressive disorders: language disorders which affect the formulation of grammatic utterances

expressive language: the formulation and production of language

external otitis: an infection of the skin of the external auditory canal

feasibility: the cost of obtaining, giving, and scoring a test

Fetal Alcohol Effect: a condition in which some effects of Fetal Alcohol Syndrome are demonstrated, without the total condition

Fetal Alcohol Syndrome: a disorder characterized by a pattern of anomalies in the children of drinking mothers

flaccid paralysis: an inability to move the muscles because the neural impulses needed for muscle contraction are lacking

fovea: the most sensitive spot on the retina in the eye because it possesses a rich supply of light sensitive cells.

generalized seizures: epileptic seizures that are bilateral and symmetrical, without local onset in the brain

genius: a particular aptitude or capacity in any area; extremely rare intellectual powers

gifted: a generic term that encompasses individuals of high intellectual ability, high talents, outstanding creativity, and pronounced leadership qualities

glaucoma: an eye pathology caused by increased intraocular pressure resulting in the slow death of nerve fibres

glial cells: cells that support and nourish the neurons

grand mal seizure: one of the most common forms of epileptic seizure, characterized by distinct stages, and loss of consciousness

group intelligence tests: intelligence tests designed for administration to specific age-ranges of children

group therapy: procedures that include the simultaneous treatment of several children, usually in the same age range

handicapped: those who have difficulty adjusting to the environment because of intellectual, physical, emotional, or social problems

hard-of-hearing: individuals who, generally with the use of a hearing aid, have residual hearing sufficient to enable successful processing of linguistic information through audition

hearing impairment: a generic term indicating a hearing disability that may range in severity from mild to profound. It includes the sub sets of deaf and hard-of-hearing.

hemisphericity: a person's tendency to rely more on one cerebral hemisphere to process certain types of information

hereditary anomalies: anomalies in the genes, that may be passed on to subsequent generations

hertz (Hz): the measurement unit for the frequency of sound

high risk: children who may, in future, develop some problem that will affect their functioning

homebound instruction: individual tutoring for children unable to attend school for extended periods, usually because of illness

hospital instruction: individual or group tutoring for hospitalized youngsters

hydrocephalus: a condition characterized by an excessive accumulation of cerebrospinal fluid in the brain due to an obstruction of its flow

hyperglycemia: a state of abnormally high blood-glucose levels

hyperopia: a refractive visual error; farsightedness

hypertonia: flaccid or loose muscles

hypoactivity: a state of unnatural non-activity

hypoglycemia: insulin reaction; a state of abnormally low levels of glucose in the blood

hypothalamus: the part of the brain that is important in the control of the internal environment of the body

idiopathic epilepsy: epilepsy of unknown origin

incidence: the number of new cases of a particular condition ascertained over a given period of time, usually a year

incus: one of the small bones of the ossicular chain in the middle ear, also called the anvil

individual psychotherapy: implies a transaction between the client and the therapist in which attitudes and feelings are discussed and probed

instrumental response recording: audiological methods that use electrical responses

intelligence quotient: the level of intelligence estimated on the ratio of mental age to chronological age

interpersonal-interactive approach: an intervention for language-disordered students which develops the child's communicative competence

intervention: the application of professional skills to maintain or improve a child's potential and functioning

inventories: lists of skills in specific subject or behavioural areas

itinerant teachers: specially trained educators who provide individual assistance to exceptional children for specific periods during the normal school schedule

Jacksonian seizure: a form of partial epileptic seizure characterized by motor symptoms without impaired consciousness

juvenile arthritis: similar to the adult form; sometimes called Still's disease

labelling: categorizing children on the basis of their primary disability

Landouzy-Dejerine muscular dystrophy: a type of muscular dystrophy characterized by slow degeneration of the muscles of the face and shoulder girdle

laterality: an awareness within the body of the difference between left and right

leadership: the ability to effect positive and productive change among other people that is self-enhancing or group-enhancing

learned helplessness: emerges when individuals have no faith that their efforts will result in desired outcomes

legal blindness: an acuity measure of 20/200 or less in the better eye with the best correction, or visual acuity of more than 20/200 if the widest diameter of the field of vision subtends an angle no greater than 20 degrees

life skills: the skills that promote self-care. They include basic hygiene, grooming, self-dressing, mobility, and housekeeping

limb deficiencies: the loss or absence of entire limbs or parts of limbs

low birth-weight babies: those born at less than 2,500 grams

macular retinal degeneration: an eye pathology that results in extremely poor central vision

mainstreaming: the temporal, instructional, and social integration of eligible exceptional children with their normal peers to the greatest extent possible

malleus: one of the small bones of the ossicular chain in the middle ear, also called the hammer

manualists: those who view deafness as a human difference that requires its own language

maturational lags: occur when children fail to reach developmental milestones

meatus: the external canal of the ear, extending from the pinna to the tympanic membrane

meninges: the coverings of the brain and spinal cord

meningitis: a childhood disease, of which there are many types, generally characterized by high fever. Many sequelae, including deafness, blindness and mental retardation.

mental age: the correspondence of the tasks a child can perform at a certain age to an age scale and chronological age

mental retardation: significantly subcoverage general intellectual functioning resulting in, or associated with, impairments in adaptive behaviour, and manifested during the developmental period

metabolic disorders: inborn errors of metabolism. The normal chemistry of the cell is altered by the inability to provide or dispose of a critical chemical or protein.

metocognition: basic learning strategies

microcephaly: a condition characterized by small head circumference. Brain development is often impaired by the abnormally small cranium.

midline defects: clefts which result from failure of parts of the embryo to fuse completely

minimal brain dysfunction: implies slight damage or injury to the brain that hinders its most efficient functioning

miscue: an error when a reader misinterprets semantic, syntactic, or graphenic cues to predict events that do not occur in the text

miscue analysis: a diagnostic measure in reading instruction

mobility: the knowledge of how to get from one place to another

monozygotic twins: identical twins

Moro reflex: an infant reflex in which the child demonstrates a startle movement that affects face, arms, trunk, legs, and eyes

morphemes: meaningful groupings of phonemes

mosaicism: a form of Down's syndrome in which there is a faulty distribution of chromosomes in later cell divisions, resulting in some body cells having a Trisomy condition

motor cells: part of the neural network. Motor cells activate responses to the outside world.

modality processing techniques: an intervention for learning-disabled students which focuses on teaching to the strongest learning modality

motor planning: the ability to plan a new motor task

multiple dependent handicapped: severely mentally handicapped individuals who also have sensory and/or physical anomalies

multiple sclerosis: a neurological disorder of unknown cause, characterized by slowly progressive scarring or hardening of the myelin coat of the nerve cells in the brain and spinal cord

multisensory impaired: a generic term used to define children with sight and hearing handicaps, developmental delays, and neurological impairments

muscular dystrophy: a group of inherited conditions characterized by degeneration of muscle fibres without neurological deficit

musculoskeletal impairments: conditions that impede bodily movements in the absence of damage to the central nervous system

mutism: the total absence of language

myelin: a white, fatty sheath which coats the axons

myopia: a refractive visual error; nearsightedness

myringotomy: a surgical procedure in which the ear drum is punctured in order to drain excess fluid from the middle ear

near acuity: the ability of the eye to see at close range

neologisms: nonsense words and phrases created by severely emotionally disturbed youngsters

neurons: nerve cells that are the basic units of neurological function

non-categorical approaches: An educational method that states that the functional behaviour of a child is the most important factor in the child's educational program. Traditional labels are displaced.

normalization: the philosophical belief that all exceptional individuals, no matter what their level and type of handicap, should be provided with an education and living environment as close to normal as possible

normal distribution: a continuum of scores that vary from the average score by predictable amounts

nystagmus: a disturbance of ocular mobility in which there is a rhythmic involuntary movement of the eyes

objectivity: when, on a test, there is only one correct response for each question

object perception: the ability to perceive objects at close range

occipital lobe: the part of the brain associated with vision

omissions: refers to speech disorders in which sounds are omitted

operations: terms used by J.B. Guilford to express the methods people use to process information

opthalmologist: a medical doctor who specializes in treatment of the eye

optic nerve atrophy: an eye pathology which results from damage to the fibres of the optic nerve

optometrist: a professional who measures and checks visual functions, and prescribes corrective lenses

oral/aural approach: educational method for hearing-impaired students that stresses speech, speech reading, and amplification

oral window: a drum which forms the entrance to the inner ear

oralists: those who view deafness as a human handicap to be overcome through the development of speech and speech reading

orientation: the knowledge of one's own location in space

orthotic: an instrument that replaces a relatively non-functional part of the body

otitis media: a condition in which the mucosol lining of the middle ear becomes inflamed, and the cavity filled with fluid

otosclerosis: destruction of the capsular bone in the middle ear and the growth of a weblike bone that attaches to, and restricts, the stapes

partial seizures: epileptic seizures that begin locally and may or may not cause alterations in consciousness

perception: the use of the senses to recognize, discriminate, and interpret stimuli

performance-oriented approach: an approach for language-disordered students which stresses modifying, decreasing, or increasing language behaviours

perseverate: inappropriate repetition of an action

petit mal seizures: one of the most common forms of epiletic seizure, characterized by absence, but no loss of consciousness

phobia: an anxiety reaction that is specific to one stimulus

phocomelia: a congenital deformity in which parts of limbs or entire limbs are missing or very short

phonemes: the smallest functional units of spoken language

phonetics: description of the speech sounds of a language

phonology: the sound system of a language

physical abuse: non-accidental physical injury to a child

physically disabled students: those who have a physical impairment other than a visual or hearing loss

physical neglect: the failure of caretakers to meet a child's basic physical needs

pinna: the cartilage structure on the side of the head which forms the outer ear

play audiometry: an audiometric method in which the child is conditioned to respond to specific sounds as part of a game

post-lingual deafness: deafness which occurs after the development of speech and language

postmature babies: those born two weeks or more beyond the expected due date

pragmatics: the way in which language is used

prebycusis: progressive nerve deterioration; the most common form of auditory defect in adults

precocity: remarkable early development

pre-lingual deafness: deafness which occurs in children prior to the development of speech and language

premature babies: those born at less than thirty-seven weeks gestation

prematurity: refers to a gestation period of thirty-seven weeks or less

presbyopia: a refractive visual error in which the lens of the eye loses its ability to accommodate to near objects; onset usually due to aging

prescription cane: white, collapsible cane specially designed for blind persons

prevalence: the total number of existing cases of a condition, old and new

products: term used by J.P. Guilford to express the forms and structures that people use to organize information

prosody: the stress, rhythm, and pitch patterns of a language

prostheses: functional devices that substitute for missing body parts

psychological processing: how an individual interprets sensory information and puts it to meaningful intellectual use

psychomotor seizure: a form of partial epileptic seizure characterized by relatively complex, organized movements and sometimes accompanied by clouding of consciousness and amnesia

reception class: a class made up entirely of students who require intense training in the dominant language

receptive disorders: language disorders which interfere with the comprehension of spoken language

receptor cells: part of the neural network; they provide sensory information

recidivist: anyone incarcerated for new charges within two years of release from prison

refraction: the ability of the eye to accommodate and focus incoming light stimuli

regular classroom: a normal placement that provides the exceptional child with the maximum integration with peers

rehabilitation: procedures that endeavour to restore the individual to normal or optimal functioning

related services: those services that permit an exceptional child to benefit from special education

reliability: the consistency of a test; whether it produces the same results on different occasions under the same circumstances

remediation: helping children to overcome, or compensate for, specific deficits in learning and development

residential schools: large, often provincially funded institutions, for students with serious learning and behaviour problems

resource room: an administrative arrangement that is the bridge between the self-contained classroom and the regular classroom

retinal detachment: a condition in which the outer layer of the retina separates from the inner portion

retinitis pigmentosa: a hereditary disease that causes degeneration of retinal tissue and loss of peripheral vision

retrolental fibroplasia: an eye pathology caused by oxygen damage to immature blood vessels, and resulting in severe visual impairment or total blindness

rigidity: a rare type of cerebral palsy

Rochester method: an oral approach to educating hearing impaired pupils that uses speech, speech reading, amplification, and simultaneous finger spelling

rods: light sensitive nerve cells found in the retina of the eye

rubella, maternal: an airborne virus that is most virulent if the mother is affected during the first trimester of pregnancy

screening: the process of identifying children who are at-risk for an exceptional condition

self-contained special classes: classes designed for exceptional children, usually those with more serious problems

semantics: the meaning of language

sensiro-neural losses: hearing loss caused by abnormal sense organs or a defective auditory nerve

sensitivity: the ability of an educational test to discriminate between any two factors

sensory integration: the ability to perceive and connect sensory information

sexual abuse: sexual involvement imposed on a child by an adult

social anomie: a lack of entrenched societal norms and values

social intervention: includes a spectrum of child welfare services when applied to exceptional children

spastic cerebral palsy: a condition characterized by slow, laborious, and poorly coordinated voluntary movement, which affects about half of the cerebral palsied population

special classrooms: self-contained classes for exceptional children, usually located in the regular school

special day schools: schools that provide special education services, usually to specific groups of exceptional children

special education: instruction that is specially designed to meet the unique needs of the exceptional child

speech audiometry: an audiometric technique which assesses the ability to hear and understand speech

speech defects: speech disorders that interfere with communication

speech detection: the level at which an individual can detect, but not necessarily understand, speech

speech reading: the skill of understanding speech through watching the lips and facial expressions

speech reception threshold: the level at which an individual can first understand speech

spina bifida: a congenital midline defect of the spinal column, in which one or more vertebrae fail to close during embryological development

spina bifida meningocele: a type of spina bifida in which the membranes surrounding the spinal cord protrude from the plane of the spine, forming a sac containing cerebrospinal fluid

spina bifida occulta: the mildest form of spina bifida; sometimes characterized by a clump of hair on the skin covering the area of the cleft

spina bifida myelomeningocele: the most serious form of spina bifida in which the protruding sac contains parts of the spinal cord and cerebrospinal fluid

spondees: two-syllable words that have equal stress on each syllable

spork: an orthotic device, a combined spoon and fork, used with motorically dysfunctioning individuals

stapes: one of the small bones of the ossicular chain in the middle ear. Also called the stirrup.

strabismus: a disturbance of ocular motility which occurs when the muscles of the eye are not synchronized

Strauss syndrome: a group of behaviours characteristic of learning-disabled children. The five major components are hyper-activity, hyper-emotionalism, impulsiveness, distractibility, and perseveration.

stretch reflex: a primitive reflex, apparent in newborns, that disappears during infancy

stuttering: a speech disorder characterized by blocking, repetition, or prolongation of sounds, words, phrases, or syllables

substitutions: refers to speech disorders in which one consonant is replaced by another

supportive therapy: a broad range of interventions that help children accommodate to their particular disabilities

sweep test: an audiometric screening procedure

symptomatic epilepsy: epilepsy in individuals who show strong evidence of brain damage

syntax: the organizational principles underlying linguistic expression

syntax based program: a program for language-disordered youngsters that stresses teaching the child syntax and specific language structures

talent: specific dimensions of a skill in an area such as music, visual arts, or drama, athletics, or particular academic domains

talented: individuals who possess skills in areas such as music, visual arts, drama, athletics, or academics

tangible reinforcer operant conditioning audiometry: a technique that uses tactile rather than visual cues

task analysis: analysing the behavioural components and prerequisite skills of a task

teacher nomination: a screening procedure in which teachers identify specific children; often used in the identification of gifted and talented pupils

teratogens: agents that interfere with normal embryological or fetal development

teratology: the study of agents that interfere with normal embryological or fetal development

thalamus: part of the brain involved in transmission of sensations

therapy: the treatment of an illness or a disabling condition

threshold of hearing: the level at which an individual can first detect a sound

tinnitus: high-pitched throbbing or ringing in the ears

token economies: behaviour intervention systems in which children earn tokens that can be traded in for reinforcers (rewards)

Total Communication: an approach to educating hearing-impaired pupils that uses speech, speech reading, and amplification, along with the simultaneous use of a school-based manual system

toxemias: a group of common pregnancy disorders are believed to be related to maternal nutrition

transition programs: approaches to educating culturally different children which focus on providing English instruction while preserving the original language

translocation: a form of Down's syndrome in which some chromosomal material from the twenty-first pair of chromosomes attaches to another chromosome

tremors: a rare type of cerebral palsy

Trisonomy 21: the most common form of Down's syndrome in which the twenty-first pair of chromosomes actually contains three chromosomes

tympanic membrane: a tough, lightly stretched membrane that separates the outer from the middle ear

unilateral hearing impairment: hearing loss in one ear only

Usher's syndrome: a condition characterized by hearing loss and progressive visual impairment

vestibular mechanism: three fluid-filled semi-circular canals in the inner ear that serve as organs of balance

visual efficiency: how well an individual is able to use residual vision

visually evoked responses: a technique that records the reception of light images by the visual cortex

visual field: the angle of view

visually reinforced audiometry: the technique of combining visual stimulation with an auditory stimulus

withdrawal classes: classes which provide immigrant children with the opportunity to learn English while still being part of the school

workshop: a term designating a wide range of work situations and rehabilitation programs for handicapped individuals

AUTHOR INDEX

SUBJECT INDEX